MASTER · A · MESIKHTA · SERIES

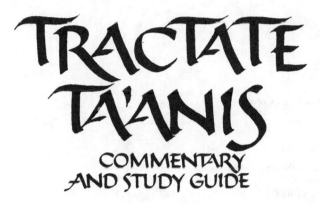

TRACTATE TA'ANIS

COMMENTARY AND STUDY GUIDE

NACHMAN COHEN

TORAH LISHMAH INSTITUTE
New York
1984 – 5744

Distributed by:

PHILIPP FELDHEIM Inc
96 East Broadway
New York, N.Y. 10002

FELDHEIM PUBLISHERS
Jerusalem

ISBN 0-87306-922-6

Library of Congress Cataloging in Publication Number: 84-51783

Torah Lishmah Institute
25 Clifton Avenue
Yonkers, New York 10705

Printed by Moriah Offset

Preface

In my twenty years as a yeshiva *menahel* I measured the success of a school by two yardsticks: How did it increase Torah values in its student body and how successful was it in inculcating in its graduates the need to make Torah study a lifelong pursuit.

Yet even yeshivos who meet these standards have many alumni who do not continue their "learning" once they have left the sacred halls of the Yeshiva. This is certainly the case with regard to the study of *G'mara*.

There are many reasons why former yeshiva students do not study *G'mara*. Some have not mastered the ability to study a Talmudic text on their own. Others need direction in understanding *rishonim* and *acharonim*. Still others are unable to derive on their own the fullness of a *sugya* or the significance of *aggadita*. Finally, there are those who are truly capable of all of the above but do not learn because of their business and professional obligations. Because of the foregoing some people shy away from learning *G'mara* while others dutifully study *G'mara* but do not find any real satisfaction.

This work is intended to meet the needs of these groupings. Herein, the student is given a **summary outline** which crystalizes the salient points of the *daf* and is excellent for review. Where appropriate, **background material** is introduced. The **analysis** of the commentaries are outlined and explained. The **sequence analysis** of the *aggadita* is illuminated. Finally, *overviews* serve to give the reader a broad understanding of the underpinnings of the *halakha*.

The *sefer* has been written primarily for those with a background in *G'mara* and rishonim. The level of material is intermediate to advanced although the cumbersome *shaklah v'taryia* has been omitted. (Nevertheless, anyone wishing to study the G'mara— even in translation—can derive a great deal of information and insight from this work.) The treatise is not meant to be a substitute for Talmud. Rather, it is written and sequenced so as to accompany the natural progression of Talmud study. That is, first the basic material is set down. This is followed by the study of the commentaries, and, thereafter, an overview of the whole topic is given.

The work is not meant to be exhaustive. Many important points have been left out. Intricate arguments made by *acharonim* are omitted. (It was felt that the reader would find this too cumbersome, and those who wished could handle the original texts.) Points which are discussed more fully in other tractates are also excluded. The *aggadita* is not outlined. (This was seen to be superfluous). Nevertheless within its guidelines the work is quite comprehensive and a thorough study of the material will allow the reader to **master the *Mesikhta*.**

I wish to thank: my brother, **Shaye David** for researching several section of this work; **HaRav Mordechai Gifter**, Rosh haYeshiva of the Telshe Yeshiva, **HaRav Yaacov Weinberg**, Rosh Yeshiva, Ner Israel, and **Rabbi Mordechai Willig** for reading the text and offering me advice and encouragement.

Most of all, I wish to thank my *aishes chayil*, **Esther Faige**, for her constant help, concern and encouragement.

Yonkers, New York — Nachman Cohen

11 Menchem Av 5744
The fourth yahrzeit of my
father-in-law's passing.

Preface to the Second Edition

I am grateful for the manner in which the first printing of this volume was accepted by the public. In the present edition, I have included the original text of the tractate as well as the original text of *M'gilas Ta'anis*.

I wish in particular to thank my wife, Esther Faige, who worked untiringly in the preparation of this volume, which she has rededicated to the memory of her beloved father, R. Chaim b. Yisrael, z'l.

Finally, I wish to express my *hakaras hatov* to the Almighty. Without Him nothing I do would be possible.

Yonkers, New York — Nachman Cohen
Tammuz 5748

Second Edition, 1988

Dedicated to the memory of
my beloved father in law

CHAIM MOSTEL ZT"L

who as president of
The Beth Jacob School of the East Bronx, Inc
and
Netzach Israel Jewish Center, Inc.
for over three decades
and as a
Member of the Board of the
Young Israel of Forest Hills,
and as an Advisor of
Om Publishing Company
played a substantial role
in the advancement of Torah study
to the American scene.

מרדכי גיפטער
ישיבת טלז
RABBI MORDECAI GIFTER
28570 NUTWOOD LANE
WICKLIFFE, OHIO 44092

בע"ה יג מנחם-אב תשנ"ג

מע"כ ידידי הנעלה הרה"ג מנחם כהן נ"י, שלום וברכה נצחי
ומבשה"ט

אקוה שהספר שהנהו מכין לדפוס, תשקוף וביאורים
באגדות למס' תענית, יהא לדבר תועלת בזמננו שמלבד
הנפרה והשינות גודרה לשחד מצוה רבה היא
להביא את דבר ה' לבתי ישראל שקשה להם, גם א"א
להם, להבין הדברים במקורם. ובדברים אלה במקורם,
הם הם ורק הם מקור הברכה לירא ה'.

יהא ה' בעזרו לברכו על המעשה, להוציא
מתח"י דבר נאה ומתוקן.

מנאי, אוהב ומוקיר לומדי ומלמדי תורת ה',
מרדכי גיפטר

ישיבת נר ישראל

NER ISRAEL RABBINICAL COLLEGE

MT. WILSON LANE / BALTIMORE, MARYLAND 21208 / 484-7200

ב"ה

זכינו לראות בימינו שאיפה חדשה בכל תפוצות
ישראל להכנס לפני ולפנים בלימוד התורה בהבנה
עמוקה. והנה הרב הגאון מוהר"ר נחמן הכהן שליט"א
ויצר מפתחות למסור בידי הלומדים המושגים של [illegible] בדרך
סידור ופיתוח הענינים בצורה ברורה.
זכה לעשות מלאכה גדולה ומסורה לה[illegible] ויה"ר שיזכה ל
יזכה להוציא לאור חיבורו הנהדר ויזכה לרבים הצמאים
לדבר ד'.

בתפלה שנזכה לראות בהגדלת תורה הק'

שמואל יעקב וינברג

Contents

Section D

***Ta'anis*: Chapter Two**

Ta'anis: Chapter Four

Introduction

"Everyone talks about the weather, but no one can do a thing about it." This well known maxim is diametrically opposed to the teachings of Judaism. It is the Torah's belief that climactic conditions are entirely dependent upon the deeds of man. The Torah records this correlation in a number of places.

In the *Kriyas Shema* we read—

> And it shall come to pass, if you hearken diligently to my commandments...that I will give you the rain of your land in its due season...and I will send grass in thy fields for thy cattle...Take heed to yourselves, that your heart be not deceived, and you turn aside , and serve other gods, and worship them and the Lord's anger be inflamed against you, and He shut up the heaven and there be no rain, and the land yield not its fruit (*Deut.* 11:10-17).

In the beginning of *parshas B'chukosai* the Torah states—

> If you walk in my statutes and keep my commandments, and do them; then, I will give you rain in due season, and the land shall yield its increase, and the trees of the land shall yield their fruit ...But if you will not hearken to me, and will not do all these commands...I will make your skies like iron, and your earth like brass: and your strength shall be spent in vain: for your land shall not yield her increase, neither shall the trees of the land yield their fruit (*Leviticus* 26).

Tractate *Ta'anis* explicates this principle. The laws found in this tractate, coupled with the aggadic literature are aimed at sensitizing man to the fact that all that befalls him—including "Natural Phenomema"— has its source in Heaven, and that God generates events based upon man's actions. To the extent that man follows the commandments, he will be blessed. If "Nature" turns against him, man must realize that "Nature" is but a manifestation of God's Will.

Included in the Torah's directives regarding climactic conditions is the rule that man should pray for blessed rain in its season and that if there is a drought, he is obligated by the Torah to blow *shofar/chatzotzeros* (trumpets). The Rabbis instituted that fasting should take place as well.

Accordingly, this tractate is divided into two main sections: prayers for rain (pages 2-10) and the procedure for fasting and blowing (*masri'in*) (pages 11-31). Of this latter section, pages 10-18 deal with Rain Fasts, pages 18-26 discuss Fasts called for other tragedies, and pages 26-31 review the laws pertaining to the Fast of the *Ma'amados* and 9 Av. As per the Talmud's normal procedure it digresses from time to time to discuss other material.

KEY TO SYMBOLS AND TRANSLITERATION

For purposes of easy identification, each *ma'amar* is numbered. Square brackets, i.e., [ ], are used to identify the sayings found in the *Mishna* and *G'mara*. Pointed brackets, i.e., < >, are used to number the positions of the *rishonim* and *acharonim*. When referring to a *ma'amar* within the same chapter only the bracket number is used. When citing a statement in another chapter, or section, the appropriate identification is placed before the bracket. Thus, ID-[23], refers to the statement to be found in Chapter I, Section D.

I have chosen to use the hybrid transliteration pattern which is presently in vogue in works of this kind. Consonants follow the Ashkenazic pronounciation, and vowels the Sephardic. ח is rendered as *"ch"*; כ is transliterated as *"kh"*.

Ta'anis: Chapter One

SECTION A

Suggestion for Study

The first ten pages of this tractate deal with the prayers that are offered for rain. These "prayers" are divided into two components: *hazkarah* (invoking God's attribute of causing rain) and *sh'elah* (praying that it rain [appropriately]). The positions of the *tannaim* in this matter are dispersed throughout these ten pages. We suggest that you isolate these statements and study them as a unit (reviewing the "Summary Outlines" will aid you in locating these statements). On page 9 there is a review chart which outlines the tannaitic positions of when *morid hageshem*, is begun and on page 27 there is chart of the various positions of the *rishonim* regarding when *sh'elah* is to begin. Page 22 contain a list of the *amoraic* positions of when *sh'elah* is to cease and there is a full discussion beginning on page 12 regarding what is to be done when a person omitted or included *sh'elah* and *hazkarah* improperly. Finally, the laws of *hazkarah* and *sh'elah* in locales whose seasonal fluctuations differ from *Eretz Israel* are discussed beginning on page 28.

After reviewing this material, we turn your attention to the following overviews: *Halakhic* Justification of Praying for Rain; Importance of Tal; and The Relationship Between *Hazkarah* and *Sh'elah*.

Summary Outline

Mishna 2a

[1] On which day do we begin reciting גבורות גשמים (מוריד הגשם)? (See [12].)

[2] R. Eliezer: On the first day of *Sukkos*;
[3] R. Yehoshua: On the last day of *Sukkos*.

We do not mention rain on *Sukkos* because were it to rain on Sukkos this would be a negative sign. (The Jerusalem Talmud text reads, "It is not a blessed sign.")

[4] We do not ask for rain (*sho'alim*) until right before the rainy season.
[5] R. Yehudah: *Hazkarah* begins during *musaf* on the eighth day of *Sukkos*. *Hazkarah* continues until and including *shacharis* on the first day of *Pesach*.

Mishna 5a

[6] When does *sh'elah* (טל ומטר) conclude?
[7] R. Yehudah: It is said until *Pesach* passes עד שיעבור הפסח; (See [59]-[62].)
[8] R. Meir: It is recited until the end of Nisan.

Mishna 10a

[9] Tanna Kamma: *Sh'elah* begins on 3 Cheshvon.
[10] R. Gamliel: *Sh'elah* begins on 7 Cheshvon, i.e., 15 days after *Sukkos*.

Summary Outline: 2a

G'mara

[11] *Mishna Rosh Hashanah* establishes that "On *Sukkos* there is a judgment regarding water." Given that rain does not fall automatically, prayer is necessary. To this end, the *Mishna* inquires when this prayer should commence.
[12] R. Yochanan: Rain in the *Mishna* is assigned the adjective גבורות since it falls powerfully.
[13] The Talmud interprets the expression "to serve Him (ולעבדו) with **all** your heart," as referring to *t'fillah*. (We truly serve God when we believe in our inner souls that He is the **sole** source of all that which occurs in the universe.)

The juxtaposition of the verses "To love the Lord your God and to serve him (ולעבדו) with all your heart," and "That I will give the rain of your land in its season..." serves to teach that prayer is a prerequisite to rain. (See Overview: The *Halakhic* Justification in Praying for Rain.)

[14] R. Yochanan: There are three areas in which God retains exclusive control:

1. Rain
2. Childbirth
3. Resurrection

[15] In Israel a fourth category was included:

4. Sustenance

[16] R. Yochanan [14] subsumes sustenance under the rubric of rain. (*M'romei Sadeh*: Eventhough on 9a R. Yochanan distinguishes rain and sustenance, they, nevertheless, are the same in the sense that God maintains control over them both.)

Overview

The *Halakhic* Justification in Praying for Rain

The G'mara [13] finds it necessary to raise the question: How is it known that we are to pray for rain? This question seems superfluous. In what way is rain unique that it requires a special derivation that prayer is appropriate? No such question arises with regard to any other request made in *sh'moneh esreh**

We believe the answer lies in the following: All of our requests involve Divine action. In the case of rain, one must wonder if God has allowed Himself the freedom to act. Specifically, the Midrash tells us that when God created the world, He established the "Laws of Nature." These "laws" were made immutable **even to God**, that is, God did not empower Himself to modify these "laws." This rule is inviolable to such an extent that the only way God was "permitted" to do miracles, such as splitting the *yam*, was to make a pre-condition when He created the world that when necessary, He would be allowed to suspend the Laws of Nature to carry out this act. (*Breishis Rabbah* 5:4)

Based upon the above, there is a very strong theological question as to God's "right" to produce rain, given that causing precipitation when none should have fallen by "natural" means requires a violation of the laws of physics. (*Parshas D'rakhim* (31) cites an opinion that rainfall is to be considered a miracle.) For this reason, the G'mara considers a *s'vara*

**S'fas Emes* explains that the *G'mara's* question is, "How is it known that if one omits *morid hageshem* that he has to repeat the *Sh'moneh Esreh*?" *Keren Orah* interprets the *G'mara's* question to be, "Why is *hazkarah* necessary?

(logical argument) insufficient to derive that one may pray for rain; it requires support for this from a Biblical verse. [13] utilizes Scripture to conclude that when God created the world, He established it, such that, the "natural" order takes into account the prayers and deeds of the Jewish people.

Praying for Rain Within the Scheme of Modern Physics

Note: This section is reserved for readers with a scientific background.

It is important to note that the difficulty mentioned above arises only if we adopt the model of Classical Physics. In this scheme, the laws of the universe are deterministic. Students of Modern Physics know that after the postulation of Heisenberg's Uncertainty Principle, the physical laws of the universe are seen to be, merely, probabilistic. In practical terms, this means that one cannot speak of events, such as, passing one solid object through another, as being physically impossible; they must be considered merely to be improbable. As such, praying for rain when the meteorological conditions indicate that no rain will fall does not constitute a prayer for something which is physically impossible—only highly improbable.

Moreover, the indeterminism of Quantum Mechanics offers us a possible model for the mechanism which connects Torah study and the performance of *mitzvos* with occurrences in the Physical World. Distinctions between Quantum and Classical Mechanics arise for the most part on the sub-atomic level. With regard to macroscopic events, the two systems converge. This is because the probability for this convergence is overwhelming. Nevertheless, the possibility—as slight as it might be—exists for even a macroscopic event to "violate" Classical Physics.

Are the Law of Modern Physics Indeterministic?

We have stated as fact that Modern Physics believes the Universe to be indeterministic. However, this issue has been fiercely debated by Physicists and Philosophers of Science. The predominant group believes that the Universe is intrinsically indeterministic. Others, including Einstein, adopted the view that "Heisenberg's indeterminism" is only a consequence of our inability to measure simultaneously conjugate coordinates, but, intrinsically, the Universe is deterministic. To this end, these Philosophers of Science postulated the existence of a "hidden variable" which generates the deterministic Universe. The Hidden Variable Theory corresponds to Judaism's model of the physical universe presented by *Yad haK'tana*.

The Duality of Models in Judaism

While physicists speak of the Quantum Mechanical Model as being the more precise physical model and the Classical Model being a useful tool which in most cases "predicts" physical events accurately, *Yad haK'tana* posits a similar duality in Judaism's metaphysical superstructure. On the one hand, God established the Laws of Physics, on the other, *hashgacha pratis* (Divine providence). While for the most part, physical events correspond to the Laws of Physics, the latter is imprecise, for it fails to take into account the "hidden variable." The "hidden variable" is mankind's righteousness. The latter causes events to occur which "violate" the Laws of Physics. This "violation," however, is in concert with the more correct system of *hashgacha pratis*.

Rain and the actions of man

Interestingly, researchers have found with regard to the advent of rain that they cannot, yet, define *the* factor which causes precipitation to occur. Within the extent of current research it is possible for there to be two exactly "similar" situations in which it will rain in one and not in the other. Based upon this, it can be said that the actions of *Klal Yisrael* are the hidden variable which cause rain to fall. Prayer may, and indeed must, be said for rain because in creating the world, God set down the Universal Law, such that, the prayers and actions of the Jewish people are the "hidden variable" which can overcome the "physics" of the situation. This is the force of [13].

Summary Outline 2b & 3a

[17] R. Avuhu: R. Eliezer derives that *hazkarah* begins on the first day of *Sukkos* from *lulav* (not from נסוך המים [water libation]). (The connection is this: The *lulav* [four species] requires water for its growth. The Torah's directive to take the *lulav*—"which cannot exist without water" and whose function it is "to serve as a supplication for rain"— on the first day of *Sukkos* indicates that from this day onward it is appropriate to pray for rain.)

a. Some say R. Avuhu knew this by tradition;
b. Some say he derived this from [18].

[18] *Braisa*: When does *hazkarah* begin?

a. R. Eliezer: On the day the *lulav* is first taken;
b. R. Yehoshua: When the *lulav* is set aside (i.e., it no longer used);
c. (R. Eliezer): Optionally, a person may be *mazkir* through the year.

d. Rebbe: *Hazkarah* ceases concurrently with *sh'elah*.

e. R. Yehudah b. B'seira: From the second day of *Sukkos*;

The Torah's hint for נסוך המים (wherein the extra letters מ, י, מ [מים: water] are inserted into the text of the Sacrificial offerings of *Sukkos*) (Num. 29:17-35) begins on the second day of *Sukkos*.

f. R. Akiva: From the sixth day of *Sukkos*.

On the sixth day the Torah speaks of two libations, i.e., wine and water.

Digression: If, as stated, which *tanna* subscribes to the *Mishna* (*Sukkah* 4:1) that states, נסוך המים is performed all seven days of *Sukkos*?"

It is R. Yehoshua. He believes that the law of נסוך המים is known through הלכה למשה מסיני. (Rashi: It also could follow R. Eliezer.) (See below.)

[19] R. Yehoshua b. B'seira follows R. Yehudah [5].

Analysis: 2b-3a

Import of *Halakha l'Moshe MiSinai*

In analyzing the positions of the *tannaim vis a vis* when *hazkarah* begins, one question stands out. If *Sukkos* is the time that the judgment on the Earth's water supply is made, why, according to R. Yehoshua, should we not begin *hazkarah* during this *yom tov*? True, rain on *Sukkos* would be a סימן קללה, but the fact that it is a יום הדין should outweigh this consideration.

We believe that R. Yehoshua's position is motivated by the fact that נסוך המים is derived via an הלכה למשה מסיני. The difference between a law which is stated or derived from the Torah and one which is known מסיני is that in the former cases one could deduce other *halakhic* conclusions from this law, whereas in the latter case this may not be done.

In effect, the *limud* to be derived from נסוך המים being ordained מסיני is that while a judgment regarding rain is being carried forth on *Sukkos*, you, who are obligated to sit in a *Sukkah*, **must not** openly mention the attribute of rain. The Almighty has set forth the necessary procedures for the judgment to be made in your favor.

Summary Outline: 4a & b

[18]* Re: [4]

a. Rava: This is R. Yehoshua's view and אין שואלין means אין מזכירין.

b. Abaye: It could follow R. Eliezer; it refers to *sh'elah*.

[19]* Re: [4]: Second version

Rava posits [18b].*

Chart

Tannaitic Positions Regarding the Commencement of *Hazkarah*

Tanna	Day	Starting Prayer
R. Eliezer [2]	1st Day of Sukkos	Shacharis[1], Musaf[2]
R. Yehoshua [3]	Sh'mini Atzeres	Ma'ariv[3], Shacharis[4], Musaf[5]
R. Yehudah [5]	Sh'mini Atzeres	Musaf
R. Yehoshua [18B]	Hoshana Rabbah Sh'mini Atzeres	Minha[6] Ma'ariv[7], Schacharis[8], Musaf[9]
R. Yehudah b. B'seira [18e]	2nd Day of Sukkos	Ma'ariv[10]
R. Akiva [18f]	6th Day of Sukkos	Ma'ariv

1. Rashi (3a), Tosefos (2b), Talmid haRamban, Ran, Riv'van and S'fas Emes.
2. Ramban (See *Tosefos Yom Tov*).
3. Ritva, *Ohr Zaru'a, Riv'van, Nimukei Yosef, G'vuros Ari.*
4. Rashi (3a), Ran, Talmid haRamban, Riv'van, and *Chazzon Ish*.
5. Ramban (See *Tosefos Yom Tov), Jerusalem Talmud.*
6. R. Chananel (4a), R. Gershom (4a), Rashi (2b,3a) and Ritva.
7. Tosefos, Rashi (4a) [See Rav Reinsburg (2b)].
8. *Tosefos Rid.*
9. *Jerusalem Talmud.*
10. *G'vuros Ari.*

Analysis

(1) is derived from [18a].

(2), (5) and (9) are derived from Jerusalem Talmud [20]-[25]. A second reason is found in [32]. No mention is made of R. Eliezer's position in this matter. However, as the *G'mara* is silent on this point, it would appear that it is plausible that he agrees with R. Yehudah in this matter.

(3) is derived as follows. As the day begins at night, so too, should the *t'fillah*.

(4) derives from two points:

a. *musaf* is ruled out from the *G'mara's* comment on (3a) that R. Yehoshua of the *Mishna* and [19] are different.

b. If R. Yehoshua ruled that one was to begin at *ma'ariv*, he would have used the unambiguous term *leil*.

(6): This is the literal meaning of [18b]. This is bolstered by interpreting Rava's opinion [19a] that *morid hageshem* and *tal u'matar* are begun on *Hoshana Rabbah*.

(7) assumes that *Hoshana Rabbah* can be ruled out because rain on this day would be a *siman k'lalah*. The Babylonian Talmud disagrees with the Jerusalem Talmud ([22] and [24]).

(8) maintains that R. Yehoshua of *Mishna* and *Braisa* hold equivalent positions. While no commentary adopts this position we list it because of its possibility.

(10) believes that *nisuch hamayim* occurs at night. Also, if *hazkarah* should begin at *musaf*, the *G'mara* would have been more explicit.

Summary Outline: Jerusalem Talmud 1:1, 1:2

Announcing מוריד הגשם/הטל

With regard to the reason that מוריד הגשם/הטל is begun on *musaf* whereas all other changes in *t'fillah* commence at *ma'ariv*, the *Midrash Aggada* (cited in Talmid HaRamban, p. 12) states that a person does not gain his composure until *musaf*. The Jerusalem Talmud offers other reasons. One reason [27] requires that an announcement be made before this *t'fillah* can commence. While this law is not to be found in the Babylonian Talmud it is quoted for purposes of *halakha* in the *Shulchan Arukh*. It is to this G'mara that we now turn.

Jerusalem Talmud (1:1)

[20] R. Yehoshua: [*Hazkarah* begins] when the *lulav* is put down (presumably on *Hoshana Rabbah*).

[21] R. Mana: A *lulav* is *kasher* the entire day. (Thus, *hazkarah* does not begin on *Hoshana Rabbah*).

[22] Why don't we begin *hazkarah* at *ma'ariv*?

[23] Not everyone is present. (People not present will not realize they must be *mazkir*.)

[24] Why don't we begin at *shacharis*?

[25] He [those not present for *ma'ariv*] will think that *hazkarah* began at night. (Thus next year the person would begin *hazkarah* at night, or would mistakingly pray an additional *sh'moneh esreh* for *shacharis*.)

[26] R. Chiyya b. Maria: This is how your father, R. Yona, would explain it.

[27] R. Chagai/R. Pdas: An individual may not be *mazkir* until the *sh'liach tzibbur* has been *mazkir*.

[28] R. Simon/R. Yehoshua b. Levi: In the *sh'liach tzibbur* this is dependent (We put in no punctuation as rishonim dispute whether this is a declarative or an interrogative sentence. See below.)

[29] R. Mana to R. Chagai: Do you argue [(presumably) with [8]]?

[30] R. Chaga: "No!" ; [8] refers to *geshem*, [9] to *tal*.

[31] Once they stood up to pray it is as if it was "mentioned" by the *sh'liach tzibbur*.

1:2

[32] R. Avun/R. Yochanan: R. Yehudah's reason is so that the festivals "go out" with the recitation of *tal*.

Analysis

<1> a. R. Amram Gaon: Only the *shliach tzibbur* begins מוריד הגשם for *musaf*. This is based upon both the language of the *Mishnah*, *"he who is the chazzan recites"* and [27]. Other *rishonim* maintain that the congregation recites מוריד הגשם at *musaf*.

b. Ravia: Based on [27] a person who is sick and prays at home should not *daven musaf* until such time that the congregation prays *musaf*.

c. Ra'avad: [27] applies to *geshem* and *tal*.

This position seems to contradict [30]. *Bach* resolves this by explaining that in [30], R. Chagai is presenting R. Simon's position. He, however, does not make this distinction. Ra'avad follows R. Chagai. *Taz* explains that [30] refers to an individual who prays. R. Simon distinguishes *tal* from *geshem* in the latter situation.

Problem of those who do not say מוריד הטל in the summer

A problem arises for people who do not say מוריד הטל in the summer. Given the Ra'avad's position how should these people conduct themselves during *musaf*? *Poskim* feel it is improper to announce that we should cease saying מוריד הגשם; as rain is considered a blessing (see 19a). For this reason they conclude that the congregation should recite מוריד הגשם in *musaf*.

Shulchan haTahor, however, offers a novel solution. He argues that just as the *chazzan* says מוריד הטל in his *t'fillah* although this is not done throughout the year, so too, should the congregation. There is a good deal of merit to this suggestion as per [32]. (We make this point from the perspective of theory. People should not change the custom of their congregations in this matter.)

Summary Outline: 3 a & b; Jerusalem Talmud

Mentioning the Attributes of *Tal* and *Ruchos* (Winds)

Babylonian Talmud

[33] *Braisa*(3a): The rabbis did *not* require the mentioning of *tal* and *ruchos*; if one wishes, he *may* mention these.

[34] R. Yochanan(3a): The reason is that *tal* and *ruchos* are never withheld.

Even though Eliyahu asked God to withhold dew as well as rain (because of the wickedness of King Achav) God never went along with Eliyahu's ban on dew (I Kings 17). Nevertheless, God did withhold dew of *blessing*.

[35]

If a person—	משיב הרוח	מוריד הגשם
Said in Non-rainy season	Need *not* repeat *t'fillah*	Mush repeat *t'fillah*
Omitted in rainy season	Need *not* repeat *t'fillah*	Must repeat *t'fillah*

[36] R. Yochanan(4b): If a person said *He causeth the wind to pass and the dew to disappear*—he need not repeat the *t'fillah*.

[37] *G'mara*(4b): Early clouds [which come before the rain] are *never* withheld. Late clouds [which follow the rain] can be withheld.

[38] *G'mara*(4b): Regular winds are never withheld, but extraordinary winds [which are necessary for winnowing] are withheld.

Jerusalem Talmud

[39] (1:1) Concerning whether God withheld dew as per Eliyahu's request: This is disputed between R. Yossi and Rabbanan. It is unknown who held which position.

[40] R. Shimon b. Lakish(1:1): From the time of Avraham, dew was never withheld.

[41] R. Shmuel b. Nachman(1:1): Rain will fall when a *tzaddik* prays for it; dew does not fall as the result of the prayers of any man; God never withholds it.

[42] R. Zera/R. Chanina(1:1):

a. If a person mentioned *tal* in the rainy season (but not *geshem*) he does *not* repeat the *t'fillah*.
b. If he mentions rain in the non-rainy season he *must* repeat the *t'fillah*.

[43] *G'mara*(1:1): [42] is distinguished from [33] in that in [33] there was simply an omission; in [42] the prayer inserted is *"mikal."* Commentaries offer different interpretations of this word. See below.

[44] *G'mara*(1:1): If a person in the rainy season neglected to mention both rain and dew the *t'fillah* has to be repeated.

Analysis

<2> Regarding [42a]:

a. The *halakha* according to *Rif, Rambam, Ramban and Shulchan Arukh* follows [42a].
b. Ra'avad claims that the Babylonian Talmud disagrees with [42a] as per [33]. Nevertheless, Ra'avad is subservient to Rif's opinion.

Note: Aside from the technical derivation made by Ra'avad in arriving at his conclusion that the two *Talmudim* argue, we believe, that there is another strong reason to adopt this view. Namely the Babylonian Talmud posits that dew is never withheld [34]; whereas the Jerusalem Talmud cites an *amora* who believes that *tal* is sometimes completely withheld. It follows, therefrom, that for the Babylonian Talmud the prayer is completely irrelevant. This is not so as far as the Jerusalem Talmud is concerned. The prayer serves an important function—it requests a commodity which is sometimes withheld. This is the basis for [42a]. For a fuller explanation see the Overview: Significance of *Tal*.

c. *Tal* serves instead of *geshem*—

1. *Beis Yosef*: Because praise concerning something which was necessary for the world was offered;
2. *Taz*: Because both are essential for the "life of the world."

<3> **Ran: On the customs regarding the mentioning of dew, wind and clouds**

In the following chart we have outlined when and where prayers for wind, clouds and dew are inserted into our *t'fillos*:

	Dew	Wind	Clouds
Summer	*Hazkarah*	X	X
Rainy Season	*Sh'elah*	*Hazkarah*	X

Ran's Analysis

a. Dew is—

1. Mentioned either as a *hazkarah* or *sh'elah* throughout the year because it is constantly beneficial;
2. Said **either** as *hazkarah* **or** *sh'elah* but not both to show that its being mentioned is voluntary; as per [33];
3. Included as *sh'elah* in the rainy season while for wind there is merely *hazkarah*. This is because dew is more beneficial than wind. (Rambam's *nusach* contains the *hazkarah* for *tal* throughout the year.)

b. Wind is—

1. Mentioned (*hazkarah*) in the wintertime because in that season it serves to dry the ground;
2. Not mentioned in the summertime because during this season it is potentially destructive.

c. Clouds are—

Not mentioned in the *t'fillah* at all because their benefit is not readily discernible.

<4> Customs regarding saying מוריד הטל in the summertime

a. נוסח ספרד does recite *tal* based on [42a].

This has the advantage that if one forgot to recite מוריד הגשם in the fall, he need not repeat the *t'fillah* because of [42a].

b. נוסח אשכנז (except for those who follow the Vilna Gaon) does not recite *tal* based upon [33].

<5> Regarding the inclusion of the words משיב הרוח in the summer time for those who follow <4a>—

a. *Bach and Magen Avraham*: It is said by those in <4a>;

b. *L'vushe S'rad*: It is *not* said because of [35a].

"Need not repeat" implies that *ab initio* it should not be said.

<6> Regarding one who recited *tal* and *geshem* in the summer

a. Ran: The *t'fillah* need not be repeated.

This is based upon response [43] to [42]. In [43] the G'mara distinguishes [42] from [33] and does not utilize the reason that rain in the summer is a curse; for in most instances it is not.

The reason that in [42b] the *t'fillah* must be repeated is because the person by-passed praying for *tal* which is always beneficial and in its place prayed for something (rain) which is sometimes harmful.

b. Rosh: *T'fillah* must be repeated.

Based on [42a].

c. The *halakha* follows Rosh.

<7> Regarding one who recited מוריד הגשם in the Summertime

a. If he did not complete the second *brakha* he begins the *brakha* over. This rectifies the false statement he made.

b. Rambam seems to indicate that he must return to the beginning of the *t'fillah*.

c. Vilna Ga'on follows [b].

d. *Mishna Brurah* follows [a]. (If he said בא״י he should say למדני חוקיך and return to the the beginning of the *brakha* (i.e., אתה גבור).

Summary Outline: 3b

One Who Forgets to Say מוריד הגשם During Rainy Season

[45] R. Yochanan (3a): If someone forgot to say מוריד הגשם in the rainy season he must repeat the *t'fillah*.

[46] *B'rakhos* 29a

a. R. Tanchum/R. Asi—

(1) Forgot מוריד הגשם : Must repeat;
(2) Forgot טל ומטר: Need *not* repeat.

b. Question: *Braisa*

(1) Forgot מוריד הגשם: must repeat;
(2) Forgot טל ומטר: must repeat.

c. Answer: [a2] concerns one who realizes his omission before he reaches שומע תפלה ; he recites טל ומטר in שומע תפלה . [b2] concerns one who did not recite טל ומטר at any point in the *Sh'moneh Esreh*.

Jerusalem Talmud (1:1)

[47] R. Zera/R.Huna: If he forgot either טל ומטר or מוריד הגשם he could include it in שומע תפלה The reason: If *sh'elah* may be included in שומע תפלה, *hazkarah* certainly can.

Analysis

<8> There is a general consensus that [46] and [47] dispute with regard to מוריד הגשם. The Babylonian Talmud's view is that only *sh'elah* (beseechment) may be included in שומע תפלה but not *hazkarah* (praise). As the *halakha* is in accordance with the Babylonian Talmud, the procedure for one who forgot to say מוריד הגשם is as follows:

a. If he remembers in the middle of מכלכל חיים—

(1) Raviah: He says מוריד הגשם and repeats מכלכל חיים ;
(2) Rosh: He says מוריד הגשם and continues from the point he was up to in the *brakha*—because the Rabbis did not establish a definite point in the *brakha* for reciting מוריד הגשם .

Mishna B'rurah agrees as does *Bach, Shulchan Arukh Harav. Mishna Brurah* adds that if the person already said

ונאמן אתה—he says מוריד הגשם and then begins ונאמן אתה.

b. If a person finished the *brakha* but did not start the next *brakha*—

Raviah: He inserts מוריד הגשם and continues the *t'fillah*;

Mishna Brurah reluctantly follows Ravia. (See *Biyur Halakha*).

c. If one said בא״י but did not recite the end of the *brakha*, he should say למדני חוקיך, משיב הָרוּח, and ונאמן אתה...

d. Once a person started אתה קדוש he must return to the beginning of the *t'fillah*.

Sequence Analysis: 3b-4a

Comparison of Rain to Torah; Vegetation to Man

On 4a the *G'mara* "digresses" from its discussion of the laws and properties of rain. This digression is of great significance, for it underscores a theme which is basic to the Tractate, "...for man is a tree of the field." (Deut. 20:19) If one desires to have an insight in the growth patterns of human beings, he need only investigate the growth of vegetation. In what follows, we demonstrate that there exists a clear parallel between the *ma'amarim* on 3b which describe the properties of rain and those on 4a which describe the properties of a young *talmid chakham*.

[48] Winds after rain can have either a good or bad effect based upon their intensity.	[53] Rava: (Young tal.): The *middos* he develops after his learning is as crucial as his learning.
After Rain	**After learning Torah**
[49] Wind is as beneficial as was the rain.	[54] Rava: As above.
[50] Cloudiness is as beneficial as was the rain.	[55] Rava: It is good for a *talmid chakham* to be as strong as iron. [A cloud is symbolic of a heaven which is as unyielding as iron.]
[51] Sun is twice as beneficial as was the rain.	[56] Revina: A *talmid chakham* should conduct himself in an easygoing manner. [It is extremely beneficial for a *talmid chakham* to possess a personality which is as cheerful as the sun.]

[52]Snow is five times as beneficial to the mountains as rain is to the earth.

[57]The written Torah is compared to rain; the oral Torah to snow (the water as the Torah is concealed in this form). The written Torah was given with "five *kolos*." The oral Torah is comparable to it. (*Ohr haTorah, Nakh*, p. 682.)

Sequence Analysis: 7a

The aggadic literature on 7a continues to develop the striking relationship which exists between rain and the Torah, as well as, between trees and man. This relationship can be put in the form of a mathematical proportion—

Rain::Torah = Tree::Man

Using this relationship, the *G'mara* cites a sequence of *ma'amarim* which begin with properties of rain and its relationship to the growth of vegetation and then moves on to the properties of Torah and the conditions whereby it be administered to properly develop a *talmid chakham*. We shall walk you through the ensuing cases and point out the general development of the theme.

Torah is equivalent to Rain: This is established by R. Yehudah:

[58] **A rainy day is equivalent to day Torah was given.**

The verse R. Yehudah cites (Deut. 32:2) discusses four types of rainfall. The *Sifri and G'mara* (19b) go into detail in explaining that rains of given intensities can be beneficial to some forms of vegetation but not others. Thus, drizzle is beneficial for vegetables, but does not benefit trees substantially. On the other hand, a heavy downpour is good for trees but can destroy saplings.

Drawing on the verse, "Man is as the tree of the field," (Deut. 20:19) Rava applies the analogy: As rain can be good or bad depending upon the recipient, so too—

[59] **If a person is a proper *talmid chakham* the Torah will benefit him; if not it will destroy him.**

If aside from his scholarship he is also a *tzaddik* then as a fruitbearing tree—

[60] R. Yochanan: **Eat of his fruit.**

If, on the other hand, he is not a *tzaddik*, albeit he is a *talmid chakham*, compare him to the **non-fruit-bearing tree** (for his inner decay prevents him from producing proper students)—

R. Yochanan: **At "times of war" tear him down* [in "peace time" do not learn from him"].**

Building of a Proper *Talmid Chakham*

Having compared **a man to a tree**, the Talmud next draws upon other analogies in nature to explicate how a *talmid chakham* is to be developed.

Early Training

[61] R. Chanina: [As we find in nature] iron sharpens iron, so too, a *talmid chakham* [should not grow up in a vacuum. Rather he] is [to be] sharpened by another *talmid chakham*.

Intermediate Training

[62] Rabbah b. b. Channah: [Even after a young *talmid chakham* has acquired the proper methodology, just as in nature] A fire can not be maintained except when a number of twigs are placed together, so too, [a student who possesses the fire of] Torah requires a group to maintain its [his] strength.

At an Advanced Level

[63] R. Yosi b. Chanina: A *talmid chakham* who studies alone arrives at foolish conclusions and thereby sins. [A *talmid chakham* must keep in contact with other *talmidei chakhamim*.]

"Learning" is Advanced through Students

Not only is contact with other *talmidei chakhamim* important, but one must seek to develop students because—

[64] R. Chanina: I learned a great deal from my Masters and colleagues, but I learned the most from my students.

Continuity of Torah Through Students

[65] R. Chanina b. Papa and R. Chanina b. Chama: If a person has a pious student, he should go to the student's home to teach him

*Even though Deut. 20:19) permits cutting down only non-fruit producing trees, Rambam (*M'lakhim 6:9) explains that it refers to a fruit-bearing tree whose produce has waned.*

Torah if for some reason the student can not come to him. [This is not true if the student lacks the necessary piety.]

Another Relationship Between Torah and Water

[66] R. Chanina b. Idi and R. Oshiya: [As water seeks the lowest level] Torah [seeks the humblest souls and] can only be acquired and maintained by those who are humble.

Aggadita: 4a

Young *Talmid Chakham*

[67] **Rava: A Rabbinical student is like a sprout which grows under a rock; once it sprouts forth it continues to grow.**

Rashi: Once he has made a name for himself, the young *talmid chakham* will continue to grow in stature.

R. Chananel: He will burst forth all at once.

Analysis

Rava's *ma'amar* teaches a number of important lessons:

1. In the growth pattern, it is natural for stagnation to occur at pivotal points.

A first grader finds it tremendously difficult to put together the sounds of the vowels and consonants and feels frustrated because he is not making progress. A student beginning Rashi finds great difficulty in reading without "dots." A high school/beis midrash student has difficulty understanding *rishonim* and *acharonim*. All these students can become very frustrated because they do not believe they are making any progress at all. Rava's *ma'amar* underscores that they should not lose heart; they are experiencing the normal growth pattern.

The learning process runs parallel to the time/temperature curve of water. When one heats ice, each calorie of energy added causes an increase in temperature. This continues until the water has reached a temperature of 32 degrees Fahrenheit. At this point, for a given amount of added energy there is no temperature rise. The same phenomenon occurs at the boiling point (212 degrees).

At these temperatures, a first-time observer would posit that indeed nothing was happening; added heat could not cause an additional temperature rise. But, in reality, at these temperatures what is actually happening is that chemical bonds are being broken within the molecules. Thus, while outwardly nothing seems to be happening, internally the body is preparing for its new status.

When a student begins a new area of intellectual pursuit— no matter what level of student he is—his initial progress is bound to be slow. Rava emphasizes that this should not be a source of frustration. The student must internalize that while unobserved, even to himself, each and every day he is making very important progress. Each moment, a great deal of inner potential is being built up. Once this is accomplished he will be ready to soar ever higher.

2. It takes many years to develop one's individual perspective (*derekh*) towards learning.

In the formative years, a student has to master a great deal of material. A good part of what he studies is mere rote. He must master a myriad of *halakhos, memros, and machloksim*. Most often, he loses sight of the forest because of the trees. However, once he begins to put all of these into place and understands how they are inter-related, his understanding no longer grows linearly but exponentially.

Aggadita: 4a

[68] **Rava: If a young Rabbinical student is overexcited; this is caused by the study of Torah.**

Rashi explains that a young *talmid chakham* becomes excited because he has a much broader perspective of life and a deeper understanding of things than most other people. This causes him to take things more seriously.

A person who studies Torah does not view events as singular occurrences. Rather, he is trained to be sensitive to the consequences of events. For this reason, he is much more likely to get excited over things which he clearly sees to be greatly beneficial or detrimental, while others cannot understand, "what is he getting so excited about."

While some look negatively on this, it must be realized that this quality is crucial to the essence of a *talmid chakham*. This is pointed out in the next *ma'amar*.

[69] **R. Ashi: Any *talmid chakham* who is not as strong as iron is not a *talmid chakham*.**

One who studies Torah must be cautious and certain before adopting a particular opinion, but once done, he must be very strong about proposing and defending his views, especially where the honor of Torah is concerned. Yet —

[70] Revina: Nevertheless, a person must learn to conduct himself in an easy going manner.

Revina makes the following two points—

1. As a person matures he must learn how to handle his emotions so that they do not get in the way of his carrying out his goals. Often, a person who is overemotional is not effective in convincing others of the correctness of his position.
2. As a person matures, he learns when to debate and when to remain silent or to acquiesce. This gives his views greater weight on issues he deems truly significant.

[71] Re: [4]

a. Rava: This is R. Yehoshua's view and אין שואלין means אין מזכירין."

b. Abaye: It could follow R. Eliezer; it refers to *sh'elah*.

[72] Re: [4]: Second version

Rava posits [71b].

Summary Outline: 4b

The G'mara deals with an apparent contradiction between R. Yehudah's statement in the first and second *mishnayos* with regard to the question—

Until when in the year does one ask for rain (*sh'elah*)?

[73] R. Yehudah in Mishna (2a)[R.Y.$_1$]: Until and including *shacharis* on the first day of *Pesach*.

[74] R. Yehudah in Mishna (5a)[R.Y.$_2$]: עד שיעבור הפסח (literally: Until the passing of *Pesach*).*

Several answers are offered—

	[73] concerns—	[74] concerns—
[75] R. Chisda	*Hazkarah*	*Sh'elah*

[76] Ula	There exist two versions of R. Yehudah	
[77] R. Yosef	*Hazkarah*	*Sh'elah*; which was said during *shacharis* of the 1st day of *Pesach* by a "translator."**
[78] Rabbah	*Hazkarah*	*Sh'elah*; which was said until *musaf**** of 14 Nisan; the time of the offering of the pascal lamb.

* *G'vuros Ari*: Eventhough for purposes of *Halakah* this term is defined with regard to vows applicable "until the rains cease" (*N'darim* 62b) as the end of *Pesach*, given that the rainfall this late in the season is not of great benefit [75], [77] and [78] maintain there is no reason to pray for rain after *Pesach*.

** *G'vuros Ari*: If a person inadvertently recites the weekday *sh'moneh esreh* on *Yom Tov* and realized his mistake while reciting ברך עלינו he does not recite טל ומטר.

*** R. Gershom believes it was said during *mincha* as well.

Analysis

Regarding R. Chisda [75]

Ula questions R. Chisda's answer. Ula considers it unjustifiable for there to be *sh'elah* without *hazkarah*.

In the Overview: Significance of *Tal*, the reason is given as to why the recitation of *tal* is begun on the first day of Pesach. Based upon that analysis it can be argued that R. Chisda adopts the view that beginning on Pesach, מוריד הגשם should be replaced by מוריד הטל. In addition, R. Chisda follows the Jerusalem Talmud [42] which states that if one mentions מוריד הטל instead of מוריד הגשם he need not repeat the *t'fillah*.

There is a second possibility. Ula's question is based upon the notion that asking, *sh'elah*, must be preceded or succeeded by praise; as is the case in *t'fillah*. This position is rejected by R. Chisda. He maintains that *hazkarah* need only precede *sh'elah*, but need not accompany or follow it. (See *G'ra y. B'rakhos* 4:4)

Regarding R. Yosef [77]:

R. Yosef understands [74] to refer to the *shacharis* service *Pesach morning. The term "יעבור" is associated with the chazzan* יעבור לפני התבה.

Rabbah asks, "But there is no *brakha* in which to recite טל ומטר on Yom Tov?

R. Yosef replies that this is done by the מתורגמן (translator).

Rishonim explain this as follows:

a. Rashi, R. Gershom: The מתורגמן incorporates טל ומטר as part of the sermon. See *S'dei Chemed* (5:231:12) regarding the recitation of הטוב והמטיב on a new *shul*; R. David Katz incorporated this *brákha* in the sermon.

b. R. Chananel: The מתורגמן is appointed by the *beis din* to offer needed prayers.

Regarding Rabbah [78]

One must wonder about not saying טל ומטר at *mincha* on 14 Nisan eventhough מוריד הגשם will continue to be said until *musaf* on the 15th. We maintain that this is consistent with R. Yehudah's *halakhic* position.

In *Pesachim*, R. Yehudah disputes R. Shimon in the following issues—

a. R. Yehudah believes that the observance of *Pesach* in Egypt was for an entire week;
R. Shimon is of the opinion that it was only one day.

b. R. Yehudah believes that בל יראה is applicable starting on the 14th at noon;
R. Shimon believes it begins at night.

R. Shlomo Kluger in his Hagadah, *Ma'aseh Y'de Yotzer* explains the dispute between Ben Zoma and the Chakhamim regarding whether the third paragraph of *sh'ma* will be recited in the Messianic Era to revolve about whether Jews who were taken out Egypt were redeemed because of their own merit or because God had to redeem them so that they would not become unsalvageable. If they were worthy then *G'ulas Mitzrayim* was completed; any future redemption is completely independent of *Y'tziyas Mitzrayim* so there is no point in mentioning Egypt at the time of the future redemption. This is not the case if they were not worthy when they were redeemed from Egypt. In the latter case, the Messianic Redemption is the culmination of *Y'tziyas Mitzrayim* and, as such, will be lauded at the time of *Mashi'ach*.

We believe that R. Yehudah and R. Shimon argue on this very same point. R. Yehudah believes that the nation was worthy of redemption. Thus the observance of *Pesach* in Egypt was seven days, and the offering of the pascal lamb was an integral part of the Festival. Thus בל יראה begins at this point.

R. Shimon disagrees. He believes that *Pesach* and *Chag haMatzos* are two different Festivals. In Egypt only *Pesach* was celebrated. The nation was not ready for *Chag haMatzos*; God gave the *mitzvah* of the pascal lamb to afford them a *mitzvah* in whose merit they could be temporarily redeemed. Thus בל יראה is tied strictly to *Chag haMatzos*.

According to R. Yehudah, the *k'dushah* of *Pesach* begins at noon on the 14th. With the coming of *Pesach* the rainy season has ended. Nevertheless, one continues the *hazkarah* because praise should extend beyond *sh'elah*, as we see from the model of the *sh'moneh esreh*.

Summary Outline/Rishonim: 4b, 6a, 10a

Halakha With Regard to *Sh'elah* and *Hazkarah*

Note: The *ma'amarim* with regard to the *halakha* of when *sh'elah* and *hazkarah* commence are dispersed over a number of pages. We suggest that you study these statements as a unit. The following is a collection of the statements and the analysis of the commentaries.

4b

[79] R. Asi/R. Yochanan: *Halakah* is as R. Yehudah [5] (hazkarah begins *Sh'mini Atzeres*).

[80] R. Eliezer/R. Yochanan (6a): *Halakah* is as R. Gamliel [86b] (*sh'elah* begins on 7 Cheshvon).

[81] R. Yochanan: The commencement and cessation of both *hazkarah* and *sh'ela* are on the same day.

[82] Question: [79-81] contradict each other (R. Yochanan is the author of all three. This motivates the *G'mara*'s second response. According to the text which considers R. Eliezer the author of [80], the crux of the question is that R. Chisda was the rebbe of R. Eliezer. The *G'mara's* response is that he was, in fact, a *talmid-chaver* of R. Eliezer. Hence, they could disagree. (*M'nachem Meishiv Nefesh/HaGahos Seder haDoros*)

[83] Answer 1: [79] is applicable in Israel; [80] in Babylonia (there, crops are left out to dry during the month of Tishri; the rains would be detrimental.)

[84] Answer 2: [79] is applicable today; [80] applied when the Temple stood.

6a

[85]

First Rain—

a. R. Meir: 3 Cheshvon;
b. R. Yehudah: 7 Cheshvon;
c. R. Yosi: 17 Cheshvon.

10a

[86] *Sh'elah* begins—

a. Tanna Kamma: 3 Cheshvon
b. R. Gamliel: 7 Cheshvon

[87] R. Elazar: *Halakha* is as R. Gamliel.
[88] Chanania: In Babylonia *sh'elah* begins 60 days after the equinox.
[89] The *halakha* follows [88].
[90] Is "60th days" inclusive of the 60th day?

a. Rav: Yes;
b. Shmuel: No;
c. R. Papa: The *halakha* follows Rav [a].

Analysis

<9> Rashi:

Re: [83] In Babylonia *hazkarah* and *sh'elah* begin on 7 Cheshvon; in Israel *hazkarah* begins on *Sh'mini Atzeres*.
Re: [84] At the time of the Temple, *hazkarah* and *sh'elah* were not recited until 7 Cheshvon. Today we are *mazkir* on *Sh'mini Atzeres*.

<10> Ran:

Re [86]: R. Gamliel said *sh'elah* begins on 7 Cheshvon because of the *o ieh regel*. This reason does not apply today. If so why should *sh'elah* still commence on 7 Cheshvon? Even after the *churban* people used to gather at the sight of the *Mikdash* on the *r'galim*.

An alternate possibility is that there are three gradations with regard to when *sh'elah* begins. Namely—

a. Babylonia: 60 days after the equinox;
b. Israel: Immediately after *Sukkos*;
c. A place where they dry out crops: 7 Cheshvon.

Ran reports that setting three times for the commencement of *sh'elah* is contrary to the view of Rif and Rambam.

<11> *Chazzon Ish*: According to [83], [85b] speaks of Babylonia. This is in contrast to [87]. Also Rashi <9> is difficult in that he claims *sh'elah* can take place immediately after *Sukkos* which is contrary to [85].

Answer: R. Yehudah believes one can be *sho'el* immediately after *Sukkos* as there is no longer the question of grave financial loss. R. Meir, however, postpones *sh'elah* until 3 Cheshvon because for him this is the start of the rainy season. R. Gamliel waits until 7 Cheshvon because of the *oleh regel*.

<12> *Bach* (R.H. 581): *Hazkarah* and *n'tilas lulav* commence on *Sukkos* even though the rainy season begins some time after this because it is important that *Klal Yisrael* begin to entreat God at a time when they are free of sin.

Chart and Analysis: 4b, 6a, 10a

Dates for Beginning *Sh'elah* in our Times

Israel	23 Tishri	Ran*, Ritvah, Hashlama, Talmid haRamban
	7 Cheshvon	Rif, Rambam, Geonim, Shulchan Arukh
Babylonia	60 days after autumnal equinox	All agree
Diaspora (other than Babylonia)	23 Tishri; 7 Cheshvon (Depending upon conditions)	Ran, Meiri, Custom of Narvonne, Rosh, Hashlama
	60 days after equinox	Rif, Rambam,Talmid haRamban Riv'van, Ritva Shulchan Arukh**

* Unless there are *oleh regel* (even in our times).

** If one erred and was *sho'el* after 7 Cheshvon he need not repeat the *sh'moneh esreh*. *(Shulchan Arukh HaRav and Shulchan HaTahor.)*

Analysis

The varying views stem from alternative interpretations of the *G'mara*. These are as follows:

Alternative 1 (Ran, *Hashlamah*, Custom of Narvonne):

a. In Israel, *sh'elah* begins 23 Tishri (from [84]);

b. In Babylonia, *sh'elah* begins 60 days after autumnal equinox (from [87]);
c. Places which need rain but for extenuating circumstances cannot ask on 23 Tishri, postpone asking until 7 Cheshvon.

[84] does not negate [83] it just offers another possible answer. Thus, [86] and [87] are, also, not contradictory opinions. [86] speaks of places in the diaspora which need rain more frequently than Babylonia.

Alternative 2 (Ritva):

a. Israel: *Sh'elah* begins 23 Tishri (from [84]);
b. Babylonia: *Sh'elah* begins 60 days after equinox (from [87]);
c. Other places: *Sh'elah* begins either 23 Tishri or 60 days after Autumnal Equinox.

[84] negates [83]. R. Gamliel speaks only of *Eretz Yisrael* during the Temple period. [87] is the only alternative date to 23 Tishri. Locales are free to choose either of these alternatives.

Alternative 3 (Rif, Rambam):

a. Israel : *Sh'elah* begins on 7 Cheshvon;
b. Diaspora: *Sh'elah* begins 60 days after equinox.

Chazzon Ish explains this position as follows: R. Gamliel [80, 86] and Chanania [87] dispute. The essence of their dispute turns on the question of whether one should begin *sh'elah* at the time of the rainy season or only when it is needed. Chanania believes it is only to be asked for when needed. Thus in Babylonia it should not be asked for until 60 days after the equinox. R. Gamliel believes it should be asked for at once. Nevertheless, when there are extenuating circumstances, such that the rain would cause problems then asking for it may be postponed.

We follow Chanania for purposes of *halakha*. Thus, we adopt the view that one should not ask for rain until the rainy season. For Israel this is the time of First Rain (*R'viyah Rishonah*). Rambam and Rif follow R. Yehudah's view in this matter; that First Rain occurs on 7 Cheshvon.

Summary Outline: 14b

Ninveh: Rain

[91] Ninveites asked Rebbe: As our location requires rain in the summer are we considered as individuals (and we thus pray for rain in

שומע תפלה) or as a congregation (and pray for rain in ברך עלינו)?

[92] Rebbe: [Even though you are a municipality, with regard to טל ומטר] you are considered to be individuals.

[93] Question on Rebbe from the following *braisa*: R. Yehudah: These laws apply only when Jews are in Israel and the seasons are regular. (Thus Ninveh should be considered as an independent community.)

[94] Answer: Rebbe has the status of a *tanna* and may disagree with a statement in a *braisa*.

[95] R. Nachman: They [the Ninveites] pray for rain in ברך עלינו (they are considered a congregation).

[96] R. Sheshes: They recite the prayer in שומע תפלה.

[97] *Halakha*: They recite the prayer in שומע תפלה.

Analysis

<13> R. Gershom and Rashi understands [93] to refer to the "order of fasts." R. Chananel believes that it refers to the schedule for praying for rain.

<14> The following question is advanced by the *rishonim*: Based on *Avodah Zara* 8a which states that if someone is in need of sustenance he may add a personal prayer in ברך עלינו why are the Ninveites restricted to reciting טל ומטר in שומע תפלה?

Ran, Talmid haRamban: In the case of sustenance, the individual's prayers do not negatively impinge on others. Rain during the summer, however, is a detriment to others. Therefore, individuals may not pray in the name of the entire congregation. A prayer inserted in שומע תפלה is understood to be a personal prayer and it is, thus, not a prayer directed towards others.

Miktam/Hashlamah: Praying for sustenance is a natural extension of ברך עלינו. Praying for rain is a factor which is external to פרנסה. Under the circumstances it may not be added in this *brakha*.

<15> Rid: [92] applies only to asking for rain (*sh'elah*). *Hazkarah*, however, may only be recited until *Pesach*.

<16> With regard to an entire country which needs rain—

Rosh distinguishes between a city and a country. If a country requires rain one may pray for it in ברך עלינו. *Magid Mishna* disagrees. He rules that as far as prayers for rain are concerned we totally follow the normal needs of the land of Israel. With regard to fasting, however, each locality is to carry on its own schedule of fasts depending upon the specific needs of that location.

Overview

Relationship Between *Hazkarah* and *Sh'elah*

In the *Mishna*, we find a dispute between various *tannaim* with regard to the question of when one begins to say *hazkarah* for rain and when *sh'elah* begins. Yet, all agree that *hazkarah* is a prerequisite to *sh'elah*. We shall presently explore the reason for this.

The first three blessings of the *sh'moneh esreh* are referred to as blessings of praise. In these blessings, God's attributes are enumerated. Yet, no attempt is made to catalogue all of the Almighty's attributes. On the contrary, the Talmud relates (*B'rakhos* 33b) that R. Chanina admonished a *sh'li'ach tzibbur* who included in the *sh'moneh esreh* the praises—האדיר, והעזוז, והראוי, והחזק,והאמיץ, והודאי, והנכבד(Majestic, Powerful, Awful, Strong, Fearless, Sure and Honored). He said to him, "Have you concluded all the praise of your master?" We, human beings, are incapable of explicating all of God's attributes. To this end, we have no right to include praises randomly, for, then, the impression would be given that God's praiseworthiness was limited to the extent of that praise.

The praises enumerated in the first blessing of the *sh'moneh esreh* are the attributes invoked in the Torah by our Patriarchs when praying or offering praise. The אנשי כנסת הגדולה chose to incorporate these attributes because they represent the manner and extent to which our forebearers understood God. It is only in these manifestations that we, their disciples, can relate to God.

The praises catalogued in the second blessing, אתה גבור , are also not arbitrary, nor are they an attempt at completeness. Rather, it is our belief, that *only* those attributes are included which demonstrate God's potential to fulfil a request that we will later make in the *t'fillah* (see below). Thus, *hazkaros* vary in accordance with *sh'elos*. If the *sh'elah* is seasonal, so too, is the *hazkarah*.

During the עשרת ימי תשובה when we must recognize God as the King who carries forth judgment המלך המשפט it is necessary to make the change in the third blessing from הא-ל הקדוש to המלך הקדוש On *Rosh Hashanah* and *Yom Kippur* we insert, ובכן תן פחדך, ובכן תן כבוד,ובכן צדיקים in the third blessing because these correspond to the blessings of מלכיות, זכרונות, שופרות (See *Beis Yosef/Kol Bo* : R.H. 582) So, too, in the case of rain, we may only recite the attribute of rain when we are going to ask for it. (R. Eliezer, a student of Shammai disagrees. Bet Shammai generates its *halakha* from the perspective of the Ideal Realm. On this level, God bestows His blessings in their proper time independent of when a given attribute is invoked.)

In the chart (p. 49B), we indicate how each attribute mentioned in the second *brakha* serves as the basis for a specific request that we intend to make in the "middle" thirteen *brakhos*.

Overview

Significance of *Tal*

Tal Should be recited on *Yom Tov*

We are well aware of the importance of *geshem* (rain); thus we understand the significance of praying for *geshem*. The function of *tal* is not as clear to us, and we tend to minimize its importance. Yet, the Jerusalem Talmud considers the *hazkarah* of *tal* to be significant. It explain that the reason we postpone the *hazkarah* of *geshem* until the last day of *Sukkos* and cease the *hazkarah* of *geshem* on the first day of *Pesach* is because it is important that *tal* be recited during the festival(שיצא המועדות בטל).

The importance of the recitation of *tal* during the Festivals is underscored by R. Huna's approach to R. Yehudah's position regarding the cessation of *hazkarah*. In response to the seeming contradiction between R. Yehudah's view in the first and second Mishnayos [see 5 & 7] R. Huna explains that it is R. Yehudah's belief that while *sh'elah* (טל ומטר) continues to be recited through *Pesach, hazkarah* ceases on the very first day. Aside from the question that is leveled against R. Huna from Ula, namely, "**How** could there be *sh'elah* without *hazkarah*?" [a] more basic question exists. Given that R. Yehudah believes that the rainy season extends to the end of *Pesach*, **Why** should *hazkarah* not be recited so long as *sh'elah* is recited? A full exposition will follow. For now, suffice it to say that R. Yehudah adopts the view that the recitation of *tal on yom tov* is so significant that it supercedes the *hazkarah* for *geshem* [32].

How could *Tal* be significant if it need not be recited?

We have indicated that being *mazkir tal* is of great significance. But this is contradicted by the *braisa* on 3a [33]. This *braisa* states that *tal* need not be recited. R. Chanina explains that this is because *tal* is never withheld. How can this law be reconciled with the Jerusalem Talmud's view that the recitation of *tal* is significant?

Furthermore, the *braisa* makes another law in the Jerusalem Talmud very difficult to understand. The latter rules that if someone in the rainy season substituted the *hazkarah* of מוריד הטל , he need not repeat the *sh'moneh esreh*. Given the Babylonian Talmud's view, Why should the recitation of something which need not be said at all exempt one from praying for something which is required? Furthermore, what relationship exists between *tal* and *geshem* that the *hazkarah* of one can exempt the other? This question is heightened when it is realized that this *halakha* does not follow with regard to *sh'elah*. In the latter case, most rishonim agree that *sh'elah* for *tal* cannot exempt one of his obligation to be *sho'el* for *geshem*. Why should there be a difference between *sh'elah* and *hazkarah*?

The Talmudim Argue as to Whether *Tal* is Withheld

The Jerusalem Talmud cites a dispute which serves to clarify its position with regard to *tal*. As opposed to R. Chanina's view that *tal* is never withheld, the Jerusalem Talmud cites a dispute in which an amora adopts the view that *tal* can be withheld. As such, the *hazkarah* of *tal* is not merely perfunctory; it is not merely the recitation of an attribute which is never withheld, but one which can be withheld. Thus, the status of *hazkaras tal* in the Jerusalem Talmud is greater than it is in the Babylonian Talmud. Yet it remains for us to understand why *hazkaras tal* can replace *hazkaras geshem*.

Difference Between *Tal* and *Tal Shel Brakha*

We have suggested that the Bavli and Yerushalmi disagree as to whether *tal* is withheld. R. Chanina states in the Bavli that it is withheld. The Yerushalmi cites a view that it is withheld and that this serves as the basis for the view that *hazkarah* of *tal* can exempt *hazkarah* of *geshem*. The difficulty of the premise as stated is that the author of the latter view which is stated in the Yerushalmi is none other than R. Chanina. Based on this we would suggest that R. Chanina's view is based upon the distinction made in the Bavli, namely, that *tal* is never withheld; what is withheld is *tal shel brakha*. Thus, all agree that *tal* in some form is never withheld. With this distinction cited, we can return to the previous question.

Tal* is Ontologically Greater than *Geshem

The status of *tal vis-a-vis geshem* is to be found in a pericope on 4a. R. Shmuel b. Nachmeni reports in the name of R. Yochanan that three people prayed improperly but, were answered properly: Eliezer, Shaul and Yiftach. R. Berekhya adds a fourth—the Nation of Israel. In their prayers, the Nation of Israel pleaded to God that He be as *geshem* to the nation. God answered that He would be as *tal* to the Jewish people. He reasoned as follows: Why should I relate to you as something which is sometimes given and sometimes withheld (i.e., *geshem*), I would rather relate to you as something which is never withheld (i.e., *tal*). How are we to understand God's response? What is the import of relating to us as *tal* or *geshem*?

God relates to the nation of Israel on two planes: *G'vurah* and *chesed* also known as *mida'as hadin and mida'as harachamim*. The difference in approach is that *g'vurah* and *din* require that God mete out to the nation of Israel their just dessert in accordance with their actions: reward for good deeds punishment for bad deeds. However, there is another level which God manifests at times. This level is that of the *middos* of *chesed* and *rachamim*. These *middos* dictate that God be gracious unto us even when we are undeserving. Ontologically, *chesed* is on a higher plane than *din*.

R. Berekhya's example points up the difference between *tal* and *matar*. *Tal* is equivalent to *chesed*; *geshem* to *din*. *Chesed* is ontologically prior to *din* and can override it.

Having reached this conclusion we can understand why it is that the *hazkarah* for *tal* exempts geshem, but the *sh'elah* for *tal* does not. In the case of *hazkarah* when we invoke the attribute of *tal* we are in effect calling on a higher attribute than that of *geshem*. We are beckoning God to treat us with his attribute of *chesed*. This *hazkarah* which invokes a higher attribute exempts the need to invoke a lower attribute. Where *sh'elah* is involved this is not the case. In the latter case it is physical rain which is needed and dew will not suffice.

A Deeper Understanding of *Tal* and its Relation to the *Yamim Tovim*

We will now turn our attention to the relationship of *tal* to the *yamim tovim*, specifically *Pesach*. First we must introduce several pericopes.

On 6a the G'mara cites a dispute among tannaim as to when the "Three Rains" of *yoreh* will fall. The opinions are as follows:

	Rain I	Rain II	Rain III
R. Meir	3 Cheshvon	7 Cheshvon	17 Cheshvon
R. Yehuda	7 Cheshvon	17 Cheshvon	23 Cheshvon
R. Yossi	17 Cheshvon	23 Cheshvon	1 Kislev

The whole pericope presents us with difficulties. To begin with, there is no source which informs us that there are "Three Fasts" for *yoreh*. Secondly, How are the dates arrived at? Are they derived empirically, or through some other manner? If the latter, what is the significance of these dates?

From the Jerusalem Talmud it appears that the dates are not empirically derived but are based upon Scripture. It makes a point of noting that the one date that all three tanna'im agree on is 17 Cheshvon; the day of the Flood (of Noah). We believe that each *tanna* bases himself upon his interpretation of the flood episode. For our purposes we will explain R. Yossi's position. [We do this because the other interpretations require kabbalistic explanations. See Ohr haTorah, *B'reishis* 1268-94 and App. R. Yossi interprets the Biblical sequence of the Flood as follows:

Originally, God intended to bring the Flood on 17 Cheshvon. However, He postponed this for a week in deference to the memory of Mesushelach, the *tzaddik* who died precisely at this time. The rains, therefore, began to fall on 23 Cheshvon. Yet, the rain that fell for the first seven days was blessed rain. God hoped that during this period the world would repent and that they would reap the benefit of this rain. It was only after they did not repent that God brought on the torrential and destructive Flood Rains. Thus, these three dates—17 Cheshvon, 23 Cheshvon and 1 Kislev were days designated as Rain Days.

The Midrash tells us that these rains not only fell on these days during the year of the Flood, but that it continued each and every year until the Beis haMikdash was built. To this end, the month after Tishri was originally called *Mabul* and when the Mikdash was built and the rain ceased to fall continuously during this month the name of the month was changed to *Bul*—the first letter—*"mem"* was dropped. (See *Pri Tzaddik, Parshas Noah*)

Tannaim Dispute the Dates of the *Mabul*

In our discussion we have assumed that the Flood occurred during Cheshvon, but this is actually disputed by *tannaim*. The dispute turns about the question, When was the world created? R. Eliezer and R. Yehoshua dispute as follows: (*R.H.* 10b-11a)

	R. Eliezer	R. Yehoshua
World Created	Tishri	Nisan
Birth of Avos	Tishri	Nisan
Birth of Yitzchak	Nisan	Nisan
Sarah, Rachel and Chanah conceived	Tishri	Tishri
Worked ceased in Egypt	Tishri	Tishri
Egyptian Redemption	Nisan	Nisan
Messianic Redemption	Tishri	Nisan

The G'mara in Rosh Hashana goes on to say that R. Eliezer who is of the opinion that the world was created in Tishri believes that the *Mabul* occurred in Tishri. R. Yehoshua, on the other hand, is of the opinion that the *Mabul* took place in Iyar. We will pursue R. Yehoshua's position since it will illuminate the relationship between *tal* and *Pesach*.

Mann first fell on 16 Iyar

Since the date of the Flood has intrinsic significance in R. Eliezer's scheme , so too, the date of the Flood has significance in R. Yehoshua's scheme. Its importance is to be derived from the Biblical account of the *mann*. The Torah tells us that the *mann* fell for the first time on 16 Iyar. [The day difference arises because depending upon the number of days in Nisan the thirty-first day after 15 Nisan could fall on 16 or 17 Iyar.] With regard to *mann* the Torah uses the expression "behold I will cause the *mann* to rain upon you from Heaven."

Relationship Between *Tal* and *Mann*

The fact that *mann* began to fall on this day takes on added significance once it is realized that there is a very strong relationship between *mann* and *tal*. Firstly, the Torah tells us that *tal* fell with the *mann*. Secondly, Chazal tie *tal* and *mann* together in that both are the food of the angels and they both fall whether deserved or undeserved.

The Characteristic of Nisan is Chesed

Above we recorded a dispute between R. Eliezer and R. Yehoshua with regard to whether a number of events occurred in Nisan or Tishri. One cannot help but wonder, what difference does it make? To be sure, we would be concerned about when the future redemption will take place, but what difference does it make whether the world was created in Nisan or Tishri especially since the date which is ascribed to Creation is arbitrary. Also, what is the relationship between past and future redemptions, if any?

To understand the significance of this dispute we must investigate the differences inherent between Nisan and Tishri. Tishri is the month in which Rosh Hashanah falls. During this month the entire world is judged. The characteristic of this month is *din*. Nisan, on the other hand, is the month of Israel's redemption. It is the month characterized by chesed. R. Eliezer's dispute with R. Yehoshua goes much further than the historical question of when the world was created. It deals with the question of which *middah* is greater *g'vurah* or *chesed.*

R. Eliezer is of the opinion that *g'vurah* is the ultimate *middah*. (This is consistent with his being a student of Beis Shammai.) This is manifested by the world being created in the month of Judgment. While God found it necessary for the Jewish people to be redeemed in Nisan this is because they needed that respite so God showed them mercy. This is only a temporary measure. The Messianic redemption can only come about if the Jewish people repent. Thus, the redemption will take place— appropriately in Tishri.

[The source for this division between the Egyptian and Messianic redemption is the Flood narration. There, according to R. Eliezer, we are told that Noah's ship rested on the mountain on 1 Nisan even though the Earth only became habitable in Tishri. According to R. Yehoshua, the ship's resting took place on 1 Tishri. This corresponds to the *p'kidah* (remembrance) of the Matriarchs on this day as well as the cessation of work in Egypt.]

R. Yehoshua, on the other hand, is of the opinion that the highest attribute is that of *chesed*. This is indicated by the world's being created in Nisan and all redemptions taking place in Nisan. The *chesed* of Nisan is so great that the future redemption will come about whether or not *Klal Yisrael* repents.

[Because of the basic difference of characteristic between the two months, R. Eliezer posits that *t'shuvah* will be required before redemption and R. Yehoshua does not. (San. 98a) Also, their dispute between the relationship between *chesed* and *g'vurah* is the same as their dispute between *lev* (heart) and *rosh* (mind). (*Midrash Mishle* 1)

Tal and Pesach

We can finally understand the reason that we begin to say *morid hatal* on Pesach. Pesach, the night of redemption, is the time of year during which the attribute of *chesed* reaches epitome. *Pirkei R. Eliezer* (Ch. 32) and Targum Yonasan, (Gen. 27:1) write that it was because "the Heavenly windows open up and pour forth *tal*" that Yitzchak waited for this night to bless his son, Esav—who he knew was otherwise unworthy and undeserving of the *brakhos*. To this end, as the "higher" attribute is existent at this point in the year—while it might still be the rainy season—we invoke this attribute and not that of *geshem*. The same is true of *Sukkos*. As it is a Yom Tov—a time of *chesed*—we seek to beseech God with this attribute as much as possible. We, thus, recite *"morid hatal"* throughout Sukkos except for a part of the last day and all of Pesach aside from part of the first day.

SECTION B

Sequence Analysis

R. Yitzchak's Statements

The G'mara lists a series of statements by R. Yitzchak which were precipitated by questions from R. Nachman who sought to understand certain Scriptural verses. In each instance R. Yitzchak drew upon R. Yochanan's explanation. We will review these statements (for simplicity we omit the verses; for this see Talmud) and indicate the reason for the order of their placement:

[1] In the time of Yo'el, God accelerated the growth process; grain, which normally takes six months to grow, grew in eleven days;
[2] God caused a seven year famine in the land;
[3] I [God] will not arrive in "Heavenly" Jerusalem until I arrive in "Earthly" Jerusalem;
[4] Idolatry causes the wicked to burn in Gehenna;
[5] The evil of idolatry is two-fold; the abandonment of God substituted by worship of a meaningless force;
[6] God caused Shmu'el to die young so that he would not witness the death of Sha'ul; (*S'fas Emes*: Shmu'el died at his appointed time. God, however, caused him to age prematurely so that people would not say he died young because he had sinned.)
[7] Ya'akov never died.

Analysis:

The significance of the sequence is as follows:

[1] and [2] indicate that man has no control over the vegetable kingdom. Ultimately, God maintains complete control over this domain. He can withhold growth [2] or he can accelerate growth [1]. Nevertheless, God places the destiny of the world in the hands of man. This is shown by statements [3-5]. The worship of idols prevents the world's redemption. Even the Name of God will not be completely unified until man has perfected himself [5].

Finally [6] and [7] emphasize a theme which is recurrent in this chapter (see p. 4a and 6a); God controls the lifespan of man as He does nature ("For man is as the tree of the field"). Those who support people who God despises will have their lives curtailed [6]; those who believe in God will live eternally [7].

Summary Outline: 6a&b

Yoreh and *Malkosh*

[8] *Yoreh* falls in Cheshvon. It is so called because—

a. It warns people to plaster their roofs, gather their fruits, and attend to all their needs (*"yoreh"* is defined as "it teaches").
b. It saturates the ground and waters it down to its depths (*"yoreh"* is defined as stemming from the root רוה).
c. It falls gently. (*"yoreh"* is defined as "to teach." Good teaching is done gently and with patience.)

[9] *Malkosh* falls in Nisan. It is so called because—

a. Shmuel: It removes the stubbornness of Israel; [If there is no *malkosh*-rain people repent]. (This explanation of *"malkosh"* is derived by dividing it into two words "מל" (to remove), "קשיות" (stiffneckedness).)
b. D'vei R. Yishma'el: It helps fill the stalks with grain; (*"malkosh"* is understood to be a conjunction of מלא (to fill) and קש (stalk).)
c. It falls both on the ears and the stalks (*"malkosh"* is composed of the two words, מלילות (ears) and קשין (stalks)).

The Timetable for the Three Rainfalls of *Yoreh*

Tannaim posit that there are three periods of *yoreh*. They dispute when these occur. Their dispute is as follows:

R. Meir: 3, 7 and 17th of Cheshvon;
R. Yehudah: 7, 17 and 23rd of Cheshvon;
R. Yosi: 17 and 23rd of Cheshvon and *Rosh Chodesh Kislev*.

See Overview: Significance of *Tal* for the importance of these dates.

Halakhic Function of the Three Rainfalls

The dates of the rainfalls listed above have the following *halakhic* significance—

[10] First Rainfall:

This date establishes the time wherein the recitation of *tal u'matar* commences.

[11] Second Rainfall:

a. R. Zera: This is the date people have in mind when they use the term "rainfall" in **vows.** (E.g., as in the vow "I will abstain from fruit until the rain comes.")

b. R. Z'vid: From this date forward **olives** left in the field are no longer considered to be "left for the poor." (Lev. 23:22) (That is, even the rich may again partake of these olives) [The Torah prohibits these fruits only so long as the poor intend to claim it. Thereafter, they no longer have exclusive rights on these olives.]

c. R. Papa: From this date forward people may no longer walk on **private paths.** [During the summer months, travelers are permitted on some roads which cut across private property. This is prohibited during the rainy season as it is detrimental to the crops.]

d. R. Nachman b. Yitzchak: Beginning this date people must begin making available to the public produce which grew during the Sabbatical year. [One may retain dominion over crops in the Sabbatical Year only so long as the wild variety is available.]

[12] Third Rainfall

This date establishes when fasting must commence for lack of rain.

[13] The amount of rain considered sufficient enough not to fast—

a. R. Avuhu: Occurs when the First Rainfall penetrates one-handbreadth of soil;

b. Jerusalem Talmud: When there is enough rain during the Second Rainfall to use the soil to form a stopper for a cask.

[14] Circumstances when there is no curse of *v'atzar* ("He will hold back the heavens from giving rain"): (Deut. 11:17)

a. R. Chisda : When it rains enough to make the soil a stopper for a cask;

b. R. Chisda: If it rains before the recitation of *sh'ma* (even if the total accumulation was not sufficient);

c. Abaye: [b] applies [only] if the rain falls before the evening *sh'ma*.(If it rains at night it is not beneficial.)

[15] Rain in Teves: Blessing or Curse?

a. R. Yehudah: [If it had rained previously] it is best if no rain falls during Teves because—

1. People can attend to their gardens;
2. Students can travel to school;
3. The grain will not become subject to blast.

b. R. Chisda: If it did not rain before this, the rain is necessary and beneficial.

Summary Outline: 6b

Blessing for Rain

[16] R. Avuhu: One recites the blessing for rain when it rains to the extent that the accumulated rain rebounds to meet every additional drop of rain that falls.

[17] Rav: The blessing is מודים אנחנו לך.

[18] R. Papa: The *brakha* concludes ורב ההודאות, א-ל ההודאות.

B'rakhos 58b

[19] R. Avuhu, *Braisa*: On rain the blessing is הטוב והמטיב. (This is contrary to [17].)

Answers:

a. [17] speaks of when he saw the rain; [19] when he heard about it.
b. Both speak when he saw it rain. [17] applies when it rained a little; [19] when it rained a great deal.
c. Both speak where it rained sufficiently. [19] applies when he owns the land; [17] when he does not.

Analysis

<1> Shulchan Arukh:
The blessing is reserved for lands where it does not rain throughout the year. It is recited even if the rainfall was insufficient. [Beis Yosef] The blessing is made in all lands when it rains during a drought.

[19] is said when one owns a field with a partner [even his wife and/or children]. If he is the sole owner of the field, the blessing he recites is שהחיינו. The foregoing applies whether he saw it rain in his field or just heard about it. [17] is recited if he does not own a field. *Shitah M'kubetzes* writes that this blessing applies even if he heard that it rained in a given province. *Mishna B'rurah* rules that given that this last point is disputed, it is best not to recite the blessing unless he actually saw it rain.

Introduction

Pages 7a-10a are composed of aggadic literature. At first glance this material seems to be disjointed and irrelevant to the topic at hand. In the pages that follow we will explain the reason for the sequence, in addition to the rationale of individual *ma'amarim*. To extract the maximum benefit from our analysis we suggest that you read our analysis of these pages, study and review the text of the G'mara, and then reread the analysis.

Summary Outline: 7a-8a

The Exaltedness of Rainy Days and the Reasons Rain is Withheld

Following is a catalogue of the exaltedness of rainy days and the reasons for which rain is withheld. This list derives from statements found in the G'mara on Pages 7a-8b. The outline below follows the Talmud's sequence. One of the difficulties which we will resolve in the next section is the basis for this sequence, including the reason that the G'mara interrupts its discussion of the significance of rainy days to discuss the reason that rain is withheld.

[20] A Rainy Day is as great as the day of—

a. R. Avuhu (7a): [Greater than] תחיית המתים (Resurrection);
b. R. Yosef (7a): תחיית המתים;
c. R. Yehudah (7a): כיום שנתנה בו תורה (Revelation);
d. Rava (7a): [Greater than] [יותר מ]יום שנתנה בו תורה;
e. R. Chama b. Chanina (7b): כיום שנבראו שמים וארץ (Creation).

A rainy Day is so great—

f. R. Oshiya (7b): Salvation is increased thereon.

Rain is withheld because—

g. R. Tanchum (7b): The nation is worthy of annihilation*;
h. R. Chisda (7b): People withhold תרומות and מעשרות;
i. R. Shimon b. Pazi (7b): People speak לשון הרע (slander);
j. R. Hamnuna (7b): People are עזי פנים (brazen);
k. R. Ketinah (7b): People neglect Torah study;
l. R. Ami (7b): People steal.

* On (7b) the *G'mara* states that it does not rain unless the sins of Israel have been forgiven. *S'fas Emes* explains that if Israel's sins are forgiven then rain falls מאוצר הטוב. If their sins have not been forgiven, but they are not worthy of annihilation the rain which falls is not מאוצר הטוב.

It does rain when—

m. R. Ami (8a): People are honest in their business dealings.

Rainy days are so exalted that –

n. R. Yitzchak (8b): Even pocket money [business transactions] is [are] blessed;

o. R. Yochanan (8b): It is equivalent to the day of קבוץ גליות (Day of the Ingathering of the Exiled).

Sequence Analysis: 7a-8b

In analyzing the foregoing sequence of *ma'amarim* a striking result emerges. Namely, that the order corresponds to that of the *sh'moneh esreh*. A point of further interest is that *ma'amarim* 7-13 which are a seeming digression, actually correspond to sections of the *brakha* of *Anenu*. The latter *brakha* is inserted on fast days in the repetition of the *sh'moneh esreh* between the blessings of ראה נא and רפאנו. We proceed to explicate the correlation.

Reason	*B'rakha/Phrase*
תחיית המתים	אתה גבור־ מחיה מתים
קבלת התורה	השיבנו־ לתורתך
יום שנבראו שמים וארץ	השיבנו־ והחזירנו בתשובה (השיבנו ה׳ אליך ונשובה חדש ימינו כקדם :כימי קדם:)
ישועה	ראה נא: וגאלנו
חייב כליה	עננו־ כי בצרה גדולה אנחנו

בטול תרומות ומעשרות	עננו־ אל תפן אל רשענו *y. B'rakhos* 9:2 derives retribution in this case from the phrase, המביט לארץ ותרעד Both verbs refer to vision.
לשון הרע	עננו־ אל תסתר פניך ממנו [This is equivalent retribution based upon the verse cited in the Talmud which refers to *lashon harah* as *lashon seiser*. Thus do not hide your face over a sin carried out clandestinely.]
עזי פנים	עננו־ אל תתעלם (Do not absent yourself.) [Concerning a person who is haughty God declares] "he and I can not reside together." (*Soteh* 4b)
בטול תורה	עננו־ היה נא קרוב לשועתנו (Be close [to listen] to our pleas.) [This is based upon the saying in y. *B'rakhos* אם תעזבנו יום יומים אעזביך (If you forsake me [by not studing Torah] for one day, I will remove myself from you [a distance of] two days.)]
גזל	עננו־ יהי נא חסדך לנחמנו (Thievery brought the Flood. Only God's *chesed* will prevent the evil decree.)

((At this point the G'mara *interjects a number of statements which underscore the importance of prayer and the remedies for various transgressions listed above. [See below: "Reasons Rain is Withheld and Remedies."]))*

ברך עלינו (This blessing concerns business.)	אנשי אמנה
ברך עלינו	מעות שבכיס

(At this point the G'mara *interjects a number of statements which relate to the blessings of* Barekh Alenu. *[See below:* Barekh Alenu.*])*

תקע בשופר: ושא נס לקבץ גליותנו	קבוץ גליות

Having shown the correspondence between the *ma'amarim* in the G'mara and the order of the *sh'moneh esreh* (and in later sections we show that the sequence of the *aggadita* through page 10 follows the sequence of the *sh'moneh esreh*) we might ask, Why does the G'mara choose this sequence? We believe the answer is two-fold.

On 2a the G'mara is troubled by the question "How do we know that one must include God's attribute of מוריד הגשם in the *t'fillah*?" Through these *ma'amarim* the G'mara indicates that God's attribute of bestowing rain requires at least as great if not a greater measure of Divine Mercy than all of His other attributes.

Beyond this, the G'mara includes this *aggadita* immediately before the section which deals with fasting for rain to indicate the special significance and meaning of these *brakhos* on this particular occasion. That is, the אנשי כנסת הגדולה set down a standard *t'fillah* text which was meant to serve for all occasions. This G'mara explicates the *kavanos* (thoughts) which one should have in mind while reciting the *sh'moneh esreh* on this day. Specifically, while reciting *brakhos* which recall God's attributes which are "as great as the giving of rain" one should have in mind that "in addition to the specific request we are presently making [e.g., wisdom, forgiveness, health, etc.] we ask that He grant us rain, for without rain we cannot survive to benefit from other manifestations of Your bounty. In addition, the G'mara indicates the sins for which we should repent while saying Anenu.

Overview

Exaltedness of Rain

Amoraim give rainy days an exalted status. They are considered to be either equal to or greater than תחיית המתים (Resurrection), יום שנתנה בו תורה (day Torah was given), יום שנבראו שמים וארץ Creation, and קבוץ גליות (Ingathering of the Exiled). Verses aside, what is the connection?

The doctrine of מדה כנגד מדה is the guiding principle. Each of the categories mentioned above involves creation and rebirth in one form or another. The day of *Kabbalas haTorah* is included because the Torah is the center of creation and Revelation served as the culmination of Creation.

Isaiah 55:9-10 explicates the significance of rain, as well as, the relationship between rain and the words of God (the Torah):

> For as the rain comes down, and the snow from heaven, and returns not there, but waters the earth, and makes it bring forth and bud, that it may give seed to the sower, and bread to the eater; so shall my word be that goes out of my mouth: it shall not return to me void, but it shall accomplish that which I please, and it shall prosper in that for which I sent it.

Isaiah defines the greatness of rain as that force which sustains the Earth and allows it to thrive. For this reason it is as great as Creation. For, as important as it is to create, it is as important to sustain that which one creates. For without constant sustenance that which one creates will not thrive, possibly, even ceasing to exist, and the creation will have been for naught.

(This is contrary to the giving habits of many individuals. People often give lavishly to building funds of institutions, but do not give funds for maintenance costs. This most often undoes much of the good for which the original funds were given. For, when institutions are starved such that they do not have the necessary operating costs, they are forced to run their programs well below the level necessary for creativity and sometimes even below the level which is considered acceptable.)

For the same reason a rainy day is greater than the day the Torah was given. Rain affords man life; life allows for Torah study. Man's learning of the Torah is of greater significance than the *giving* of the Torah. Therefore, the day which enables continued Torah study is greater than the day the Torah was given.

(This is consistent with R. Tzadok haKohen's explanation of this *ma'amar*. (*Pri Tzadik* 5:262) He argues that *Yom haGeshamim* is *Sh'mini Atzeres*; the day on which we begin to ask for rain. It was the day that the wellsprings of the Oral Torah open which afford us a greater opportunity of understanding the Written Torah. Thus, the *ma'amar* states that *Yom haGeshamim* (*Shmini Atzeres*) is greater than the day the Torah was *given (Sh'vu'os)*.)

There is, however, a deeper level on which these comparisons are to be understood. *Chazal* equate the physical and spiritual realms. We mentioned above that the Torah compares man to a tree. This is not just a symbolic comparison. Our Rabbis believe that there is a one to one correspondence between the spiritual and physical realms. If rain is withheld it means the nation has sinned. Rabbis would not fast on a cloudy day because this indicated the existence of a barrier between God and man. On rainy days the potential for understanding Torah is increased. Thus, a rainy day is greater than the day of *Kabbalas haTorah* because the *chesed* of God exuded on this day allows man an extra measure of understanding of the holy Torah.

Overview

Reasons for Rain: מדה כנגד מדה

Honesty in business dealings is one of the precipitants of rain. (8a) Included in the reason for rain not falling are: people not giving *t'rumos and ma'aseros*, speaking *lashon harah* and *gezel*. (7b) The underlying rationale for these reasons is the doctrine of מדה כנגד מדה People who believe that their sustenance comes solely from God are rewarded by God granting them sustenance. Those who suffer a lack of faith have their sustenance withheld.

God grants rain to man when he appreciates that ultimately his sustenance stems from God. Those who refuse to give the *t'rumah and ma'aser* gifts do so because they are afraid to give away **their** hard earned possessions. This is because they believe their acquisition of wealth is due solely to their own efforts and abilities. They do not believe that God had a hand in it or that He takes and gives wealth as He sees fit.

Stealing is motivated by this same lack of faith; so is slandering. The slanderer believes that he lacks, because others have. He is convinced that the other person is the source of his deprivation. For this reason he vents his feeling against the other person. Were he to have proper faith he would internalize the fact that God can grant **each** person on Earth as much worldly goods as He sees fit. A person of true faith thus seeks only to help his friend and never to speak out against him.

Lack of faith is also the root cause of brazenness. A person who truly believes in God knows that he has nothing to be brazen about, since ultimately, all of his qualities and advantages are gifts of God.

Neglect of Torah study is also listed as a reason for rain being withheld. The correlation is as follows: Torah is the world's spiritual nourishment. Without it, the universe is bereft of its function. Lacking purpose, there is no reason for the physical world to exist. Hence, God withholds water—one of the substances most necessary for the continuance of life.

Summary Outline/Sequence Analysis: 7b-8a

Reasons Rain is Withheld and Remedies

7b sets down a number of reasons for which rain is withheld. These have been outlined above. Surprisingly, the G'mara digresses for a whole page before continuing to discuss the exaltedness of rain. We shall demonstrate below that this "digression" is nothing other than a series of *ma'amarim* which chart out remedies for the transgressions that lead rain to be withheld. The *ma'amar* and its author are bracketed.

Reason rain is withheld	**The Remedy is—**
1. Jews worthy of annihilation	a. [R. Ami: *dor m'kulkal*] Pray for/do act of mercy.
2. Withholding *t'rumos and ma'aseros*	b. [R. Ami: *Gezel*] Prayer.*
3. People speak *lashon harah*	c. [R. Lakish: Snake] Realize you gain nothing from your slander.
4. *Azeh Panim*	d. [Rava: Student who is an an *Az panim* does not learn because his Rebbe does not think kindly of him] have friends intercede by praying for you.
5. *Bitul torah*	e. [R. Lakish: If you do not know Torah because you did not study hard] Increase your study hours and your diligence.

* Sfas Emes: The prayers of the righteous will help even if the stolen object has not been returned. *Keren Orah* disagrees.

Advanced Analysis

Reason for sequence a-e and inclusions

Questions:

a. Given the explanation that (a)-(e) are the remedies of (1)-(5) why are they not listed in the same sequence as (1)-(5)?

b. Why are the following two *ma'amarim* included between (d) and (e)?

(6) R. Ami: A person must pray or get someone to pray for him, but that person should not become haughty because his prayers were answered.

(7) Rava: Two *talmidei chakhamim* should not be haughty towards each other.

Answer: [b] is listed first because it deals with *gezel*. *Gezel* is present in all sins. In commiting any sin, a person utilizes the strength God gives him for the purpose of performing *mitzvos* and illegally diverts these strengths to the performance of *aveiros*.

(a) follows (b) for it corresponds to (1).

(c) follows (a) because R. Lakish is cited first and then Rava—who is the author of [d].

(d) is next because it quotes the same verse as does (b).

(6) is inserted here since it follows naturally from (d); (d) suggests that a person get friends to intercede on his behalf with his Rebbe, (6) suggests that a person secure an individual to intercede on his behalf with God (through *t'fillah*).

(7) is the natural continuation of (6). (6) points out that those whose prayers are answered should not be haughty; (7) emphasizes that those who are accomplished *talmidei chakhamim* should not be haughty.

Sequence Analysis: 8a&b

Barekh Alenu

Following the *G'mara's* discussion regarding the remedies for various transgressions, the *G'mara* moves on to introduce pericopes which follow the sequence of the *brakha*, ברך עלינו. The following chart explicates this relationship.

Statement	Section of *B'rakha*
R. Ami: Rain falls for people who are honest in business.	ברך עלינו This is a general opening who are honest in business. statement which relates to the essence of .
R. Ami: Those who are answered are those who have **belief in God.**	ה׳ אלקינו
(R. Yochanan: But know that the righteous are sometimes not answered because God judges them very carefully.)	
R. Lakish/Bar Kaparah: Crops pass through the same stages as a woman who gives birth. There is the possibility of not conceiving (no rain); miscarrying (foul growth); or giving birth to a still born (attack of pestilence when the crop is near to ripe).	כל מיני תבואתה לטובה (The implication being that while the crop can grow it might not be a good crop.)
R. Shmuel b. Nahmeni: Rain should fall beneficially—it should not be destructive; strong rain for the trees; light rain for the vegetables rain for the reservoirs.	ותן טל ומטר לברכה (This implies that it can also rain destructively; we pray for beneficial rain.
R. Shmuel b. Nachmeni: When there is famine and plague pray that God rid the famine; "When God provides sustenance (*sov'ah*) it is meant solely for the living."	ושבענו מטוביך (The prayer being invoked is that we live to enjoy the food.)
R. Yitzchak: Rain on Erev Shabbos is a curse even when the rain is sorely needed. Rabbah b. Shelah: A rainy day is as bad as Judgment Day.	וברך שנתנו כשנים הטובות (This prayer speaks of "good years." In good years rain falls precisely when and where it is needed.)
R. Yitzchak: A Rainy Day is great—even a *prutah* in the pocket is blessed.	General recap of the essence of the *brakha*. Representative of the closing (*chasimah*).

Sequence Analysis: 8b-9b

Continuation of Correspondence Between Sequence of *Ma'amarim* and the *Sh'moneh Esreh*

Statement	Section of *b'rakha*
R. Yochanan: A Rainy day is as great as the Day of Ingathering (קבוץ גליות).	תקע בשופר: ושא נס לקבץ גליותנו
R. Yochanan: Even armies do not fight on rainy days.	השיבה שופטינו: והסר ממנו יגון ואנחה
R. Yochanan: Rain is withheld when pledges to charity are not redeemed.	ולמלשינים: (Those who sin with their mouths.)
R. Yochanan: If you give *ma'aser* you will become rich. Reish Lakish: You may test God concerning this.	על הצדיקים: ותן שכר טוב לכל הבוטחים בשמך
R. Yochanan: Rain falls for the needs of even one individual. יפתח ה׳ לך את אוצרו הטוב	על הצדיקים: ותן שכר טוב (See *Parshas D'rakhim* 31 concerning אוצר הטוב.)
R. Yochanan: *Parnasa* is given only in the merit of the congregation. A leader [Moshe] is equivalent to the whole congregation.	את צמח: וקרנו תרום בישועתיך This is the only *t'fillah* in which we pray for an individual. This is because he is equivalent to the whole congregation.

Correspondence Between Attributes and Supplication

See page 30

Praise	*B'rakha*
אתה גבור	אתה חונן: דעת (אני בינה לי גבורה) (משלי ח:י״ד)
מחיה מתים	השיבנו: והחזירנו בתשובה [Would that God did not accept our repentance, we would not be alive.] נפש חוטאת היא תמות (עז יח:ד)
רב להושיע	ראה נא־ וגאלנו
מוריד הגשם מכלכל חיים	ברך עלינו: ותן טל ומטר את כל מיני תבואתה לטובה
מחיה מתים ברחמים	שמע קולנו: ורחם עלינו (That this *b'rakha* refers to *t'chiyas ha'meisim* follows from the Rambam's sequence of— 1. Building the *Mikdash*: ולירושלים עירך 2. The coming of *Mashi'ach*: את צמח 3. *T'chiyas ha'meisim*. תחיית המתים
סומך נופלים	תקע בשופר: וקבצנו יחד As per the verse ואולך אתכם קוממיות
רופא חולים	רפאנו
מתיר אסורים	סלח לנו Freedom from our spiritual prison.
ומקים אמונתו	על הצדיקים: שכר טוב לכל הבוטחים בשמך
בעל גבורות	ולירושלים עירך: (לא למענכם...אלא למען שמי)
מלך	השיבה שופטינו: ומלוך עלינו
מצמיח ישועה	את צמח דוד

SECTION C

Introduction

Thus far, the tractate has dealt with the laws pertaining to praying for rain under normal conditions. The *Mishna* now moves on to discuss the procedure when rain is withheld. This involves a sequence of Fasts (the term is capitalized to connote a *halakhic* category; not the mere abstinence from food), the *halakhic* guidelines of these Fasts and the special procedures to be followed.

Summary Outline: 10a&b

Y'chidim

Mishna:

[1] If it does not rain by 17 Cheshvon, *y'chidim* fast three Fasts. The Fasts begin in the morning.

[2] If it does not rain by Rosh Chodesh Kislev, the populace fasts three Fasts. These Fasts begin in the morning with only food and drink being prohibited.

G'mara

[3] R. Huna: "*y'chidim*" in [1] are the Rabbis.

[4] R. Huna: The sequence of the *y'chidim's* Fasts is Monday, Thursday, Monday.

Even though the supposed reason for not beginning on Thursday is that it might lead to elevated food prices (*Braisa*$_1$) and this would not occur if only *y'chidim* fast, R. Huna posits, nevertheless, that the law applies to this case as well. (See<2>.)

[5] *Braisa*$_2$: Although *y'chidim* have begun their Fast sequence, Fasts are suspended for Rosh Chodesh or any day mentioned in *M'gilas Ta'anis*. (See <3> and <4>.)

[6] *Braisa*$_3$: (As per our text): Every *talmid chakham* is to consider himself a *yachid*.

Definitions:

a. *Yachid*: Anyone who could be appointed a *parness*.
b. *Talmid*: Anyone who can answer an *halakhic* question even in *Tractate Kallah* (alt. reading: Tractate d'Kallah). (See <7>.)

[7] *Braisa*$_4$:

a. R. Meir: Not every one who wishes may act as a *yachid*; "A *talmid* may." (See below.)

b. R. Yosi: He [anyone] may [act as a *yachid*].

[8] *Braisa*$_5$:

a. R. Shimon b. Elazer: same as R. Meir [7a].

b. R. Shimon b. Gamliel: One may not behave like a *yachid* where he will receive undeserved honor. Concerning actions involving pain, any person may conduct himself as a *yachid*.

***Shabbos* 114a**

[9] a. R. Yochanan: What level of *talmid chakham* is to be chosen as a *parness*? Someone who is asked a question in any (alt.: every) place—even *M'sekhes [d']Kallah*. (See <7>.)

b. He who knows one *m'sekhes* can be chosen to be a local leader. He who knows *shas* can be chosen to be a *rosh mesivta*.

Analysis

<1> Re: [1]: The date 17 Cheshvon is problematic in that this is the date of the Third Rainfall according to R. Meir (6a). R. Yosi (6a) rules that the *y'chidim* begin fasting on Rosh Chodesh Kislev. R. Chisda rules that the *halakha* follows R. Yosi.

Nonetheless, Rif and Rambam rule that the fasting begins on 17 Cheshvon. They follow the second approach on 6a, namely, that R. Chisda's remarks are directed to another end— establishing the *halakha* of *hazkarah* in accordance with R. Gamliel. Thus, as there is no definitive statement in the *G'mara* in support of R. Yossi, we follow R. Meir whose view is supported by a *stam (anonymous) Mishna*.

Yet, this resolution is not without difficulty. Generally, where there are two versions of a statement Rif gives credence to the one which is cited by the editor of the G'mara and not the one cited by a particular rabbi. Based upon this, Ran and Ritva would rule that the *y'chidim* should begin fasting on Rosh Chodesh Kislev; however, they defer to the Rif.

Ritva suggests that Rif and Rambam were swayed by the rule that the *halakha* is in accordance with an anonymous mishna (R. Yochanan, Shabbos 46a). R. Yehonatan of Luniel explains that R. Gamliel agrees with R. Yosi, although First Rain does not fall until 17 Cheshvon, R. Gamliel believes that one should begin praying for rain on 7 Cheshvon. If so, it can be argued that according to this view, the function of Three Rains is other than that stated in the *G'mara*. Namely, the First Rain date (17 Cheshvon) establishes the time that the *y'chidim* should begin fasting; the Second Rain is as stated in the *G'mara*; and the Third Rain (Rosh Chodesh Kislev) is when everyone should fast.

<2> Re: [4]: R. Huna's answer implies that there is a significance to fasting specifically on Mondays and Thursdays independent of "fear of raising food prices." (Ritva believes that even in the case of *y'chidim* one need be concerned about "raising the prices.") See Chapter 3 for a full discussion on this point.

Eshkol: In our day, when there is no market day, fasting may commence on Thursday. R. Elberg'loni prohibits it, nonetheless.

<3> Re: [5]: This law applies specifically to *y'chidim*. The status of a congregation *vis-a-vis* this issue is discussed at the end of Chapter 2.

<4> Re: [5]: This law seems to run counter to the law of אסור כולל (umbrella prohibition) [y. *Sh'vu'os*3:4], wherein vows made to prohibit an object which is both voluntary and required are declared valid (e.g., he who prohibited himself from eating *matzah* all year long may not eat *matzah* on Passover).

Ra'avad makes the following distinction. The declaration of the *beit din* to fast cannot be considered an אסור כולל, since the *beis din* never truly binds the person to the entire sequence of fasts. For, were it to rain sufficiently during any part of the sequence, the subsequent fasts would be suspended.

Others suggest that this case is different from *matzah* in that a person who prohibits himself from eating *matzah* realizes that this includes the first night of Pesah. Thus, his statement is considered an אסור כולל. However, one who vows regarding fasting probably does not take note of the days listed in *M'gilas Ta'anis*, and thus does not include them in his vow.

<5> Re: [3]: Riv'van equates *"rabbanan"* to "גדולי הדור" Others have the textual reading *"talmidei chakhamim."*

<6> Re: [7a]: Rashi's reading "A *talmid chakham* may act as a *yachid*." Thus, [7b] rules that even one who is not a *talmid chakam* may fast.

Rashi (second version): "Neither may he act as a *talmid*." This means that one who is not worthy may not dress in the attire of a *talmid chakham*.

<7> Re: [6]: As noted, there are two readings. R. Chananel's reading is d'Kallah. The import of [6] is that for purposes of being declared a *talmid chakham* it is enough if someone is erudite in *any* part of *Shas*; even those sections which are commonly stud-

ied during the *Kallah* (the two months during the year—Elul and Adar—during which the populace gathered to study.) The second text reads *"Tractate Kallah."* This refers to the minor tractate which is composed of *braisos*. This tractate has two properties. It is easy and it was hardly ever studied. This fact coupled with a lack of clarity by what is meant by בכל מקום in the statement "a *talmid chakham* is one who can answer questions בכל מקום," gives rise to two interpretations. בכל מקום "from **any** place," i.e., even from the easiest tractate—thus the reference to *Tractate Kallah*. Alternatively, "בכל מקום" can mean "from **every** place." In this sense *Tractate Kallah* is used to indicate that a true *talmid chakham* who is picked as a *parness* must know **all** of Shas including the remotest segment (See Ran).

[9] rules that only one who knows *M'sekhes Kallah* may be chosen a *parness*. In this pericope, a person with these qualifications is merely considered to be a *talmid chakham*. [9], therefore, seems to be at odds with [6]. Tosefos explains that in [9] Talmid is used as someone who knows all of Shas "even Tractate Kallah." In [6], we speak of a *talmid* who knows only *Tractate Kallah*. Talmid haRamban explains that [6] speaks of someone who can **merely identify** that a *braisa* comes from *Tractate Kallah*; he is considered a *talmid*. [9] refers to someone who **can explain in depth** a *braisa* found in *Tractate Kallah*; he can be chosen as a *parness*. (See Ritva note 361).

Tashbatz (Responsa: V. 1: 32) explains [(b & c] as follows: [9b] refers to appointing a person as a judge. [9c] concerns appointing a rosh mesivta.

<8> R. Yochanan's *Shita*

It should be pointed out that in determining the qualifications of a *parness*, R. Yochanan's opinion is not universally adopted. In Shabbos 3a, R. Chiyyah admonishes Rav for asking R. Yehudah haNasi a question from a section of the Shas which was not being studied at the academy. R. Chiyyah told him that his question was out of order —for perhaps R. Yehudah haNasi would not have known the answer. Based on R. Yochanan's premise this admonition is problematic. By definition, a rosh mesivta must be able to answer *any* question from *any* part of Shas at *any* time.

We propose the following solution: The Talmud notes that there are two ways in which *talmidei chakhamim* distinguish themselves. There are those who have encyclopedic knowledge (*sinai*) and there are those who have great conceptual abilities (*oker harim*). In Shas we find that both the *sinai* and *oker harim* were partial to their personal approach to Torah study. Each type preferred his own specialty. Thus, in *Gittin* 6b, R. Yosef, who was a *sinai* does not consider R. Avimi a *talmid chakham* because he was unfamiliar with an *halakhic* statement of R. Yitzchak. Abaye, an *oker harim*, disagrees. He argues that ignorance of a statement made by an amora does not in any way indicate that a person is not a *talmid chakham*. The determinant of being a *talmid chakham* is whether one has the ability to analyze a problem properly. To this end, R. Yochanan, a *sinai*, defined a *talmid chakham* as one who is a *sinai*. He, also, required each *parness* to be a *sinai*. Rebbe, on the other hand, an *oker harim*, considered the properties of *oker harim* to be paramount. As such, it is possible for one to be a rosh mesivta without being a *sinai*.

Aggadita: 10b-11a

Communal Responsibility

The Mishna states that *"y'chidim"* (specific individuals; as explained above) begin to fast for the congregation approximately two weeks before the congregation itself is required to fast. This becomes the focal point for much aggadic discussion concerning the individual's relations and responsibility to the community.

The issue is the crux of the tannaitic dispute on the right of non-*y'chidim* to fast on those days designated for *y'chidim*. The *G'mara* concludes with the opinion of R. Yosi and R. Shimon b. Gamliel that he may do so because "it is not an advantage to him but a hardship" (Translation Soncino). An alternate text reads "[As this is] an action involving hardship, he [a non-*yachid*] may include himself."

The conclusion to be drawn from the opinion of these *tannaim* is that while *y'chidim* are **required** to fast, non-*y'chidim* should be encouraged to fast because this would increase their sensitivity to the needs of the community. It is important that each person be trained to understand that **he** is a vital member of the community. All too often, people feel that the concern for the *tzibbur* lies solely in the hands of the Rabbanim. To counteract this outlook, R. Yosi and R. Shimon b. Gamliel encourage people to join the *y'chidim* in these first fasts.

The *aggadita* which follows elaborates on the importance of people feeling compassion for the rest of the community. It, also, explicates the negative results which befall members of the community who are oblivious to its needs.

Ma'amar	**Explanation**
[10] [One who fasts and the problem passes is required to complete his fast.]	The *G'mara* cites this statement because it generally quotes an entire *braisa*. The significant statement in the *braisa* for this discussion is [11].

[11] A person is required to fast both if he enters a place where fasting is being observed (even if no Fast was proclaimed in his home town) or, if while visiting another locale, the members of his home town declare a Fast.*

A person has two communal obligations:
1. to his home community;
2. to the community he is visiting.

[12] One who accidentally eats on a Fast Day—should not be seen in public ("he should not be as a groom among mourners").**

Sensitivity to the *tzibbur* includes abstaining from anything which causes people to be disheartened.

[Note: the following ma'amarim *are included because a proof was cited for [12] in that Ya'akov sent his children to Egypt for food even though they had enough food. Ya'akov did this so that the local citizenry should not feel that he was insensitive to their plight. As their trip to Egypt was mentioned the* G'mara *now discusses some aspects of that trip, as well as, certain laws pertaining to travel some of which are related to the topics mentioned above.]*

a. ***Al tirg'zu baderekh***:

Don't study (in a rigorous manner) while travelling on the road since you might get lost. Non-complicated Torah studies, however, should be reviewed on the road.

R. Gershom explains that people who see you debating will think that you are a quarrelsome group and disassociate themselves from you.

b. One should not take large steps [this causes a deficiency in one's eye-sight].
c. Enter and leave town during daylight hours. [As a precaution against robbers and potholes.]
d. R. Yehudah/R. Chiyyah: When travelling do not eat more than famine rations [because]—

1) Consuming large quantities of food when walking a great deal leads to health problems. (The law would not apply to someone who rides in a couch or on a boat.)

2) If one is not careful, he might exhaust his food supply before reaching his destination. (The law does not apply to situations in which food is readily available on the road.)

[13] One who eats little during famine years is saved from an unnatural death.

The person who is sensitive to the plight of the community is rewarded.

* Tosefos: He must complete that Fast. Rashi: He must complete the series of Fasts.
** It is only if he was not *m'kabel ta'anis* that he may continue eating.

[14] One should not have intercourse during famine years (unless he has not fulfilled *pru u'rvu*). (As Levi's wife had no other children she was permitted to have relations in the midst of the famine. (*S'fas Emes*))

This law is reserved for *y'chidim*. It demonstrates the extent to which one must "feel" the communal plight. Even when no one is aware of his actions, the *yachid's* compassion for the *tzibbur* does not allow him to partake in personal pleasure.

[15] Do not separate yourself from the *tzibbur*. He who does will not witness the community's salvation.

A separatist is not considered a member of that *tzibbur*. Therefore, he is not included in any blessings Heaven bestows on it.

[16] A person should not eat and drink in private and say *shalom alay nafshi* (I need only look after myself). This is punishable by early demise.

This teaches that not only is the person who follows [15] not blessed, but he is, in fact, punished.

[17] Who testifies? walls/angels/n'shama/limbs.

[17] underscores the assurance of accountability for transgressing [15].

[18] א-ל אמונה (God is trustworthy) because a *tzaddik* is punished in this world;
ואין עול: the wicked are punished in the future world;
צדיק וישר: when he dies, a man who is judged for his actions will affirm that the judgment is correct.

צדוק הדין: Each person acknowledges that the final judgment that he receives is correct.

Summary Outline: 11a, 22b

Status of Fasting

[19] Shmuel: He who fasts is considered a Sinner.

This is based upon R. Elazar Hakapar's statement wherein a *nazir* is considered a sinner. Given that he who voluntarily abstains only from wine is considered a sinner, how much more so is he who fasts [and abstains from everything]. (The term *kadosh* refers to having his hair grow long.)

(*Keren Orah*: Rambam explains that this only refers to a person who fasts constantly. *Shalo"h*: It refers to someone who has never sinned. A person who fasts as part of the *t'shuvah* process is not considered a sinner and is obligated to fast so long as he is physically able.)

[20] R. Elazar: He who fasts is considered a *kadosh* (a sanctified person).

R. Elazar derives this from *nazir*. The Torah calls a *nazir* "*kadosh*." (The *nazir* referred to as a Sinner (see [19]) is one who defiled himself through contact with the dead.)

(*Shalo"h*: This refers even to a person who never sinned—for fasting reverses the sin of Adam haRishon.)

[21] Question: R. Elazar: A person should always act as if God dwells within him.

[22] Answer: [20] speaks of one who can not bear self affliction; [21] with one for whom fasting is not problematic.

[23] Reish Lakish: One who fasts is considered a *chasid*.

[24] R. Sheshes: The dogs should devour a young scholar who fasts.

[25] R. Yirmiyah b. Aba: The only *ta'anis tzibbur* in Babylonia is 9 Av.

[26] R. Yirmiya b. Aba/Reish Lakish: A *talmid chakham* may not fast as this will lessen his Heavenly work.

22b

[27] For a city surrounded by Gentiles, or in danger of being flooded, etc.—

a. Tanna Kamma: An individual may fast,
b. R. Yosi: He may not as he might become dependent upon assistance from others and they will not show mercy towards him;

Rav: R. Yosi's view is based upon the Biblical obligation of sustaining one's physical body.

Summary Outline: 11b-12b

General Laws of Fasting

[28] R. Zeira/R. Huna:

a. An individual who has undertaken to fast, although he eats and drinks a whole night may say *Anenu* on the next day. (See <10>.)
b. If he fasted on a particular day and he prolonged the Fast into the evening he may not say *Anenu* at *ma'ariv* or even during the next day

c. Abaye: The reason is this: In [a] the person was *m'kabel ta'anis* (verbally proclaimed the fast) in [b] he did not. [Abstention from food does not mean one is fasting. Rather, a day becomes a Fast Day when it is so designated previous to the day. (See [33].)

[29] *Halakha*:

a. One may fast "for hours." (Explained below.)
b. He who fasts "for hours" may say *anenu*. (See <13>.)

[30] R. Chisda: "Fasting for hours"—

a. means that one does not eat until the evening; occurs when one decided in the middle of the day to fast.

[31] R. Chisda: For a Fast to be valid it must be maintained until the evening. (See <11>.)

[32] (Certain "fasts" mentioned in the *G'mara* are not really Fasts in that they do not comply with the rules of Fast Days. Those who "fast" on these days intend, merely, to participate as much as possible in the anguish of the congregation (לצעורי נפשיה) as in the case of the *anshei mishmar,*or to sidestep some difficult social situation as in the case of R. Yochanan who did not wish to eat in the house of the *Nasi*.)

[33] Shmuel: Any fast which was not proclaimed in the afternoon before the fast is not a valid Fast.

Rabah b. Shelah: He who fasts without proclaiming it is compared to a bellows filled with wind.

[34] At which point does one "proclaim" the Fast—

a. Rav: At any point in the afternoon; (see <14>)
b. Shmuel: During the *mincha* prayer. (See <15-19> and Appendix I.)

[35] Until when may one eat preceding a Fast which begins in the morning?—

a. Rebbe: Until dawn (עמוד השחר); (see <20>)
b. R. Eliezer b. Shimon: Until the cock crows. (See <25>.)

[36] There are further restrictions:

a. (Version I): Abaye: If one has finished his meal [and has removed all food from the table (interpretation of braisa)] on the eve before the Fast, he may no longer eat.
b. (Version II): Rava: He may eat until he falls asleep. If he merely dozes [(מתנמנם; defined by R. Ashi as one who answers when asked who he can not recall an argument but remembers it if he is reminded of it] he may eat. (See <22-24>.)

[37] R. K'hana/Rav: One who accepts a *ta'anis yachid* may not wear shoes: we are concerned about the possibility that he, inadvertantly, accepted upon himself the laws of a *ta'anis tzibbur*.

Raba b. Shila: He may not wear shoes unless he says explicitly, "I hereby accept upon myself a *ta'anis yachid*." (See <27>.)

This view was followed by "Rabbanan," Abaye and Rava (they wore shoes without soles), and Mar Zutra (who exchanged his left and right shoes).

R. Ashi's students wore shoes. They followed Shmuel [38].

[38] Shmuel: There is no Public Fast in Babylon except for 9 Av. (See <26>.)

Exchanging a Fast Day

[39] (Version I): R. Yehudah/Rav: A person may exchange a Fast Day (i.e., he may eat on a day he intended to fast and make up for it on another day).

a. Shmuel (version I): Is this, then, as a vow which he can repay on another day? (see below)
b. Shmuel (version 2): This is as a vow which can be repaid on another day.

[40] R. Yehoshua b. Rav Idi (from an occurrence): One may not "exchange" a *ta'anis chalom (fast for a bad dream)*.

R. Chisdah: A ta'anis chalom must be observed on the day of the dream.

R. Yosef: Even [if that day is] the Sabbath.

G'mara: Nevertheless, if one fasts on Shabbos, he must fast another day for the transgression of fasting on Shabbos.

Analysis

<10> Re: [28]: The textual reading in our G'mara speaks of someone who intended to fast but one day. Rif and R. Chananel among other have the reading, "An individual who accepted upon himself two days." The outcome is the same according to both readings.

Miktam: [28b] speaks of the case wherein a person decided during the night to fast that entire night and the next day. He still does not pray *anenu*.

Ta'anis Sha'os

<11> Re: [30] & [31]:

a. R. Chananel: Before statement [4], R. Chananel's text includes the additional words, "R. Chisda *l'ta'amei" (follows his halakhic* approach). Thus, [30] & [31] are not understood to be independent statements. [30] draws support from [31].

b. Rashi/Rid: *Ta'anis sha'os* requires that one fast the entire day. It is called *"sha'os"* (Fast for Hours) for the following reason—as opposed to an ordinary Fast the person did not have the intention on the day before the Fast to fast the entire next day. Rather, the day begun with the person not eating, and thereafter, he decided to fast.

c. Rambam: It is considered *ta'anis sha'os* if one eats in the morning and fasts the latter part of the day. (Ran explains that Rambam could have R. Chananel's text, <a>. As such [31] modifies [30], such that, even though [30] implies that one need fast the entire day this is not so. Instead [30] teaches that if the person fasted an entire day and albeit he did not accept the fast on the previous day—as per [33] & [34]—his "fast" has the status of a *ta'anit sha'os*.

Talmid haRamban explains that the function of [31] is to indicate that even though there is a valid notion of fasting for *"sha'os,"* if someone made a *neder* declaring, "Behold I will fast," we rule that he meant to adopt an all day fast. Explaining [31] in this manner means that there is no indication by R. Chisda that one need fast an entire day to fulfil *ta'anis sha'os*.

Rambam follows the Jerusalem Talmud, [41]. The latter also considers a *ta'anis sha'os* to be valid even where one fasted in the morning but ate in the afternoon. This is the basis of our custom to proclaim Half-day Fasts.

d. *Miktam*/Ra'avad: [30] involves the case wherein one afternoon a person was *m'kabel* to fast until noon the next day, and at noon time, he decided to fast the entire day. [30] teaches that this is considered a valid fast—even though fasting a half day, by itself, has no status as a *ta'anis* (as per [31]).

From [31] we learn that if a person was *m'kabel ta'anis* for the second half of the day this *ta'anis sha'os* is valid only if he also did not eat that morning.

e. *Hashlamah* One fulfils his *neder* (promise) to fast on a given day if he follows the procedure outlined in [d].

f. Rashi: [29a] means that if he declared that he would fast a certain number of hours he may not eat during these hours.

Ritva elaborates on this. He explains that the *chiddush* in this law is that a *neder l'hisanos* (a vow to fast) is not considered a regular vow. With regard to a regular vow there is no question but that a person has the right to stipulate the exact type of prohibition he wishes to undertake and then he is obliged to fulfill that provision. But *nidrei ta'anis* are classified as *nidrei hekdesh*. As such, the G'mara wishes to know whether a fast declared "for hours" has any status under the rubric of "*nidrei hekdesh*."

During which *T'fillos* Is *Anenu* recited on *Ta'aniyos*?

[42] *Shabbas 24a: Tanni* R. Oshiya: "...on Fast Days and *ma'amodos, arvis, shacharis and mincha, anenu* is recited in "*shome'ah t'fillah*." There is no mention of the fast in *kiddush* or *birkas hamazon*.

[43] Jerusalem Talmud: R. Yona/Rav: Even an individual adds *anenu*.

R. Z'era/R. Huna: כליל שבת ויומו (i.e. *arvis, shacharis, mincha* [Rif]). (See <12>.)

Analysis

<12> a. Ba'al haMa'or: Rav [43] follows R. K'hana's opinion [37] that even in the diaspora one observes Fasts with all the severity of a *ta'anis tzibbur*. Therefore, he rules that one says *anenu* for *ma'ariv*. Given that we rule as Shmuel [38] that in the diaspora there are no Fasts, except 9 Av, which begin at night, *anenu* is not recited until the next day. [42] likewise refers to Fasts that begin at night.

b. Ramban *(Milchamos)*: *Anenu* is said at ma'ariv. [37] does not prove otherwise. [37a] merely indicates that one who accepts upon himself a *ta'anis yachid* must observe the "five *inuyim*," but he does not begin his fast until the morning. [43] also discusses fasts which begin in the morning as is evidenced by the statement that one should not include *anenu* in *birkas hamazon*. Presumably this refers to Fasts that begin at night. An objection might be brought from [28a] wherein it is stated that he begins to say *anenu* on the next day (למחר). This is not a strong objection. The term "מחר" is used for the ruling in [28b] that even though one fasted the entire night, for *shacharis* he may still not say *anenu*. [It is interesting to note that Rashi's text does not include the word "למחר." See *Shabbos* 24a and Ravia 857.]

c. Miktam: Supports Ramban [b]. He cites a Tosefta [not found in our texts] which states explicitly, "There are times that one does not fast and says *anenu*, for example, at *ma'ariv*."

d. Rishonim who follow [b]: Riv'van, Rif, Ritva, Talmid Ramban.

e. Rishonim that follow [a]: R. Yehonatan Miluniel.

Note

a. Rishonim (Rashi [*Shabbos* 24], Tosefos) point out that we no longer say *anenu* for any t'fillah except *mincha*. The reason: we fear that the person will be forced to eat and it will turn out *ex post facto* that he lied in his prayer. *Miktam* posits that under the circumstances the prayer would be invalid. Talmid haRamban writes that a person who is sure that he will be able to fast may recite *anenu* even for *shacharis*.

b. Miktam maintains that during our "Four Fasts" *anenu* is to be recited for *shacharis* as well. This follows from *Miktam*'s reason stated in [a]. As the "Four Fasts" retain the status of a *ta'anis tzibbur* even if the person eats, there is no reason why *anenu* should not be recited.

c. All agree that the *shli'ach tzibbur* recites *anenu* during *shacharis* on the "Four Fasts" "to publicize the fast." Here there is no concern that an individual might eat as surely, at least some members the congregation will fast the entire day.

Parameters for *Anenu* during a *Ta'anis Sha'os*

<13> a. Ritva: Inorder to say *anenu* one must be *m'kabel ta'anis* in the *t'fillah* before the *ta'anis*. (This is because [29b] is absent from the text of the Ritva as it is absent from the texts of B'hag, R. Amram Gaon and Machzor Vitri.)

b. Rambam rules that the person says *anenu* even though he was not *m'kabel ta'anis* at a previous *t'fillah*. Ritvah suggests that while Rambam follows Shmuel [34b] with regard to a full day Fast, he follows Rav [34a] with regard to a *ta'anis sha'os*.

Kabbalas Ta'anis

<14> Re: Rav [34a]:

a. R. Yehonatan MiLuniel: The afternoon is meant specifically. This is because it is immediately prior to the beginning of the Fast. Thus, *kabbalas ta'anis* during the morning previous to the Fast is an invalid *Kabbalah*.

b. Ritva: *Kabbalah* may precede the Fast by many days. His proof for this is derived from the *G'mara's* proof from the statement in *M'gilaṣ Ta'anis* "Any man that has been subject to a Fast previous to this "*ye'asar*." This is understood to mean, "he should bind himself [beyond his previous boundedness] ."

Were it that Rav insisted that it is only during the preceding afternoon that one could accept a Fast,then this would not be a proof to Rav. As it serves as a proof indicates that Rav allows the Fast to be accepted many days in advance—as is the case with any *neder* of *mitzvah*.

Shmuel requires the Fast to be accepted immediately prior to the day because he does not consider this *kabbalah* to be a real *neder mitzvah*. To this end, the *kabbalah* is to be understood as being similar to recitation of *kiddush* which is to be made concurrent with the acceptance of the day.

c. Mordechai: It may be said anytime during the afternoon *except* during the *t'fillah*.

<15> Re: Shmuel [34b]:

a. Rashi and other Rishonim: *Kabbalah* may be made only during *t'fillas mincha* or it is invalid;

b. Ritva, Mordecai: בדיעבד it may be said anytime during the afternoon (i.e., Shmuel agree with Rav בדיעבד).

Kabbalas Ta'anis

	In PM only		In *mincha*	
	Rav	Shmuel	Rav	Shmuel
Rashi	Yes	Yes	Also	Only
Mordecai	Yes	Yes	No	Also
Ritva	No	Yes No[1]	Also	Only[2]

1. For purposes of being obligated to fast.
2. For purposes of saying anenu.

Analysis of <14> & <15>

The significance of limiting the acceptance of a Fast to the preceding afternoon—which would not be the case if we were dealing with an ordinary vow, or even a *neder mitzvah*—is that, with regard to Fast Days, there exists the dictum of "קדשו צום" (sanctify the Fast) [12b]. To encompass the whole day, the sanctification announcement need be made prior to the day. As with Shabbos and Yom Tov the pronouncement cannot be made sooner than the preceding afternoon since it is at this time that the potential properties of the succeeding day begin to make their presence felt.

The significance of limiting *kabbalah* to *t'fillas mincha* is that the sanctification of the Fast קדשו צום is most appropriately made during the *t'fillah*—as is the case with regard to *Shabbos and Yom Tov*.

According to the Ritva <14b> Rav and Shmuel consider *kabbalas ta'anis* to be a a *neder mitzvah* (a vow to perform a commandment). A *neder mitzvah* may be made many days in advance of the performance of the *mitzvah*. Shmuel, however, is also concerned with the element of קדשו צום. To this end, he insists that a second *kabbalah* be made during *t'fillas mincha*. If this was not done, Shmuel requires the person to fast because of his original vow but does not permit him to say *anenu* because he did not properly sanctify the day and give it the significance of a Fast Day.

The Mordechai explains that Shmuel is more inclusive than Rav. Shmuel permits *kabbalas hata'anis* **even** during the *t'fillah*; Rav does not. Rav believes that *kabbalas ta'anis* is not appropriate to *t'fillah*. It is considered to be merely *sichas chulin* (mundane speech) [See Bach 573]. Shmuel disagrees; *kabbalas ta'anis* serves the function of truly elevating the nature of the day.

<16> Re: [34b] : The *nusach* of "*kabbalah*?"

a. *Miktam*: ענני אלקי בתענית שאעשה למחר
b. *Orchos Chayim, Kol Bo/Ri*: הריני בתענית יחיד למחר
c. Riv'van: יהי רצון שתהא תעניתי שאתענה למחר מקובלת
d. R. Yehonatan Miluniel: The person should first add supplications for salvation from the particular problem at hand. At the conclusion of these supplications he should add, "and because of this [specific reason] I am fasting tomorrow."
e. Rambam (*Ta'anis* 1:10): *Haga'os Maimonis* writes that Rambam requires the recitation of *anenu*. This is not mentioned in our text.

<17> Re: [34b]: Where is "*kabbalah*" added in *sh'moneh esreh?*

Weekdays

a. R. Yehonatan, Ritvah: שומע תפלה;
b. Rashi, Talmid haRamban: Before אלקי נצור.

On Shabbos/Yom Tov

a. Tosefos (*Avodah Zara* 34a) : Before אלקי נצור.

<18> May one say *anenu* if there was not a proper *kabbalah*?

a. Ritva: Shmuel agrees that one who "accepts" the Fast in the afternoon but not during the *t'fillah* must fast. Nevertheless, in this case, Shmuel would be of the opinion that he may not say *anenu*.

b. Tosefos (*Avodah Zarah* 34a): R. Tam, *Agur*: If there was merely *kabbalah b'lev* and/or this did not take place until the evening of the Fast, the Fast is valid and he may recite *anenu*. Shmuel's law is only לכתחלה

<19> The *Halakha*—

a. Rif, Rambam, Ritva: Is in accordance with Shmuel;
b. Others (cited in Ritva): Is in accordance with Rav;
c. *Shulchan Arukh*: Is in accordance with Shmuel.

Summary Outline: 12a

Until when can he eat?

[44] Jerusalem Talmud: R. Yehudah N'siyah (Grandson of Rebbe) entered N'tzivin on the eve of Yom Kippur. Even though he had completed his pre-fast meal he was prevailed upon to eat again.

[45] Jerusalem Talmud: If he declared (*hisnah*) that he intended to eat again then [even if he went to sleep or cleared the table] he may eat again.

Analysis

<20> The *halakha* follows Rebbe [35a]. (Rif, Rashi)

<21> Otzar HaGeonim, Rambam, Ritva: This law applies both to a *ta'anis yachid* and a *ta'anis tzibbur*.

<22> a. Rashi: The *Halakha* follows Version II [36b] that the sole determinant is sleep. (Also, Rif as explained by Talmid haRamban, Rambam, Vilna Gaon, *Sefer haBatim, Bal haTzroros*.)

b. R. Chananel: *Halakha* follows Version I [36a] that the sole determinant is clearing the table.

c. Rif (As explained by Ran, Milchamos, Ritva and Rosh) : *Halakha* follows Version II. However Version II follows the view that the only time you cannot continue eating is if the person both went to sleep *and* cleaned the table. If either component is absent he may continue his meal.

d. Ra'avad is stringent. He rules that a person may not eat if either he finished eating or he went to sleep. (Rid's text reads, "If he fell asleep in the *middle of his meal* he may no longer eat.")

There are several ingredients which motivate the *rishonim* in this matter. The first concerns the question of what is the status of a half-day Fast. Specifically, is this a Fast which was לכתחלה meant to be a half-day Fast or was it truly meant to be a 24 hour Fast, but, because the Rabbis felt that this would be too burdensome upon the congregation, they only decreed that the Fast span the daylight hours? (This can be said to be the basis of the dispute as to whether one should recite *anenu* at *ma'ariv* on a half-day Fast. See <12>.) The second concerns the question of whether by the mechanism of *kabbalah* one may extend a *ta'anis tzibbur*. According to Tur (O.H. 592), Ra'avad rules that *kabbalah* of a *ta'anis* can extend the fast and this *kabbalah* can be passive in nature. Hence, he is stringent about the case in point. Rif, on the other hand, requires an active *kabbalah*. This should mean that since there was no active *kabbalah* in this case that the person should be able to eat until עלות השחר in any case. However, we suggest that the Rif interprets Abaye and Rava's law [36] to be based on the fact that half-day Fasts were really meant to be full day Fasts (Ritva). The Rabbis only allowed eating at night begrudgingly. Therefore, where the person shows conclusively that he no longer intends to eat we require him to fast from that point on.

<23> Do "Conditions" help?

If a person makes a condition that he intends to eat again even if he cleans the table and/or falls asleep—

a. Ritva: We abide by his "condition."
b. Magid Mishnah (1:1), haBatim, Tashbatz (114) (Note 501 Ritva): As no mention is made in the Babylonian Talmud regarding "conditions" we must assume that a condition would not help. [See a full discussion on this point in Note 501 in Ritva.]

   This follows from our explanation above that a "condition" would not change the status of Abaye/Rava's law. We showed that the Rabbis only begrudgingly permitted people to eat at night. As such, their *"heter"* only extended to one evening meal and/or until one fell asleep.

<24> Fasts which begin at night: Until when may a person eat?

a. Gaon (cited in Rif): Until sunset (Ritva: even if he stopped eating beforehand);
b. Rif: [a] is qualified thus: so long as he was not *m'kabel ta'anis*. No distinction is made between eating and drinking. (Also Miktam, Rambam, Ra'avad [based on Ta'anis 28: "Once one

eats the *seudah hamafsekes* Erev 9 Av the laws of 9 Av apply." The latter is only true for 9 Av, not other fasts. Thus, on other Fast Days, it is only with kabbalah that eating and drinking become prohibited]).

c. Ramban: Tosefes (adding to the day) does not exist with respect to these Fast Days [See *P'sachim* 54b]. Thus under all circumstances [even if he made a "condition"] he may eat and drink until בין השמשות (twilight).

<25> When does the day begin

Kra HaGever—

a. Talmid Ramban: This refers to the first crow of the cock;
b. R. Yehonatan miLuniel: This refers to the time people begin waking up.

The dispute between Rebbe and R. Shimon b. Gamliel is based upon whether objective or subjective factors are to be followed. Rebbe rules that the fast begins at the moment that the day begins which is עלות השחר. R. Shimon b. Gamliel rules that the fast begins at the time *people* begin to wake up.

<26> Re: [38]: One who accepts a Fast Day

a. Rashi (*P'sachim* 54b): Shmuel refers to the ban of the five ענוים. Also, [38] only applies to Fasts for rain and specifically in Babylonia. The reason is that the need for rain in Babylonia is never as drastic as in Israel, because, in the former, there is normally a sufficient amount of rainfall.

R. Yehonatan miLuniel concurs with Rashi's reason. He states that [38] refers to Fasts which start in the evening and he only addresses the question of wearing shoes. It was common even in Babylonia to fast "forty or fifty days [for other reasons] until God answered their prayers."

b. Ra'avad: Shmuel's law refers to *the prohibition against work*. The reason for this is that *they were poor in Babylonia*; thus, this restriction could not be imposed upon them. If it applied to washing, the reason for being lax in Babylonia is because the atmospheric conditions require that a person wash constantly.

c. Ritva: Disagrees with Rashi's analysis. If, as per Rashi, What does "except for 9 Av" mean? There are still "Public Fast Days" which can be declared for reasons other than rain? During these fasts, the five ענוים were observed (R. Yehudah Nesiyah (14b)). Ritva, therefore, adopts the following explanation also advanced by the Ramban:

Ramban: [38] applies to all Fasts. It also applies throughout the

Diaspora. The reason for [38] is that one could not have a *ta'anis tzibbur* because there was no *nasi* in Babylonia. The presence of a *nasi* is necessary for it is only he who can impose a Fast upon all Israel unilaterally. This reason is stated explicitly in the Jerusalem Talmud 2:1.

d. Geonim/Ritva: Nevertheless, in Babylonia there is *neilah* "24 brakhos" and shofar. The last is independent of the severity of the Fast. It is determined only by the time being סוף בקשת רחמים.

<27> To avoid the Dilemma of [37]

a. *Hashlama*: The person should say "Behold! I accept upon myself a *ta'anis yachid.*" (Also, Tosefos 12b)
b. Ravia, Rosh, Ritva : We no longer need be concerned about [37] because the *halakha* follows [38]. [37] applies only at such time that *ta'anis tzibbur* is practiced.

Notwithstanding, 9 Av is still considered a *ta'anis tzibbur* because it has its origin in the Prophets.

c. Thus, today all Fast Days only involve abstinence from eating and drinking.

<28> Lan b'ta'aniso[39]:

a. Ritva: [39] (Rav) applies even when one wishes to exchange a specific day which was designated as a Fast Day. (Also Ra'ah, Rashbah [*Shabbos 11a], Ra'avad, Ran, Riv'van Ohr Zaru'ah, Rashi and Riva [as per Ohr Zaru'ah].)*
b. Rambam: [39] applies only to a non-designated day (i.e., X declared, "I will fast ten days," but did not specify which ten days. Anticipating that today would be one of these days, he began fasting. He may exchange this day for another. (Rif *[Tshuvos301] Ri Miluniel)*
c. Rosh: [39] applies even when one said, "I will fast on ***this*** day" so long as this is not a special day such as a *yahrzeit*. (Also, *T'rumas haDeshen* 275)

<29> Circumstances for which one is permitted to exchange a fast

a. Ritva: A Fast may be exchanged to attend a voluntary function. He derives this from the incident with R. Yehoshua b. Idi [40] where the latter was merely invited to dine with people. In that case there were no extenuating circumstances.

(The rationale is that *kabbalas ta'anis* is not a regular vow but a *neder mitzvah* similar to "I will give *this* coin to *tzedakah.*" In the latter case the person may exchange the coin for another)

b. R. Chananel: A fast may be exchanged only when the person is in pain. [40] speaks of this prototype.

c. Rif/Rambam: It may be exchanged if a person is called on to attend a סעודת מצוה or a meal in honor of a great scholar.

d. R. Yehonatan miLuniel: Adds to [b] and [c] the need to attend a סעודת מריעות (friendly gathering) because of *darkei shalom* (to stay on friendly terms).

<30> Rationale for exchanging a Fast

a. Ritva: A fast may be exchanged because the *kabbalas ta'anis* is not a regular vow but a *neder mitzvah*. The person's vow—while it might have sounded specific—was not directed at a specific day. Rather, it was a person's call to pour out his heart and soul before God. Thus, it may be done on any day.

R. Yosef Rosen offers the following insight. The person who adopts a fast does not intend to say, "I prohibit myself from eating and drinking on *this* [particular] day." Rather, he means to say, "This day shall be unto me a fast day." The difference is this. In the first alternative the person is pronouncing a regular vow against eating and drinking on a certain day. As such, it may not be altered without it being rescinded (*hataras n'darim*) In the latter case the person is not prohibiting himself from eating and drinking. Rather, he is accepting a *ta'anis* upon himself—not eating and drinking is a secondary consequence of a *ta'anis*. Accepting a *ta'anis* is an expression of the desire to do a *mitzvah*. This expression does not fall under the rubric of *nidrei issur* but *nidrei mitzvah*.

<31> Re: [39a&b]:

a. Ritva: [39a] believes that *kabbalas hata'anis* is a *neder mitzvah*. It is to anguish over his sins. Because of this, where this brings about difficulty, it may be absolved. [39b] likewise considers *kabbalas ta'anis* a *neder mitzvah*. However, it must be repaid as would any other *neder mitzvah*.

SECTION D

Summary Outline: 12b

Second [Middle] Series of Fasts

Mishna

[1] a. Fasting is observed night and day.
b. Work is prohibited. (See <10c>.)
c. Eating, washing, annointing, wearing shoes and copulation are prohibited.
d. Bathhouses are closed.

Note: The balance of this mishna is listed in later sections together with the G'mara which modifies it.

G'mara

[2] R. Chisda/R. Yirmiya b. Aba: *M'lakha* (work) is prohibited on a Fast Day based upon the verse, "Sanctify a Fast." (*Yo'el* 1:14)

[3] R. Zera: "Gather the Elders" (*Yo'el* 1:14)—just as the Elders [Sanhedrin] gather only during the day, so too, fasting is limited to the daylight hours.

[4] R. Huna: The Elders gathered on the morning of a Fast Day.

[5] Abaye: Until noon [of a Fast Day], they [the Elders] examined their deeds; the next quarter day they read from the Torah and Prophets, and the last quarter of the day they prayed.

Summary Outline: 13a&b

Washing on Fast Days

[6] Rifram b. Papa/R. Chisda:

a. On a communal day of mourning, for example, Tisha b'Av and Mourning—
Washing in **hot or cold water is *prohibited*.**

b. On a day such as a Public Fast in which *ta'anug* (pleasure) was prohibited—

Washing in **hot water is *prohibited*;**
Washing in **cold water is *permitted*.**

[7] R. Idi b. Avin:

A proof for [6] is that the *Mishna* requires the bath houses [warm water] to be closed. Thus cold water is permissible.

[8] *Braisa* [B_1]:

a. Those obligated to immerse [*t'villah*] **may do so** in the usual fashion on **both 9 Av and Yom Kippur**.

b. R. Chanina, Deputy High Priest: Our House of God merits that a man should forego an immersion once a year.

[9] While [8a] could speak of **cold water**, R. Channa b. K'tina posits that it discusses a *mikveh* heated with the **Natural Hot springs of Tiberias**. Based on this R. Papa explains that [8b] speaks of a place in which there are no cold water *mikva'os*; since immersion in a cold water *mikveh* would be permissible.

[10] *Braisa* [B_2]:
When they said work is prohibited...[on a Public Fast Day];
When they said wearing shoes was prohibited;
When they said washing—

The whole body is *prohibited*;
Hands, feet and face (hereafter "parts") are *permitted*.

"This is true with regard to those placed under a ban and to mourners."

[11] R. Sheshes/R. Chisda (13b): A mourner *may not* stick his hand in **warm water**.

[12] G'mara:

a. Based on [11], [10] should speak of **cold water**.

b. No! It speaks of **warm water**, but the reference to mourner does not apply to the case of washing.

[13] Question: R. Aba Kohen/R. Yossi Kohen: R. Yosi b. Chanina washed in **cold water** all seven days he was in mourning.

[14] Answer: [13] speaks of consecutive bereavements

[15] Rava (R_1): A mourner is *permitted* to wash **in cold water** all seven days similar to his being permitted to eat meat and drink wine.

[16] Rava (R_2): A mourner is *prohibited* from washing in **cold water** all seven days. Wine and meat are *permitted* only because these counteract his fears.

[17] *Halakha*:
Mourner: Washing—
Whole body: *Prohibited* in **water of any kind**;
Parts of body: *Prohibited* in **warm water**;
Permitted in **cold water**;
Annointing is prohibited except to remove dirt.

Note: Before analyzing this G'mara we shall compare it to several others dealing with this topic.

[18] R. Eliezer (*P'sachim* 54b): A person may not place his hand in water either on 9 Av or Yom Kippur.

[19] R. Yehoshua b. Levi (*Yoma* 78a)— would soak a towel in water on Erev Yom Kippur and would allow it to dry out. On the morrow he would wipe his hands, feet and face.

On Erev 9 Av he would soak a towel in water. The next morning he would wipe his eyes with it.

[20] The following was the custom of R. Yehoshua b. Levi: (*Yoma* 8:1)

a. Fast day: He would wash parts of his body in the usual manner [i.e., **warm water**];
b. Tisha b'Av: He would wash his hands and pass them over his face;
c. Yom Kippur: He washed his hands; dried them on a towel; and then passed the towel over his face.

Advanced Analysis

Aspects of key statements are unknown. This leads to alternate interpretations. We shall first analyze the G'mara on our own and then investigate how this compares to the analysis of the commentaries.

(1) [6], [15] and [16] are unclear as to whether they speak of Parts or of the Whole Body.

(2) [11] indicates that R. Chisda prohibits a mourner from washing parts of his body in **warm water**. Thus, [6] should be understood to prohibit even washing Parts. This leaves open the question of whether [6b] permits washing the whole or just parts of the body in **cold** water.

B_2, [10], permits Parts. For it to correspond with [11] and [6] only alternative [12b] which speaks of hot water and distinguishes this case from mourners is acceptable.

Summary

From [11]: For a mourner: Parts are prohibited in warm water and are permitted in cold water.

Thus [6a] which prohibits washing in even cold water deals with washing the entire body.

From [12b]: On a Fast Day: One may not wash his whole body in warm water, but he may wash parts of his body in warm water.

[6b] speaks of washing the entire body. (This is the only alternative.)

R. Chisda: As per [12b]							
Fast Day				Mourner/9 Av			
Whole		Parts		Whole		Parts	
Wrm	Cld	Wrm	Cld	Wrm	Cld	Wrm	Cld
No	Yes	Yes	Yes	No	No	No	Yes

(3) Regarding Rava $_1$, [15], it appears that Rava agrees with R. Chisda in prohibiting a mourner from placing his hands into warm water. Rava does not, however, make a distinction between mourning and Fast Days. Consequently, he would adopt [12a] and allow only Parts of the body to be washed in **cold water**. As such, his view is aligned with the *hilkh'sa*.

Summary

From [11]: Mourners may not wash parts of their body in warm water, but may do so using cold water.

From [12a]: On a Fast Day: Parts of the body may be washed with cold water but not the entire body.

Therefore, one may not wash even parts of his body in warm water.

[15]—discusses a mourner, but it is unclear whether the ruling applies to the whole or parts of the body.

From [10] and [12]: "The same is true for mourners," it is derived that a mourner may not wash his whole body in cold water.

Rava$_1$: As per [12]							
Fast Day				Mourner/9 Av			
Whole		Parts		Whole		Parts	
Wrm	Cld	Wrm	Cld	Wrm	Cld	Wrm	Cld
No	No	No	Yes	No	No	No	Yes

Rava$_1$ as outlined above corresponds to [20]. [20] permits a person to wash his hands even on Tisha b'Av.

(4) With regard to Rava$_2$, [16], it would seem that he prohibits a mourner from washing any part of his body even in cold water (R. Chisda and Rava$_1$ permit the washing of parts in cold water; this is the only way in which this position would be different than the other two.) He also agrees with R. Eliezer [18] who obviously prohibits **even cold water.** With regard to [10] he would ascribe to alternative [12a] as per the simple meaning of [10].

Rava$_2$: As per [12a]

Fast Day				**Mourner/9 Av**			
Whole		**Parts**		**Whole**		**Parts**	
Wrm	**Cld**	**Wrm**	**Cld**	**Wrm**	**Cld**	**Wrm**	**Cld**
No	**No**	**No**	**Yes**	**No**	**No**	**No**	**No**

Rava$_2$ corresponds to R. Eliezer's position, which prohibits a person from placing his hand in **cold water** on Tisha b'Av [13], and on Fast Days he permits only the washing of parts of the body in cold water.

Analysis: Rishonim

<1> The Rishonim divide into two groups.

Miktam and R. Yitzhak of Milinsh follow the position just outlined. Namely R. Chisda [11] argues with R. Eliezer [20] (P'sachim 54b). The latter prohibits one to stick his hands even into **cold** water on Tisha b'Av, the latter permits this to be done.

Ritva, Talmid haRamban and Hashlama take the view that R. Chisda does not argue with R. Eliezer. He, too, prohibits one to wash even his face in cold water on Tisha b'Av. Given that [6] speaks of washing parts of the body, then on a fast day, one could not wash his full body even in cold water. Ritva's text does not contain [11]. The question from [10] is simply that R. Chisda equates the laws of washing for a mourner to that of 9 Av, whereas the *braisa* [10] equates the laws of mourners to that of a Public Fast Day. According to Ritva, R. Chisda's view is as follows:

R. Chisda							
Fast Day				Mourner/9 Av			
Whole		Parts		Whole		Parts	
Wrm	Cld	Wrm	Cld	Wrm	Cld	Wrm	Cld
No	Yes	Yes	Yes	No	No	No	No

Ritva understands that $Rava_1$ [15] makes his comment with regard to the washing of the entire body. He disagrees with R. Chisda that the washing restrictions upon a mourner are equivalent to those prevailing during a Public Fast Day. According to his opinion the statement in the *braisa* [10] "this is true...[for] mourners" is true as it stands.

$Rava_1$							
Fast Day				Mourner/9 Av			
Whole		Parts		Whole		Parts	
Wrm	Cld	Wrm	Cld	Wrm	Cld	Wrm	Cld
No	Yes	Yes	Yes	No	Yes	Yes	Yes

$Rava_2$ also adopts the view that the laws of 9 Av are more stringent with regard to washing than are the restrictions for a mourner. He interprets [16] to refer to the washing of the whole body. $Rava_2$'s position is as follows:

Rava$_2$							
Fast Day				Mourner/9 Av			
Whole		Parts		Whole		Parts	
Wrm	Cld	Wrm	Cld	Wrm	Cld	Wrm	Cld
No	Yes	Yes	Yes	No	No	Yes	Yes

The Ritva therefore makes a three way distinction—

1. 9 Av represents mourning for a very public tragedy. As such, its laws are most stringent. To wit, one may not wash parts of his body even in cold water.
2. Mourning commemorates one's personal loss. In the broad scope this is a lesser tragedy than 9 Av. The laws are, therefore, less stringent. One may wash parts of his body in cold water.
3. On a Public Fast Day when only *ta'anug* is prohibited one may wash his whole body in cold water and parts of his body in warm water.

Summary Outline: 13b

Annenu

[21] R. Yehudah: An individual who proclaims a personal Fast Day includes *anenu* in his prayers; as a separate *brakha* between ראה נא and רפאנו.

[22] R. Yitchak (Yosef), R. Sheshes: Argues that an individual may not add a *brakha* to the *sh'moneh esreh*. Rather *anenu* is included as part of שומע תפלה.

[23] Question: Braisa: No distinction exists between an individual (*yachid*) and congregation (*tzibbur*) except that an individual prays eighteen blessings and the congregation nineteen.

"Yachid" must refer to *ta'anis yachid* and *"tzibbur"* must refer to *ta'anis tzibbur*. Thus on a private Fast only eighteen blessings are recited. Hence *anenu* is said in שומע תפלה.

[24] No! It is possible that [23] speaks only of a public Fast, *"yachid"* refers to the individual recitation of the *sh'moneh esreh; "tzibbur"* to the repetition of the *shli'ach tzibbur*.

[25] A digression is made to discuss the parameters of when the "Twenty-Four Blessings" are recited. (See II-<2>.)

[26] Conclusion

a. Rav: Anenu is said between ראה נא and רפאנו.

b. R. Yanai b. R. Yishmael: It is recited in שומע תפלה.

c. *Halakha*: It is recited in שומע תפלה.

[27] *Shabbos* 24a: Braisa: One says *anenu* in אלקי נצור .

Analysis

<2> *Miktam/Ra'avad, Hashlamah, Talmid haRamban*: Amoraim argue only in the case of an individual who accepted upon himself a private Fast with the stringencies of a public Fast. If he merely accepted a private fast all agree as per [7] that *anenu* is said in שומע תפלה.

Where does the *sh'liach tzibbur* say *anenu* on public fasts?

<3> Rid, Talmid haRamban : The *sh'liach tzibbur* says *anenu* as a separate *brakha* and concludes העונה בעת צרה.

Eshkol: An individual who is repeating the *sh'moneh esreh* with the *chazzan* does not say *anenu* as a separate *brakha*.

Agur: To say *anenu* as a separate *brakha* ten people must be fasting.

Agur: A person who is not fasting may act as a *sh'liach tzibbur* on a Fast day and recite *anenu* if there is no one else present who knows how to *daven*.

Where does the *sh'liach tzibbur* say *anenu* on private fasts?

<4> Talmid haRamban: The *sh'liach tzibbur* does not say anenu as a separate *brakha* on a *ta'anis yachid* even if there is a *minyan* of "fasters."

He rejects the opinion of those who hold that an individual praying in a *minyan* may say *anenu* as a separate blessing. Were this a viable option [23] could have been explained thereby.

Where does the *sh'liach tzibbur* say *anenu* on *Shabbos*?

<5> Geonim, Ritva: An individual says it before אלקי נצור.

Jerusalem Talmud: In the situation wherein a congregation may fast on Rosh Chodesh, the *sh'liach tzibbur* inserts *anenu* as an independent blessing after הא-ל הקדוש.

HaManhig, Bha"g, Tosefos and Rosh (*B'rakhos* 31b): When one recites *anenu* before אלקי נצור he concludes it with a blessing (*chosem bibrakha*). This is not problematic since it is unusual and because it is being recited after the *sh'moneh esreh*. R. Amram, Rif and Rambam disagree.

Summary Outline: 14a

Pregnant and Nursing Mothers

[28] Three Braisos are listed which appear contradictory. R. Ashi resolves this apparent contradiction by explaining that pregnant and nursing mothers fast only during the middle three fasts.

Analysis

<6> Rishonim explain that pregnant and nursing mothers do not fast during the first three fasts because the danger is not yet that acute. They also do not fast during the last seven fasts as the requirements are too demanding.

Rambam disagrees with the above interpretation. He maintains that pregnant and nursing mother fast *only* on the Last Fasts.

[29] The outline of *masri'in* begins with III-[4]. The analysis follows.

Summary Outline: 14a-15a

[30] *Mishna*: Third [Last] Series of [Seven] Fasts

a. All of the laws of the Middle Fasts are applicable;
b. *Shofar/chatzotzeros* are sounded; (See Chapter 3.)
c. Stores are closed. (See [33].)

Maximum number of Fasts for catastrophies other than rain

[31] Braisa:

a. Rebbe: The *beis din* should never declare more than thirteen Fasts; as this is an excessive burden for the congregation. (See <7>.)
b. R. Shimon b. Gamliel: There is no maximum number of Fasts.

[32] R. Yehuda N'siyah and R. Yochanan follow R. Shimon b. Gamliel. R. Ami follows Rebbe.

[33] *Braisa*: Closing Stores

a. On Monday the stores open towards evening.
b. On Thursday they are open the whole day (for *Shabbos* buying).
c. If a store has two doors, the proprietor opens one and keeps the other closed. (See <9>.)
d. If there is a stand in front of the door he may open the door in the usual way.

[34] *Mishna*; After the thirteen fasts are completed—

a. Business dealings are restricted;
b. Building and planting, and marriage are restricted; (see [35a])
c. Greeting people is prohibited; (see 35b);
d. *Y'chidim* continue to fast until the end of Nisan;
e. If it rains after Nisan it is a סימן קללה (curse).

[35] G'mara:

a. re: [34a and b] Braisa: In [34b] it is pursuits of joy which are prohibited; the prohibition against "building" refers to the building of a house for the marriage feast of one's son; that against planting refers to the building of a royal banquet hall [or the planting of a tree which will later be used for making a wedding canopy.]
b. re: [34c] Braisa: If one is greeted by an *am ha'aretz* who is ignorant of the law, he may return the salutation in a solemn manner.
c. The people are to sit as mourners, as people placed under a ban.
d. re: [34d]: R. Elazar: an important person should not be נופל על פניו (fall on his face in prayer) or wear sack-cloth unless he can be assured that he will be answered.

R. Elazar: Not all may be נופל על פניהם (as did Moshe and Aharon) or rend their garments (as did Yehoshua and Kalev). (R. Zera argues that Yehoshua also was נופל על פניו.)

R. Elazar: In the Messianic era only kings will stand before Israel, whereas princes will prostrate themselves. (R. Zera argues that princes will rise and prostrate themselves.)

R. Nachman b. Yitzchak: In the Messianic era *tzaddikim* will "see the light" and the upright will be invested with joy.

Analysis: 14b

<7> Thirteen Fast Limit

There are two different textual readings:

a. The Standard Text:

R. Yehudah wishes to declare more than thirteen fasts for catastrophies other than rain. R. Ami declares that thirteen is the maximum number of fasts that can be called. R. Yochanan—R. Ami's Rebbe—is shown to disagree. He argues that thirteen is only a maximum with regard to rain (because after that the predominant rainy season is over [see R. Gershom]). A braisa is then cited to show that this point is disputed by *tannaim*.

b. Rif's text: (See Rivav, Ran, Talmid haRamban and Ritva)

The situation of R. Yehudah Nesiyah (whether it involved rain fasts or not) is unclear. R. Ami explains to him that one does not declare more than thirteen fasts as this is overly burdensome on the congregation. R. Yochanan then delimits this restriction to Fasts announced for lack of rain.

The outcome does not change according to either text. **One may call more than thirteen fasts in non-rain situations.** The Ritvah writes that even in Fasts for rain one may declare more than thirteen Fasts in regions where there is a prolonged rainy season.

The tannaitic and amoraic dispute centers about the question of whether there is an intrinsic importance to not going beyond **thirteen** fasts or is this number just arrived at merely through external considerations—there is only time for thirteen Fasts within the height of the rainy season. Those who argue that there should only be a maximum of thirteen fasts do so on the basis that the number "thirteen" is reminiscent of the thirteen attributes of mercy. As we find, that the Fast sequences are divided into three and seven— numbers associated with *taharah*—so, too, the total number of Fasts should total a number which symbolizes mercy and forgiveness.

<8> Sequence of non-rain fasts

a. Ran: All fasts no matter what their severity must proceed on the basis of a sequence of 3, 3, 7.

b. Ritva: The order of 3, 3, 7 is only to be followed when the severity of the problem is progressive. Otherwise Fasts are to be held as needed on Mondays and Thursdays.

Closing stores

<9> Rashi: [33c&d] refers to Monday. Even on Monday, if the store has two doors the proprietor may keep one door completely open.

Rashi states that the rationale for not keeping food stores open is that it would cause people grief.

Concerning [33d], Rashi explains that the stand prevents people on the street from seeing the open door. While he is silent about [33c] it would seem that it is referring to the situation in which the second door does not face the street (a back door). This door may be kept open.

The difficulty with this approach is that the *G'mara* should then have been more explicit about its concern for things being seen from the street.

<10> Riv'van/Rambam: [33c] refers to Thursday. It is only on Thursday that one door may be opened completely. Similarly [33d] refers to Thursday.

Thus [33c & d] delimit the *heter* to open Thursday. While the store must be open לכבוד שבת the appearance of its being open should be minimized.

Falling Prostrate

<11> Re: [35d]: The following limitation is found in the Jerusalem Talmud (As cited by the Ran, Miktam and Riv'van): "This prohibition applies only to a person who prays in public." We find that R. Akiva used to fall prostrate when he prayed privately (*B'rachos* 31a).

A second opinion is cited in the name of the Jerusalem Talmud. The law applies only when one is praying "for the congregation's needs." This reading is supported by Ra'avad (*Hil. T'fillah 5:14), and Tosefos, M'gilah (20b). Ran, M'iri, and Rosh combine the reasons. That is, the law applies only to one who prays in public for the congregation. This second opinion is not found in our editions of the Jerusalem Talmud. (See Hirshler.)*

Rishonim list several reasons for this law—

1. It will be a great disgrace if he is not answered; (Rashi)
2. He will appear haughty in the eyes of the congregation; (Rid, Talmid haRamban)
3. If he is not secure in his piety (בטוח בחסידות) perhaps he will not be answered; Heaven's name will be disgraced and he will be suspected of not being truly pious. (*Miktam*)

Summary Outline: 14b

Restrictions on Building

[36] Jerusalem Talmud: If a wall is hazardous it must be knocked down and rebuilt.

Analysis

<12> Ran: The combination of statements in the Bavli and Yerushalmi serve to delimit the scope of prohibited work. [36] prohibits any non-essential work from being done. By implication, [35a] only prohibits joyous pursuits, but permits necessary work.

R. Hai Gaon observes that since the *Mishna* equates business pursuits to building a house for a marriage feast he deduces that just as business refers to a voluntary pursuit, so, too, does the case of marriage. Thus, where marriage is a *halakhic* necessity—where one must fulfil the *mitzvah* of *p'ru u'r'vu*—he may even build a house for a marriage feast.

<13> Riv'van: In [36] the wall in question is a hazard. The Rabbis permit him to rebuild it during this period for, if not, he might not wish to knock it down.

Taz (O.H. 551) permits a wall to be knocked down even for only economic considerations.

<14> Rid—seems to have a contrary text. Specifically, he writes that it is *only* building which is for a joyous activity which may be performed.

R. M. Hirshler suggests that the Rid agrees with the other texts. He merely refers to the law which prohibits work during the Middle Fasts. Concerning this he writes that it is only routine work which is prohibited; work done for the performance of a *mitzvah* is permitted. He derives this from R. Chananel's explanation to the G'mara on *M'gilah* 5b. (See notes to *Piskei Rid*, p. 22. n. 88.)

Ta'anis: Chapter Two

Introduction

Having set down the sequence and general laws of fasting in Chapter One, the Talmud goes on to review the actual procedure of the *t'fillos* on Fast Days (see below as to when this procedure is applicable). The *Mishna* discusses the distinction between the procedure in and out of the Temple. This leads to a review of the fasting procedures of those who were involved in the Temple service, i.e., *anshei mishmar* and *anshei ma'amad*. (We postpone an analysis of these laws until the last chapter as this enables us to study the laws pertaining to the *Mikdash* as one unit.)

It has been assumed that Rain Fasts may be declared on any day. The *Mishna* continues with a study of the days that one is not permitted to fast. These are the days listed in *M'gilas Ta'anis*. The *Mishna* then states that no Fast sequence may begin on Thursday. Finally, the *Mishna* grapples with the question of a Fast Sequence which conflicts with *M'gilas Ta'anis*.

Summary Outline: 15a-16a

Mishna:

[1] The procedure on Fast Days is the following:

a. The ark is removed to the open space (*rechov*) of the city.
b. Ashes (*efer makleh*) are put—

(1) On the ark; (Rambam: and on the *sifrei Torah* (S.E.))
(2) The *nasi*'s head; (See [9] & [11].)
(3) The *av beis din*'s head.

c. Each person puts ashes on his own head. (See 10.)
d. The Elder admonished the congregation. (See below.)
e. They recited the *amidah* with six extra *brakhos*.

[See "Additional Six *Brakhos*" for a full description of these *brakhos*.]

[2] *Anshei mishmar (kohanim* who were obligated to work in the *Mikdash* on the week but not on the day of the Fast):

Series of Fast	First	Middle	Last
a) R. Yehoshua	Fast but do not complete	Fast	Fast
b) Chakhamim	Do not Fast	Fast but do not complete	Fast

[3] *Anshei beis av (kohanim* who were obligated to work in the *Mikdash* on the day of a Fast):

Series of fast	First	Middle	Last
a) R. Yehoshua	Do not Fast	Fast but do not complete*	Fast
b) Chakhamim	Do not Fast	Do not Fast	Fast but do not complete*

* They ate after midday (*S'fas Emes*).

[4] *Anshei mishmar* and *anshei beis av*: With regard to drinking wine and haircuts: This is discussed in Chapter 4.
[5] Re: *M'gilas Ta'anis*: See p. 102
[6] Conclusion of Mishna: See p. 110

G'mara:

[7] *Braisa:* During the First and Middle Fasts the *t'fillah* was carried on in the *shul*. During the Last Fasts it took place in the *rechov*.
[8] R. Papa: The *Mishna*, also, refers only to the Last Fasts.

[9] The ashes are put first on the head of the *nasi* [1b(2)] to indicate his importance. It is as if they would say to him "You are worthy enough to pray on our behalf for mercy."

[10] R. Aba of Kisri: [The reason that the *nasi* and *av beis din* have ashes put on their head is that] One cannot compare self inflicted embarrassment to imposed embarrassment.

[11] The ashes are placed on the forehead, where the *t'fillin* are normally placed.

Summary Outline: 15a&b, 16a, 19a 23a, y. Ta'anis 2:1

Procedure for a *Ta'anis Tzibbur*

The *Mishna* spells out the procedure to be followed on a *ta'anis tzibbur*. Following is its rationale as given in the *Bavli and Yerushalmi*.

[12] Congregation prays in the street

a. R. Chiya b Abba (TB): "We prayed in private quarters and were not answered let us embarrass ourselves by praying in public."
b. Reish Lakish (TB): This is considered symbolic exile; let it be an atonement for our sins.
c. R. Yehoshua b. Levi (TY): "Because we prayed privately and were not answered let us go into the street and make it known."

[13] Torah's are taken into the street

R. Yehoshua b. Levi (TB)/R. Chiya b. Bo (TY): We possess a precious secret gift and it has become disgraced through our actions.

[14] Sack-cloth is worn

R. Chiya b. Aba (TB): "We are as lowly as animals."

[15] Ashes are placed upon everyone's head

a. (TB): "We are as dust."
b. (TB)/(TY): As a remembrance of the Binding of Yitzchak.
c. (TY): As a remembrance of Avraham.

[16] Congregation visits cemetery

a. (TB)/(TY) R. Levi: "We are as dead."
b. (TB): So that the dead can pray for them.

[17] Blowing *Shofar*

R. Ya'akov (TY): "Think of us as crying animals."

Overview

Two Approaches to Prayer

An analysis of the reasons given in the *G'mara* reveals two distinct patterns. [12a&b], [14], [15a], [16a] and [17] all adopt the *tzaddok hadin* approach; if tragedy befalls the Jewish people it is because they have sinned. The only proper response is to approach God with profound humility.

This same approach is taken by almost all the Prophets in their prayers. A prime example is found in the following excerpts of a prayer offered by Nechemia. (8:6-33)

> Thou are Lord alone; thou hast made heaven, the heaven of heavens, with all their host, the earth, and all things that are in it, the seas and that is therein...Thou..who didst choose Avram, and didst bring him out of Ur Kasdim...and Thou didst see the conflict of our fathers in Egypt, and didst hear their cry by the sea of Suf...and Thou didst divide the sea before them...and Thou didst lead them with a pillar of cloud by day and Thou dist come down on Mount Sinai, and didst speak with them from Heaven and gavest them right judgments and good Toros, good statutes and commandments: and Thou didst make known to them thy holy Sabbath...
>
> But they and our fathers dealt arrogantly...and they refused to obey...they hardened their necks, and...appointed a captain to return to their bondage...they were disobedient...and they cast thy Torah behind their backs, and slew thy prophets...
>
> **Yet Thou are just in all that is brought upon us; for Thou hast done right, but we have done wickedly.**

There is, however, a second approach to prayer which is indicated by the second set of reasons posited in the Talmud. [12c] sets forth a challenge to God. We have indeed prayed, but *You did not answer us*—we now challenge You *publicly*. Likewise [15b & c] and [16b] take the very forward approach that we can approach God through strength given our familial background and the merit of our Elders (*z'khus avos*).

Chuni Ha'Magal approached God through Strength

This latter, rather astonishing, approach to prayer, is found accented in Chapter Three. The Talmud relates the story of Chuni, the Circle Drawer. Chuni was very forceful and demanding when he prayed to God. His name resulted from having once given God an ultimatum while praying. Setting down a circle of rocks around him, he proclaimed, "God, your children have turned to me as I am an integral member of your household (*ben bayis*). I swear by Your Great Name that I will not move from here until You have shown

Mercy towards your children!" His audacity was evidenced when it started to drizzle instead of rain; and Chuni boldly proclaimed, "This is not the type of rain for which I prayed!"

Chuni's manner of praying embarrassed the Nasi, Shimon b. Shetach. He proclaimed, " Were it not that you are Chuni, I would place you in *nidduy*...but what can I do to you [given that] you sin before God [and nevertheless] He carries out your will."

Prayer From Strength is not for Everyone

The remarks of Shimon b. Shetach as well as the formula adopted by the Prophets indicate that not everyone is at liberty to pray "from Strength." The *G'mara* relates (24a) that Levi beseeched God "from Strength" and was punished. The question is, Who may pray to God in this manner?

Interestingly, Chuni's privileged status was familial. The Jerusalem Talmud notes that his grandfather successfully prayed for rain in this manner and the Babylonian Talmud reports that his two grandsons, Abba Chilkiya and Channan haNechbah were, also, answered whenever they prayed for rain.

A Clue is to be found in Chuni's Prayer

Two seemingly extraneous points mentioned by Chuni unlock the puzzle. Chuni states, "I am considered a House-member (*ben bayis*)," and "This is the nation that you brought up from Egypt." The latter appears out of place given that it occurred more than a thousand years previously.

What is the import of the first statement? A perusal of the Torah reveals that this appellation was used for only one other person, *Moshe Rabbenu*. Regarding Moshe we are told, "My servant Moshe...is the trusted one in all my house. With him I speak mouth to mouth..." (Numbers 11:7,8) Moshe prayed "from Strength." When the Jews sinned with the golden calf, Moshe accosted God saying, "Why are you angry God at the nation that you **took from Egypt**?" Truly God had a great deal to be angry about given that the Jewish people had just committed the gravest of sins shortly after Revelation. Yet, Moshe seemed oblivious to this in his prayers.

Further we find that Moshe also employed Chuni's tactics. When told he could not enter Israel, Moshe drew a circle and said I will remain herein until this decree is rescinded (Midrash Rabbah, D'varim 11:6). Thus Chuni followed the pattern set forth by Moshe Rabbenu. What gave only Chuni and his family this right?

Chuni's lineage and the importance of *z'khus avos*

Midrash Tanchuma (Va'era) reveals the answer. Chuni was a direct descendent of Moshe. His family was then considered to be "house-members" of God. To this end, they could implore God and He would respond to them. When Chuni uttered the words, "Your nation that you took from Egypt," he was merely reminding God of Moshe's prayer following the sin of the golden calf when Moshe used the same expression.

This teaches us a very important lesson. Regarding prayer, certain people are intrinsically more privileged than others. This is because they possess *z'khus avos*. This is echoed in the *G'mara*, "One cannot compare the prayer of a *tzaddik* whose father was a *tzaddik* and one whose father was wicked." (*Y'vamos* 64a)

Summary Outline: 15a

Earnestness of the T'shuvah of Ninveh

A dispute exists between the two Talmudim as to the ernestness of the people of Ninveh.

Jerusalem Talmud

[18] R. Shimon b Lakish: Ninveh's *t'shuvah* was one of trickery.

[19] R. Huna/R. Shimon b. Chalfusah: They placed suckling calves on the inside [of the corral] and their mothers on the outside. Each cried for the other. They [the Ninveites] said [to God] if you have no mercy on us we will not have mercy upon them.

[20] "They called out to God forcefully":

R. Shimon b. Chalfusa: *Chutzpa* accomplishes its aim when it is for the good, certainly when one uses it to approach God.

[21] *From the plunder which was in their hands*

R. Yochanan: The plunder which was visible [in their palms] they returned. That which was hidden away in the closets was not returned.

Babylonian Talmud

[22] Same as [19].

[23] "They called out to God forcefully":

What did they say? ...If one is submissive and the other is not, one is righteous and the other is not, which of them should yield?

[24] "From the plunder in their hands"

Shmuel: Even if one had stolen a beam and built it into his castle, he razed the entire castle to the ground and returned the beam to its owner.

Overview

T'shuvah of Ninveh

The Jerusalem Talmud, [18] and [19], posits that the people of Ninveh did not truly repent. This is in contradistinction to the Babylonian Talmud which indicates [24] that their *t'shuvah* was indeed complete. The position adopted by the Jerusalem Talmud is that incomplete *t'shuvah* is significant. Chasam Sofer writes that this is the lesson that Adam learned from Cain (*Toras Moshe*: *Nitzavim* p. 68). When Cain returned from his judgment, Adam asked him what had occurred. Cain answered I did *t'shuvah* and it was accepted. Adam responded, "I did not realize the strength of *t'shuvah*." Chasam Sofer explains that Adam's remarks were made in line with R. P'rakyia's interpretation that Cain came forth from the Lord in a devious manner. Adam said, I did not realize that non-complete repentance would be accepted. This view is also cited by Sadia Gaon and is in marked divergence from the Rambam who rules that a *ba'al t'shuvah* is only one about whom God would testify that his *t'shuvah* is so complete that he would never commit this crime again.

From the fact that [19] and [20] are placed between [18] and [21] which underscore the non-seriousness with which Ninveh repented, the Jerusalem Talmud understands that [19] and [20] are also acts of non-serious repentance. [19] and [21] are the incidents that are alluded to in [18]; [20] explains that notwithstanding, these actions are accepted by God. In effect [20] states that God will accept a plea—although that plea is stated irreverently—so long as it is true and meant to further a good cause. Since this is crucial to our understanding of the Jerusalem Talmud's approach, we shall elaborate.

It is difficult enough to understand the reason that God necessarily accepts the repentance of those who sin against Him Willfully. It is more difficult to understand how He can give any credence to a repentance which is only half-hearted. We believe the following to be its basis:

When a community outwardly manifests a desire to do *t'shuvah* in a situation similar to Ninveh, while lacking the necessary commitment, desire or fortitude to undertake a complete change of lifestyle, the effort alone affirms some belief in God. Although not a firm belief, God considers the very act of turning to Him to be very important; as it paves the way for real *t'shuvah* at a later time. Secondly, *"t'shuvah shelo lishma"* does not necessarily indicate an unwillingness to repent. Rather, it shows a personal inability to repent fully. In either case, God considers this first step of man to be very important.

The Babylonian Talmud essentially disagrees with the approach of the Jerusalem Talmud. There is no hint in the Babylonian Talmud that Ninveh's *t'shuvah* was of anything but the highest order. [24] is in direct disagreement with [21] and no parallel of [18] exists. To this end, [22] which is the equivalent of [19] is obviously understood differently.

We believe the Babylonian Talmud's interpretation of [19] to be as follows: Ninveh was saying to God, "We are like the calves who have been separated from their parents. A barrier has been set up between us. We want You, we beckon for You. True, we might not be deserving, but You are the Father of Mercy. You ask us to be good and merciful. Yet if You do not show Your countless Mercy to us, then we have no role-model which will teach us how to be merciful." (See Rashi)

[23] differs from [20]. [20] called [19] *chutzpah*. [23] considers [22] to simply be an action which calls on God to be merciful.

The moral derived from the Jerusalem Talmud is to be tolerant of those who attempt *t'shuvah* but have difficulty doing complete *t'shuvah* (to a great extent all of mankind faces this problem). From the Babylonian Talmud one learns that we have the right to implore God to manifest His Mercy even when we are undeserving.

Overview

The Need for Fasting

The Elder said before them words of admonition, "It does not say with regard to the people of Ninveh, 'And God saw their sack-cloth and fasts' but, 'God saw their good deeds.'"

This pericope underscores that *t'shuvah* is the key element in the fasting process. This is reiterated by the prophet Isaiah in the *Yom Kippur haftarah* reading (Chapter 58):

> Why have they fasted, say they, and thou seest not? Why have we afflicted our soul, and thou takest no knowledge? Behold, in the day of your fast you pursue your business, and exact all your payments. Behold you fast for strife and debate, and to smite with the fist of wickedness: you fast not this day to make your voice heard on high. Is such the fast that I have chosen? a day for a man to afflict his soul? is it to bow down his head like a bulrush, and to spread sack-cloth and ashes under him? wilt thou call this a fast, and an acceptable day to the Lord? Is not this rather the fast that I have chosen? to loose the chains of wickedness, to undo the bands of the yoke, and to let the oppressed go free, and to break every yoke? Is it not to share thy bread with the hungry, and thou bring the poor that are cast out to thy house? when thou seest the naked, that thou cover him; and thou hide not thyself from thy own flesh.

The strong question which remains is, If the purpose of a fast is *t'shuvah*, why is *fasting* necessary?

One very obvious and true answer is that fasting leads man to think about *t'shuvah*. Thus, someone who fasts begins to realize his mortality. While healthy and strong, man all to easily thinks of himself as invincible. By just abstaining from food and drink for but a few hours a person feels weak and frail. This gets him to think about the human condition and his place in the world. Thus, fasting is a good medium through which to bring a man to do *t'shuvah*.

A more basic reason is as follows: We must realize that there are in fact two components in the *t'shuvah* process. One is that we truly repent our actions. The other is that we committed wrongs which exacted their tolls. We are obligated to compensate for our actions.

Mishna Bava Kamma states that when a person injured someone he must compensate him for the damage; but he also must apologize. When we sin against God we assume that we have not caused any damage. This is untrue. When man sins he not only adversely effects the spiritual world, but the physical world as well. This is underscored in our own Tractate (23a):

> In their season: [This means that rain would fall only] on the eve of Wednesdays and Sabbaths. For so it happened in the days of Shimon b. Shetach. [At that time] rain fell on the eve of Wednesdays and Sabbaths so that the grains of wheat came up as large as kidneys and the grain of barley like the stones of olives, and of the lentils like the golden *denari* and they stored specimens of them for future generations in order to make known unto them the ill effects of sin, as it is said, *Your iniquities have turned away these things and your sins have withholden good from you*." Likewise we found that it happened during the days of Herod when the people were occupied with the rebuilding of the Temple. [At that time] rain fell during the night but in the morning the wind blew and the clouds dispersed and the sun shone so that the people were able to go out to their work, and then they knew that they were engaged in sacred work.

Because he has done damage to the physical world, man is obligated to pay restitution.

Beyond this when a person sins, he has transgressed the commandments of the Almighty. In the time of the Temple he would have been able to compensate through the bringing of an animal sacrifice (*korban*). This sacrifice would have stood in the person's stead. Instead of the person being punished corporeally for his sins, God permitted this affliction to be passed on to the *korban*. Naturally, this would atone for the person's sins only if he did *t'shuvah*.

R. Yishmael points out (Yoma 86a) that while we no longer bring *korbanos*, God still exacts compensation for particular sins. Thus, if a person did an action wherein the Torah exacts a particular punishment, while this punishment is no longer meted out by the Courts, God, Himself, exacts these punishments—be it through the medium of fire, water, asphyxiation, pestilence or other means.

Today, while it is no longer possible for a person to bring offerings to obvert bodily retribution, fasting serves this function. If a person fasts it is seen as if he sacrificed his own flesh and blood upon the altar. Thus, fasting carries out the portion of the *t'shuvah* process which calls for restitution.

Aggadita: 15a

Admonishment

The elder said before them words of admonishment:

1. My brothers! It does not say with regard to the people of Ninveh that God saw their sackcloth and fasts, but *God saw their deeds, that they repented*.
2. In the Scriptures it is written, "Rend thy hearts and not thy garments".

The elder cited two verses for the following reason: *T'shuvah* contains two aspects: remorse for past deeds and resolve not to repeat this action again.

We often find individuals who outwardly profess to do *t'shuvah* and are sincerely sorry about their past deeds. Yet they can not truly bring themselves to resolve not to continue to transgress. (1) teaches that a person's *t'shuvah* must be so resolute that God, Himself, must be willing to testify that he will not transgress in the future.

On the other hand, there are people who make a true resolve to repent and will in fact not transgress in the future, yet because of this, they fail to see the need to be remorseful over their past deeds. They fail to see the need for being sorry for their transgressions. For these individuals, (2) teaches that in addition to any resolve about the future one must be truly sorry about past transgressions; for by having committed these transgressions, man has contributed to the spiritual pollution of the cosmos. This can only be corrected if man realizes and repents for the damage that his sin brought.

Summary Outline: 15a, 16a&b, 24a,25a

Halakhic Qualifications of a *Sh'liach Tzibbur*

[25] The *Mishna* is very precise about the qualities that a *sh'liach tzibbur* for a *ta'anis* should possess. The *sh'liach tzibbur* should–

a. be an elder (*zaken*);
b. be a *chakham*;
c. have an imposing physical stature;
d. be fluent in prayers;
e. have a large family and no means of support;
f. have a "clean" house: both in terms of finances and transgressions; (Rambam: This refers to the person and his household.)

g. not have a bad reputation as a youth;
h. be meek;
i. be acceptable to the congregation;
j. be skilled in chanting;
k. have a pleasant voice.

With regard to priorities: (>="precedes")

(1) [d] >[a], [b] and [c];
(2) [a]>[b]>[c];
(3) Where the person possesses properties [d-k]; one should also look for [c] if possible;
(4) There does not seem to be an order of priorities set within [e]-[k]. Perhaps they are listed in descending order.

Example(s) of–

[a] is found on 25b. In this case, R. Eliezer, the Rosh Mesivta, was the *sh'liach tzibbur.*

(2) is found on 25b, wherein R. Eliezer, the Elder, preceded R. Akiva.

(1) are found on 24a, wherein R. Ilfa prayed in the presence of Rebbe; Elementary school teacher before Rav.

Aggadita: Jerusalem Talmud

God's Choice for *Sh'liach Tzibbur*

In light of the above there are three very astounding stories regarding choices for *sh'liach tzibbur* related in the Jerusalem Talmud (1:4).

1. A person came before a relative of R. Yanai and asked him for support. He replied, "Why should you need support? Your father had a good deal of money held by X." The man responded, "I heard that the money might have been acquired improperly. I will not use it."

   The Rabbi remarked, "You are worthy to pray for us."

2. The Rabbis received a vision–Palan the donkey driver should be the *chazzan*. Asked what was his merit, Palan told of an incident where a woman hired him to transport her somewhere. On the road she began to cry. When asked why, she responded that her husband had been imprisoned and that the only way she could raise the money to redeem him was by becoming a prostitute. To prevent this Palan sold his donkey and gave her the proceeds.

   The Rabbis proclaimed, "You are worthy to pray for us."

3. R. Avuhu received a vision–P'natkeka should pray for rain. P'natkeka, a cabaret owner, was actually a procurer. Astounded, R. Avuhu asked

what meritorious deed he had done. He related that a Jewish girl wished to become a prostitute. When he asked why. She responded it was so that she could redeem her husband from prison. Rather than see this happen he sold his bed and bed-roll and gave her the money.

R. Avuhu proclaimed, "You are truly worthy to pray for us."

Analysis

The foregoing occurrences served the following ends:

1. **The Rabbis are taught the greatness of even the simplest Jew.**

   No Jew can be underestimated with regard to the greatness of his deeds. (Perhaps the G'mara wishes to underscore that in their *divrei k'vushim* the Rabbis should not belittle the congregation too much.)

2. **In reckoning *mitzvos* versus *aveiros* it is not a question of quantity but quality.**

   P'natkeka continued his former lifestyle, and he certainly did not fulfil the *halakhic* requirements outlined above—thus, he could not be chosen to lead the congregation. Nevertheless, he was chosen by God.

3. **These events point up the relationship between rain and *emunah* with regard to one's source of sustenance.**

   All three cases deal with money matters. In all three cases, the principals were willing to forego monetary gains or chance losses. They placed their economic faith in God. They thus deserved to be answered when praying for sustenance. (See Overview: *Middah K'neged Middah*.)

Aggadita: 10b, 12b, 15a, 25b, y. *Ta'anis* 2:1

Not Allowing Routine to Become Rut

R. Zera (16a): **The first time** I saw ashes spread out on the *aron* my whole body shook.

R. Zera (y. *Ta'anis* 2:1): **Each time** I saw this happen my body shook.

The difference between these two different versions is very significant. Talmud Bavli's version addresses the human condition—man's capacity to reduce very significant emotional events to the mundane. Modern man has been recipient of the greatest of miracles; nevertheless, he has developed the capacity of taking all of these wonders in stride.

The Psalmist pronounces accurately, "The Heavens declare the glory of

God." Yet, part of humanity does not recognize God. Why? Many explain that the answer is found in the very next verse, "Each day it utters speech." Were man to witness a sunrise once in a lifetime or once in fifty years he would be thunderstruck by this event, but, as it occurs everyday, he takes this in stride.

Importance of Rote

God has blessed man with the capacity to perform actions involuntarily, thereby expanding his ability. If it were necessary to think about breathing or about raising our hands, little time would be left for anything else. A beginner driver must fully concentrate on driving and can do nothing else while driving. However, once he has mastered driving, he can easily listen to the radio, carry on a conversation or even dictate a letter while driving. This is true of many other areas of life. Once we have carried on a procedure often enough and have mastered its technique we need not think about it.

God has given us the gift of executing actions without thinking about them. Yet, this self-same blessing has negative aspects as well. Having no need to concentrate on actions or occurrences after mastering or being familiar with their patterns, we usually do not give these occurrences our full attention. Subconsciously we say, "I am very familiar with that." Thus we most often act without thinking. This is one important aspect of R. Zera's declaration, "It was *only* the first time that I saw the Torah in ashes that my body shook." (I, too, can testify that while in Israel when visiting several Holocaust memorials, the **first time** I saw the display of a Torah being used as a book cover and as a banjo cover, my body shook involuntarily. Yet, when in a different museum I subsequently saw the same display my reaction while still strong, was not nearly as intense.)

Overcoming Rote

Given the problem, what is its solution? The Rabbinic response is, be aware of the problem and consciously attempt to overcome it. One way of doing this is by introducing variety. To this end, the thirteen Fasts were set up in a sequence of increased severity.

Another approach is by raising the significance of events to the conscious level by means of Shock Therapy. Thus, R. Nachman when unable to make it rain (24a) proclaimed, "Take Nachman and throw him from the roof." Similarly, when R. Eliezer (25b) realized that it did not rain after thirteen Fasts he called out to his congregants, "Did you prepare graves for yourselves?" In unnerving them, he made them conscious of their actions. This consciousness-raising technique caused them to repent; thereby causing their prayers to be answered.

The Rabbis employed other devices, as well. One example found in the *Shulchan Arukh* concerns the reading of *Kol Nidre* and *Eikha*. In both cases, we are instructed to read each ensuing reading louder than the one before. This helps overcome rote.

We, too, must be aware of this problem, as it effects us daily, and take measures to overcome it. As an example, if a person finds that his *t'fillah* is becoming *k'va*, he might try *davening* from a different *siddur* or changing the pace of his *t'fillah*. The same is true with regard to other *mitzvos*. Where necessary, do *mitzvos* in a manner in which you are forced to consciously think about the *mitzvah* you are performing.

Summary Outline and Analysis: 15a, 16b, 17a

Additional Six *Brakhos*

[26] There are six additional *Brakhos* which are added after ראה נא. Following is the procedure from ראה נא as per Rashi:

I. ראה נא:

Regular *Brakha* is said; special prayers are added; the following ending is added: He who answered Avraham on Mount Moriah should listen... בא״ה גואל ישראל (Redeemer of Israel).
Congregation: Amen
Chazzan (shamash): "Blow a *t'kiyah*"
Shofar/chatzotzeros: T'kiyah, t'ru'ah, t'kiyah

Note: See p.128 for an analysis of when each or both are blown.

(In the Temple: The ending of the *brakha* is: בא״ה אלקי ישראל מן העולם עד העולם בא״י גואל ישראל (Blessed be the Lord, God of Israel from everlasting to everlasting. Blessed be the Lord, Redeemer of Israel).
Congregation: ברוך שם כבוד וגו׳ ; Blessed be the Name of His glorious kingdom forever and ever.
Chazzan/shofar/chatzotzeros: Same
Sh'liach Tzibbur: Repeats, "He who answered..."

II. זכרונות (Rememberances): Same as on *Rosh Hashanah*.

Brakha Ending: He who answered Our Forefathers at *Yam Suf*...Who Rememberest All Forgotten Things (זוכר הנשכחות).

[Note: Procedure is as outlined above for both in and out of the Temple except for the order of *shofar/chatzotzeros* blowing.]

Shofar: T'ru'ah/t'kiyah/t'ru'ah

Rashi: It is appropriate to end זכרונות with mention of the Egyptian exodus, because the Jews had practically given up hope when God redeemed them.

R. Yehudah substitutes: רעב כי יהיה (I Kings 8:37-53). *G'vuros Ari*: But he retain the same חתימת הברכה . *S'fas Emes:* He believes that זכרונות are dependent upon מלכיות ; hence they can only be recited on Rosh Hashanah. *Keren Orah*: R. Yehudah argues just in the case of Rain Fasts (Ran).

This is appropriate to Fast days for it spells out all of the catastrophies for which we fast. See Relationship between King Solomon's Prayer and *Mishna*.

III. שופרות : As on Rosh Hashanah.

Brakha Ending: He who answered Yehoshua at Gilgal...Who hearest the trumpet blasts (שומע תרועה).
Shofar: T'kiyah, t'ru'ah, t'kiyah

Rashi: While still camped at Gilgal, God felled Jericho through the blowing of the *shofar*.

R. Yehudah substitutes דבר ה' אל ירמיהו (Jer. 35) which deals with drought.

IV. Psalm 120: אל ה' בצרה לי ("In my distress I called the Lord")

Brakha Ending: He who answered Shmuel in Mitzpah... Who harkenesth to cries (שומע צעקה).
Shofar: T'ru'ah, t'kiyah, t'ru'ah

Rashi: Shmuel in Mitzpah was in a difficult situation (צרה). Ending corresponds to the verse ויצעק אל ה' . (I Sam. 7:9)

V. Psalm 121: אשא עיני אל ההרים (I lift my eyes to the mountains)

Brakha Ending: He who answered Eliyahu at Carmel... He hearkenest unto Prayer (שומע תפלה).
Shofar: T'kiyah, t'ru'ah, t'kiyah

Rashi: Eliyahu looked up at Mount Carmel ["The Mountains"] and asked for salvation. Ending corresponds to his prayer (עננו). (I Kings 18:37)

Note: According to *G'mara* 17a some reverse the endings of [IV] and [V]. An explanation is found in the *G'mara* for this.

VI. Psalm 130: ממעמקים (Out of the depths I have cried to Thee...)

Brakha Ending: He who answered Yonah in the belly of the Fish...The one who answereth you in time of trouble (העונה בעת צרה)
Shofar: T'ru'ah, t'kiyah, t'ru'ah

Rashi: Psalm corresponds to the "depths" of the fish. *Brakha* ending corresponds to " קראתי מצרה לי ." (Yona 2:3)

VII. Psalm 102: תפלה לעני כי יעטף " (A prayer for the afflicted, when he faints...)

Brakha Ending: He who answered David and Shlomo in Jerusalem...Who Hast Mercy upon the Land.
Shofar: T'kiyah, t'ru'ah, t'kiyah

Rashi: David was helped at the time when famine struck the land (II Sam. 21); Shlomo is invoked because of his prayer that God help the nation when there is no rain. (I Kings 8). *Brakha* ending corresponds to the psalm in that the latter speaks to the situation of a drought.

<1> Interpretation of *Rambam*

Rambam makes several changes in the above procedure:

a. *Nusach* (Text of the blessings):

He believes that זכרונות , שופרות and the psalms listed in the *Mishna*, as well as, additional beseechments were all to be said as part of the blessing of ראה נא

In the ensuing six *brakhos*, beseechments, as well as citations from verses that are appropriate to these *brakhos*, are to be included.

b. *Chatzotzeros*:

Outside of the *Mikdash*, *chatzotzeros* and not *shofar* are to be blown, but not during the *t'fillah*, rather at **the end of the *t'fillah***.

c. *Mikdash*:

The *chatzotzeros/shofar* were/was sounded after the *brakha*. After the congregation said ברוך שם כבוד וגו' the *chazzan* then said *mi she'ana* after which the *chatzotzeros/shofar* was sounded a second time. [Ran is unsure whether in the *Mikdash* מי שענה was said once or twice. If indeed it was repeated, or it was delayed until after the recitation of ברוך שם כבוד וגו' , it was so the *chatzotzeros/shofar* blowing would be in proximity to the ברוך שם כבוד וגו' and not to the specific contents of the *brakha*.

R. Yosef Rosen (*Hafla'ah* p. 109) writes that מי שענה had to have been said before the *brakha* because one cannot recite a blessing immediately after the recitation of Scripture. (y. *B'rakhos* 1:8)]

Analysis

The Basis of the Rambam-Rashi Dispute

The *Mishna* notes that R. Chalafta and R. Channania b. Tradyon followed the procedure of the Temple in Tzipori and Sikhni respectively. When told of this, the Rabbis responded, this procedure is limited to the Eastern Gate of the Temple Mount.

Rishonim disagree on exactly which point the Rabbis negated in R. Chalafta's procedure. Rashi maintains that the Rabbis disagreed with his saying *barukh shem* outside the Temple. *Rambam* believes that they disagreed with R. Chalafta's blowing the *chatzotzeros* or *shofar* for each of the six/seven *brakhos* of the *sh'moneh esreh*. R. Gershom/Ran explain that the displeasure was over the recitation of *mi she'ana* after the *brakha*.

Rambam follows the *Mishna* and the first *braisa* (16b). (See full discussion on this point by *Keren Orah*.) In either version, no mention is made of "blowing" during the *sh'moneh esreh* except in the Temple. Nevertheless, *Rambam* obligates blowing the *chatzotzeros* even outside of the Temple. However, he posits that this blowing is to be independent of the *t'fillah*.

[Note: *Ra'avad* makes a similar distinction. 14a cites that *the shofar* was blown " symbolizing Jericho." But, what about *chatzotzeros?* They were blown during the *r'fillah,* while the *shofar* was blown after the *t'fillah*.]

R. Yosef Rosen utilizes this distinction to answer the question on 14a, wherein it is stated that 18 blasts are sounded. Given that there are seven points at which blasts are sounded, and three sounds are produced for each blessing then there are 21 sounds produced. He answers, that in the *Mikdash* 21 blasts were sounded; 14a, however, refers to the territories. There, the *shofar/chatzoteros* were sounded after the *t'fillah*. As such, only 18 blasts were sounded.] (*Sfas Emes* offers an alternate interpretation. See III-[6].)

Rashi, on the other hand, accents that part of the *braisa* which differentiates the *Mikdash* and the territories *vis a vis* the recitation of *amen*. R. Gershom/Ran disagree with this latter approach in that had R. Chalafta insisted on saying *barukh Shem* he would have done so on all occassions not just on Fast Days. Regarding the blowing of *shofar* during the *t'fillah*, these *rishonim* find no reason to distinguish between the *Mikdash* and territories.

Summary Outline and Analysis: 15a, 16b, 17a

Relationship Between *Shofar* and *Brakha*

In some *brakhos*, the *t'kiyah* is emphasized (i.e., two *t'kiyos* are sounded); in others, the *t'ru'ah* is emphasized. Aside simply from this being the natural sequence, it also conforms to the essence of each *brakha*. The *t'kiyah* is sounded for the proclamation of Kingship and at times of redemption. The *t'ru'ah* is sounded for the purpose of beseechment. The correspondence between the *brakha* and *shofar*-sound is described below.

1. גואל ישראל : *T'kiyah*; **Redemption.**
2. זוכר הנשכחות : T'ru'ah; We **beseech** God that he remember His past covenants with us.
3. שומע תפלה : *T'kiyah*; *Shoferos* speaks of the future **redemption.**
4. שומע צעקה : *T'ru'ah*; The tone of Psalm 120 is completely that of **be-**

seechment, as is the meaning of *tze'akah*.

5. שומע תפלה : *T'kiyah*; Psalm 121 speaks in positive terms of God's watching over the nation.
6. העונה בעת צרה : *T'ru'ah*; This note is appropriately sounded *b'es tazarah*.
7. מרחם על הארץ: T'kiyah; The *T'kiyah* is appropriately sounded in honor of the mention of **Kings David and Shlomo**.

Overview

Correspondence of the Seven *Brakhos* to the Seven Mystical Spheres

1. חסד : Avraham was characterized by חסד ; *"Give truth to Yaakov,* חסד *to Avraham."* (Mich. 7:20) The attribute of חסד is being granted something undeserved and unsolicited. God, at Mount Moriah, answered Abraham—not to sacrifice Yitzchak— eventhough Avraham made no such request.
2. גבורה : *Yam Suf; God redeemed Israel at Yam Suf* through Strength. (*B'rakhos* 58a) One explanation is that the redemption took place even though the Jews were unworthy. To go against the obvious truth required God to manifest גבורה.
3. תפארת: Yehoshua at Gilgal. (*B'rakhos* 58a) תפארת means beauty. In broader terms, " התפאר עלי " (Ex. 8:5) means "challenge me," "Ask of me something you think I cannot do." Also Prv. 20:29 תפארת בחורים כוחם (the beauty, i.e., impressiveness, of young men is their strength). Thus, the functional interpretation of תפארת is that it is something which is impressive but unessential. While the Jews were at Gilgal, God sank the walls of Jericho, and stopped the revolution of the sun at Givon. These acts were unessential for winning the wars but served to underscore the glory of God.
4. נצח: Shmuel uttered the words נצח ישראל לא ישקר (15:29) He related to God on this level.
5. הוד : Eliyahu. הוד represents inner as opposed to outer beauty (Malbim). At Carmel *at the moment* that the Jews shouted ה' הוא האלקים they expressed this belief with true inner belief.
6. יסוד : Yonah; This attribute is synonymous with Yona's praying to God while in the fish. The Gaon of Vilna, based on the *Zohar* explains that Yona refers to the *n'shamah*, "בן אמתי" to that which derives directly from God (the essence of Truth). R. Tzadok haKohen (*Pri Tzadik 1:50*) explains that one possesses the attribute of יסוד when the intrinsic relationship with God is so strong that no matter how low he sinks spiritually his feelings for God will always remain, albeit, at times it will be hidden away. This is precisely the attribute demonstrated by Yona.

7. מלכות : Kings David and Shlomo were earthly manifestations of God's kingship מלכותא דארעא כעין מלכותא דרקיעא.

Analysis: 26a

Twenty Four Blessings

<2> When said:

a. R. Chananel (quoted by Ran): Only at *neilah*.
b. Ran: They were not said *shacharis*. He is not clear about whether it was said both for *mincha* and *neilah*.
c. R. Zerachia: They were said during an added *t'fillah* (*musaf*).
d. Tur (quotes *Siddur of Geonim*): They were said for *shacharis, mincha and neilah*.

Torah Reading

Eshkol: The Torah reading during the Seven Fasts varied. They corresponded to the order of the Seven Blessings. To wit—

Fast	Torah Reading	Correspondence to Brakha	Haftorah
I	ויהי בימים הרבים (שמות א׳)	This is the begining of the Redemption	דרשו ה׳ בהמצאו (ישעי׳ נ״ה)
II	מה תצעק אלי (שמות י״ד)	This concerns the miracle at Yam Suf	שובה ישראל (הושע ו״ד)
III	סע משה (שמות ט״ו)	God sweetened the waters and showered the heavens with Mann which lasted until after Jericho after which they ate the produce of the land.	גם אתה (יואל ב׳)
IV	ראה אתה (שמות ל״ג)	This parsha concerns 13 Attributes. Sh'muel was on a level comparable to Moshe.	לכן יחכה ה׳ (ישעי׳ ל׳)
V	בחוקתי (ויקרא כ״ו)	Eliyahu was answered at Mount Karmel. We pray that the blessings said at Mount Sinai be bestowed upon us.	ויאמר אליהו התשבי (מל׳ א׳: י״ז)
VI	ואתה ישראל (דברים י׳)	Yonah said, "I fear God." This parsha states that Rainfall is contingent on fear of God.	אל דברי הבצורת (ירמי׳ י״ד)

VII	והיה אם שמוע תשמע (דברים כ״ח)	We pray that God bestow upon us the blessings enumerated in this parsha as He did in the days ofKings David and Sh'lomo.	ויהי רעב בארץ (שמו׳ ב׳: כ״א)

Background Information

M'gilas Ta'anis

M'gilas Ta'anis is a listing of thirty six days during which significant joyous events occurred (mostly during the time of the Second Temple) and the rabbis prohibited fasting and in some cases eulogies. According to *Shabbos* 13b it was written by Chanania b. Chizkia and his associates. This was one of the few documents, aside from the *Tanakh* which was permitted to be written. While many study about it while learning the Talmud, relatively few have studied it and know it is extant. As an aid to the student we include it. (A copy and commentary of the *braisos* of *M'gilas Ta'anis* is found in *Otzar ha'Igeres*, R. J. Epstein, (New York: Torat haAdam Publishing Company, 1968).

The following are days listed in *M'gilas Ta'anis* during which one may not fast because of the joyous events which occurred. On some of these days fasting is prohibited, on others neither fasting nor eulogies are permitted.

1-8 Nisan (~E)	During these days the Rabbis overruled the Baitusim as follows: The Daily Sacrifice *(Korban Tamid)* had to be a communal offering and not an individual offering.
8-21 Nisan (~E)	The Rabbis overruled the Baitusim as follows: The Forty-nine day count from which the celebration of *Sh'vu'os* is determined begins on First Intermediate Day of *Pesach* and not the Sunday following the first day of Passover.
7 Iyar (~E)	On this day the walls of Jerusalem were completely rebuilt.
14 Iyar (~E)	*Pesach Sheni*
23 Iyar	The Bnei Hikra were driven out of Jerusalem (The City of David) by the Macabees. Previously, the Bnei Hikra did not permit entrance or exit from the city.

27 Iyar	Foreign tax-collectors were forced out of Jerusalem.
14 Sivan	The capture of Migdal Tzur
15-16 Sivan	Gentile inhabitants of Bet She'an and Bikah were exiled.
25 Sivan	The walls of Shomron were recaptured.
25 Sivan	Tax-collectors left Jerusalem.
14 Tamuz (~E)	Book of Decrees was abolished.
15 Av (~E)	Time of the major Wood-offerings (26a).
24 Av	Jewish Courts were restored.
7 Elul (~E)	The dedication of the walls rebuilt around Jerusalem.
17 Elul	Romans left Jerusalem.
22 Elul	Killed *m'shumadim*.
3 Tishri	God's name was able to be used in documents (this had been forbidden by the Greeks). This was later stopped by the Rabbis because after these deeds were not needed they would be disgarded.
23 Cheshvon	The brothels that the Greeks put in the Temple were destroyed.
25 Cheshvon	The recapturing of Shomron.
27 Cheshvon	The Rabbis were victorious over the *Tz'dukim* regarding the offering of *soles* for the altar.
3 Kislev	Removal of Greek Idols from the Temple.
7 Kislev	Death of [the wicked] King Herod.
21 Kislev	Har Grizim Day. Alexander decided not to destroy Jerusalem. He bowed before Shimon the *Tzadik*.
25 Kislev (~E)	Chanukah begins on this day and continues for a total of eight days.
28 Teves	Shimon b. Shetah wrested the Sanhedrin from the hands of the *Tz'dukim*.
2 Shvat (~E)	Death of the [wicked] King Yanai.

22 Shvat (~E)	The plan to bring an idol into the Temple was averted
28 Shvat	Antiochus was removed from Jerusalem.
8, 9 Adar	Day of *T'ru'ah* for rain (took place on a different year than 20 Adar.)
12 Adar	Turyanos Day (18b)
13 Adar	Nikanor Day (18b)
14, 15 Adar	Purim
16 Adar (~E)	The rebuilding of Jerusalem's walls began.
17 Adar	Rabbis who fled Yanai's persecution were saved from massacre in Kalkis and Bet Zavdin.
20 Adar	Chuni prayed for rain and was answered. (19a)
28 Adar (~E)	Greek decree against Torah study was abolished.

Summary Outline: 15b 17b-18b, 12a

Mishna (15b)

[27] a. Any day on which *M'gilas Ta'anis* prohibits—

	Eulogies		Fasting	
Day—	Before	Following	Before	Following
R.Meir	No	Yes	Yes	Yes
R. Yosi	No	No	No	Yes

G'mara (17b-18b)

[28] *M'gilas Ta'anis*: 1-8 Nisan eulogies are prohibited; Daily Offering (*Tamid*) established.

[29] Rav: 1 Nisan is mentioned even though fasting is otherwise prohibited so as to prohibit the day before *Rosh Chodesh* [27]. Ordinarily on the day before *Rosh Chodesh* one is permitted to

fast because days designated as joyous days by the Torah need not be strengthened, i.e., the populous accepts these days without question.

[30] *M'gilas Ta'anis*: 8-22 Nisan eulogies are prohibited; Rabbis convinced *Baitusim* of the proper date for *Sh'vu'os*.

[31] R. Papa: The dates of *Pesach* (which occurred from 15-22 Nisan) are included in these dates so as to prohibit the day after *Pesach*.

[32] *M'gilas Ta'anis* thus follows R. Yosi [27].

[33] If so, why list 1 Nisan? If to prohibit fasting on 29 Adar it is already known to be prohibited since it follows 28 Adar (the day the decree against Torah study was lifted) [as R. Yosi prohibits fasting on the succeeding day]?

a. Abaye: It is necessary for the case in which Adar has thirty days.
b. R. Ashi: While R. Yosi prohibits fasting on the succeeding day, he permits eulogies. Listing 29 Adar between two days listed in *M'gilas Ta'anis* serves to prohibit this day even for eulogies.

[34] Why is 8 Nisan mentioned twice? In case for some reason one set of days [e.g., 1-8 Nisan] is cancelled, the 8th would retain its status because of the other set of dates [e.g., 8-22 Nisan].

[35] Answer in [34] could be used for [30].

[36] The *Halakha* is in accordance with—

a. Rav: R. Yosi;
b. Shmuel: R. Shimon b. Gamliel (see [37]), he is most lenient.

[37] R. Shimon b. Gamliel: Both on the day before and after a day mentioned in *M'gilas Ta'anis* one is permitted to...

[38] R. Yochanan: *Halakha* follows R. Yossi.

R. Chiyyah: This refers only to not fasting. With regard to eulogies he follows R. Meir.

R. Yochanan's position with regard to both eulogies and fasting is—

1. the previous day is forbidden;
2. the succeeding day is permitted.

[39] Question: With regard to *M'gilas Ester* a Braisa states—
"In places where it may be read early [people in small villages may read it as early as 11 Adar] one may still eulogize and fast on these days." When can this apply? Since 13 Adar is Nikanor Day and 12 Adar is Tarianus Day (see above) one may certainly not fast on these days. Rather, the *braisa* must speak of 11 Adar. If so, the *braisa* permits fasting. Whereas from [38], R. Yochanan prohibits fasting on this day.

[40] Answer: The *braisa* refers to fasting on 11 Adar when the *M'gilah* was read on 12 Adar. This became permissible because Tarianus day was repealed.

R. Nachman once proclaimed a Public Fast on 12 Adar. When the Rabbis objected he responded, "This day has been repealed because of the assassination of the brothers Shma'ya and Ahiyah which took place on this day."

[41] R. Ashi: Once the 12th was repealed one can not prohibit this day because it is "the day preceding Nikanor day."

12a

[42] *M'gilas Ta'anis*: Anyone who has undertaken a Fast before the incidence of the festive days is forbidden from breaking his Fast. For example, he who decided to fast every Monday and Thursday and a *M'gilas Ta'anis* Day falls on Monday or Thursday, then if his vow came before the prohibition of fasting then he may fast. If the proclamation came first then he may not fast. (See <7> and <8>.)

Tractate Rosh Hashana 18b-19a

[43] The status of *M'gilas Ta'anis*—

a. Rav, R. Chanina: It has been repealed; (This is similar to the Four Public Fasts. During the time of the Temple they were Festivals now they are Fast Days.)
b. R. Yochanan, Reish Lakish: It has not been repealed. (These days can not be compared to the Fast Days. The latter's differing modes is dependent upon the status of the Temple. Not so these other days; they are independent of the Temple.)

[44] R. Kahana questions Rav: It occurred that a Fast Day was declared on Chanukah in Lod. R. Eliezer disregarded it by washing; R. Yehoshua by taking a haircut. They then decreed that the group had to fast for fasting on Chanukah.

Chanukah, however, is one of the days listed in *M'gilas Ta'anis*! Thus we see that *M'gilas Ta'anis* was not repealed.

[45] Answer: R. Yosef: Chanukah's status is different than anything mentioned in *M'gilas Ta'anis* because of the *mitzvos* associated with these days.
[46] Abaye questions: Let the *mitzvos* be repealed!
[47] R. Yosef answers: The day cannot be repealed because of the public awareness and celebration of the day. (Rashi: People consider it to be as significant as a Biblical festival.)

[48] R. Acha questions: The Rabbis in the period of Yochanan Kohen Gadol declared 3 Tishri a feast day. (They prevailed on the populace to no longer put God's name in contracts). As per Rav, the *M'gilah* was abolished earlier, Why add new dates?

[49] Answer: Rav agrees that the abolishment of *M'gilas Ta'anis* took place only after the destruction of the Temple.

[50] Question: How could 3 Tishri be a feast if it is the day G'dalia was murdered? As per the G'mara the Fast of G'dalia was considered a festival when the Temple stood as per Zacharia.

[51] Answer: [48] serves to prohibit fasting on 2 Tishri as per [27]. This is not accomplished by it being G'dalia Day or the day after *Rosh Chodesh* as both of these days have their source in the Bible. As such, their observance is firm and hence one ordinarily may fast and eulogize on the days preceding and succeeding them.

[52] R. Tuvi b. Masna questions: 28 Adar (see [33]) was declared a festival during the days of Yehuda b. Shamua (a student of R. Meir). R. Meir lived after the destruction of the Temple. If *M'gilas Ta'anis* was abolished after the destruction of the Temple as per [49] why did they declare a new joyous day?

[53] The answer: It is not just amoraim who dispute whether *M'gilas Ta'anis* was repealed; it is disputed, also, by Tannaim.

a. R. Meir: *M'gilas Ta'anis* applies today.
b. R. Yosi: It only applied during the time of the Temple; a time of peace and tranquility.

[54] *Halakha*: *M'gilas Ta'anis* was abolished except for Chanukah and Purim.

Analysis: 17b-18b

Status of *Chanukah* and *Purim* in Light of the Suspension of *M'gilas Ta'anis*

<3> Question: According to [54], *M'gilas Ta'anis* was abolished except for *Chanukah* and *Purim*. Following from [38] (because in a dispute between R. Yochanan and Shmuel, [36b], the *halakha* follows R. Yochanan]) the *halakha* is that one may not fast the day before *Purim* or *Chanukah*. If so, how are we permitted to fast on *Ta'anis Ester*?

Answers:

a. Ramban/*Hashlamah*: 13 Adar was originally celebrated as Nikanor Day. With the abolition of *M'gilas Ta'anis* this was no longer true. From [41] we learn that on a day which was once commemorated and was since abolished fasting cannot be prohibited because it is a day which precedes another day which is being commemorated.

Ran argues that a distinction can be made between our situation and [40] which involves Tarianus Day. In the case of [40] the day lost its status because of a particular tragedy which took place thereon. Nikanor Day lost its status as part of the general abolition of *M'gilas Ta'anis*. As such, the case can be made that while Tarianus Day should not be commemorated, in and of itself, 13 Adar may still be observed as being the day before *Purim*.)

b. R. Albageloni: Since *M'gilas Ta'anis* was rescinded, the Rabbis are as lenient as possible regarding the *M'gilah's* rulings. Under the circumstances they follow Shmuel [36b] and permit fasting the day before *Purim*.

c. Miktam/Ritva/Ra'avad (*hasagos*): [54] merely indicates that *Chanukah* and *Purim* themselves were not rescinded. Yet, the preceding and suceeding days were rescinded.

d. Ra'avad/Miktam: Fasting on 13 Adar is not in violation of *M'gilas Ta'anis* because this fast is in a different category. It was declared by the Rabbis as part of the *takana* of *Purim* (דברי הצומות וזעקתם). *The fasting is to be viewed as "the beginning of the rejoicing."*

(Ran counters: 13 Adar was never established as a permanent Fast Day. " דברי הצומות*" refers to the four Fast Days established to mourn for the destruction of the Temple, and* וזעקתם *refers to Ester's Fasts. Nevertheless, from Mesekhes Sof'rim* it appears that no set day was established.

(Question: If 13 Adar was established as a Fast Day, how could it simultaneously be declared Nikanor Day (a joyous day)?

Answer: During the days of the Second Temple it was not necessary to fast on these days because these were times of peace.

Question: Given that 13 Adar is the day before *Purim* what did Nikanor Day add?

Answer: Jerusalem Talmud states that on this day eulogies became prohibited. This was not the case previously.)

e. Ran (Tr. Rosh Hashanah)/R. Zerachia HaLevi: Fasting is permitted on 13 Adar because *Purim* is *divrei kabbalah* which as per [28] need not be strenghened.

(Ran in *Tractate Ta'anis* cites the Jerusalem Talmud which states that the 13th was originally prohibited as a fast day because of *Purim*.)

f. R. Ephraim (quoted by Bal HaMa'or) has a different text. In his reading of [27] fasting is taken to be more stringent than eulogies. Thus there are days in which there may be eulogies but not fasting. He asserts that the *halakha* follows R. Yosi—because R. Ashi [6b] supports R. Yosi. R. Yosi—according to his reading—for days in which both eulogies and fasting is prohibited (such as *Purim*) prohibits eulogies on the preceding and succeeding days. With regard to fasting the prohibition only involves the following day not the preceding day. Therefore we may fast on 13 Adar.

The other rishonim negate this text for it changes the readings of both the Mishna and R. Ashi. Also because they feel that the prohibition of eulogies is a stronger prohibition than fasting. The latter involves a negation of respect to the living and deceased. Only on the most joyous of days is this respect to be abrogated.

g. An interesting distinction is made by the *Bal Hama'or.* He argues that 14 Adar was established through *divrei kabbalah*. Those for whom 14 Adar is the main day of *Purim* may fast on 13 Adar based upon [2]. Those who observe *Purim* on 15 Adar are only prohibited on the 14th from eulogies and fasting due to the edict of *M'gilas Ta'anis*. As such they may not fast on 13 Adar, because "it is a day before a *M'gilas Ta'anis* Day."

The Ra'avad disagrees with this analysis. He argues that both days were established as special days in all locations because of the original miracle and not because of *M'gilas Ta'anis*.

R. Tzvi Pesach Frank discusses the *halakhic* import of this *Bal Ha'Maor* for those who live in Jerusalem. He cites the *Pri Chodosh* who agrees with *Ba'al haMa'or*, but writes that it is, nevertheless, the custom to fast on 13 Adar in Jerusalem.

<4> Ra'avad: Although *M'gilas Ta'anis* has been rescinded this is only with regard to private Fasts. With regard to public Fasts [13a] indicates that were it not for the unusual tragedy which occurred on 12 Adar, a fast would not have been proclaimed on this day despite the abolition of *M'gilas Ta'anis*.

Ran: [44] is a counterproof to the Ra'avad. The *g'mara* considers R. Eliezer and R. Yehoshua's action in disregarding the fast proclaimed on *Chanukah* to be a problem only for those who posit that *M'gilas Ta'anis* was not rescinded. For those who believe that it was rescinded, fasting is permitted on *M'gilas Ta'anis* Days. This is contrary to the Ra'avad.

Ra'avad could respond: The G'mara **could have** answered that even if *M'gilas Ta'anis* were rescinded the fast should not have been proclaimed. However, the G'mara gives a more powerful answer, "*M'gilas Ta'anis* was not suspended for *Chanukah*." Thus, not even Private Fasts may be observed on *Chanukah*.

Summary Outline: Mishna 15b, 18b, 12a

Mishna 15b

[55] A Fast sequence may not begin on Thursday lest it cause a rise in food prices.

[56] Tanna Kamma: [55] refers just to the First Series. The Middle Series of Fasts may begin on Thursday.

R. Yosi: [55] is applicable to all the Fast Series.

[57] Fasts may not be declared on *Rosh Chodesh, Chanukah or Purim*.

[58] If a Fast sequence was begun and will fall out on a day mentioned in [57]—

a. R. Gamliel: They fast;
b. R. Meir: R. Gamliel agrees that while they fast they do not complete their Fasts.

[59] The same rule applies for 9 Av that falls out on Friday.

18b

[60] In [58] "begun" means—

a. R. Aha: They already fasted three Fasts;
b. R. Asi: Even if they fasted only one Fast.

[61] [59] follows R. Meir [58b]. The Chakhamim rule that the Fast is completed.

[62] Mar Zutra/R. Huna: The *halakha* is that if 9 Av falls on Friday we complete the fast.

12a

[63] *M'gilas Ta'anis*: Any person who accepted a Fast upon himself before the *M'gilas Ta'anis* Day was declared, may fast.

For example, one who declared that he would fast every Monday and Thursday throughout the year and included in these days were days enumerated in *M'gillas Ta'anis*—

a. If his vow preceded "our decree" then he fasts on these days; (see <7>)
b. If "our decree" was first, he does not fast.

Analysis

<5> Prohibition against Fasting on *Rosh Chodesh*

Ritva: Fasting is prohibited on *Rosh Chodesh* because it is called a מועד. Nevertheless, because the terms משתה ושמחה are not associated with *Rosh Chodesh* if a Fast sequence had begun it may continue. In any case, the prohibition is Rabbinic in nature.

<6> When Do Congregational Vows Supercede *Rosh Chodesh, Chanukah and Purim*?

Ritva: The *beis din* should not schedule fasts which will knowingly conflict with *Rosh Chodesh, Chanukah and Purim*. However, if, unknowingly, they schedule a series of Fasts, such that, one happens to fall on *Rosh Chodesh* then fasting is permitted. [The reason being that the decree of *beis din* is viewed as an אסור כולל (an umbrella vow which incorporates the permissible and prohibited)]. Within this framework, R. Acha still requires that *Rosh Chodesh* fall on the fourth Fast; R. Yosi is satisfied if it is the second Fast.

Ritva quotes an alternate view which espouses that the *beis din* may knowingly incorporate a series of fasts such that one will fall on *Rosh Chodesh*. This is based upon their textual reading of [58] which is that one may not establish a series in which the "first" day is *Rosh Chodesh*. Ritva rejects this view.

Ritva does, however, permit a series of fast in which the second sequence will be begun on *Rosh Chodesh* because he views the second series as being completely independent of the first.

<7> When Does an Individual's Vow Supercede a Day in *M'gilasTa'anis*?

a. Rashi: [63] is an historical comment. It refers to the time when *M'gilas Ta'anis* was being written.
b. R. Gershom: [Second Interpretation]: An individual's vow may supercede days in *M'gilas Ta'anis* if they were made at a time in which it could not be determined that they would necessarily fall on one of the *M'gilas Ta'anis* Days. Specifically, in the time

in which *Rosh Chodesh* was determined visually, if a man vowed that he would fast on a day in a future month the vow would supercede *M'gilas Ta'anis*, because when the person vowed, he had no certain knowledge of the correlation between days (i.e., Monday, Tuesday, etc.) and dates.

Summary Outline: Jerusalem Talmud

Torah Reading when Fasting Occurs on Rosh Chodesh

Jerusalem Talmud: 2:14

[64] R. Yosi: They read ברכות וקללות." (The reading of Fast Days]
[65] R. Mana: They read this in order to indicate that it is a Fast Day.
[66] But, this is known by the fact that they say *tachanun*?
[67] The opposite is the case. *Tachanun* is said so that people will remember that the Torah reading is ברכות וקללות.
[68] R. Yudin of Zk'put'kia/R. Yuda b. Pazi: The *beis va'ad which declared Rosh Chodesh* read the *Rosh Chodesh* reading.

Analysis

<8> Ran: Although [66] indicates that they said *tachanun* on *Rosh Chodesh*which would imply that *tachanun* should be said even if 10 Teves falls on Friday our custom is to delete *tachanun*. This is not contradictory.*Tachanun* was said in [66] to indicate the Torah reading; this is not necessary in our case.

With regard to the Torah reading on a *Rosh Chodesh*-Fast Day morning, the Bavli and Yerushalmi argue. Based on 12b the Bavli posits that there was no morning Torah reading on a fast. Therefore, in the case being discussed there would be no reason to replace the standard *Rosh Chodesh* reading.

<9> Riv'van: We derive from the *ma'amados* (see Chapter 4) that when a Public Fast falls on Friday there is no afternoon Torah reading.

Background Information

Additional Fast Days Mentioned in the *Shulchan Arukh*

Following is a list of Fast Days mentioned in the *Shulchan Aurkh. Mishna B'rurah* writes that Beis Yosef quotes *rishonim* who feel that it is improper to fast on the days enumerated below which fall on Rosh Chodesh. *The Ramah writes that one who fasts on* Rosh Chodesh *should not complete his fast. However, there are those who believe that these dates were established in the Talmudic period and, therefore, the pious (בעלי נפש) should fast on these days.*

1 Nisan	The children of Aharon died.
10 Nisan	Miriam died; the well ceased.
26 Nisan	Yehoshua died.
10 Iyar	Eli and his two sons died and the aron was captured.
28 Iyar	Shmu'el Died.
23 Sivan	Yeravam prevented *bikurim* from being brought to the Temple.
25 Sivan	R. Shimon b. Gamliel, R. Yishma'el and R. Chanina, S'gan Kohen were murdered.
27 Sivan	R. Chanania b. Tradian was burned with Sefer Torah.
1 Av	Aharon died.
18 Av	*Ner Ma'aravi* was extinguished in the time of Achaz[Some say 17 Av].
17 Elul	*M'raglim* died. [Some say 7 Elul].
5 Tishri	R. Akiva was captured.
7 Tishri	It was decided that our forefathers would be killed because of the worshipping of the Golden Calf.
7 Cheshvon	King Tzidkiyahu was blinded; his children killed.
28 Kislev	King Yehoyakim burned Yirmiyahu's*Eikha* scroll.
8 Teves	Ptolemy had the Torah translated into Greek.
9 Teves	Reason unknown [*Shulchan Arukh*]. Ezra died [*Selichos]*.
5 Sh'vat	*Elders of Yehoshua died.*
23 Sh'vat	*Tribes waged war against Binyamin over the Pilegesh of Givah incident.*

7 Adar	*Moshe* died.
9 Adar	*The Beis Shammai-Bes Hillel disputes occurred.*

In addition, there are those who believe that a decree exists to fast every Monday and Thursday to mourn the destruction of the *Beis haMikdash*, the Torah which was burned and the desecration of God's Name. It is a custom among some who cannot fast to refrain from wine and meat on these days and their preceding nights [*Mishna B'rurah*].

Some fast on the Friday of *Parshas Chukkas* because twenty cartons of *s'farim* were burned in France (Tanya). In Poland it was the custom to fast on 20 Sivan because of the destructions during *Tach v'Tat (Mishna B'rurah*).

Ta'anis: Chapter Three

Introduction

Thus far, the Talmud has dealt solely with fasting due to a lack of rain. The *Mishna* now expands this to include other reasons for which Fasts are proclaimed. Thereafter, the *Mishna* and *G'mara* indicate how and under what circumstances the prayers of the righteous are answered. (We show below that the *aggadita* is not just a rambling of stories. Rather, it is a fabric woven to show the parameters whereby the Leaders and the congregation interact to bring rain.) Finally, the chapter ends with the procedure to be followed if, in fact, rain falls during a Rain Fast.

Suggestions for Study

Because this chapter has a great deal of *aggadita* which is dispersed among the text, we have chosen to veer from the Summary Outline pattern that we follow in the other chapters. Rather, we integrate the halakhic material of the *Mishna* and *G'mara* so that these can be studied as a unit. After this has been done the aggadic material is studied.

We suggest that in studying this chapter you first review all of the halakhic material and then study the outlines and analysis found herein.

Summary Outline

Reasons For Which to Fast/Blow *Chatzotzeros*/or *Shofar*

In the previous chapters the Talmud set down the sequence of Rain Fasts and the progression of their severity. In Chapter 3 the Talmud explains that for other types of crises wherein the danger is more imminent Fasts are to be held every Monday and Thursday: until the danger ceases; the condition has passed (19b); or the situation is beyond help (*rishonim*). These Fasts have the halakic severities of the last 7 fasts for rain. Following are a variety of reasons—culled from the Mishna and *G'mara*—for which fasts are proclaimed and/or *chatzotzeros/shofar* are/is blown, and the range of people to whom these procedures apply. [A full discussion on *chatzotzeros* is found below.]

[1] Catastrophies which are limited to the people affected

a. Seeds are planted but do not grow. (19a)

b. An unusual change occurs in a growing crop. (Mishna 18b)

If the crops wither completely, there is no fasting even when the seeds shot into stalks. (R. Nachman; 19a)

c. Forty days elapse between the first and second rainfall. (Mishna 18b)

d. Rain falls for crops but not for trees. (Mishna 18b)—

That is, it falls gently but not heavily. (19b)

e. Rain falls for trees but not for crops. (Mishna 18b)—

That is, it falls heavily but not gently. (19b)

f. Rain falls for crops and trees but not for cisterns, ditches and caves.(Mishna 18b)—

That is, it falls heavily and gently but not in great volume. (19b)

g. Rain falls for cisterns, ditches and caves but not for crops and trees. (19b)—

That is, it rains torrentially. (19a)

h. Beginning on *P'ros haPesach* if there is not enough rain for the trees to flower. (19b)

"P'ros haPesach" refers to—
Rashi: The middle of *Pesach*;
Miktam Rambam, Riv'van, M'iri: *Rosh Chodesh Nisan*.
G'vuros Ari: Erev Rosh Hashanah.

i. Beginning *P'ros haChag (Sukkos)* if there is not enough water for the cisterns, wells and ditches. (19b)

"P'ros Chag haSukkos" refers to the—
Miktam: First of Tishri;
Rambam: Beginning of *Sukkos*.

Jerusalem Talmud's text reads: *"P'ros ha'Atzeres."*

j. If there is no drinking water. (19b)

Rambam: One could pray for rain even in the summer time.

Halakhic Procedure:

In all of the above cases the Mishna writes, *"masri'in miyad"* (The *chatzotzeros/shofar* are/is blown immediately). *Rishonim* dispute the import of this term. See <1> and <2> for a full discussion of the views of the *rishonim*.

[2] **Catastrophies which are of concern to surrounding cities**

a. One city received enough rain; its neighbor did not. (*Mishna* 19a)
b. A city suffered from *dever* (plague).(*Mishna* 19a) [Parameters are defined below.]
c. The buildings in a city collapsed (*mapoles*) due to high winds or an earthquake. (Mishna 19a) [Parameters are defined below.]
d. Croup. (19b) [Parameters are defined below.]

Halakhic Procedure:

a. People in the location suffering from the catastrophe must Fast and blow *shofar/chatzotzeros;*
b. People in other areas of the same country—

1. Tanna Kamma: Must Fast but do not blow *shofar/chatzotzeros;*
2. R. Akiva: Must blow *shofar/chatzotzeros* but not Fast.

c. People in other countries(even those in close proximity to the area struck)—

1. Rashi, Tosefos, Ran: Need not fast;
2. R. Chananel, Meiri, Riv'van): Must fast. (See <3>.)

PARAMETERS OF *DEVER*

Number of deaths needed for it to be declared *dever*

a. *Mishna: In a city which fields an army of 500 people 3 people must die on three consecutive days for it to be classified as dever.*

(R. Chananel and R. Gershom interpret this as 9 people die in three days; Rashi's interpretation is that 3 people die over a three day period)

b. *G'mara* (21 a & b): For larger cities the ratio remains the same.

Time Parameter

If said deaths occurred in less than three days—

a. *Braisa* (21a): This is not considered *dever;*
b. R. Nachman b. R. Chisda: It is classified as *dever.*

Who is counted in the number of deaths?

a. Geonim, Rambam: Children, woman and the elderly are not included [because the expression "that fields an army" is used].
b. *Miktam*: Woman are included in the number.
c. R. Yehudah (21b): If pigs die from *dever* they are included in the number [for their intestines are similar to those of human beings].
d. If heathens die of *dever*—

    1. Tosefos: They count;
    2. *Miktam*: They do not count. [See <3>.]

PARAMETERS OF *MAPOLES*

Condition of buildings

The buildings which collapsed must have been substantial and not have had structural defects. They must have fallen from gale or hurricane winds or as a result of an earthquake.

Number of houses which must collapse for it to be classified *mapoles*

Ritva: Probably three houses must fall. This number is independent of the size of the city.

CROUP

Definition

a. It must be fatal. (19b)
b. Rambam: As opposed to *dever*, it is declared croup where any number of sicknesses combine to cause deaths.

Number of deaths necessary for it to be declared croup

Ritva: A minimum of three deaths are required for these deaths to be classified as croup. However, as opposed to *dever*, there are no time restrictions in this case.

[3] Catastrophies which can spread throughout the whole country

a. Blasts (שדפון) (*Mishna*)

Even the sighting of a minimal amount is considered a catastrophe.

b. Mildew (ירקון) [as per Rambam; according to Rashi it is a human illness]. (*Mishna*)

Minimal affliction necessary to be classified a "Catastrophe"

[a] *Mishna* and *G'mara* (22b): The amount which will fill an oven.
[b] R. Akiva (22a): The most minimal amount.

Rambam: [a] defines [b]; that is, [a] is the minimum measurement.

Rashi: [a] is the requirement for blowing *chatzotzeros*; [b] is the requirement for fasting.

Alternatively, there is no minimum requirement as per [b]; [a] is just the account of a factual story.

c. Locust (ארבה): Even if just one wing was sighted.
d. Crickets (חסיל): Even if just one wing was sighted. (22a)
e. Wild beasts (חיה רעה) (*Mishna*). This is not considered worthy of fasting unless their attacks are clearly "sent from Heaven" (משולחת).

The following are the criteria established by the *G'mara* to determine whether a beast was משולחת:

It is considered if the animal (was)	משולחת	Not משולחת
Seen in the city	Day*	Night
Seen in field		Day/night
Seen in field near reedland and—	Ran	Stood
Saw two men (day) in an open field and—	Stood	Hid/ran away

S'fas Emes: R. Yosi (*Mishna*) interprets the case in *Ever haYarden* as occurring in the city; therefore, 'being sighted' is enough to declare a Fast.

Tore apart two men**(in reedland)	Ate one or neither (Tosefos)	Ate two or neither (R. Chananel)
In a House in a desolate area	Took child from crib on roof	
Poisonous snakes, scorpions, flies hornets	(Ra'avad, Tur Rambam per B.Y.)	Rambam

f. Sword

Even if an army merely passes through the land to do battle someplace else. (22a)

Rambam: The law applies where the foreign army intends to wage war, to conquer land, exact a tax or proselytize

Halakhic Procedure:

In all of the above cases the *Mishna* prescribes מתריעין בכל מקום (literally everyplace).*** (See<3>.)

Chart: 17b

Relationship Between Mishna and the Prayer of King Solomon at the Founding of the *Beis HaMikdash*

Solomon's Prayer (I Kings Ch. 8)	*Mishna*
V. 33: When heaven is shut up, and there is no rain because they sinned against you,	No rain

** The reason it is necessary for there to be two people is because the verse, "And the fear of you and the dread of you shall be upon every beast of the earth" is written in plural.

*** *Sfas Emes*: In the case of a hostile army which passes through the land to attack another country *shofar* blowing is restricted to the immediate locale of the army.

V. 37: If there be famine in the land,	**Plagues which lead to famine e.g., sprouts turn, maladies due to non-normal rainfall**
if there be pestilence דבר	**דבר**
	מפולת *
blasting שדפון	**שדפון**
mildew ירקון	**ירקון**
locust ארבה	**ארבה**
crickets חסיל	**חסיל**
Wild Animal חיה רעה	**חיה רעה**
if their enemy besiege them in the land of their cities;	**חרב**
whatever plague, whatever sickness there be.	
V. 48: And they return to thee with all their heart... and pray to thee...then hear thou their prayer.	

* Perhaps mapoles might be derived from the extra word ba'Aretz which indicates a disaster in the land (e.g., earthquake, hurricane or flood. Chayah ra'ah might be considered a conquering army. Compare Yo'el 1:6.

Introduction to Analysis

Before discussing the views of the *rishonim* regarding the blowing of *chatzotzeros/shofar* we present the following background material.

Chatzotzeros

And if you go to war in your land against the enemy that oppresses you, then you shall blow an alarm with the trumpets (*chatzotzeros*; and you shall be remembered before the Lord your God, and you shall be saved from your enemies. Also in the day of your gladness, and in your solemn days, and in the beginnings of your months, you shall blow with the trumpets over your burnt offerings, and over the sacrifices of your peace offerings; that they may be to you for a memorial before your God: I am the Lord your God.

Numbers 10:9-10

With *chatzotzeros* and sound of the *shofar* make a joyful noise before the Lord the King.

Psalms 98:6

And if you go to war in your land: Both if you go to war against them or if they go to war against you.

Scripture speaks of the War of Gog and Magog...the Torah states "And you shall be saved from your enemies"; which war is it that the Jews will win and there will not be any servitude thereafter only the War of Gog and Magog...

R. Akiva says, "I only can derive the War of Gog and Magog, how do I derive blasts, mildew, a woman who has trouble delivering in child-birth and a ship which is in danger of sinking, Scripture states, "On the trouble which troubles you" (*tzar ha'tzorer*); [this includes] any other trouble which might befall you.

Sifre B'ha'alos'kha Piska 18

It is a positive commandment in the Torah to cry out (*litz'ok*) and blow the *chatzotzeros* for every problem which befalls the congregation...for example drought, plague, locusts, etc. you should cry out and blow [the *chatzotzeros*].

And this is [included] in the *t'shuvah* [Repentance] process: At a time when catastrophe befalls you and you pray and blow all will know that this occurred because of your bad deeds...and this will cause the trouble to subside.

But if they do not pray or blow, but say that this occurrence is natural and coincidental, this is a barbarian attitude which will cause them to further cling to their evil ways, and more tragedies will befall them, behold it is written in the Torah, "If thou goest with me [as if it were] in happenstance, then I shall treat you with the wrath of happenstance", i.e.,if when I bring trouble upon you, so that you repent if you think of it as a natural occurrence I will cause more such occurrences upon you.

Rabbinic edict requires fasting for any communal distress which occurs until Heaven is merciful. During these Fast-Days prayers are said, beseechments and the *chatzotzeros* alone are blown. In the Temple both the *chatzotzeros* and the *shofar* are blown... [this] only in the Temple as it is written, with *chatzotzeros and shofar* you should blow before the King, God.

Rambam, *Yad: Hilkhos Ta'anis* 1:1-4

Analysis

<1> *Masri'in*

The halakhic response to the catastrophies enumerated in [1] and [3] is *masri'in* (we blow) and *masri'in miyad* (we blow immediately). No mention is made of fasting. *Rishonim* debate whether fasting is prescribed or not. Rambam believes that fasting is required. This position is found in *Tanakh*. The prophet Yo'el proclaimed a public Fast because of the coming of *arbeh* and *ch'sil* (*Yo'el* Ch 1 & 2); Yehoshafat because of a military threat (II Chron. 32). Rambam believes the term *"masri'in"* was used to indicate that *chatzotzeros/shofar* should be blasted, but certainly not to rule out fasting.

Ra'avad, on the other hand, posits that *"masri'in"* is meant to be defined literally; *"masri'in"* to the exclusion of *misanin*. The obvious question arises, Why should there be no fasting given the precedent of

Tanakh, especially given that in the first two chapters we find Fasts being called in less severe situations?

The extent to which the *chatzotzeros* are to be blown is debated in *Sifri*. (See above) *Tanna Kamma* is of the opinion that the *chatzotzeros* are only to be blown during times of war. For all other dilemmas *chatzotzeros* are not blown.

Not so R. Akiva. It is his opinion that *chatzotzeros* are blown for all real or potential catastrophies that befall the nation. With regard to fasting, R. Akiva [2] believes that fasting was only instituted for those who are presently feeling the effects of the tragedy and not those who might be effected in the future. *Chatzotzeros*, however, are to be blown [Biblically] by all.

Ra'avad believes that [1] and [3] are the views of R. Akiva. [1] and [3] concern people not directly effected (This makes the expression, "For these one blows **in every place**" more meaningful.) For this reason there is *masri'in* but not *misanin*.

The reason the *Mishna* addresses itself to even those not directly effected is because it wishes to present standard *halakhos* which will apply universally. This is in keeping with the pattern that it has adopted up until this point. Hitherto, all of the *halakhos* which were presented, applied equally to all Jews residing in Israel. The *Mishna* wishes to continue this pattern. Thereafter, it discusses situations in which the *halakha* varies for different people depending upon their circumstances.

Rambam, on the other hand, rules in accordance with the *Chakhamim* of the Mishna that the surrounding cities fast but do not blow. At first glance, this seems to be at variance with his own ruling that blowing "for all troubles" is a *mitzvah* from the Torah.

Rambam, however, maintains the view that the Biblical *mitzvah* **is only applicable in the place facing the problem**. Wanting the *Mishna* to correspond to the *halakha*, he interprets [1] to be referring to the place of the catastrophe; interpreting *masri'in* to mean fast and blow. (This is difficult because the term *"masri'in"* is then ambiguous, being used in the *Mishna* in two differing ways. It is also difficult because it turns out that this position is at variance with both positions mentioned in the *Sifri*.)

<2> *Masri'in Miyad*

The term *"masri'in miyad"* [3] is understood differently by *rishonim*. Some take the view that this is delimited in the *G'mara* (19b) by the statement, "and what is [meant by] immediately? Monday, Thursday and Monday." For these *rishonim*, there are no Fast sequences other than Monday, Thursday, Monday.

It is possible, however, to take the *G'mara's* question as applying only to Rain Fasts. This has support in that the statement on (19b) comes immediately after a discussion of Rain Fasts. In other situations, however, one would blow/fast on any and every day; in some cases, even on *Shabbos*.

Still another possibility is found in the Jerusalem Talmud. Namely, that limiting Fasts to Mondays and Thursdays is solely the view of Rav. [Rav's view would be based upon the intrinsic properties of time. (See Appendix I)] R. Yehudah (14a), on the other hand, would permit fasting on all days except for sequential Rain Fasts.

The question remains, Why are Rain Fasts limited to Mondays and Thursdays? The creations of Monday and Thursday both involved water. Monday was the day in which God separated the waters and Thursday was the day in which the fish—creatures of the sea—were blessed (heard from R. Yochanan Zweig). To this end, prayers for rain should be limited to these two days. This is not the case with regard to other maladies.

<3> *Masri'in b'khol makom*

The reason that the *Mishna* prescribes blowing thoughout the land is that these catastrophies are *"makos m'ha'lkhos"* (conditions which spread). People in the country struck must fast and/or blow *shofar/chatzotzeros* for they must fear that the catastrophe will spread to their province. Thus, Shmuel who lived in Nehardea decreed a Fast because there was a plague in Bei Chuza'i even though this was quite distant from his vicinity. He did this saying, "Is there, then, a natural barrier which would prevent the plague from spreading (21b)?"

Rishonim debate whether people living in different countries need to fast or blow *shofar/chatzotzeros* when a neighboring country is plagued with a *makah m'halekhes* in situations wherein no natural barriers exist to prevent the spread of the catastrophe. Some rishonim, basing themselves upon the *Tosefta* which states, "For a *makah m'halekhes* in Suria they do not fast in Israel, [for a *makah m'halekhes*] in Israel they do not fast in Suria," rule that even in the case of *makah m'halekhes* the observance of fasting/blowing is limited to the country being struck. These rishonim interpret the statement "And for all of these one only fasts in their הפרכיה (19b)" [Rashi, Tosefos, Ran and Ritva all explain הפרכיה as meaning "that country"] to apply even to the case of *makah m'halekhes*.

The rationale for this is our belief that all bona fide catastrophies emanate solely from God and not from the forces of "Nature." To this end, while there might not be any physical barriers which would prevent a catastrophe from spreading, those living in other countries need not be concerned because **each nation is judged on its own independent merits.** These rishonim would take the position that the death of gentiles do not count when determining *dever* because their death does not indicate that there is a *g'zeirah* (decree) against *Bnei Yisrael*.

Other *rishonim*, however, interpret בכל מקום literally. They believe that where one deals with a natural or medical phenomenon which is likely to spread one must fast/blow to the furthest ends of the Earth. In Rashi's words, "If it [the plague] is seen in Aspamia (presumably Spain) then they need to fast in Babylonia."

These *rishonim* interpret הפרכיה to mean "that locale" (Riv'van: The locale which is lacking in [water]; Meiri: מחוז; R. Chananel: אנשי מקום; R. Gershom: שכונה), or limit the applicability of the statement in 19b to cases involving lack of rain (in these instances, as the problem is self-contained, it is not necessary for those living out of the area to fast) and find no other source in the Babylonian Talmud which limits fasting/blowing to a particular country.

Summary Outline

Masri'in

[4] I-[D:30b] States that on the Last Rain Fasts, *masri'in*.

[5] What is the meaning of *"masri'in"* in this context?

a. R. Yehudah: They blow *shofar*;
b. Rav: They pray *anenu*.

Rashi: The *anenu* referred to is עננו אלוקינו עננו

[6] Question: *Braisa*: No less than seven Fast Days are called during which 10 "התרועות are blown." (*Sfas Emes*: The blowing began after ראה נא as a prelude to the additional *brakha*. There was no blowing **after** *the last brakha*.) This is symbolized by Jericho. [At Jericho they used *shofros*.] If so התרעה definitely refers to *shofar*.

[7] Answer: Rav agrees that *"masri'in"* can and does also refer to *shofar*, but R. Yehudah disagrees that it can refer to *anenu*.

[8] Question: *Braisa*: For all other catastrophies, such as, itch, locust, flies, hornets, gnats and the invasion of snakes and scorpions they were not *masri'in*, but צועקים. [If צעקה means that they prayed, *"masri'in"* must mean that they blew *shofar*.]

[9] Answer: The matter is disputed by *tannaim*.

Braisa:

a. Tanna Kamma: For the following reason *masri'in* on *Shabbos*: a city under siege; a city inundated by flood; and a ship sinking at sea;
b. R. Yosi: [For these] לעזרה אבל לא לצעקה.
As on *Shabbos* one may not blow *shofar*, *masri'in in [a] must refer to anenu*. (See<4>.)

Analysis

<4> *Masri'in b'Shabbos*

The *G'mara* (14a) establishes that *"masri'in"* means "they pray." The interpretation "They blow [*chatzotzeros*]" is ruled out since one may not blow shofar on *Shabbos*. This, however, does not appear to be universally accepted.[1]

On the statement made by one of the sons of R. Papa, *"masri'in* even on Shabbos to relieve the epidemic of itching," Rashi comments, "*"Masri'in* through prayer, ***shofar and chatzotzeros***." The Jerusalem Talmud 3:8 also concludes that the *Tanna Kamma* requires the *shofar* to be blown on *Shabbos*.

From what has been said above <1>, the distinction rests in the function of the *mitzvah* of *chatzotzeros*. According to R. Akiva, the *chatzotzeros* are supposed to be sounded— Biblically speaking—for all types of travail. As such, he would advocate the *shofar* be blown even on *Shabbos*—especially since there is no need to decree, given that *shofar*-blowing is not a *m'lakha* and, also, that it is a *mitzvah* relegated solely to *beis din* (Rabbinic Court); as such there is no reason to fear Sabbath violation.[2]

Yet, Rambam while postulating that *chatzotzeros* are indeed a Biblical *mitzvah*, nonetheless, rules that the *chatzotzeros* may not be blown on *Shabbos*. The reason being that he considers the blowing of *chatzotzeros* to be merely a *hekhsher-mitzvah* [*mitzvah* prerequisite]. It serves as an announcement that God has acted justly in this matter, and that we repent our sins. Given that *chatzotzeros* are only a *hekhsher mitzvah they may not be blown on Shabbos*. *Smag* concurs. For this reason, he does not include the blowing of *chatzotzeros* to be one of the "613 *mitzvos*." Nevertheless, those who posit that *chatzotzeros* are a Biblical *mitzvah* advocate that the *chatzotzeros* **be blown on *Shabbos***.

Perhaps, this is precisely the point about which R. Yehudah [5a] and Rav [5b] disagree. R. Yehudah posits that the blowing of *chatzotzeros* is a *mitzvah* while Rav believes that it is only a *hekhsher mitzvah* which must be accompanied by prayer and repentance. For this reason, it may not be blown on *Shabbos*.

This understanding of Rav and R. Yehudah permits an insight into the manner in which these *amoraim* interpret the term *"miyad"* (immediately) found in the *Mishna*. The Babylonian Talmud gives the impression that all agree *"miyad"* is not to be taken literally. Rather it means "Mondays and Thursdays." This is somewhat puzzling given that the danger is immediate and only blowing is involved [according to Ra'avad]. The Jerusalem Talmud allows us to understand that this point is debated by *amoraim*. It does this by identifying Rav as the author of the statement, "One is only to fast/blow on Mondays and Thursdays." For Rav it makes sense to limit the procedure to two times a week, for he believes that *masri'in* is merely a call for fasting and repentance. The latter is too much of a burden to exact more than twice a week. Not so, Rav Yehudah (or *Tanna Kamma* על אלו מתריעין). *He believes the blowing of chatzotzeros* is a *mitzvah*-act in and of itself. As such, it is to be done on all days of the week including *Shabbos*.

1. See Bach O.H. 289 who offers the possibility that Rambam believes that the *halakha* does not follow this G'mara and one may blow shofar on Shabbos. His ultimate rejection of this possibility is in consequence of his interpretation of the Tur and not the merits of the hypothesis.

2. This point is discussed extensively by R. Yehudah Ya'aleh (Responsa O.H. 183) and Maharam Shik (Responsa O.H. 292). R. Yehuda Ya'aleh maintains that the notion of "perhaps he will carry it into a public domain" is not the same as with regard to blowing *shofar* on *Shabbos-Rosh Hashanah*. There, the Rabbis leveled a decree since each Jew has the personal obligation to perform the *mitzvah*. [We fear that in his zeal, a person who does not know the laws of *shofar* might forget that it is *Shabbos* and go to ask an authority the laws of *shofar*; thereby carrying the *shofar* in the public domain.] This fear is not applicable here given that it is the *kohanim* who blow the *chatzotzeros* [and they are not suspected of unwittingly violating the Shabbos] and there are no specifics regarding the blowing [i.e., there are no set amount of blasts or specific sounds that must be blown]. The concern is that a person in the city under siege will forget it is Shabbos and carry the *shofar* in the public domain.

Maharam Shik disagrees with R. Yehudah Ya'aleh's conclusion: Why does he believe that the fear is that the tumult will cause individuals to carry the *shofar* into the public domain when 1) among the catastrophies listed for blowing *chatzotzeros* there is "pregnant women who can't deliver—there is no tumult in this case—and 2) there is no Biblical public domain in most areas that we need be concerned about carrying.

Maharam Shik explains the reason for not blowing *shofar* on *Shabbos* as follows: The Biblical *mitzvah* of blowing *chatzotzeros* is relegated only to those people directly involved in the catastrophe. These people **may blow the *chatzotzeros* on *Shabbos*.** (In the text we maintain that this point is disputed between Rambam and Ra'avad.) Rav and R. Yehudah argue in the situation of those who are not directly involved in the catastrophe. In this case the G'mara assumes that they may not blow the *chatzotzeros* on *Shabbos*.

Analysis

<5>*Masri'in b'Shabbos:* לעזרה אבל לא לצעקה

a. Geonim: One may pray that God help the people in their time of need, but he is forbidden to pray on *Shabbos* that he should not be struck by this tragedy.
b. R. Gershom: People may pray privately, but not publicly concerning this matter.
c. Rashi, Talmid haRamban, Riv'van: : One may call others to help, but one may not pray—as there is uncertainty as to whether the prayers will be answered.
d. R. Yehonatan miluniel: One may pray for those struck, but not bemoan their plight.

<6> Why is *"masri'in"* mentioned in this case and not Fasting?

a. Ramban: Because the surrounding cities need fast only when the people who are in trouble also fast. When they can not fast the others are exempt.

b. Ran: Because the fasts mentioned in the *Mishna* are limited to those held on Mondays and Thursdays. The dangers mentioned in the *Mishna* are such that an immediate response is necessary. The fasting sequence is thus inappropriate.

c. Ritva: *Rishonim* understand that there is no distinction between *Shabbos* and the weekday in this matter. Under all circumstances an individual may choose to fast but no fast may be imposed upon the congregation. The reason is that non-participants fast only if they are concerned that the problem will effect them. If not, there is no obligation for them to fast. However, they should pray for them. This prayer is to be offered world wide, but only during the week. In the case in point wherein the principals involved are harried and can not fast themselves, others may pray for them even on Shabbos. (Compare both Ritvah on p. 20a and 22b).

<7> Praying on *Shabbos* for those who are endangered

Question: Re: [3]. Why should one not be permitted to pray even if he is not sure that his prayers will be answered? The *halakha* is that to save a soul one may violate the Shabbos even if it is not clear that this violation will accomplish its mission!

Answer:

R. Yehudah Ya'aleh: The laws regarding violating *Shabbos* for *piku'ach nefesh* apply only where one employs natural means. The law does not apply to invoking Heaven's help. Thus, one may not give *tzedakah* (charity) on Shabbos in the hope that this will save someone's life.

This is difficult, for if this were true, one should not even be able to pray privately. Yet, Rashi in his second interpretation permits this. This objection is made by Maharam Shik (*Responsa O.H.* 292). See his responsa for an alternative answer.

<8> Why do we no longer blow shofar or chatzotzeros on Fast days?

Magen Avraham (*Orach Chayim* 576) asks why we do not blow on Fast Days? Several answers are applicable. Before stating them we must first study the issue of what is to be blown on Fast days.

In the above quoted pericope, Rambam posits that on Fast days, except in the *Mikdash*, it is the *chatzotzeros* alone which are blown. Rambam derives this from *Rosh Hashanah* 26b-27a:

The *Mishna* states:

> On [Communal] Fast Days they used [two] curved *shofros* of rams, the mouths of which were overlaid with silver. There were two *chatzotzeros* between them; a short blast was made with the *shofros* and a long one with the *chatzotzeros*, because the religious duty of the day was [to be performed] with the *chatzotzeros*.

A *Braisa* delimits the above law:

> When is it said [that the *shofar* and *chatzotzeros* are sounded together] this is only in the Temple; outside of the Temple where the *chatzotzeros* are blasted, the *shofar* is not sounded, where the *shofar* is blasted the *chatzotzeros* are not.

From the above, Rambam (and R. Zerachia haLevi: *Ba'al haMa'or)* derives that on Fast Days, outside the Temple, the *shofar* is not blown alongside the *chatzotzeros*. Rather the latter is blown by itself, "for the *mitzvah* of the day is the *chatzotzeros*."

Others disagree. R. Zerachiah states that the *Geonim* in their responsa report that it was the ***shofar*** which was blown on Fast Days. Ramban explains this position as follows: The proponents of this view base themselves primarily on *Ta'anis* 14a. The *G'mara* in defining the term *"masri'im"* states that it refers to *shofar*. To strengthen the fact that the use of this term is not arbitrary, the Talmud goes on to say, "the symbolism for this is Jericho." In Jericho *shofros* were blown by Joshua to fell the walls.

According to this school of thought,the above-quoted *Braisa* is independent of the *Mishna* and is interpreted as follows: "Where the *shofar* is blown" refers to Rosh Hashanah and Fast Days; "Where the *chatzotzeros* are blown" refers exclusively to wars. Based upon Numbers 10:9 *chatzotzeros* are limited exclusively to wars which effect all of Israel. Ramban concludes that on other occasions either 1) only the *shofar* may be blown or 2) the *shofar* or *chatzotzeros* may be blown.

Based upon the above we can approach *Magen Avraham*'s question. With regard to Rambam's view that *chatzotzeros* must be blown, R. Moshe Feinstien (*Iggrot Moshe* O.H., vol. I, 169) explains that it is also Rambam's view that the *chatzotzeros* which must be used are those of the *Mikdash* and they must be blown by *bona fide kohanim*. Lacking both of these elements *chatzotzeros* can no longer be blown. Other commentaries would give the following responses to *Magen Avraham*'s question. *Chinukh and Arukh haShulchan* rule that *chatzotzeros* need only be blown when the Temple stands. *Smag*'s view is that *chatzotzeros* are merely a voluntary measure which is meant to bring people to repent.

The reason *shofar* is not blown on Fast Days is unclear. *Pri M'gadim* suggests that *shofar*-blowing is limited to the land of Israel. *Chidah* asks, "If so why is the *shofar* not blown today in Israel? In fact, *Tzitz Eliezer* (v. 11, 16) cites *Sh'vileh David* who posits that it is the custom to blow *shofar* in Israel today. I, personally, observed a S'fardic group, in the presence of a former chief Rabbi, blow *shofros* at the *kosel* after *mincha* on 17 Tammuz.

Summary Outline: 19a&b

בצורת and כפנה

[10] R. Nachman: During a famine if supplies can be brought—

a. By sea this condition is classified as a בצורת;
b. Over land this condition is classified as a כפנה.

[11] R. Chanina:

a. If wheat sells for 1 *se'ah* per *sela* (currency) and is obtainable, this is classified as a בצורת;
b. If wheat sells for 4 *se'ah* per *selah* but the wheat is unobtainable this is classified as a כפנה.

[12] R. Yochanan:

a. Inflation—wherein prices are high but people acquire money easily—is considered בצורת;
b. Depression—where prices are low but money is not easily obtainable—is considered כפנה.

Analysis

<9> Tosefos (19a) distinguishes between בצורת as it is used in the Mishna and G'mara. The Mishna discusses a situation which has the potential of leading to widespread hunger. The G'mara uses the term with regard to a self-contained situation.

Amoraim's definition of כפנה.

a. R. Chanina: The determinant of when things have reached the כפנה stage is availability of food, not price;
b. R. Nachman: It is accessibility of food. Even if wheat is obtainable, but only under great difficulty, this is considered כפנה;
c. R. Yochanan: The determinant is price, not availability.

R. Nachman and R. Chanina believe that Fast Days are declared only when God's bounty has been withheld. If food is available—even if prices are so prohibitive that most individuals do not have the funds to purchase the food—no Fast is declared.

R. Yochanan adopts a more expansive perspective. Even if God has bestowed His bounty upon the world, so long as it is unobtainable because of its cost, it is considered as if the produce has been completely withheld. This condition calls for fasting.

Summary Outline: Mishna 19a, 25b-26a, 10b

Mishna

[13] If during a Rain Fast sufficient rain fell—

a. Tanna Kamma: Before sunrise they do not fast;
After sunrise they fast.

b. R. Eliezer: Before noon they do not fast;
After Noon they fast.

[14] In Lod they declared a Rain Fast. Before noon of the Fast Day it rained. R. Tarfon declared that a festival be declared and during *mincha* they recited *hallel*.

G'mara: 25b

[15] *Braisa*: If, during a Rain Fast, sufficient rain fell—

a. R. Meir: Before sunrise, they do not fast;
After sunrise, they fast. (See Appendix I.)

b. R. Yehudah: Before noon, they do not fast;
After noon, they fast;

c. R. Yosi: Before 9 hours, they do not fast;
After 9 hours, they fast.*

[16] R. Ami follows R. Yehudah [15b].

[17] Re: [14]: Abaye, Rava: They waited until *mincha* to recite *hallel hagadol* for it should only be recited after one has eaten.

[18] Question: In M'chuzzah, where a similar incident occurred, they recited *hallel hagadol* immediately.

[19] Answer: This was done because the people of M'chuzzah were known to become inebriated.

* This is based on the fact that for princes who get up in the third hour, their "sixth hour" is Nine Hours. Based on this *Magen Avraham (O.H. 157) rules that on Shabbos* when one must eat before the "sixth hour" that this time is determined from when the person arises.

11b

[20] Braisa: If someone is fasting for a given catastrophe or illness and the danger has passed the person is obligated to complete the fast.

Overview

Relationship Between the Stature of the Leader and that of the Congregation with Regard to Prayers for Rain

The *aggadic* literature of Tractate *Ta'anis* reveals within its fabric of stories a very interesting calculus, namely, in order that it rain a given level of merit is called for. This is the net positive resultant merit of the congregation and its leaders. At times, the leader's merit is so great that regardless of the congregation's level, the leader's merit outweighs their negativeness. At times, the masses' negativeness outweighs the merit of the leader. At other times, the merit of both the people and the scholars are needed to bring rain. What follows are examples of the various type cases cited in the G'mara.

Rain falls solely due to the merit/need of an individual

R. Yochanan (9a), R. Lakish (9b) : Rain will fall for the needs/merit of one individual.

This case deals with the situation in which an individual is judged totally on his own merit. Rashi explains that this individual planted his crops later than the other farmers in his area, or he resided in a city of gentiles.

In the above case only positive and no negative forces are at work.

Rain falls solely on the merit of the tzaddik

1. Chuni ha'ma'agal (18a, 23a)
2. Nakdimon b. Gurion (20a)
3. Abba Chilkiya; Chuni's grandson (23a)
4. Chanan ha'Nechba; Chuni's grandson(23b)
5. R. Yona; father of R. Mani(23b)

Leader requires humility; but rain falls in his merit

1. R. Yehuda HaNasi (24a)
2. R. Nachman (24a)
3. R. Papa (24b): This case differs from the two above in that R. Papa was embarrassed by others.
4. R. Eliezer/R. Akiva (25b): R. Akiva was listened to because he was מעביר על מדותיו .

Leader requires congregation

1. R. Huna/R.Chisda (23b): Called for public fasting.
2. R. Chama b. Chanina (25a): R. Yehoshua b. Levi could bring rain by himself because he is greater than I am. I require your [the congregation's] assistance.
3. R. Eliezer (25b)

Congregation and Leader require Righteous person

1. Ilfah (24a): The supplier of wine for *kiddush and havdalah* caused the rain. Neither Rebbi nor the congregation had enough merit.
2. Teacher (24a) : His merit was his dedication to the children. Neither Rav nor the congregation had enough merit.

Congregation serves as a negative force

1. Rabbah (24a): "What can the leader do when the generation does not act properly?"

Aggadita: 19b-20a

Nakdimon b. Guryon

Understanding the nuances of this story requires attention to details:*

a. Nakdimon did not pray for rain until ridiculed by the Heathen;
b. Nakdimon asked God to reimburse him for performing a *mitzvah*. By what right did he do this?
c. Nakdimon asked for the sun to shine after it allegedly set. How could he pray for a miracle?
d. In his prayer Nakdimon pleads, "Show that there are people in the world who love You?" What is the significance of this remark?

Taken together, the above comments cast light upon the story. Nakdimon had no intention of praying to God for rain so that he might recoup his money. He had paid for the wells strictly because a *mitzvah* was involved. His *only* reason for praying when he did was because of the heathen's ridicule. He sensed that the heathen was scoffing at the God of Israel. He was saying to Nakdimon, "The God of Israel is not the one who causes rain. If it did not rain a whole year it will not rain now." Sensing a *chillul haShem* (a desecration of the Divine Name) Nakdimon felt it necessary to pray for rain.

Once it rained, the heathen agreed that God brought the rains because of Nakdimon. Yet, at this point, he served up another challenge. God can change the course of Nature, but He can not battle Truth itself.

*See *Keren Orah*

Given that it rained after sunset there is no way that He can make the money rightfully yours.

To this, Nakdimon approached God with the following plea. God, I am not someone who worships You just through fear. I worship You through love. In the latter case it is stated, "A *tzaddik* decrees and God fulfils [the *tzaddik's* wish]." (*Mishlei Yisrael* 4940; see also *Shabbos* 59b) So that people might learn the greatness You bestow upon those You truly love, move things in a manner that I may legally be exempt from paying the heathen. God responded to his prayer.

Sequence Analysis: 20b-22a

For Whom the Walls Stand

The *G'mara* has just discussed the need to fast if well structured secure walls are felled by the likes of a tornado or earthquake. The purpose of fasting is to demonstrate belief that this occurred only because it was the Will of Heaven. Now, the Talmud, in a series of *ma'amarim* which span the next two pages, demonstrates that just as healthy walls will collapse when people sin, so too, dilapidated structures which, by the laws of physics, should collapse remain intact in the merit of a righteous person.

A dilapidated wall will not cave in on the righteous

1. The merit of R. Adda b. Ahava was so great (see below) that Rav and Shmuel were willing to walk with him under a dilapidated wall in Naharda'ah that they would never walk under when alone.
2. R. Huna also relied on R. Ada b. Ahava to remove wine from a dilapidated house.
3. The house caved in immediately after Nachum *Ish Gam Zu* left.*

(The Rabbis need be concerned about the danger presented by dilapidated structures.)

4. In threatening weather, R. Huna used to survey the city and order the demolition of any structure which was unsafe.)

A *tzaddik* who gives up full time Torah study in order to earn a living is no longer protected from the dangers of condemned structures.

5. Story of Ilfa and R. Yochanan.

* *G'vuros Ari*: The rule "[A person] may not rely on a miracle' did not apply in this case, as Nachum entered the house when it was not in danger of collapse.

"THE RIGHTEOUS" ARE NOT LIMITED TO SCHOLARS

The *Mishna* couples falling walls with the plague. On its discussion regarding the latter, it emphasizes that even the merit of simple people can avert catastrophies. The following pericopes explicate this principle:

Righteous people need not be of rabbinic descent

6. Discussion of R. Nachman b. Yitzchak with R. Nachman b. R. Chisdah.

Catastrophies are averted because of the merit of "ordinary" righteous people.

7. Sura was spared a plague in the merit of a man who lent shovels and spades for funerals.*
8. Derokeres was saved from fire in the merit of a woman who [on Fridays] would heat her oven and permit others to make use of it. (See below)

The merit of "ordinary" people.

9. Abba the cupper would receive greetings from the Heavenly Academy daily, whereas Abaye would receive such greetings only on Friday afternoons, and Rava only on Yom Kippur Eve. (See below.)
10. R. Beroka Choza'ah was told by Elija the Prophet of three people who merit the World to Come—
    a. A jailor who acted as a Gentile, but who saved imprisoned Jewish women from sin, and informed the rabbis of any impending decrees;
    b. Two jesters who cheered people up and who helped avert/or patch up quarrels.

Aggadita: 20a&b

Things Are Not Always the Way They Seem

The *G'mara* quotes a series of verses and ends with a story all of which revolve about one theme: Things are not what they seem.

1. R. Yehudah/Rav: In Lam. (1:17) it is written, "And Jerusalem is among them as one with Niddah-uncleanness."

A seeming curse is actually a blessing. Just as one with Niddah uncleanness will eventually become clean and permitted to return to her husband, so too, Jerusalem will be reinstated.

* *Sfas Emes*: From the *G'mara* we learn that a *tzaddik* who is so great that he will not be punished along with the congregation will not save the congregation in the case cited.

2. R. Yehudah: She [Jerusalem] is become like a widow. (Lam.1:1)	A seeming curse is a blessing in disguise. She is not a real widow; her husband will return. So too, Israel [God*] will return.
3. R. Yehudah: "Therefore have I also made you contemptible and base before all the people." (Mal. 2:9)	Because of your downtrodden state your people will not be appointed to do compromising work, i.e., overseers of rivers and tax officers.
4. R. Yehudah/Rav: "For the Lord will smite Israel as a reed is shaken in the water" (I Kings 14:15)	Comparing Israel to a reed is better than to a cedar tree. The former never will become uprooted and will survive; the latter can become completely uprooted.
5. R. Elazar b. Shimon studied and was haughty. He shamed an ugly person who said to him, "Why don't you complain to the Maker [God].' The latter would not forgive him until the townsfolk pleaded that he should.	R. Elazar could be compared to a cedar. He had studied Torah and mastered it. His strength was his weakness. His "perfection" did not permit him to accept "imperfection." Therefore, he sinned. An "ugly" person is seemingly cursed, but his ugliness prevents him from sinning. Also, as per R. Yehoshua b. Chanania (7a) "If I were uglier I would have accomplished more in my Torah studies." Thus, things are not what they seem to be. Therefore, R. Elazar b. Shimon lauded the reed over the cedar.
6. On that day R. Elazar b. Shimon entered the Bet Midrash and taught "A person should be as a reed etc."	*Zoharei HaShas* explains that this teaches one should immediately rectify any sin that he has committed.

Aggadita: 20b

R. Ada b. Ahava's Longevity

R. Ada b. Ahava gives the following reason for his longevity: I never—

a. Displayed impatience in my house;
b. Walked before anyone greater than myself;
c. Meditated Torah in unclean places;

*(R. M. Schneerson, (L.S., 9:147): Even when God "chased out" Israel, it was merely an outer manifestation. "Da'ato lahzor" indicates that He watches over Israel b'hester (from behind the scene). Thus even now He is Israel's "husband."

d. Walked four cubits without being involved in Torah study or without wearing t'fillin;
e. Slept, even for short durations, in the beis hamedrash;
f. Rejoiced at the disgrace of my friends;
g. Called my friends by nicknames.

It must be understood why R. Ada b. Ahava considered the above to be reasons for longevity. In the Torah we find that longevity is promised for three acts: Honoring Father and Mother; "Sending away the mother"; and Torah study.

With regard to Honoring Father and Mother, Zohar explains that aside from the literal interpretation of the verse, the terms "father" and "mother" are to be understood as follows: "Father" is the Almighty; "Mother" refers to Israel. [c, d, e] fall into the former category; [a, b, f, g] the latter. In all cases the underlying reason for longevity is sensitivity to and true respect and awareness of the intrinsic worth of Torah, mitzvos and K'lal Yisra'el.

It is to be noted that in the case of *Torah and mitzvos* longevity is not a consequence of learning Torah or performing *mitzvos*. Rather, it is due to the respect one shows for the system. The מדה כנגד מדה in this, we believe, to be the following: A person who internalizes the fact that *Torah and mitzvos* are the reality of life תורה ומצוות...כי הם חיינו (ma'ariv service) is blessed with long life to indulge in *Torah and mitzvos*.

Aggadita: 20b

R. Huna and Communal Responsibility

From R. Huna one learns the scope of Rabbinic responsibility. R. Huna was concerned with the **physical** needs of the townsfolk to the following extent:

1. He condemned delapidated structures and, if necessary, personally financed the rebuilding costs;
2. He would protect merchants by purchasing surplus food and dumping it into the river. [He did not want to give the food to the poor lest they would depend on this subsidy and would not trouble to buy food on their own.] (*From this we can learn that it is sometimes correct to waste food.*)

   He did this to insure—

   a. a proper supply of food in future weeks;
   b. stable food prices;
3. He provided the populace with new drugs that they could not afford;
4. At mealtime he opened his doors to the needy.

Aggadita: 21a

Leaving Yeshiva: Ilfah and R.Yochanan

The story of Ilfah and R. Yochanan is repeated annually in yeshivos. It highlights the question, Should I remain in the yeshiva and make Torah studies my sole pursuit or should I leave the yeshiva and enter the world of business and professions? The sequence of the story is as follows:

1. Both R. Yochanan and Ilfa studied in the yeshiva, on a very advanced level, but they were very poor;
2. Both decided that they should leave yeshiva to earn a livelihood;
3. They lunched under a faulty wall;
4. One angel wanted to cave the wall in, "For they are forsaking Eternal life for mundane life";
5. The other angel prevented it, "One is destined for greatness";
6. Only R. Yochanan heard this conversation; he returned to yeshiva; eventually became Rosh Yeshiva;
7. After some time Ilfa returned; taunted by the townsfolk he demonstrated that he was indeed a great scholar.

Analysis

The episode reveals the following situation and dilemma:

1. Both R. Yochanan and Ilfa were *roshei yeshiva* material; (The case is not whether one should leave yeshiva after high school.)
2. Neither wanted to leave yeshiva on principle. The reason was solely financial;
3. It is unclear about whom the angel was referring. Perhaps Ilfa was greater than R. Yochanan. Surely he proved his learning ability.

Moral

Notwithstanding the above doubts the story does reveal one very important point—for someone to grow up to become a *gadol ha'dor* or a *rosh yeshiva/mesivta* it is necessary for him to devote himself to it on a full time basis over many years. The knowledge required of a *gadol* is enormous. Not only is the material diverse and wide ranging, but also one must obtain the status of expert in all areas of Jewish law. This can not be accomplished with anything less than a full-time pursuit.

Also, one can only be appointed a *rosh yeshiva* if he has demonstrated his willingness to sacrifice himself completely for the sake of Torah. This is important for the purposes of role model. Students are perennially faced with the R. Yochanan-Ilfah dilemma. The forces drawing them away from yeshiva are often overwhelming. For the student to gather the conviction to stay and study Torah he must be exposed to someone who, himself, has been *moser nefesh* for Torah study. This quality is more important than learning ability. Ilfa might have been a greater *lamdan* (scholar) nevertheless, because he did not display R. Yochanan's *mesiras nefesh* for Torah study he could not be appointed rosh yeshiva.

Aggadita: 21a

Nachum *Ish Gam Zu*: What is Good?

Nachum was noted for one thing, he believed all occurrences were for the good.* In *Chazzon Ish*, R. Korelitz points up that the term *bitachon* (trust in God) is often misunderstood. People think that *bitachon* means that if one observes the *mitzvos*, he may trust in God that nothing bad will befall him. Not so, says R. Korelitz. Rather, *bitachon* is the steadfast belief that whatever befalls man is brought about by God for the ultimate well-being of man. The fact that we sometimes do not understand the Divine Will is the reason *bitachon* (trust) is necessary. We, in effect, must trust God's judgment in these matters.

Nachum mastered the attribute of *bitachon*. He internalized that all which occurred was God's Will and that it was, therefore, for the good. This is the message he sought to inculcate in the Rabbis. Even with regard to his own physical "misfortune"—which his students thought to be a curse—Nachum pointed out, "Woe unto me if you did not see me in this condition!"

However, Nachum's achievement was also the cause of his sinning. In training himself to see everything as a benevolent act of God, Nachum learned to downgrade or redefine the severity of situations. While this attribute is commendable it often leads to inaction; for if things are not really so bad there is no need to change the *status quo*.

Nachum's mistake was his not distinguishing between situations which effected him from those which effected others. In the former case, *tzaddok hadin* is admirable; in the latter it is detrimental. When he saw the pauper, Nachum hesitated for a slight moment, improperly thinking to himself, "Things are not so bad." In this short moment, the man bent over and died.

For this reason Nachum told his students, "Woe unto me if you did not see me in this condition," for you, too, might then have repeated my sin.

*R. M. Schneerson of Lubavitch: R. Akiva stated the same expression in aramaic, "*kol d'avid Rachmana l'tav avid.*" *(B'rakhos 60b)* The latter expression refers to situations in which the outcome is positive, but the intermediate steps brings pain and anguish. "*Gam zu l'tova*" applies when all aspects of an incident are understood to be for the best. Each *tanna* uses an expression which is appropriate to his situation. Nachum lived closer to (or at) the time of the Temple. Then God's presence was manifest and everything was seen to be for the good. R. Akiva, his student, lived at a time of political upheaval. When he lived, the most he could state was, '[Even though 'bad things' are occurring, in the end] these events are for the best. (*Likutei Sichos* 2:395)

Aggadita: 20b

Not Praying for an Abundance of Blessing: Israel and the Diaspora

The *Mishna* rules that we are prohibited from praying that rain should not fall. R. Yohanan explains that this is because it is improper to pray to avert an abundance of blessing. Rami b. R. Yud states that this law is only applicable in Israel; in the diaspora, one has the right to pray to avert an overabundance of rain.

Keren Orah explains. The land of Israel is directly overseen by God. With regard to the Almighty it is written, "No evil can manifest from God." If an overabundance of blessing turns out to be a curse, it is not because it is truly a curse, but rather our shortcomings do not enable us to properly accept this goodness. This is not the case with regard to the diaspora. These lands are under the aegis of various ministering angels. Angels are empowered to bring forth cursed events. Thus, an overabundance of rain in the diaspora is not to be seen as an unappreciated blessing, but rather as a true curse.

Aggadita: 21b & 22a

Aba Umnah The Heavenly Academy and Engendering Peace

When there is peace below the blessings from heaven become manifest on earth. Aba, the blood letter, carried on his profession in a way which engendered peace. To this end, he was blessed with daily greetings from the Heavenly Academy.

By being discrete with regard to the medical treatment of female patients, he increased peace in the world. This is derived from Pinchas. When the latter carried forth his heroism in killing Zimri and Kazbi who were involved in forbidden copulation, God bestowed upon him the blessing "of Peace." Thus, he who is careful in these matters is so blessed. (Keren Orah)

He further engendered good will in not embarrassing people who could not afford to pay; freely treating young scholars, as well as subsidizing them, and always giving people the benefit of the doubt.

While no mention is made in the Talmud with regard to Abaye's merit, it can be seen from B'rakhos 17a that Abaye concentrated on peace, as well.

> A favorite saying of Abaye was: A man should always be subtle in the fear of Heaven...and one should always strive to be on the

> best terms with his brethren and his relatives and with all men and even with the heathen in the street, inorder that he may be beloved above and well-liked below and be acceptable to his fellow creatures.

That same G'mara also specifies Rava's desire for familial peace and affection—although it is clear that he does not concentrate on the furtherment of peace to the degree of Abaye.

> A favorite saying of Rava was: The goal of wisdom is repentance and good deeds, so that a man should not study Torah and Mishnah and then despise his father, mother, teacher and his superior in wisdom and rank.

Aggadita 22b, 23a, 25b & 9b

Blessed Rains

The main message of this tractate, as pointed out above, is that God controls the climate and that what occurs is directly related to our belief, Torah study and good deeds. To this end, the G'mara reiterates the extent to which God will bestow His blessings upon us if we observe His commandments:

a. Rain will fall in the exact right amount; (22b: 49-50)
b. It will fall immediately when it is asked for; literally when מוריד הגשם is uttered; (25b:43-52)
c. It will fall exactly where needed even down to the exact blade of grass; (9b:8-16)
d. It will fall at a time when it is most convenient, e.g., Friday night; (23a:1-3, 8-12)
e. Fruit will grow to giant proportions. (23a:4-5)

If there is any variance from the aforesaid, it is only because man has sinned. (23a:5)

Aggadita: 23a

Chuni: Companionship and Effectiveness

The most tragic part of Chuni's life is when he returns after seventy years and was not accepted by the Rabbis of the time. Not being accepted, he prays for death, to which Rava proclaims, "Either companionship or death."

From the above, we may learn the following:

a. Leaders who are appropriate in one setting might not be suitable in another.
b. More than anything, man needs companionship. At times we think that we do not need the support and love of others, but without these, life, itself, is not worth living.

Chanan ha'Nechbah: The Righteous Must be Implored

It is told that when the world required rain the Rabbis sent in young children to implore Chanan to pray. Why was the subterfuge necessary and why did he not pray for rain even before asked? Similarly, the question applies to R. Ami's *ma'amar* (8a). Why did he not pray for rain **before** he was asked by the congregation?

Undoubtably, the חסיד had been praying throughout. Nevertheless, his prayers alone were insufficient to bring rain. A correquisite is that the congregation humble themselves. In this pericope this is manifest in two ways. Firstly, by the mere fact that the Elders realized that no matter how much they prayed, their merit was insufficient to bring rain and they had no other recourse but to approach the גדול הדור. Secondly, sending children—those who are completely earnest and free of sin—as their emissaries is an admission that they lack these important qualities. This leads to shame, humility and ultimately *t'shuvah*. For this reason the prayers of the חסיד שבדור would now be answered.

Sequence Analysis: 23b-24a

R. Zrikah points out to R. Safra the difference between the stout-hearted Israeli Rabbis (*t'kifim*) and the pious men of Babylonia (*chasidim*); the first were answered even when they prayed privately, the latter only when they prayed publicly. While not explicitly stated, we believe, that in the *ma'amarim* which follow, the *G'mara* goes on to explain both the stout-heartedness and the greatness of the Israeli Rabbis.

a. R. Yona is an Israeli-*takif*. His prayers were answered even when said privately.
b. R. Yosi of Yokeres is most likely R. Yosi b. Zvida who was a Palestinian amora, a very good friend and business associate of R. Yona. As can be seen from the story below, he, too, was a *takif*.
c. R. Elazar ish Birtah is most likely R. Elazar ish Birtosa. He was a *tanna*. It is unknown where Birtosa was. Being a *tanna* he no doubt lived in Israel.

The stories of these masters explains their greatness and the reason their prayers were answered. On the one hand, they were extremely punctilious about *halakha*. Simultaneously, they were very open in doing acts of *chesed*.

In choosing R. Elazar for its final example in this series, the *G'mara* adds another dimension to the reason the Israeli rabbis were answered when they prayed for rain. In Avos 3:8, R. Elazar states,

> Give Him [God] his for you and your possessions are his.

We have pointed out above that people are answered in their prayers for rain in proportion to their belief that all sustenance essentially comes from God. The Talmud establishes here that this belief was embodied by R. Elazar. No doubt the other Rabbis mentioned also bore living testimony to R. Elazar's *ma'amar*, and for this reason their prayers were answered.

Summary Outline: 23b-24a

R. Yosi of Yokeres

R. Yosi was very stern—

a. His son caused a fig tree to bear its fruit early and, thereby, troubled God unnecessarily. He prayed that his son die prematurely;
b. His daughter caused people anguish because of her beauty, she, also, served as a possible source of sin. He prayed that she die;
c. Even his donkey was punctilious about the constricts of the law.

Aggadita

R. Mani

R. Mani asked—

a. His father to use miraculous means to cause the members of the Patriarch's household not to annoy him;
b. R. Yitzhak b. Eliashiv to pray that the rich members of his [R. Mani's] father-in-law's family become poor [because they treated him with disdain]. When this was accomplished he asked him to pray that they become rich again [because they were asking him for support];
c. R. Yitzhak b. Eliashiv to pray that his [R. Mani's] wife become beautiful. Then, he got him to pray that she become ugly [because she had become domineering].

After this experience, R. Yitzhak b. Eliashiv refused to perform these feats again.

The lesson to be learned is that a person should not expect miracles to rid him of his basic problems. The *avodah* (life's work) of man—which will lead to the perfection of humanity—is to learn to live with the vicissitudes of life. Miracles can bring about abrupt changes in circumstances, but they cannot solve the problems man faces in his daily existence. This, he must do on his own.

R. Eliezer b. Birsah

R. Eliezer was excessively charitable. Charity collectors fled **from him** for fear that he would give them all of his money. He even gave away his daughter's wedding dowry. While free with giving his money away he was strict about not benefitting from items produced miraculously.

Summary Outline: 24b-25a

[21] R. Mari—would not allow people to use grain that was produced miraculously.

[22] Rava—proclaimed a fast in Hagrunia. He asked the people if any had a dream that night. When told of a good dream, he asked the people to pray, and it rained.

[23] Rava—was asked by Shapur Malkah in the summer months to cause it to rain. To accomplish a *kiddush haShem* (sanctification of God's name) he beseeched Heaven and it rained. His deceased father appeared to him and admonished him for troubling Heaven. He, also, warned him to change his seat in the *beis midrash*. The next day, knives were found on his regular seat.

Analysis

This story is connected with the two previous stories:

a. [23] demonstrates that Rava did not need the merit of the congregation to bring rain. Nevertheless, in [22] he purposely involved the congregation in the process.

b. [23], also, demonstrates that when a person relies on miracles it does not please heaven.

Summary Outline

[24] R. Chanina b. Dosa

The following stories of R. Chanina must be viewed as a unit:

a. He could make it rain at will;

b. His wife often had miracles occur;

c. [The reason he could perform miracles at will was because on his level there was no distinction between the miraculous and nature; nature was a miracle. This is the meaning of his statement] To his daughter, "He who makes oil light will make vinegar light;

d. [Nevertheless, as in [23] (Story of the golden pedestal which came from Heaven)], he learned, if Heaven gives a miraculous gift it causes a dimunition in one's future reward.

[25] R. Elazar b. Pdas—was poor. God told him he would remake the world for him; *perhaps* he would be born in a more prosperous times.

Analysis

This is a continuation of the stories surrounding R. Chanina. Notice in both cases, God brings about miracles to help saintly people, but does not provide sustenance through natural means. This is in concert with Bava Metzia which proclaims "the giving of sustenance is the most difficult of feats."

Aggadita: 25b

R. Eliezer and R. Akiva

R. Eliezer prayed for rain and was not answered. R. Akiva merely said אבינו מלכינו and was answered. A *bas kol* called forth, "Not because one is greater than the other, but because one is forebearing, the other not."

R. Yisrael Salanter explains the *bas kol* as follows: R. Eliezer was a student of Beis Shammai; R. Akiva of Beis Hillel. Each school had its approach to worshipping God. Beis Shammai was unrelenting when it came to standards. Beis Hillel was forebearing. Each approach was Divinely sanctioned as being correct. Yet, when it comes to answering one's prayers one is answered on the basis of one's own attributes. Given R. Eliezer's strict standards, Heaven could not relent and give rain when the congregation was not worthy. Not so if R. Akiva, the disciple of Beis Hillel, prayed. His prayers would be answered because his manner of worship allowed for mercy and kindness.

The Jerusalem Talmud continues the story: R. Akiva told his Rebbe, R. Eliezer, that his prayer was not answered because God wishes those that he especially loves to continue praying to Him. This principle is well known. It is the reason why all of the Matriarchs (except Leah) were originally barren.

Ta'anis: Chapter Four

Introduction

This chapter centers on the *Mikdash*. The laws of *n'siyas kapayim, ma'amados and korban eitzim* are included. Its place in this tractate is three-fold: the number of times there is *n'siyas kapayim* on a Fast Day is disputed; the *anshei ma'amad* fasted four times per week; and we fast four times a year in commemoration of the destruction of the Temple. After reviewing these laws, the tractate ends with a description of the merriment which took place in the Temple on 15 Av and a fervent prayer that the Temple will be built "speedily in our days" (*kein y'hi ratzon*).

We begin a study of the chapter with all of the laws of *kohanim* found in the Tractate.

Summary Outline: 26, 17a

Kohanim

Birkas kohanim/n'siyas kapayim

Mishna

[1] There are three categories of day during which *kohanim* bless the people four times a day; *shacharis, musaf, mincha neilah*. They are : Fast Days, *ma'amados* (explained below) and Yom Kippur.

G'mara

[2] [1] is to be read that there are three "categories of day" during which the *Kohanim* bless the people **during each prayer**. (This

change was made in light of the fact that there is no *musaf*-prayer on Fast days or *ma'amados*.)

[3] R. Nachman: [1] follows R. Meir. (See below.)

[4] Biblically, *n'siyat kapayim* is to be recited during each *t'fillah*. The Rabbis prohibited *n'siyas kapayim* during *mincha* since people may be inebriated and, thus, prohibited from performing *birkas kohanim*. *Tannaim* dispute the status of *birkas kohanim* on Fast Days when there is no need to be concerned about drunkenness. Their positions are tabulated below.

Birkas Kohanim

	Mincha	*Neilah*	
R. Meir	yes	yes	People know it is a Fast Day, and drunkedness is not a problem.
R. Yehudah	no	no	The decree applies on all days.
R. Yosi	no	yes	The decree was meant to apply only to *mincha*. It does not extend to *neilah* which is only prayed on Fast Days.

[5] *Halakha*

a. Rav: The *halakha* follows R. Meir.

b. R. Yochanan: The people followed (נהגו) R. Meir. The status of נהגו is that no public pronouncement is made to follow this procedure. However, if someone asks, he is advised to perform *n'siyas kapayim*.

c. Rava: The custom (מנהג) is as R. Meir. This means, a verdict is not rendered in favor of R. Meir. However, if one follows R. Meir, then we do not nullify the action.

d. R. Nachman: The *halakha* follows R. Yosi.

e. G'mara: The *halakha* follows R. Yosi.

[6] *Kohanim*, in fact, perform *birkas kohanim* during *mincha* of Fast Days since *mincha* on Fast Days is prayed very close to sunset. (Throughout the year, *mincha* was customarily *davened* earlier in the day.) In this regard *mincha* is similar to *neilah*.

Status of a *kohen* who drinks wine

[7] One who has drunk wine may not perform *birkas kohanim*

Bar Kapara: This is derived from the juxtaposition between the laws of *birkas kohanim* and *nazir*. (The G'mara concludes that this is only an *asmakhta*.)

17a

[8] *Kohanim* who are part of the *mishmar* may not drink wine during the day for the entire week they serve in the Temple. They may, however, drink wine during the evenings. (G'mara: Lest the work be too much for the *bet av* and they be asked to serve on that day. Rashi: The night is not a problem. Given that the offerings are brought during the day the *kohanim* know by nightfall whether they will be called on to assist.)

[9] *Kohanim* who are part of the *beis av* (the people who actually perform the service on a given day) may not drink wine either during the day or the following evening. (G'mara: Because they are called on to serve day and night.)

[10] It is said: Any *kohen* today who knows his *beis av* should not drink wine on the day his *beis av* is to serve in the Temple, lest the Temple be built on that day and he be called to serve.

If he knows his *Mishmar* he may not drink wine that whole week.

If he knows neither [his *beis av* or *mishmar*] he may not drink wine the year round.

[11] Rebbi: I concur. Yet this decree has been abandoned because of the length of time that the Temple has not been rebuilt. (Rambam: [10] and [11] refer to the time of the *Mikdash*. See Rashi.)

[12] Abaye: Today's *kohanim* rely on Rebbe [11].

[13] Rami b. Aba: If one drank wine, after sleeping a little or walking the distance of a *mil*, he may perform *birkas kohanim*.

[14] R. Nachman/Rabba b. Avuhu: [13] discusses the situation where just a *r'vi'is* was drunk. If a person drank more than a *r'vi'is* of wine, then walking and sleeping have negative effects.

[15] R. Ashi: *Avodah* performed by a drunk is invalid.

[16] Braisa: A drunk who performs *avodah* incurs the death penalty. (Lev. 10:9)

Kohanim: Haircuts

[17] There is a *mitzvah* for a—

a. King to have a haircut each day;

[R. Aba b. Z'vidah: Thine eyes shall see the king in his beauty (Isa. 33:17)]

b. *Kohen Gadol to take a haircut each Friday;*

[R. Shmuel b. Yitzchak: So that each new mishmar would see him at his best.]

c. *Kohen* once a month.

This is derived from a *gzeira shava* made between *kohen* and *nazir.* In both sections the term *"pera"* is used. In the case of *nazir* the Torah demands that he grow his hair for thirty days. In the case of *kohen*, the Torah demands that he not let his hair grow for more than thirty days without it being cut.

[18] Haircuts are only required of those who perform the Temple service.

No decree was enacted requiring *kohanim* in the Post-Temple Era to take haircuts (see above) because—

a. One can quickly cut his hair if necessary;
b. A person who performs the *avodah* with long hair does not invalidate that *avodah*. [One who does the *avodah* while drunk invalidates that *avodah*. (As per R. Ashi above)]

Analysis

***Birkas Kohanim*—**

<1> On *mincha* of Fast Days

re: [6]: *Rishonim* rule that the only Fasts during which there is *n'siyas kapayim* for *mincha* are those in which *neilah* is not recited. On these Fasts, *mincha* is *davened* immediately prior to sunset. Throughout the year, *mincha* is *davened* earlier in the day. Due to this time difference, people will not extrapolate any procedure carried on during this *mincha* and apply it to *mincha* throughout the year.

On a Fast in which *neilah* is recited, *mincha* is said at the regular time. For this reason, *n'siyas kapayim* is not performed.

Chazzon Ish posits that, nowadays when *mincha* throughout the year is prayed toward sunset, whereas on a Fast Day it is prayed in the early afternoon, *n'siyas kapayim* may be performed even in the early afternoon.

<2> On *mincha* of Yom Kippur

Rishonim dispute the status of *birkas kohanim* for *mincha* on *Yom Kippur*. There are three positions in this matter. *B'hag* (as quoted by the Tur) rules that there is *birkas kohanim* because the *selichos* recited during *mincha* cause *n'siyas kapayim* to take place near sunset. (Interestingly, in our editions of the *B'hag* it is not stated that there is *n'siyas kapayim* on *mincha* of *Yom Kippur*.)

R. Amram Gaon rules that there is no *n'siyas kapayim* during this *mincha*. Were a *kohen* to ascend the *bima* he would be asked to descend. Rambam takes an intermediate position. He rules that there is no *n'siyas kapayim*. However, if a *kohen* ascends we allow him to perform *n'siyas kapayim*.

This dispute leads to another difference of opinion with regard to whether *Elokeinu...barkhenu babrakha* is recited. Bach records that it is **customary** to recite it, but that this is contrary to the *halakha* which is that we do not perform *n'siyas kapayim*.

Haga'os Maimonis substantiates the custom on the basis that if a *kohen* ascends he does recite the blessings.

<3> On *mincha* of a half-day Fast

R. Yerucham writes that on a half-day Fast, since one can eat in the afternoon, *Elokeinu* is not said. Magen Avraham states that given that were a *kohen* to ascend he could perform *n'siyas kapayim*, *Elokeinu* should be recited.

Summary Outline: 26a, 27a-28a

Mishmaros and Ma'amados

Definition of *Mishmaros*

Biblically, it appears from the G'mara that a *kohen* is entitled to do the *avodah* in the Temple at any time. (See <1>.) Since this would be very unwieldy, assuming an overabundance of *kohanim, mishmaros* (Watches) were established wherein only specific families were permitted to work in the Temple on given weeks. Each *mishmar* worked in the Temple for one week at a time on a rotating basis. The *mishmar* worked from *Shabbos* to *Shabbos*.

[18] Braisa$_1$ & R. Chama b. Guria/Rav:

a. Moshe decreed that there be 8 *mishmaros*—4 from Elazar's family and 4 from Itamar's.
b. Shmuel increased the number to 16.
c. King David increased the number to 24 (I Chronicles 26); 8 from Elazar and 16 from Itamar.

[9] *Braisa*$_2$
a. Moshe decreed 16 *mishmaros*; 8 from Elazar and 8 from Itamar.
b. Shmuel and Kind David increased the number to 24.

[20] *Braisa*$_3$:

During the Second Commonwealth many prominent families of *kohanim* preferred not to return to Israel from the exile. The Rabbis created the 24 *mishmaros* from the four families that returned, proclaiming that these families will forever take precedence over the others. If and when the others return, their "*mishmaros*" will be incorporated in the rotation of the original four.

Definition of and reason for *ma'amados*

[21] *Mishna*: When an offering is brought, it is proper that its owners be present. As such, the daily (*tamid*) offering which was collectively owned by all of Israel required representatives. The Rabbis instituted that a group of *yisra'elim* (Israelites) be present when the offering was made.

[22] The *ma'amados* were divided in accordance to *mishmaros*. Members of the *ma'amados* served for a week at a time.

What did the *ma'amad* do?

[23] One part of the *ma'amad* served in Jerusalem as stated.

One part supplied the other with food.

One part of the *ma'amad* stayed in its home area and prayed that the sacrifice be accepted.

Torah Reading

[24] Each day they read from readings in the CreationChapter—

Sunday:	Day One and Two
Monday:	DayTwo and Three
Tuesday:	Day Three and Four
Wednesday:	Day Four and Five
Thursday:	Day Five and Six
Friday:	Day Six and *Shabbos*

[25] The Creation Chapter is read to signify that the world exists only in the merit of (or for the sake of) the sacrificial service. When the Temple is not extant, the world survives because of those who utter the Biblical verses of the *korbanos* (27b). [This revelation

was given to Avraham during the Covenant of the Pieces.]

[26] For the smaller paragraphs, only one person was called. For the larger, two people were called.

(For a full discussion of this point see Tractate M'gilah)

[27] They read from the Torah after *shacharis* and *musaf*. (See <8>.)

At *mincha*–

a. Tanna Kamma: One person reads the same reading orally for the entire congregation.
b. R. Yosi: Each person reads the reading orally to himself.

Situations in which *ma'amados* are abrogated

[28] On a day in which *hallel* is recited there is no *ma'amad* for *shacharis*. [The need to say *hallel* supercedes the *ma'amad*.] (See <11>.)

[29] R. Akiva:

a. On a day in which there is a *musaf*-offering there is no *ma'amad* for *neilah*. (This is because the *musaf*-offering involves many animals; the process is thus time-consuming.)
b. On a day in which there is a wood-offering (*korban eitzim*) there is no *ma'amad* for *mincha*.

[30] Ben Azai/R. Yehoshua

a. Where there is *musaf*-offering there is no *ma'amad* for *mincha*.
b. When there is a wood-offering there is no *ma'amad* for *neilah*.

Analysis

<4> **On the origin of *Mishmaros*:**

Ritva:

a. From both *Braisos* [18] and [19] it appears that the concept of *mishmaros* was instituted by Moshe and that it is **Rabbinic** in nature.
b. *Sifri (Shoftim Piska* 169) explains *l'vad mimkarav al ha'avos* (Deut. 18:8) to mean that the Torah mandates that each family give up its rights to work in the *Mikdash* at all times in return for having exclusive rights at other times. Thus, *mishmaros* are of **Biblical** origin.
c. *Braisa of 32 Middos of R. Eliezer b. R. Yosi haG'lili*: From *Numbers* 8:26 it is derived that the **Torah** designates that *l'vi'im* be divided into *mishmaros*.

From I Chronicles 24:19 it is known that *kohanim* were divided up into 24 *mishmaros* from the time of Moshe; this division was **Biblical**.

d. Conclusion:
The *concept* of dividing *kohanim* and *l'vi'im* into *mishmaros* is **Biblical**. The *exact manner* in which the division should take place is **Rabbinic**.

<5> The composition of the *ma'amados*

a. Rashi: The *ma'amados* consisted of *kohanim, l'vi'im and yisraelim*. (See Rashi on Mishna and (27a).) (*G'vuros Ari*: A *korban tzibbur* [certainly the *korban tamid*] which is offered without there being a *ma'amad* is *pasul*. *S'fas Emes* disagrees.)
b. Piskei Rid: The *ma'amad* was a subsection of *kohanim, l'vi'im and yisraelim* of every *mishmar* that resided permanently in Jerusalem. The *kohanim* and *l'vi'im* of every *mishmar* went up to Jerusalem at the appointed time. The yisraelim who lived outside Jerusalem did not ascend to Jerusalem. They relied upon those who lived in Jerusalem.
c. Ritva: The *ma'amad* consisted solely of *yisraelim*

<6> What did the yisraelim of the *ma'amad* do?

We must distinguish between the *ma'amad* of Jerusalem and the others.

I. Jerusalem *Ma'amad*:

a. Rashi: They used to cut the wood and draw the water.
b. R. Yehonatan of Luniel: They stood by when the *korban* was offered.
c. Tosefos Rid: "In Jerusalem there was no *ma'amad*." Rather, they stood in the *Mikdash* and prayed that the *korban* be accepted"

[a] and [b] rule that part of the ma'amad's procedure was to fast and read the Torah as per [24]. Talmid haRamban agrees. Rid disagrees. Riv'van explicitly states that the group in Jerusalem did not fast. This appears at first sight to be contrary to the Jerusalem Talmud which notes that parts of the Sanhedrin fasted in rotation with the *anshei ma'amad*. Nevertheless, one could say that the Sanhedrin fasted alongside those in the provinces.

I. Non-Jerusalem *ma'amados*

The *ma'amad*—

a. Read the Torah
b. Fasted

c. Prayed that the *korban* be accepted

(1) Ra'avad: Their prayer was said in the *rechov* as per R. Menachem b. R. Yosi, "the [*rechov*] has sanctity since they pray there on Fast Days and *ma'amados*. (*M'gilah* 26a)

(2) Ritva: They prayed in *shul*. The reason for praying in the *rechov*—to publicize that our prayers for rain have not been answered—does not apply here.

<7> The Number of prayers recited by the *ma'amad*

a. Rambam, R. Z'rakhia haLevi : They prayed five *t'fillos* per day including *musaf* and *neilah*.

(This is based upon the Jerusalem Talmud which states that *ma'amados* prayed four *t'fillos* excluding *ma'ariv*. Another basis for this is [29]. The latter implies that there was a *ma'amad* for *musaf* even when there was no *korban musaf*.)

b. Other Rishonim: They prayed four *t'fillos* per day; They *davened neilah* but not *musaf*.

<8> Torah Reading

a. After *shacharis* and after *musaf*, they read from a *Sefer Torah*. [According to Rambam this means everyday; to the others, on a day in which there was no *korban musaf*. Rid, because of <10a>, deletes the words "after *musaf*." *Keren Orah* distinguishes between the *ma'amad* in Jerusalem and the others.]

b. At *mincha* they read the Torah portion by heart as per [27]. (R. Yehonatan: to lighten the burden of the Fast.) (No mention is made whether the reading is before or after *mincha*. Ordinarily, we would think that it is before *mincha* as per our custom. This can be questioned, however, based upon the fact that the *musaf* reading took place **after** *musaf*. Yet, Nechemia 9:3 would support the contention that the Torah reading preceded the *t'fillah*.)

Keren Orah explains the dispute in [27] as follows: *Tanna Kama* maintains that anything which is the *seder hayom* (service of the day) may be read by heart. This is similar to the reading of the *kohen gadol* on *Yom Kippur-mincha*. R. Yosi prohibits an oral public reading, but maintains that the prohibition against reciting Scripture by heart is limited to public readings.

c. At *neilah*—

Rashi Rambam in *Yad*: There was no Torah reading.

R. Yehonatan, Rambam in *Mishnayos*: A reading took place but it was by heart as per [27].

<9> Regarding the suspension of *ma'amados* as per [29&30]

This was done—

a. *Otzar haGeonim*, Tosefos Rid: So as to highlight the importance of these days.
b. Rashi: Because these various activities are time consuming and there was not sufficient time to do both.

According to [a] the suspension was throughout the land (Tosefos Rid). According to [b] it was only in Jerusalem.

<10> Regarding [29 & 30]: What was suspended when there "was no *ma'amad*?"

a. Rid: They did not gather at all; there was no Torah reading;
b. R. Yehonatan miLuniel: The group met as always and read the Torah; for this there was always sufficient time. Rather, when there was "no *ma'amad*" it was the extra *techinos and selichos* which were said exclusively by the *anshei ma'amad* which was suspended.

<11> On a day of *korban eitzim*,who did not have *ma'amad*?

a. R. Yehonatan: The **whole** *ma'amad* was suspended. On this happy occassion everyone joined in congratulating the participating family and thus there was no time to also conduct a *ma'amad*.
b. Ritva/Ra'avad: **Just the family** that brought the *korban* who were also members of that *ma'amad* did not join the *ma'amad* on that day.

<12> Re: *Neilah*

a. Ritva: They *davened neilah* only on days that the *ma'amad* fasted.
b. Ran/"Some posit": *Neilah* was *davened* even on days in which no fasting took place.

<13> *Neilah* on the Four Fast Days

The Mishna lists Fast Days as one of the times during which one prays *neilah*. We proceed to delimit this statement. *P'sachim* 54b states explicitly that *neilah* is not said on 9 Av. (Rashi states that it is optional but not obligatory. Tosefos states that while not obligatory, one who prays *neilah* on 9 Av has fulfilled a *mitzvah*.) Based on this it is derived that this is also the case for the other three Fasts which commemorate the destruction of the Temple (10 Teves, 17 Tammuz and the Fast of Gedalia). *Rishonim* explain that *neilah* is only to be recited for Fasts of Beseechment not those which were established to commemorate mournful events.

<14> *Neilah* on Rain Fasts

The "Fast Days" referred to in the *Mishna* are those which are proclaimed in times of trouble. *Rishonim* debate over which set of Rain Fasts, *neilah* is recited. There are those who postpone saying *neilah* until the Middle Fasts—they reason that it should be said only when there is a full 24 hour fast. Others, however, posit that it should be said even during the first set of Fasts. They bring proof of this from the fact that the *anshei ma'amad* did not fast 24-hour fasts and yet *davened neilah*. The first group counters that it is only with regard to the length of the fast that *anshei ma'amad* are lenient because they must fast four days in a row. With regard to other *halakhos*, however, they observe the severities of the Middle Fasts immediately.

<15> *Neilah* outside Israel

Ritva states that in theory one should recite *neilah* even for Public Fasts held outside of Israel. In this regard it should be the same as the law regarding the "24 Blessings." Nevertheless, the custom in Spain was not to recite *neilah*. He explains that this was due to the fact that with regard to *neilah* one requires a *bona fide* Public Fast. As per *Ta'anis* 12b, fasts in the diaspora do not acquire this status. (Ran compares these fasts to the "first" set of fasts, for which he rules there is no *neilah*.) They recited the "24 blessings." The latter, is not a completely separate prayer, but an extension of an existing prayer. As such, it may be recited, albeit, the fast does not meet the requirements of an official *ta'anis tzibbur*.

<16> *Neilah* on Sundays and Fridays

Rishonim differ on the status *neilah* on Sundays and Fridays. We believe that the dispute centers about the question: is *neilah* prayed by the *anshei ma'amad* because they are fasting—therefore, on days in which there is no fasting it should not be said—or because the sanctity of each and every day when experienced on the level of the *anshei ma'amad* calls for the *neilah* prayer—according to this view *neilah* is as the *k'dushah* of Yom Kippur. (*Ohr HaTorah: D'varim*, 1506)

We find a similar querie put forth by R. Akivah Eiger (Tshuvos O.H. 24) as to the reason for reading the Torah on *mincha* of Yom Kippur.]

Overview of *Ma'amados*

Having summarized the G'mara and rishonim on the subject of *ma'amados*, we shall proceed to utilize this information to obtain a better understanding of the nature and purpose of *ma'amados*.

R. Moshe Iserliss in *Olas R'iyah* maintains that the main function of *korbanos* is to emphasize to man his mortality and indeed the total finiteness of the universe. This is done by showing how life can be annihilated and the molecules which compose a body revert back to their original state.

R. Shneur Zalman of Ladi (*Likutei Torah* 4:154) uses this notion as a springboard. There is nothing, he reminds us, other than God. With creation, the universe appears to exist. The *korban* is the medium whereby we indicate that there is none other than He; the *korban* symbolizes the abolition of all that which exists. Burning the *korban* on the altar is not, however, to be seen as a negative act of desparation. Rather, it is the positive act wherein man dedicates all that which is at his disposal to God.

This, too, was the function of the *anshei ma'amad*. The G'mara (27b) explains that the reason for reading the parshiyos of creation during the *ma'amados* was to establish, reiterate and teach that the world existed and continues to exist only in the merit of the *korbanos* which are brought each and every day. [At the time when the *mikdash* no longer stands, this role is taken over by the saying and studying of the laws of *korbanos*.]

Yet, we must explain why the *anshei ma'amad* fasted. Indeed given that in some sense the *korban* brought on that day was theirs, they should not have been permitted to fast. We must also understand why they prayed an extra *t'fillah* each day; according to the Rambam they prayed two extra *t'fillos*.

As the *sh'luchim of Klal Yisrael* for the bringing of this *korban*, the *anshei ma'amad* were elevated to high levels of *avodah*. This enabled them to pray that the *korban* be accepted on the level of "*shanim kadmoniyos*" (*Ohr haTorah: Bamidbar,* 1110); the highest of levels. In this vein, the fasting of the *anshei ma'amad* is not to be seen as a contradiction to the *simcha* of bringing a *korban*. Rather, this fasting was a complement to their *simcha*. This fasting was indicative of their spiritual attainment: as we find in the case of Moshe who fasted while on Mount Sinai. To approach the *Sh'khinah*, Moshe waited seven days so that the food within him be completely digested. (*Yoma* 6b)

Their extra *t'fillos* were also a consequence of their level of *avodah*. Just as the *k'dushah* of Yom Kippur elevates man to the point wherein he worships God on the level of "*lifnei haShem titharu*," and this obligates the fifth *t'filah* (*Ohr HaTorah: D'varim*, 1508), so too, *anshei ma'amad* were on a spiritual level which required five *t'fillos* per day.

Summary Outline: 26a, 28a&b

Korban Eitzim

[31] Braisa$_1$ (28a): At the beginning of the Second Commonwealth when the Temple was dedicated, there was no wood for the altar. Several families (listed below) donated wood for the altar. The prophets among them declared that in later years even if there was sufficient wood for the altar the *eitzim* of these families would be used for the altar on the anniversary of the date they first offered the wood.

[32] Mishna (26a): Following are the dates for the *korban eitzim*:

1. 1 Nissan	Family of Orah b. Yehudah
2. 20 Tammuz	Family of David b. Yehudah
3. 5 Av	Family of Parush b. Yehudah
4. 7 Av	Family of Yonadav b. Rekev
5. 10 Av	Family of Sanah b. Binyamin
6. 15 Av	Family of Zesuh b. Yehudah, *Kohanim, L'vi'im*, all who do not know their tribe, *B'nei gonve ali* (see [33]) and *Bnei kotzei k'tziyos* (see [33])
7. 20 Av	Family of Pachas Mo'av b. Yehudah
8. 20 Elul	Family of Adin b. Yehudah
9. 1 Teves	Family of Parush b. Yehudah (2nd time)

[33] Braisa$_2$ (28):

B'nei Gonve Ali and *Bnei Kotzetzei K'tziyos* were those people who through subterfuge brought *Bikurim* (First Fruits) to Jerusalem and wood for the altar at a time when this was forbidden by the governing authorities.

[34] R. Meir: Fam. of Pachas Mo'av = Fam. of David b. Yehudah
R. Yosi: Fam. of Pachas Mo'av = Fam. of Yo'av b. Tzruyah

[35] R. Yehudah: Fam. of Adin = Fam. of David b. Yehudah
R. Yosi: Fam. of Adin = Fam. of Yo'av b. Tzruyah

[36] There is a second version of R. Yosi's opinion which negates that Pachas Moav is a descendant of either Yo'av or David.

Analysis

R. M. Schneerson (*Likutei Sichos* 4:1106, 9:86): Re: [34]: This family was, in fact, descended from both David and Yo'av. The dispute concerns: through whose attributes (David or Yo'av) was this family able to attain the spiritual height to bring the wood offering on this important day. [71f] teaches that from 15 Av no more wood could be cut to be used on the *mizbe'ach* (altar). Thus any wood brought on this day had to be cut previously. The families in charge of bringing the offerings after 15 Av possessed a commodity (kosher wood) which was otherwise unobtainable. This they donated to the *Mikdash* not only for the public offerings, but also for voluntary and sin-offerings. (This required the ability to properly predict the amount of wood to pre-cut.) R. Meir and R. Yosi dispute from which ancestor did they inherit this concern for *K'lal Yisrael*.

Sanhedrin 49a states, "Were it not David's [Torah study] Yo'av would not have been victorious in battle, were it not for Yo'av['s battles] David would not have been able to be immersed in Torah." Torah study is a pursuit involving an entity which is separate and apart from this world. It obtains from a higher realm. The spreading of God's Name through battle involves one literally in the most physical aspects of the world.

R. Meir (see Appendix I), whose level of *avodah* (worship of God), was as Adam before the sin, lauds Torah study as that which raised up the spiritual level of the family of Pachas Mo'av. R. Yosi, who generates *halakha* from a this-worldly perspective, (the numerical value of his name is *teva* (Nature)) accents the fact that man's *avodah* in life is to separate out the good from the evil which is manifest in the physical realm. This was Yo'av's primary concern. This concern gave his descendants the ability to think beyond themselves and be concerned with the good of others.

[35] indicates that this same family (Pachas Mo'av) brought an offering on 20 Elul but were then referred to as the Family of Adin. The reason for this is that there are two ways in which a Jew can help another Jew. Corresponding to Elul, a month in which God manifests Mercy, there is the Jew who considers himself to be perfect, who is, nonetheless, willing to be pliant, *adin*, (see R. Chananel, *M.K.* 16b) and to give of his own to help another Jew atone for his sins. Corresponding to Av, the month of recompense, this same "perfect" Jew realizes that his perfection might just be superficial; that he might, in fact, be Pachas Mo'av, a descendant of Ruth the Moabite, and that he is truly on a low spiritual level. From this vantage point he helps other Jews because he realizes they might be more worthy than he.

Summary Outline: *Rosh Hashanah* 18b

The Four Fasts

This tractate mentions but two of the four Public Fasts which were observed by those in the Babylonian exile. Zekaria refers to these fasts as "the Fast of the Fourth Month...Fifth Month...Seventh Month ...Tenth Month." (Zek. 8:19). For the sake of completeness we will now review several *ma'amarim* from Tractate Rosh Hashana which deal with this topic. This will be followed by an analysis of the conceptual significance of these fasts.

Which dates of the months mentioned by Zekharia are the fasts to be held?

[39] Braisa:

a. R. Akiva:

Fourth Month—is 9 Tammuz (Date the Walls of Jerusalem were breached).

Fifth Month—is 9 Av (Date Temple was destroyed).

Seventh Month—is 3 Tishri (Anniversary of Gedalia's murder).

Tenth Month—10 Teves (Date Babylonians began the siege of Jerusalem).

b. R. Shimon: He agrees with R. Akiva regarding (1)-(3).

Tenth Month—The date the news of the Temple's destruction reached Babylonia.

Regarding the Universality of these Fasts

[2] Zekharia in his enumeration of these days (8:19) refers to them both as Fasts and as Festivals. Amora'im dispute the *halakhic* significance of this.

a. R. Huna b. Bizna/R. Shimon Chasidah: During times of peace these should be Festive Days; when there is no peace then they are to be Fast Days.

b. R. Papa: During times of peace these should be Festive days; during times when there are decrees against the Jewish people they should be Fast Days; when there is neither full peace or decrees then fasting is optional.

Overview

In analyzing the Fast Days enumerated by Zekharia we find that each of these dates represents a milestone in the destruction of Jerusalem, *the Beis haMikdash* and Davidic rule. While these events are significant enough to establish *b'chiyah l'doros* (Eternal mourning) we believe that more is involved.

The Mishna enumerates that five tragedies occurred on 17 Tammuz and five on 9 Av. One can argue that this repetition of tragedy was merely coincidental. However, this is certainly not the Talmud's view. In arriving at the date that the Second Temple was destroyed the Talmud concludes that it must have been 9 Av because *"m'galglin zkhus l'yom zakai v'chiyuv l'yom chayav"* (good things happen on good day and bad things occur on bad days). Before analyzing this statement it must be pointed out that this is the sole criterion the Talmud bases itself on with regard to this determination. As proof to this we offer the fact that with regard to deriving a source that the *tamid* ceased to be brought on 17 Tammuz or that Apus'tmus burned a Torah on this date, or that Betar was razed on 9 Av the Talmud states that these are known "by tradition" (*G'mara*). This is not the case with regard to the destruction of the Second Temple. This is "known" merely through the reasoning that if the First Temple was destroyed on this day, so too, must have been the Second. For the Talmud to be so certain of its position means that it relies heavily on the mechanism of *"m'gal'g'lim."* It is to this that we turn.

"M'gal'g'lim" is based upon the rabbinic view of time. This view is that time is heterogeneous, that is, different times have different properties. The properties of each day are unique. Thus, the "time" of Shabbos is different from the "time" of *chol* (weekday). Even specific hours of a particular day have unique properties. Thus, far from a day being a passive entity which in no way influences events, the "time-properties" of the day, in fact, generate events. Days with positive properties generate "good" events, those with negative properties generate "bad" events.

A question arises: Were 'days' invested with these properties from Creation? Certainly, some days, such as Shabbos, were given initial properties. However, from the G'mara it can be seen that at least R. Yochanan is of the belief that Man can invest days with properties. Thus he states with regard to 9 Av, "[God says] because you cried [on 9 Av in the desert] without just cause, behold I will make you cry [on this date] throughout the generations."

Given that Days have properties, when Chazal tell us that five things occurred on 17 Tammuz and 9 Av we must understand that the Talmud is asking us to seek out the common denominator of these events. This is important, for once found, we can derive the unique property potentials of these days. This allows us to properly identify and repent the particular sin for which this day makes us vulnerable. Repentance, it will be recalled, is the main goal of a fast.

We turn now to analyzing the tragedies of each of the Four Fasts to determine the unique properties of these days in an effort to determine the specific *t'shuvah* which is required on these days.

17 TAMMUZ

According to the *Mishna* five tragedies befell the Jewish people on 17 Tammuz: Moshe broke the *luchos* (Ten Commandments); the *tamid* ceased to be brought; The Walls of Jerusalem were breached; Apust-'mus burned the Torah; and an idol was put in the Temple. If we analyze these events with the goal of finding a common thread what emerges is that all of these events turn about a duality: the Jewish people were deprived of Torah because they worshipped idolatry.

Moshe broke the *luchos* because the Jewish people worshipped the golden calf. The *tamid* which ceased being offered on this day is a sacrifice which was instituted to atone for the golden calf. Its being interrupted on this day indicates that in their actions/thoughts, B'nei Yisrael were not cleansed of the sin of Idolatry. Chazal tell us that one of the major sins of Jerusalem at the time of the destruction of the First Temple was that of Idolatry. Apus't'mus' burning the Torah and Menashe's putting the idol in the Temple are explicit examples of the iniquities indicated.

Realizing that we are judged for this flaw on 17 Tammuz, we must repent, specifically, for this failing during the Fast. We must bolster up our faith in God. Even an implicit lack of faith—that is, even if we continue to believe in Him - but lack faith in our *g'dolei hador* <"for we have no idea of what happened to Moshe, the man who took us out of Egypt" > — ultimately leads man to the worship of idolatry. For the worshipping of idolatry in its broadest sense includes the belief that some force other than God—be it social, political or economic—ultimately determines world events.

Idolatry is not only reprehensible but it is a sin which does not permit Torah to infiltrate a person's being. It is for this reason that Moshe had to withhold the *luchos*. On 17 Tammuz this point must be taken to heart. We truly want to study and observe Torah. Yet, we have the mistaken idea that Torah can co-exist with other beliefs. This is not so.

When a dentist fills a cavity, he must drill until all signs of decay are eradicated; for decay which remains under a filling will just keep destroying the tooth. In the same way, Torah can not be built upon a decaying foundation. On 17 Tammuz we must completely eradicate any vestige of "idolatry" which might be part of us so as to allow the entance of Torah into our being.

9 AV

Five catastrophic events occurred on 9 Av: The *dor midbar* (desert generation) were told that they would not be permitted to enter Israel: the two Temples were destroyed: the city of Betar was captured: and Jerusalem was razed. Each of these events involve *galus* (exile). In each case the catastrophe served as the end of an era which caused wandering from place to place and caused the generation involved to see their fate sealed.

The root cause for this end is lack of faith in God. This lack of faith goes deeper than that of 17 Tammuz and, therefore, its consequence is greater. 17 Tammuz dealt with a subtle complaint that God's messenger had mysteriously disappeared. There is never any open statement that Israel did not trust in God. 9 Av was different. When the Jews heard the message of the spies they truly believed that God could not deliver them from their enemies. Because they lacked this faith, they became unworthy of *Eretz Israel* which is only reserved for people who believe that "God's eyes are directed there from the beginning to the end of the year."

It is this lack of faith which we must counteract on 9 Av. One way in which this can be brought about is through our realization of the level to which we are removed from God. We must take the *9 Av* Torah reading seriously. There, it is stated that from the realization of your trevail and oppression you will seek to return to God. On His part we are told God will not forget His covenant with the *avos*(patriarchs). Thus 9 Av gives us the impetus to reach the high spiritual level mentioned in the reading—"You were shown to know that God is Elokim, there is none other than He" (*Ata har'esa la'da'as...*). (Deut. 4:35)

FAST OF GEDALIA

The Talmud in Rosh Hashanah reveals to us the significance of this Fast. It is the only one of the Four Fasts which does not directly involve the Beis HaMikdash. It is meant to teach us that "The day on which a *tzaddik* is killed is to be considered as much of a tragedy as the day on which the Temple was destroyed."

All too often it is the case that people are able to relate to structures being sanctified but cannot relate to people being sacred. Judaism believes that a human being *qua* human being is sacred in that he is a *tzelem Elokim* (in the image of God); how much more so a tzaddik. By proclaiming a Fast in a series which is a memorial for the destruction of the Temple, Chazal underscore the importance of the *tzaddik*.

On this Fast Day which occurs during the *Aseres Y'mai Tshuvah* it is important for us to internalize the function of this fast. Specifically, it must be a day in which we examine how we treat others. We must be especially concerned about the way in which we might have played a role in "killing" people through the grave iniquities of *lashon harah* or *lifnei iver*.

10 TEVES

10 Teves falls during the winter (in the Northern Hemisphere) on a very short day, not in the "season" of Fasts. It is a Fast which can easily be forgotten and, in fact, is often forgotten. This characteristic, we believe, is precisely the one for which this day calls upon us to atone.

Historically, the day is the one which marks the beginning of the siege of Jerusalem. People have a tendency not to pay attention to beginnings. They usually can not forsee the problem that small seemingly insignificant actions can have. It took two and a half years from the beginning of the siege, to fell Jerusalem. In other areas it might take even longer for decay to make its presence felt and even longer to cause a structure to topple. Thus, it is only the truly clever person who can see the *nolad* (potential danger). This Fast serves to keep us aware that if we are vigilant about things not starting off wrong then we will not have to worry about final destructions and exiles.

Halakhically, Avudraham (*Hil. Ta'anis*) underscores the significance of this Fast—the root cause of the subsequent Fasts—by ruling that were it to fall on *Shabbos* one must still fast. This is based on the verse (*Yeh. 24:2)* wherein the term *"be'etzem hayom hazeh"* is used to describe the events of 10 Teves. This same term is used with regard to *Yom Kippur*. (See R. M. Schneerson, *Likutei Sichos*, v. 15, pp. 420-1.)

Summary Outline: 26, 28b

[37] Torah Reading: A full discussion on this subject is reserved for Tractate *M'gillah*.

Hallel: A discussion on this subject is reserved for Tractate *B'rakhos*.

17 Tammuz

[38] Five things occurred on 17 Tammuz—

(1) Moshe broke the first set of the Ten Commandments

Moshe went up to Mt. Sinai 7 Sivan. He stayed there for forty days and nights and came down thereafter—on the 17th of Tammuz. According to the Tanna Kamma he went up on Sunday. According to R. Yosi he went up on Shabbat.

(2)The daily offering (korban tamid) ceased to be offered.

This is known by tradition. (28b) (Rambam maintains that this occurred during the First Temple; Rashi posits that is occurred during the Second Temple. (See *G'vuros Ari.*))

(3) The Walls of Jerusalem were breached.

Braisa and Rava (28b): This refers to the destruction of the Second Commonwealth. Based upon Jer. 52 during the First Commonwealth the walls of Jerusalem were breached on 9 Tammuz. (See Overview: Four Fasts.)

(4) Apustimus burned the Torah:This date is known by tradition.
(5) An Idol was placed in the Temple: Based on Daniel 9 & 12 there were two idols but one fell upon the other and broke its hands. (Rava: 28b)

9 Av

[39] Five things occurred on 9 Av—

(1) It was decreed that the Jews who left Egypt would not be permitted to enter Israel.
(2) First Temple was destroyed;

a. According to II Kings 25 the Temple was destroyed on 7 Av.
b. According to Jeremiah 52 the Temple was destroyed on 10 Av.
c. The G'mara resolves the apparent contradiction as follows: On the 7th the Babylonians entered the Temple. On the afternoon of 9 Av they set fire to the Temple. The Temple continued to burn through 10 Av. (See Jerusalem Talmud 4:5. One version states that the Temple was destroyed on 1 Av.)
d. R.Yochanan: I would have established the fast on the 10 Av.*
e. Rabbis: [The fast was established on 9 Av because] The beginning of a tragedy is when it is most painful.
f. The Temple was destroyed on *motza'ei Shabbos*, after the Sabbatical year, during the *mishmar* of Y'hoyariv.

(3) Second Temple was destroyed;

This is deduced because God causes good things to happen on good days and bad things on bad days.

* *G'vuros Ari*: The major portion of the First Temple was burned on 10 Av; the Second on 9 Av. We follow the events of the Second Temple in this matter.

(4) Beytar was captured; (See Jerusalem Talmud for full exposition)

This is known by tradition.

(5) Jerusalem was razed.

This is known by tradition.
(R. Chananel)

Significance of Time

From (3) one can derive that the G'mara believes that time is heterogeneous, i.e., different times have different properties, and that because of this there is more of a propensity that certain events are more likely to occur at specific times during the year. This notion appears again in [41]-[42]. (The author is presently planning to publish a *sefer*, IY"H, devoted specifically to the notion of time in the Talmud.)

Laws of the Days Preceding 9 Av

Month of Av

[41] Mishna: With the arrival of Av joy diminishes.
[42] R. Yehudah b. R. Shmu'el b. Shilas/Rav (29a):

As when Av enters we diminish joy, so too, when Adar enters we increase joy.

Legal disputes with non-Jews should be settled in Adar but not Av (if possible).

[43] Mishna: One may not wash clothes or take a haircut; these are permitted on Thursday in honor of the *Shabbos*.
[44] Braisa$_1$ (29b):

One may not take a haircut or wash clothes—

a. R. Meir: From 1 Av through 9 Av. (This is based on the verse "I shall rid all her joy [from] her festival ...(Rosh Chodesh.") *Hoshea* 2:13)
b. R. Yehudah: The entire month of Av. (This is based on the verse, "I shall rid ...joy [from] ...her month." *Hoshea* 2:13)
c. R. Shimon b. Gamliel: During the entire week that the fast occurs (This is derived from the verse, "I shall rid...joy [from]...her week." *Hoshea* 2:13) (See Appendix I.)

Week of 9 Av

[45] Braisa$_2$:

a. If 9 Av falls on Sunday one may wash clothes during the entire preceding week.

b. If 9 Av falls on Monday through Thursday, then on the days of the week preceding the Fast it is prohibited to wash clothes; on the day's following the Fast it is permitted.
c. If 9 Av falls on Friday one may wash clothes on Thursday. If he did not wash them on Thursday he may wash them late Friday afternoon (9 Av). (Abaye was oppossed to this.) (See <26>.)

[46] Rava: The *halakha* is in accordance with the leniencies of of R. Shimon b. Gamliel and R. Meir (that is, it is forbidden to wash or take a haircut from the beginning of the week in which 9 Av falls until the culmination of the fast.)

[47] R. Nachman/R. Elazar: One may wash clothes during the week of 9 Av, provided he has no intention of wearing the clothes until after 9 Av.

R. Sheshes: Washing is prohibited under all circumstances.

A proof may be brought by the fact that the fullers of Rav's household were idle during this week. Thus they did not wash items which were to be used after the Fast.

[48] R. Ham'nuna (29b): [3] seems to be a proof for R. Nachman. Washing on Thursday for *kavod Shabbos* implies that the clothes are not to be worn on Thursday but *Shabbos*. Thus, in other circumstances washing a garment to wear after the Fast is prohibited.

[49] Not necessarily! [43] speaks of a person who has only one garment (He will wear it immediately).

R. Yochanan: He who owns only one garment may wash it on *Chol haMo'ed*.

[50] Braisa$_3$:

a. One may not wash before 9 Av even for wearing after 9 Av.
b. *Gihutz* (pressing or using soap) in Babylonia is as effective as plain washing done in Israel.
c. *Gihutz* is ineffective with regard to linen garments.

[51] [50a] refutes R. Nachman [47].

[52] R. Yitzchak b. Guryah/R. Yochanan:

Nothwithstanding [50c] one may still not wear these garments during the week of 9 Av.

[53] The prohibition of wearing clothes that were washed during the week of 9 Av applies—

a. Rav: Only before the fast;
b. Shmuel: Even after the fast (rules as [44c]).

Analysis

Washing clothes during the week of 9 Av

<18> Clothes washed before week of 9 Av

S'fas Emes/Rosh: R. Nachman [47a] prohibits the wearing of clothes which were washed before the week of 9 Av. For if not, then [49] would be difficult. Given that he intends to wear the clothes on *Shabbos* he should be able to wash it on any other day. *G'vuros Ari* disagrees.

The *halakha*—

Rif: Is in accordance with R. Sheshes [47b].

<19> Washing in Babylonia/Diaspora

a. Ran, Ra'avad: The implication of [50b] is that only *gihutz* is prohibited; *kibus* (plain washing) is permitted. [50c] teaches that with regard to *gihutz* it is only woolen garments which are prohibited; whereas linen garments are permitted (see c). The reason: because they never really can be rehabilitated to look "like new." [52] teaches that while some washing may be done during this week one may not wear clothes that have been washed during this week.

b. Rosh: The reason linen garments may be washed is that they are worn as undergarments and will immediately become soiled due to perspiration. (Thus linen outer garments could not undergo *gihutz*.)

c. Ritva: New linen garments may not be washed even according to the first interpretation of the Ran.

d. R. Yehonatan miLuniel: Some say linen garments may undergo *gihutz* because if this is not permitted people will refrain from wearing them. Others distinguish between under and outer garments

e. Talmid HaRamban, Hashlama. One may not be *m'gahetz* even if *kibus* was done on the previous week. Diaspora "*kibus*" (washing in cold water) is permitted because it is only performed as a stop gap operation (*m'lekhes arai*). This is also the opinion of the Ra'avad.

f. Nimukei Yosef: *Kibus* is prohibited because it draws one's attention away from the period of mourning.

Some say that only old clothes can undergo *gihutz*. New clothes may not for they can be completely restored through the *gihutz* process.

<20> Definition of *Gihutz*:

a. R. Yehudah b. Avraham, Chakham HaKolel, Ritva : Pressing.
b. R. Yehonatan miLuniel, Talmid haRamban: Washing with soap (*mei ha'efer*) and warm water.

<21> Does [10b] mean Babylonia specifically or the whole Diaspora?

Ran, Rambam, Ravia, Ritva : The basis of the leniency is that the water quality in Babylonia is such that the clothes washed there do not become sufficiently clean. This is limited to Babylonia and other areas whose water has similar properties. In other places the law does not apply.

<22> Clothes which were previously washed but not worn

Ran: [52] implies that clothes which were washed the previous week but were not worn are prohibited. The prohibition is both for men and women. It extends not only to clothes but also to sheets and tablecloths (Ritva claims that this law also applies to mourners. This is contrary to Rashi in *Mo'ed Katan* 24b.)

<23> Hair cutting during the week of 9 Av

a. R. Yehonatan miLuniel: One may not take a haircut.
b. Ran, Talmid haRamban: The laws which apply to a mourner apply here. One may not take a haircut or cut one's beard. [His prohibition might be even more general, for he writes *"v'kol se'ar she'bo"* (Lit.: any hair he possesses). However, if one's beard interferes with his eating then he may cut it. (Also Ritva)
c. Ri'az: It is customary not to cut one's hair beginning 17 Tammuz.

<24> Washing one's body during the week of 9 Av

a. Ran: No mention of this is made in the Talmud. It is, therefore, permitted to wash even one's whole body in warm water.

   The pious (*tz'nu'im*), however, abstained from washing during this week.

<25> Making new clothes

Shiltei Giborim/Shb"t: The making of new clothes is prohibited. The prohibition is based upon Jerusalem Talmud *P'sachim* 4: "It is a valid custom not to weave from [Rosh Chodesh] Av."

<26> Washing if 9 Av falls on Thursday

Ritva, Ramban: Even if 9 Av falls on Thursday washing is prohibited. [45c] concerns 9 Av which falls on Friday.

In the latter case, Abaye cursed the person for not washing on Thursday, thereby being forced to wash on Friday afternoon which was 9 Av.

Summary Outline: 30a

Last Meal before 9 Av

[54] Mishna.

On the Eve of 9 Av one may not eat—

a. Tanna Kamma:

1. *Shnei Tavshilin* (Two courses) [defined below]
2. Meat
3. Wine

b. R. Shimon b. Gamliel:

He should change from his normal custom.

[55] *Braisa*$_1$: Chakhamim:

He should change his custom and minimize the eating of meat and wine.

[56] Braisa$_2$: R. Shimon b. Gamliel:

If it is his custom he may eat radish or savoury after his meal.

[57] R. Yehudah: [54a] applies only if the following two conditions apply—

1. The meal is eaten in the afternoon;
2. It is the last meal before 9 Av.

[58] R. Yehudah: re [54b]: If one is used to: eating two *Tavshilin* he should eat one; eating with ten people he should eat with five; drink ten cups he should drink five.

[59] Tanna: Yet one may eat pickled (salted 2 days and a night) meat and wine in the first stage of fermentation.

[60] Rav: R. Yehudah b. Ilaiy's custom on the eve of 9 Av was to sit between the baking and cooking ovens and eat dry bread, and salt and water, and deport himself as if a near relation lie dead before him.

[61] Braisa$_3$:

If 9 Av falls on Shabbos(so the fast is Sunday) or Sunday, one may eat on Shabbos afternoon as sumptuous a meal as he desires (even if it is as great as the feast of King Solomon).

[62] Braisa$_4$:

a. Tanna Kamma:

During any meal observed for 9 Av one may not have meat, wine **or wash himself**.

b. R. Yishmael b. Yosi/R. Yosi

So long as one is permitted to eat he may wash himself.

Prohibitions of 9 Av

[63] Braisa:

a. R. Meir

That which is prohibited to a mourner is prohibited on 9 Av—

(1) Eating, drinking, washing, annointing, cohabitation;
(2) Torah study (This is prohibited because it brings joy);

He may, however, study that with which he is unfamiliar or not used to, as well as, Lamentations, Job and the sad sections of Jeremiah.

(3) School children may be taught on 9 Av.

b. R. Yehudah

(1) One may not study even those areas of Torah unfamiliar to him;
(2) Children may not be taught Torah.

[64] Mishna (*P'sachim*)

(a) With regard to working on 9 Av, one may work in locales wherein it is the custom to work. But he may not work where it is the custom to refrain from working.
(b) A *talmid chakham* should not work on 9 Av even in areas where it is customary to work.
(c) R. Shimon b. Gamliel: Everyone should strive to act as a *talmid chakham* in this matter.

[65] Braisa:

(a) R. Shimon b. Gamliel: Whoever eats and drinks on 9 Av it is as if he did so on Yom Kippur.
(b) R. Akiva: Whoever does work on 9 Av will not derive pleasure therefrom.
(c) Chakhamim: Whoever works and does not mourn for Jerusalem will not share in its joy.

[66] Overturning Beds

All agree that beds should be overturned when the person is able to sleep thereon without tremendous discomfort. Those for whom this would be an excessive discomfort (e.g., pregnant woman) need not overturn their beds.

Beds not slept on—

(a) R. Yehudah: Should be turned over;
(b) Chakhamim: Need not be turned over;
(c) Rava: The *halakha* follows Chakhamim.

Analysis: 30a

Last Meal

<27> ***Shnei tavshilin***

Sar Shalom: *Shnei Tavshilin* are prohibited because this indicates a demonstration of respect for self. This is improper for one mourning the destruction of the Temple.

<28> **Definition and parameters of *shnei tavshilin***

a. R. Hai Gaon (*Shiltei haGiborim*): E.g., Rice and *dochen*
b. Ritz Ge'utz (Shiltei haGiborim): E.g., Beans and vegetables;

Nevertheless, if this is a standard manner of preparing a dish throughout the year it is permissible.

c. Ran, Ramban

Anything cooked together in one pot is considered one *tavshil*. The reason: No feeling of importance (*chashivus*) is afforded to things cooked together.

d. Some permit cooked fruits because they can be eaten raw. Thus, their being cooked is superfluous.

e. Rosh: Two foods which can be eaten raw, e.g. milk and cheese, may be cooked and eaten together;
f. Ra'avad: Disagrees with [e];
g. Geonim, R. Yehonasan miLuniel, Ritva: The prohibition of *shnei tavshilin* applies even for one food which was prepared two different ways, e.g., roasted and cooked.

<29> ***Seudah hamafsekes***

a. Ramban: The *seudah hamafsekes* is defined as the last regular meal (*seudas k'va*) that a person intends to eat before 9 Av. Thus, even if a person intends to eat a light meal before 9 Av it is the regular meal which is considered the *seudah hamafsekes*. It follows that it is improper for people to eat meat at the last regular meal, on the basis that they will follow this with another light meal.

b. Sar Shalom: *seudah hamafsekes* may be eaten before *mincha* and one may eat and drink after its completion.

<30> Eating Meat

a. *Otzar haGeonim*: Eating meat is prohibited only at the *seudah hamafsekes* (the last meal). Some are more stringent. "We have never eaten meat on [any part of] 9 Av."

Agur: Ravia permits chicken to be eaten at the *seudah*. Mordechai: Prohibits chicken from *Rosh Chodesh*.

b. *Shiltei haGiborim*: Some texts include in [41] "meat should not be eaten nor wine drunk." Based on this there are communities which abstain from meat during the week of 9 Av. Others extend this prohibition to Rosh Chodesh Av.

c. Ri'az: Some abstain from meat starting on 17 Tammuz. *HaPardes*/R. Sadia traces this to the association of the three week fasts mentioned in Daniel with the Three Weeks. They consider abstention of meat to be symbolic of fasting.

<31> Eat Salted meat/unfermented wine for *seudah hamafsekes*

a. *Avi Ha'ezri*: There is no *simcha* (joy) in eating meat kept longer than three days, nor in eating the meat of fowl (*Chagigah*). These, therefore, may be eaten at the *seudah hamafsekes* (Also Riv'van—it is no longer considered meat. *Nimukei Yosef* explains that meat spoils after three days.)

b. *Shiltei haGiborim*: These products are prohibited. The reason: The criterion is not whether there is *simcha* in eating the meat or drinking the wine. Rather, the Rabbis wish to increase the awareness for the mourning period.

Sma"k: Today salted meat is prohibited given that the majority of meat today is of this type. [Presumably he does not want the law mentioned in the G'mara to be forgotten.]

<32> Poskim: Re: *Seudah hamafsekes*

a. *Tur*: There are those who permit salted meat and poultry at the *seudah hamafsekes* (R. Shv"t). Nevertheless, it is best to prohibit it so as to increase the feeling of mourning. With regard to *shnei tavshilin* he follows Rosh [e]. He, also, permits eggs mixed into fish. (As per *Bach*.)

b. *Beis Yosef*: Follows Ra'avad [f]. The reason: Being served a number of dishes one's pleasure and feeling of importance is increased.

c. Ramah: One should reduce his liquid intake and not eat condiments (radish and salted foods) during the *seudah*.

d. *Magen Avraham*: One should refrain from drinking beer unless he feels feeble. Rashal permits beer if it is a person's normal custom to drink beer at his meals.

e. *Sha'arei T'shuva*: Vinegar pickles are prohibited. He disagrees with those who prohibit coffee. He permits the use of vinegar.

f. Vilna Gaon: Discourages the eating of radishes based on [60'].

<33> Customs of *seudah hamafsekes*

a. *Shiltei haGiborim*: Some people eat lentils at this meal.

b. R. Shrira Gaon: *Birkas hamazon* is not said with a *m'zuman*.

c. *Mishna B'rurah*: If it is one's custom to say *birkas hamazon "al hakos"* even when he *bentches* privately he may do so over beer.

Analysis

<34> Washing *Erev* 9 Av during/after the *seudah hamafsekes*

a. Ramban: The rationale for [62a] is as follows: The pleasure derived from washing and annointing continue into 9 Av. Therefore, these activities are prohibited. Wearing shoes, on the other hand, is permitted, because its pleasure does not persist beyond the moment.

b. Rosh: is perplexed by Ramban's interpretation. The latter allows eating after the *seudah* which indicates that the laws of 9 Av are not yet applicable, but at the same time prohibits washing and annointing.

Keren Orah responds. According to Ramban partial *aveilus* begins at the *seudah hamafsekes* given that one is enjoined against eating meat or drinking wine. As such, washing and annointing are also prohibited.

c. Ra'avad: [62a] is based upon the belief that one may not eat after the *seudah hamafsekes*. *Keren Orah* explains that this is because abstention from meat and wine at the *seudah* is tantamount to *kabbalas ta'anis*. (See *Keren Orah* as to whether Rif and Ra'avad disagree on whether one may not eat before a *ta'anis tzibbur* after he was *m'kabel ta'anis*.

d. Ran: The *Halakha* follows [47a].

<35> Not wearing shoes

a. *Geonim*: The prohibition against wearing shoes applies throughout the day.
b. *Nimukei Yosef*: It applies only to shoes which are composed of leather.
c. *Avi haEzri (Shiltei haGiborim)*: In the Diaspora one need only remove his shoes in the Jewish quarter.
d. *Ateres Z'keinim*: If one must wear shoes he should fill them with earth.
e. *Shibolei haLeket*: When 9 Av fell or was observed beginning *Motzei Shabbos*: those who were stringent went to *shul* barefoot; Rabbanim wore shoes to *shul l'kavod Shabbos*; the *sh'li'ach tzibbur* tooks his shoes off before *Borkhu* so that his prayers would not be confused and the rest of the congregation took their shoes off after *Borkhu*.

<36> Conjugal Relations if 9 Av falls on Shabbos

a. R. Yitzhak miVina, Ramah : Conjugal relations are prohibited on this Shabbos because it has the same status as one whose relative must be buried on *Yom Tov*.
b. Rosh, Ramban, *Shulchan Arukh*, Gaon of Vilna: They are permitted as per Tosefta.
c. R. Meir of Rothenburg: They are permitted. Nevertheless, abstenance is commendable.
d. *Bach*: Today the custom is to refrain. (*Maharal*)
e. R. A. of Tirna: The *shamash* announces "Private things are applicable."
f. *Sh'loh*: If one's immersion night falls on this Shabbos the lenient view can be relied on.
g. *Haga'os Maimonis*: Married couples should not sleep in the same bed.
h. *Magen Avraham*: Married couples may not touch each other at night but it is permissible during the day.

Arukh haShulchan: It is permissible for them to touch both during the day and the evening.

<37> Last meal when 9 Av falls out on Shabbos or Sunday

a. Rashi: He may eat anything.
b. Ran: No innuyim apply.

c. R. Sar Shalom: We refrain from eating meat. The third Shabbos meal may be eaten before the *seudah hamafsekes*.
d. Rosh ate meat at this meal. R. K'lonimos ate meat, but sat "b'da'avon nefesh" (despondent).
e. Shibbolei haLeket/R. Yitzchak b. Yehudah: Made hamotzi on two chalos.
f. R. M'shulam: Ate alone.

Summary Outline: 30a

Washing on 9 Av

[67] **Yoma 78: Ze'ira b. Chama: It was R. Yehoshua b. Levi's custom that on** *erev Tisha b'Av* he soaked a towel in water and on the next morning he would pass it over his eyes.

Analysis

<38>

a. Ran: One may wash in the regular manner for the purpose of *t'fillah* as this is a *mitzvah* and is in the same category as *t'villah*. (Also Ritva: (1) does not refer to *t'fillah*. Talmid haRamban)
b. Rambam: As there is no washing on 9 Av one does not recite the blessing *al n'tilas yadayim*.
c. Tur: An immersion of *mitzvah (t'villas mitzvah)* may be performed on 9 Av. One may wash for *t'fillah*. Otherwise, putting one's hand in cold water is prohibited. After relieving one's self, one may wash his hands and recite *al n'tilas yadayim*.
d. *Beis Yosef*: We no longer permit immersions on 9 Av even for *t'villas mitzvah*. (Ri: In the time of the Mikdash it was important to immerse on time because they handled *taharos*.)

   Only an *ist'nis* may wipe his face with a damp cloth

   While theoretically it might be proper for a Rebbe to pass through a stream of water to reach his student, in practice, this is not done.

e. *Bach*: Eventhough *Ta'anis 12a* would seem to indicate that one may wash parts of his body in cold water, the Tur follows Rosh and prohibts this. (See discussion on 12a.)
f. *Shulchan Arukh* 544):

   One may not put his hand even in cold water nor may one immerse even for a *t'villas mitzvah*. One may however wash parts of the body that become covered with dirt. In the morning one washes his hands until the knuckles and may pass his dried hands over his eyes. One may go through a stream of water to greet his Rebbe and return home. He may also pass through a stream of water to guard his produce but may not return through the stream.

g. *Magen Avraham*: One may rinse off meat on 9 Av eventhough his hands will thereby become wet.

h. Vilna Gaon: One may wash his hands on 9 Av.This is especially true with regard to washing before one prays. (So also *Arukh haShulchan*.

i. *Mishna B'rurah*: One should say *al n'tilas yadayim* for *t'fillah* after he relieved himself, not otherwise.

j. *Mateh Yehudah*: A person may wash his hands for *mincha*.

k. *Arukh haShulchan*: With regard to [67], we must distinguish Yom Kippur in which it is important to have a clear head, and 9 Av during which it is better if the person is anguished.

<39> Washing on the afternoon of 9 Av

a. *Ateres Z'keinim*: There was a custom established by the Elders that women could wash their hair during the afternoon of 9 Av as a symbol for the coming of the *Moshi'ach*.

<40> A Bride/Groom whose *shivas y'mei hamishteh* falls on a public Fast Day

If the *shivas y'mei hamishteh* of a couple falls on a Public Fast Day—

Nimukei Yosef: The couple must fast. This is because a public fast period pushes aside the couple's private period of joy. Moreover, this is indicated by the verse, "Would that I conjur up Jerusalem above my personal joys." (Psalms)

Torah Study on and before 9 Av

What may be studied

a. *Beis Yosef*: The Chapter *Eilu M'galchim (Mo'ed Katan* 3) may be studied (Ri)—as no passages of joy are found therein and the chapter deals primarily with rebuke (*tokhacha*).

The interpretation of *Eikha* may be studied but not that of I'yov [Job] (R. Peretz). Maharal permits studying the interpretations of I'yov and Yirmiyahu (Jeremiah). *Shulchan Arukh* concurs. Nevertheless, one may not expound on these interpretations in a public forum.

(When 9 Av falls on Shabbos or Sunday, *Chasan Sofer* permits the Rabbi to speak publicly about the sidra and haftarah only until noon.)

Magen Avraham: The Torah reader may preview the reading; one may not study the prophesies concerning the catastrophies which will befall the gentiles.

<42> *Ma'avir Sidrah*

a. *Minhagim*: Permits one to be *ma'avir sidrah* on Shabbos
b. *Taz*: If 9 Av falls on Thursday one may be *ma'avir sidrah* if this is his normal practice.

<43> *T'hilim*

a. *Magen Avraham*: In Pozna they prohibited the saying of Psalms the whole day of 9 Av. In *Magen Avraham's* area they recited *T'hillim* in the afternoon.

<44> Torah study on the eve of 9 Av

Darkei Moshe: Maharil prohibits Torah study past noon on erev 9 Av even on Shabbos. Thus the weekly study of *Pirkei Avos* must be suspended.

In the Talmud there is absolutely no prohibition against Torah study before 9 Av itself. The purpose of the prohibition is meant to serve as a "guard" against Torah study on 9 Av. Chasan Sofer explains that this prohibition exists because that which a person studies remains in his thoughts. To prevent this from happening on 9 Av we ask people to abstain beginning the previous noon.

R. Meir of Lublin argues that it is excessive for this decree to extend to the case of 9 Av which falls on Shabbat or Sunday. For in this circumstance none of the other restrictions apply. The Gaon of Vilna is also strongly against this prohibition, arguing that a person can only learn that which his heart desires—it is enough that there exists a prohibition on 9 Av; there is no reason for this to be expanded upon.

<45> Manner of study

a. No public exposition of Torah study should be undertaken (see above).
b. Magen Avraham: One should not study with others. *Dagul Me'r'vava* disagrees arguing that where the people need his aid with regard to things which may be studied on 9 Av, a person may give it.
c. Shulchan Arukh: One may not even study [non-permissible

Torah studies] mentally (The joy of studying is independent of studying aloud.)

Maharil: One may study Torah mentally.

d. One may not render legal decisions unless circumstances do not permit a postponement.

<46> Studying with children

Taz: The prohibition against teaching children is not due to the pleasure they derive from learning new things but rather because of the satisfaction of the teacher who is himself reviewing this material.

Arukh haShulchan disagrees with this. He argues that the teacher is permitted to teach bacause it is for the good of the community (rabim tzrikhim lo). He explains that the prohibition against teaching children is due to the fact that while on the surface students might not be delighted by school the pure Jewish soul within them derives pleasure from being exposed to Torah.

With regard to the Tannaitic dispute—

Arukh HaShulchan: R. Meir permits children to be taught because at least in the short run they are pained by having to master new passages. R. Yehudah prohibits them to be taught because of the joy experienced by their inner soul.

Taz: R. Yehudah's prohibition is based upon the notion that one is prohibited in mourning from doing something which will give pleasure at a later time. Thus a woman may not take a facial even though she does not appear sightly while the process is going on because she will be delighted by the results. Here, too, the children may not be taught now because they will later look back and appreciate that they were taught this material.

G'vuros Ari argues that according to R. Meir it is wrong not to teach Torah to children on 9 Av for the following reasons: Children are not obligated in mourning on 9 Av, thus there is no iniquity in their learning Torah. Beyond this, it would be ironic to suspend Torah study to commemorate the destruction of the Temple when it is well known that school children may not suspend their Torah study even to help build the Temple.

9 Av which falls on Sunday

<47> *T'fillah*

a. *HaPardes*: *Tzidkatekha* is omitted on *Shabbos-mincha*; *Shibbolei haLeket*: In Speyer it was said in Mayence it was recited.

b. R. Hai, R. Tzemach: *V'yhi no'am* is not said.

c. R. Tzemach: *V'ata kadosh* is said except for the verse *va'ani zos b'risi*.

<48> *Havdalah*

a. Ran, Ramban, Ritva: During this week *havdalah* is not recited over wine. Since *havdalah* may not be recited over wine on 9 Av it may not be recited on any ensuing day. Also, on 9 Av, people are considered *aniyim* (impoverished). Based on *B'rakhos* when the congregation is impoverished, *havdalah* said during the *t'fillah* suffices.

b. B'HaG: On Saturday night, *havdalah* is made in *t'fillah*. On Sunday night, *havdalah* is recited on wine. Some claim that one may make *havdalah* the whole week. (*P'sachim* 107a)

c. *Shiltei haGiborim*: The custom follows *B"HaG*.

d. R. Meir of Rotenburg, *Hagahos Maimonis*, *Beis Yosef*: On Saturday night a blessing is made on the fire (*boreh m'orei ha'esh*).

e. *Taz, Beis Yosef*: This [d] is done before the recitation of "*Eikha*." This is based upon the phrase, "God has placed me in darkness."

f. *Shulchan Arukh*: No blessing is made over spices, since these give pleasure.

g. *Mishna B'rurah*: If someone did not recite *havdalah* in the *t'fillah*, he need not repeat the *sh'moneh esreh*.

h. *Arukh HaShulchan*: On Sunday night, *havdalah should not be recited over wine.*

i. *Eshkol*: On Sunday night, R. Shalom of Noitz put his shoes on before reciting *havdalah; Mahara"g put them on after havdalah.*

<49> *Milah*

a. Ritva: If a *bris milah* falls on 9 Av, no blessing is made over the wine, but a blessing is made for the myrtle.

<50> Sick Person

a. *Sha'arei T'shuvah*: If someone must eat on 9 Av he should make *havdalah* over wine immediately on Motza'ei Shabbos.
b. *Gan haMelekh*: If one made *havdalah in the t'fillah, he should not recite it over wine.*
c. *Shibbolei haLeket*/R. Avigdor: A sick person does not recite *nachem* in the *birkas hamazon*. The Gaon of Vilna adopts this view.

Ramah/MaHaril: He does recite *Nachem*.

<51> Seder Hayom

a. *Shibbolei Haleket*: Some begin sitting on the floor after *borkhu*. Others wait until after the *sh'moneh esreh*.
b. *HaPardes: Tiskabel* was said before but not after *Kinos. This is based on the verse, "gam ki ashave'ah sasam t'filasi."*

Shibbolei haLeket: In Mayence *tiskabel was omitted even before Kinos*.

c. R. Hai Gaon: It is a correct custom to take the Torah out without a cover (possibly this is the source for our removing the ark cover) and to say *ashrei in the afternoon but not in the morning*.
d. Ritva, *Shibbolei Haleket, Itur*: *She'asah li kol tzorki* is said, even though shoes are not worn. Ra'ah disagrees.
e. *Shibbolei haLeket*: *T'fillin may be worn on 9 Av. 9 Av is to be compared to the second day of mourning. A mourner wears t'fillin* on his second day of mourning.

Agur/Maharam: *T'fillin* are not worn. The *Minhag Ashkenaz* was to wear *t'fillin* for *mincha*.

f. Rashi: In Spire they wore *talitos*;
Agur/Maharam: A *talis* is not worn.
g. Tur, Ramban, Ritva: Some people prohibit the reading of the *korbanos*. (*Shibbolei haLeket*: One starts the *t'filah* at *"barukh she'amar* and omits " *vayosha* and the *shirah*.") Ramban permits this because it is *seder hayom*. This is also the view of the *Shulchan Arukh* and *Aruk haShulkhan*.
h. R. Amram: The custom of the *Yeshivos* was to say *selichos* and *anenu* on 9 Av.

Shibolei haLeket disagrees. On 9 Av they said *Kinos*.

i. *Shibbolei haLeket*: The Torah is not read on the *bimah*. Rather it is read in a corner of the *shul* while being held in someone's arms. *"Gadlu"* is not said, nor is *"V'sigaleh."*

HaPardes: The Torah is read from the *bimah*.

j. *Shibolei haLeket*: *Vay'chal* is not to be read in the morning so as not to pronounce the *Yud Gimmel Middos* (The Thirteen Attributes of Mercy). Some say that at *mincha "vay'chal"* is read and *selichos* are recited.

k. "Va'ani zot briti" is omitted.

l. *Shibbolei haLeket*: Some say *tiskabel* and *lam'netze'ach* in the morning. This they argue follows from the fact that the main *aveilus* is at night. They base this on the verse *"kumi roni ba'laila"* (Awake and wail at night). Others believe that this verse does not negate mourning during the day. Thus they do not say *tiskabel* even in the morning.

Summary Outline

Nachem

[68] Jerusalem Talmud: R. Acha: On 9 Av an individual says *nachem* in the blessing of *r'tzeh*, since it concerns a future request.

Analysis

<53> Where in *sh'moneh esreh* is *nachem* recited?

a. Geonim: It is said in *l'Y'rushalayim irchah*, during each *t'fillah*. This blessing pertains to the rebuilding of Jerusalem and it is thus an appropriate place to include this prayer. [His text reads *rachem*.]

Arukh Hashulchan explains that the Jerusalem Talmud follows the view that *l'Y'rushalayim irkah* was fused with *es tzemach*, in which case it was inappropriate to recite this lament in the same blessing wherein one prays for the coming of the Messiah [See Tosefos Rid p. 14]. Since we divide the blessings, it is more appropriate to say *nachem* in *l'Y'rushalayim*.

b. R. Hai Gaon: It is said only at *mincha* and if it is omitted, the *t'fillah* need not be repeated.

c. Ritva: It is recited in *l'Y'rushalayim*. [68] follows the view that the congregation asks for its needs in *R'tzeh*.

d. R. Yehonatan of Luniel: It is said in *R'tzeh*.

e. *Shiltei haGiborim*: Some had the custom to say *rachem* during ma'ariv and shacharis, and nachem during *mincha*.

f. Rosh: Questions the custom of reciting *nachem* only during *mincha*.

g. Ritvah: *Nachem* should be said in all of the *t'fillos*.
f. Ramah: The custom is to say it only at *mincha*.
i. *Mishna B'rurah*: It is the custom in Jerusalem to say *nachem* during all of the *t'fillos*. [This is no longer the custom.]

<54> If one erred and forgot to say *nachem* in *l'Y'rushalayim*

a. R. Gershon b. Shlomo: He says it in *modim*.
b. *Taz*: [a] contains a textual error. It should read in *r'tzeh*; as a beseechment for the future is involved. However, it is best to say it in *shome'ah t'fillah*.
c. *Mishna B'rurah*: Concurs with *Taz* [b].

<55> One who fasts on 10 Av

a. *Magen Avraham/Sh'loh*: He says*Nachem* in all of the *t'fillos*.

(R. Moshe Feinstein (O.H. V.3, pp. 394-5): If someone said *Nachem* on any other day of the year, the *sh'moneh esreh* need not be repeated, since we require consolation throughout the entire year for the destruction of the *Beis haMikdash*. Nevertheless, it is improper to say this prayer on days during which *tachanun* is not recited. In addition, one should not say *nachem* throughout the year as *Chazal* did not indicate that this prayer should be recited throughout the year.)

Summary Outline

Mishna

[69] R. Shimon b. Gamliel: There were no greater *Yamim Tovim* than *Yom Kippur* and 15 Av.

G'mara

[70] *Yom Kippur* is great because it is a day of atonement.
[71] Why is 15 Av so important?

a. Shmuel: It was the day that the Tribes were able to intermarry [and not be worried about inheritance passing from one tribe to another];
b. R. Nachman: It was the day that Binyamin was allowed to intermarry with the other tribes [after the incident of the *Pilegesh* of Givah];
c. R. Yochanan: It was the day that the *dor midbar* (desert generation) stopped dying;
d. Ula: It was the day Hoshea removed the guards that prevented Jews from being *oleh regel*;

e. R. Masna: It was the day that the dead of Betar were allowed to be buried;
f. Rabbah, R. Yosef: It was the day they stopped cutting wood for the altar.

R. Eliezer haGadol: This is because from this date forward the sun no longer dries the wood sufficiently [and it is feared that these trees contain worms].

R. Menasia: 15 Av is called the Day of the Breaking of the Sickle (*Tavar Magal*]).

[72] From 15 Av onward, people increase their evening hours of Torah study, and will be rewarded with increased life.

[73] [*Mishna*: On 15 Av the Jerusalemite girls would borrow cloths] so as not to embarrass those who lacked nice clothing. (The Babylonian and Jerusalem Talmuds argue over the order the borrowing took. See *Likutei Sichos*: 4:1336.)

[74] R. Elazar: Even clothes which were never worn were ritually cleaned.

[75] The pretty girls would say, "Set your eyes on beauty..." The girls from noble families would say, "Look for a good family..." The ugly ones said, "Carry off your purchase in the Name of Heaven..." (See *Likutei Sichos* Vol. X11, no. 41.)

[76] Ula Bira'ah/R. Elazar: In the days to come God will make a circle for the righteous in *Gan Eden* and He will sit in their midst, and every one will point a finger towards Him, as it is said, "...Lo this (*zeh*)is our God (*Elokeinu*) ...this (*zeh*) is the Lord (*Havayah*) for whom we waited, we will be glad and rejoice in His salvation." (Isa. 25:9)

Overview

Siyum

R. M. Schneerson, the Lubavitcher Rebbe, in a brilliant *siyum* on this Tractate makes the following points:

The *G'mara* underscores the greatness of 15 Av through [76]. The latter depicts the scene which will take place during the era of *t'chiyas hameisim* (resurrection). At that time, man will "see" (comprehend) God with even greater clarity than at *Yam Suf*. At *Yam Suf*, Israel was able to comprehend the imminent aspect of God—*zeh KELI v'anveyhu*—at *t'chiyas hameisim* they will also comprehend the transcendent aspect of God. Thus they could proclaim *"hiney ELOKEINU zeh"* and *"Zeh HAVAYA kivinu lo."*

The greatness of the period of *t'chiyas hameisim* is also depicted by the righteous sitting in a circle about God. There are no prominent or secondary points along a circle. Thus, during this era the equality of all will be stressed. Given that this equality is based upon the unification of God, it leads to forgiveness (the term *m'chol* means both a circle and forgiveness), peace and joy. A fascimile of this occurs on Yom Kippur. Because on this day *Klal Yisrael* are like angels and they unify God's Name on a very high level, forgiveness, friendship and joy ensue (as per [69]).

15 Av is also a day of great joy because the properties ofthis day generate unity. This is portrayed in [71:a-f].

a. On this day *Klal Yisrael* became unified in the Sinai Desert. Until the point when the *dor midbar* stopped dying, there was a disunity among the living. They were divided into those who would enter the land and those who would not. From 15 Av, all the living had the common bond that they would enter the land of Israel.
b. *Klal Yisrael* was further unified on this day because the tribe of Binyamin was no longer discriminated against; they were permitted to intermarry with the other tribes.
c. The prohibition given to the daughters of Tzelafchad was rescinded on 15 Av. Thus, the tribes were permitted to intermarry with each other and not be concerned about inheritance rights.
d. In the time of Hoshea, *Klal Yisrael* were reunited on this day in the sense that all were able to worship God as one in the *Beis haMikdash*.
e. The burying of the dead of Betar—a city who rejoiced at the destruction of Jerusalem—indicated that a unity was being reestablished even with those who had passed on to the *olam ha'emes*.
f. The *korban eitzim* on this day was offered for *kohanim, l'vi'im and all those who did not know their tribes*. This, too, served to unite all of *K'lal Yisrael*

[72] concludes that on this day Torah study should be increased. Torah study is the common unifying force in the nation of Israel.Whereas,with regard to *mitzvos* there are differences in obligations, the obligation of Torah study is the same for all.

The end of the Tractate is tied to its beginning in the following sense: The tractate concludes with the portrayal of the era of *t'chiyas hameisim*. The beginning of the tractate deals with the falling of rain. I-[14-15] indicate that Rain and t'chiyas hameisim are related.

The bond is further strengthened in that we follow R. Yehoshua I-[3] and are not *mazkir* rain until the last day of *Sukkos* eventhough he also believes that *Hazkarah* should begin on the first day. His reason being, that we should not even mention something which can disrupt the blessings of the *Yom Tov*. R. Yehoshua's desire to maintain peace and harmony without any disruptions is the essence of the *m'chol* (circle) of the righteous.

Let us hope and pray that on that day—*yom shetzadikim yoshvim v'atroseihem biydeihem v'nehenim miziv ha'shekinah*— each and all of us are meritorious to attend, *v'y'hi chelkeinu imahem*.

Appendix I

R. Meir, Rav and R. Huna *l'Shitasam*

In the *M'sekhta* there are a number of disputes whose basis is not dealt with by the commentaries. Because it would have been to cumbersome to explain the basis for each dispute as it came up we have chosen instead to explain them as a unit. The basis of our approach is that when presenting a *halakhic* opinion a *tanna/amora* does not arrive at his position *ad hoc*, but in consequence of a well thought out perspective from which all of his legal decisions are rendered. (One of the goals of **Torah Lishma Institute** is to explicate the *shitos* of Talmudic Rabbis. A work presently in preparation reviews the basis of the Beis Shammai/Beis Hillel disputes.)

We begin by noting that Rav was a student of R. Meir and R. Huna was a student of Rav. We assume that unless otherwise stated each follows the *halakhic shita* of his Rebbe.

R. Meir is considered the *tanna* who generates his *halakhic* decisions based upon the Ideal Man—Adam before the sin. [See *Tosefos Chadashim, Avos* 1:1; *Pri Tzaddik, Ma'amar* 6.] This is understood to be the interpretation of the *ma'amar* which states that in R. Meir's *Torah* the word *"ohr"* in *kosnos ohr* [regarding the clothes God made for Adam] is written with an *"aleph"* (meaning that God girded him with light [knowledge] as opposed to 'clothes made of hide').

Based upon this cosmic perspective, R. Meir emphasizes the goodness in this world and views evil occurrences as temporary abberations. **R. Huna cites Rav who cites R. Meir** as saying, "A person should train himself to say,'Whatever God does is for the best.'" (*B'rakhos* 60b) Similarly, R. Meir disputes R. Yehudah. (*Sifri Ha'azinu* 32:5) The former posits that *Yisra'el* only has the status of *banim* (God's Children) (Deut. 14:1) when they are free of sin. R. Meir counters that this status is eternal and is independent of *Yisra'el's* actions. Even in the case where people die as *r'sha'im* (wicked), their minor children enter *olam ha'bah*. (*Avos d'R. Natan* 36:41)

This explains R. Meir's position with regard to 9 Av. Firstly, it is his view that one need only mourn from the beginning of the month until the fast. [Rav's statement, *"k'shem k'she'misheniknas Av m'ma'atin b'simchah, kak mishinichnas Adar marbim b'simchah," IV-[41] follows R. Meir's position that the mourning begins at the beginning of the month.]*

*Thereafter, no mourning need be carried forth IV-[44]. This view is echoed by Rav IV-[53]. The reason for this is, as stated, R. Meir believes that all that happened is for the good. Thus, there is no reason to mourn the Mikdash*except for purposes of *t'shuvah*; since *t'shuvah* would cause the *Mikdash*to be returned. Thus we mourn prior to 9 Av, but once the day has passed, we demonstrate our faith that "even this was for the good." (In mourning the *Mikdash* one has to indicate the objective loss that its destruction brought about, namely, the lack of *korbanos*. For this reason, R. Meir prohibits wine and meat at the *seudah hamafsekes* <others say he prohibits these from *Rosh Chodesh Av*>.) According to *Sfas Emes*, R. Meir interprets the verse thus: "*Chagah*"—the *aveilus* continues until 9 Av; "*Chodshah*"—it begins on *Rosh Chodesh*; "*Shabbata*"—the observances are increased during the week 9 Av falls.

(R. Yehudah IV-[44] agrees with R. Meir with regard to the beginning of the mourning period, but based upon his position above, he believes that the whole month carries with it inherent potential for evil occurrences. The dispute between, R. Meir, R. Yehudah and R. Shimon b.Gamliel as follows:

The week is the temporal structure about which God created the world. The month is the temporal structure about which God structured the Jewish people [as evidenced by the fact that the very first *mitzvah* given to them as a nation was to consecrate the First Month]. In viewing the *churban* R. Yehudah accents the loss the *Mikdash* was to *K'lal Yisrael*. R. Shimon b. Gamliel accents its loss to the entire world. He reports the statement in the name of R. Yehoshua, "From the time of the Temple's destruction there is not one day free of curses; blessed *Tal* no longer falls and the good taste has been removed from the fruit." (*Soteh* 9:12) R. Yehoshua (according to some R. Yehoshua b. Levi) states explicitly, "Would that the nations of the world knew how much they benefited from the *Beis haMikdash* they would have protected it with tents and forts." (*VaYikra Rabbah 1:11; Bamidbar Rabbah 1:3*))

Another consequence of R. Meir's position is his belief that it is permissible to teach youngsters Torah on 9 Av. As they have not been exposed to sin and they need not repent [see above: the children of the wicked enter Gan Eden] there is no reason for them to be kept from Torah study. (By extension this would mean that they need not observe any of the other signs of mourning. This view is echoed by R. Moshe ibn Habib in his commentary on *Yoma* (*Tosefos Yom haKipurim*, p. 46) that there is no training (*hinukh*) of youngsters on 9 Av. R. Moshe Feinstein (*Igros Moshe Yoreh De'ah* 11) writes that R. Yehudah's prohibition against children's studying Torah on 9 Av is based upon the fact that they must mourn the destruction of the Temple. In this he disagrees with *G'vuros Ari*.

R. Meir also authors the view that speech has intrinsic significance. Thus if someone mistakingly declares an animal "the tenth," R. Meir believes that this animal possesses all of the properties of an animal which is truly "the tenth." This coupled with his belief of the importance of an individual ["For an individual who repents God forgives the entire world" (*Yoma* 86b)] motivate Rav and R. Huna I:D-[26] to adopt the position that an individual may say *Anenu* as an independent blessing [it will be remembered that R. Huna posits that an individual may say *k'dushah* (*B'rakhos* 21b) which some interpret to mean even when he is *davening* privately]. It also allows Rav to maintain that *kabbalas ta'anis* (*Kadshu Tzom*) I:D-[34] may be made independent of *t'fillah*. Also, that if one accepts a fast upon himself, while *ta'anis tzibbur* is not prevalent in Bablylonia, we must be concerned that he might have meant to accept a *ta'anis tzibbur* I:D-[37].

R. Meir's *halakhic* perspective leads him to the position that time is heterogeneous; various times possess different intrinsic properties. Thus once a day has been invested with certain properties it remains that way eternally. Thus, *M'gilas Ta'anis* Days remain special forever. II-[53]. This is also the reason that one may not continue his fast into *Shabbos* II-[58]. The various rulings regarding days preceeding *M'gilas Ta'anis Days* is dependent upon the level of joy with which these days were originally invested.

The immutable objective status obtained by a particular day is what motivates R. Meir III-[15] to adopt the position that once a Fast has begun, even if it rains the Fast must still continue the rest of the day. The intrinsic properties which can be given time is, also, what motivates R. Huna to rule that he who fasts *l'sha'os* may recite *anenu* I:C-[28].

R. Meir's perspective also causes him to be lenient about *n'siyas kapayim* IV-[4]. On the level upon which he generates *halakhah* there is no reason to extend a decree because of the fear that people are ignorant about the reason for the decree.

Finally, he believes the three rain days are 3, 7 and 17 Cheshvon for the following reason. 17 Cheshvon was the day of the Flood. The property of the month is rain. Rain is a sign of forgiveness. (8b) This forgiveness need correspond to the days of *ha'za'ah*, i.e. the third and seventh day. (We refer the reader to *Ohr haTorah (Breishis* pp. 1286-94) for the basis of R. Yehudah's position.)

מתני'

מאימתי

מזכירין גבורות גשמים רבי אליעזר אומר מיום טוב הראשון של חג ר' יהושע אומר מיום טוב האחרון של חג. אמר לו ר' יהושע הואיל ואין הגשמים אלא סימן קללה בחג למה הוא מזכיר אמר לו ר' אליעזר אף אני לא אמרתי לשאול אלא להזכיר משיב הרוח ומוריד הגשם בעונתו אמר לו א"כ לעולם יהא מזכיר אין שואלין את הגשמים אלא סמוך לגשמים ר' יהודה אומר העובר לפני התיבה ביו"ט האחרון של חג האחרון מזכיר הראשון אינו מזכיר ביו"ט הראשון של פסח הראשון מזכיר האחרון אינו מזכיר: גמ' *תנא היכא קאי דקתני מאימתי תנא התם קאי דקתני *מזכירין גבורות גשמים בתחיית המתים ושואלין בברכת השנים והבדלה בחונן הדעת וקתני מאימתי מזכירין גבורות גשמים וליתני התם מ"ש דשבקיה עד הכא אלא תנא מראש השנה סליק דתנן *ובחג נידונין על המים ואיידי דתנא ובחג נידונין על המים תנא מאימתי מזכירין גבורות גשמים וליתני מאימתי מזכירין על הגשמים מאי גבורות גשמים א"ר יוחנן מפני שיורדין בגבורה שנאמר *°עושה גדולות (א) עד אין חקר ונפלאות עד אין מספר וכתיב °הנותן מטר על פני ארץ ושולח מים על פני חוצות מאי משמע אמר רבה בר שילא אתיא חקר חקר מברייתו של עולם כתיב הכא עושה גדולות עד אין חקר וכתיב התם °הלא ידעת אם לא שמעת אלהי עולם ה' בורא קצות הארץ לא ייעף ולא ייגע אין חקר לתבונתו (ב) וכתיב °מכין הרים בכחו נאזר בגבורה ומנא לן דבתפלה דתניא °לאהבה את ה' אלהיכם ולעבדו בכל לבבכם איזו היא עבודה שהיא בלב הוי אומר זו תפלה וכתיב בתריה °ונתתי מטר ארצכם בעתו יורה ומלקוש אמר ר' יוחנן *ג' מפתחות בידו של הקב"ה שלא נמסרו ביד שליח ואלו הן מפתח של (ג) גשמים ומפתח של חיה ומפתח של תחיית המתים מפתח של גשמים דכתיב °יפתח ה' לך את אוצרו הטוב את השמים לתת מטר ארצך בעתו מפתח של חיה מנין דכתיב °ויזכור אלהים את רחל וישמע אליה

רש"י

מאימתי מזכירין גבורות גשמים. שאומר משיב הרוח ומוריד הגשם ובגמרא מפרש טעמא אמאי קרי ליה גבורות גשמים מפני שיורדין בגבורה שנאמר עושה גדולות וגו': סימן קללה בחג הן. כדאמרינן במס' סוכה בפרק הישן (דף כח:) מאימתי מותר לפנות משתסרח המקפה משל לעבד שבא למזוג כוס לרבו ושפך לו קיתון על פניו וא"ל אי אפשי בשמושך כלומר כשהגשמים יורדין לסוכה הכל יוצאין ונראה שאין הקב"ה חפץ שנשתמש לפניו ואמאי מתחילין להזכיר גבורות גשמים בחג ונראה שהוא מתפלל שיבא מטר בחג: לא אמרתי לשאול. שיתפלל על הגשמים בחג כגון ותן טל ומטר: אלא להזכיר. שמתחיל להזכיר בחג גבורות של מקום שמוריד גשמים: בעונתו. כלומר בזמנו: אם כן. ואמאי פוסק בפסח מלהזכיר: **גמ'** תנא היכא קאי. כלומר מדקתני מאימתי מכלל דפשיטא ליה להאי תנא דחייבים להזכיר והיכא חזינן דמחייב להזכיר: התם קאי. מזכירין גבורות גשמים כו' במסכת ברכות: (וליתני התם. במסכת ברכות סמוך דתני מזכירין ליתני מאימתי): מ"ש דשבקיה עד הכא. כלומר האי דקתני הכא בסדר מועד מאימתי ליתני התם (ד) דקתני מזכירין במסכת ברכות הייט סדר זרעים: עד הכא. עד סדר מועד: אלא. לא תימא דהא דקתני מאימתי דהתם קאי דתנא מר"ה השנה סליק ששניהן בסדר אחד הן להכי לא מצי למימר מאי שנא דשבקיה עד הכא: (בחג. הוי דין על המים ומשום דתני מאימתי הוי דין על המים קתני נמי אימתי זמן הזכרה) (ה): ואיידי דתני בחג נידונין. כלומר אגב דתנא בחג נידונין על המים קסבר בנפשיה הואיל ונידונין בחג על המים ש"מ בעינן להזכיר ענינא דמיא לרצויי על המים דליהו לברכה להכי קתני מאימתי מזכירין: כתיב עושה גדולות (ו) עד אין חקר. אלמא דכתיב חקר בגשמים וכתיב חקר בברייתו של עולם מה ברייתו של עולם כתיב ביה גבורה אף גשמים הוי כמאן דכתיב ביה גבורה: ואמר רבי יוחנן שלש מפתחות. הייט שלא נמסרו לשליח אחד ביחד (ז): יפתח ה'. ולא שליח:

כי

תוספות

מאימתי. מיום טוב האחרון של חג. שמיני דלא יתבון בסוכה ואפילו האידנא איט אלא מדרבנן משום ספיקא ואע"ג דבקיאין בקביעא דירחא גזרה שמא יחזור הדבר לקלקולו או משום מנהג אבותינו בידינו כדאי' פ"ק דביצה (דף ד:) ולכן מדכרינן אבל כל שבעה לא שהגשמים בימי סוכה סימן קללה הן כדתנן פרק שני דסוכה (דף כח:) משל לעבד וכו': **אם** כן. אם אתה אומר מזכירין אע"פ שאין שואלין הואיל ומשמע בעונתו אף בקיץ יזכירו ומה אתה נותן סימן מי"ט הראשון ור' אליעזר אומר בברייתא בגמרא כל הקיץ אם בא להזכיר מזכיר דלעולם בעונתו משמע מיהו עד השתא לא רמי עליה חובה אבל בי"ט ראשון חובה לרצות לפני שאלה שכל הבא לבקש מקדים ומרצה ואסימן קללה לא קפדינן ורבי יהושע קפיד: **התם** קאי. פירוש בסדר זרעים בברכות פרק אין עומדין (דף לג.) וליתני התם מאי שנא כו' כלומר אמאי תנא הכא במועד מאי דתני התם בסדר זרעים: **אלא** תנא מראש השנה קא סליק. פירוש ור"ה הויא בסדר מועד ואם תאמר ולכתי ליתני בסדר זרעים וי"ל דהכא עיקר דאמר בחג נידונין על המים והורחא דמילתא לרצות לפני שאלה לכך שביק עד הכא אבל בסדר זרעים (ח) אומרים מזכירין גבורות גשמים אפשר דמשמע לעולם כמו תחיית המתים או הבדלה בחונן הדעת: **וליתני** מאימתי מזכירין (ט) גשמים מאי גבורות גשמים אמר ר' יוחנן שיורדין בגבורה. תימה התם בברכות פ' אין עומדין (שם) קתני כי הכא מזכירין גבורות גשמים ושואלין הגשמים וכו' אמאי לא קא מקשה כמו הכא וליתני מזכירין על הגשמים מאי גבורות ויש לומר שאני הכא דהוי עיקר סדר של גשמים באיזה זמן מתחילין לאומרו ומאימתי פוסקין מלאומרו ומשום הכי פריך הכא טפי מהתם: **וכתיב** מכין הרים בכחו נאזר בגבורה. וזה גבי בריאת עולם וכי היכי דהאי חקר' בבריאת העולם רוצה לומר בגבורות כמו כן הכא גבי גשמים האי חקר נמי רוצה לומר גבורות אכן יש להקשות אמאי נקט גבורות טפי מכח וכמו כן הוה ליה למימר מאימתי מזכירין כח גשמים או ליתני גדולות גשמים וי"ל דמן הדין נקט גבורות משום טעמא דאיכא כח ואיכא גדולה אי נמי משום דהברכה מתחלת בגבורה להכי נקט גבורות: **שלשה** מפתחות שלא נמסרו לשליח. וא"ת והא אמרינן (סנהדרין דף קיג.) דמפתח הגשמים (י) נמסרין לאליהו וכן מפתח של תחיית המתים וכן לאלישע דכתיב (מלכים א יז) ויאמר אליהו חי ה' וגו' דהכ"נ אומר בפירקין לקמן (דף כג.) וי"ל דהא דקאמר שלא נמסרו לשליח איט ר"ל שלא נמסרו מעולם דהא של תחיית המתים ושל גשמים נמסרו אלא לא נמסרו לשליח להיות לעולם ממונה עליהם: **וישמע** אליה אלהים ויפתח את רחמה. פירוש שהוא בעצמו עשה וא"ת מהכא משמע דליכא אלא שלשה מפתחות וא"כ יש להקשות והא כתיב (ירמיה נ) פתח ה' את אוצרו ויוצא את כלי זעמו ומשמע נמי שלא נמסרו לשליח וכמו ההיא וישמע אליה אלהים וגו' וא"כ אמאי לא חשיב לה וי"ל דלא חשיב כי אם אותן מפתחות של טובה ולהכי לא קא חשיב מפתח של זעם וא"ת דמשמע מהאי קרא דפתח ה' שלא נמסר מפתח של זעם לשליח והא אמרינן (פסחים דף קיח.) יורקמי שר של ברד הוי וי"ל מכלי זעם אחרינא קאמר שלא נמסרו לשליח אבל משום ברד לא דאותו של ברד נמסרו:

איבעיא

עין משפט נר מצוה

א א ב ג מיי' פ"ב מהלכות תפלה הלכה טו סמג עשין יט טוש"ע א"ח סי' קיד סעיף א:

ב ד מיי' שם הלכה טז וסמ"ג שם טוש"ע א"ח סי' קיז סעיף א:

ג ה מיי' שם הלכה יב וסמג שם טוש"ע א"ח סי' רצד סעיף א:

רבינו חננאל

(אידי) [אהרא] דתנן במתניתין מאימתי מזכירין גבורות גשמים מקשי תנא היכא קאי דקתני מאימתי כלומר מי הזכיר שנזכיר גבורות גשמים עד שיאמר מאימתי. ושנינן תנא מר"ה סליק דתנן ובחג נידונין על המים. ולפיכך תנא הכא מאימתי מזכירין גבורות גשמים. ואמאי תני גבורות כלומר מה גבורה יש בגשמים. וא"ר יוחנן שיורדין בגבורה שנאמר בענין המטר עושה גדולות עד אין חקר ונמר חקר חקר מברייתו של עולם שנאמר בורא קצות הארץ אין חקר לתבונתו. וכתיב מכין הרים בכחו נאזר בגבורה. מיכן סמכו לומר גבורות גשמים ויפריש במתני' בתפלה ואמרי' ומנא לן שלא תהא הזכרה זו אלא בתפלה. ופשטנא מדכתיב [ולעבדו] בכל לבבכם וגו' ונתתי מטר ארצכם בעתו יורה ומלקוש וגו'. ודייקינן איזו היא [עבודה] בלב שבשבילה המטר יורד הוי אומר זו תפלה. וא"ר יוחנן שלשה מפתחות לא נמסרו לשליח אלא הם בידו של הקב"ה. מפתח גשמים שנאמר יפתח ה' לך את אוצרו הטוב את השמים וגו'. מפתח של חיה

רבינו גרשום מאור הגולה

מאימתי מזכירין גבורות גשמים. שאומ' מוריד הגשם: מאחר שהגשמים סימן קללת הוא בחג כדאמרן בסוכה משל לעבד שמשמש לרבו והפך לו רבו קיתון על פניו כלומר שאינו חפץ בו אף כך כשיורדין גשמים בחג יוצאין הכל מן הסוכה ונראה שאין חפץ הקב"ה שישבו בסוכה ואמאי מתחיל להזכיר גבורות גשמים ונראה שהוא מתפלל שירדו גשמים בחג: לא אמרתי לישאל שיתפלל על הגשמים בחג אלא להזכיר. שמתחיל להזכיר בחג *) גבורות של גשמים מקום שמוריד גשמים בעונתם לאחר החג כשצריכין: אם כן לעולם יהא מזכיר אפי' בימות החמה שמוריד גשמים בעונתן: גמ' התם קאי מזכירין כו' במס' ברכות: וליתני התם במס' [ברכות] סמוך לדתני מזכירין כו' ליתני מאימתי מ"ש דשבקיה עד הכא כלומר מי קתני הכא בסדר מועד מאימתי אמאי דתני מזכירין במס' ברכות דהיינו בסדר זרעים. תנא מר"ה סליקי ששניהם בסדר אחד הן להכי לא מצי למימר מ"ש דשבקיה עד הכא. כתיב עושה גדולות עד אין חקר אלמא דכתיב חקר בגשמים וכתיב חקר בברייתו של עולם מה בברייתו של עולם כתיב ביה גבורה אף בגשמים הוי כמו דכתיב גבורה: שלא נמסרו שלשתן ביחד ביד שליח. יפתח ה' ולא שליח

כי

*) מלא"ס רצ"ל גבורות של מקום שמוריד גשמים וכו'.

מסורת הש"ס

ר"ה טז.

[ברכות לג.]

שם לג.

ר"ה טז.

[נ"ל עושה גדולות ואין חקר נפלאות עד אין מספר (איוב ה ט) וכן הגי' למהרש"א ע"ש וגם לקמן ח: ודף לא. ובפי' הרמב"ם מ"ס דברכות לריכין לגי' עד אין חקר בלא לנסח ע"ש דרך סג"ל]

שם

סנהדרין קיג.

דברים כח

בראשית ל

הגהות הב"ח

(א) גמ' שנאמר עושה גדולות ואין חקר נפלאות כו' כצ"ל ותיבת עד נמחק וכ"ב (איוב ה): (ב) שם ואין חקר לתבונתו נותן ליעף כח וכתיב מכין הרים: (ג) שם ואלו הן. מפתח של חיה ומפתח של גשמים ומפתח של תחיית המתים מפתח של חיה מנין דכתיב ויזכור אלהים את רחל וישמע אליה אלהים ויפתח את רחמה מפתח של גשמים מנין דכתיב יפתח ה' לך גו' מטר ארצך כו'. מפתח של תחיית המתים וכו' כצ"ל: (ד) רש"י ד"ה מאי שנא כו' ליתני התם היכא דתני כו' סדר זרעים ואמאי שבקיה עד הכא כו' כצ"ל והד"א: (ה) ד"ה בחג כו' זמן הזכרה ליתנא אחרינא ואיידי דתני כו' כצ"ל והד"א: (ו) ד"ה כתיב עושה גדולות ואין חקר כו': (ז) ד"ה ואמר כו' ביחד. נ"ב דקא קשיא ליה קושיית התוס': (ח) תוס' ד"ה אלא כו' אבל בסדר זרעים דתני מזכירין כצ"ל: (ט) ד"ה וליתני מאימתי מזכירין על הגשמים כו' פרק אין עומדין דקתני כי הכא מזכירין גבורות גשמים ושואלין וכו' אמאי לא כו' כצ"ל ותיבת הגשמים נמחק: (י) ד"ה שלשה כו' דמפתח הגשמים נמסר לאליהו:

עין משפט נר מצוה

ד א מיי' פ"ז מהלכות מעשה הקרבנות הלכה פ:

אליה אלהים ויפתח את רחמה מפתח של תחיית המתים מנין דכתיב °וידעתם כי אני ה' בפתחי את קברותיכם במערבא אמרי אף מפתח של פרנסה דכתיב °פותח את ידך וגו' ור' יוחנן מאי טעמא לא קא חשיב להא אמר לך גשמים (א) היינו פרנסה: ר' אליעזר אומר מיום טוב הראשון של חג כו': איבעיא להו ר' אליעזר מהיכא גמיר לה מלולב גמר לה או מניסוך המים גמר לה מלולב גמר לה מה לולב ביום אף הזכרה ביום או דלמא מניסוך המים גמר לה מה ניסוך המים מאורתא *דאמר מר *°ומנחתם ונסכיהם אפילו בלילה אף הזכרה מאורתא תא שמע דאמר רבי אבהו לא למדה ר' אליעזר אלא מלולב איכא דאמרי ר' אבהו גמרא גמיר לה ואיכא דאמרי מתניתא שמיע ליה מאי היא דתניא מאימתי מזכירין על הגשמים *רבי אליעזר אומר משעת נטילת לולב *ר' יהושע אומר משעת הנחתו א"ר אליעזר הואיל וארבעת מינין הללו אינן באין אלא לרצות על המים וכשם שארבע מינין הללו אי אפשר בהם בלא מים כך אי אפשר לעולם בלא מים אמר לו ר' יהושע והלא גשמים בחג אינו אלא סימן קללה אמר לו ר' אליעזר אף אני לא אמרתי לשאול אלא להזכיר וכשם שתחיית המתים מזכיר כל השנה כולה ואינה אלא בזמנה כך מזכירים גבורות גשמים כל השנה ואינן אלא בזמנן לפיכך אם בא להזכיר כל השנה כולה מזכיר רבי אומר אני משעה שמפסיק לשאלה כך מפסיק להזכרה ר' יהודה בן בתירה אומר בשני בחג הוא מזכיר ר' עקיבא אומר בששי בחג הוא מזכיר ר' יהודה משום ר' יהושע אומר העובר לפני התיבה ביום טוב האחרון של חג האחרון מזכיר הראשון אינו מזכיר ביום טוב ראשון של פסח הראשון מזכיר האחרון אינו מזכיר שפיר קאמר ליה ר"א לרבי יהושע אמר לך רבי יהושע בשלמא תחיית המתים מזכיר דכולי יומא ומניה הוא אלא גשמים כל אימת דאתיין זמנייהו היא והתנן *יצא ניסן וירדו גשמים סימן קללה הם שנאמר °הלא קציר חטים היום וגו' ר' יהודה בן בתירה אומר בשני בחג הוא מזכיר מ"ט דרבי יהודה בן בתירה דתניא *רבי יהודה בן בתירה אומר נאמר בשני °ונסכיהם ונאמר בששי ונסכיה ונאמר בשביעי כמשפטם הרי מ"ם יו"ד מ"ם הרי כאן מים מכאן רמז לניסוך המים מן התורה ומאי שנא בשני דנקט דכי רמיזי להו בקרא בשני הוא דרמיזי הלכך בשני מדכרינן רבי עקיבא אומר בששי בחג הוא מזכיר שנאמר בששי ונסכיה *בשני ניסוכין הכתוב מדבר אחד ניסוך המים ואחד ניסוך היין ואימא תרוייהו דחמרא סבר לה כר' יהודה בן בתירה דאמר רמיזי מיא

רש"י

איבעיא להו רבי אליעזר מהיכא גמיר לה מלולב גמיר מה לולב ביום וכו'. פי' ולולב האי רצוי דמים וגדל על המים או דלמא מניסוך גמר לה פי' ונפקא מינה (ה) אי מלולב גמר לה אבל ניסוך המים סבירא ליה דלאו ביום ראשון הוא או מניסוך המים קא גמר לה דסבירא ליה דניסוך המים ביום ראשון הוא אי נמי דאי מלולב גמר הוה דווקא ביום שנאמר (ויקרא כג) ולקחתם לכם ביום אבל אי מנסוך הוה אפילו בלילה ולענין זה אהאי דאמר מר ומנחתם ונסכיהם (ו) בלילה אף וכו' פירוש דאע"ג דניסוך קרבנות לא הוי עד לאחר הקרבת קרבנותיהם ואם כן היאך קריבי נסכים בלילה רוצה לומר בלילה שניה והניסוך החג דהוי ממים מצי למהוי בלילה ראשונה ואע"ג דאמרינן במסכת יומא בפ' בראשונה (דף כו:) *אמר רב ואיתימא ר' יוחנן אין מנסכים מים בחג אלא בתמיד של שחר וא"כ לא הוי בלילה ראשונה דהא איכא אלא ביום יש לומר דאינו חייב לנסך אלא בתמיד של שחר מכל מקום אי בעי עביד ליה בליליא: **דאמר** רבי אבהו לא למדה רבי אליעזר אלא מלולב. פירוש וסבירא ליה דניסוך לא הוי עד בשני: **משעת** נטילת לולב. פירוש דהיינו תחילת יום ראשון של סוכות ורבי יהושע אומר משעת הנחתו פירוש לאורתא דמוצאי שביעי של סוכות שמניחין בו את הלולב: **משעה** שמפסיקין לישאל. ותן טל ומטר בברכת השנים פוסקין מלהזכיר מוריד הגשם בתחיית המתים: **העובר** לפני התיבה בי"ט של חג האחרון מזכיר וכו'. פי' האחרון שמתפלל תפלת מוסף הראשון אינו מזכיר פירוש שמתפלל שחרית אינו מזכיר ובירושלמי קאמר אמאי אינו מזכיר מאורתא פירוש מתפלת ערבית ומשני דלית תמן כל עמא ולדכרו בצפרא פירוש בתפלת שחרית ומשני דהוו סברי דהוו מדכרו ליה מאורתא: **מים**. מ"ם מנסכיהם דכתיב בשני ויו"ד דכתיב בששי ונסכיה ומ"ם שבשביעי כתיב כמשפטם והוי מים (ז) טעמא דרבי עקיבא בששי ונסכיה דמשמע תרי נסכים הלכך בששי בחג הוא מזכיר גבורות גשמים:

תוספות

כי אני ה'. ולא שליח: פותח את ידך. ולא שליח: גשמים נמי הייט פרנסה. (ג) וככר תשבנא ליה: מלולב גמר לה. שדומה ללולב שכשם שאי אפשר לאלו ארבע מינין בלא גשמים ובאין לרצות על המים כדאמרינן בסוכה *כך אי אפשר לעולם בלא מים: מה לולב ביום. שמתחילין ליטול ביום ראשון אף הזכרה נמי ביום כלומר שאין מזכירין בלילי יום טוב הראשון עד למחר: מה ניסוך המים מאורתא. כדאשכחן במס' סוכה (דף מח:) שממלאין הכלי מים לניסוך המים בלילה ויש ספרים דכתיב בהו דאמר מר ומנחתם ונסכיהם בלילה (ג) שמקריבין הקרבנות ביום יכולין להביא המנחות והנסכים בלילה אף האי ניסוך המים נמי יכול לנסך בלילה: אף הזכרה נמי מאורתא. שבלילי י"ט הראשון קאמר ר' אליעזר שמתחילין להזכיר גבורות גשמים: גמרא גמיר לה. רבי אבהו דרבי אליעזר לא למדה אלא מלולב: *) מתניתין שמיע ליה. דרבי אליעזר גמר מלולב: משעת הנחתו. מיום שמברכין בו באחרונה דהייט בשביעי א]: ארבעה מינין הללו. שבלולב ואתרוג: כך גשמים. יהא מזכיר כל השנה אפילו בימות החמה אם הוא רוצה יהא מזכיר: משעה שפוסק מלשאול. שבפסח פוסק מלומר ותן טל ומטר פוסק מלהזכיר גבורות גשמים והשתא לא מצית למימר אם בא להזכיר כל השנה כולה מזכיר אלא בימות החמה אינו מזכיר הואיל ואין זמנו אף בחג אינו מזכיר הואיל ולא סימן ברכה הן: האחרון. המתפלל תפלת מוסף: הראשון. המתפלל תפלת יוצר: אינו מזכיר. ושוב אין מזכירין: שפיר קאמר ליה ר' אליעזר לר' יהושע. דאמר כי היכי דמזכירין תחיית המתים כל השנה ואף על גב דלא מטא זמנייהו כך מזכירין גבורות גשמים אם רוצה כל השנה ובחג נמי אע"ג דלאו סימן ברכה הן מזכירין הואיל ואין שואלין: כל אימת דאתיין זמנייהו הוא. וכיון דלאו זמניה הוא אין מזכירין והוא הדין בחג: בשני ונסכיהם. ושני ננסכה וכיון דבשני אייתר מ"ם לדרשה להכי מתחילין להזכיר בשני: בשני ניסוכין הכתוב מדבר. שני ניסוכין על קרבן אחד אבל ונסכיהם (ד) משמע הרבה דבקרבנות הרבה לכן לא הוה דריש רבי עקיבא מונסכיהם: סבר לה כרבי יהודה. דמ"ם יו"ד מ"ם מרבה ניסוך המים:

*) נ"ל מתניתא

רבינו חננאל

שנאמר וישמע אליה אלהים ויפתח את רחמה. מפתח של תחיית המתים שנאמר וידעתם כי אני ה' בפתחי את קברותיכם וגו'. גשמים היינו פרנסה ומשום שרגשמים חשובים כתחיית המתים קבעו ברכה זו בתחיית המתים: פיסקא ר' אליעזר אומר מיו"ט הראשון של חג מזכיר. [איבעיא להו אי מלילי יו"ט הראשון מזכיר] וגמר לה מניסוך דאתקש ניסוך המים לניסוך היין דאמר מר ומנחתם ונסכיהם (מלילי יו"ם טו"ב הראשו"ן מזכי"ר) אפילו בלילה. פירושו בתמורה בתחלת פרק יש בקרבנות. או מלולב גמר לה דכתיב ולקחתם לכם ביום ולא בלילה ופשטנא מהא דתניא מאימתי מזכירין של הגשמים. ר' אליעזר אומר משעת נטילת לולב. ר' יהושע אומר משעת הנחתו. א"ר אליעזר הואיל וארבעת מינים הללו אינם באין [אלא] לרצות המים כו'. שפיר קאמר ליה רבי אליעזר לר' יהושע אני לא אמרתי לשאל אלא להזכיר כשם שתחיית המתים מזכיר כל השנה ואינה אלא בזמנה כך גשמים מזכיר ואינן אלא בזמנן. ואמרינן ר' יהושע פריך הכי מה לתחיית המתים שמזכיר בכל יום דכל יומא זימניה היא אלא גשמים אטו כל יומא זימנייהו הוא. והתנן יצא ניסן וירדו גשמים סימן קללה היא ר' יהודה בן בתירה אומר בשני של חג הוא מוכיר. וגמר לה מניסוך דכתיב בשני ונסכיהם מדכתיב מ"ם יתירה דהוה ליה למכתב ונסכה וכתיב ונסכיהם. ובששי כתיב יוד יתירה דכתיב ונסכיה. ובשביעי כמשפטם. כתיב מ' יתירה. סימן לניסוך המים מן התורה. וכי רמיזי מיום שני רמיזי הלכך מיום שני מזכיר. ר' עקיבא אומר בששי בחג הוא מזכיר. ר' עקיבא נמי אית ליה סימן לניסוך המים. מיהו דייק מדכתיב ביום הששי. ונסכיה. בשני ניסוכין הכתוב מדבר ניסוך מים וניסוך יין

לפנינו ליתא ר' אבא ולא תימא כמי בר חמא ולא תיתא ר' יוחנן

רבינו גרשום

כי אני ה' ולא שליח פותח את ידך ולא שליח. גשמים נמי היינו פרנסה וכבר השיבנא ליה: **פיסקא** מלולב גמר לה שדומה ללולב שכשם שאי אפשר לאילו בלא מים כך אי אפשר לעולם בלא מים מה לולב ביום שמתחיל ליטול ביום ראשון אף הזכרה ביום (בו' צ"ל כלומר) שאינו מתחיל להזכיר בלילי יו"ם ראשון עד למחר. מה ניסוך המים מאורתא כדאשכחן במס' סוכה שממלאין המים לניסוך המים בלילה ויש ספרים שכתוב בהן [דאמר מר] מנחתם ונסכיהם בלילה שמקריבין קרבן ביום יכולין להביא המנחה והנסכים בלילה אף האי ניסוך המים יכולין לנסך בלילה. אף הזכרה נמי מאורתא שבלילי יו"ם הראשון קאמר ר' אליעזר שמזכירין להזכיר גבורות גשמים. גמרא גמיר לה ר' אבהו דר' אליעזר לא למדה אלא מלולב. מתניתין שמיעה ליה דר' אליעזר גמר מלולב: משעת הנחתו מיום שמברכין בו באחרונה דהיינו בשביעי. ארבעת מינין הללו שבלולב ואתרוג: כך גשמים יהא מזכיר כל השנה אפי' בימות החמה אם הוא רוצה אף בחג נמי אם הוא רוצה יהא מוכיר. משעה שפוסק מלשאול שבפסח פוסק מלומר ותן טל ומטר פוסק מלהזכיר גבורת הגשמים ועכשיו לא מצית למימר אם בא להזכיר כל השנה מזכיר אלא בימות החמה אינו מזכיר הואיל ואין זמנו אף בחג אינו מזכיר הואיל ולאו זמן ברכה הוא. האחרון המתפלל תפלת מוסף. הראשון המתפלל (תפלת) יוצר: מזכיר ושוב אינו מזכיר. שפיר קאמר ליה ר' אליעזר לר"י דכי היכי דמזכירין תחיית המתים כל השנה אע"ג דלא זמניה כך מזכירין גבורות גשמים אם רוצה כל השנה ובחג נמי אע"ג דלאו סימן ברכה הוא מזכירין. סימן קללה הוא וכיון דלאו זמנה אין מזכירין וה"ה בחג: נאמר בשני ונסכיהם דמני בנסכה וכיון דבשני אתרבי מ' לדרשה דמים לפיכך מתחיל להזכיר בשני: בשני ניסוכין הכתוב מדבר שני ניסוכין על קרבן אחד ונסכיהם משמע ניסוכין הרבה דקרבנות הרבה. סבר לה כר"י דמרבה ניסוך המים

הגהות הב"ח

(א) גמ' אמר לך גשמים נמי הייט פרנסה: (ב) רש"י ד"ה גשמים נמי הייט פרנסה שזורעים ופירות גדלים מהם לפרנסת העולם וככר תשבנא ליה: (ג) ד"ה מה ניסוך כו' ונסכיהם בלילה אפילו בלילה דאע"ס שמקריבין הקרבנות: (ד) ד"ה בשני ניסוכין כו' אבל ונסכיהם דמשמע הרבה ניסוכין בקרבנות הרבה: (ה) תוס' ד"ה איבעיא כו' ונפקא מינה דאי מלולב גמר לה כו' דס"ל דניסוך המים נמי ביום ראשון הוא: (ו) בא"ד ומנחתם ונסכיהם אפילו בלילה וכו' פי' דאע"ג כו' וא"כ האיך קריבי נכסים בלילה אלא י"ל בלילה שניה מ"מ הניסוך דחג דהוי ממים כו' כנ"ל: (ז) ד"ה מים כו' וטעמא דר"ע דכתיב בששי ונסכים:

הגהות מהר"ב רנשבורג

א] רש"י ד"ה משעת הנחתו וכו' דהייט בשביעי. כ"כ וכן פרש"י לקמן דף ג ע"א בד"ה אלא ר' יהושע היא וכו' דהייט בשביעי וכו' עכ"ל. וצ"ע דלקמן דף ד סע"א פרש"י בד"ה ר' יהושע היא וכו' דהייט יום שמיני וכו' עכ"ל. וכן משמע מדברי הש"ס שם ודו"ק. שוב ראיתי דלק"מ דמ"ש רש"י בשביעי על שעת הנחת לולב אמר אבל ההזכרה היא לאורתא דשמיני וכמ"ש תוס' ד"ה משעת נטילה וכן נלמד ממהרש"א לקמן דף ג ע"א ד"ה גמ' יעוש"ה:

מסורת הש"ס

[דף לז: ע"ש תוס' ד"ה כדי] · תמורה יד. [זבחים ח: חד] מנחות מה: נב. · [לקמן ד.] · [שם] · לקמן יב: · שבת קט. · זבחים קי:

תורה אור

יחזקאל לז · תהלים קמה · במדבר כח · ש"א יב · במדבר כט

אי סבר לה כרבי יהודה בן בתירה נימא כוותיה קסבר רבי עקיבא כי כתיב ניסוך יתירא בששי הוא דכתיב תניא ר' נתן אומר בקדש הסך נסך שכר לה' בשני ניסוכין הכתוב מדבר אחד ניסוך המים ואחד ניסוך היין אימא תרוייהו דחמרא אם כן ליכתוב קרא או הסך הסך או נסך נסך מאי הסך נסך שמעת מינה חד דמיא וחד דחמרא אלא הא דתנן **ניסוך המים כל ז' מני אי ר' יהושע נימא חד יומא אי ר"ע תרי יומי אי ר' יהודה ב"ב שיתא יומי לעולם ר' יהודה ב"ב היא וס"ל כר' יהודה דמתני' דתנן *רבי יהודה אומר בלוג היה מנסך כל שמונה ומפיק ראשון ומעייל שמיני ומאי שנא ראשה דלא דכי רמיזי מים בשני הוא דרמיזי שמיני נמי כי רמיזי מים בשביעי הוא דרמיזי אלא רבי יהושע היא וניסוך המים כל שבעה הלכתא גמירי לה *דאמר ר' אמי א"ר יוחנן משום ר' נחוניא איש בקעת בית חורתן עשר נטיעות ערבה וניסוך המים הלכה למשה מסיני: רבי יהודה אומר משום רבי יהושע העובר לפני התיבה ביום טוב האחרון של חג האחרון מזכיר הראשון אינו מזכיר ביום טוב הראשון של פסח הראשון מזכיר האחרון אינו מזכיר: הי רבי יהושע אילימא רבי יהושע דמתניתין הא אמר ביום טוב האחרון של חג הוא מזכיר אלא ר' יהושע דברייתא האמר משעת הנחתו ותו הא דתניא ר' יהודה אומר משום בן בתירה העובר לפני התיבה ביום טוב האחרון של חג האחרון מזכיר הי בן בתירה אילימא רבי יהודה בן בתירה הא אמר בשני בחג הוא מזכיר אמר רב נחמן בר יצחק (א) תהא ברבי יהושע בן בתירה זמנין דקרי ליה בשמיה וזימנין דקרי ליה בשמיה דאבא והא מקמי דליסמכוהו והא לבתר דליסמכוהו תנא בטל וברוחות לא חייבו חכמים להזכיר ואם בא להזכיר מזכיר מ"ט א"ר חנינא לפי שאין נעצרין וטל מנלן דלא מיעצר דכתיב ויאמר אליהו התשבי מתושבי גלעד אל אחאב חי ה' אלהי ישראל אשר עמדתי לפניו אם יהיה השנים האלה טל ומטר כי אם לפי דברי וכתיב לך הראה אל אחאב ואתנה מטר על פני האדמה ואילו טל לא קאמר ליה מאי טעמא משום

דלא

רש"י

אי סבר לה כר' יהודה. לימא כר"י. שהזכיר בשני: ניסוך יתירא בששי כתיב. כלומר ונסכיה דמרבי תרי ניסוכין כתיב בששי להכי אמר בששי מתחיל להזכיר ולהאי מ"ם מים יו"ד מ"ם מים דלא מצינו למימר תרוייהו דיין: או הסך הסך או נסך נסך. מדשני קרא בדיבוריה ש"מ תרתי: אי ר"ע תרי יומי הוו. ותו לא דהא אמר (ג) ונסכיה דהיינו בששי מרבה ניסוך המים: וסבר לה כר' יהודה דמתניתין. דאמר בלוג היה מנסך כל שמונה לא סבר כוותיה במה דאמר כל שמונה מנסך אלא במה דאמר בשמיני מנסך וכיון דבשמיני מנסך משכחת לה לרבי יהודה [ב"ב] דאמר בשני מתחילין לניסוך המים כל שבעה: (ג) דמפיק ראשון ומעייל שמיני. משיב בעל הגמרא מי מצי אמר רבי יהודה דבשמיני מנסך: מאי שנא. דקאמר דבראשון אינו מזכיר דכי רמיזי מיא בשני הוא דרמיזי דמונסכיהם מרבה ניסוך המים שמיני נמי מי מצי אמר דמנסך הא שביעי אמר רחמנא דמ"ם יו"ד מ"ם מים כתיב בשביעי דסוף קרא דניסוך המים בשביעי כתיב כמשפטם ולא בשמיני: אלא ר' יהושע היא. דאמר משעת הנחתו (ד) [דהיינו בשביעי] מזכיר ואעפ"כ סבר דניסוך המים כל שבעה דגמרא גמיר לה הלכה למשה מסיני דניסוך המים כל שבעה והאי כר"א אתי שפיר אבל כרבי יהודה בן בתירה וכר"ע לא מיתוקמא אלא להכי לא פסיק לה כר' אליעזר דהא לא מיבעיא אי ר' אליעזר סבירא ליה הכי דהואי לרבי אליעזר אתי שפיר והא דקא מוקים כר' יהושע רבותא קמשמע לן אבל כר"י בן בתירה וכר"ע לא מיתוקמא דרבי יהודה יליף מונסכיה בשני ונסכיהם ס' אלמא דסבר דניסוך המים לא הוו אלא ו' ימים דהיינו לא מפיק ראשון ומעייל שמיני משום האי פירכא דפריך לעיל לא אתי כרבי יהודה ורבי עקיבא יליף מנסכיה שנאמר בששי אלמא דסבר דניסוך המים לא הוו אלא תרי יומי אבל כרבי יהושע מיתוקמא דפסיק אין מזכירין אלא ביו"ט האחרון דגשמים בחג סימן קללה אבל ניסוך המים הוי כל שבעה דגמרא גמיר לה: עשר נטיעות. המפוזרות בתוך בית סאה חורשין כל בית סאה ערב שביעית עד ר"ה אע"ג דשאר שדות אין חורשין לפני שביעית ל' יום זה חורשין דהואיל ואם אין חורשין סביבן מפסידין: וניסוך המים. כל שבעה: ר' יהודה אומר משום רבי יהושע העובר לפני התיבה ביו"ט האחרון של חג כו'. כמין אמר מר הוא כלומר אמריק לעיל ר' יהודה אומר: הי רבי יהושע אילימא רבי יהושע דמתני' (ה) מיו"ט האחרון הוא מזכיר. דראשון נמי המתפלל תפלה יוצר מזכיר ואילו הכא תני בראשון אינו מזכיר: האמר משעת הנחתו. דהיינו בשביעי והכא קתני יו"ט האחרון של חג דהיינו בשמיני: ותו הא דתניא. במכילתא אחריתי ר' יהודה אומר משום בן בתירה העובר לפני התיבה בי"ט אחרון של חג האחרון מזכיר הראשון אינו מזכיר: (אלא) אמר רב נחמן בר יצחק תהא. תרוייהו הא דבעית הי ר' יהושע והא דבעית הי בן בתירה היא דהאי דקאמר ר' יהודה לעיל משום ר' יהושע והדר קאמר משום בן בתירה תהא תרוייהו ר' יהושע בן בתירה ולא קשיא זמנין קרו ליה בשמיה דאבוה בן בתירה וזמנין דקרו ליה בשמיה דידיה ר' יהושע: מקמי דליסמכוהו. לא הוה חשוב וקרו ליה בשמיה דאבוה והאי דקרו ליה בשמיה דנפשיה ר' יהושע היינו לבתר דסמכוהו: בטל וברוחות. משיב הרוח ומוריד הטל לא חייבוהו חכמים להזכיר אפילו בימות הגשמים: לפי שאינן נעצרין. שאלמלא (ו) כן אין העולם מתקיים והאי דאמרינן בתפלה משיב הרוח ומוריד הגשם לאו משום חיוב אלא חוק גשם הוא מזכיר [א] דטל ורוחות משיבות לארץ לתקנה ולנגבה כדכתיב דיקא דבתר מיטרא כמיטרא: ואילו טל לא קאמר. ואתנה טל ומטר אלא מטר בלבד:

תוספות

אי רבי יהודה בן בתירה. דאמר בשני בחג הוא מזכיר שית יומי הוו א"כ לא יהיה הניסוך כי אם ששה ימים: עשר נטיעות. פירש"י (ז) נטיעות מפוזרות בבית סאה חורש כל בית סאה בשבילן דכל נטיעה יונקת ודוחקא מבית סאה היה צריך לגם יכול לחרוש עד ר"ה של שביעית דהוו שפיר אוקומי אילנא שרי אבל יותר מבית סאה אינו חורש אלא כדי צרכן דהואיל ומפוזרות ביותר מבית סאה קיימי שפיר ובפחות מיכן למה קיימי וליעקר קיימי ודוחקא נטיעות אמר דחורשין בשבילן עד ראש השנה אבל אילנות אסור דאורייתא כל אלול ומדרבנן *פסח ועצרת תקון בשדה הלבן עד פסח מותר אבל מפסח ולהלן אסור ושדה אילן עד עצרת מותר מכאן ואילך אסור: ערבה. שמקיפין את המזבח וניסוך המים הלכה למשה מסיני כולהו: ויאמר אליהו התשבי מתושבי גלעד. לכך נקרא מתושבי גלעד לפי שהרגו ישראל אנשי יבש גלעד על מעשה פילגש בגבעה ולא נשאר ביבש גלעד כי אם מעט אנשים מן המיושבים בעיר כי כל השאר היו עם אספסוף לכך מעיד כי אליהו מן התושבים כך שמעתי מהר"י פרוש"י משם הר"י בה"ר יצחק ממגנצא: בטל וברוחות לא חייבו חכמים להזכיר. משיב הרוח ומוריד הטל ס' לפיכך אין קפידא לומר מוריד הטל אפילו בימות החמה אך שלא יאמר מוריד הגשם והכי הלכתא ואם לא אמר בימות הגשמים כי אם מוריד הגשם ודילג משיב הרוח ומוריד הטל אין מחזירין: ואילו טל לא מיעצר. ומיהו נראה דגבי גדעון (שופטים ו) כשאמר (ח) על הארץ יהיה טל ועל הגיזה יהיה חורב כתיב ויעש כן אבל כשאמר על הארץ יהיה חורב ועל הגזה יהיה טל כתיב ויהי כן כלומר דעל הגיזה היה הטל אבל לא כתיב ויעש כן משמע דעל הארץ היה טל דטל לא מיעצר ע"כ בנוסח שלפני ועוד מצאתי כשאמרו על כל הארץ יהיה טל כתיב ויעש אלהים כן וכשאמר טל יהיה על הגיזה לבדה (ט) ועל כל הארץ יהיה חרב כתיב ויהי כן ולא הזכיר בזה הש"י וטעמו אשר אומר כי הוא זה כי אין הש"י מזכיר שמו על הרעה כי אם יהיה חורב על כל הארץ תהיה רעת יושבי בה וכתיב (שמות כ) בכל המקום אשר אזכיר את שמי אבוא אליך וברכתיך אבל כשאמר על כל הארץ (י) יהיה טל כתיב ויעש אלהים וכדומה לזה (בראשית א) ויקרא אלהים לאור יום ולחשך קרא לילה וגבי חשך לא הזכיר השם יתברך וכן במעשה דברות אחרונות (שמות כ) מלא תרצח ואילך לא הזכיר הש"י הכל הולך אל מקום אחד משל למלך שבנה דירה נאה והגיח לצייר מגיע לפני כל חדרי הבית אלמלי בית הכסא מקום הטינוף:

בימות

רבינו חננאל

יין. ודכי כתיב ניסוך יתירה בששי כתי' הלכך בששי מזכיר. ואקשינן אלא הא דתנן ניסוך המים שבעה מני אי ר' יהודה בן בתירה האומר ניסוך המים מיום שני של חג מתחיל משעה שמזכיר הלא משכחת אלא ששה אי ר' עקיבא תרי יומי הוו כר' כל אחד משעה ששומ' פי' מזכיר משעה שהוא מתחיל ימי הניסוך ואסיקנא הא דתנן ניסוך המים ז' גמרא הוא דאמר משמיה דר' יוחנן ערבה ביום השביעי של חג. וניסוך המים שבעת ימי החג. ועשר נטיעות (משורות) [מפורזות] בבית סאה חורשין כל בית סאה בשבילן כבר פירשנוהו. ואלו כולן גמרא בידינו כי הל"מ הם. ותרויינהו הכי א"ר יהודה משום ר' יהושע בן בתירה העובר לפני התיבה ביו"ט אחרון של חג האחרון מזכיר. פי' המתפלל במוסף הוא מזכיר בתחיית המתים מוריד הגשם. [והמתפלל שחרית אינו מזכיר וביו"ט הראשון של פסח] המתפלל שחרית מזכיר מוריד הגשם ופוסק. והמתפלל במוסף אינו מזכיר כלל. וכן הלכתא (ד)גרסינן בירושלמי א"ר יוחנן הלכה כר' יהודה שאמר משום ר' יהודה בן בתירה. ומ"ט דר' יהודה [כרי שיהא] המועדות בטל. מפני שהטל סימן יפה לעולם. אם לא הזכיר גשמים בתחיית המתים ולא שאלה בברכת השנים מחזירין אותו. והכן הוא החזר בו ויחזיר כמו שפי' בר"ה אם עקר את רגליו חוזר בתחלה. ואם לאו חוזר לעבודה. והכא אם עקר את רגליו חוזר בתחלה ואם לאו חוזר לשומע תפלה *) (וכן

א"ר יהודה קודם שיסמך בישיבה היו קורין אותו בן בתירה). מתוך ה' דברים נגאלו ישראל ממצרים. מתוך צרה שנאמר ויאנחו בני ישראל מן העבודה. מתוך צוותה שנאמר נאקתם. מתוך זכות אבות שנאמר ויזכור אלהים את בריתו וגו'. מתוך תשובה שנאמר וירא אלהים את בני ישראל וגו'. מתוך הקץ שנאמר וידע אלהים. וכן הם מפורשים בענין בצר לך ומצאוך. וכן בענין וירא בצר להם בשמעו את רנתם. אסור ליחיד להזכיר עד שיזכיר ש"צ ויאמר מוריד הגשם קטן לצלותא כמו שיזכיר ש"צ דסי וזוכרין הצבור ביחיד אע"פ שלא סקמי ש"צ: תנא [illegible] ואלו טל לא ארכר. למיטרא

דלא

עין משפט נר מצוה

ה א מיי' פ"ז מהלכות תמידין הלכה ו [illegible]

ו ב מיי' פ"ג מהלכות שמיטה ויובל הלכה ט [illegible]

ז ג מיי' פ"ו מהלכות לולב הלכה כב:

ח ד מיי' פ"י מהלכות תמידין הלכה ו:

ט ה מיי' פ"ב מהלכות תפלה הלכה [illegible]

[גליונות רש"י [illegible]]

מסורת הש"ס

סוכה מב: | שם מה: | מו"ק ג: | סוכה לד. [illegible]

הגהות הב"ח

(א) גמ' אמר רב נחמן בר יצחק תהא תרוייהו ברבי יהושע בן בתירה: (ב) רש"י ד"ה [illegible] (ג) ד"ה [illegible] (ד) ד"ה אלא [illegible] (ה) ד"ה [illegible] (ו) ד"ה [illegible]

(ו) ד"ה לפי שאינן נעצרין שאלמלא נעצרין אין העולם כו' לאו משום חיוב דרוח אלא חיוב גשם הוא מזכיר: (ז) תוס' ד"ה עשר נטיעות פי' רש"י עשר נטיעות המפוזרות כו' דאוקמי אילנא ושרי אבל יותר: (ח) ד"ה ואילו וכו' דגבי גדעון כשאמר יהי נא חרב אל הגזה כו' כתיב ויעש כן אבל כשאמר טל יהיה על הגזה כתוב ויהי כן כלומר דעל הארץ היה טל כו' כנ"ל: (ט) באו"ד ועל כל הארץ חרב כתיב כו' כנ"ל ותיבת יהיה נמחק:

*) [illegible] ולא חייבו חכמים להזכיר שאינן נעצרין כמו המספר דכתיב חי ה' אם יהיה טל ומטר כי אם לפי דברי. וכתיב לך הראה אל אחאב ואתנה מטר על פני האדמה. ואלו טל לא אדכר. [illegible] נראה שכצבור שייך למעלה וכצ"ל ותריגנא הכי אמר ר"י משום ריב"ע וקודם שנסמך כשיבה היו קורין אותו בן בתירה.

רבינו גרשום

[illegible]

הגהות הגר"א

[א] רש"י ד"ה לפי כו'. מזכיר דרוחות פותלת כצ"ל:

גליון הש"ס

[illegible]

עין משפט נר מצוה

[illegible]

מסורת הש"ס

[illegible]

בימות החמה אמר משיב הרוח אין מחזירין אותו מוריד הגשם מחזירין אותו. אבל אם דילג אלא אמר לא גשם ולא טל אין מחזירין ובימות הגשמים לא אמר משיב הרוח אין מחזירין אותו לא אמר מוריד הגשם מחזירין אותו אבן אם אמר מוריד הטל בימות הגשמים אין מחזירין ואם ספק אם הזכיר אם לאו אם איט זכור (ג) שלא אמר שום דבר בימות הגשמים כל ל' יום חזקה מה שהוא למוד הוא אומר ומחזירין מספק כל ל' יום וכן זכרט ומי כמוך וכתוב לחיים שאומרים מן הכסה עד יום הכפורים מספק מחזירין ירושלמי גשם רבי חנינא היה שייך בגשם והזכיר טל אין מחזירין אותו בטל והזכיר של גשמים מחזירין אותו והתניא בטל וברוחות לא חייבו חכמים להזכיר ואם בא להזכיר מזכיר לא דמי ההוא דמלי ומיקל להאי דלא מלי ולא מיקל ומפרש רביט נתנאל (ד) טוב [illegible] מכשהוא מזכיר גשם לפי שהגשמים סימן קללה בימות החמה היה שייך בטל לא הזכיר לא טל ולא גשם אין מחזירין אותו והדין להפך במוריד הגשם דאמר בירושלמי בגשם והזכיר של טל אין מחזירין אותו והתניא אם לא שאל בברכת השנים או שלא אמר גבורות גשמים מחזירין בההוא דלא הזכיר כלל לא טל ולא מטר ומשם הר"ם שאין לומר בימות החמה משיב הרוח דהא אמר רבי חנינא בימות החמה אמר משיב הרוח אין מחזירין אותו מכלל דלכתחילה אין לאומרו ומשום הכי אמר הר"י בשם א"ז לעולם בין בימות החמה בין בימות הגשמים מוריד הטל דלעולם לא אתי לידי ספק אמר ספק לא אמר והיכא דלא מזכיר בגבורות מזכיר בשומע תפלה דהכי קאמר בירושלמי ומה שאלה שהיא מדוחק אומר בש"ת הזכרה שהיא מרווח לא כ"ש וכי היכי דשואלין בש"ת הוא מזכיר בש"ת ואפילו (ה) הזכיר קודם שומע תפלה איט אומר עד שיגיע לש"ת והיכא דלא אמר בשומע תפלה אי זוקק קודם שעקר רגליו חוזר לש"ת ואי לא חוזר לראש בין לא אמר מוריד הגשם ובין לא אמר ותן טל ומטר (ומחזירין) וכן הפסק והני מילי ביחיד אבל שליח צבור פסק רביט יהודה דאין מחזירין לפי דאין מחזירין שליח צבור אלא משום ג' דברים מתחיית המתים ומבונה ירושלים ומברכת ולמלשינים משום דנראה ככופר שמעתי מפי רבי שלמה לא דמי (ו) מלי ומיקל למאן דלא מלי ולא מיקל פירוש מיקל כמו מקלל כלומר שאין מחזירין אם לא אמר ותן טל ומטר:

הא בחרפי. פי' הא דאמר נעצרים היינו בחריפי כלומר בפירות המתבכרות וכו' אבל באפלי במאוחרות לא מיעצרי:

רוחות ארוחות לא קשיא הא ברוח וכו'. וה"ה דמצי לשטויי הא בחריפי הא באפלי אלא שפיר קא משני ליה הא ברוח מצויה וכו': **שניות** למטר. שניות במעלה כדאמרי אינשי משנה למלך:

הא דאתא ניחא. פי' כשיורדות בנחת תשובה כאן ברזיא כלומר בחוזק ואז אינה טובה:

גילהי דליליא. פי' זריחת הלילה שקורין לניסו"ר בלע"ז:

ושמשא דביני קרחי. פי' כמו דבר קרחה שמכאן ומכאן יורדין הגשמים והשמש זורח באמצע זה דשמש לא מעלי:

עורפילא

ארץ כשיאמר לשלג הוה ארץ הרי הוא כגשם מטר וגשם מטרות והרי יש כאן חמשה:

תורה אור

דלא מיעצר וכי מאחר דלא מיעצר אליהו אשתבועי למה ליה הכי קא"ל אפילו טל דברכה נמי לא אתי וליהדריה לטל דברכה משום דלא מינכרא מילתא (*אלא) רוחות מנא לן דלא מיעצרי *א"ר יהושע בן לוי דאמר קרא °כי כארבע רוחות השמים פרשתי אתכם נאם ה' מאי קאמר להו אילימא הכי קאמר להו הקב"ה לישראל דבדרתינכו בארבע רוחי דעלמא אי הכי כארבע בארבע מיבעי ליה אלא הכי קאמר כשם שאי אפשר לעולם בלא רוחות כך א"א לעולם בלא ישראל א"ר חנינא *הלכך בימות החמה ואמר משיב הרוח אין מחזירין אותו אמר מוריד הגשם מחזירין אותו בימות הגשמים לא אמר משיב הרוח אין מחזירין אותו לא אמר מוריד הגשם מחזירין אותו ולא עוד אלא אפילו אמר מעביר הרוח ומפריח הטל אין מחזירין אותו תנא בעבים וברוחות לא חייבו חכמים להזכיר ואם בא להזכיר מזכיר מ"ט משום דלא מיעצרי ולא מיעצרי והתני רב יוסף °ועצר את השמים מן העבים ומן הרוחות אתה אומר מן העבים ומן הרוחות או אינו אלא מן המטר כשהוא אומר ולא יהיה מטר הרי מטר אמור הא מה אני מקיים ועצר את השמים מן העבים ומן הרוחות קשיא רוחות ארוחות קשיא עבים אעבים עבים אעבים לא קשיא הא בחרפי הא באפלי רוחות ארוחות לא קשיא הא ברוח מצויה הא ברוח שאינה מצויה רוח שאינה מצויה חזיא לבי דרי אפשר בנפוותא תנא העבים והרוחות שניות למטר היכי דמי אמר עולא ואיתימא רבי יהודה דבתר מיטרא למיטרא דמעליותא היא והכתיב °יתן ה' את מטר ארצך אבק ועפר ואמר עולא ואיתימא רב יהודה זיקא דבתר מטרא לא קשיא הא דאתא ניחא הא דאתא רזיא (ואי בעית אימא) הא דמעלה אבק הא דלא מעלה אבק ואמר רב יהודה זיקא דבתר מיטרא כמיטרא עיבא דבתר מיטרא כמיטרא שימשא דבתר מיטרא כתרי מטרי למעוטי מאי למעוטי גילהי דליליא ושמשא דביני קרחי אמר רבא מעלי תלגא לטורי כחמשה מטרי לארעא שנאמר °כי לשלג יאמר הוא ארץ וגשם מטר וגשם מטרות עוזו ואמר רבא תלגא לטורי מטרא רזיא לאילני מטרא ניחא לפירי עורפילא

ולא מיעצר. לעולם אפילו באותן שנים: אישתבועי למה ליה. (א) אם יהיה השנים האלה טל ומטר כי אם לפי דברי הא לא נעצר: אפילו טל דברכה. שילמיה שום למה: וליהדריה לטל דברכה. ולימא ואתנה טל ומטר · דלא מינכרא מילתא. והא טל הוה מעיקרא ולא היה אחאב הרשע מודה בחזירה דטל של ברכה דאי הוה אומר ואתנה טל ומטר היה אחאב מקנטרו ואומר לו שלא נעצר: אלא דמכניפנא לכו מד' רוחי עלמא לא גרסינן דהא פרשתי אתכם כתיב בקרא ואיכא למימר דגרם ליה והכי משתמע קרא כי מד' רוחות השמים שפרשתי אתכם משם אקבצכם ואיכא לשון בעלמא הוא דלא כתיב קיבוץ בקרא: כשם שא"א לעולם בלא רוחות. שלא יתקיים מרוב הבל וחמימות: בלא ישראל. שאין העולם מתקיים אלא בשביל ישראל והכי אמר קרא כי כד' רוחות השמים פרשתי אתכם [illegible] (ירמיה לג) אם לא בריתי יומם ולילה חקות שמים וארץ לא שמתי: בימות החמה. מניסן עד החג: משיב הרוח אין מחזירין אותו. דבלאו הכי לא מיעצר: מוריד הגשם מחזירין אותו. דמיעצר וכיון דבעא אמיטרא לא התפלל תפלתו כהוגן וחוזר לראש הברכה ואומרה בלא מוריד הגשם לפי שהגשמים בקיץ סימן קללה הן מפני הקציר: מעביר הרוח. שלא ינשב: ומפריח הטל. שלא ירד: אין מחזירין אותו. דלא מיעצרי: בעבים. מקשר עבים: למימרא דלא מיעצרי. לפיכך לא חייבוהו להזכיר: בחרפי. עבים בכירות הבאים לפני המטר אינן עצורות: באפלי. הבאות מאוחרות לאחר המטר דשניות למטר הן כדלקמן ובהנהו כתיב ועצר וכיון דאין טלם נעצרות לא חייבו להזכיר: שאינה מצויה. כתיב ועצר ואפ"ה לא חייבוהו להזכיר דסגי ליה במצויה רוחות לא מצי לתרוצי הא בחרפי הא באפלי דרוח בין במטר בין בלא מטר לא מיעצר כגון רוח מצויה: רוח שאינה מצויה נמי חזיא לבי דרי. [illegible] וכחייב להזכיר: אפשר בנפוותא. וו"ן בלע"ז בנפה וכברה: שניות. כמעט שמועילות כמטר עצמו: מאי היא. (ב) אי זה עבים ורוחות קאמר דשניות למטר: אמר עולא ואיתימא רב יהודה דבתר מיטרא. עבים ורוחות שלאחר המטר: זיקא ל"ג הכא: יתן ה' את מטר ארצך אבק ועפר וגו': זיקא דבתר מיטרא. שהרוח מעלה אבק אחר הגשמים ונדבק בתבואה: ה"ג הא דאתא ניחא הא דאתא רזיא. כשירד בנחת איט מעלה אבק: רזיא. בכח ולא גרסינן ואי בעית אימא הא והא ט' אלא ה"ג הא דמעלה אבק הא דלא מעלה אבק והיט הך: כמיטרא. שניות למטר כדקתני בתוספתא: למעוטי מאי. מאחר דטלהו כמיטרא מאי קממעטינן דהוי בתריה ולא הוי כמיטרא: גילהי דליליא. אישלושטר"א בלע"ז בגילהי הוה קאי במס' (פסחים דף יג.) ורוב גילהי בליליא שכיח: וביומא שמשא דביני קרחי. שבין העבים שנראה במקום אחד אורה ובמקום אחר מעונן כקרח שיש לו שערות במקום אחד וקרחה במקום אחר: מעלי תלגא לטורי. וכ"ש לבקעה אלא הרים אין להם גשמים אלא שלג שהגשמים יורדין למטה ואין ההר שותה מהן ועוד שלג שבעמקים נמס והולך מפני החום ששולט שם כמים הוא אבל בהרים קרוי שלג: כחמשה מיטרי לארעא. דהכי משמע קרא כי לשלג יאמר הוא ארץ והרי יש כאן חמשה: מיטרא ניחא. שיורד בנחת יפה לפירות התבואה: עורפילא

רבינו חננאל

דלא מיעצרי. וכן הרוחות לא מיעצרי. דכתיב כי כארבע רוחות השמים פרשתי אתכם. א"ר חנינא בימות החמה אמר משיב הרוח אין מחזירין אותו. אמר מוריד הגשם מחזירין אותו בימות הגשמים לא אמר משיב הרוח אין מחזירין אותו. לא אמר מוריד הגשם מחזירין אותו ולא עוד אלא אפילו אמר מעביר הרוח ומפריח הטל אין מחזירין אותו לפי שאינן נעצרין. תנא בעבים וברוחות [illegible] להזכיר. ואם בא להזכיר מזכיר. איני והא תני רב יוסף ועצר את השמים מן העבים ומן הרוחות ושנינן [עבים אעבים ל"ק] חרפי אין נעצרים. אפלי נעצרים משום דשעלי [illegible]

רבינו גרשום

[illegible]

הגהות הב"ח

[illegible]

[illegible]

שורפילא · גשמים דקים כך שמן כדלקמן : אפי' לפרצידא דתותי קלא. הגרעין שתחת גושה של קרקע : מהניא· שמתחיל לבלבן ולעלות מיד: שורו פילי · שסותם סדקי הארץ נ"א שמגדלת ומצמחת הגרעינין העומדין בסדקי הקרקע : צורבא מרבנן · בחור חריף כמו ביעי דצריבן במסכת ביצה (דף ז·) תלמיד חכם זקן לא קרי צורבא אלא הבא מרבנן קרי ליה : כיון דנבט נבט · שמתחיל לבלבן ולעלות עולה למעלה כך תלמיד חכם כיון שיצא שמו הולך וגדל למעלה : אורייתא מרתחא ליה · שיש לו רוחב לב מתוך תורתו ומשים ללבו יותר משאר בני אדם וקמ"ל דחייבין לדונו לכף זכות : כאש · שמחמם כל גופו : בוניה · תלמידי חכמים מקיימי עולם בבנייניהו : ברזל · קפדנים וקשים כברזל : שלשה שאלו כו' · משום דרבי ברכיה מיירי בגשמים לקמן נקט לה : ובנות אנשי העיר יוצאות והיה הנערה · משמע הנערה היוצאה תחילה מן העיר ויאמר לה השקיני (ג) לא היה מנחש : אפי' חיגרת אפי' סומא · לפי שלא פירש בשאילתו ואפשר שתהיה בעלת מום ולא יבין בה אליעזר ויקחנה : (אלא) השיבוהו כהוגן · וזימן לו רבקה : דבר טמא · כלב או חזיר : והיינו דאמר להו נביא כו' · מדגלי ביה קרא ואמר הצרי אין בגלעד [אלמא דלא הוי ניחא קמי שמיא כדאמרינן הצרי אין בגלעד] פנחס היה שם והיה יכול להתיר נדרו אלא שלא רצה יפתח לילך אצלו (ד) והוא לא רצה לבוא אצל יפתח בבראשית רבה* : וכתיב אשר לא צויתי · בירמיה כתיב בפרשת בקבוק ובנו את במות (*התופת אשר בגיא בן הנם) לשרוף את (בנותיהם ואת) בניהם באש אשר לא [צויתי ולא] דברתי ולא עלתה על לבי שלא תאמרו הלא צוה כמו כן הקב"ה ליפתח ומישע ואברהם כי מעולם לא צויתי למישע לשרוף את בנו באש דכתיב ויקח את בנו הבכור אשר ימלך תחתיו ויעלהו עולה על החומה ולשמים נתכוון כסבור היה לרצות להקב"ה והאי דכתיב* על שרפו עצמות מלך אדום לשיד מילתא אחרינא הוא ולא דברתי ליפתח (ה) מימים ימימה ותהי חק בישראל ובתרגום מזכיר פנחס לגנאי ויפתח לגנאי אלמא לא היה הקב"ה רוצה בבתו שהרי מזכירים לגנאי לפי שלא הלכו זה אצל זה לבטל הנדר ה"ג ולא עלתה על לבי זה יצחק בן אברהם כלומר שאע"פ שצויתי לו מעולם לא עלתה על לבי לשחוט בנו אלא לנסותו מפני קטיגורו היינו שטן כדאמר בסנהדרין בהאחנקין (דף פט:) ויהי אחר הדברים האלה אחר דבריו של שטן וכו' ואית דלא גרסינן האי ולא עלתה על לבי "דטעי בקרא אחרינא דלא כתב אלא אשר לא צויתי ולא דברתי (ירמיה ז' פסוק כא) ובפרשת בקבוק כתיב כל הני שלשה אשר לא צויתי ולא דברתי ולא עלתה על לבי · בתנחומא אשר לא צויתי זו בתו של יפתח אע"פ שצויתי לו תורה ומלות מטה זו לא צויתי עליו ולא דברתי זה בנו של מישע מלך מואב והלא מישע נכרי הוא ולא חולין הוא לי לדבר עמו אפילו דיבור בעלמא · ובאגדה קא חשיב כלב בהדייהו אשר יכה את קרית ספר ולכדה וגו' ורבי יונתן דלא חשיב ליה דבגמרא פשיט ליה להאי קרא בהלכות שנשתכחו בימי אבלו של משה כדאמרינן בתמורה (דף טז·) ואין לחוש שתשרה רוח הקדש על עבד ועל ממזר כדאמרינן בנדרים (דף לח·) שאין שכינה שורה כו' מפי רבי· וגדעון ששאל למטע טל מעל הארץ ובגזה לבדה יהיה אין זה שלא כהוגן ומה תקלה יש אם יחסר העולם טל לילה אחת לבד מפי רבי : ויבוא כגשם לנו · פעמים ·אינו מתבקש שהוא סימן קללה בקיץ : (ו) דבר המתבקש לעולם · טל אפילו בימות החמה : פעמים נראה · כשהוא ערום נראה זרועו וכנגד לבו ואינו נראה כשהוא לבוש והכף נראית כל שעה שהיד נראית לעינים וי"ל על כפים (ז) על השמים טורח אדם שהוא בכסא וכן נשא לבבנו אל כפים (איכה ג) מפי רבי : (ח) ה"ג סברוה שאלה והזכרה חדא מילתא היא · כלומר הא דקתני אין שואלין את הגשמים היינו אין מזכירין את הגשמים : ומאן תנא · דאמר סמוך לימות הגשמים מזכירין אבל לא קודם לכן : רבי יהושע היא · דאמר משעת הנחת לולב הוא מזכיר דהיינו יום שמיני והוא סמוך לגשמים דמן החג ואילך הוא זמן גשמים :

עורפילא אפילו לפרצידא דתותי קלא מהניא ליה מאי עורפילא עורו פילי ואמר רבא האי צורבא מרבנן דמי לפרצידא דתותי קלא דכיון דנבט נבט ואמר רבא האי צורבא מרבנן דרתח אורייתא הוא דקא מרתחא ליה שנאמר °הלא כה דברי כאש נאם ה' ואמר רב אשי *כל ת"ח שאינו קשה כברזל אינו ת"ח שנא' °וכפטיש יפוצץ סלע א"ל רבי אבא לרב אשי אתון מהתם מתניתו לה אנן מהכא מתנינן לה דכתיב °ארץ אשר אבניה ברזל אל תקרי אבניה אלא בוניה אמר רבינא אפ"ה מיבעי ליה לאיניש למילף נפשיה בניחותא שנאמר °והסר כעס מלבך וגו' א"ר שמואל בר נחמני אמר רבי יונתן שלשה שאלו שלא כהוגן לשנים *השיבוהו כהוגן לאחד השיבוהו שלא כהוגן ואלו הן אליעזר עבד אברהם ושאול בן קיש ויפתח הגלעדי אליעזר עבד אברהם דכתיב (א) °והיה הנערה אשר אומר אליה הטי נא כדך וגו' יכול אפי' חיגרת אפי' סומא השיבו כהוגן ונזדמנה לו רבקה שאול בן קיש דכתיב °והיה האיש אשר יכנו יעשרנו המלך עושר גדול ואת בתו יתן לו יכול אפי' עבד אפילו ממזר השיבו כהוגן ונזדמן לו דוד יפתח הגלעדי דכתיב °והיה היוצא אשר יצא מדלתי ביתי וגו' יכול אפילו דבר טמא השיבו שלא כהוגן נזדמנה לו בתו והיינו דקאמר להו נביא לישראל °הצרי אין בגלעד אם רופא אין שם וכתיב °אשר לא צויתי ולא דברתי ולא עלתה על לבי אשר לא צויתי זה בנו של מישע מלך מואב שנאמר *°ויקח את בנו הבכור אשר ימלך תחתיו ויעלהו עולה ולא דברתי (ג) זה יפתח ולא עלתה על לבי זה יצחק בן אברהם אמר רבי ברכיה אף כנסת ישראל שאלה שלא כהוגן והקב"ה השיבה כהוגן שנא' °ונדעה נרדפה לדעת את ה' כשחר נכון מוצאו ויבוא כגשם לנו אמר לה הקב"ה בתי את שואלת דבר שפעמים מתבקש ופעמים אינו מתבקש אבל אני אהיה לך דבר המתבקש לעולם שנאמר °אהיה כטל לישראל ועוד שאלה שלא כהוגן אמרה לפניו רבש"ע °שימני כחותם על לבך כחותם על זרועך א"ל הקב"ה בתי את שואלת דבר שפעמים נראה ופעמים אינו נראה אבל אני אעשה לך דבר שנראה לעולם שנאמר °הן על כפים חקותיך : אין שואלין את הגשמים כו' : סברוה שאלה והזכרה חדא מילתא היא מאן תנא אמר רבא °ר' יהושע היא דאמר *משעת הנחתו א"ל אביי אפילו תימא רבי אליעזר שאלה לחוד והזכרה לחוד ואיכא דאמרי לימא רבי

ירמיה כג · שם · דברים ח · קהלת יא · בראשית כד · שמואל א יז · שופטים יא · ירמיה ח · ירמיה יט · מלכים ב ג · הושע ו · הושע יד · שיר השירים ח · ישעיה מט

עורפילא. היינו גשם דק אפילו לפרצידא דתותי קלא מהניא פי' פרצידא זו גרעין שהוא מתחת האבן היינו כמו חטה שמתחת הקרקע : מאי עורפילא עורו פילי · פי' מעורכן ומלמיהן פילי פי' אותן העומדים בסדקי הארץ : שלשה שאלו שלא כהוגן · אליעזר שאול ויפתח וא"ת אמאי לא חשיב כלב בן יפונה שאמר אשר יכה את קרית ספר ולכדה ונתתי לו את עכסה בתי לאשה אמאי לא פריך כמו הכא יכול ממזר או עבד וי"ל דהא דקאמר כלב שיתן לו (ס) הקב"ה כל מי שיכול לחזור אותן הלכות ששכחו בימי אבלו של משה אתן לו עכסה בתי וי"מ דלכך נקראת *עכסה שכל הרואה אותה כועס על אשתו וזהו ודאי משום צניעות יתירה דקא חזו בה והיה סומך דזכותה וזכות דידיה מסייע דלא מזדווגין לה אלא כפי מעשיה כדאיתא בסוטה (דף ב·) דאין מזווגין וכו' : יכול אפי' חיגרת או סומא · תימה אמאי לא נקט הכא גבי אליעזר עבד אברהם כמו דקאמר גבי שאול בסמוך יכול אפי' ממזרת או שפחה וכו' ואמר רש"י משום דגבי אליעזר לא שייך עדיין ממזרת דהא לא נתנה תורה אי נמי דגבי אשה לא דייק עלמא אלא ליופי וא"ת היכי קאמר דשאל אליעזר שלא כהוגן והא לא אמר אלא אשר אומר אליה הטי נא כדך ואם יראה שתהא חיגרת או סומא לא יאמר לה וי"ל דה"פ יכול אפילו חיגרת ואפילו סומא יכול אפי' חיגרת שיהיה לה אפילו רגל של עץ והוא לא יהא רואה או סומא כגון שיש לה עינים יפים ואינה רואה כלל : והיינו דקאמר להו נביא לישראל הצרי אין בגלעד אם רופא אין שם · כלומר להתיר נדרו ליפתח והא הוה פנחס ואמאי לא הלך יפתח אצלו להתיר נדרו אלא מתוך גסות רוחו אמר לא אלך אצלו שאני שופט ונגיד אלא יבא אצלי ופנחס אמר ליתי גבאי דאנא כהנא ועל ידי תהא פטורה שהייתי (י) שורה ומתיר הנדר ופוטר אותה ולבסוף נענשו שניהם יפתח נענש שנפלו אבריו קודם מיתה כדכתיב ויקבר בערי גלעד ופנחס נענש דכתיב לפנים היה ה' עמו* :

[כל זה ליתא במ"צ סוף סדר בחקותי]

[פי' תוספות סוכה נב. ד"ה אם ברזל]

[נ"ל השיבום יעב"ץ]

רש"א

[פ' חיי שרה]

נ"ל בכבל

רש"א

[סנהדרין לט:]

[עמוס ב]

[לעיל ב:]

[נ"ל משום דטעו ולי"ס כרש"י שבפי"]

רבינו חננאל

לפירות : עורו פילי . פי' הטפה היורדת בכח מערערת פילא כמו פילחא כדכתיב כמו פולח ובוקע בארץ·אפי' לפרצידא דתותי קלא . פי' שתחת האבן צומח *)וכן ת"ח דומה לפרי תחת האבן (ששואב שואב) וכיון שצומח [צומח] בבת אחת . צורבא מרבנן דרתחא אורייתא מרתחא ליה שנאמר הלא כה דברי כאש : אמר רב שמואל בר נחמני א"ר יונתן ג' שאלו שלא כהוגן אליעזר שאול ויפתח . ומצינו בבראשית רבה ד' הן ששאלו שלא כהוגן אליעזר שאול ויפתח וכלב ופשטיה כיון דשאול וכלב שוין דתרווייהו נתינת [בתם חשיב] להו כאחד . לפיכך תני הכא שלשה: אין שואלין הגשמים כיון ששנינו כאן שאילת הגשמים סמוך לגשמים היא הוצרכנו לומר סברוה שאלה והזכרה ביום אחד הן הניחא לר' יהושע דאמר משעת הנחתו מזכיר ומיד שואל כי אין שאלה אלא בתפלת החול בי"ח בברכת השנים אלא לר' אליעזר קשיא ושנינן הזכרה לחוד ושאלה לחוד לזמן אחר ולאו כי הדדי :

*) עי' מ"ש בפירוש רבינו לקמן ריש פ"ג ושייך כאן .

רבינו גרשום

עורפילא· מיטרא דקה׳ פרצידא גרגר׳ דתותי קלא. תחת קרקע קשה: עורו פילי התעוררו בקעים כלומר שמכנים המטר דקה בבקעים ומוציא התבואה שבהם: כיון דנבט שבקע ויוצא אף ת"ח כיון שיוצא שמו בעולם שוב הולך וגדול בכל שעה : שאינו קשה כברזל . שאינו קשה לרצות׳ הצרי אין בגלעד כלומר שהיה יכול לילך אצל אליהו ומתיר לו נדרו׳ : על לבי זה יצחק שלא היה בלבו של הקב"ה שישחטהו אלא בפה כדי לנסותו : על כפים חקותיך . וידים נראין לעולם : אין שואלין את הגשמים . ותן טל ומטר : ר' יהודה אמר האחרון מזכיר . גבורת גשמים וה"ה דשואלין ותן טל ומטר : מאן תנא דהתחלת שאלה והזכרה מצי למיהוי ביום אחד : דאמר משעת הנחתו דהיינו בשביעי מתחילין להזכיר שהוא חולו של מועד מצי להתחיל לשאול בברכת השנים שהרי מתפללין אתה חונן . דאי ר' אליעזר כיון דאמר בראשון מתחיל להזכיר לא מצי למיהוי התחלת הזכרה והתחלת שאלה ביום אחד דביו"ט ראשון ליכא שאלה שהרי אין מתפללין בו אתה חונן ולא מצי למישאל אלא בברכת השנים אפי' תימא דקתני אין שואלין ר' אליעזר היא ולא תימא שאלה והזכרה כהדדי .

גליון הש"ס

גמ' ר"י היא דאמר משנת הנחתו . תמוה לי אמאי נקט ר"י דברייתא ולא נקט ר"י דמתני' מיו"ט האחרון הח"כ מאלאי כעזיה בספר סמכרים לריא"ז דמחק זה וכנ"ל סתם מני ר"י היא :

הגהות הב"ח

(א) גמ' אליעזר עבד אברהם דכתיב ובנות אנשי העיר יוצאות וגו' והיה הנערה אשר : (ב) שם ולא דברתי זו בתו של יפתח : (ג) רש"י ד"ה ובנות כו' השקיני נא כיון מנחש : (ד) ד"ה והיינו כו' יפתח לילך אצלו מתוך גסות רוחו אמר לא אלך אצלו שאני שופט ונגיד ופנחס לא טיה רוצה לבא אצל יפתח שהוא עניה כנ"ל: (ה) ד"ה וכתיב כו' ולא דברתי ליפתח שאמר מימים ימימה כו' ולית דלא גרסי כו': (ו) ד"ה ויבוא כו' קללה בקיץ הס"ד ואח"כ מה"ד טל דבר המתבקש לעולם אפילו בימות : (ז) ד"ה פעמים כו' וי"ש לומר על כפים השמים כו' כנ"ל ותיבת על נמחק : (ח) בא"ד מפי רבי הס"ד ואח"כ מה"ד שאלה והזכרה כו' ותיבות ה"ג סברוה נמחק ונ"ב וכן פי' למאי דקאמר שאלה וכו' : (ס) תוס' ד"ה שלשה וכו' שיתן לו כתו סכי קאמר כל מי וכו' : (י) שם ד"ה והיינו וכו' שהייתי מורה ומתיר :

יא א מיי' פ"ב מהל' תפלה הל' טז סמג עשין יט טוש"ע א"ח סי' קיז סעיף א:

רבי יהושע היא דאמר משעת הנחתו אמר רבא אפילו תימא רבי אליעזר שאלה לחוד והזכרה לחוד: רבי יהודה אומר העובר לפני התיבה כו': ורמינהו *עד מתי שואלין את הגשמים (א) ר' יהודה אומר עד שיעבור הפסח ר' מאיר אומר עד שיעבור ניסן אמר רב חסדא לא קשיא כאן לשאול כאן להזכיר מישאל שאיל ואזיל להזכיר ביו"ט הראשון פסיק אמר עולא הא דרב חסדא קשיא *°כחומץ לשינים וכעשן לעינים ומה במקום שאינו שואל מזכיר במקום ששואל אינו דין שיהא מזכיר אלא אמר עולא תרי תנאי אליבא דר' יהודה רב יוסף אמר מאי עד שיעבור הפסח עד שיעבור שליח צבור ראשון היורד ביו"ט ראשון של פסח א"ל אביי שאלה ביו"ט מי איכא א"ל אין שואל מתורגמן וכי מתורגמן שואל דבר שאינו צריך לצבור אלא מחוורתא כדעולא רבה אמר מאי עד שיעבור הפסח עד שיעבור זמן שחיטת הפסח וכתחילתו כן סופו מה תחילתו מזכיר אע"פ שאינו שואל אף סופו מזכיר אע"פ שאינו שואל א"ל אביי בשלמא תחילתו מזכיר (ג) הזכרה נמי ריצוי שאלה היא אלא סופו מאי ריצוי שאלה איכא אלא מחוורתא כדעולא *) א"ר אסי א"ר יוחנן הלכה כר' יהודה א"ל ר' זירא לר' אסי ומי אמר רבי יוחנן הכי והתנן *בשלשה במרחשון שואלין את הגשמים רבן גמליאל אומר בשבעה בו *וא"ר אלעזר **הלכה כרבן גמליאל א"ל **) גברא אגברא קא רמית איבעית אימא לא קשיא כאן לשאול כאן להזכיר והאמר ר' יוחנן במקום ששואל מזכיר ההוא להפסקה איתמר והאמר ר' יוחנן התחיל להזכיר מתחיל לשאול פסק מלשאול פסק מלהזכיר אלא לא קשיא *הא לן הא להו מאי שנא לדידן דאית לן פירי בדברא לדידהו נמי אית להו עולי רגלים כי קא"ר יוחנן בזמן שאין בית המקדש קיים השתא דאתית להכי הא והא לדידהו ולא קשיא כאן בזמן שבית המקדש קיים °כאן בזמן שאין בית המקדש קיים ואנן דאית לן תרי יומי היכי עבדינן אמר רב מתחיל במוספין ופוסק במנחה ערבית ושחרית וחוזר במוספין אמר להו שמואל פוקו ואמרו ליה לאבא אחר שעשיתו קודש תעשהו חול אלא אמר שמואל מתחיל במוספין ובמנחה ופוסק ערבית ושחרית וחוזר ומתחיל במוספין

*) גי' הרא"ש א"ר יוסי בר חנינא הלכה כו' **) [ב"ק מג: סנהדרין כט: ל: חולין נג:]

רבא

רש"י

הכי גרסינן ואיכא דאמרי לימא ר' יהושע היא אפי' תימא רבי אליעזר כו' · ולא גרסינן סברוה שאלה לחוד והזכרה לחוד דהא לא משתמע ממתני': עד אימתי שואלין את הגשמים · בסוף ימות הגשמים: עד שיעבור הפסח · דאמרינן כל חולו של מועד ותן טל ומטר: עד שילא ניסן · וכדמפיק טעמא במתני': הכי גרסינן אמר רב חסדא כאן לשאול כאן להזכיר מישאל שאיל ואזיל והזכרה ביו"ט ראשון פוסק · לשאול שואל והולך עד שיעבור הפסח כדקתני עד מתי שואלין כו' להזכיר אינו מזכיר אלא בתפלת יוצר של יו"ט ראשון: במקום שאינו שואל · ביו"ט האחרון של חג שאינו מתפלל תפלתו תפלת חול דאין שאלה אלא בברכת השנים: מזכיר · גבורות גשמים כדאמר רבי יהודה האחרון מזכיר: במקום שהוא שואל · בחולו של מועד של פסח: תרי תנאי · חד אמר עד שיעבור [...] ואמר שאלה עד הפסח והזכרה שיכול להזכיר ביו"ט מזכיר ביו"ט הראשון של פסח בתפלת יוצר ובמוספין פוסק: רב יוסף אמר · האי דקתני עד אימתי שואלין עד שיעבור כו' ה"ק עד שיעבור שליח צבור כו' והיינו כאידך רבי יהודה דמתני' דאמר הראשון מזכיר האחרון אינו מזכיר: שאלה ביו"ט מי איכא · וכי מתפלל הוא תפלת חול שאתה אומר עד שיעבור הפסח דהיינו (ג) זמן שליח צבור של תפלת יו"ט הראשון של פסח: אמר ליה אין שאלה דמתורגמן · בדרשה שהוא דורש אומר ברכת שאלה לבדה: דבר שאינו צריך לצבור · דכיון דזמן הפסקה הוא לאו אורח ארעא למישאל בצבור דבר שאינו צריך: עד שיעבור זמן שחיטת פסח · (ד) חצות יום דארבעה עשר עד שיעבור חצות דהיינו כל תפלת יוצר ואשמעינן ר' יהודה דבמנחה דערבי פסחים אע"ג דמצלין תפלת חול מפסיקין ולא יאמר ותן טל ומטר ואע"ג דמדכרינן עד למחר במוספין פוסק השאלה בתפלת מנחה של ערב יו"ט הראשון והזכרה שיכול להזכיר ביום טוב מזכיר עד תפלת מוסף של יום טוב הראשון: כתחילתו · שהוא מזכיר תחלה ביום טוב אחרון של חג ואינו שואל עד לאחר. התם (ה) כך [...] ערב יו"ט הראשון ומזכיר עד מוסף של יו"ט ראשון והכא ליכא למיפרך שאלה ביו"ט מי איכא: דהזכרה נמי צורך שאלה היא · שמרצה תחלה לפי שא"א לו לשאול ביו"ט וכיון דאיכא שאלה אבתריה מזכיר הוא לרצויי בעלמא: אבל סופו · למה הוא מזכיר הואיל ואינו צריך לשאול מכאן ואילך הא כיון דאפסקה מאתמול גלית אדעתך דלא ניחא לך בהו ואמאי מזכיר: הלכה כרבי יהודה · דאמר העובר לפני התיבה וכו': מי אמר רבי יוחנן הכי · דהלכה כרבי יהודה דמזכיר ביו"ט האחרון: בשלשה במרחשון · הכי קים להו דהוה זמן גשמים כו': הלכה כרבן גמליאל · דאינו שואל עד שבעה במרחשון וקא ס"ד דבמקום שהוא שואל מזכיר עד דמשני לקמן: כאן לשאול · בשבעה במרחשון: כאן להזכיר · מיו"ט האחרון ור' יוחנן אית ליה דרבי אלעזר: והא א"ר יוחנן במקום ששואל מזכיר · (ו) במקום שאינו שואל אינו מזכיר והיכי א"ר יוחנן דהלכה כר' יהודה שמזכיר ביו"ט האחרון הא ליכא שאלה דאין אומר ברכת השנים ביו"ט: להפסקה איתמר · דכשהוא מפסיק לשאלה בערב הפסח פוסק נמי להזכרה דהכי משמע במקום ששואל מזכיר: והא תרוייהו איתמר · התחלה והפסקה: יתחיל לשאול · דהיינו בחול שיכול לשאול: פסק מלשאול · בערב הפסח פוסק מלהזכיר אלמא לא סבירא ליה כרבי יהודה והיכי אמר הלכה כמותו: הא לן והא להו · לבני בבל שיש לנו תבואה ופירות בשדה כל תשרי אין מזכירין עד שבעה במרחשון ושם שואלים כדאמר רבי יוחנן מתחיל להזכיר מתחיל לשאול: והא להו · לבני ארץ ישראל דקוצרין בניסן ואוספין בתשרי מזכירין ביו"ט האחרון כרבי יהודה דאמר רב אסי הלכה כמותו: בדברא. מדבר כלומר בשדות: אית להו עולי רגלים · ואם ירדו להן גשמים קשה להן בחזירתן: אלא כי א"ר יוחנן · הלכה כר' יהודה דמזכיר מיו"ט האחרון כו' בזמן שאין בהמ"ק קיים וליכא עולי רגלים מזכיר: כאן בזמן שבית המקדש קיים. דאיכא עולי רגלים אינו מזכיר עד ז' במרחשון: אנן דאית לן תרי יומי · שני ימים טובים אחרונים שמיני ספק שביעי ותשיעי ספק שמיני לרבי יהודה דאמר מיו"ט האחרון באיזה מהן מזכיר: מתחיל במוסף · של שמיני ספק שביעי דשמא יו"ט האחרון הוא: ופוסק במנחה · שמא שביעי חול הוא ואין זמן הזכרה עד מוסף של מחר: ופוסק נמי בערבית ושחרית · של תשיעי ספק שמיני: לאבא · חברי: לאחר שעשיתו קודש · לשמיני ספק שביעי שהזכרת בו גבורות גשמים כרבי יהודה מיו"ט האחרון: תעשהו חול · בתמיה שמפסיק במנחה של אותו היום: ופוסק ערבית ושחרית · דלאו היינו תפלה של אותו היום:

רבא

תוספות

ואמר ר' אלעזר הלכה כר"ג ואמר דאין שואלין עד שבעה וכו' · פירוש ולית אמרת הלכה כר' יהודה בהא דקאמר במתני' רבי יהודה אומר העובר לפני התיבה בי"ט האחרון של חג האחרון מזכיר והראשון אינו מזכיר ומדמינן לעיל שאלה להזכרה דפריך ורמינהו עד מתי שואלין את הגשמים עד שיעבור וכו' ומשני גברא אגברא וכו': והא אמר רבי יוחנן במקום ששואלין הגשמים מזכיר · ומשני ההוא להפסקה פי' דבמקום שמפסיק מלשאול מפסיק מלהזכיר אבל מתחיל קודם להזכיר וטעמא הוי דהזכרה הוה ריצוי שאלה ומש"ה ליכא חששא אם מזכיר קודם: הא לן · פירוש לבני בבל (ז) [א] עד לאחר שבעה במרחשון דאית נהו פירי בדברא ובארץ ליכא חששא דהא יכולים פירותיהן להיות יבשים בלא הולכה למדבר: והא להו · כי המתחיל להזכיר יתחיל לשאול:

רבא

רבינו חננאל

פיסקא ר' יהודה אומר העובר לפני התיבה ורמינן עלה עד [...] ר' יהודה אומר עד שיעבור הפסח ומשני רב חסדא פוסק מלהזכיר מיום הראשון של פסח ושואל עד שיעבור הפסח. וזהו כחומץ לשינים (וכעשן) שקהה לשינים וכעשן לעינים. ומשני עולא תרי תנאי ואליבא דר' יהודה [רב יוסף אמר כו'] ואקשינן ושאלה ביו"ט מי איכא ופריק אין לשאול מתורגמן ומדלא דחי לה ואמר מי איכא תורגמן בצלותא שמעינן מינה דבי דינא הוו מוקמי מתורגמן לישאל מלתא דהוה צריכא להו לפיכך אמר אפשר להוא לשאל בערבית ושחרית של יו"ט יהי רצון מלפניך ה' אלהינו שתתן טל ומטר על פני האדמה: רבה אמר מאי עד שיעבור הפסח עד שיעבור זמן שחיטת הפסח. פי' שואלין את הגשמים עד ערב הפסח זמן שחיטת הפסח ופוסק ומזכיר עד מנחה ואע"פ שפוסק מלישאל עדיין מזכיר ליל ט"ו ושחרית ביו"ט ופוסק נמצא מזכיר באחרי שפסק מלשאל כתחלתו מה תחלתו מזכיר אע"פ [...] ודחה לה אביי בשלמא תחלתו מזכיר כי הוא ריצוי לשאלה. כלומר להבא עוד צריך לשאל. אלא סיפא הזכרה בלא שאלה למה כו' אלא מחוורתא כדעולא. דאמר תרי תנאי אליבא דר' יהודה: א"ר אסי א"ר יוחנן הלכה כר' יהודה דקתני העובר לפני התיבה ביו"ט האחרון של חג האחרון מזכיר. פירוש ש"ץ המתפלל מוסף הוא מזכיר מוריד הגשם ומזכיר והולך עד יו"ט הראשון של פסח בתפלת שחרית ואח"כ פוסק. ואקשינן איני דהלכתא כר' יהודה והאמר ר' אלעזר הלכתא כר"ג דתני בשבעה במרחשון שואלין את הגשמים ושנינן רבי אלעזר קא רמית אר' יוחנן. איבעית אימא הלכה כר' יהודה להזכיר כלומר מזכירין מיו"ט (הראשון) [האחרון] של (פסח) [חג] והלכתא כר"ג לשאל שאין שואלין את הגשמים ואין אומרים ותן טל ומטר אלא בז' במרחשון ונדחית זו דהא בהדיא לית ליה לר' יוחנן הפסקה בין הזכרה לשאלה דאמר ר' יוחנן התחיל להזכיר ישאל פסק מלשאל יפסק מלהזכיר. אלא לא קשיא הא דר' יוחנן לבני ארץ ישראל והא דאמר רבי אלעזר עד ז' במרחשון לבני בבל משום דאית להו פירא בדברא והמטר מפסידם ואקשינן בני ארץ ישראל נמי יש להם עולי רגלים. ואם ישאלו מיום טוב (הראשון) [האחרון] של חג ירד המטר נמצא המטר מעכבן בחזירתן ואוקימנא בזמן הזה דליכא בית המקדש [...]

רבינו גרשום

אלא שאלה לחוד והזכרה לחוד דמזכירין ביום ראשון ושואלין בחולו של מועד. אמר רבא [אפילו תימא] ר' אליעזר היא דאמר הזכרה ביו"ט הראשון ולא מצי למישאל ביה שהרי אין מתפלל אתה חונן· דראשון מזכיר וה"ה שואל· ר"י אמר עד שיעבור הפסח והיכי אמר במתני' שאינו שואל אלא עד יום ראשון של פסח כאן לשאול כאן להזכיר. הא דאמר ר' יהודה במתניתין הראשון מזכיר ביו"ט ראשון של פסח היינו להזכיר אבל לשאל יכול לשאל עד שיעבור הפסח: במקום שאינו שואל מזכיר· שהרי מתחיל להזכיר בחג ואינו שואל עד ששים בתקופה: מקום שהוא שואל דקאמרת דשואל עד שיעבור הפסח: על אחת כמה וכמה שיזכיר (ומתרץ) [והיכי תריץ] רב חסדא דרבי יהודה קאמר שאינו מזכיר אלא עד יום ראשון של פסח וה"ה לשאלה *) דפרכת האמר ר' יהודה ששואל עד שיעבור הפסח תרי תנאי ואליבא דר"י: עד שיעבור ש"ץ ראשון של יו"ט ראשון היינו נמי כדאמר ר' יהודה במתניתין הראשון [מזכיר האחרון] אינו מזכיר וה"ה לשאלה: שאלה ביו"ט מי איכא דקאמרת דקאמר ר' יהודה ביו"ט ראשון שואל והא אינו מתפלל אתה חונן והיאך אמר שאלה בברכת השנים. שואל במתורגמן המתורגמן [...] ביו"ט של פסח אומר שאלה בדרשה: דבר שאינו צריך לצבור כלומר שאין הצבור שואלין בתפלה ישאל המתורגמן אלא כדעולא דלא תריץ ליה עד שיעבור ש"ץ אלא לאחר הפסח ממש: עד זמן שחיטת פסח דהיינו י"ד אבל ביו"ט ראשון אינו שואל והאי דקאמר ר' יהודה במתניתין הראשון היינו להזכרה ולא לשאלה מה תחלתו מזכיר אע"פ שאינו שואל שמזכיר בחג ואינו [...] ששים בתקופה: אף סופו מזכיר. עד יום ראשון ואינו שואל אלא עד י"ד: דהזכרה נמי ריצוי [...] היא כלומר להכי מזכיר בחג הואיל ועתיד לשאול בששים בתקופה שלאחריו. מאי ריצוי שאלה [...] **) עדיין הוא עתיד לשאול אלא מכיון שפסק מלשאול שוב אינו מזכיר אלא כדעולא דתריץ עד [...] הפסח ממש והא דא"ר יהודה במתני' עד יום ראשון של פסח ***) היינו להזכרה ולא לשאלה [...] יהודה דאמר מזכיר ביום אחרון של חג וה"ה לשאלה כאן לשאול כאן להזכיר הא דאמר ר' יוחנן [...]

*) נראה דצ"ל אלא אמר עולא הא דפרכת וכו'. **) נראה דצ"ל והא הו אינו עתיד לישאל וכו'. ***) כדכר תמוה דהא תי' זה כבר דחי הגמ' לעיל ושולא הא מתרץ דתרי תנאי אליבא דר"י [...]

הגהות הב"ח

(א) גמ' ר' יהודה אומר וכו' [...]

הגהות הגר"א

[א] תוס' ד"ה הא לן פי' לבני בבל אין שואלין עד שבעה. כצ"ל (ועמ"ש רבינו גאו"ח ריש סימן קי"ז):

גליון הש"ס

גמ' כאן בזמן שאין בית המקדש קיים. עי' יומא דף יג ע"א תוס' ד"ה כלכה:

(ס) ד"ה כתחילתו כו' לאחר החג הס"ד ואח"כ מה"ד כך בסופו אינו שואל בליל[י] ערב יו"ט: (ו) ד"ה והא אמר כו' מזכיר הא במקום: (ז) תוס' ד"ה הא לן פי' לבני בבל אין מזכירין [...] במרחשון דאית להו פירי בדברא כי המתחיל להזכיר יתחיל לשאול והא להו פי' לבני א"י ליכא חש[שא] יכולים כו' כצ"ל וד"ה והא להו נמחק:

רבא אמר כיון שהתחיל שוב אינו פוסק וכן אמר רב ששת כיון שהתחיל שוב אינו פוסק ואף רב הדר ביה דאמר רב חננאל אמר רב מונה עשרים ואחד יום כדרך שמונה עשרה ימים מר"ה עד יוה"כ *ומתחיל וכיון שהתחיל שוב אינו פוסק °והלכתא כיון שהתחיל שוב אינו פוסק: **מתני'** *עד מתי שואלין את הגשמים ר' יהודה אומר עד שיעבור הפסח ר' *מאיר אומר עד שיצא ניסן שנאמר °ויורד לכם גשם מורה ומלקוש בראשון: **גמ'** א"ל רב נחמן לר' יצחק יורה בניסן (א) יורה במרחשון הוא (*דתנן) *יורה במרחשון ומלקוש בניסן א"ל הכי אמר רבי יוחנן בימי יואל בן פתואל נתקיים מקרא זה דכתיב ביה °יתר הגזם אכל הארבה וגו' אותה שנה יצא אדר ולא ירדו גשמים ירדה להם רביעה ראשונה באחד בניסן אמר להם נביא לישראל צאו וזרעו אמרו לו מי שיש לו קב חטים או קבים שעורין יאכלנו ויחיה או יזרענו וימות אמר להם אעפ"כ צאו וזרעו נעשה להם נס ונתגלה להם מה שבכתלין ומה שבחורי נמלים יצאו וזרעו שני ושלישי ורביעי וירדה להם רביעה שניה בחמשה בניסן הקריבו עומר בששה עשר בניסן נמצאת תבואה הגדילה בששה חדשים גדילה באחד עשר יום נמצא עומר הקרב מתבואה של ששה חדשים קרב מתבואה של אחד עשר יום ועל אותו הדור הוא אומר °הזורעים בדמעה ברנה יקצרו הלך ילך ובכה נושא משך הזרע וגו' מאי הלך ילך ובכה נושא משך וגו' א"ר יהודה שור כשהוא חורש הולך ובוכה ובחזירתו אוכל חזיז מן התלם וזהו בא יבא ברנה מאי נושא אלומותיו א"ר חסדא ואמרי לה במתניתא תנא קנה זרת שיבולת זרתים א"ל רב נחמן לר' יצחק מאי דכתיב °כי קרא ה' לרעב וגם בא אל הארץ שבע שנים בהנך שבע שנים מאי אכול א"ל הכי אמר רבי יוחנן שנה ראשונה אכלו מה שבבתים שניה אכלו מה שבשדות שלישית בשר בהמה טהורה רביעית בשר בהמה טמאה חמישית בשר שקצים ורמשים ששית בשר בניהם ובנותיהם שביעית בשר זרועותיהם לקיים מה שנאמר °איש בשר זרועו יאכלו וא"ל רב נחמן לר' יצחק מאי דכתיב °בקרבך קדוש ולא אבוא בעיר משום דבקרבך קדוש לא אבוא בעיר א"ל הכי א"ר יוחנן אמר הקב"ה לא אבוא בירושלים של מעלה עד שאבוא לירושלים של מטה ומי איכא ירושלים למעלה אין דכתיב °ירושלם הבנויה כעיר שחוברה לה יחדיו וא"ל רב נחמן לר' יצחק מאי דכתיב °ובאחת יבערו ויכסלו מוסר הבלים עץ הוא א"ל הכי א"ר יוחנן אחת היא שמבערת רשעים בגיהנם מאי היא ע"ז כתיב הכא מוסר הבלים עץ הוא וכתיב התם °הבל המה מעשה תעתועים וא"ל רב נחמן לר' יצחק מ"ד °כי שתים רעות עשה עמי תרתין הוא דהוו עשרין *וארבע שביקא להו א"ל הכי א"ר יוחנן אחת שהיא שקולה

רבא אמר כיון שהתחיל · בשמיני ספק שביעי שוב אינו פוסק: הדר ביה · ממאי דאמר פוסק: מונה כ"א יום · מראש השנה עד שמיני ספק שביעי של חג כדרך שמונה מר"ה עד יוה"כ י' ימים שמתחיל למנות מיום ראשון של ר"ה ומזכיר מכאן ואילך וזהו שמזכיר בשמיני ספק שביעי שהוא כ"ב שוב אינו תורה אור פוסק והא דמתחילין אנו למנות מיום א' דהא דאנו עושין ב' ימים לאו משום ספק דשמא עיברו לאלול דהא אנן בקיאין בקביעא דירחא אלא משום דמנהג אבותינו בידינו ל"א מונה כ"א יום כדרך שמונה ס' כלומר אם עיברו אלול לא יחשוב מיום ראשון של ר"ה כ"א יום שאם כן לא ימלאו בידו אלא כ' ובליס (ג) ביום טוב שביעי יום נטילת ערבה אלא מיום שמתחילין למנות עשרה ימים לעשות בעשירי יוה"כ יתחיל למנות באלו שבכך לא יטעה שיום הכפורים יום אחד לבד וידע מהיכן התחילו למנות לו וביום שכלין כ"א (ג) דהיינו ביום טוב אחרון מתחיל להזכיר וכיון שהתחיל שוב אינו פוסק: א"ל רב נחמן לרב יצחק יורה בניסן הוא · דכתיב ויורד לכם גשם מורה ומלקוש בראשון בתמיה: והא במרחשון הוא · כדתניא לקמן ובספרי הוא: יורה ומלקוש · מפרש לקמן: אמר ליה · ודאי במרחשון הוא ומקרא זה בימי יואל בן פתואל נתקיים שיורה ומלקוש היה בראשון ע"י נס שהיה רעב שבע שנים דכתיב כי קרא ה' לרעב וגם בא אל הארץ שבע שנים וכתיב יתר הגזם אכל הארבה וגו': הכי גרסינן יצא אדר ולא ירדו גשמים · ולא זרעו רוב אדר לא גרסינן: רביעה ראשונה · התחלת גשמים ולקמן (דף ו:) מפרש רביעה שמרביע את הארץ: או יזרענו וימות · ברעב קודם שתגדל התבואה החדשה שלא יהיה לו מה יאכל: נעשה להם נס כו' · והיינו דכתיב ושלמתי לכם את השנים אשר אכל הארבה וגו': נתגלה להם תבואה שבחורי נמלים ומה שבכתלים · שאגרו העכברים: יצאו וזרעו · (ד) וזרעו מה שבידם: שני · בניסן ושלישי ורביעי ומה שמצאו אכלו ולאחר שזרעו ירדו להם גשמים בה' בניסן והקריבו עומר בט"ז בניסן מאותה תבואה חדשה: הגדילה בששה חדשים · מתשרי ועד ניסן: בי"א יום · מחמשה בניסן עד ט"ז: הזורעים בדמעה ברנה יקצורו · שלא היה להן מה לאכול: מאי הלך ילך ובכה · אם לבני אדם כבר נאמר הזורעים בדמעה ברנה יקצורו אלא על השור הכתוב אומר: בהליכתו · לחרוש התלם: ובחזירתו אוכל חזיז · שחת מן התלם שזרעו בהליכתן שכשהוא זורע מיד מתחלת ליגדל: מאי בא יבוא ברנה נושא אלומותיו · אם מפני התבואה שיש להם לאכול הרי כבר אמור ברנה יקצורו: שבולת זרתים · זהו נס גדול מה שאין כן דרך כל תבואה שהקנה פי שלשה וארבעה בשבולת: כי קרא ה' לרעב · בימי יהורם בן אחאב נאמר: מה שבשדות · ספיחים ומה שנשתייר בשדות: אכלו בשר בניהם · מקראם: משום דבקרבך קדוש · *שאתה מטיב מעשיך לא יבא הקב"ה בעיר: לא אבא בירושלים כו' · והכי קאמר עד שיהא בקרבך קדוש למטה דהיינו ירושלים לא אבוא בעיר שלמעלה: ירושלים הבנויה כעיר שחוברה לה יחדיו · ירושלים שלמטה תהא בנויה כעיר שחוברה לה שהיא כיוצא בה חבירתה ודוגמתה מכלל דאיכא ירושלים אחריתי והיכן אם לא למעלה: ובאחת יבערו ויכסלו מוסר הבלים עץ הוא · אי לאו גזרה שוה היה משמע אטומים כעץ לקבל מוסר ולשוא היו לוקין: באחת · עבירה שהן עושין יתבערו הכסילים רשעים: עשרים *וארבעה שביקא להו · בתמיה בפרשת התשפוט (יחזקאל כב) כ"ד עבירות שעברו ל"א שעברו על כ"ד ספרים: שקולה

ובחזירתו אוכל חזיז מן התלם וכו' · וקשיא הא דקאמר לעיל נמצא הגדילה בששה חדשים גדילה באחד עשר יום הוה ליה למימר גדילה בתליסר *ובי"ד יומי שהרי מיד מתחלת ליגדל ושמא י"ל דלכל המאוחרת שנזרעה בשלישית קאמר נמצא גדילה בי"א יום ול"ע:

לא אבוא בעיר · פירוש בעיר ר"ל בעיר ממש וי"מ פשטיה דקרא בעיר בשנאה כלומר לא אבוא בשנאה ועיר הוי ל' שנאה כמו ומלאו פני תבל ערים (ישעיה יד):

רבא אמר כיון שהתחיל שוב אינו פוסק · כלומר כיון שהתחיל ביום ראשון של (ה) אחרונים שוב אינו פוסק וכן הפסק:

יורה במרחשון הוא · פי' אקרא דכתיב ויורד לכם גשם מורה ומלקוש בראשון פריך דמתני' אפשר לתרך דאמלקוש קסמיך אבל ביורה מודה דבמרחשון:

רבינו חננאל

ואסקוה [מונה] כ"א יום מר"ה ועד יו"ט האחרון של חג ומתחיל להזכיר ביו"ט האחרון כדרך שמונה י' ימים מר"ה ועד יוה"כ והעשירי הוא יוה"כ. ומתחיל להזכיר וכיון שמתחיל שוב אינו פוסק וכן הלכה: מתני' עד מתי שואלין את הגשמים כו' א) הא אסיק' לשמעתא כי ש"ץ היורד לפני התיבה ביו"ט הראשון של פסח מזכיר מוריד הגשם ופוסק מלהזכיר והיורד במוסף אינו מזכיר ב) כיון שא"ר מאיר עד שיצא ניסן שנא' ויורד לכם גשם מורה ומלקוש בראשון ואקשינן והא מורה במרחשון הוא ומלקוש בניסן ושנינן בימי יואל בן פתואל ג) (ש"מ) [נאמר] מורה בניסן שיצא אדר ולא ירדו גשמים. ירד רביעה ראשונה באחד בניסן אמר להם הנביא צאו וזרעו נעשה להן נס ונתגלה להם החטים שאוגרין הנמלין בחורין ובכתלים ולקחו אותן וזרעו ירדה להן רביעה שנייה בחמשה בניסן וצמחו זרעים והקריבו העומר בי"ו בניסן. נמצאת תבואה הגדילה בו' חדשים גידלה בי"א יום על אותו דור נאמר הזורעים בדמעה ברנה יקצורו השור שהיה בהליכתו הולך כמו בוכה. בחזירתו היה אוכל חזיז. בא יבא ברנה [נושא] אלומותיו קנה זרת שבולת שתים. א"ל רב נחמן לר' יצחק הא דכתיב כי קרא ה' לרעב וגו' אותן ז' שנים מאי אכול א"ל הכי א"ר יוחנן שנה ראשונה אכלו מה שבבתים שניה אכלו מה שבשדות כו'. ותוב בעא מיניה בקרבך קדוש ולא אבוא בעיר א"ל הקדוש ברוך הוא לישראל שאינו בא בירושלים של מעלה עד שיבנה להם ירושלים של מטה וישרה שכינתו הקדושה בקרבם. ותוב בעא מיניה מ"ד ובאחת יבערו ויכסלו וגו'. א"ל אחת היא שמבערת הרשעים לגיהנם ומאי ניהי ע"ז. ותוב בעא מיניה מ"ד כי שתים רעות עשה עמי וגו' תרתי בלחוד הוא דעבוד. כ"ב שביקא להו יש מי שמפרש וכי יש עבירה הכתובה בכ"ד ספרים כלומר במקרא שלא עשו אותה ואמאי כתיב כי שתים רעות (וכ"ב דמתמה. כלומר וכי הניחו כ"ד ספרים עבירה הכתובה בהם שלא עשו אותה) ואנו קבלנו מרבותינו כי אלו הן כ"ד חטאות בכאן הם המפורשים בתלמוד א"י בפרק אלו שאין להם חלק ד) יש מן החכמים המפרשים שהיו אומרים כ"ד רעות אלו הן הנדברות בהאי קרא אותי עזבו מקור מים חיים. לחצוב להם. עזבך את ה' אלהיך. רעתך ומשובותיך ולא פחדתי אליך לא אעבור צועה זונה נהפכת נכתם עונך לא נטמאתי דרכך בגיא אהבתי זרים ואחריהם אלך הובישו המה מלכיהם שריהם כהניהם ונביאיהם אומרים לעץ אבי אתה ולאבן את ילדתנו כי פנו אלי עורף מספר עריך היו אלהיך אלו כ"ד רעות א"ר יוחנן לא גלו ישראל עד שנעשו כ"ד כתות של מינים שנאמר בן אדם שולח אני אותך וגו' אל גוי המורד לא נאמר אלא גוי המורדים ומצאנו במדרש חזית א"ר יוחנן כ"ד חטאות הוכיח יחזקאל הנביא את ישראל בפרשת התשפוט את עיר הדמים אלו הן עיר שופכת דם ועשתה גלולים טמאת השם רבת המהומה איש לזרועו היו בך למען שפוך דם ה) אב ואם הקלו בך לגר עשו בעושק בתוכך יתום ואלמנה הונו בך קדשי בזית ואת שבתותי חללת אנשי רכיל היו בך ואל ההרים אכלו בך זמה עשו בתוכך ערות אב גלה בך טמאת הנדה ענו בך ואיש את אשת רעהו עשה תועבה ואיש את כלתו טמא בזמה ואיש את אחותו בת אביו ענה בך שוחד לקחו בך נשך ותרבית לקחת ותבצעי רעיך בעשק ואותי שכחת נאם ה' ועל כולם לא חתם אלא על הגזל והנה הכיתי כפי אל בצעך אשר עשית ועל דמך אשר היו בתוכך. היעמוד לבך אם תחזקנה ידיך לימים אשר אני עושה אותך

א) נראה דר"ל דאסיקנא לעיל דאין הלכה כר"י דקך מתני' רק כאידך דר"י דש"ץ היורד וכו'. ב) נראה דצ"ל ר"מ אומר עד שיצא וכו'. ג) אולי צ"ל בימי יואל בן פתואל ירד מורה בניסן. ד) כאן נ"ל מ"ש א"ר לא גלו ישראל וכו'. ה) אב ואם נתקבים לג' וכן יתום ואלמנה כ"ה בערוך.

עין משפט נר מצוה: יב א ב מיי' פ"ב מהל' תפלה הל' טו טוש"ע א"ח סימן קיד סעיף ג ד:

מסורת הש"ס: לעיל ד: | [ג' רי"ף ורא"ש יוסי] | [נ"ל דתניא] [לקמן ו.] | יואל א | דברים יא | תהלים קכו | מ"כ ח | ישעיה ט | הושע יא | תהלים קכב | ירמיה י | שם | שם ב | ג' רש"א וכי"ע | [ס"א ותרתי] [וכן גירסת הערוך עשרין וכו'] | [בתמיה משום דבקרבך קדוש] | [ס"א ושתים]

הגהות הב"ח: (א) גמ' יורה בניסן הוא יורה במרחשון הוא: (ב) רש"י ד"ה מונה כו' אלא כ' ובליס ביום שביעי יום כו' כצ"ל ותיבת טוב נמחק: (ג) בא"ד דהיינו ביו"ט אחרון. נ"ב כלומר עד ליל יו"ט ולא ליל יו"ט בכלל: (ד) ד"ה יצאו וזרעו מה שבידם כצ"ל ותיבת וזרעו נמחק: (ה) תוס' ד"ה רבא כו' ביום ראשון של שני ימים אחרונים שוב:

רבינו גרשום

כר' יהודה היינו להזכרה שמתחיל להזכיר בחג והא דאמר ר' אלעזר הלכה כר"ג היינו לשאלה · והאמר ר' יוחנן במקום שהוא שואל מזכיר אלמא הא דאמר ר' יוחנן הלכה כר' יהודה היינו בין לשאול בין להזכיר דכי הדדי נינהו וקשיא הלכתא אהלכתא: ההוא להפסקה. כלומר הא דאמר מקום שהוא שואל הוא מזכיר היינו להפסקה כלומר שפוסק מלשאול ומלהזכיר ביום ראשון של פסח אבל להתחלה מתחיל בחג ושואל בשבעה במרחשון: הא לן והא להו הא דאמר הלכה כר"ג דאינו שואל עד שבעה במרחשון היינו להו לבני בבל דאית להו פירי בדברא ואין צריכין לגשמים עד ז' במרחשון והא דאמר הלכה כר' יהודה מזכיר ושואל לן בא"י דלית לן פירי בדברא: אית להו עולי רגלים ואם יורדין גשמים בג' *) אינן יכולין לחזור מפני הגשמים: כי קאמר ר' יוחנן הלכה כר' יהודה דשואל ומזכיר בחג בזמן שאין בית המקדש קיים דליכא עולי רגלים והא דאמר הלכה כר"ג בזמן שביהמ"ק קיים ובז' במרחשון כבר הזרו · ואנו דאית לן תרי יומי [שמיני] ואחרון של חג: היכי עבדינן הא אחד מהן חול הוא ובאיזה יום יתחיל לשאול. מתחיל במוספין של יום ראשון מימים האחרונים ופוסק במנחה דשמא חול הוא וערבית ושחרית ביום האחרון לגמרי. לאחר שעשיתו קדש ששאלת במוסף אלמא דקדש הוא תעשהו חול שאין אתה מזכיר במנחה: ופוסק ערבית שהרי היא הכנסה דיום אחרון ושחרית ושואל במוסף כמו שעשה אתמול דקדש הוא ואמר דאחרון שואל: כיון שהתחיל לשאול במוסף דיום ראשון שוב אינו פוסק אלא שואל במנחה בשחרית ובערבית ומוסף וכו' ואף רב הדר ביה ואמר כיון שהתחיל שוב אינו פוסק. מונה כ"א בתשרי דהיינו ראשון של אהרון ויתחיל לשאול ושוב אינו פוסק: כדרך שמונה מר"ה ועד יוה"כ. יורה ומלקוש בראשון האי ראשון היינו ניסן. בימי יואל נתקיים מקרא הזה יורה בראשון ולעולם יורה במרחשון הוא: שני ושלישי ורביעי בניסן נמצא תבואה שרגילה להתגדל בו' חדשים גדילה בי"א יום מרביעי דניסן עד יום י"ו בו שמקריבין בו העומר: כשהשור הולך לזרוע בוכה שרעב. מהו אלומותיו דמשמע תרי דקנה זרת ושיבולת שתי זרתות: אמר הקב"ה לא אכנס בירושלים של מעלה דהכי משמע עד שבקרבך קדוש שיבנה ירושלים למטה לא אכנס לירושלים של מעלה: יחדיו משמע תרי ירושלים. ומנלן דהאי אחת משמע ע"ז כתיב הכא מוסר הבלים עץ הוא. עשרים וארבעה שביקא להו כלומר והלא עברו על עשרים וארבעה ספרים

ע"א

*) אולי צ"ל בג' במרחשון או דצ"ל בחג אינן יכולין לחזור וכו'.

רבינו חננאל

אני ה' דברתי ועשיתי. והפיצותי אותך בגוים וזריתיך בארצות והתימותי טומאתך ממך ונחלת בך לעיני גוים וידעת כי אני ה'. א"ל הכי אמר ר' יוחנן עבירה אחת שיש בה שתי רעות ומאי נינהו ע"ז שנאמר כי שתים רעות עשה עמי אותי עזבו והלכו אל הגלולים כי עברו איי כתיים גו' עד ועמי המיר כבודו בלא יועיל. ותוב בעא מיניה כתיב ויהי כי זקן שמואל מי קא סיב כולי האי והאמר מר במסכת מועד במשקין מת בן חמשים שנה זו היא מיתתו של שמואל הרמתי. א"ל הכי אמר ר' יוחנן זקנה הקפיץ הקב"ה עליו שנאמר (ויהי כי זקן שמואל) נחמתי כי המלכתי את שאול למלך. ויחר לשמואל ויזעק אל ה' כל הלילה אמר לפניו רבש"ע שקלתני כמשה ואהרן כו'. ועד מי גרם לשאול לישב שתי שנים ומחצה בגבעה תפלתו של שמואל הרמתי. וכי מידחי גברא מקמי גברא אין שנאמר חצבתי בנביאים הרגתים באמרי פי במעשיהם לא נאמר אלא באמרי פי אלמא מדחי גברא מקמי גברא. אין אומרים דבר הלכה בסעודה שמא יקדים קנה לושט ויבא לידי סכנה (ותתקל הסעודה) בתר דסעיד א"ל הכי אמר ר' יוחנן יעקב אבינו לא מת שנאמר כי הנני מושיעך מרחוק ואת זרעך מארץ שבים וגו' מקיש יעקב לזרעו מה זרעו בחיים אף הוא בחיים.

רבינו גרשום

ע"א עשרים ושש עבירות כתיבי באותה פרשה התשפט התשפט: ומאי נינהו ע"ז דכתיב פן תשחיתון ועשיתם פסל [illegible] השחתה אינו אלא דבר ערוה וע"ז. ע"א. מאי נינהו ע"ז כלומר כשהוא עובד הני תרי ע"ז דקדריים וכותיים ומנלן דהאי קרא כי שתים רעות משמע ע"ז כתיב הכא כו': לא בטלו מעשה ידיהן בחייהן. משכן: מרנני כל עם אבתריה. דאמרי לפי שחטא מת בחור. קפצה עליו זקנה דלא רנני עליה דסבר זקן הוא. אלא באמרי פי כגון שמואל: ביודעה ומכירה: שמורה הבריות לפי שהוא ספר הראשון: שיורד בנחת כמו עושה הוראה לבניו בנחת: ששופף את הגרנות. דמשמע יורה כחץ: שמפיל אילנות. דמשמע *) מתוך סלקישה: סקאן. צלצל: שמל ששיותן. שכשאינו יורה מתענין ומתפללין: או אינו יורה אלא בכסליו: בעתו. היינו י"ז במרחשון: בביורה גרסינן. עד שיגיע ר"ח כסליו כדאמר דאין מתענין אלא עד הש לישית שאינה

*) אולי צ"ל דכן משמע לשון מלקוש.

גמרא

שקולה כשתים ומאי נינהו ע"ז דכתיב °כי שתים רעות עשה עמי אותי עזבו מקור מים חיים לחצוב להם בארות בארות נשברים וכתיב בהו °כי עברו איי כתיים וראו וקדר שלחו והתבוננו מאד וגו' ההימיר גוי אלהים והמה לא אלהים ועמי המיר כבודו בלא יועיל תנא כותיים עובדים לאש וקדריים עובדין למים ואע"פ שיודעים שהמים מכבין את האש לא המירו אלהיהם ועמי המיר *כבודי בלא יועיל וא"ל רב נחמן לר' יצחק מ"ד °ויהי כאשר זקן שמואל ומי סיב שמואל כולי האי והא בר נ"ב הוה דאמר מר *מת בנ"ב שנה זהו מיתתו של שמואל הרמתי וא"ל חבי ור"י יוחנן *וקנה קפצה עליו [illegible] °נחמתי כי המלכתי את שאול אמר לפניו רבש"ע שקלתני כמשה ואהרן *דכתיב °משה ואהרן בכהניו ושמואל בקוראי שמו מה משה ואהרן לא בטלו מעשה ידיהם בחייהם אף אני לא יתבטל מעשה ידי בחיי אמר הקב"ה היכי אעביד לימות שאול לא קא שביק שמואל לימות שמואל אדזוטר מרנני אבתריה לא לימות שאול ולא לימות שמואל כבר הגיעה מלכות דוד *ואין מלכות נוגעת בחברתה אפילו כמלא נימא אמר הקב"ה אקפיץ עליו זקנה היינו דכתיב °ושאול יושב בגבעה תחת האשל ברמה *וכי מה ענין גבעה אצל רמה אלא לומר לך מי גרם לשאול שישב בגבעה שתי שנים ומחצה תפלתו של שמואל הרמתי ומי מידחי גברא מקמי גברא אין דא"ר שמואל בר נחמני א"ר (*יוחנן) מ"ד °על כן חצבתי בנביאים הרגתים באמרי פי במעשיהם לא נאמר אלא באמרי פי אלמא מידחי גברא מקמי גברא רב נחמן ור' יצחק הוו יתבי בסעודתא א"ל רב נחמן לר' יצחק לימא מר מילתא א"ל הכי א"ר יוחנן אין מסיחין בסעודה שמא יקדים קנה לוושט ויבא לידי סכנה בתר דסעוד א"ל הכי א"ר יוחנן יעקב אבינו לא מת א"ל וכי בכדי ספדו ספדנייא וחנטו חנטייא וקברו קברייא א"ל מקרא אני דורש שנאמר °ואתה אל תירא עבדי יעקב נאם ה' ואל תחת ישראל כי הנני מושיעך מרחוק ואת זרעך מארץ שבים מקיש הוא לזרעו מה זרעו בחיים אף הוא בחיים א"ר יצחק *כל האומר רחב רחב מיד נקרי א"ל רב נחמן אנא אמינא ולא איכפת לי א"ל כי קאמינא ביודעה ובמכירה *(יבמזכיר את שמה) כי הוו מיפטרי מהדדי א"ל ליברכן מר אמר ליה אמשול לך משל למה"ד לאדם שהיה הולך במדבר והיה רעב ועיף וצמא ומצא אילן שפירותיו מתוקין וצילו נאה ואמת המים עוברת תחתיו אכל מפירותיו ושתה ממימיו וישב בצילו וכשביקש לילך אמר אילן אילן במה אברכך אם אומר לך שיהו פירותיך מתוקין הרי פירותיך מתוקין שיהא צילך נאה הרי צילך נאה שתהא אמת המים עוברת תחתיך הרי אמת המים עוברת תחתיך אלא יהי רצון שכל נטיעות שנוטעין ממך יהיו

תוספות

ומי סיב שמואל והא בר נ"ב שנין הוה וכו' · ועתה (*אפי') היו שמואל נ"ב שנה שהרי בשנה ראשונה שהיה עלי ממונה לכ"ג נולד שמואל כדכתיב (שמואל א א) ועלי יושב כלומר אותו יום נתיישב ונתמנה ועלי היה נביא ושופט ארבעים שנה כדמפרש בקרא ושמואל היה נביא ושופט י' שנים קודם מלכות שאול כדאיתא בסדר עולם נמצא שהיה שמואל בן מ"ט שנה כשפסק מלהיות שופט וחצי שנה שבשנה ראשונה שהיה עלי נביא נולד ותרתין שנין ופלגא דשאול המלך הרי נ"ב שנין ולהכי קא פריך ומי סיב ומורי ש"י חשיב הני ארבעים שנה דעלי קודם שנשבה הארון ובאותו יום שנשבה מת כדכתיב ויהי כהזכירו ארון האלהים ויפול אחורנית ותשבר מפרקתו וגו' והארון היה בבית אבינדב בגבעה עשרים שנה כדכתיב (שמואל א ז) וירבו הימים ויהיו עשרים שנה וינהו כל בית ישראל אחרי ה' ומיד כשמלך דוד דירושלים דהיינו לאחר [illegible] בחברון שבע שנים ומחצה הביאו לשם לא ותשוב ארבעים שהיה עלי עם עשרים שנה שהיה הארון בבית אבינדב היינו ששים נמצא שהיה ששים שנה משנולד שמואל עד שבא הארון בירושלים אע"ג דנולד בשנה הראשונה א"כ נכי לפחות חצי שנה *דהריון אותן שבעה חדשים (ג)היה הארון בשדה פלשתים דלא קא חשיב ומלי' להגהו דשעת הריון נמצא שהיה שמונה שנים ממיתת שמואל עד שבא הארון לירושלים שהרי היה ששה חדשים ממיתת שמואל קודם שמשחו דוד למלך בחברון ומלך שם שבע שנים ומחצה ומיד מלך בירושלים והביא הארון ועתה הסר שמונה שנים מן ששים שנים שהיה משנולד שמואל עד הבאת הארון וישאר נ"ב שנים: **יעקב** אבינו לא מת · וכן משמע (ד) דכתיב ויגוע ולא כתיב וימת כדמפרש בסוטה (דף יג·) גבי מעשה דחושים:

ביודעה ומכירה קאמינא · פי' ביודעה שבא עליה ומכירה שראה אותה:

רש"י

ששקולה כשתים · דכותיים וקדריים כדמפרש שהרעו משניהן לא הביטו מהן דכותיים וקדרים (א) אע"פ שיראתם פחותה לא רצו להמיר ועמי המירו באחר ולא עוד אלא בלא יועיל: והאמר מר · במועד קטן (דף כח·) זו מיתתו של שמואל הרמתי (ב) ולא *כרת היא במסכת שמחות (פ"ג) מפרש מת בכך שנים זו היא מיתת כרת בכך וכך זו היא מיתת אסכרה: ימיו של שמואל נ"ב שנה · דכתיב עד יגמל הנער וגו' היבירי"ר בלע"ז וכ"ד חדשים נקרא תינוק וכתיב (שמואל א א) וישב שם עד עולם עולמו של לוי חמשים שנה שנאמר (במדבר ח) ומבן חמשים שנה ישוב מצבא העבודה (*בבכורות) ירושלמי ובסדר עולם תמצא כשני דפין תוספת על זה: קפצה · הלבין שערו: נחמתי · ורצה הקב"ה להורגו מיד: שקלתני כמשה ואהרן דכתיב משה ואהרן בכהניו ושמואל בקוראי שמו וגו' · שוין הן: מעשה ידיהן · יהושע אף הוא היה תלמידו של אהרן כדאמרי' בעירובין (דף נד:) יצא משה ושנה להן אהרן פירקו: כי זוטר · בחור: מרנני כולי עלמא אבתריה · דאמרי מדמית זוטר שמא ח"ו עבירה היתה בו: וכי מה ענין גבעת בנימין אצל רמה · בהר אפרים: שישב ב' שנים ומחצה · כדמפרש בסדר עולם שמלך מחלית שנת עשתי עשרה ושנים עשרה ושלשה עשר ושמואל מת בתוך שנת שלש עשרה לסוף שמונה חדשים: מי מידחי גברא כו' · דאידחי שמואל מקמי דוד: במעשיהם לא נאמר · דמשמע בעבור חטא: אלא באמרי פי · מפני דבר שגזרתי כגון האי מעשה דשמואל: שמא יקדים קנה · כשיוציא הקול נפתח אותו כובע שעל פי הקנה ונכנס בו המאכל ומסתכן ולפיכך לא אומר לך כלום מאכל ומשתה הולך דרך הושט: ה"ג לימא לן מר מידי · ולא גרסינן חד לחבריה: לא מת · אלא חי הוא לעולם: בכדי · וכי בחנם ספדו ספדיא וחנטו חנטיא דכתיב ביה (בראשית נ) ויחנטו (אותו) ויספדו (לו): מקרא אני דורש · והאי דחנטו חנטיא [illegible] בחיים · כשהוא מקבץ את ישראל מארץ שבים החיים הוא מקבץ שהן בשבי שהמתים אינן בשבי: אף הוא בחיים · שיביאנו בגולה כדי לגאול את בניו לעיניו כמו שמליטו במצרים וירא ישראל וגו' ודרשינן ישראל סבא ודחנטו חנטיא נדמה להם שמת אבל חי היה: כל האומר רחב רחב מיד נקרי · נעשה בעל קרי: לא איכפת לי · איני חושש: ביודעה · היינו נמי מכירה: כי הוו מיפטר. רב נחמן מרב יצחק: והיה צילו נאה · שזה צריך לאדם עייף לנוח תחתיו: ופירותיו מתוקין · לרעב: ואמת המים · לצמא:

תורה אור

ירמיה ב · שם · ש"א ח · שם טו · תהלים צט · ש"א כב · הושע יג · ירמיה ל

מסורת הש"ס

[נ"ל מיתת כרת] [נ"ל בכורים פ"ב ע"ש] [נ"ל כבודו] מו"ק כח. [שנה מנ.] [עמ"ש תוס' גיטין סח. ד"ה וכתיב] [ברכות מח: וש"נ] [תוספתא דסוטה פי"א] [נ"ל יוחנן]

הגהות הב"ח

(א) רש"י ד"ה ששקולה כו'. נ"ב מלשונם"י משמע שהיה גורס כותיים עובדים למים וקדריים עובדין לאש וכ"ה בילקוט ע"ש: (ב) ד"ה והאמר מר כו' של שמואל הרמתי כרת היא במס' שמחות מפרש מת בכך וכך שנים כו' כנ"ל והיבת ולא נמחק: (ג) תוס' ד"ה ומי כו' אותן שבעה חדשים שהיה הארון כו' דשעת הריון ונמצא שהיו שמונה: (ד) ד"ה יעקב כו' וכן משמע מדכתיב ויגוע:

יג א מיי' פ"י מהלכות נדרים הל' יא ופ"א מהלכות מתנות עניים הלכה יא סמג לאוין רמב טוש"ע י"ד סי' רכ סעיף יח :
יד ב מיי' פ"ב מהלכות תפלה הלכה טז סמג עשין יט טוש"ע א"ח סי' קיז סעיף א :

תורה אור

יהיו כמותך אף אתה במה אברכך אם בתורה הרי (א) תורה אם בעושר הרי עושר אם בבנים הרי בנים אלא יהי רצון *שיהו צאצאי מעיך כמותך : ת"ר יורה שמורה את הבריות להטיח גגותיהן ולהכניס את פירותיהן ולעשות כל צרכיהן (ג) דבר אחר שמרוה את הארץ ומשקה עד תהום שנאמר °תלמיה רוה נחת גדודיה ברביבים תמוגגנה צמחה תברך (תהלים סה) דבר אחר יורה שיורד בנחת ואינו יורד בזעף או אינו יורה אלא שמשיר את הפירות ומשטיף את הזרעים ומשטיף את האילנות ת"ל מלקוש מה מלקוש לברכה אף יורה לברכה או אינו מלקוש אלא שמפיל את הבתים ומשבר את האילנות ומעלה את הסקאין ת"ל יורה מה יורה לברכה אף מלקוש לברכה ויורה גופיה מנלן דכתיב °ובני ציון גילו ושמחו בה' אלהיכם כי נתן לכם את המורה לצדקה ויורד לכם גשם מורה ומלקוש בראשון (יואל ב) : ת"ר *יורה במרחשון ומלקוש בניסן אתה אומר יורה במרחשון ומלקוש בניסן או אינו אלא יורה בתשרי ומלקוש באייר ת"ל בעתו מלקוש אמר רב נהילאי בר אידי אמר שמואל דבר שמל קשיותיהן של ישראל דבי ר' ישמעאל תנא דבר שממלא תבואה בקשיה במתניתא תנא דבר שיורד על המלילות ועל הקשין ת"ר יורה במרחשון ומלקוש בניסן אתה אומר יורה במרחשון או אינו אלא בחדש כסליו ת"ל °בעתו יורה ומלקוש (דברים יא) מה מלקוש בעתו אף יורה בעתו (*כיון שיצא ניסן וירדו גשמים אינו סימן ברכה) תניא אידך יורה במרחשון ומלקוש בניסן דברי ר"מ וחכמים אומרים יורה בכסליו *מאן חכמים אמר רב חסדא ר' יוסי היא דתניא *) איזו היא רביעה ראשונה הבכירה בשלשה במרחשון בינונית בשבעה בו אפילה בשבעה עשר בו דברי ר"מ ר' יהודה אומר בשבעה ובי"ז ובעשרים ושלשה *ר' יוסי אומר בי"ז ובעשרים ושלשה ובראש חדש כסליו וכן היה ר' יוסי אומר אין היחידים מתענין עד שיגיע ראש חדש כסליו אמר רב חסדא הלכה כר' יוסי אמימר מתני להא דרב חסדא בהא לישנא *בשלשה במרחשון שואלין את הגשמים רבן גמליאל אומר בשבעה בו אמר רב חסדא °הלכה כרבן גמליאל כמאן *אולא הא דתניא רשב"ג אומר גשמים שירדו שבעה ימים זה אחר זה אתה מונה בהן רביעה ראשונה ושניה ושלישית כמאן כר' יוסי אמר רב חסדא הלכה כר' יוסי בשלמא רביעה ראשונה לשאול שלישית להתענות שניה למאי אמר ר' זירא *לנדרים דתנן הנודר

מלקוש לברכה או אינו אלא שמפיל הבתים ומשבר האילנות וכו' · ל"ע אמאי לא קאמר ומשבר הגרעות ומשיר את הפירות כדלעיל : **גשמים** שירדו ז' ימים זה אחר זה ולא פסקו אתה מונה בהן רביעה ראשונה ושניה · כיון דלא פסקו ז' ימים דאין בין י"ז לכ"ג אלא ז' ימים י"ז י"ח י"ט כ' כ"א כ"ב כ"ג אבל לא גרסינן ושלישית שהרי אם יתחיל בכ"ג וירדו ז' ימים רצופים (ז) אכתי לא תמלא רביעה שלישית דאיכא ח' ימים מכ"ג עד ר"ח כסליו ואגשי גרנוב"א גורסין גשמים שירדו ז' ימים זה אחר זה אתה מונה בהם רביעה שניה ושלישית כגון הגשמים התחילו באמצע היום וירדו ז' ימים רצופים א"כ ירדו עד חצי יום של ר"ח מעת לעת :

דאלי

רש"י

יהיו כמותך · בתורה ולעושר וכבוד : יורה · ונתתי מטר ארצכם בעתו יורה ומלקוש (דברים יא) : יורה · רביעה ראשונה היורדת במרחשון כדלקמן למה נקרא יורה שמורה להן להטיח גגותיהן בטיח של טיט שלא יטפו גשמים בבית : ולהכניס פירותיהן שהניחו בשדות לייבשן עד עכשיו : כל צרכיהן · שאר דברים הצריכים לימות הגשמים : שיורד בנחת · והכי משמע יורה כאדם שמורה לתלמידיו בנחת דכתיב (קהלת ט) דברי חכמים בנחת נשמעים אי נמי לשון חץ יורה ההולך ביושר ואינו נוטה לכאן ולכאן לשון אחר שמתשין לארץ ואינו יורד בזעף בספרי : תלמיה רוה · כשאתה מרוה תלמי חרישה של ארץ ישראל : נחת הוא לגדודיה · בני אדם הייתי פשט המקרא ולקמיה *דריש שאפי' גייסות פוסקות בו : ה"ג או אינו אלא שטוטף את הזרעים · כלומר דעד השתא אמרינן יורה לברכה או אינו אלא יורה לשון קללה כמו ירה יירה (שמות יט) שסוכר הכל או לשון חץ היורה והכי משמע קרא והיה אם שמוע תשמעו אל מצותי וגו' ואם לאו ונתתי מטר ארצכם יורה לרעה מלתא בעלמא הוא ואורחא דברייתא למתני כי האי גוונא : משיר פירותיהן · שעודן באילן כגון אתרוגים או רמונים או סופי תאנים ולא גרסינן שוטף את הגרעות דגרעות (ג) במרחשון ליכא : מה מלקוש לברכה · שא"א לדורשו לשבר גרעות ולהשיר פירות שאינם מצויים באותו הפרק ואי אתה יכול לדורשו אלא לטובה שיורד על המלילות ועל הקשין וממלא את התבואה בקשיה : הדר אמר דלמא מלקוש קללה הוא והכי משמע שמל וקשה כלומר מל את הבתים והאילנות שמפילן ומשברן וקשה .לתבואה : שמעלה סקאים · וברכה דקרא למילוי מים בורות שיחין ומערות גימגום : שמפיל את הבתים ומשמעו כדלקמן שמל קשיותן של ישראל אי נמי שמל דבר הקשה תוקף ומשבר את הבתים כלומר אין בו תקלת גרעות והשרת פירות לפי שא"א לו : סקאי · מין ארבה כדמתרגם הגלגל (דברים כח) סקאה ומלקוש לשון ארבה כמו והנה לקש אחר גזי המלך (עמוס ז) : את המורה לצדקה · אלמא יורה לטובה : ה"ג או אינו אלא יורה בתשרי ומלקוש באייר · שיש עדין מלילות וקשין : ת"ל בעתו · יורה במרחשון ומלקוש בניסן שכך היא העת והזמן ויפה הוא כדלקמן דזמן רביעה ראשונה במרחשון הוא אית ספרים דקתני בהו או אינו אלא בכסליו דזמן יורה בכסליו הוא וכרבנן דפליגי עליה דר"מ לקמן ת"ל בעתו יורה ומלקוש מה מלקוש בעתו אף יורה בעתו דמלקוש זהו שיורד על המלילות ועל הקשין והוא ניסן שיש בו קשין ומלילות : דבר שמל קשיותן של ישראל · שכשאינו יורד חוזרין ישראל בתשובה ומתענין ופושטין לדקות : מלילות · ראשי שיבולות שאדם מולל בידו כדכתיב (דברים כג) וקטפת מלילות בידך : וקשין · קנה : שממלא התבואה בקשיה · ומשלימה : (ד) הי רביעה · איזה זמן רביעה : בכירה · ראשונה ולקמן מפרש למאי הלכתא ניהו יורה יש בו ג' זמני גשמים : אפילה · אחרונה כמו כי אפילות הנה (שמות ט) : ר' יהודה אומר · בכירה בז' במרחשון וביטנית בי"ז ואפילה בכ"ג וכולהו הני תלתא יורה קרי להו : אין היחידים מתענין כו' · דאמרי' בסמוך שלישית להתענות והואיל וזמן שלישית בר"ח חדש הוא אין ליחידים להתענות (ה) : יחידים · חסידים והכי אמרי' במתני' לקמן (דף י) הגיע י"ז במרחשון ולא ירדו גשמים התחילו היחידים להתענות שמכאן ואילך זמן רביעה אפילה לר"מ דסתם מתני' ר"מ וה"ג אמר ר' יוסי דאין מתענין עד ר"ח כסליו דהיינו רביעה אפילה והיינו כחכמים דאמרי יורה בכסליו : אמר רב חסדא הלכה כר' יוסי · ואמימר תני להא דאמר רב חסדא הלכה כרבן גמליאל דאינו שואל עד ז' במרחשון : ז' ימים בזה אחר זה · שירדו גשמים (ו) עכשיו א] ופסקו עד יום שביעי וירדו ז' ימים זה אחר זה אתה מונה בהן ראשונה ושניה ושלישית : כר' יוסי · דאליבא דר' יוסי הכי הוו בין רביעה ראשונה ושניה או שניה ושלישית דראשונה בי"ז ושניה בכ"ג דהיינו ז' ימים עם שנים ימי רביעה ומכ"ג עד ל' ז' ימים בלא יום רביעה אחרונה דלכולהו תנאי לא הוי הכי דלר"מ דאמר ראשונה בג' ושניה בז' ליכא בין זו לזו אלא ארבעה ימים בין שניה לשלישית יש י' ימים ולר' יהודה בין ראשונה לשניה י' ימים אבל בין שניה לשלישית יש ב] *) יותר : נראה לרבי דהכי גרסינן אמר רב חסדא הלכה כר' יהודה דאמר בכירה בז' במרחשון ואז מתחילין לשאול כדלקמן (דף י.) : ראשונה לשאול · מכאן ואילך ותן טל ומטר : שלישית להתענות · שאם לא ירדו גשמים עד זמן רביעה שלישית אפי' פעם אחת מתענין היחידים שני וחמישי ושני :

*) ס"א ז' ימים

הטודר

[ב"מ קו.] · דף ה: · [לעיל ב.] · [פירקין ס. וש"נ] · [נדרים סג. פ"ג תוספתא פ"א] · [לקמן י. (וש"נ)] · [נדרים סג. פ"ג תוספתא פ"א]

רבינו חננאל

רש"א מ"ז ופי' מלקוש ולפי' גבי או אינו אלא מלקוש באייר ת"ל בעתו שייך למיתני נמי הכי כיון שיצא ניסן כו'

מורה ומלקוש . מורה שמורה את הבריות להטיח גגותיהן ולהכניס פירותיהן מלקוש שמל קשיותיהן של ישראל · תנא דבר שיורד על המלילות ועל הקשין וממלא התבואה בקשיה: ת"ר מורה במרחשון ומלקוש בניסן דברי ר' מאיר וחכמים אומרים מורה בחדש כסלו. מאן חכמים אמר רב חסדא ר' יוסי היא . דתניא מאימתי זמן רביעה . ר' מאיר אומר בכירה בשלשה בינונית בשבעה אפילה בי"ז . ר' יהודה אומר בשבעה ובשבעה עשר ובעשרים ושלשה. ר' יוסי אומר בי"ז ובכ"ג ובר"ח כסלו וכן היה ר' יוסי אומר אין היחידים מתענין עד שיגיע ר"ח כסלו· כמאן אולא הא דתניא רשב"ג אומר גשמים שירדו ז' ימים זה אחר זה אתה מונה רביעה ראשונה ושניה ושלישית כמאן כר' יוסי פי' כגון שהתחילו הגשמים לירד ביום הראשון מחצי יום וכשתחשוב ז' ימים משת לעת אתה מוצא מקצת סיום השביעי להשלמת ז' ימים ולא תמצא מאלו התנאים בז' ימים למנות בהן רביעה ראשונה ושניה או שניה ושלישית אלא לר' יוסי בלבד דאי ר"מ ראשונה ושניה משכחת לה שניה ושלישית לא משכחת לה דהוא בין שניה ושלישית י' ימים ואי לר' יהודה שניה ושלישית הוא משכחת לה ראשונה ושניה לא משכחת לה דהוא לדבריו י' ימים בין הראשונה לשניה אבל ר' יוסי דאמר ראשונה בי"ז שניה בכ"ג הנה ו' ימים ביניהם . אתה מונה בהן ראשונה ושניה ואם התחילו הגשמים בחצי היום בכ"ג יום למרחשון נמצא עד ר"ח כסליו ו' ימים ומקצת היום של יום ראשון אתה משלימן מיום ראשון של חדש כסלו נמצאת מונה להן שניה ושלישית והוא שהיה (ר' א') [ר"ח] מרחשון חסר כי בשלשה איתא בפיר' בתוספתא שהיה ר' יוסי אומר בכירה בי"ז בינונית בכ"ג. אפילה בל'. אמר רב חסדא הלכה כר' יוסי ואמרינן בשלמא רביעה ראשונה לשאול ותן טל ומטר כר' מאיר דאמר בכירה בג' במרחשון דתנן בג' במרחשון שואלין את הגשמים שלישית להתענות כדתנן הגיע י"ז במרחשון ולא ירדו גשמים התחילו היחידים מתענין אלא רביעה שניה למאי פירוש כיון מתחלת רביעה ראשונה עד שלישית כולן ימי שאלה הן למה נקראת שניה והביאו טעם ר' זירא ורב זביד

הגהות הב"ח

(א) גמ' אם בתורה הרי יש לך תורה ואם בגדולה הרי יש לך גדולה ואם בכבוד הרי יש לך כבוד ואם בעושר הרי יש לך עושר אם בבנים הרי יש לך בנים אלא יהי רצון שיהו כל צאצאי מעיך: (ב) שם ולעשות כל צרכיהן ד"א יורה שיורד בנחת ואינו יורד בזעף ד"א שמרוה את הארץ כו' צמחה תברך או אינו יורה בו' את הזרעים ומשבר את הגרעות ת"ל יורה ומלקוש מה מלקוש לברכה : (ג) רש"י ד"ה משיר כו' דגרעות במרחשון ליכא וברכה דקרא למילוי בורות שיחין ומערות גימגו"ם הס"ד ואח"כ מה"ד יורה ומלקוש אם מלקוש לטובה יורה נמי לטובה ליכא מה מלקוש לברכה שא"א כו' התבואה בקשיה ומה"ד הדר אמר וכו' וקשה לתבואה שמעלה סקאים הס"ד ואח"כ מה"ד שמפיל את כו' ומשבר את הבתים ואילנות ואין בו תקלת כו' כצ"ל ותיבת כלומר נמחק : (ד) ד"ה הי רביעה נ"ל איזוהי רביעה : (ה) ד"ה אין היחידים כו' אין ליחידים להתענות אלא משלישית ואילך והכי אמרינן במתני' לקמן וכו' דאמרי יורה בכסליו הס"ד ואח"כ מה"ד ואמימר תני להא דאמר כו' כצ"ל ותיבות אמר רב חסדא הלכה כר' יוסי נמחק : (ו) ד"ה ז' ימים כו' שירדו הגשמים מכשיו ולא פסקו עד : (ז) תום' ד"ה גשמים כו' ז' ימים רצופים א"כ ירדו עד חצי יום אכתי לא תמלא :

רבינו גרשום

שאינה יורדת : כמאן כר' יוסי דאמר ראשונה בי"ז ושניה בכ"ג הרי ראשונה ושניה בז' ימים : עד שתרד רביעה ראשונה אינה חשובה כלום :

גליון הש"ס

גמ' לנדרים דתנן. עמוס לי דאמרו לא נקט נמי לשכירות בתים דקתני בריתא דמתני' שם כמשכיר בית לחבירו עד הגשמים עד שתרד רביעה שניה :

הגהות מהר"ב רנשבורג

א] רש"י ד"ה שבעה ימים זה אחר זה וכו' שירדו גשמים ופסקו וכו' צ"ל ולא פסקו : ב] ד"ה כר' יוסי וכו' אבל בין שניה לשלישית יש יותר נ"ל אין יותר

***[א]הנודר עד הגשמים (א) *משירדו גשמים עד שתרד רביעה שניה** רב זביד אמר לזיתים דתנן *[ג]מאימתי כל אדם מותרין בלקט בשכחה ובפאה משילכו הנמושות בפרט ובעוללות משילכו עניים בכרם ויבואו בזיתים משתרד רביעה שניה מאי נמושות אמר ר' יוחנן סבי דאזלי *אתיגרא ר"ל אמר לקוטי בתר לקוטי רב פפא אמר כדי להלך בשבילי הרשות דאמר מר *[ג]מהלכין כל אדם בשבילי הרשות עד שתרד רביעה שניה רב נחמן בר יצחק אמר לבער פירות שביעית *דתנן *עד מתי נהגין ושורפין בתבן ובקש של שביעית עד שתרד רביעה שניה מאי טעמא דכתיב °ולבהמתך ולחיה אשר בארצך [ד]כל זמן שחיה אוכלת בשדה האכל לבהמתך בבית כלה *לחיה מן השדה כלה לבהמתך מן חבית אמר רבי אבהו מאי לשון רביעה דבר שרובע את הקרקע כדרב יהודה דאמר רב יהודה מיטרא בעלה דארעא הוא שנאמר °כי כאשר ירד הגשם והשלג מן השמים ושמה לא ישוב כי אם הרוה את הארץ והולידה והצמיחה ואמר רבי אבהו רביעה ראשונה כדי שתרד בקרקע טפח שניה כדי לגוף בה פי חבית אמר רב חסדא גשמים שירדו כדי לגוף בהן פי חבית אין בהן משום ועצר ואמר רב חסדא גשמים שירדו קודם ועצר אין בהן משום ועצר אמר אביי לא אמרן אלא קודם ועצר דאורתא אבל קודם ועצר דצפרא יש בהן משום ועצר דאמר רב יהודה בר יצחק *הני ענני דצפרא לית בהו מששא דכתיב °מה אעשה לך אפרים מה אעשה לך יהודה וחסדכם כענן בקר וגו' א"ל רב פפא לאביי והא אמרי אינשי במפתח בבי מיטרא בר חמרא מוך שקך וגני לא קשיא הא דקטיר בעיבא הא דקטיר בעננא אמר רב יהודה טבא לשתא דטבת ארמלתא איכא דאמרי דלא ביירי תרביצי ואיכא דאמרי דלא שקיל שודפנא איני והאמר רב חסדא טבא לשתא דטבת מנוולתא לא קשיא הא דאתא מיטרא מעיקרא הא דלא אתא מיטרא מעיקרא ואמר רב חסדא גשמים שירדו על מקצת מדינה ועל מקצת מדינה לא ירדו אין בהן משום ועצר איני והכתיב °וגם אנכי מנעתי מכם את הגשם בעוד שלשה חדשים לקציר והמטרתי על עיר אחת ועל עיר אחת לא אמטיר חלקה אחת תמטר וגו' *ואמר רב יהודה אמר רב שתיהן לקללה לא קשיא הא דאתא טובא הא דאתא כדמבעי ליה אמר רב אשי דיקא נמי דכתיב תמטר תהא מקום מטר ש"מ א"ר אבהו *[ה]מאימתי מברכין על הגשמים משיצא חתן לקראת כלה [ו]מאי מברך אמר רב יהודה אמר רב *מודים אנחנו לך ה' אלהינו על כל טפה וטפה שהורדת לנו ור' יוחנן מסיים בה הכי אילו פינו מלא שירה כים ולשוננו רנה כהמון גליו כו' עד [א]אל יעזבונו רחמיך ה' אלהינו ולא עזבונו ברוך רוב ההודאות ולא כל ההודאות אמר רבא אימא אל ההודאות אמר רב פפא [ז]הלכך נימרינהו לתרווייהו

רש"י

הנודר עד הגשמים · דאמר קונם אם אהנה מדבר זה עד הגשמים: **עד שתרד רביעה שניה** · בנדרים הולכין אחר לשון בני אדם ואין קורין גשמים לראשונה עד שתרד שניה שמכאן ואילך מקולקלות הדרכים ומאוסות מפני הגשמים ל"א עד הגשמים משמע תרי דהיינו רביעה שניה: **כל אדם** · אפילו העשירים: *) **פרט**. לא תפאר אחריך (דברים כד) לא תטול תפארתו ממנו: **משילכו הנמושות** · בשדה דמכאן ואילך נתייאשו שאר העניים לפי שיודעין אם נשאר לקט שכחה ופאה נמושות נטלום: **נמושות** · לשון ממשש: **משילכו עניים בכרם ויבאו** · כלומר שלקטו וחזרו ובאו פעם שניה והשתא מסחי דעתייהו עניים: **משתרד רביעה שניה** · דעד ההיא שעתא לקטו הכל: **דאזלי אתיגרא** · הולכין בנחת ומעייני טפי מחזיק בפלך (שמואל ב ג) מתרגמא אתיגרא: **לקוטי בתר לקוטי** · עני מוליך בנו אחריו שנוהג ואילך [illegible] עניים מללקט: ה"ג **רב פפא אמר לשבילי הרשות** · כלומר שיש רשות מב"ד לעוברי דרכים לקצר שבילן לילך בשדות: **עד שתרד רביעה שניה** · שמכאן ואילך גדלה התבואה וקשה לה דישת הרגל דאמר מר בפרק מרובה* בתנאים שהתנה יהושע מהלכין בשבילי הרשות וכו': **בתבן וקש של שביעית** · ספיחים שגדלו בשביעית דיש בהן איסור שביעית או תבואה שגדלה בשביעית לאחר שנכנסה: **כלה לחיה מן השדה** · לשון זכר כמו (בראשית יח) עשו כלה כלומר כלה האוכל: **כלה לבהמתך** · כמו כלה בחימה כלה ואיננו (תהלים נט) ומשירדה רביעה שניה מכאן ואילך אין תבן וקש בשדות שהגשמים עושין אותן זבל: **והולידה** · כאדם שמוליד: **גשמים ברביעה ראשונה** · אם באין כל כך שנימס הקרקע (ב) יפין הן ואין צריך להתענות: **לגוף בה פי חבית** · שעושה מן המים עד שנעשה טיחוח כל כך שיכול לעשות מגופת חבית בלא תוספת מים: **אין בהם משום ועצר** · אין זו קללה של ועצר את השמים: **קודם ועצר** · קודם זמן ק"ש דכתיב ביה ועצר את השמים אע"פ שלא יהיה רוב גשמים: **אבל ירדו קודם ועצר דצפרא יש בהן משום ועצר** · הואיל ולא ירדו ביום ואין יפין לעולם: **לית בהו מששא** · ואין שנתן מתברכת: **וחסדכם כענן בקר** · שאין בו ממש: **מיטרא במיפתח בבי** · אם יורדין בבקר כשפותחין הפתחים יקפל החמר שמוכר תבואה את שקו ליכנס לישן מפני שהשנה מתברכת ויהיה שובע בעולם ולא *ישתכר במכירת תבואתו אלמא יפין הן: **דקטיר בעיבא** · אם נתקשרו שמים בעננים עבים ולא קלושים אין בהם משום ועצר: **דקטיר בעננא** · שהיא קלושה מעב אין בו ממש: **טבא לשתא** · אשריה כלומר טובה יש לשנה דטבת ארמלתא שאין גשמים יורדין בה להרביע את הארץ: **איכא דאמרי דלא ביירי תרבילי** · אותן מקומות שמרבילין בהן תורה אינן בורות מפני שהדרכים יפין הן והולכין התלמידים ממקום למקום ללמוד תורה ל"א לא ביירי תרבילי גנות שאינן גדילין על רוב מים כגון כרשינין: **לא שקיל שודפנא** · אין השדפון נאחז ומתדבק בתבואה: **מנוולתא** · שהדרכים מנוולים בטיט מפני הגשמים: **הא דאתא מיטרא מעיקרא** · שירדו הגשמים בזמנן במרחשון וירדו אף בטבת רעים הן שכבר די לעולם בגשמים של מרחשון: **דלא אתא מיטרא מעיקרא** · טבא לשתא דטבת מנוולתא לשון אחר הא דאתא מיטרא מעיקרא טבא דמנוולתא: **אין בהם משום ועצר** · דאותן של קצת מדינה שירדו להן גשמים מוכרין לאחרים: **ואמר רב יהודה אמר רב שתיהן לקללה** · אותן שירדו ואותן שלא ירדו מפני שרוב גשמים קלקלו את תבואתם: **הא דאיכא מיטרא טובא** · יותר מדאי שתיהן לקללה: **כדמבעי ליה** · אין בהן משום ועצר שקצת מדינה הספק לקצת מדינה: **תמטר תהא מקום מטר** · כלומר יותר מדאי: **מאימתי מברכין על הגשמים** · בפרק הרואה (ברכות דף נט·) אמרינן על הגשמים אומר הטוב והמטיב והתם (דף נט·) פרכינן הך ברכה דתקון לה רבנן *ומשנינן לה הא דחזא מיחזא והא דשמע משמע: **חתן לקראת כלה** · שירדו כל כך שכשהטפה נופלת יוצאה אחרת ובולטת כנגדה מפי מורי ל"א שהשווקין מקלחין מים שוק מקלח וזה מקלח כנגדו: **רוב ההודאות** · כלומר רוב ההודאות אתה קורא להקב"ה ולא כל ההודאות והכי משמע ברוך אתה ברוב ההודאות ולא בכל אלא כך חותם בא"י אמ"ה אל ההודאות דמשמע כל ההודאות:

למימרינהו

תוספות

דאזלי אתיגרא · פי' שהולכים במקלות ונשענים עליהם ואמר דתרגומא מחזיק בפלך דכתיב *גבי יואב הוי באתיגרא:

בשבילי הרשות · פי' בדרך שעשוי דרך השדות והכרמים:

עד שתרד רביעה שניה · מכאן ואילך מזקי להו:

עד מתי נהגין ושורפין בתבן ובקש של שביעית · פירוש בשנה שמינית וכו' וס"ל כמ"ד ספיחי זרעים מותרים ולר' עקיבא דאמר ספיחי זרעים אסורים מקרא דהן לא נזרע ולא נאסוף כדיתפרש במסכת פסחים פרק מקום שנהגו (דף נא:) צ"ל דמוקי לה ולבהמתך ולחיה וגו' בספיחי אילנות ולאו דוקא תבואה קאמר אלא כגון תבואת הכרם דהיינו אילנות אבל ספיחי זרעים אסורים:

לא אמרן אלא קודם ועצר דאורתא · כלומר שירדו גשמים קודם ק"ש של ערבית אבל קודם של שחרית יש בהם משום ועצר כדאמר רב שמואל בר רב יצחק:

איכא דאמרי לא ביירי תרבילי · שאין הגנות ריקים מזרעים:

וכל

עין משפט נר מצוה

[שמואל ב ג]

טו א מיי' פי"ג מהלכות נדרים הלכה יא סמג לאוין רמב טוש"ע י"ד סימן רכ סעיף יח:

נדרים סב: שביעית פ"ט מ"ו

פאה פ"ח מ"א ב"מ כא:

טז ב מיי' פ"א מהלכות מתנות עניים הלכה יא:

יז ג מיי' פ"ה מהלכות נזקי ממון הלכה ד טור ח"מ סי' רעד:

[הערוך בערך גד ובערך נמב גרס' אתינרא פי"ש שמניא ראיה מתרגום]

יח ד מיי' פ"ז מהלכות שמטה ויובל הל' א סמג עשין קמח:

[במשנה דשביעית איתא מאימתי כו' משתרד רביעה כו' עי' ר"ש שם [illegible]]

יט ה מיי' פ"י מהלכות ברכות הלכה ו סמג עשין כז טוש"ע א"ח סי' רכא סעיף א:

כ ו ז מיי' שם הלכה ה טוש"ע שם סעיף ב:

רבינו חננאל

למאי הלכתא. (למאי הלכתא) נקראת שניה. ובפרק ג' פירש כי רביעה א' וב' לשאול ג' להתענות וכן הלכתא. וא"ר זירא שניה לנודר דתניא הנודר עד הגשמים עד שתרד רביעה שניה רב זביד אמר לזיתים. דתניא מאימתי כל אדם מותרין בלקט שכחה ופאה משילכו הנמושית בפרט ובעוללות משילכו עניים בכרם ויבאו בזיתים עד שתרד רביעה שניה. סבי דאזלו אתגרא. זקנים המהלכים במשענת בנתיבי בני רה"ר. מאי לשון רביעה שרובע לקרקע כדרב יהודה דאמר מטרא בעלה דארעא היא שנאמר והולידה והצמיחה. רביעה [ראשונה] כדי שתרד בקרקע טפח. שניה כדי לגוף בה פי חבית: אמר רב חסדא גשמים שירדו כדי לגוף בה פי חבית אין בהם משום ועצר· וכן גשמים שירדו קודם ועצר. פי' קודם ק"ש שכתוב בה ועצר את השמים. אמר אביי לא אמרן אלא קודם קרית של ערב אבל קודם שמע דצפרא יש בהן משום ועצר כלומר המטר היורד בשחר אינו כלום ועובר הוא כדכתיב חסדכם כענן בקר והני מילי במטר דקטיר בעננא. והוא שעבר והולך. אבל אם נתקשרו שמים בעבים בבקר אינו פוסק אותו היום מטר וזהו האמור בר חמרא מוך שקך וגני. הצע השק שלך ושכב שאין לך היום הליכה. וטוביא רישתא דטבת ארמלתא דלא ביירא תרביצי. כגון הא דגרסי' (ב"ב ז.) חד מסיא תרביצא וחד מסיא אספלידרא. וי"א דלא ביירי תרביצי בליירי מלשון בורה כדכתיב והארסה לא תשם ומתרגמינן וארעא לא תבור כלומר שהשקה ונשאר בה לחלוחית עדיין (משתיב) תורשין אותה וזורעין אותה היינו דלא ביירי תרביצי. פי' סבת ארמלתא שלא ירדו גשמים בטבת שהגשמים הם בעל לארץ שנאמר והולידה והצמיחה (הן) [אין] סניחין *) האכסדרא בורא (שדה) בור שוכנין בה מפני שלא באו גשמים ליכנס בבית אלא יושבין באכסדראות כמו אלמנה שאין לה ישיבת בית איכא דאמרי דלא שקיל שיבתנא כלומר לא נסתלק החום אלא ישינים בפתחים מפני חוזק החום איני כי טוב היא כאשר לא יבא הכפור בטבת והאמר רב חסדא טבא דטבת מטולתא כלומר בעת שידו בני אדם מטנפים את רגליהם ובבגדיהם בטיט בזה טובת השנה ושנינן אם היו גשמים במרחשון ובטלו הטוב שלא יהיו בטבת גשמים ואם לא היו גשמים במרחשון וכסלו (הוו ביה תשתא) [טוביא דשתא] דטבת מטולתא. ועוד א' גשמים שירדו על מקצת מדינה אין בהם משום ועצר איני והכתיב חלקה אחת תמטר וחלקה אשר לא תמטיר עליה תיבש ואמר רב שתיהן לקללה ושנינן אי אתא טובא ומתכנשין תמן מיא לקללה. כדכתיב [תמטר] שם יהיה המטר כנס כלומר נקיים שם המים כנו

*) זהו פי' ב' ומ"ש למעלה כגון הא דגרסי' כו' עד אספלידה שייך לכאן.

רבינו גרשום

מאימתי כל אדם מותרין בלקט בשכחה ובפאה של בעה"ב המוציא לקט שכחה ופאה יכול ליקח. משילכו הנמושות שכבר הסיתו עניים סרעתן. אתיגרא בטורח שכבר לא השאירו כלום: שבילי הרשות דרכים שהם ברשות היחיד בשדות *) ברביעה שניה כבר כלה לחיה: שניה אין צריך אלא כדי שיכול ללוש מהן עפר לגוף פי החבית. אין בהן משום ועצר. כלומר דיש בהן משום ברכה. קודם ועצר דק"ש · סוף קפל חסוך כלומר שכל היום יורד מטר: עיבא עבים עבות הן של ברכה ובהכי אמרו מוך שקך תגי: ענני קטנים. ארמלתא שאין יורד גשמים' לא ביירי תרביצי אין חריבין בתי מדרשות שיכולין תלמידים לבוא שאין מעכבין להן גשמים ובטבת יש להם פנאי יותר מכל ימות השנה ע"א שאין מפסידין הגנות: דאתא מיטרא מעיקרא. קודם טבת ובטבת (נמי אתי טוביה אי ומוקפין) הוי ארמלתא: הא כתיב והמטרתי ** לפורענות: הא דאתא טובא אין בהן משום ועצר דברכה הוי. דאתא כדבעי כלומר ועיר הוי קללה דיקא נמי דקרא בודיר מיטרא כתיב: תמטר תהא מקום מטר כל דהו: משיצא חתן לקראת כלה. משיצא

סים

*) נראה דצ"ל עד מתי נהגין וכו' עד שתרד רביעה שניה שאז כבר כלה לחיה. **) נ"ע ואולי אמר רב שתיהן לפורענות.

מסורת הש"ס

[נ"ל עד שיהיו קראיה במשנה נדרים סב: ועי' במשנה ז פ"ט דשביעית]

*) [נ"ל פאה ר"ל בזית עי' חולין קלא:]

ב"ק פא.

[פסחים נב. נדה נא:]

[ב"ק דף פא.]

ברכות נט. ע"ש

[עם בברכות פרש"י בע"א פ"ש]

הגהות הב"ח

(א) גמ' הנודר עד הגשמים עד שיהו גשמים עד שתרד: (ב) רש"י ד"ה גשמים שנימס הקרקע בעומק טפח יפין הן:

ברכות נט: וע"ש

[גי' רי"ף וא"ר מודים וגי' רא"ש א"ר חנא]

הגהות הגר"א

[א] גמ' כהמון גליו כו' עד נ"ב וימליכו את שמך מלכנו כ"ה גירסת הרי"ף וש"ס:

גליון הש"ס רש"י ד"ה מאימתי מברכים כו' ומשגיח לה כה דתני מחוי. ק"ל הא דחיק שם כן מירוצא ומסקינן אידי ואידי דמתני כאן דאתא טובא וכו' ול"ע:

תורה אור

*נימרינהו לתרוייהו אל ההודאות ורוב ההודאות אמר ר' אבהו גדול יום הגשמים מתחיית המתים דאילו תחיית המתים לצדיקים ואילו גשמים בין לצדיקים בין לרשעים ופליגא דרב יוסף דאמר רב יוסף *מתוך שהיא שקולה כתחיית המתים קבעוה בתחיית המתים אמר רב יהודה גדול יום הגשמים כיום שניתנה בו תורה שנא' °יערף כמטר לקחי ואין לקח אלא תורה שנא' °כי לקח טוב נתתי לכם תורתי אל תעזובו רבא אמר יותר מיום שניתנה בו תורה שנאמר יערף כמטר לקחי *מי נתלה במי הוי אומר קטן נתלה בגדול רבא רמי כתיב יערף כמטר לקחי וכתיב תזל כטל אמרתי אם תלמיד חכם הגון הוא כטל ואם לאו עורפהו כמטר תניא היה ר' בנאה אומר כל העוסק בתורה לשמה תורתו נעשית לו סם חיים שנאמר °עץ חיים היא למחזיקים בה ואומר °רפאות תהי לשרך ואומר °כי מוצאי מצא חיים וכל העוסק בתורה שלא לשמה נעשית לו סם המות שנאמר יערף כמטר לקחי ואין עריפה אלא הריגה שנאמר °וערפו שם את העגלה בנחל א"ל ר' ירמיה לר' זירא ליתי מר ליתני א"ל חליש לבאי ולא יכילנא לימא מר מילתא דאגדתא א"ל הכי אמר ר' יוחנן מאי דכתיב °כי האדם עץ השדה וכי אדם עץ שדה הוא אלא משום דכתיב °כי ממנו תאכל ואותו לא תכרת וכתיב אותו תשחית וכרת הא כיצד אם ת"ח הגון הוא ממנו תאכל ואותו לא תכרת ואם לאו אותו תשחית וכרת אמר רבי חמא (*אמר רבי) חנינא מאי דכתיב °ברזל בברזל יחד לומר לך מה ברזל זה אחד מחדד את חבירו אף שני תלמידי חכמים מחדדין זה את זה בהלכה אמר רבה בר בר חנה למה נמשלו דברי תורה כאש שנאמר °הלא כה דברי כאש נאם ה' לומר לך מה אש אינו דולק יחידי אף דברי תורה אין מתקיימין ביחידי והיינו דאמר רבי יוסי בר חנינא *מאי דכתיב °חרב אל הבדים ונואלו חרב על שונאיהן של תלמידי חכמים שעוסקין בד בבד בתורה ולא עוד אלא שמטפשין שנאמר ונואלו ולא עוד אלא שחוטאין כתיב הכא ונואלו וכתיב התם °אשר נואלנו ואשר חטאנו ואיבעית אימא מהכא °נואלו שרי צוען [וגו'] והתעו את מצרים אמר רב נחמן בר יצחק למה נמשלו דברי תורה כעץ שנאמר °עץ חיים היא למחזיקים בה לומר לך מה עץ קטן מדליק את הגדול אף תלמידי חכמים קטנים מחדדים את הגדולים והיינו דאמר ר' חנינא *הרבה למדתי מרבותי ומחבירי יותר מרבותי ומתלמידי יותר מכולן רבי חנינא בר פפא רמי כתיב °לקראת צמא התיו מים וכתיב °הוי כל צמא לכו למים אם תלמיד הגון הוא לקראת צמא התיו מים ואי לא הוי כל צמא לכו למים רבי חנינא בר חמא רמי כתיב °יפוצו מעינותיך חוצה וכתיב °יהיו לך לבדך *אם תלמיד הגון הוא יפוצו מעינותיך חוצה ואם לאו יהיו לך לבדך (*ואמר) רבי חנינא בר אידי [י]למה נמשלו דברי תורה למים דכתיב הוי כל צמא לכו למים לומר לך מה מים מניחין מקום גבוה והולכין למקום נמוך אף דברי תורה אין מתקיימין אלא במי שדעתו שפלה *ואמר רבי אושעיא למה נמשלו דברי תורה לשלשה משקין הללו במים וביין ובחלב דכתיב הוי כל צמא לכו למים וכתיב °לכו שברו ואכלו ולכו שברו בלא כסף ובלא מחיר יין וחלב לומר לך מה שלשה משקין הללו אין מתקיימין אלא בפחות שבכלים אף דברי תורה אין מתקיימין אלא במי שדעתו שפלה (א) כדאמרה ליה *ברתיה דקיסר לר' יהושע בן חנניה אי *חכמה מפוארה בכלי מכוער אמר לה אביך רמי חמרא במני דפחרא אמרה ליה אלא במאי נירמי אמר לה אתון דחשביתו רמו במאני דהבא וכספא אזלה ואמרה ליה לאבוה רמייא לחמרא במני דהבא וכספא ותקיף אתו ואמרו ליה אמר לה לברתיה מאן אמר לך הכי אמרה ליה רבי יהושע בן חנניה קריוהו אמר ליה הכי אמאי אמרת לה הכי אמר ליה כי היכי דאמרה לי אמרי לה והא איכא שפירי דגמירי

אי

רש"י

למימרינהו לתרוייהו · ברוך אתה ברוב ההודאות במרבית ההודאות האל של כל ההודאות משמע ומתחלה היה משמע רוב ממש ולא מרובות וכמו כן בישתבח אל מלך גדול בתשבחות אל ההודאות · מפי רבי : (ג) רשעי עובדי כוכבים אינן חיין כי תולעתם לא תמות ואשם לא תכבה (ישעיה סו) : ופליגא דרב יוסף · דאיהו אמר כתחיית המתים ולא יותר שבה חיים בני אדם שהתבואה גדילה בו : כמטר לקחי. השוה לקח למטר : יערף · כמו אף שמיו יערפו טל (דברים לג) ושחקים ירעפו טל (משלי ג) שהיא מרבה הפירות : כתיב תזל כטל · דמשמע נחת : ערפיהו כמטר · הרגהו : לשמה · משום כאשר צוני ה' אלהי ולא כדי להקרות רבי : לא יכילנא · למיגמר : וכי אדם עץ השדה · אלא מקיש אדם לעץ השדה מה עץ השדה אם עץ מאכל הוא ממנו תאכל ואותו לא תכרות כך תלמידי חכמים אם הגון הוא ממנו תאכל למוד הימנו ואם לאו אותו תשחית סור מעליו : ברזל בברזל יחד · ואיש יחד פני רעהו מה ברזל זה אחד מחדד את חבירו כגון סכין על גבי הבירתה : אינה דולקת יחידי · עץ אחד אינה דולקת אלא ב' או ג' ביחד : יחידי · בלא חבר שיחדדנו : שמוסיפין טפשות דכתיב (ג) נואלנו · אשר נואלנו מתרגם דאיטפשנא : שחוטאין · דכתיב נואלו גבי חטאנו : ואיבעית אימא מהכא נואלו שרי צוען וגו' והתעו את מצרים · ותועה היינו חוטא : תורה כעץ · דכתיב עץ חיים היא למחזיקים בה כשמדליק את האור מצית את העצים דקין תחלה : קטנים מחדדין · ששואלין כל שעה : התיו · משמע להוליך לו מים : וכתיב לכו למים · ילך הוא עצמו : אם תלמיד (חכם) הגון · שרוצה ללמוד ממך מצוה לרב לילך אצלו במקומו : ואם לאו · ילך הוא אצל הרב : יפוצו מעינותיך חוצה · אם הגון הוא אמור לו (ד) סתרי תורה : ואם לאו יהיו לך לבדך · ואין לזרים אתך : שלשה משקים הללו · מים יין וחלב (ה) זו התורה שאינו טוען בה כלום ויודעה ולומדה: בפחות שבכלים · במאני דפחרא (ו) : במאני דפחרא · בדרך שחוק אמר ימרמז מה את אומרת לי והלא אביך טוען יין בכלים מכוערין של חרס : ואלא במאי נירמיה · אם לא בשל חרס הא כולי עלמא עבדי הכי : ותקיף · החמיץ : כי היכי דאמרה לי · אי חכמה מפוארה בכלי מכוער הכי אמרי לה (ז) דיין משתמר בכלי מכוער אף התורה מתקיימת בי יותר משאלו הייתי נאה :

תוספות

וכל העוסק בתורה שלא לשמה תורתו נעשית לו סם המות · וקשה והלא אמרינן (פסחים דף נ:) לעולם יעסוק אדם בתורה אע"ג שאינה לשמה שמתוך שלא לשמה בא לשמה ויש לומר דהכי שלא לשמה הוי דמה שאמרינן לעולם יעסוק בתורה אפילו שלא לשמה היינו כלומר כדי שיקרא רבי או כדי שיכבדוהו ומה שאמרינן הכא כל העוסק בתורה שלא לשמה נעשה לו סם המות היינו מי שלומד לקנטר*:

אם תלמיד חכם הגון ממנו תאכל· פירוש למוד לפניו ואותו לא תכרות כלומר לא תפרד ממנו לילך לפני רב אחר ואם לאו לא תלמוד לפניו והא דאמרינן דלומדים מת"ח אע"פ שאינו הגון כר"מ שהיה לומד לפני אחר במסכת חגיגה (דף טו·) היינו דוקא תלמיד חכם (אחר) יכול ללמוד לפניו לפי שלא ילמוד ממעשיו אבל אם אינו תלמיד חכם אינו רשאי ללמוד לפניו :

אף דברי תורה וכו' · וכן נמי אמרינן בעירובין פ' כילד מעברין (דף נה·) לא בשמים היא ולא מעבר לים היא כלומר לא תמצא התורה במי שמגביה עצמו כשמים שדעתו גבוה ולא בסוחרים ההולכים במדינת הים בעבר הים *דאי ספרא לא סייפא ואי סייפא לא ספרא °והכי נמי איתא התם לא בסחרנין ולא בתגרין ולא *באיסטרולגין כלומר באותן שרואין בכוכבים אמרו ליה לשמואל והא מר איסטרולוגוס הוא אמר להו תיתי לי דלא מעיינא בהו אלא בעידן דנפקא *למיא פירוש להטיל מים ולא אגי מבטל לעלמי :

אי הוו סנו הוו חכימי טפי·(ח) פי' אם היו שונאים היופי הוו תלמידי חכמים ביותר :

ברכות נט: [מגילה כח:] | מגילה כח. | [ברכות לג.] | [כ"ע יג.] | [נ"ל ברבי] | ברכות סג: מכות י. ע"ש | [מכות י. ע"ש] | [נ"ל אמר] | נ"ל אמר | ינוביל נג | נדרים נ: ע"ש [עי' פרש"י] בע"ן עז: ס"ד ספת איתא אוכמא]

[ברכות לג.] [ל"ע כתובות] [ע"ע מ"ה] [פ"ח] [ב"ב]

גליון הש"ס

תוס' ד"ה אף ד"ה וכו' והכי איתא התם במדרש דברים רבה פ"ח :

עין משפט נר מצוה

כא א מיי' פ"ד מהל' ת"ת הל' א טוש"ע י"ד סימן רמו סעיף ז :

כב ב מיי' שם פ"ג הלכה ט :

רבינו חננאל

שנתון במקום האשבורן. אבל אם באו כרבעו לה לברכה : משיצא חתן לקראת כלה . כשתרד הטיפה על הקרקע שכבר ירד בו ממר טפלת כמין אבעבועין היו מברכין ברכת גשמים : א"ר אבהו גדול יום הגשמים כיום שנתנה בו תורה כו' . כל העוסק בתורה לשמה נעשית לו סם חיים שנאמר עץ חיים היא למחזיקים בה והמתעסק שלא לשמה נעשית לו סם המות שנאמר יערוף כמטר לקחי ואין עריפה אלא הריגה א"ר יוחנן כתיב כי האדם עץ השדה אם ת"ח הוא הגון ממנו תאכל ואותו לא תכרות . ואם אינו הגון אותו תשחית וכרת . דברי תורה אין מתקיימין ביחידי שנאמר חרב על הבדים ונואלו . והקטנים מחדדים את הגדולים כו'. ומתלמידי יותר מכולם . (למה)

[אין זה בעירובין אלא במדרש פ' נצבים איתא קצת מזה]

[במדרש הנ"ל איתא לבית המים]

צ"ין לע"ג

רבינו גרשום

מים התחתונים לקראת מים העליונים כדרך שיבא חתן לקראת כלה : ששקולה כתחיית המתים ששניהם חיים לעולם·אלא להכי כתיב כי האדם [עץ השדה] שת"ח נמשל בו וממנו תאכל . כלומר שיכול להבין בתורה : אותו תשחית וכרת שהתורה משחתת בו . נואלו שרי צוען . והרי הן היו רופאין:בפחות שבכלים.

הגהות הב"ח

(א) גמ' אלא במי שדעתו שפלה עליו כדאמרה ליה כו' בכלי מכוער אמר לה אי בת מלכא אבוך במאי רמי חמרא אמרה ליה במאני דפחרא אמר לה כ"ע במאני דפחרא ואבוך במאני דפחרא אמרה ליה אלא במאי נירמי אמר לה כגון אהון דחשביתון רמו: (ב) רש"י ד"ה (רשעי עובדי כוכבים) תא"מ ונ"ב ס"א רשעים : (ג) ד"ה שמוסיפין טפשות דכתיב אשר נואלנו מתרגם כו'·כצ"ל: (ד) ד"ה יפוצו כו' אמור לו (סתרי תורה) תא"מ ונ"ב ס"א דברי תורה: (ה) ד"ה שלשה כו' מים יין וחלב בלא כסף זו התורה מי שאינו טוען: (ו) ד"ה בפחות כו' דפחרא הס"ד ואח"כ מה"ד י"ל אי בת מלכה את כו' כשהיה אמר : (ז) ד"ה כי היכי כו' הכי אמרי לה כי היכי דיין משתמר : (ח) תוס' ד"ה אי הוו כו' פי' אם היו שונאים כ"ב ולהאי פירושא ניחא מסוגיא דיעקב ודרכי אכהו אבל לפרש"י קשיא :

בראתים לא נאמר אלא בראתיו · פי' דמשמע דמהדר אגשם ואם כן משום דגדול יום הגשמים כיום שנברא בו שמים וארץ משתבח ביה הקב"ה אי הוה כתיב בראתים הוה משמע דאהדר אשמים וארץ: **פנים** נזעמים לשון סתר · פירוש בשביל לשון שקר שאומר לשון הרע הרוח צפון תבטל הגשם והייט פנים נזעמים: **מותר** לקרותו רשע · אף על גב דאמרי' בקדושין (דף כח·) הקורא לחבירו רשע יורד עמו לחייו לזה מותר דודאי נכשל בעבירה ועומד במורדו דהכרת פניו ענתה בו: **בהורין** · לשון בהרות טרוק"ש בלע"ז: אם

אי הוו סנו · אותם נאים שהם חכמים: טפי הוו גמירי · שאי אפשר לנאה להשפיל דעתו ובא לידי שכחה: בהיסח הדעת · שאם לא ישמרם יפה יהו נשפכין או טפל לתוך דבר מאוס ונפסלים מלשתות כדבר קל יותר משמן ודבש שמתוך שהן עבים לפה הפסולת למעלה ואפשר לאדם ליטול העליון וזורקו לחוץ והתחתון בר ונקי מה שאין כן במשקה לנטל שהוא עב קלי"ר בלע"ז: בהיסח הדעת · אם אינו מחזירם תמיד: ·שנאמר הרעיפו שמים ממעל ושחקים יזלו צדק תפתח ארץ ויפרו ישע וצדקה תצמיח יחד אני ה' בראתיו בראתים לא נאמר · דמשמע אשחקים יזלו קאי אלא אני ה' בראתיו לטל ומטר שמע מינה שמשתבח ומתפאר (ג) הקב"ה במטר השמים: ישועה פרה ורבה בו · מלילי זכות נכנסין לפניו ביום הגשמים שנזכר לישועה מתוך שעת רצון הוא לישנא דקרא ויפרו ישע ואימתי [illegible] ארצך · במים: נשאת עון עמך · מיד: ה"ג א"ל מר זעירי מדיהבת לרבינא כו' · זעירי סתם היה מן הראשונים ורבינא סוף הוראה לא ראו זה את זה: ואתה תשמע השמים וגו' · ואומר ונתת מטר על ארצך בתפלה השלמה: ציה גם חום יגזלו מימי שלג · כשציה גם חום גוזלין מימות השלג שאין יורדין מטר כמשפטם בידוע ששאול חטאו: ולא יהיה מטר · וסמיך ליה ואבדתם: ציה · דריש לשון צווי דברים שצויתי אתכם בימות החמה תרומות ומעשרות גזלו מימי שלג את המטר: רוח צפון תחולל גשם ופנים נזעמים לשון *שקר · תחולל תבטל כמו לא יחל דברו (במדבר ל) כדאמרי' ביבמות (דף עב·) דרוח צפון ברור הוא ומביא אורה לעולם מה שגשמים נעצרין ופנים נזעמין שמראה הקב"ה שאינו מביא מטר לעולם מפני לשון שקר רכילות ופשט המקרא כשם שרוח צפון תחולל גשם כך פנים נזעמים מפני לשון שקר: וימנעו רביבים · משום דמאכת הכלם שהיה בך עזות היא · משמע כבר נכשל: העז איש · שיש בו עזות פנים אמור לו רשע בפניו ואין בו משום מלקות כדאמרי' במסכת קדושין (דף כח·) ומשום דבר זה בלבד מותר לקרותו רשע: מותר לשנאותו · אע"ג דכתיב ואהבת לרעך כמוך: ועז פניו ישונא · ועז כתיב חסר ו' מי שהוא עז פנים ישנא בשו"א *): ימך · כמי שאין בו כח להוריד טל ומטר: ועתה לא ראו אור . מפני שלא ראו אור של תורה: אפילו כשהשמים בהורין · כמו בהרת מטמר בעבים ורוצה להוריד גשמים רוח עברה ותטהרם

אי הוו סנו טפי הוו גמירי דבר אחר מה שלשה משקין הללו אין נפסלין אלא בהיסח הדעת אף דברי תורה אין משתכחין אלא בהיסח הדעת אמר רבי חמא בר' חנינא גדול יום הגשמים (א) כיום שנבראו שמים וארץ שנאמר °הרעיפו שמים ממעל ושחקים יזלו צדק תפתח ארץ ויפרו ישע וצדקה תצמיח יחד אני ה' בראתיו בראתים לא נאמר אלא בראתיו אמר רב אושעיא גדול יום הגשמים שאפי' ישועה פרה ורבה בו שנאמר תפתח ארץ ויפרו ישע אמר רבי תנחום בר חנילאי אין הגשמים יורדים אלא א"כ נמחלו עונותיהן של ישראל שנאמר °רצית ה' ארצך שבת שבות יעקב נשאת עון עמך כסית כל חטאתם סלה א"ל זעירי מדיהבת לרבינא אתון מהכא מתניתו לה אנן מהכא מתנינן לה °ואתה תשמע השמים וסלחת לחטאת וגו' אמר ר' תנחום בריה דרבי חייא איש כפר עכו אין הגשמים נעצרין אא"כ נתחייבו שונאיהן של ישראל כליה שנאמר °ציה גם חום יגזלו מימי שלג שאול חטאו א"ל זעירי מדיהבת לרבינא אתון מהכא מתניתו לה אנן מהכא מתנינן לה °ועצר את (ג) השמים ואבדתם מהרה אמר רב חסדא אין הגשמים נעצרין אלא בשביל ביטול תרומות ומעשרות שנאמר ציה גם חום יגזלו מימי שלג מאי משמע *תנא דבי רבי ישמעאל בשביל דברים שצויתי אתכם בימות החמה ולא עשיתם יגזלו מכם מימי שלג בימות הגשמים אמר רבי שמעון בן פזי אין הגשמים נעצרין אלא בשביל מספרי לשון הרע שנאמר °רוח צפון תחולל גשם ופנים נזעמים לשון סתר אמר רב סלא אמר רב המנונא אין הגשמים נעצרין אלא בשביל עזי פנים שנאמר °וימנעו רביבים ומלקוש לא היה ומצח אשה זונה היה לך וגו' ואמר רב סלא אמר רב המנונא כל אדם שיש לו עזות פנים סוף נכשל בעבירה שנאמר ומצח אשה זונה היה לך רב נחמן אמר בידוע שנכשל בעבירה שנאמר היה לך ולא נאמר יהיה לך אמר רבה בר רב הונא כל אדם שיש לו עזות פנים מותר לקרותו רשע שנאמר °העז איש רשע בפניו רב נחמן בר יצחק אמר מותר לשנאותו שנאמר °ועז פניו ישונא אל תקרי ישונא אלא ישנא אמר רב קטינא אין הגשמים נעצרין אלא בשביל ביטול תורה שנאמר °בעצלתים ימך המקרה *בשביל עצלות שהיה בישראל שלא עסקו בתורה נעשה שונאו של הקב"ה מך ואין מך אלא עני שנאמר °ואם מך הוא מערכך ואין מקרה אלא הקב"ה שנאמר °המקרה במים עליותיו רב יוסף אמר מהכא °ועתה לא ראו אור בהיר הוא בשחקים ורוח עברה ותטהרם ואין אור אלא תורה שנאמר °כי נר מצוה ותורה אור בהיר הוא בשחקים תנא דבי ר' ישמעאל אפילו בשעה שרקיע נעשה בהורין בהורין להוריד טל ומטר רוח עברה ותטהרם אמר ר' אמי אין הגשמים נעצרין אלא בעון גזל שנאמר °על כפים כסה אור בעון כפים כסה אור ואין כפים אלא חמס שנאמר °ומן החמס אשר בכפיהם ואין אור אלא מטר שנאמר °יפיץ ענן אורו מאי תקנתיה ירבה בתפלה שנאמר °ויצו עליה במפגיע *ואין פגיעה אלא תפלה שנאמר °ואתה אל תתפלל בעד העם הזה [וגו'] ואל תפגע בי וא"ר אמי מאי דכתיב °אם קהה הברזל והוא לא פנים קלקל אם ראית רקיע שקיהה כברזל מלהוריד טל ומטר בשביל מעשה הדור שהן מקולקלין שנא' והוא לא פנים קלקל מה תקנתן יתגברו ברחמים שנא' °וחילים יגבר ויתרון הכשיר חכמה כל שכן אם הוכשרו מעשיהן מעיקרא ריש לקיש אמר אם ראית תלמיד שלמודו

מפוזרת העבים: (ד) המלאך אף ברי שמו יפיץ ענן אורו גשם שלו: וילו · הקדוש ברוך הוא: עליה · על הגשם שתרד: במפגיע · כשיתפלל עליה כמו ואל תפגע בי: קהה הברזל · כמו הקהה את שיניו *ושיני בנים תקהינה (ירמיה לא): והוא לא פנים קלקל · שקלקלו הדור: וכ"ש אם הוכשרו מעשיהן · קודם לכן והכי משמע ויתרון הכשיר שהכשיר לחכמה אם הכשירו מעשיהן מתחילה שיבואו הגשמים יותר מבחיילים יגבר שהן מגבירין חיילים ועומדין בתפלה בזמן שקלקלו:

*) [נ"ל בצי"ן שמאלית וא' עי' מהרש"א בח"א]

שבת נב: [נ"ל סתר] [מגילה יא.] [לקמן ח. ברכות כו: סוטה יד. סנהדרין לה:] [נבהגדרס של פסח]

רבינו חננאל

אין הגשמים יורדין בעולם אא"כ נמחלו עונותיהם של ישראל שנאמר רצית ה' ארצך וגו' נשאת עון עמך וגו' ואתה תשמע השמים וסלחת לחטאת עבדיך ועמך ישראל כי תורם את הדרך הטובה אשר ילכו בה ונתתה מטר על ארצך אשר נתת לעמך לנחלה. אין הגשמים נעצרים אא"כ נתחייבו שונאי ישראל כלייה כו' או בשביל תרומות ומעשרות . ובשביל מספרי לשה"ר . ובשביל עזי פנים . וכל מי שיש לו עזות פנים וראי נכשל בעבירה . ומותר לקרותו רשע שנאמר העז איש רשע בפניו ומותר לשנאותו [שנאמר] ועז פניו ישנא א"ת ישונה אלא ישנא · אין הגשמים נעצרים אלא בעון גזל שנאמר על כפים כסה אור ואין רחוח אלא גזל שנאמר ומן החמס אשר בכפיהם . וכן נמי נעצרים בשביל ישראל שמעשיהם מקולקלין · והוא לא פנים קלקל

רבינו גרשום

כלי תרס: נפסלין בהיסח הדעת . כלומר מפסידין כשאין משתמרין' אלא בראתיו · דהיינו בריית עולם: שצויתי אתכם בימות החמה היינו תרומות ומעשרות: שנאמר ומצח שהוא עז פנים מיד אשה זונה היית לך ועז פניו שמעיו פניו ישנא: ימוך שאינו נותן מטר: כהרים בהרים נדודים:

ויקרא כו

הגהות הב"ח

(א) גמרא גדול יום [illegible] ס"א ר"ים: (ב) שם יעצר את השמים ולא יהיה עשר והאבדתם: (ג) רש"י ד"ה שנאמר כו' ומתפאר בו הקב"ה (ומביא גשמים) הא"מ ונ"ב ס"א אין זה ולספרינו דגרסי גדול יום הגשמים מיום שנבראו כו' ניחא ומכריח ממה שמגיה שמים אלמא דגדול מיום: (ד) ד"ה אפי' כו' המלאך אף ברי . נ"ב לשון רש"י בא"וב אף ברי שם מלאך הממונה על העננים והוא יפיץ ענן מפרו של המקום:

שלמודו קשה עליו כברזל בשביל משנתו שאינה סדורה עליו שנאמר °והוא לא פנים קלקל מאי תקנתיה ירבה בישיבה שנאמר °וחילים יגבר ויתרון הכשיר חכמה כ"ש אם משנתו סדורה לו מעיקרא כי הא דריש לקיש הוה מסדר מתני' ארבעין זמנין כנגד מ' יום שניתנה תורה ועייל לקמיה דר' יוחנן רב אדא בר אהבה מסדר מתני' עשרין וארבע זמנין כנגד תורה נביאים וכתובים ועייל לקמיה דרבא רבא אמר אם ראית תלמיד שלמודו קשה עליו כברזל בשביל רבו שאינו מסביר לו פנים שנאמר והוא לא פנים קלקל מאי תקנתיה ירבה עליו רעים שנאמר וחילים יגבר ויתרון הכשיר חכמה כ"ש אם הוכשרו מעשיו בפני רבו מעיקרא ואמר ר' אמי מאי דכתיב °אם ישוך הנחש בלא לחש ואין יתרון לבעל הלשון אם ראית דור שהשמים משתכין (א) כנחשת מלהוריד טל ומטר בשביל לוחשי לחישות שאין בדור מאי תקנתן ילכו אצל מי שיודע ללחוש דכתיב °יגיד עליו רעו ואין יתרון לבעל הלשון ומי שאפשר לו ללחוש ואינו לוחש מה הנאה יש לו ואם לחש ולא נענה מאי תקנתיה ילך אצל חסיד שבדור וירבה עליו בתפלה שנאמר °ויצו עליה במפגיע *ואין פגיעה אלא תפלה שנאמר °ואתה אל תתפלל בעד העם הזה ואל תשא בעדם רנה ותפלה ואל תפגע בי ואם לחש ועלתה בידו ומגיס דעתו עליו מביא אף לעולם שנאמר °מקנה אף על עולה רבא אמר שני ת"ח שיושבין בעיר אחת ואין נוחין זה לזה בהלכה מתקנאין באף ומעלין אותו שנאמר מקנה אף על עולה *אמר ר"ל מאי דכתיב אם ישוך הנחש בלא לחש ואין יתרון לבעל הלשון לעתיד לבא מתקבצות ובאות כל החיות אצל הנחש ואומרים לו ארי דורס ואוכל זאב טורף ואוכל אתה מה הנאה יש לך אמר להם ואין יתרון לבעל הלשון אמר רבי אמי אין תפלתו של אדם נשמעת אלא אם כן משים נפשו בכפו שנאמר °נשא לבבנו אל כפים [*איני והא] אוקים שמואל אמורא עליה ודריש °ויפתוהו בפיהם ובלשונם יכזבו לו ולבם לא נכון עמו ולא נאמנו בבריתו ואף על פי כן °והוא רחום יכפר עון וגו' *לא קשיא כאן ביחיד כאן בציבור אמר ר' אמי אין גשמים יורדין אלא בשביל בעלי אמנה שנאמר °אמת מארץ תצמח וצדק משמים נשקף וא"ר אמי בא וראה כמה גדולים בעלי אמנה מניין מחולדה ובור ומה המאמין בחולדה ובור כך המאמין בהקב"ה עאכ"ו אמר רבי יוחנן כל המצדיק את עצמו מלמטה מצדיקין עליו הדין מלמעלה שנאמר אמת מארץ תצמח וצדק משמים נשקף רבי חייא בר אבין אמר רב הונא מהכא °וכיראתך עברתך ריש לקיש אמר מהכא °פגעת את שש ועושה צדק בדרכיך יזכרוך הן אתה קצפת ונחטא בהם עולם ונושע אמר ריב"ל כל השמח ביסורין שבאין עליו מביא ישועה לעולם שנאמר בהם עולם ונושע אמר ריש לקיש מאי דכתיב °ועצר את השמים בשעה שהשמים נעצרין מלהוריד (*טל ומטר) דומה לאשה שמחבלת ואינה יולדת והיינו דאמר ריש לקיש משום בר קפרא נאמרה עצירה בגשמים ונאמרה עצירה באשה נאמרה

רש"י

שלמודו קשה עליו כברזל · שקשה הוא לו מרוב קושיות בשביל משנתו שאינה סדורה לו ואינו זוכר מה כתיב בה ולפיכך אינו יודע לפרק אי נמי שגורסה בטעות פוטר על החיוב ומחייב על הפטור ומקשי עלה מדוכתא אחריתי והכי משמע קרא והוא לא (ב) שאינו יודע שמועתו מפני שפנים קלקל שקלקל במשנה שהיא קודם לגמרא: ירבה בישיבה · שיסדירו בני הישיבה משנתם שנאמר וחיילים בין תלמידים שהן חיילות חיילות: ויתרון הכשיר · כשסידר משנתו מתחילה: כנגד מ' יום שניתנה התורה · שתתקיים בידו והדר עייל קמיה דר' יוחנן למיגמר גמרא: כנגד תנ"ך · שהן כ"ד ספרים: שפנים קלקל · שהראה לו פנים רעות: ירבה עליו רעים · לפייס הימנו שיסבור לו פנים: משתכין עליו כנחשת · מאדימין פנים כעין רודיל"א כדאמרי' בבבא מציעא (דף כו.) דשחיך טפי שהעלה חלודה שנעגרין (*מלהוליד) טל ומטר: לוחשי לחישות · בשביל שאין מתפללים תפלה בלחש: יגיד עליו רעו · יתפלל עליו חבירו וגבי גשמים כתיב באיוב: ואין יתרון לבעל הלשון · כלומר מה הנאה יש לבעל הלשון שיודע ללחוש ואינו לוחש: מקנה אף על עולה · מקנה אף מי שמגיס דעתו ועולה: ואין נוחין זה לזה כו' · והכי משמע בשביל שצריך להגיד זה לזה ולהיות נוחין בהלכה ואינן עושין מקנה מתקנאים מתגרים באף ומעלים אותו ומביאים אותו עליהן · ויש גורסין ונוחין זה לזה בהלכה מתקנאים באף וכו' משיגיד עליו רעו שנוחין זה לזה מתקנאים באף ומעלים אותו מעליהם: ארי דורס ואוכל · מיד ואינו מתירא: טורף ואוכל · שמוליך לחוריו ואוכל שם שמפחד מן הבריות ולשלן יש להם הנאה: ולך מה הנאה יש לך · שאתה נושך בני אדם והורגן והוא אומר מה יתרון לבעל הלשון שמספר לשון הרע אע"פ שאין לו הנאה ולפיכך מביאו (ג) הקב"ה בדין אלא נחש כדי שיתביישו מפני שהשיא אדם הראשון ומתביישין עמו מספרי לשון הרע: ולבם לא נכון עמו · עם הקב"ה: ואעפ"כ כתוב בסמוך והוא רחום יכפר עון ושומע תפלתם והיכי אמרת שאין תפלתם נשמעת אא"כ משים נפשו בכפו כלומר שנפשו מכוונת בכפו (ד): בצבור · תפלתם נשמעת ואע"פ שאין לב כולם שלם כדכתיב ויפתוהו בפיהם בדברים לי' רבים: ביחיד · אינו אלא א"כ לבו מכוון: בזמן שאמת מארץ תצמח · שיש אמונה במשא ומתן אז צדק משמים נשקף דהיינו גשמים שהן צדקה: מחולדה ובור · שהמיתו שני בני אדם מלוי הוא באגדה (ה) מעשה בבחור אחד שנתן אמונתו לריבה אחת שישאנה אמרה מי מעיד והיה שם בור אחד וחולדה אמר הבחור בור וחולדה עדים בדבר לימים עבר על אמונתו ונשא אחרת והוליד שני בנים אחד נפל לבור ומת וא' נשכתו חולדה ומת אמרה לו אשתו מה מעשה הוא זה שבניו מתים במיתה משונה ואמר לה כך וכך היה המעשה: המאמין בהקדוש ברוך הוא · שמשימו עד בינו לבין חבירו על אחת כמה וכמה: המצדיק עצמו · שמכשיר ומקשט מעשיו: מצדיקין עליו · מדקדקין עמו אפילו כחוט השערה יותר משאילו מקלקל מעשיו כדי למרק עונותיו: שנאמר אמת מארץ תצמח · אז צדק משמים נשקף צדקה אין כתיב כאן אלא צדק דמשמע דין: וכיראתך עברתך · על מי שהוא ירא אותך אתה מחזיק עברתך כדי למרק עונותיו ופשט המקרא מי יודע עוז אפך מי יודע עוז וכח למצוא אותו לגוס מפניך ביום אפך וכיראתך עברתך כשם שאתה יראוי ומפוחד כך יש להתיירא ולהתפחד מעברתך: פגעת את שש ועושה צדק · במי ששמח ועושה צדק שהן העושים כך בדרכיך יזכירוך אתה פוגע בו אם חוטא כלום כמו ויפגע בו וימת · קרא הכי הוא פגעת את שש ועושה צדק והן העושין כך בדרכיך יזכירוך בהוטם דרכים שאתה מייסרן ביסורין יזכירוך לטובה ואומרים הן אתה קצפת בשביל שחטאנו בהם עולם ונשע בשבילם טשע לעולם הבא: שמחבלת · כמו חבלי יולדה אף השמים עושין כן וקשה לעולם ועל חטא הוא: נאמרה

תוספות

אם ראית דור שהשמים משתכין עליו כנחשת מלהוריד גשם עליו וכו' · מכאן מוכיח ר"ת דהא דאמרי' בבבא בתרא (דף יט. ושם) אין טומנין בסלעים מ"ט משום דמשתכי ליה לקדירה ר"ל משתכי מקלקלים המאכל שבקדירה ובלע"ז אורמשי"ר והא דאמר לקדירה לאו דוקא לקדירה אלא למאכל שבקדירה דהכי נמי קאמר (שבת דף יח:) האי קדרה חייתא שרי ואין לפרש כפרש"י שפי' התם משתכי משברים הקדירה דא"כ מאי קאמר הכא שהשמים משתכין (ו) ר"ל שהשמים משתברין אלא ודאי משתכים ר"ל מעלין חלודה כמו דבר שבטל ממלאכתו ימים רבים ומחליד ובלע"ז ראולי"ר: **ואי** לוחש ועלתה בידו ומגיס דעתו מביא אף לעולם שנאמר יגיד עליו ריעו וגו' · כלומר אם יגיד עליו ריעו שעל ידו באו הגשמים והוא מגיס דעתו מקנה אף עולה כלומר הוא קונה אף ועולה כלומר אם עולה שמגיס דעתו עליו הוא מקנה האף:

בחולדה ובור כך בהקב"ה על אחת כמה וכמה · פי' מאמין בחולדה ובור מעשה היה בנערה אחת היתה רוצה לילך לבית אביה והיה בור בדרך ונפלה ובא בחור אחד ואמר אם אני אעליך תנשאי לי אמרה לו הן ונשבעו ביניהן שהוא לא ישא אשה אחרת והיא לא תנשא לאיש אחר ואמרו מי מעיד בינינו והיתה חולדה אחת הולכה לפני הבור ואמרו אלו שנים בור וחולדה יהיו עדים בינינו והלכו לדרכם והיא עמדה בשבועתה והוא נשא אשה אחרת וילדה בן באת חולדה ונשכתו ומת וילדה לו בן שני ונפל לבור ומת אמרה לו אשתו מה זה המעשה שהגיע לנו שלא כשאר בני אדם נזכר השבועה וסיפר לאשתו כל המעשה אמרה לו א"כ חזור וקחנה וכתב לה גט והלך ונשא את הבתולה והיינו דאמרי המאמין בבור וחולדה שהעמידו עדותן : וגטמה

רבינו חננאל

תלמיד שתלמודו קשה עליו מפני שאין רבו מסביר לו פנים בהלכה: אם ראית הגשמים נעצרים ומתכסין שאין בדור לוחש לחישות כראוי כו'. ואין הגשמים יורדין אלא בשביל בעלי אמונה שנאמר אמת מארץ תצמח א"ר יוחנן כל המצדיק עצמו מלמטה ומחזיק דרך החסידות אפילו מעט אם יפח מדקדקין עליו מלמעלה ולוקחין הדין ממנו שנאמר אמת מארץ תצמח וצדק משמים נשקף. ועוד מהכא וכיראתך עברתך. לפי דקדוקן ביראתך כן מדקדקין עליהם בעברתך ועוד מהכא בדרכיך יזכרוך. כפי דרכך מזכירין אותך מלמעלה. אריב"ל כל ששמח ביסורין הבאין עליו מביא ישועה לעולם שנאמר הן אתה קצפת ונחטא בהם עולם ונושע. הן קצפת והכית אותנו בשביל חטאתינו שחטאנו ששמחנו בהן כלומר הודינו כי הכאה זו בשביל עונותינו היא עולם ונושע ראויה זו להיות ישועה לעולם. א"ר שמעון בן לקיש נאמרה עצירה

רבינו גרשום

וכ"ש היכא דהוכשרו מעשיהם מעיקרא דהיינו יתרון הכשר והוא לא פנים קלקל שלא הראה פנים במשנה קלקל בתלמוד: והוא לא פנים. שאין רבו מסביר לו פנים ירבה עליו רעים. לרצות את רבו שיסביר לו פנים: משתכין. מהליך: לוחשי לחישות. שיודעין להתפלל ואין מתפללין: מקנה שמגיס דעתו אף על עולה מעלה כעס על העולם: ומעלי אותו שמסלקין אותו מן העולם: מה הנאה יש לך. שאתה נושך ואינך אוכל. כאן ביחיד. נשא לבבנו: כאן בצבור. ויפתוהו בפיהם: מצדיקים עליו מלמעלה כדכתיב וסביביו נשערה מאד:

הגהות הב"ח

(א) גמ' דור שהשמים משתכין עליו כנחשת מלהוריד כו' לחישות שאין באותו הדור מאי: (ב) רש"י ד"ה שלמודו כו' משמע קרא והוא לא פנים קלקל שאינו יודע: (ג) ד"ה ולך כו' מביאו הקב"ה בדין (אלא נחש) תא"מ וכ"ב סיא אינו ולגירסא שלפנינו נ"ל מביאן: (ד) ד"ה ואעפ"כ כו' מכוונת בכפו מכוון הס"ד נ"ב כלומר עם כפו: (ה) ד"ה מחולדה כו' מעשה בבחור אחד. נ"ב עי' בערוך ערך חלד מבאר המעשה באריכות: (ו) תוס' ד"ה אם כו' קאמר הכא שהשמים משתכין שאין ר"ל שהשמים:

[ג"י מלהוריד]
[לעיל ז: וש"נ]
[ילקוט איתא ספר]

נאמרה עצירה באשה שנאמר °כי עצר עצר ה' בעד כל רחם ונאמרה עצירה בגשמים דכתיב °ועצר את השמים נאמר לידה באשה ונאמר לידה בגשמים נאמר לידה באשה דכתיב °ותהר ותלד בן ונאמר לידה בגשמים דכתיב °והולידה והצמיחה נאמר פקידה באשה ונאמר פקידה בגשמים נאמר פקידה באשה דכתיב °וה' פקד את שרה ונאמר פקידה בגשמים דכתיב °פקדת הארץ ותשקקה רבת תעשרנה פלג אלהים מלא מים מאי פלג אלהים מלא מים תנא כמין קובה יש ברקיע שממנה גשמים יוצאין אמר רבי שמואל בר נחמני מאי דכתיב °אם לשבט אם לארצו אם לחסד ימציאהו אם לשבט בהרים ובגבעות אם לחסד ימציאהו לארצו בשדות ובכרמים אם לשבט לאילנות אם לארצו לזרעים אם לחסד ימציאהו בורות שיחין ומערות בימי רבי שמואל בר נחמני הוה כפנא ומותנא אמרי היכי נעביד [א]ניבעי רחמי אתרתי לא אפשר אלא ליבעי רחמי אמותנא וכפנא ניסבול אמר להו ר' שמואל בר נחמני [ב]ניבעי רחמי אכפנא דכי יהיב רחמנא שובעא לחיי הוא דיהיב דכתיב °פותח את ידך ומשביע לכל חי רצון ומנלן דלא מצלינן אתרתי דכתיב °ונצומה ונבקשה מאלהינו על זאת מכלל דאיכא אחריתי במערבא אמרי משמיה דר' חגי מהכא °ורחמין למבעא מן קדם אלה שמיא על רזא דנא מכלל דאיכא אחריתי בימי ר' זירא גזור גזרה וגזור דלא למיתב בתעניתא אמר להו ר' זירא [ג]נקבליה עילוון ולכי בטיל הגזירה ליתביה אמרי ליה מנא לך הא אמר להו דכתיב °ויאמר אלי אל תירא דניאל כי מן היום הראשון אשר נתת את לבך להבין ולהתענות לפני אלהיך נשמעו דבריך אמר רבי יצחק אפילו שנים כשני אליהו וירדו גשמים בערבי שבתות אינן אלא סימן קללה היינו *דאמר רבה בר שילא *קשה יומא דמיטרא כיומא דדינא אמר אמימר אי לא דצריך לברייתא בעינן רחמי ומבטלינן ליה ואמר רבי יצחק שמש בשבת צדקה לעניים שנאמר °וזרחה לכם יראי שמי שמש צדקה ומרפא ואמר רבי יצחק גדול יום הגשמים שאפילו פרוטה שבכיס מתברכת בו שנאמר °לתת מטר ארצך בעתו ולברך את כל מעשה ידיך ואמר רבי יצחק *אין הברכה מצויה אלא בדבר הסמוי מן העין שנאמר °יצו ה' אתך את הברכה באסמיך תנא דבי ר' ישמעאל אין הברכה מצויה אלא בדבר שאין העין שולטת בו שנאמר יצו ה' אתך את הברכה באסמיך ת"ר [ד]הנכנס למוד את גרנו אומר יר"מ ה' אלהינו שתשלח ברכה במעשה ידינו התחיל למוד אומר ברוך השולח ברכה בכרי הזה מדד ואח"כ בירך הרי זו תפלת שוא לפי שאין הברכה מצויה לא בדבר השקול ולא בדבר המדוד ולא בדבר המנוי אלא בדבר הסמוי מן העין: קיבוץ גייסות צדקה (*מעשה) פרנס סימן: אמר רבי יוחנן גדול יום הגשמים כיום קבוץ גליות שנאמר °שובה ה' את שביתנו כאפיקים בנגב ואין אפיקים אלא מטר שנאמר °ויראו אפיקי ים ואמר רבי יוחנן גדול יום הגשמים שאפילו גייסות פוסקות בו שנאמר °תלמיה רוה נחת גדודיה ואמר רבי יוחנן אין הגשמים נעצרין אלא בשביל פוסקי צדקה ברבים ואין נותנין שנאמר °נשיאים ורוח וגשם אין איש מתהלל במתת שקר וא"ר יוחנן מאי דכתיב

עשר

רש"י

נאמרה עצירה באשה כו' · כלומר על כולן מבקשים רחמים: פלג · בריכה: כמין קובה · אבל מלא מים: אם לשבט · אם גזר הקב"ה רוב גשמים לרעה אז יורדים בכח כשבט שמכה בכח וחזרו בתשובה הקב"ה מורידן על הרים וגבעות מקום שאין שם איש: אבל אם לחסד · שיורדין בנחת ימציאהו לארצו לארץ ישראל: אתרתי · לא בעינן רחמי אהדדי כדלקמן: נבעי רחמי אכפנא · דליתיב שובעא ומותנא ליבטל ממילא: דכי יהיב רחמנא שובעא לחיי הוא דיהיב · לחיים ולא למתים דאינו מביא שובעא כדי להמית בני אדם אלא כדי שיחיו: משביע לכל חי רצון · שובע נותן לבני אדם חיים: על זאת · על חדא משמע בעזרא כתיב: על רזא דנא · בדניאל כתיב: דלא ליתבו בתעניתא · דלא בעו דליתי ברכה לעולם בשבילן: ניקבל עילוון · יומי תעניתא דמשום קבלה מהני לן [illegible] ומנלן דעבדינן הכי. כלומר דמהני אי עבדינן הכי: אשר נתת לבך להתענות לפני אלהיך נשמעו דבריך · אלמא מסקיבל עליו נשמעו דבריו: כשני אליהו · בימי אחאב שהיה העולם צריך לגשמים דכתיב (מלכים א יז) אם יהיה השנים האלה טל ומטר כי אם לפי דברי: סימן קללה · שבני אדם צריכים לחזר בשוק לקנות סעודת שבת (א): קשי יומי דמיטרא · שאין בני אדם יכולין לעשות צרכיהן: כיומא דדינא · שני וחמישי שמתקבצין בני אדם לדון עם חבריהן כתקנת עזרא שיש הומות וקולות ואוושות ביום הגשמים כיום הדין ובערב שבת כל שכן דקשי מיטרא: והיינו דאמר ר' שילא: ומבטלינהו לירידת גשמים שטורחין בני אדם ואינן יכולין לצאת ולבא: צדקה לעניים · שמתעדנין בה ונוח להן יום ברור ומתחממין בה ביום הגינה: יראי שמי · שומרי שבת: פרוטה שבכיס · אפי' מעשה ידים שאינן צריכים לגשמים מתברכין: ברוך השולח ברכה · (*שיפוע) ומזכיר בה מלכות ואזכרה ככל הברכות כולן: הרי זו תפלת שוא · (ג) ושוב אין ברכה נכנסת בה: בדבר הסמוי מן העין · שאינו יודע הסכום: כאפיקים · כאפיקי נחלים: בנגב · (ג) יבשה והנה חרבו מתרגמינן נגיבו: אפיקי ים · מולאי (ד) ים אלמא אפיק לשון מים ואפיקים בנגב נמי לשון גשמים: גייסות · חיילות כשארץ מרווה תלמי הארץ בגשם מיד גדודים נוחין כדלקמן: פוסקי צדקה ברבים · בשם ולפנים ואורחא דמילתא נקט שאין אדם עשוי לפסוק צדקה בינו לבין עצמו ואינו נותן: נשיאים ורוח · באין לעולם כאילו גשמים יורדין ואינן יורדין בשביל האיש המתהלל במתת שקר דכשם שהוא עושה לפנים ומחניף את העניים אף שמים מחניפין את הארץ שמראין נשיאים ורוח וגשם אין אי נמי אין קאי אשלשתם דמכל אלו נעצרין:

ליטקא

תוספות

ונצומה ונבקשה מאלהינו · ויעתר לנו פירוש מדקאמר על [זאת] משמע דאיכא מילתא אחריתא וכן פירש בסמוך על דנא: **אלא** בדבר הסמוי מן העין שנאמר יצו ה' וגו' · תימה דאמרינן פרק כל הבשר (חולין דף קה:) גבי הני שקולאי דדרו חביתא דחמרא בעו לאתפוחי אותבוהו תותי מרזיבא פקע חביתא ומפרש שם בשביל השד שהיה שם עד דאכפייה מר בר רב אשי לשד לשלם אמר ליה שידא למר בר רב אשי ליקבע לי מר זימנא דאיזיל ואשלים קבע ליה זימנא כי מטא זימניה איעכב ואמר ליה אמאי לא אתית בזמנך אמר ליה כל מידי דצייר וחתים וכייל ומני לית לן רשות למישקל מיניה אלמא בדבר המדוד והמנוי לית ליה רשות למשקל מיניה ובדבר הסמוי אית ליה רשות אלמא אין ברכה בדבר הסמוי וי"ל דלא קשה מידי דהא דקאמר התם (*) היינו [illegible] הפקר ולא דבר דכייל ומנוי או צייר וחתים היינו בשביל דאין ברכה מצויה בהגי ולית בהו דבר הפקר והאי דבעלים ניגהו אלא בדבר הסמוי והיינו מטעם דהברכה מצויה בדבר הסמוי ומה שמתברכה בשביל הברכה אית להו רשות למישקל בסמוי דהייט כמו הפקר שאין לשום אדם זכות בו אי נמי הכא מיירי בדבר המנוי והמדוד בלא צייר וחתים ובהא אית להו רשותא והתם מיירי במדוד ומנוי וכייל וצייר וחתים ובהא לית להו רשותא: **גדול** יום גשמים כיום קיבוץ גליות שנאמר שובה ה' את שביתנו כאפיקים בנגב וגו' · ואם תאמר אמאי לא קאמר גדול יום הגשמים יותר מקיבוץ גליות דהא כאפיקים בנגב כתיב ומי נתלה במי קטן נתלה בגדול שאפיקים גדולים מיום קיבוץ גליות דהכי נמי אמר (לעיל דף ז:) יערוף כמטר לקחי מי נתלה במי קטן נתלה בגדול וי"ל דה"פ אנו מתפללים הכי שובה ה' את שביתנו כאפיקים היורדין בנגב שגדול יום קיבוץ כאפיקים בנגב א"כ עשה עמנו לטובה אוה בקבוץ גליות בהיות כי זה כמו זה ואפיקים בנגב תחדש בכל יום כיום קיבוץ גליות אבל יותר לא:

עשר

עין משפט נר מצוה

כג א ב טוש"ע א"ח סי' תקעו סעיף טו:

כד ג שם סימן תקעה סעיף ג:

כה ד מיי' פ"י מהל' ברכות הלכה כב סמג עשין כו טוש"ע א"ח סימן רל סעיף ג:

רבינו חננאל

ולידה ופקידה באשה וכנגדן ברקיע ובארץ. פקידה שנאמר פקדת ארץ ותשוקקה. לידה שנאמר והולידה והצמיחה עצירה שנא' ועצר את השמים תנא [illegible] ומשם גשמים יורדים שנאמר פלג אלהים מלא מים: הוה כפנא ומותנא אמרי לא אפשר למבעי רחמי אתרתי דכתיב ונצומה ונבקשה מאלהינו על זאת. במערבא אמרי ורחמין למיבעי מן קדם אלהא על רזא דנא. מכלל דאיכא (אחר) אחריתי: אלא מיבעי רחמי אכפנא (ומותנא נסבול) דכי יהב רחמנא שובעא לחיי הוא דיהיב שנאמר פותח את ידך ומשביע לכל חי רצון. בימי רבי זירא גזור שמדא ומנעום מלקבוע תענית א"ר זירא ניקבליה עלוון מהשתא ולכי בטיל שמדא ניתוב בתעניתא שנאמר ויאמר אלי אל תירא דניאל כי מן היום אשר נתת לבך להבין ולהתענות וגו'. גשמים (בלילי)[בערבי] שבתות אפילו [illegible] סימן קללה הן. אין הברכה מצויה לא בדבר המדוד ולא בדבר המנוי ולא בדבר השקול אלא בדבר הסמוי מן העין שנאמר יצו ה' אתך את הברכה באסמיך וגו'. א"ר יוחנן אין הגשמים נעצרין אלא בשביל פוסקי צדקה ברבים ואינם נותנים שנאמר נשיאים ורוח וגשם אין וגו'.

רבינו גרשום

אם לשבט דאתי ברזיא: להרים שילך על ההרים: אם לחסד שיורד בנחת ימציאהו ליישוב: צדקה לעניים שמתחממין שהן ערומים: בערבי שבתות סימן קללה הוא שאין יכולין לטרוח לכבוד שבת.*) כרעבד לאבוך · שנעשה גל של עצמות:

*) עיין לדף ט.

הגהות הב"ח

(א) רש"י ד"ה סימן כו' סעודת שבת הס"ד ואחר כך מה"ד והיינו דאמר ר' שילא קשי יומי דמיטרא שאין כו' עד כ"ש דקשי מיטרא מה"ד ומבטלינהו לירידת גשמים כו': (ב) ד"ה הרי זו תפלת שוא. דשוב אין ברכה: (ג) ד"ה בנגב. לשון יובש והנה חרבו: (ד) ד"ה אפיקי ים. מולאי מים אלמא כו' כצ"ל: (ס) תוס' ד"ה אלא כו' דהא דקאמר התם הכי הייט טעמא:

מסורת הש"ס

[נ"ל ושפע]

ב"מ סה.

עיין נכרי"ך בע"י פירושו

ב"מ מב.

[נ"ל מעשה]

ב"ב ט

(דברים יד) עשר תעשר *עשר בשביל שתתעשר אשכחיה ר' יוחנן לינוקא דריש לקיש אמר ליה אימא לי פסוקיך א"ל עשר תעשר א"ל ומאי עשר תעשר א"ל עשר בשביל שתתעשר אמר ליה מנא לך א"ל זיל נסי אמר ליה ומי שרי לנסוייה להקב"ה והכתיב (שם ו) לא תנסו את ה' א"ל הכי אמר רבי הושעיא (מלאכי ג) חוץ מזו שנאמר הביאו את כל המעשר אל בית האוצר ויהי טרף בביתי ובחנוני נא בזאת אמר ה' צבאות אם לא אפתח לכם את ארובות השמים והריקותי לכם ברכה עד בלי די *מאי עד בלי די אמר רמי בר חמא אמר רב עד שיבלו שפתותיכם מלומר די א"ל אי הות מטי התם להאי פסוקא לא הוית צריכנא לך ולהושעיא רבך ותו אשכחיה ר' יוחנן לינוקיה דריש (משלי יט) לקיש דיתיב ואמר אולת אדם תסלף דרכו ועל ה' יזעף לבו יתיב רבי יוחנן וקא מתמה אמר מי איכא מידי דכתיבי בכתובי דלא רמיזי באורייתא א"ל אטו הא מי לא רמיזי (בראשית מב) והכתיב ויצא לבם ויחרדו איש אל אחיו לאמר מה זאת עשה אלהים לנו דל עיניה וחזא ביה אתיא אימיה אפיקתיה אמרה ליה תא מקמיה דלא ליעבד לך כדעבד לאבוך (*א"ר) יוחנן מטר בשביל יחיד פרנסה בשביל רבים מטר בשביל יחיד דכתיב (דברים כח) יפתח ה' לך את אוצרו הטוב לתת מטר ארצך פרנסה בשביל רבים דכתיב (שמות טז) הנני ממטיר לכם לחם מיתיבי ר' יוסי בר' יהודה אומר שלשה פרנסים טובים עמדו לישראל אלו הן משה ואהרן ומרים וג' מתנות טובות ניתנו על ידם ואלו הן באר וענן ומן באר בזכות מרים עמוד ענן בזכות אהרן מן בזכות משה (במדבר כ) מתה מרים נסתלק הבאר שנאמר ותמת שם מרים וכתיב בתריה ולא היה מים לעדה וחזרה בזכות שניהן מת אהרן נסתלקו ענני (שם כא) כבוד שנאמר וישמע הכנעני מלך ערד *מה שמועה שמע שמע שמת אהרן ונסתלקו ענני כבוד וכסבור ניתנה לו (שם כ) רשות להלחם בישראל והיינו דכתיב ויראו כל העדה כי גוע אהרן אמר ר' אבהו אל תקרי ויראו אלא וייראו כדדריש ר"ל *דאר"ל כי משמש בארבע לשונות אי דלמא אלא *דהא חזרו שניהם בזכות משה מת משה (זכריה יא) נסתלקו כולן שנאמר ואכחיד את שלשת הרועים בירח אחד וכי בירח אחד מתו והלא מרים מתה בניסן ואהרן באב ומשה באדר אלא מלמד שנתבטלו ג' מתנות טובות שנתנו על ידן ונסתלקו כולן בירח אחד אלמא אשכחן פרנסה בשביל יחיד שאני משה *כיון דלרבים הוא בעי כרבים דמי רב הונא בר מנוח ורב שמואל בר אידי ורב חייא מווסתניא הוו שכיחי קמיה דרבא כי נח נפשיה דרבא אתו לקמיה דרב פפא כל אימת דהוה אמר להו שמעתא ולא הוה מסתברא להו הוו מרמזי אהדדי חלש דעתיה אקרויה

רש"י

ליטקא דריש לקיש · בן אחותו של ר' יוחנן ולאחר מיתתו של ריש לקיש כדמוכח לקמן : אמר · ינוקא לר' יוחנן מאי עשר תעשר : א"ל ינוקא · והכתיב לא תנסו : שיבלו · כלומר שייגעו דוורלא"ש בלע"ז : אי הוה מטינא להתם · להאי קרא דהביאו את כל המעשר הוה ידעית ליה ממילא : לר' הושעיא רבך · דאמרית לי משמיה : אולת אדם תסלף דרכו ועל ה' יזעף לבו · כשאדם חוטא מסלף דרכו שבאין עליו פגעים ועל השם יזעף לבו שכועס ואומר מפני מה אירע לי פגע זה: ולא רמזה · משה באורייתא שהחומש הוא יסוד נביאים וכתובים ובכולן יש סמך למצוא מן התורה : דלי עיניה · רבי יוחנן שהיו עפעפיו מכסין את עיניו ומגביהן במזלגי דכספא בבבא קמא בפ' אחרון (דף קיז·) שהיה רוצה לראותו מפני שהוא חריף : דלא ליעביד לך כדעבד לאבוך · שלא יתן עיניו בך כמו שנתן באביך והמיתו בבבא מציעא (דף פד·) : מטר בשביל יחיד · שאם א"צ מטר אלא לאדם אחד כגון שזרע אחר זמן זריעת בני אדם או שדר בעיר שכולה נכרים וצריך למטר בא בזכותו (א) ופרנסה שפע טובה ומחיה לכל העולם אינו בא לעולם בזכות אחד אלא בשביל רבים שאם רבים צריכין שובע שתשלח ברכה בתבואה הקב"ה עושה אם זכו אבל יחיד הצריך שיתברכו תבואותיו אין הקב"ה משנה בעבורו דין השנה אלא כפי ברכותיה ואע"פ שמוריד *) בשביל יחיד מטר זה להשקות תבואותיו שלא יהו גרועות משל אחרים אבל לעשות שדהו כשדה שובע לא : מטר ארצך · של אחד משמע : ממטיר לכם · לשון רבים : בארה של מרים · סלע ובין ממנו מים והיה מתגלגל והולך עם ישראל והוא הסלע שבו הכה משה שלא היה רוצה להזיל מימיו בשבילו לפי שמתה מרים : ונסתלקו ענני כבוד · ענני רקיע וענני עשן ושאר עננים אינן של כבוד : חזרה בזכות שניהן · שכן כתיב ודברתם שניכם אל הסלע ונתן מימיו : כי משמש ארבע לשונות · אי דלמא אלא דהא · כל מקום שצריך לדרוש כי בין לענין דרשה בין למשמעות המקרא תוכל לשנותו באחד מהני ארבע לשונות דלשון כי משמש בעולם וכן וכד וכרם ואוי בכלל הני ד' הן והאי דכי גוע אהרן משתמש בלשון דהא ושמעינן מינה טעמא דקרא דמה טעם נתראו דהא מית שהרי מת אהרן וריש לקיש לא אתי למימר דלא מתרגמין שום כי בעולם אלא (ב) מהני לשונות אלא אפי' מתרגם א] דלמא אזי דרשינן משמעותיה כמשמעות דהא ומאן דמתרגם וחזיאו כל כנישתא דהא מית טועה הוא דאם כן ואתחזיאו מיבעי ליה ויראו כל העדה במשקל ויראו ראשי הבדים וירפו המים ויעלו מעל משכן קרח : חזרו שניהם בזכות משה · מדכתיב ואכחיד את שלשת הרועים פשיטא לן דבדידהו משתעי שלא מצינו פרנסים לישראל שלשה כאחד אלא הם : מתה בניסן · שנאמר (במדבר כ) ויבואו בני ישראל כל העדה מדבר צין בחדש הראשון וישב העם בקדש ותמת שם מרים ותקבר שם (*בפרה) אדומה : אהרן מת . באחד לחדש*: מוסתניא · מאותו מקום: אחוו להדדי · מראין ומבינין זה לזה דלא סלקא להו שמעתא כרבא :

*) בשביל זה מטר להשקות רש"א .

תוספות

עשר תעשר · הכי איתא בסיפרי עשר תעשר את כל תבואת זרעך היוצא השדה שנה שנה אין לי אלא תבואת זרעך שחייב במעשר רבית ופרקמטיא וכל שאר רווחים מנין ת"ל את כל דהוה מצי למימר את תבואתך מאי כל לרבות רבית ופרקמטיא וכל דבר שמרויח בו והכי נמי איכא בהגדה *היוצא השדה שנה [שנה] כלומר אם לא תעשר שדך כהוגן לא יהיה לך אלא היוצא מן השדה כלומר לא יעשה שדך אלא כפי מעשרות שהיו קודם לכן דהיינו היוצא מן השדה כלומר מה שהיית רגיל להוציא למעשר מן השדה ומעשה באדם אחד שהיה עשיר והיה לו שדה שעשתה אלף כור והיה אותו עשיר נוטל ק' כורין למעשר ומפריש כל שנה ושנה וכן עשה כל ימיו כשחלה למות קרא לבנו ואמר לו בני דע שהשדה זו שאני מוריש לך עושה בכל שנה ושנה אלף כורין הזהר שתפריש ק' כורין כאשר עשיתי ומת אותו האיש ועמד הבן במקומו ועשה השדה אלף כורין כאשר היה עושה בחיי האב והפריש ממנה ק' כורין בשנה שניה נסתכל וראה הבן שמעשר היה דבר גדול ואמר שלא יפריש לשנה אחרת נתמעט השדה ולא עשה כי אם מאה כורין נצטער עליו ושמעו קרוביו שכך מיעט ולא הפריש מעשר באו כולם אלנו מלובשים לבנים ושמחים אמר להם כמדומה לי שאתם שמחים בקלקלתי אמרו לו נצטער עליך כי גרמת לך כל הרעה הזאת ומפני מה לא הפרשת מעשר כראוי היטב בא וראה כי מתחלה כשבא השדה לידך היית בעל הבית והקב"ה כהן שהיה המעשר חלקו ליתן לעניים ועכשיו שלא הפרשת חלקו לו היה הקב"ה בעל הבית ואתה כהן שאין שדך עושה (ג) מה שהיה עושה מתחלה אלף כורין והפריש לך מאה כורין והיינו דכתיב (במדבר ה) ואיש את קדשיו לו יהיו כלומר *כשאינו מפריש כהוגן לא יהיה לו אלא הקדשים כלומר המעשר ועל זה אמרו חכמים המעכב מעשרותיו לסוף בא שלא יהיה לו אלא אחד מעשר כדכתיב (ישעיה ה) וזרע חומר יעשה איפה דהיינו המעשר דאיפה ג' סאין ובחומר יש (לו) ל' סאין וכן כתיב *כי עשרת צמדי כרם יעשו בת אחת וה"ר נתן האופניא"ל פי' *היוצא מן השדה כלומר ואם לאו שאין אתה מפריש העישור יהיה לאותו היוצא לשדה דהיינו עשו הרשע כלומר שיקחוהו העובדי כוכבים :

רבינו חננאל

עשר תעשר כלומ' עשר כדי שירבה קנייניך ותעשר עוד פעמי' אחרים . ואמרינן שרי למינ' והכי יוכר : לא תנסו את ה' א"ל : ושנינן חוץ מזו שנא' הביאו וגו' ובחנוני בזאת וגו' כתיב : אולת אדם תסלף דרכו ה' יזעף לבו . כיוצא בתורה דכתיב ויחרדו איש אל אחיו לאמר מה זאת עשה אלהים לנו. א"ר יוחנן מטר בזכות יחיד שנאמר [illegible] ארצך בעתו ר"ל אמר כהנא שאלו מה' מטר וגו' ותניא ומטר גשם יתן להם לאיש יכול לכל השדות שלו ת"ל בשדה. יכול לכל השדה ת"ל עשב השדה וכדר' דניאל ברי' רב קטינא דהוה סייר גינתיה ואמר האי משרא בעי מיא והאי משרא לא בעי מיא ואתי מטרא : [illegible] משרא דאמר בעי [illegible] פרנסה בשביל רבי' שנאמר הנני ממטיר לכם לחם מן השמים וגו' . ואקשינן משה רבינו יחידי הוה (וקמא) [וקאמר] כי המן ירד בזכותו . והענן בזכות אהרן והבאר בזכות מרים . והיינן כיון שמתו נסתלקו [illegible] אחד ואחד הדבר שהיה בזכותו . וחזר בשביל מרע"ה . וכיון שמת נסתלקו הכל שנאמר ואכחיד שלשת הרועים בירח אחד . ושנינן שאני משה רבינו כיון דאלים זכותיה כרבים דמי . ג' פרנסים טובים עמדו לישראל . ואלו הן משה ואהרן ומרים וג' מתנות נתן להם הקב"ה על ידם ואלו הן מן ובאר ועמוד הענן כו' : תלמידי דרבא כד נח נפשיה אתו לקמיה דרב פפא לא הוו מסתברי להו שמעתתיה הוה מרמזי להדדי חזנהו

[גם זה איתא בילקוט רמז תתנ"ג וכן בתנחומא]

[עי' ילקוט רמז תת. וכן איתא בתנחומ' פ' ראה]

הגהות הב"ח

(א) רש"י ד"ה מטר כו' בא בזכותו הס"ד ומה"ד ופרנסה כו' ואף על פי שמוריד בשביל זה מטר להשקות : (ב) ד"ה כי משמש כו' שום כי בעולם אלא באחד מהני לשונות : (ג) תוס' ד"ה עשר כו' ואתה כהן שאין שדך עושה עתה מה שהיה עושה :

[נ"ל בפרשת פרה] .

[נ"ל באחד לחדש בחדש החמישי בפ' אלה מסעי]

הגהות מהר"ב רנשבורג

[א] רש"י ד"ה כי משמש וכו' אלא אפי' מתורגם אזי כצ"ל :

[שבת קיט.]

[לקמן כב: שבת לב: מכות כג:]

[נ"ל ואמר רבי]

ר"ה ג.

גיטין ל. שבועות מט:

[פסחים לג:]

ס"א כיון דאלים זכותיה כרבים דמי

תורה אור

תלמוד

תלמוד לומר עשב · פי' שאם לא יהיו צריכים אלא לעשב אחד ירד על אותו עשב ועל שאר כל השדה לא ירדו :

נהילא מקמי מיטרא · פי' גשם דק וסימנך מהולתא פירוש שמתחילה יוצא הפסולת ואח"כ הסולת פירוש שלא היו עושין כמו דעבדינן האידנא (ג) היו כותשין החטין במכתשת עד שנקלף כל הסובין מעל החטים וכי הוו מרקדין על גבי נפה היה הפסולת הסובין שעליו יוצא לכתחילה ואחר כך היה יוצא הסולת :

חריא דעיזי · פי' ריעי של עזים שבתחילה ריעי גדול וכשהיא פוסקת מתרזת וכל דק :

ואמר רבי יוחנן מעליותיו של הקב"ה כמאן כר' יהושע · פי' כרבי יהושע דאמר כל העולם כולו ממים העליונים הם שותים דאי כרבי אליעזר הא אמר מימי אוקיינוס הוא שותה :

יקר

תורה אור

אקרויה בחלמיה °ואכחיד את שלשת הרועים למחר כי הוו מיפטרי מיניה אמר להו ליזלו רבנן *בשלמא: רב שימי בר אשי הוה שכיח קמיה דרב פפא הוה מקשי ליה טובא יומא חד חזייה דנפל על אפיה שמעיה דאמר רחמנא ליצלן מכיסופא דשימי קביל עליה שתיקותא ותו לא אקשי ליה ואף ר"ל סבר מטר בשביל יחיד דאמר ר"ל מנין למטר בשביל יחיד דכתיב °שאלו מה' מטר בעת מלקוש ה' עושה חזיזים ומטר גשם יתן להם לאיש עשב בשדה יכול לכל תלמוד לומר לאיש ותניא אי לאיש יכול לכל שדותיו ת"ל זורה או זורה יכול לכל הזורה ת"ל עשב כי הא דרב דניאל בר קטינא הוה ליה ההיא גינתא כל יומא הוה אזיל וסייר לה אמר הא מישרא בעיא מיא והא מישרא לא בעיא מיא ואתא מיטרא וקמשקי כל היכא דמיבעי ליה מיא מאי ה' עושה חזיזים א"ר יוסי (*בר) חנינא מלמד שכל צדיק וצדיק הקב"ה עושה לו חזיז בפני עצמו מאי חזיזים אמר רב יהודה פורחות אמר רבי יותנן סימן למטר פורחות מאי פורחות אמר רב פפא עיבא קלישא תותי עיבא סמיכתא אמר רב יהודה נהילא מקמי מיטרא אתי מיטרא בתר מיטרא פסיק מיטרא מקמי מיטרא אתי מיטרא וסימניך מהולתא דבתר מיטרא פסיק מיטרא וסימניך חריא דעיזי: עולא איקלע לבבל חזא פורחות אמר להו פנו מאני דהשתא אתי מיטרא לסוף לא אתי מיטרא אמר כי היכי דמשקרי בבלאי הכי משקרי מיטרייהו *עולא איקלע לבבל חזי מלא צנא דתמרי בזוזא אמר מלא צנא דדובשא בזוזא ובבלאי לא עסקי באורייתא בליליא צערוהו אמר מלא צנא דסכינא בזוזא ובבלאי עסקי באורייתא תניא* ר' אליעזר אומר כל העולם כולו ממימי אוקיינוס הוא שותה שנאמר °ואד יעלה מן הארץ והשקה את כל פני האדמה אמר לו רבי יהושע והלא מימי אוקיינוס מלוחין הן אמר לו *ממתקין בעבים ר' יהושע אומר כל העולם כולו ממים העליונים הוא שותה שנאמר °למטר השמים תשתה מים אלא מה אני מקיים ואד יעלה מן הארץ מלמד שהעננים מתגברים ועולים לרקיע ופותחין פיהן כנוד ומקבלין מי מטר שנאמר °יזקו מטר לאדו ומנוקבות הן ככברה ובאות ומחשרות מים על גבי קרקע שנאמר °חשרת מים עבי שחקים ואין בין טיפה לטיפה אלא כמלא נימא ללמדך שגדול יום הגשמים כיום שנבראו בו שמים וארץ *) שנאמר *°עושה גדולות עד אין חקר וכתיב °הנותן מטר על פני ארץ וכתיב להלן °הלא ידעת אם לא שמעת אלהי עולם ה' אין חקר לתבונתו [א] **) (וכתיב °מכין הרים בכחו וגו') כמאן אזלא הא דכתיב °משקה הרים מעליותיו וא"ר יוחנן מעליותיו של הקב"ה כמאן כרבי יהושע ור' אליעזר כיון דסלקי להתם משקה מעליותיו קרי להו דאי לא תימא הכי °אבק ועפר מן השמים היכי משכחת לה אלא כיון דמדלי להתם מן השמים קרי ליה הכא נמי כיון דסלקי להתם מעליותיו קרי ליה כמאן אזלא [הא] דא"ר חנינא °כונס כנד מי הים נותן באוצרות תהומות מי גרם לאוצרות שיתמלאו בר תהומות (א) כרבי אליעזר ור' יהושע ההוא בברייתו

*)[לעיל ב:] **) [לא גרסינן הכא עי' רש"י ד"ה ללמדך אלא לעיל ב. גרס לוה שפיר]

(זכריה יא · שם · בראשית ב · דברים יא · איוב לו · איוב לו · ישעיה מ · איוב ה · איוב ט · תהלים סה · תהלים קד · דברים כח · תהלים לג)

אקרויה · הוו מקרין אותו מקרא זה בחנום ואכחיד את שלשת הרועים בירח אחד שרוצין לעונשן בשמים משום דמכספי ליה : קבל עליו · רב שימי שתיקותא מלהקשות עוד : יכול לכל · כלומר יכול אין טתן מטר אא"כ הכל צריכין לו : ת"ל לאיש · אפילו בשביל אחד : אי לאיש יכול לכל שדותיו · כלומר אינו יורד עד שהא צריך לכל שדותיו : ת"ל שדה · אפי' אינו צריך אלא בשדה אחד : אי בשדה יכול עד שילטרך לכל השדה ת"ל עשב · אפילו אינו צריך אלא לעשב אחד (עשב) בשביל ירק אחד יורד עליו מטר : וסייר · מעיין : מישרא · ערוגה : עושה לו חזיז · לכל לדיק הבא בעולם הזה להריק לו גשמים על שדותיו כרישא בעי מאי חזיזים לשון רבים והדר בעי ומאי ניגהו חזיזים מאי ניגהו דקרי חזיזי : ה"ג עיבא קלישתא דתותי עיבא סמיכתא · דתותי עיבא כלפי הארץ : נהילא · (ב) שנו קיעות נשילא (שולין דף ולו) שהיא דקה גשמים דקים כקמחא נהילא שהיא דקה הבאין תחילה למטר ואח"כ בא מטר : אתי מיטרא · גשמים יורדין לרוב ואין פוסקין מהר אבל בא מטר תחילה ומתחילין דקין לבא פוסקין מיד : מהולתא · שמתחילה יוצא קמח דק ולבסוף סובין גסין : חריא דעיזי · ריעי של עזים בתחילה יוצאה גסה ולבסוף דקה ופוסק : דתמרי · דבש עושין מהן : ובבלאי לא עסקי · כלומר יכולין הן לעסוק תמיד שיש להן מזונות בזול ובלא טורח : (ג) מלערים · בשלשול דאמרו (גיטין דף ע·) תמרי משתגן ומשלשלן : מלא צנא דסכיני בזוזא · שמתוך שטורחין אותו בזול אוכלין מהן הרבה ומלערים אותן : ממימי אוקייטס · כלומר ממים של מטה ולא ממים של מעלה שנאמר ואד יעלה מן הארץ ששתה בארץ ועלה : מלוחין הן · °ואין תבואה גדילה מהן : יזקו מטר לאדו · רקיעין מוליאין מים לעבים : יזקו · כמו יצוקו נא לעם ויאכלו (מלכים ב ד) : חשרת מים עבי שחקים · העבים מחשרין כלומר מחשירין המים לארץ : ללמדך · אקרא דלקמן קאי ואומר מכין הרים לא גרסינן הכא : *כרבי יהושע · דאמר ממים העליונים : ואמר רבי יוחנן מעליותיו של מעלה · כלומר ממים העליונים ורבי יוחנן מים העליונים אתא לאשמועינן דא לאו רבי יוחנן האי אמילתא דהכא קאמר מעליות שהקדוש ברוך הוא עומד בהם הוא משקה אותן למטה ולעולם המים מאוקייטס : ור' אליעזר · אמר לעולם מעליותיו של הקב"ה כרבי יוחנן וכו' : תהומות · מים של מטה כדכתיב תהומות יכסיומו (שמות טו) :

בברייתו

[כע"י סגיר' לשלמא ועי' ברכות סד. ומ"ק כט.]

הגהות הגר"א

[א] גמ' (וכתיב מכין הרים בכחו וגו') תא"מ

[נ"ל בר']

פסחים פח. ע"ש

ערובין מב:

גליון הש"ס

רש"י ד"ה מלוחים ואין תבואה גדילה מהן. לא ידעתי למאי צריך לזה ולא בפסוק באנו רואים באינבם לותים:

[נ"ל עושה גדולות ואין (...) פסוק ס)]

[דיבור זה שייך בסמוך לאחר דיבור המתחיל ואמר ר' יוחנן]

רבינו חננאל

חלש דעתיה אקרויה בחלמא ואכחיד את שלשת הרועים וגו'. כי הוה מפטרי מיניה אמר להו ניזולו רבנן בשלום: רב שימי בר אשי הוה מקשי לרב פפא טובא יומא חד חזייה דנפל על אפיה ובעי רחמי ואמר רחמנא שזבן מכיסופא דשימי קביל עליה שתיקותא ותו לא אקשיה ליה. עבים הרקים נקראים חזיזים אמר רב פפא עיבא קלישתא דתותי עיבא סמיכתא ונקראות פורחות: אמר רב יהודה נהילא פי' מטר היורד רק כמו קמח. אם הם תחלת ירידת המטר ירד מטר וסימנא נפה שכיון שמתחלת לשלוט הרק פולטת סולת וצריד וביוצא. אבל אם זו נהילא באחרית מטר דע דפסק מטרא וזהו תמצית המטר וסימניך חריא דעיזא כיון שא... בא בקילוח אלא כעין שותת ספה לא נשאר בו כלום: תניא רבי אליעזר אומר כל העולם כולו ממימי אוקינוס שותה שנאמר ואד יעלה מן הארץ והשקה וגו' ואע"פ שמלוחין מתמתקים הם בעבים. ר' יהושע אומר כל העולם כולו ממים העליונים הוא שותה שנאמר למטר השמים תשתה מים והאי דכתיב ואד יעלה מן הארץ מלמד שענני כבוד מתגברות ועולות לרקיע ופותחות פיהם כנוד ומקבלות מטר שנאמר יזקו מטר לאדו ומנוקבות ככברה ומחשרות על הארץ. שנאמר חשרת מים עבי שחקים ובין ספה לספה כמלא נימא כו'.

[נ"ל מתמתקין]

רבינו גרשום

מטר אתי בשביל תפלת יחיד ולברך את מעשה ידיך שבשביל יחיד אתי מטר: יכול לכל כלומר שאינו יורד גשם א.א (...) לאיש שמוריד לו מטר בשביל תפלתו: נהילא. מטר דקה סימן דאתי מיטרא: מהולתא. שבתחלה מוציא קמח דקה ולבסוף מוציא עבה: חריא דעיזי · ריעי של עזים שמוציא ריעי לבסוף דק:

הגהות הב"ח

(א) גמ' לאוצרות שיתמלאו בר תהום וכו' כמאן כר"א: (ב) רש"י ד"ה נהילא כמו קיטמא נהילא. נ"ב בפ"ק דכתובות איתא הכי ליתא אבל כאן צריך לגרס דמדמה ליה לקמח שיש בו ... כמו גשמים וכמ"ש וסימניך מהולתא: (ג) ד"ה מלערים · נ"ל לערוב: (ד) תוס' ד"ה נהילא כו' כמו דעבדינן האידנא אלא כיון שהבין:

קרי ביה חכשרת. פי' הטל הכ"ף מן חשכת ושדי עם חשרת ויהיה חכברת כלומר שהמים בעננים מהכשרים שהעננים שותים לבסוף הם ממתקים בעבים: **טובעני** ולא יובשני. פי' מוטב להיות בארץ שהיא לחה מכשהיא יבשה:

הלכתא יום ס' כלאחר ס'. וכן עמא דבר ויום תקופה מתחיל: **אין** גוזרין תענית על הצבור בתחילה בחמישי שלא להפקיע השערים. פי' שע"י שעשו הצבור תענית יקנו מזון של חמישי ושל שבת וכשבוריס העם יוקר היא ויפקיעו השערים: איזהו

בברייתו של עולם ת"ר א"י נבראת תחילה וכל העולם כולו נברא לבסוף שנאמר עד לא עשה ארץ וחוצות א"י (א) משקה אותה הקב"ה בעצמו וכל העולם כולו ע"י שליח שנאמר הנותן מטר על פני ארץ ושולח מים על פני חוצות א"י שותה מי גשמים וכל העולם כולו מתמצית שנאמר הנותן מטר על פני ארץ וגו' א"י שותה תחילה וכל העולם כולו לבסוף שנאמר הנותן מטר על פני ארץ וגו' משל לאדם שמגבל את הגבינה נוטל את האוכל ומניח את הפסולת אמר מר ממתקן הן בעבים מנליה דא"ר יצחק בר יוסף א"ר יוחנן כתיב חשכת מים עבי שחקים וכתיב חשרת מים עבי שחקים שקול כף ושדי אריש וקרי ביה *הכשרת ור' יהושע בהני קראי מאי דריש בהו סבר לה כי הא דכי אתא רב דימי אמר אמרי במערבא נהור ענני זעירין מוהי חשוך ענני סגיין מוהי כמאן אזלא הא דתניא מים העליונים במאמר הם תלוים ופירותיהן מי גשמים שנאמר מפרי מעשיך תשבע הארץ כמאן כר' יהושע ור' אליעזר ההוא במעשה ידיו של הקב"ה הוא דכתיב אריב"ל כל העולם כולו מתמצית גן עדן הוא שותה שנאמר ונהר יוצא מעדן וגו' תנא מתמצית בית כור שיתה *תרקב: ת"ר *ארץ מצרים הויא ד' מאות פרסה על ד' מאות פרסה והוא אחד מששים בכוש וכוש אחד מששים בעולם ועולם א' מששים בגן וגן אחד מששים לעדן ועדן אחד מס' לגיהנם נמצא כל העולם כולו כביסוי קדרה לגיהנם וי"א גיהנם אין לה שיעור וי"א עדן אין לה שיעור א"ר אושעיא מאי דכתיב שוכנת על מים רבים רבת אוצרות מי גרם לבבל שיהו אוצרותיה מליאות בר הוי אומר מפני ששוכנת על מים רבים אמר רב עתירה בבל דחצדא בלא מיטרא אמר אביי נקיטינן *טובעני ולא יובשני:

מתני' *בג' במרחשון שואלין את הגשמים רבן גמליאל אומר *בשבעה בו ט"ו יום אחר החג כדי שיגיע אחרון שבישראל לנהר פרת: **גמ'** *א"ר אלעזר הלכה כרבן גמליאל תניא חנניה אומר ובגולה עד ששים בתקופה אמר רב הונא בר חייא אמר שמואל הלכה כחנניה איני והא בעו מיניה משמואל מאימת מדכרינן ותן טל ומטר אמר להו מכי מעיילי ציבי לבי טבות *רישבא דילמא אידי ואידי חד שיעורא הוא איבעיא להו יום ששים כלפני ששים או כלאחר ששים ת"ש רב אמר יום ששים כלאחר ששים ושמואל אמר יום ששים כלפני ששים א"ר נחמן בר יצחק וסימנך עילאי בעו מיא תתאי לא בעו מיא אמר רב פפא הלכתא יום ששים כלאחר ששים:

מתני' הגיע י"ז במרחשון ולא ירדו גשמים התחילו היחידים מתענין ג' תעניות אוכלין ושותין משחשיכה ומותרין במלאכה וברחיצה ובסיכה ובנעילת הסנדל ובתשמיש המטה הגיע ר"ח כסליו ולא ירדו גשמים ב"ד גוזרין שלש תעניות על הצבור אוכלין ושותין משחשיכה ומותרין במלאכה וברחיצה ובסיכה ובנעילת הסנדל ובתשמיש המטה: **גמ'** מאן יחידים אמר רב הונא רבנן ואמר רב הונא יחידים מתענין שלשה תעניות שני וחמישי ושני מאי קמשמע לן תנינא *אין גוזרין תענית על הצבור בתחילה בחמישי שלא להפקיע את השערים אלא שלש תעניות הראשונות שני וחמישי ושני מהו דתימא הני מילי צבור אבל יחיד לא קמשמע לן תניא נמי הכי כשהתחילו היחידים להתענות מתענין שני וחמישי ושני ומפסיקין בראשי חדשים ובימים

רש"י

בברייתו של עולם. כתיב שהיה כל העולם שטוף במים והקב"ה כונסן במקום אחד כמכניס מים בנאד (ג) שנתנם באוצרות דכתיב נותן באוצרות תהומות שם חול גבולו ואוצר לים: משיורי תמצית. מה שנשאר בעבים אחר שתיית': על פני ארץ. א"י: בתחילה שותה. שם יורדין הגשמים תחילה כך שמעתי: חשרת מים וחשכת מים. שני מקראות הן חד בתהלים וחד בשמואל בוידבר דוד: ה"ג שקול כף ושדי אריש. כלומר קח כף שבמלת חשכת ואדפו עם מלה הברת וקרי ביה (ג) חכשרת שממתקין ומכשירין בעבים: חשוך ענני סגיאין מימוהי. והייני דכתיב חשכת מים: נהור ענני. כשהענן קליש זעירן מימוהי ומכלל חשוך סגיאין אתה למד אבל נהור זעירין והשרת לשון השרה כמו אין שורין דיו (שבת דף יז:) כו' כדדריש ליה רבי יהושע לעיל אבל חשכת מיבעי ליה להכי ולהכי: במאמר הן תלוין. אינן נחות על שום דבר אלא מסוכנות ועומדות כמין בריכה ותלויות במאמרו של הקב"ה: ופירותיהן מי גשמים. משום לישנא דקרא נקט הכי משום דכתיב מפרי מעשיך תשבע הארץ ופירותיהם כלומר מזיעת המים שאין נחסרין כלום כדכתיב (תהלים סה) פלג אלהים מלא מים כל שעה והקרן קיימת ופירותיהן מי גשמים וכן מפורש בבראשית רבה: ונהר יוצא מעדן. (ד) סימן לדבר שגן עדן שותה מן הגשמים תחילה דכתיב ונהר יוצא מעדן להשקות את הגן וגו': תנא מתמצית בית כור. כלי שמשקין במימיו בית כור יכולין להשקות בתמציתו שיעור זריעת תרקב שהוא אחד מששים בבית כור והכי נמי עולם אחד מששים בגן עדן ודי לו בתמצית העננים המשקין את הגן (ה) גן לפני כל העולם כולו כעדן לגן: נמצא כל העולם ככיסוי קדרה. הקטן כנגד הקדרה: שוכנת על מים רבים. רבת אוצרות בא קצך אמת בצעך: שרבו אוצרותיה. שקנו עושר: מים רבים. שמשקין שדותיהן דבבל עמוקים מכל הארצות וגשמים מטפטפין ויורדין שם: עתירה בבל. עשירה היא בבל שקוצרין בה תבואה בלא מטר שאינן צריכים לגשמים: נקיטינן. דהכי (ו) הלדא בבל בלא מיטרא: דטובעני. היא מקום מצולה ורקק: ולא יובשני. שאינה יבשה: **מתני'** בשלשה במרחשון שואלין את הגשמים וכו' רבן גמליאל אומר בשבעה בו בט"ו יום אחר החג. כלומר בשבעה במרחשון הוא ט"ו אחר החג: כדי שיגיע האחרון. כלומר קודם ביאת מים לנהר פרת שהוא רחוק יותר: **גמ'** ובגולה עד ששים. ובגולה אין שואלין עד ששים בתקופה לפי שהוא מקום נמוך ואין צריכים מטר כל כך: מכי מעיילי ליבי לבי טבות רישבא. משעה שמכניסין עצים לאוצר לצורך ימות הגשמים שכן היו נוהגין לפי שהיו יודעין שזמן גשמים הוא משם והילך ולא היו יכולין לחטוב עצים ביער: רישבא. לייד עופות כמו אין פורשין *רשבים ליונים (ב"ק דף עט:) טבות שם אדם: כלפני ס'. ולא מדכרינן: כלאחר ס'. ומדכרינן: עילאי בעו מים. העומדים בהרים צריכין יותר מים מפני שהגשמים מתגלגלים ויורדין למטה: תתאי לא בעו מים. שמתכנסין כל מימי ההרים לבקעה ה"נ רב שהיה מארץ ישראל כדאמרינן בעלמא (גיטין דף ו:) מכי אתא רב לבבל וארץ ישראל גבוהה מכל הארצות משום הכי אמר כלאחר ששים ובבבל בגולה מתוך שאינן צריכין לגשמים אין שואלין עד ס' לתקופת תשרי וכן אנו נוהגים שכל מנהגינו אחר בני בבל: **מתני'** הגיע שבעה עשר וכו'. אוכלין ושותין משחשיכה שאין אוכלין מבעוד יום כיום הכפורים ותשעה באב: **גמ'** מאי קמ"ל. האי דקאמר שני וחמישי ושני: תנינא. בפירקין דלקמן (דף טו:) אין גוזרין תענית כו' שלא להפקיע את השערים שאם היו מתחילין להתענות בחמישי היו קונין למוצאי התענית שתי סעודות גדולות אחד להתענית ואחד לשבת וכשבור המוכר שרעב בא לעולם ואתי לאפקועי שערים: אפקועי. מבטל שיעור מדה הראשונה וממעטה: אבל יחידים לא. שלש תעניות שהיחידין עושין קודם לצבור אינן זקוקין להתחיל בשני דליכא אפקעת שערים משום יחידים לחודייהו והללו ג' תעניות דיחידים אינן בכלל י"ג תע[ניו]ת דצבור תדע דקא חשיב במתני' שלש ושלש ושבע: ומפסיקין בראשי חדשים. שאם חל ר"ח בשני ובחמישי לאחר שהתחילו תעניות פוסקין תעניתם: וכן

רבינו חננאל

ארץ ישראל נבראת תחלה שנאמר עד לא עשה ארץ וחוצות א"י הקב"ה משקה אותה [בעצמו] וכל העולם כולו ע"י שליח. שנאמר הנותן מטר על פני ארץ ושולח מים על פני חוצות. א"י שותה מי גשמים וכל העולם שותה תמצית שנאמר הנותן מטר וגו' משל לאדם מגבל גבינה. נוטל מאכל ומניח הפסולת: ת"ר מצרים ד' מאות פרסה על ד' מאות פרסה. ואחד מס' בכוש. וכוש אחד מס' בעולם. והעולם אחד מס' בגן. וגן אחד מס' בעדן. ועדן אחד מס' בגיהנם. נמצא כל העולם כולו ככיסוי קדירה לגיהנם. אריב"ל כל העולם מתמצית הגן הוא שותה שנאמר ונהר יוצא מעדן להשקות את הגן. תנא מתמצית בית כור שותה. תרקב. פי' התרקב הוא חצי סאה. והכור יש בו ל' סאין. נמצא א' מס' בכור. וכיון ששנה בחיצונה והעולם א' מס' בגן. נמצא [illegible] העולם. דקדק התנא [illegible] כמו שהוא העולם א' מס' בגן [illegible] (בשמונה) [בשבעה] בו. א"ר [illegible] שמואל הלכתא כחנניה. [illegible] לן יום ס' כלפני ס' ואינו [illegible] ס' וסימנך עילאי בעי מיא [illegible] מים. וסורא אתריה דרב [illegible] תחתיין נקוין המים בהן [illegible] וה' וב'. ומפסיקין בר"ח וביו"ט

הגהות הב"ח

(א) גמ' משקה אותה [illegible]

[illegible] וגו' א"י משקה אותה הקב"ה בעצמו וכו' מתמצית וכו' על פני ארץ וגו' משל לאדם שמגבל את [illegible] (ג) רש"י ד"ה בברייתו כו' כמכניס מים בנאד ונתנם באוצרות כו' ואוצר לים מה"ד שותה תחלה שם [illegible] גשמים תחלה כך שמעתי ומה"ד מתמצית משיורי מים בשאר בעבים כו' א"י מה"ד השרת כו': [illegible] ה"ג שקול כו' חכשרת. נ"ב ולהכי נקט רי"ש ולא נקט שי"ן דשי"ן הכא והכא כתיב: (ד) ד"ה [illegible] מעדן כלומר סימן לדבר כו' דכתיב קרא ונהר יוצא מעדן תחילה להשקות הגן: (ה) ד"ה הגא [illegible] את הגן הס"ד ואח"כ מה"ד גן לפני כל שלם כולו כגן עדן לעולם: (ו) ד"ה נקיטינן דהכי הוא דהלדא בבל בלא מיטרא דטיבעני כו' הד"א:

העולם כולו חלק א' מס' חלקים בגן ומתמציתו שותה כל העולם. שמתמצית ב"ה כור שותה תרקב שהרי זה התרקב א' מס' בכור כמו שהוא העולם א' מס' בגן ושותה המציתו: כתני' בג' מרחשון שואלין הגשמים ר"ג אומר (בשמונה) [בשבעה] בו. א"ר אלעזר הלכה כר"ג. תנא דחנניה אומר ובגולה עד ס' יום בתקופה. אמר שמואל הלכתא כחנניה. וזמן הכנסת עצים דבי מיבות רישבא מן השרת הוה ס' בתקופה. ואיבעיא לן יום ס' כלפני ס' ואינו שואל או כלאחר ס' ושואל. רב אמר כלפני ס' ושמואל אמר כלאחר ס' וסימנך עילאי בעי מיא תתאי לא בעי מיא. פי' נהרדעא אתריה דשמואל והיא גבוהה והן מבקשים מים. וסורא אתריה דרב והיא לגבי נהרדעא תתאה. והן אינן מבקשין מים כלומר כיון שהן תחתיין נקוין המים בהן [illegible] אצלם. אמר רב פפא הלכתא יום ס' כלאחר ס': כתני' הגיע י"ז במרחשון ולא ירדו גשמים התחילו היחידים מתענים. ואוקים רב הונא להני יחידים רבנן ומתענין ב' וה' וב'. ומפסיקין בר"ח וביו"ט

רבינו גרשום

[illegible] יהושע דאמר כמים העליונים הם. כמאן כר' אליעזר דאמר מן הארץ עולה כמר. מתמצית [illegible] תרקב. מתמצית גן עדן שותה כל העולם דכל העולם לגבי גן עדן כתרקב לפני כור תרקב הרי [illegible] ג' קבין. כור ל' סאין ותרקב חצי סאה נמצא תרקב אחד מששים בכור וכל העולם אחד מששים [illegible] רחצדא בלא מטרא כלומר שקוצרת בלא מטר כלומר שאינה צריכה מטר שיושבת כין [illegible] ע"א אצדא: טובעני ולא יובשני כלומר מיתרסי שטובעין הזרעים אבל לשלם אין מתייבשין: [illegible] בשבעה בו בכשה עשר יום אחר החג כלומר ז' במרחשון הוא ט"ו אחר החג כדי שיגיע האחרון כו' קודם הגשמים: ובגולה אין שואלין את הגשמים עד ששים בתקופה. לפי שהן במקום נמוך ואין צריכין למטר כל כך: ציבי דטבות רישבא. דהוה עשיר והיו עצים שלו מונחים ליבש בשדה עד שיכנסם במרחשון: כלפני ששים. ואין שואלין בו: או כלאחר ששים. ושואלין בו: עילאי בעו מיא רב דהוה מא"י בעי מים בששים. תתאי לא בעי מיא שמואל דהוה מבבל עד לבסוף לא בעי מיא עד ששים ואחר: אוכלין ושותין משחשכה. שאין אוכלין מבעוד יום כיוה"כ וכתשעה באב: שלא להפקיע את השערים. דבני כפרים הבאים ליום הכניסה מספקים מים ומזון לאחיהן שבכרכין

ל א ב מיי' פ"ג מהלכות תעניות הלכה א טוש"ע א"ח סי' תקעה סעיף א:

לא ג מיי' פ"ג מהלכות תעניות הלכה ט טוש"ע א"ח סי' תקעה סעיף א:

לב ד מיי' שם טוש"ע א"ח סי' תקסח סעיף ג:

לג ה מיי' שם וטוש"ע שם סעיף א:

לד ו מיי' שם וטוש"ע שם סעיף ג:

[גי' ר"י יהודה]

ובימים טובים הכתובין במגילת תענית תנו רבנן אל יאמר אדם תלמיד אני איני ראוי להיות יחיד אלא *כל תלמידי חכמים יחידים אי זהו יחיד ואיזהו תלמיד יחיד כל שראוי למנותו פרנס על הצבור תלמיד *כל ששואלין אותו דבר הלכה בלמודו ואומר ואפילו במסכת דכלה תנו רבנן לא כל הרוצה לעשות עצמו יחיד עושה תלמיד עושה דברי ר' מאיר רבי *יוסי אומר עושה וזכור לטוב לפי שאין שבח הוא לו אלא צער הוא לו תניא אידך לא *כל הרוצה לעשות עצמו יחיד עושה תלמיד עושה דברי רבי שמעון בן אלעזר רבן שמעון בן גמליאל אומר במה דברים אמורים בדבר של שבח אבל בדבר של צער עושה וזכור לטוב שאין שבח הוא לו אלא צער הוא לו: ת"ר *מי שהיה מתענה על הצרה ועברה על החולה ונתרפא הרי זה מתענה ומשלים ההולך ממקום שאין מתענין למקום שמתענין הרי זה מתענה עמהן ממקום שמתענין למקום שאין מתענין הרי זה מתענה ומשלים ישכח ואכל ושתה אל יתראה בפני הצבור ואל ינהיג עידונין בעצמו שנאמר °ויאמר יעקב לבניו למה תתראו אמר להם יעקב לבניו אל תראו עצמכם כשאתם שבעין לא בפני עשו ולא בפני ישמעאל כדי שלא יתקנאו בכם °אל תרגזו בדרך אמר רבי אלעזר אמר להם יוסף לאחיו אל תתעסקו בדבר הלכה שמא תרגזו עליכם הדרך איני והאמר ר' אלעאי בר ברכיה *שני תלמידי חכמים שמהלכים בדרך ואין בינהן דברי תורה ראויין לישרף שנאמר °ויהי המה הולכים (*הולך) ודבר והנה רכב אש וסוסי אש ויפרידו בין שניהם טעמא דאיכא דיבור הא ליכא דיבור ראויין לישרף לא קשיא הא למיגרס הא לעיוני במתניתא תנא אל תפסיעו פסיעה גסה והכניסו חמה לעיר אל תפסיעו פסיעה גסה דאמר מר *פסיעה גסה נוטלת *אחד מחמש מאות ממאור עיניו של אדם והכניסו חמה לעיר כדרב יהודה אמר רב *דאמר רב יהודה אמר רב לעולם יצא אדם בכי טוב ויכנס בכי טוב שנאמר °הבקר אור והאנשים שלחו אמר רב יהודה אמר רבי חייא °המהלך בדרך אל יאכל יותר משני רעבון מאי טעמא הכא תרגימו משום מעיינא במערבא אמרי משום מזוני מאי בינייהו איכא בינייהו דיתיב

(בראשית מב / בראשית מה / מלכים ב ב / בראשית מד)

איזהו יחיד כו' שראוי למנותו פרנס על הצבור (ד) להיות פרנס ואיזהו תלמיד כל ששואלין דבר הלכה בכל מקום וכו'. וקשה דהכא משמע דקרי תלמיד אותו שיודע להשיב כששואלין לו דבר הלכה בכל מקום ואומרה והתם אמרינן במס' שבת פרק ואלו קשרים (דף קיד.) איזהו תלמיד הראוי למנותו פרנס על הצבור כשיודע להשיב כל ששואלין (ה) דבר הלכה ואפילו במסכת כלה אלמא הראוי למנותו פרנס על הצבור הוי כשיודע להשיב והכא משמע דאותו הראוי למנותו פרנס הוי מילתא אחריתי ועוד דהכא משמע דיחיד עדיף מדקאמר בסמוך לא כל הרוצה לעשות עצמו יחיד עושה אבל הרוצה לעשות עצמו תלמיד עושה ויש לומר דיש חילוק בתלמיד דווקא כשהרב בא אל מקום אחד וכל התלמידים הללו זה שואל אל הרב ממה שהוא לומד וזה שואל ממקום אחר ואותו הרב יודע להשיב לכל התלמידים לכל אחד ואחד כפי שאלתו ואפילו במס' כלה זהו יחיד דעדיף מתלמיד דהכא ונקרא תלמיד התם בפרק אלו קשרים אותו והאי ראוי למנותו פרנס על הצבור אבל אם אינו יודע להשיב אלא במסכת שלו נקרא גם כן תלמיד ומזה מיירי הכא:

ההולך ממקום שמתענין למקום שאין מתענין הרי מתענה ומשלים. ל"ש דעתו לחזור ל"ש אין דעתו לחזור הואיל וקבל עליו התענית: **למה** תתראו. כמו שמפרש אל תראו עצמכם בפני בני עשו וכו' ויש במדרש למה תתראו פירוש למה תהיו כחושין:

אל תרגזו בדרך. ויש מדרש אל תפסיקו מדבר הלכה:

ואין ביניהם דברי תורה ראויים לישרף דכתיב ויהי המה הולכים הלוך ודבר וגו' טעמא דאיכא דבור וכו'. ויש מדרש שהם היו מדברים דברים בטלים ומש"ה ראוין לישרף: **פסיעה** גסה נוטלת אחת מחמש מאות ממאור עיניו של אדם. ואין להקשות אם כן בחמש מאות פסיעות גסות יהיה ניטל כל מאור עיניו של אדם ואם קא אזיל דלאו הכי הוה ונראה לפרש דהפסיעה ראשונה נוטל אחת מחמש מאות והפסיעה שניה נוטל פחות מן הראשונה בשניה אינה נוטלת אלא אחד מחמש מאות הנשארים כמו בעישורייתא דבי רבי (כתובות דף סח.) ר"ל העישור ממה שנשאר אבל עדיין קשה דמ"מ פסיעה ראשונה דנוטלת יותר מן השניה אלא יש לומר דלא נוטלת אלא פסיעה ראשונה דוקא ומכאן ואילך כיון דדש דש אי נמי פסיעה ראשונה נוטלת עפי מש"ס *)דכל התחלות קשות: **לעולם** יצא אדם בכי טוב. פי' בפרק קמא דפסחים (דף ב.) [וע"ע תוס' ב"ק כ:]:

משום מעיינא. פירוש משום שהבני מעיין הוי קשה להו לאכול

*) ומכילתא הביאו רש"י פ' יתרו יש פ"מ

וכן בימים טובים הכתובים במגילת תענית: תלמיד אני. ואיני חשוב כל כך כיחידים כלומר איני ראוי להתחיל תענית עם היחידים: לא כל הרוצה לעשות עצמו יחיד. לענין תענית: עושה. דנראה מגסי הרוח ותנן (אבות פ"ג משנה י) כל שרוח הבריות נוחה הימנו כו': הכי גרסינן התלמידים עושין עצמן. כדאמרינן לעיל שכל התלמידים ראויין לכך ואין בהם משום גסות הרוח: רבי יוסי אומר כל אדם. ואפילו שאינו תלמיד עושה עצמו יחיד להתענות וזכור לטוב דלצער הוא לו ולא גסות לישנא אחרינא גרסינן לא כל הרוצה לעשות עצמו יחיד עושה תלמיד עושה כלומר ולא כל הרוצה נמי לעשות עצמו תלמיד להתנהג עצמו במדת *תלמיד בחלוקו ובמטתו ולהתנאות בסודר של תלמידי חכמים ושאר דברים עושה דכל הרוצה ליטול לו את השם לא יטול ורבי יוסי אתרישא ומסתבר כי האי לישנא מדקא מהדר רבן שמעון בן גמליאל דבר של שבח אינו עושה מכלל דאיירי בשבח: על החולה ונתרפא. הוא הדין אם מת החולה בעי לקיומי נדרו: על הצרה ועברה. מתענה ומשלים ואם לאו נראה כמתנה עם קונו אם תעבור (*אתענה) ואם לאו (לא) אתענה: למקום שאין מתענין הרי זה מתענה ומשלים. כל התעניות שקבלו עליהן בני עירו דנותנין עליו חומרי המקום שיצא משם: אכל ושתה. דיעבד: אל יתראה בפניהן. שנראה כחתן בין אבלים ויתקנאו בו: ואל ינהיג עדונים בעצמו. שלא יאמר הואיל ואכלתי כל שהוא אוכל הרבה: אל תראו עצמכם. שיש לכם חטים הרבה ולא הלכו אלא בשביל דבר זה שלא להתראות בפני בני עשו שהיו לצורים ורעבים: תרגזו עליכם הדרך. התעו: לישרף בלא. דכתיב והנה סוסי אש וכתיב בההוא עניינא הלוך ודבר והכי כתביה לאשמועינן דאי לאו שהיו הולכין (א) בעומקה של הלכה לא [היו ניצולין]: הא למגרס. מבעי ליה באורחא אבל במלתא דמבעי ליה לעיוני לא: במתניתא תנא. מאי אל תרגזו בדרך אל תזיקו עצמכם בפסיעה גסה: והכניסו חמה לעיר. כשאתם לנין ושוכבין בדרך בעיירות הכניסו לעיר בעוד שהחמה זורחת: יצא אדם בכי טוב. שימתין עד שיאור כמו וירא אלהים את האור כי טוב (בראשית א): ויכנס בכי טוב. בערב בעוד שהחמה זורחת שאין ליסטין מצויין אי נמי שלא יפול בבורות ובקעים שבעיר שלא יעלילו עליו עלילות מרגל אתה או גנב: הבוקר אור והאנשים שולחו המה וחמוריהם. מיכן שילאו בכי טוב והוא הדין ליכנס בכי טוב יש ספרים דלא כתיב בהו האי קרא הלא מילתא דרב יהודה סברא הוא ולא בעי' קרא: לא יאכל יותר ממה שאוכל בשני רעבון. דאמר לקמן (דף יא.) שצריך להרעיב עצמו בשני רעבון: (הכא (ב). תלמיד זה בבלי הוא וכי משתעי בבבל קאמר הכא וכל הא לן והא להו בבבל קאמר): משום מעיינא. שלא יתחלחלו מעיו של אדם ברוב אכילתו מפני טורח הדרך יש אומרים יהיו מעיו של אדם שופכין זה לזה כעין מעיין: משום מזוני. שמא (ג) אין לו לאח"כ:

שבת קיד. קדושין מט:

[ב"ב מו:]

[תוספתא פ"א]

[תוספ' פ"ב]

[נ"ל לא התענה]

סוטה מט.

[נ"ל הולך]

[פסחים מב.]

פסחים ב. ב"ק ס: ע"ש

רבינו חננאל

ובי"ט הכתובים במגלת תענית: ת"ר לא יאמר זה איני ראוי לכך. אלא כל התלמידים ראוין לכך. איזהו יחיד כל שראוי למנותו פרנס על הצבור. ואיזה תלמיד כל ששואלין אותו הלכה בכל מקום ואומרה. פי' בכלים מקום בלימוד מקום מן התלמוד. ואפי' במס' דכלה. שמתעסקין בה כל תלמיד חכם שיודעים לשונותיה בכלה של אדר תניא לא כל הרוצה לעשות עצמו יחיד עושה שנראה ביהירות התלמידים עושין דברי ר' שמעון בן אלעזר. רשב"ג דבר של שבח אינו עושה. דבר של צער עושה. עצמו יחיד וכן ר' יוסי אומר עושה וזכור לטוב. שאינו שבח לו התענית אלא צער הוא לו: ת"ר מי שהיה מתענה על החולה ונתרפא על צער צרה ועברה מתענה ומשלים ההולך ממקום שמתענין למקום שאין מתענין וכו'. זה שאמר יוסף לאחיו אל תרגזו בדרך. אל תתעסקו בדבר הלכה שלא תתגר עליהם הדרך ואוקימנא לעיוני אבל במגרס לא. דא"ם ב' ת"ח המהלכים בדרך ואין ביניהם דברי תורה ראוין לישרף שנאמר ויהי המה הולכים הלוך ודבר והנה רכב אש וסוסי אש ויפרידו בין שניהם. במתניתא תנא אל תפסיעו פסיעה גסה שנוטלת אחד מחמש מאות במאור עיניו של אדם. והכניסו חמה לעיר. כדרב יהודה אמר רב לעולם יכנס אדם בכי טוב ויצא בכי טוב כלומר באור היום כדכתיב וירא אלהים את האור כי טוב. וכתיב הבקר אור והאנשים שלחו. משום מעיינא פי' אם יאכל הרבה יקחנו שלשול ויבא להתאחר מן השיירא.

הגהות הב"ח

(א) רש"י ד"ה לישרף בלא כו' שהיו הולכין בדבר של הלכה: (ב) ד"ה הכא תרגימו. תלמוד זה כו': (ג) ד"ה משום מזוני שמא יהיה לו לאח"כ: (ד) תוס' ד"ה איזהו כו' פרנס של הצבור ואיזהו תלמיד כו' כצ"ל ותיבות להיות פרנס נמחק: (ה) בא"ד כל ששואלין אותו דבר הלכה ואפילו:

רבינו גרשום

שבברכין וכשהן באין בחמישי לא ידעו שקבלו עליהם תענית ואין מביאין מזון אלא לצורך השבת ולוקחין הכל לצורך ליל חמישי לפי שהתענו בו ומתייקר המזון לצורך השבת אבל כשגוזרין בשני כשבאין בשני לעיר שומעין כשגוזרין תענית וכשבאין בחמישי מביאין מזון כדי לסבור ללילי חמישי ולשבת: מפסיקין בראשי חדשים אם אירעו בחמישי ושני הכתוב במגילת תענית דלא להתענאה בהון: אל יאמר תלמיד [אני] איני ראוי לכך להתענות. ר' יוסי אומר כל אדם נמי עושה עצמו וזכור לטוב: אפילו במס' כלה שאין רגילין להתעסק בו שאין שבח הוא לו שמתענה: דבר של שבח אינו עושה כגון חתן קורא ק"ש בלילה הראשון. של צער מתענה. ות"ח עושה. בין של שבח בין של צער: הרי זה מתענה ומשלים שניתנין עליו חומרי מקום שהלך לשם וחומרי מקום שיצא משם: אל יתראה בפניהם. כשהוא שבע. אל ינהיג בעצמו עידונין. שלא יאמר הואיל שאכלת כל שהוא אוכל הרבה: והן רעבין מפני הרעב: שמא ירגזו עליכם הדרך שהרואה אתכם שאתם חולקין בדבר הלכה סבור נלחמים אתם ומתרגזים

גליון הש"ס גמ' המהלך בדרך אל יאכל כו'. עי' מג"א סי' קי ס"ק י:

דיתיב בארבא אי נמי דקאזיל מאוונא לאוונא רב פפא כל פרסה ופרסה אכיל חדא ריפתא קסבר משום מעיינא אמר רב יהודה אמר רב *כל המרעיב עצמו בשני רעבון ניצל ממיתה משונה שנאמר °ברעב פדך ממות מרעב מיבעי ליה אלא הכי קאמר בשכר שמרעיב עצמו בשני רעבון ניצול ממיתה משונה אמר ריש לקיש אסור לאדם לשמש מטתו בשני רעבון שנאמר °וליוסף ילד שני בנים בטרם תבוא שנת הרעב תנא *חסוכי בנים משמשין מטותיהן בשני רעבון תנו רבנן בזמן שישראל שרויין בצער ופירש אחד מהן באין שני מלאכי השרת שמלוין לו לאדם ומניחין לו ידיהן על ראשו ואומרים פלוני זה שפירש מן הצבור אל יראה בנחמת צבור תניא אידך בזמן שהצבור שרוי בצער אל יאמר אדם אלך לביתי ואוכל ואשתה ושלום עליך נפשי ואם עושה כן עליו הכתוב אומר °והנה ששון ושמחה הרוג בקר ושחוט צאן אכול בשר ושתות יין אכול ושתו כי מחר נמות מה כתיב בתריה ונגלה באזני ה' צבאות אם יכופר העון הזה לכם עד תמותון עד כאן מדת בינונים אבל במדת רשעים מה כתיב °אתיו אקחה יין ונסבאה שכר והיה כזה יום מחר מה כתיב בתריה הצדיק אבד ואין איש שם על לב כי מפני הרעה נאסף הצדיק *אלא יצער אדם עם הצבור שכן מצינו במשה רבינו שציער עצמו עם הצבור שנאמר °וידי משה כבדים ויקחו אבן וישימו תחתיו וישב עליה וכי לא היה לו למשה כר אחת או כסת אחת לישב עליה אלא כך אמר משה הואיל וישראל שרויין בצער אף אני אהיה עמהם בצער וכל המצער עצמו עם הצבור זוכה ורואה בנחמת צבור *ושמא יאמר אדם מי מעיד בי אבני ביתו של אדם וקורות ביתו של אדם מעידים בו שנאמר °כי אבן מקיר תזעק וכפים מעץ יעננה דבי רבי שילא אמרי שני מלאכי השרת המלוין לו לאדם הן מעידין עליו שנאמר °כי מלאכיו יצוה לך רבי חידקא אומר *נשמתו של אדם היא מעידה עליו שנאמר °משוכבת חיקך שמור פתחי פיך ויש אומרים אבריו של אדם מעידים בו שנאמר °אתם עדי נאם ה' °אל אמונה ואין עול אל אמונה כשם שנפרעין מן הרשעים לעולם הבא אפילו על עבירה קלה שעושין כך נפרעין מן הצדיקים בעולם הזה על עבירה קלה שעושין ואין עול כשם שמשלמין שכר לצדיקים לעולם הבא אפילו על מצוה קלה שעושין כך משלמין שכר לרשעים בעולם הזה אפילו על מצוה קלה שעושין צדיק וישר הוא *) (אמרו בשעת) פטירתו של אדם לבית עולמו כל מעשיו (*נפטרין) לפניו ואומרים לו כך וכך עשית במקום פלוני ביום פלוני והוא אומר (*הין) ואומרים לו חתום וחותם שנאמר °ביד כל אדם יחתום ולא עוד אלא שמצדיק עליו את הדין ואומר להם יפה דנתוני לקיים מה שנאמר °למען תצדק בדברך אמר שמואל כל היושב בתענית נקרא חוטא (א) סבר כי האי תנא דתניא *ר' אלעזר הקפר ברבי אומר מה תלמוד לומר °וכפר עליו מאשר חטא על הנפש וכי באיזה נפש חטא זה אלא שציער עצמו מן היין והלא דברים קל וחומר ומה זה שלא ציער עצמו אלא מן היין נקרא חוטא המצער עצמו מכל דבר ודבר על אחת כמה וכמה ר' אלעזר אומר נקרא קדוש שנאמר °קדוש יהיה גדל פרע שער ראשו ומה זה שלא ציער עצמו אלא מדבר אחד נקרא קדוש המצער עצמו מכל דבר על אחת כמה וכמה ולשמואל הא איקרי קדוש ההוא אגידול פרע קאי ולר' אלעזר הא נקרא חוטא ההוא דסאיב נפשיה ומי אמר רבי אלעזר הכי והאמר ר' אלעזר לעולם ימוד אדם עצמו כאילו

*) [נ"ל מלמד שבשעת כך אי' בשאלתות]

רש"י

דיתיב בארבא. שהולך בספינה משום מזוני איכא משום מעיינא ליכא: מאוונא לאוונא. מקום מלון התגרים מכפר לכפר דמשתכחי מזוני וליכא למיחש למזוני ולמעיינא איכא למיחש: כל פרסה ופרסה אכל ריפתא. קסבר רב פפא הא דאמור רבנן לא ליכול טפי משום מעיינא ואיהו לא מיסתפי ממעיינא דבעל *בטן הוה ענין אחר כריסו רחבה כדאיתא בבבא מציעא (דף פד.) דקא חשיב אבריה דרב פפא וכאיש גבורתו ולפיכך יכול לאכול הרבה ואינו מזיק לו: מיתה משונה. מת בחרב וברעב וכל מיתה שאינה בידי מלאך המות כדרך כל אדם על מטתו: בשכר שמצער עצמו. כשישראל בצער: אסור לשמש מטתו בשני רעבון. דצריך אדם לנהוג לצער בעצמו: חסוכי בנים. חסירי בנים (ב) דגרסינן במנחות (דף כט:) לגבי מטרה ומי חסיכי כולי האי *שלא קיימו פריה ורביה: שני מלאכי שרת (ג) מלוין לו לאדם. אחד מימינו ואחד משמאלו דכתי' (תהלים צא) כי מלאכיו יצוה לך: הנה ששון ושמחה הרוג בקר ושחוט צאן אכול בשר ושתות יין כי מחר נמות ונגלה באזני ה' צבאות אם יכופר העון הזה לכם עד תמותון: זו מדת בינונים. שיראין מן המיתה כדכתיב בהו כי מחר נמות: אתיו אקחה יין ונסבאה שכר והיה כזה יום מחר. גדול יותר מאד: הצדיק אבד ואין איש שם על לב. מפני מה הוא מת מפני הרעה נאסף הצדיק מפני שלא יצטער הוא ברעה ואחר שהיא גזרה מלפניו כי מפני הרעה נאסף הצדיק ל"א מפני רעות של אלו הוא נאסף שאין הקב"ה רוצה שיבקש עליהם רחמים: כפים. חצי לבינה ורגלין לתחה בין שתי נדבכי העצים: הכי גרסינן אבריו של אדם הן מעידין בו שנאמר ואתם עדי לשון רבים נאם ה': מאי דכתיב אל אמונה ואין עול כשם שמשלם כו'. כך משלם לרשעים בעולם הזה כדי לטורדן מן העולם הבא וכדכתיב (דברים ז) ומשלם לשונאיו אל פניו להאבידו: ואין עול. שאין עושה (ד) דין בלא דין אמת וצדק: צדיק וישר. מצדיק הדין על הצדיקים לפרוע מהם ועושה טובה וישרות עם הרשעים לפרוע כל זכותם בעולם הזה כדי לטורדן: ביד כל אדם יחתום. כותב מעשה כל אדם ומחתים (ה) יד על כל מעשיו: למען תצדק בדברך. שהוא מצדיק עליו בדבריך שאתה מרצה לו (ו): לשמואל קדוש יהיה גדל פרע קאי. שנערו אסור בהנאה אבל הוא עצמו לא נקרא קדוש ולר' אלעזר חוטא דקאי כתרגומו מאשר חטא על הנפש פשט המקרא על שנטמא במת: וכי באיזה נפש חטא זה. מי הרג שנקרא חוטא שאין מצוה לצער עצמו כדאמרינן לדיקי (*מי) אכלי האי עלמא (והאיך) מי סני להו במס' הוריות (פ"ג דף י:): נקרא קדוש. רישיה דקרא קא דריש בשביל שמתוך כך מתמרקין עונותיו שמתענה: כאילו

תוספות

אסור לאדם לשמש מטתו בשני רעבון. ואם תאמר הרי יוכבד *נולדה בין החומות ואותו העת עת רעב היה וע"כ שימשו מטותיהן בשני רעבון ויש לומר דלכ"ע לא הוי אסור אלא למי שרוצה לנהוג עצמו בחסידות ויוסף לא שימש אבל שאר בני אדם שימשו:

אמר שמואל כל היושב בתענית נקרא חוטא. וקשיא דאמרינן בפ' החובל (ב"ק דף צא: ושם) החובל בעצמו רשאי אבל אחרים שחבלו בו חייבים ומפרש התם הא דקאמר החובל בעצמו רשאי אמר שמואל ביושב בתענית אלמא משמע דשמואל קאמר דיושב בתענית לא נקרא חוטא ויש לומר דודאי הוי חוטא כדאמרינן הכא מקל וחומר מנזיר ומה נזיר שלא ציער עצמו אלא מיין וכו' אבל מכל מקום המצוה שהוא עושה התענית גדול יותר מן העבירה ממה שהוא מצער נפשו דמצוה לנדור כדאמרינן (סוטה דף ב.) הרואה סוטה בקלקולה יזיר עצמו מן היין ומכל מקום יש קצת חטא מידי דהוה *אמתענה תענית חלום בשבת דקורעין גזר דינו ונפרעין ממנו תענית של שבת ומאי תקנתיה ליתב תעניתא לתעניתיה*: כאילו

[ואף צדיק גמור צריך לצער עצמו עם הצבור שכן מצינו במשה רבינו שציער עצמו וכו' כך אי' בשאלתות פ' ההוינו סימן קמג]

רבינו חננאל

והמרעיב עצמו בשני רעבון ניצל ממיתת משונה שנאמר ברעב פדך ממות. אסור לאדם לשמש מטתו בשני רעבון. תנא חשוכי בנים משמשין מטותיהן בשני רעבון. חייב אדם לצער עצמו עם הצבור שבזמן שפורש עצמו מן הצבור ב' מלאכי השרת המלוין אותו מניחין ידיו על ראשו ואומרים פלוני שפירש מן הצבור אל יראה בנחמת ישראל. אלא מיבעי ליה לצעורי עם הצבור שכן מצינו במרע"ה שציער עצמו עם הצבור שנאמר וידי משה כבדים וגו'. וכי לא היה לו כר או כסת לישב בה אלא רצה להצטער בצער צבור. ושמא תאמר מי מעיד בו. אבני ביתו. שנאמר כי אבן מקיר תזעק. ומלאכים השומרים אותו שנאמר כי מלאכיו יצוה לך וגו'. כתיב אל אמונה ואין עול. כשם שנפרעים מן הרשעים לעוה"ב אפילו בעבירה קלה כך נפרעין מן הצדיקים בעוה"ז וכשם שמשלמין שכר טוב בעוה"ב לצדיקים [אפי' על מצוה קלה] כך משלמין שכר טוב לרשעים אפילו על מצוה קלה בעוה"ז. בשעת פטירתו של אדם. כל מעשיו נפרשין לפניו. אומרים לו עשית במקום פלוני והוא אומר הן. אומרים לו חתום. והותם שנאמר ביד כל אדם יחתום. ולא עוד אלא שמצדיק עליו את הדין ואומר יפה דנתוני שנא' למען תצדק בדברך וגו': אמר שמואל היושב בתענית נקרא חוטא. סבר לה כר' אלעזר הקפר בר' [דאמר] בשביל שציער עצמו מן היין קראו הכתוב חוטא שנאמר וכפר עליו מאשר חטא על הנפש המצער עצמו מכל מאכל ומשתה לא כ"ש. ושפני מה כתיב בו קדוש יהיה משום (דמרבי) [דמרכי] נפשיה מטומאה*). ור' אלעזר פליג עליה דאמר המצער עצמו לשם שמים כגון תעניד וכיוצא

*) נראה מזה דרבינו היה לו גי' אחרת בכאן הטוא דמדכי נפשי' וכ"ה גי' רבינו גרשום כאן:

רבינו גרשום

ושתוים עליכם. בעיתי. לא עייני באורחא: משום מעיינא. שאם אוכל הרבה מתכבד במיעיו אינו יכול לילך. משום מזוני דלא שכיחי באורחא: דיתיב בארבא. ליכא משום מעיינא ואיתא משום מזוני. דאזיל מאונא לאונא. דשכיחי מזוני. משום מזוני ליכא משום מעיינא איכא: רב פפא הוי אכיל פני: חסוכי בנים ולא כולי עלמא: זו מדה בינונית שהרי מזכירין יום המיתה כדכתיב כי מחר נמות: ההוא דמרכי בנפשיה. כלומר שנזיר שמצער עצמו מן הטומאה קרוי קדוש ולא לישב בתענית. ההוא אשר חטא על הנפש דמסאב נפשיה על המת: כאילו קדיש שרוי בתוך מעיו ולא יתענה ר"ל

הגהות הב"ח

(א) גמ' כל היושב בתענית נקרא חוטא (סבר כי האי תנא) תא"מ ונ"ב ס"א שנאמר וכפר עליו מאשר חטא על הנפש וכי באיזה נפש חטא זה אלא שציער נפשו מן היין דתניא וכו' ולשמואל הא איקרי [...] נ"ב פירוש מדפליג אדשמואל אלמא דלשמואל לא נקרא קדוש אבל לר' אלעזר אפשר לא קשיא דלמא [...] נקרא קדוש אלא דנקרא נ"כ חוטא אבל לשמואל קשיא דמשמע לדידיה לא נקרא קדוש ואפ"ה דמודה [...] דיושב מצוה בנזירות מ"מ לא נקרא קדוש וכפר סתי פריך אר' אלעזר כה נקרא חוטא דמדפליג לשמואל אלמא דס"ל דלא נקרא חוטא: (ב) רש"י ד"ה חסוכי בנים חסירי בנים כמו דגרסינן במנחות: (ג) ד"ה שני וכו' שמלוין: (ד) ד"ה ואין עול שאין עושה דבר בלא דין: (ה) ד"ה ביד כל כו' ומחתים יד כל אדם על כל: (ו) ד"ה למען כו' שאתה מרצה לו מה"ד וכי באיזה נפש חטא זה מי הרג שנקרא חוטא הס"ד ואח"כ מה"ד אלא שציער עצמו וכו' שאין מצוה לצער עצמו כדאמרינן אמו נדיקי אי אכלי תבי עלמא וכו' עד שומעיו שמתענה הס"ד לשמואל קדוש יהיה וכו' לא נקרא קדוש הס"ד ואח"כ מה"ד ולר' אלעזר וכו' שבעטא כמה הס"ד:

עין משפט נר מצוה

לה א ב מיי' פ"ג מהל' תענית הלכה ח טוש"ע א"ח סי' תקעד סעיף ד:

לו ג שם סעיף ה:

מסורת הש"ס

ג"י רש"ל בשר

[לשון חיסור כמו לא תחסר. ערוך]

עי' בהגהת מהרי"ף שם

חגיגה טז. [פ"ש כמה שיטיים]

ג"י שם

[צ"ל נפרעין וכ"ה בשאלתות]

[צ"ל הן]

[שבועות ח. סוטה טו. כריתות כו.] ב"ק צא: נזיר יט. כב. נדרים י.

[צ"ל אין]

[ברכות לה: ולקמן יב:]

[ועי' תוס' ב"ק צא: ד"ה אלא ותוס' נזיר ב: ד"ה והאי]

עין משפט נר מצוה

לז א טוש"ע א"ח סי' תקעא סעיף א:

לח ב מיי' פ"ג מהלכות תענית הלכה יא טוש"ע א"ח סי' תקסח סעיף ו:

לט ג טוש"ע א"ח סי' תקעא סעיף ב:

מ ד מיי' פ"א מהלכות תענית הלכה י סמג עשין יג טוש"ע א"ח סי' תקסב סעיף ז:

מא ה מיי' שם הלכה יא סמג שם טור ש"ע א"ח שם סעיף ט:

מב ו מיי' שם הלכה יג טוש"ע שם סעיף י:

מג ז מיי' פ"א מהלכו' מאכלות אסורות הלכה טו סמג לאוין קמח טוש"ע י"ד סי' קלה [illegible]:

תורה אור

כאילו קדוש שרוי בתוך מעיו שנאמר °בקרבך קדוש ולא אבוא בעיר לא קשיא *הא דמצי לצעורי נפשיה הא דלא מצי לצעורי נפשיה ר"ל אמר נקרא חסיד שנאמר °גומל נפשו איש (א) (*חסיד) ועוכר שארו וגו' אמר רב ששת האי בר בי רב דיתיב בתעניתא ליכול כלבא לשירותיה אמר רבי ירמיה בר אבא *ג אין תענית צבור בבבל אלא תשעה באב בלבד (*אמר) ר' ירמיה בר אבא אמר ריש לקיש ד אין תלמיד חכם רשאי לישב בתענית מפני שממעט במלאכת שמים: אוכלין ושותין משחשיכה כו': אמר רבי זעירא אמר רב הונא ה יחיד שקיבל עליו תענית אפילו אכל ושתה כל הלילה ו למחר הוא מתפלל תפלת תענית ז לן בתעניתו (ג) אינו מתפלל של תענית אמר רב יוסף מאי קסבר רב הונא סבירא ליה אין מתענין לשעות או דלמא מתענין לשעות והמתענה לשעות אינו מתפלל תפלת תענית אמר ליה אביי לעולם קסבר רב הונא מתענין לשעות והמתענה לשעות מתפלל תפלת תענית ושאני הכא דאיכא שעות דליליא דלא קביל עליה מעיקרא *מר עוקבא איקלע לגינזק בעו מיניה מתענין לשעות או אין מתענין לשעות לא הוה בידיה קנקנין של נכרים אסורין או מותרין לא הוה בידיה *במה שימש משה כל שבעת ימי המלואים לא הוה בידיה אזל ושאיל בי מדרשא אמרו ליה ו הלכתא מתענין לשעות ומתפללין תפלת תענית ז והלכתא קנקנין של נכרים לאחר שנים עשר חדש מותרין במה שימש משה כל ז' ימי המלואים בחלוק לבן רב כהנא מתני בחלוק לבן שאין לו אימרא אמר רב חסדא

הא

רש"י

כאילו קדוש שרוי בתוך מעיו. כאילו כל מעיו קדוש ואסור להכחישן דהכי משמע בקרבך קדוש כלומר דאסור להתענות (ג) בקרבך קדוש רישיה דקרא קדריש בשביל שקדוש שרוי בגער לא אבוא בעיר של מעלה עד שאבנה ירושלים של מטה ורמיזא בעלמא הוא: הא דמצי מצער נפשיה. שיכול לסבול התענית משבחו הקב"ה אבל מי שאינו יכול להתענות נקרא חוטא: נקרא חסיד. המתענה דכתיב גומל נפשו איש חסד מפריש עצמו ממאכל ומשתה כמו ביום הגמל את יצחק (בראשית כא) שבריי"ר בלע"ז מפי מורי אי נמי גומל לשון תגמול שמשלים נפשו לקוט (ד): ועוכר שארו. המתענה ומכחיש בשרו נקרא אכזר: שממעט במלאכת שמים. חלש הוא ואינו יכול ללמוד: שירותיה. סעודתו כלבא ליכול סעודתו ולכך המתענה אינו מועיל לו אלא כמי שמתענה מפני שאין לו מה יאכל: אין תענית צבור בבבל. לענין איסורי חומרי תענית אמר ר' ירמיה למילתיה שהיו נוהגין בו כעין אבילות שהיו אוכלין מבעוד יום ואסורין בנעילת הסנדל אלא תשעה באב בלבד: יחיד שקיבל עליו תענית. מאתמול (ה) הרי אני יושב בתענית למחר אפילו אכל ושתה כל הלילה עד עמוד השחר למחר מתפלל תפלת תענית עננו: לן בתעניתו. באותו תענית שקיבל עליו שלא אכל במוצאי תעניתו ולן כל אותו הלילה לשם תענית עד הבקר: למחר אין מתפלל תפלת תענית. אינו יכול להתפלל (ו) עננו קודם שיאכל כדי לצאת ידי חובת תענית של לילה אע"פ שהוא יום אחד דכתיב (בראשית א) ויהי ערב ויהי בקר יום אחד ולקמן מפרש ואזיל מאי קסבר רב הונא מאי טעמא אין מתפלל למחר עננו: והכי גרסינן מאי קסבר רב הונא מיסבר קסבר אין מתענין לשעות או דלמא קסבר מתענין לשעות והמתענה לשעות אינו מתפלל תפלת תענית אמר אביי לעולם קסבר מתענין לשעות (*ומתפלל) תפלת תענית כו'. פירוש מאי קסבר רב הונא אין מתענין לשעות כלומר האי דקאמר למחר אין מתפלל תפלת תענית לכן אינו מתפלל דקבלת תענית זו אינו קבלה ואינו תענית כל[ל] ואם רוצה לאכול ולשתות בתוך התענית הרשות בידו דאין מקבלין תענית לשעות כגון זה שלא קיבל תענית של לילה זה מאתמול (ז) כדקתני לן בתעניתו דמשמע מאליו כשהחשיך ובא לסעוד עמד ולא אכל כלומר שהיה בדעתו לאכול עד שעבר מקצת הלילה שעה אחת או שתי שעות ואחר כך נמלך ולן בתעניתו או דלמא האי דקאמר רב הונא למחר אין מתפלל תפלת תענית לאו משום דאין מתענין לשעות דשם תענית עליו ואם רוצה לחזור בו ולטעום אחר שהתחיל בתענית אינו יכול אלא להכי אינו מתפלל תפלת תענית דסבר אין תענית של שעות חשוב וחמור כל כך שיהא צריך להתפלל עליו עננו: לעולם קסבר. בעלמא דמתענין לשעות והמתענה לשעות מתפלל תפלת תענית והכא מאי טעמא אין מתפלל תפלת תענית דשאני הכא היכא דהתענה אתמול ובלילה לן בתעניתו דלא קיבלה עילויה (ח) שלא קיבל עליו תענית זה בפני עצמו מאתמול כדרך שאר מתענין לשעות ואינו חשוב להתפלל עליו עננו: מר עוקבא איקלע לגינזק. גרסינן דאילו ר' עקיבא לא היה מסתפק לו הנך בעיי ועוד דבלשון ברייתא הוה משתעי ביה מעשה ברבי עקיבא כו' ולא בגמרא*: קנקנים של חרס. שמכניסין בהן יין לקיום אסור להשתמש בהן: במה שימש משה. דאילו באהרן כתיב בגדי כהונה דכתיב (שמות כט) והלבשתם שבשעה שהיה משה עובד אהרן היה לבוש בגדי כהונה ועבודה דמשה גזירת הכתוב הוא ובגדי כהונה לא מצינו בו ומסתמא אין הדבר כשר שהיה עובד בבגדיו של חול שיוצא בהן לשוק: לאחר שנים עשר חדש. הולך טעם יין נסך ומותרים בלא עירוי מים אבל תוך י"ב חדש צריך עירוי שלשה ימים מעת לעת: בחלוק לבן. של פשתן עשוי לשם כך: רב כהנא מתני. כי האי לישנא: בחלוק לבן שאין בו אימרא. שפה מתרגמינן אימרא (שם כח) (ט) כלומר *תחוב היה מחוץ אחד כל החלוק ולא כבגדים שלנו שבתי הידים מדובקין בבגד הגוף בתפירה כדי שלא יחשדוהו שמא בתוך שפה הוליא מעות הקודש משום שנאמר (במדבר לב) והייתם נקיים מה' ומישראל:

הא

תוספות

כאילו קדוש. הקב"ה (י) פירוש והא אמר לעיל שנקרא קדוש כלומר שהיושב בתענית נקרא קדוש ומשני לא קשיא:

גומל נפשו. פירוש שגומל חסד לנפשו שאינו מתענה נקרא חסיד:

אין תענית צבור בבבל אלא תשעה באב בלבד. פירוש שהיה להם הרבה גשמים:

יחיד שקיבל עליו תענית אע"פ שאכל ושתה כל הלילה מתפלל תפלת תענית. תימה אמאי נקט יחיד דלצבור נמי דאמרינן במתני' (לעיל דף י.) דעושין שלשה תעניות ואוכלים משחשיכה וכ"ע:

לן בתעניתו. פירוש שהתענה היום ובלילה לא אכל ולן בתעניתו אע"ג שהלילה היה מכח תענית שקיבל עליו אינו מתפלל תפלת תענית וכה"ג יש אוכל ומתפלל תפלת תענית ומפרש כמו הכא דבשחרית אומר תפלת תענית אע"פ שאכל כל הלילה ויש מתענה שאינו מתפלל כמו בערבית אע"פ שלא אכל ומפרש בהלכות גדולות דאין אומרין עננו בתפלת שחרית שמא כמלא שקרן בתפלתו דשמא לא יסיים התענית ולי נראה דלא נקרא שקרן כיון שהיה בדעתו להתענות אפילו אקרי אונס אחר כך ולא מצי לנער כפשיה לא גרע ממתענין לשעות וכן משמע מהא דתנן (לקמן דף יט.) ירדו להם גשמים קודם הנץ אינן משלימין ומסתמא משמע שאמרו תפלת תענית מכל מקום אין זה ראיה גמורה דשמא לא אמרוה ומהא דלקמן (דף יב:) גבי רב הונא בריה דרב יהושע בריה דרב אידי *דיתיב בתעניתא מדאמרו ליה ליזוף מר וליפרע ואמר להו תענית חלום הוא אמאי לא אמר מפני שאמר תפלת תענית אין זה ראיה (כ) לדברי ה"ג דלא היה דעתו להתענות מבעוד יום ולא קבל עליו וכתב הר"ן מי שלא קבל עליו מבעוד יום דאין אומר עננו אי לאו דתענית חלום הוא ונוהגים שליח צבור אומרו בשחרית כדי להודיע לעולם ולהזכיר התענית אבל יחיד אינו אומר עד המנחה [ובטור אורח חיים (סי' תקסה) אומר שליח צבור אומר בכל פעם שאי אפשר שלא יתענו קצת מקהל עכ"ל]:

רבינו חננאל

יכיוצא בו [נקרא] קדוש כדכתי' קדוש יהיה. א"כ מה ת"ל מאשר חטא על הנפש בנזיר שנטמא הכתוב מדבר ומפני שנטמא נקרא חוטא. ור"ל אמר המונע עצמו מן התענית הוא חסיד שנאמר גומל נפשו איש חסד. [illegible] לנפשו איש חסד: א"ר ירמיה אין ת"ח רשאי לסגף עצמו בתענית מפני שממעט (עצמו) במלאכת שמים. אמר רב הונא יחיד שקבל עליו תענית ב' ימים זה אחר זה אפילו אוכל ושותה כל הלילה כו'. הדין במי שקבל עליו יום אחד או ב' ימים תענית דינם אחד מיהו נוח להתלמד להבין פירושו בשני ימים מיום אחד. וכן פירושו. אדם שקבל עליי להתענות שני ושלישי והתענה יום ב' ובערב אכל ושתה למחר *) עד ביום ג' מתענה ומתפלל תפלת התענית **) אע"פ שמתענה רוב יום ג' מפני שלא קבל עליו מיום ב' להתענות יום ג' ונמצא תעניתו ביום ג' תענית שעות דהא לא קיבל תענית מאתמול. ועל זה מדקדק רב יוסף מ"ט דרב הונא. מי אמרינן קסבר רב הונא מתענה לשעות. והמתענה לשעות אינו מתפלל תפלת תענית. לפיכך אמר למחר אינו מתפלל תפלת תענית. או דלמא קסבר רב הונא אין מתענין לשעות ואינם תענית כלל. לפיכך אינו מתפלל תפלת תענית. ואמר אביי לעולם קסבר רב הונא מתענין לשעות והמתענה לשעות מתפלל תפלת תענית. ושאני הכא דלא קביל עליה מעיקרא. ועוד לא היה בדעתו להשלים תעניתו עד הערב. וקיי"ל כל תענית שלא שקעה עליו חמה לאו שמיה תענית לפיכך ***) תמצא תענית שעות. ומסתברא דמי שנזדמן לו ולא אכל עד שעבר רוב היום וכיון שראה כך הסכים לצום ולהשלימו אותו יום בתענית זהו תענית שעות ומתפלל באותה שעה שהסכים להשלימו התענית שעות תפלת תענית עננו בשומע תפלה. ודווקא אחר שקבל עליו לעצמו ****) שמתפלל תפלת תענית אבל מקודם לא: ר"ע אקלע לגינזק בעו מיניה מתענין לשעות כו' ואסיקנא הלכתא המתענה לשעות מתפלל תפלת תענית וקנקנים (שלמים) [ישנים] ששימשו בהן עובדי כוכבים ביין שלהן לאחר שישבו היין מהן אם ישארו ריקים י"ב חודש מותר לישראל להטיל בהן יין להשתמש בהן.

אמר

*) דברי רבינו כמו שהם לפנינו אין לו שום ביאור כלל ועי' בהא"ש כאן והמגא"ג י' רבינו ז"ל ופירושו באר היטב. **) חסר כאן ואולי כצ"ל לן בתעניתו כלו' אם לא קבל עליו תענית אלא יום ב' בלבד והתענה אותו היום ובלילה נמלך ולן בתעניתו למחר אין מתפלל תפלת תענית אע"פ שמתענה יום ב' ויום ג' כו' ועי' בריי"ף ובמלחמות בשם רבינו. ***) אולי צ"ל לא נקרא תענית בשום. ****) אולי צ"ל לעצמו להשלים התענית מתפלל תפלת תענית

רבינו גרשום

ר"ל אמר יושב בתענית נקרא חסיד שנא' גומל נפשו איש חסד שפירש עצמו מליכל כמו ויגמל: כסעם במלאכת שמים. שאינו יכול לעסוק בתורה: יחיד שקיבל עליו תענית. כראוי מבעוד יום. לן בתענית. ה"ק אם לא קבל מבעוד יום אלא בצפרא קבל עליה להתענות חצי היום ובחצי היום קביל עליה עד לאורתא ולן בלילה בתעניתו ולא קבל עליה כלום והתענה אף למחר אין מתפלל תפלת תענית שכבר יצא בתפלת תענית דאתמול. ושאני הכא דלא קביל עליה מאורתא כלומר באותו יום שמתענה לשעות מתפלל תפלת תענית אבל הכא דלן בתעניתו עבדיה להאי תענית שני כתענית אריכא שהוא מאתמול שעדיין לא אכל וכיון שהתפלל אתמול תפלת תענית אין צריך להתפלל היום: מתענין לשעות שמקבלין תענית ביום אע"ג דלא קביל עליה מאורתא: קנקנים של עובדי כוכבים שנשתמש בהן יין. לאחר שנים עשר חודש. לאחר שנשתמשו בו עובדי כוכבים: חלוק לבן שאין לו אימרא. שאין לו שפה כדי שלא יחשדוהו שמא באותה שפה הכניס מעות הקדש שנגב משום שנאמר והייתם נקיים

גליון הש"ס

גמ' הא דמצי לצעורי. עי' לקמן דף כב ע"ב תוד"ה ר' יוסי: שם למחר הוא מתפלל תפלת תענית. מדברי רש"י שבת כד ע"א ד"ה ערבית נראה שלא היה לרש"י שם הגי' כאן תיבת למחר:

הגהות הב"ח

(א) גמ' שנאמר גומל נפשו איש חסד אמר ר' ירמיה בר אבא אמר ריש לקיש אין ת"ח וכו' שממעט במלאכת שמים אמר רב ששת האי בר בי רב וכו' אלא תשעה באב בלבד אוכלין כו': (ב) שם לן בתעניתו למחר אינו מתפלל: (ג) רש"י ד"ה כאילו כו' דאסור להתענות הס"ד ומה"ד בקרבך קדוש כו': (ד) ד"ה נקרא כו' שמשלים נפשו לקוט הס"ד ואח"כ מה"ד ועוכר שארו וכו': (ה) ד"ה יחיד כו' כצ"ל וכד"ה: (ו) ד"ה למחר כו' אינו יכול להתפלל. נ"ב פי' אינו יכול אע"פ שרוצה להתפלל בלא חיוב ונראה דלא פירש כן אלא לאפוקי דקס"ד דאין מתענין לשעות כ"ל לרב הונא דלהוי תענית הוא אבל למ"ד דמתענין לשעות שם תענית עליו אפי' לן בתעניתו דאינו חשוב וחמור להתפלל עננו כהוראת חיוב מ"מ הרשות בידו להתפלל עננו שכרי שם תענית עליו שאסור לו לאכול: (ז) ד"ה וכ"ג מאי כו' תענית של לילה זה מאתמול. נ"ב פירוש מאתמול מזמן המנחה: (ח) ד"ה לעולם כו' דלא קיבלה עילויה. נ"ב ר"ל דלא קיבלו כלל מאתמול דאף בלילה לא קיבלו: (ט) ד"ה רב כהנא כו' (כלומר תחוב) תא"מ ונ"ב כ"ה כלי הכוב: (י) תוס' ד"ה כאילו קדוש הקב"ה שרוי בתוך מעיו ואסור להכחישן פי' והא אמרינן לעיל: (כ) ד"ה לן כו' אין זה ראיה לדברי ה"ג אלא למימר דלא היה דעתו:

[נ"ל חסר]

[לקמן יב. פסחים נד: ...] [נ"ל ואמר]

ע"ז לד. [ע"ש בתוס' ד"ה ר' עקיבא]

[עי' תוס' מגילה ו: ד"ה מאי כ"מ ותוס' סנהדרין סו: ד"ה של סיני]

[לשיטתו זה היה רב יהושע בריה דרב אידי]

[נ"ל מתענין לשעות והמתענה (ששוי ...)]

[ועמ"ש תוס' ב"ב לד. ד"ה ר"ע וכו' על דברי רש"י דהכא]

[נ"ל ארוג יעב"ץ]

הא דאמרת מתענין לשעות והוא שלא טעם כלום עד הערב א"ל אביי הא תענית מעלייתא היא לא צריכא דאימלך אימלוכי ואמר רב חסדא *כל תענית שלא שקעה עליו חמה לאו שמיה תענית מיתיבי *אנשי משמר מתענין ולא משלימין התם לצעורי נפשיה בעלמא הוא תא שמע *דא"ר אליעזר (*בן) צדוק אני מבני בניו של *סנאב בן בנימין ופעם אחת חל ט' באב להיות בשבת ודחינוהו לאחר השבת והתענינו בו ולא השלמנוהו מפני שיו"ט שלנו הוא התם נמי לצעורי נפשיה בעלמא הוא תא שמע *דאמר רבי יוחנן אהא בתענית עד שאבוא לביתי התם לשמוטיה נפשיה מבי נשיאה הוא דעבד אמר שמואל כל תענית שלא קיבל עליו מבעוד יום לאו שמיה תענית ואי יתיב מאי אמר רבה בר שילא דמי למפוחא דמליא זיקא אימת מקביל ליה רב אמר במנחה ושמואל אמר בתפלת המנחה אמר רב יוסף כוותיה דשמואל מסתברא דכתיב במגילת תענית להן כל איניש דייתי עלוהי מקדמת דנא ייסר מאי לאו ייסר עצמו בצלו לא יאסר עצמו פליגי בהא רבי חייא ורבי שמעון ברבי חד אמר ייסר וחד אמר יאסר (א) מ"ד ייסר כדאמרינן למאן דאמר יאסר מאי היא דתניא במגילת תענית כל איניש דייתי עלוהי מקדמת דנא יאסר כיצד יחיד שקיבל עליו שני וחמישי (ושני) של כל השנה כולה ואירעו בם ימים טובים הכתובים במגילת תענית אם נדרו קודם לגזרתנו יבטיל נדרו את גזרתנו ואם גזרתנו קודמת לנדרו תבטל גזרתנו את נדרו תנו רבנן *עד מתי אוכל ושותה עד שיעלה עמוד השחר דברי רבי *רבי אליעזר בר שמעון אומר עד קרות הגבר אמר *אביי לא שנו אלא שלא גמר סעודתו אבל גמר סעודתו אינו אוכל איתיביה *רבא גמר ועמד הרי זה אוכל התם כשלא סילק איכא דאמרי אמר רבא לא שנו אלא כשלא ישן אבל ישן אינו אוכל איתיביה אביי (ב) ישן ועמד הרי זה אוכל התם במתנמנם *היכי דמי מתנמנם אמר רב אשי

ניס · נים

רש"י

הא דאמרת מתענין לשעות והוא שלא טעם כלום כל אותו היום. כלומר לא אמרו במתענה שאכל בו ביום כגון שהתחיל להתענות עד חצי היום ואח"כ אכל דאין זה עינוי ואם אכל קודם חצות אין בכך כלום דאינו תענית של כלום אלא כשהשלים כל היום אע"פ שלא קיבלו עליו מאתמול ופריך אי דקבל עליו להתענות עד חצי יום והדר מתענה כל היום האי תעניתא מעלי' הוא ופשיטא דתענית גמור הוא ואפילו תפלת תענית נמי מתפלל עליו ולא איצטריך לאוקמי הלכה בהכי דזהו תענית גמור והאי מקשה סבר דהאי הלכה מתענין לשעות כמשמעו דיכול להתענות עד חצי היום מתענה קרינא ביה: לא צריכא דאמליך אימלוכי. כלומר לא היה בדעתו כלל להתענות אלא אהא ליה טרדא ולא אכל עד חצי היום וכי מטא חצי יום ממליך אמר הואיל והתעניתי עד חצי היום אתענה כל היום: שלא שקעה עליו חמה. שלא התענה עד אותה שעה: אנשי משמר. כהנים ולוים העובדין מתענין כדלקמן בפרק סדר תעניות: ולא משלימין. לפי שהן עסוקין בעבודה ואין יכולים להשלים אלמא אע"ג דאינו משלים מתענה קרי ליה: לצעורי נפשייהו. עם הצבור אבל אינו תענית לא להתפלל תפלת עננו ולא לקובעו עליו חובה כלל וכל שעה שהוא רוצה לאכול אוכל: מבני (סנאב) בן בנימין. משבט בנימין: שיו"ט שלנו היה. כדלקמן בשלשה פרקים (דף כו.) זמן עצי כהנים והעם כו' עד בחמשה באב בני פרעוש בן יהודה בעשרה בו בני (סנאב) בן בנימין שעל ידי מעשה קבעו להן חכמים להתנדב עצים ולהביא למערכה וכשמגיע זמנו מביאין אותן ומדליקין אותן על גבי המזבח אע"פ שהיו שם שאר עצים הרבה אפ"ה בשאר מתנדבי עצים דאין מבעירין אותן בזמן שיש עצים אחרים במסכת מנחות (דף קו:) אמרינן המתנדב עצים לא יפחות משני גזרין ועלים טעונין קמילה טעונים הגשה כו': דאמר רבי יוחנן. פעמים שהיה אומר אהא בתענית עד שאבוא לביתי ואי מטי לביתיה בשתים או בג' שעות ביום הוה אכיל וקרי ליה מתענה: לשמוטיה נפשיה מבי נשיאה. דלא ליטרחוהו למיכל בהדייהו שהיה מבקש הימנו שיאכל עמו היה אומר כן שלא יטריחנו לאכול עמו ומיהו לא הוי תענית שאם היה רוצה היה אוכל מיד ואין בנדרו כלום: ואי יתיב מאי. מי סליק לתענית אי לא: למפוחא. זוא המפוח שנופחין בו הנפחין את האור המתמלא ברוח אף זה נתמלא רוח שלא אכל בחנם: במנחה. בזמן המנחה ואפילו בשוק אומר הריני מחר בתענית: בתפלת המנחה. בסופה (ג) תוספת רילוי ותחנונים עד שאומר הריני מחר בתענית ודוקא נקט מנחה משום דסמוך לתחלת יום תעניתו לאפוקי תפלת יוצר ודיקא נמי מדפסיק שמואל ופליג אדרב דאמר בזמן המנחה שיעורא יתירא: כדכתיב במגילת תענית. לסוף ימים טובים הכתובים במגילת תענית כתיב בה מקדמת דנא ייסר לעיל מינה תני אלין יומיא די לא להתענאה בהון להן כל איניש דייתי עלוה תענית מן קדמת דנא לפני אלו ימים טובים כגון שקיבל עליו עשרה תעניות או עשרים ונכנסו אלו הימים בהם: ייסר בצלו. בתפלה ואי לא קבליה עליה בתפלת המנחה לא דחי להנך ימים טובים אלמא דעיקר תענית בעי לקבולי בתפלת המנחה עילויה ואי לא קבליה עילויה בתפלת המנחה לא עשה כלום: ייסר. לשון ואסרה אסר (במדבר ל): בצלו. לצלותא איכא דאמרי לשון נדר שקבל עליו להתענות כמו הרימותי ידי אל ה' (בראשית יד) דמתרגמינן ארימית ידי בצלו ואין רבי מודה. הא דקתני דכתיב משום דמגילת תענית היתה נכתבת לבד לזכרון נסים: וחד אמר יאסר. דלא הוה תני ייסר (ד) בצלו דמשמע דוקא כדאמרינן אי מקבל בתפלת המנחה אין ואי לא לא אלא יאסר דמשמע יהא אסור לאכול אי אתי עליה תענית מן קדמת דנא בין בתפלה בין שלא בתפלה: מאי היא. מאי קסבר ומשני כדתניא יחיד שקבל עליו תענית שני וחמישי של כל השנה כולה כלומר כדמפרש בהדיא אם נדרו קודם לגזרתנו כו' ולא שנא בין בתפלה בין שלא בתפלה: קודם גזרתנו. קודם שגזרו חכמים ימים טובים הללו אבל משגזרו אע"פ שהתחיל תענוותיו קודם הזמנים הללו לא דחו: עד מתי אוכל ושותה. בלילה כשמתענה למחר בכל תעניות שהוא אוכל משהחשך ואפילו בתענית יחיד קא מיירי: עד קרות הגבר. אפילו פעם ראשונה קאמר מדקאמר גבי יונא יחידי בלילה בסדר יומא (דף כא.) עד שישלש: שלא גמר סעודתו. אבל גמר דברי הכל אינו אוכל: אכל ועמד. אע"פ שבירך ועמד משולחנו חוזר ואוכל ואין בכך כלום: שלא סילק. את הטבלא דלאו עקירה היא ולא אסח דעתיה מאכילה וכסעודה אריכתא דמיא: איכא דאמרי אמר רבא כו'. והלכה כאיכא דאמרי אוכל ושותה עד שיישן קבע ועד שיעלה עמוד השחר כרבי: אבל ישן. הפסקה היא ושוב אינו אוכל: התם. לאו ישן ממש אלא מתנמנם שומליי"ר בלע"ז:

תיר

תוספות

כל תענית שלא שקעה עליו חמה לא שמיה תענית. פי' במסכת ע"ז פרק אין מעמידין (דף לד.) וכן בחלוק שאין לו אימרא פירש התם וכל הפסק דמתענין לשעות דכל תענית צריך לקבלו מבערב בתפלת המנחה בשומע תפלה ואם הוא שבת באלהי נצור וצריך שיאמר למחר אהיה בתענית יחיד כי היכי דליכא למטעי בתענית צבור: התם לצעורי נפשיה בעלמא. ואע"ג דאמרינן (ר"ה דף יח:) משחרב בית המקדש בטלה מגילת תענית והאי עובדא דרבי אליעזר בר צדוק היה לאחר חורבן דאי קודם החורבן אמרינן (שם) (ה) כיון שיש שלום אין שם גזירות המלכות האי תנא סבר דלא בטלה: יאסר. פי' יאסר באל"ף הוי לשון אסור שאסר עצמו וייסר הוי לשון הסרה כלומר יסור מן הנדר (ו) יהיה מותר לאכול למחר שיהיה יום טוב ואין להתענות: ואם גזרתנו קודם לנדרו ידחה נדרו מפני גזרתנו. אומר רש"י ידחה נדרו מכל וכל ולא ישלים אותו תענית והר"י מסופק בדבר ויש להחמיר דדוקא אותו יום לא יתענה אבל ישלים אותו ליום (ז) מחר וכן יש ליזהר שלא להתענות בראש חדש ובחנוכה ובפורים דמאלו ודאי לא בטלה מגילת תענית:

עין משפט נר מצוה

מד א ב מיי' פ"א מהל' תענית הלכה יג סמג עשין ג טוש"ע א"ח סי' תקסב סעיף י:

מה ג שם סעיף א:

מו ד מיי' פ"ו מהלכות כלי מקדש הלכה ט:

מז ה מיי' פ"א מהלכות תענית הלכה י סמג שם טוש"ע שם סעיף ט:

מח ו מיי' שם וטוש"ע שם סעיף ו:

מט ז ח מיי' שם הלכה ח סמג עשין ג טוש"ע שם סי' תקסד סעיף א:

מסורת הש"ס

לקמן טו: · עירובין מא. · תענית כו. · [נ"ל סנאה] · [נ"ל סנאה] · [ג"י רא"ש ר' אלעזר אומר] · [פסחים קז: מגילה יז: יבמות נד. נדה סג.]

[עי' תוס' פ"ז נד. ד"ה מתענין ותוס' מנחות ל ד"ה נפסל] · [נ"ל ברבי] · [נ"ל סנאה עי' תוס' עירובין מא. ד"ה מבני] · [תוספ' פ"א] פסחים ג ע"ב [עי' תוס' שבת קיח ד"ה לפי שאין] · ס"י רבא וכן הוא בה"ג · ס"י אביי

הגהות הב"ח

(א) גמ' וחד אמר יאסר בצלמא מ"ד ייסר כדאמרינן למ"ד יאסר מאי היא כדתניא במגילת תענית: (ב) שם איתיביה אביי אכל ועמד כו' זה אוכל: (ג) רש"י ד"ה בתפלת המנחה בסופה אומר הריני תוספת ריצוי: (ד) ד"ה וחד אמר יאסר לא הוה תני בצלו דמשמע דוקא: (ה) תוס' ד"ה התם כו' קודם החורבן אמרינן בזמן שיש שלום אין שם גזי' האי תנא סבר: (ו) ד"ה ייסר כו' ויהיה מותר: (ז) ד"ה ואם כו' אבל ישלים אותו ליום אחר וכן יש ליזהר:

רבינו חננאל

אמר רב חסדא הא דאמרת מתענין לשעות ומתפלל תפלת תענית והוא שלא טעם כלום עד הערב ואע"ג דאמליך אמלוכי. רב חסדא לטעמיה דאמר כל תענית שלא שקעה עליו חמה לא שמיה תענית. ואותבינן עליה הא דתנן אנשי משמר מתענין ולא משלימין. והא דאמר ר' אלעזר בר צדוק והתענו בו ולא השלמנוהו הנה תעניותם תענית אף על פי שלא שקעה עליו חמה. ומשני התם אינה תענית אלא רצו להצטער גם הם בצער צבור. ולא משום דהורת דין תענית עליהם ור' יוחנן לא הוה מסכים תענית בלבו ולא היה אומר אלא להשתמט מבי נשיאה שלא היה רוצה *לסעוד אצלם: אמר שמואל כל תענית שלא קבלה מבע"י אינה תענית אימת מקבל לה רב אמר במנחה משעה *) שיסכן לתפלת המנחה. ואפי' מתעסק במלאכתו אומר מחר אהיה בתענית. יהי רצון שתהא תפלתי ביום תעניתי מקובלת ושמואל אמר בתפלת המנחה כלומר צריך להיות כולל אלו הדברים בשומע תפלה וגו'. אמר רב יוסף כשמואל מסתברא דכתיב במגלת תענית להן כל איניש דייתי עליהו מן קדמת דנא יאסר. מאי יאסר עצמו בצלו מקודם שיקבל עליו תענית מקבל עליו בתפלתו תענית שנמצא אוסר עצמו באכילה ובשתיה בקבלתו תענית בתפלתו: פליגו בה ר' חייא ור' שמעון בר' חד תני ייסר וחד תני יאסר. מאן דתני ייסר כלומר ייסר עצמו בצלו בתפלת המנחה ואיסור אוסר על עצמו בתפלתו. ומאן דתני יאסר כדתניא להן כל איניש דייתי עלוהי [מקדמת דנא] יאסר. כיצד יחיד שקיבל עליו תענית ב' וה' (וב') של כל השנה ואירעו בהן י"ט הכתובים במגלת תענית כגון שמונת ימים שמראש חדש ניסן וכיוצא בהן דלא להתענאה בהן. אם נדרו קודם לגזרתנו ידחה נדרו את גזרתנו כו'. פי' כל איניש דייתי עליהו נדר תענית מקדמת גזרה דנא להיות היום י"ט ושיהיה אסור בתענית יאסר באכילה ובשתייה ומקיים נדרו. תניא ר"ח כסלו ולא ירדו גשמים ב"ד גוזרין ג' תעניות על הצבור אוכלין ושותין משחשכה ומותרין במלאכה כו': ת"ר עד מתי אוכלין ושותין עד שיעלה עמוד השחר דברי רבי ר"ש בן אלעזר אומר עד קרות הגבר. אמר רבה לא שנו עד שיעלה עמוד השחר אלא אם לא ישן

שנת

*) שיתכוין לצ"ל וכ"ה בערוך.

רבינו גרשום

נקיים מה' ומישראל · דקא מימלך אימלוכי]. שקיבל עליו תענית בשחרית עד הצהרים ובצהרים קבל עליו להתענות עד לאורתא. שלא שקעה עליו חמה כלומר שלא התענה כל היום עד לאורתא: לצעורי נפשיה מיכוין אבל תענית לא מיקרי אלא א"כ משלים כל היום: זמני שיו"ט שלהם היה. שמביאין בו עצים למערכה: התם לצעורי נפשייהו בעלמא מיכוונו ולא לתענית שהרי יו"ט שלהן היה: עד שאבא לביתי אלא דאין משלימין: יהם לשמוטיה נפשיה מבי נשיאה שהיה מבקש ממנו שיאכל עמו היה אומר כן כדי שלא יטריחו לאכול עמו: במנחה. בפ' עע"ת ומחצה: כל איניש דאתי עליהון שקיבל עליו תענית. מקדמת דנא קודם שהגיעו אותן ימים שאמרו חכמים במגילת תענית שלא להתענות שאירע התענית באותן ימים: מאי לאו ייסר עצמו בצלו. כלומר שייסר עצמו בתענית במה שקבל בתפלת המנחה. מאן דאמר ייסר כדאמרן דאפי' קיבל עליו התענית לאחר שנתקנו אותן ימים טובים שלא להתענות בהן אלא שקיבל עליו קודם שהגיעו שייך נפשיה בתענית ממה שקיבל עליו תענית בתפלת המנחה: אם נדרו קודמת לגזירתנו אם קיבל עליו תענית קודם שתיקנו חכמים אותן ימים טובים: תדחה גזירתנו מפני נדרו דאיסור באכילה הואיל שקיבל עליו בתפלת המנחה: אם גזירתנו קודמת לנדרו שתיקנו אותן ימים טובים קודם שקיבל זה עליו אלו תעניות תדחה נדרו מפני גזירתנו שאינו מתענה מפני אילו ימים טובים. ועוד הורה ששמע משום אב ב"ד שבירוני' אם נדרו קודמת לגזירתנו קודם שקבעו ב"ד את החדש שבו אלו ימים טובים היינו גזירתנו קבועה החדש תדחה גזירתנו מפני נדרו דהואיל כשקיבל עליו תענית לא ידע באיזה יום יארע ימים טובים אלו אבל קדם גזירתנו לנדרו שקבעו ב"ד את החדש קודם וזה שקיבל עליו תענית וכשקיבל כבר ידע באיזה יום יארע ימים טובים אלו ואעפ"כ קבל לפיכך ידחה נדרו דאינו מתענה באלו ימים טובים

עד

*נים ולא נים תיר ולא תיר דקרו ליה ועני ולא ידע אהדורי סברא וכי מדכרי ליה מדכר אמר רב כהנא אמר רב יחיד שקיבל עליו תענית אסור בנעילת הסנדל חיישינן שמא תענית צבור קיבל עליו היכי ליעבד אמר רבה בר רב שילא לימא הכי ״למחר אהא לפניך בתענית יחיד אמרו ליה רבנן לרב ששת הא קא חזינן רבנן דמסיימי מסנייהו ואתו לבי תעניתא איקפד ואמר להו דלמא מיכל נמי אכול אביי ורבא מעיילי כי מסיימי אפנתא מרימר ומר זוטרא מחלפי דימינא לשמאלא ודשמאלא לימינא רבנן דבי רב אשי נפקי כי אורחייהו סברי כי הא דאמר שמואל *אין תענית צבור בבבל אלא תשעה באב *בלבד אמר רב יהודה אמר רב ״לוה אדם תעניתו ופורע כי אמריתה קמיה דשמואל אמר לי וכי נדר קבל עליה א] דלא סגי דלא משלם לצעורי נפשיה קביל עליה אי מצי מצער נפשיה אי לא מצי לא מצער נפשיה איכא דאמרי אמר רב יהודה אמר רב לוה אדם תעניתו ופורע כי אמריתה קמיה דשמואל אמר לי פשיטא לא יהא אלא נדר נדר מי לא מצי בעי לשלומי ומיזל למחר וליומא אחרינא *רב יהושע בריה דרב אידי איקלע לבי רב אסי עבדו ליה עגלא תילתא אמרו ליה ליטעום מר מידי א״ל בתעניתא יתיבנא אמרו ליה ולוזיף מר וליפרע לא סבר מר להא דאמר רב יהודה אמר רב לוה אדם תעניתו ופורע אמר להו תענית חלום הוא ואמר רבה בר מחסיא אמר רב חמא בר גוריא אמר רב ״יפה תענית לחלום כאש לנעורת (*אמר) רב חסדא ״ובו ביום ואמר רב יוסף ״ואפילו בשבת *מאי תקנתיה ״ליתיב תעניתא לתעניתא: **מתני׳** ״עברו אלו ולא נענו בית דין גוזרין ג׳ תעניות אחרות על הצבור *אוכלין ושותין מבעוד יום ואסורין במלאכה וברחיצה ובסיכה ובנעילת הסנדל ובתשמיש המטה ונועלין את המרחצאות ״עברו אלו ולא נענו ב״ד גוזרין זוליהן, זוד שבע שהן י״ג תעניות על הצבור *הרי אלו יתרות על הראשונות שבאלו מתריעין ונועלין את החנויות *)בשני מטין עם השיכה ובחמישי מותרין מפני כבוד השבת **עברו אלו ולא נענו ממעטין במשא ומתן בבנין ובנטיעה באירוסין ובנישואין *ובשאילת שלום בין אדם לחבירו כבני אדם הנזופין למקום היחידים חוזרין ומתענין עד שיצא ניסן *יצא ניסן וירדו גשמים סימן קללה שנא׳ ״הלא קציר חטים היום וגו׳: **גמ׳** בשלמא כולהו אית בהו תענוג רחיצה וסיכה ותשמיש המטה אבל מלאכה צער הוא אמר רב חסדא אמר רב ירמיה בר אבא אמר קרא ״קדשו צום קראו עצרה אספו זקנים כעצרת מה עצרת אסור בעשיית מלאכה אף תענית אסור בעשיית מלאכה אי מה עצרת מאורתא אף תענית נמי מאורתא אמר רבי זירא לדידי מיפרשא לי מיניה דר׳ ירמיה בר אבא אמר קרא אספו זקנים דומיא דאסיפת זקנים מה אסיפת זקנים ביום אף צום נמי ביום ואימא *מטיהרא אמר רב ששא בריה דרב אידי מסייע ליה לרב הונא דאמר **)מצפרא כינופיא ״היכי עבדי אמר אביי מצפרא עד פלגא דיומא מעיינן במילי דמתא מכאן ואילך ריבעא דיומא קרינן בספרא ואפטרתא מכאן ואילך בעינן רחמי שנא׳ ״ויקומו על עמדם ויקראו בספר תורת ה׳ אלהיהם רביעית היום ורביעית מתודים ומשתחוים לה׳ אלהיהם

איפוך

*) [פרש״י על זה לקמן דף יד:]

רש״י

תיר . ער כדמתרגמינן (בראשית מא) ויקץ ואיתער : אהדורי סברא . אם צריך ממנו דבר שצריך הרהור אינו יודע לומר בעוד שמתנמנם : וכי מדכרו ליה מדכר . כזה שמעת מדכר : יחיד שקבל עליו תענית . סתם ואינו יודע איזה תענית קבל עליו אם של (א) יחיד אם של תורה אור צבור : ואסור בנעילת כו׳ . שמא תענית צבור כג׳ ״ראשונות או כז׳ אחרונות קיבל עליו : קאתו רבנן לתעניתא כו׳ . בתענית צבור וסברי לה כשמואל דאמר אין תענית צבור בבבל בפרק מקום שנהגו (פסחים דף נד:) (ב) דאסור בנעילת הסנדל וככל הני : איקפד רב ששת דלמא מיכל נמי אכלי . ופורשים מדרכי צבור ולית ליה דשמואל ואנן האידנא נהגינן כשמואל : אפנתא . אושקריפי״ש : מחלפי . ביומא דתעניתא : לצעורי בעלמא . אי מצי מצער נפשיה ואי לא (ג) לא יהא אלא (״ליומא) אחרינא : ואפילו בשבת . יכול להתענות כדי שיתבטל צער גופו : קדשו צום קראו עצרה אספו זקנים כל יושבי הארץ בית ה׳ אלהיכם וזעקו אל ה׳ : מה עצרת . שבועות ושמיני עצרת : אי מה עצרת . איסור מלאכתו מאורתא : דומיא דאסיפת זקנים ביום . דבלילה כל אחד בביתו ואין נאספין : מסייע ליה לרב הונא . הא דפשיטא לך דאסיפת זקנים ביום : דאמר מצפרא כינופיא . ביום תענית צבור מתקבצין ובאין לבית הכנסת מן הבקר : מעיינן במילי דמתא . דרישה וחקירה לבדוק במעשיהם בעסקי בני העיר אם גזל וחמס ביניהן ומפייסין אותן : (ד) היכי עבדי . מאי עבדי בכינופיא דמצפרא ובכוליה יומא דתעניתא: ריבעא דיומא. מחלות ואילך עושין ב׳ חלקים בפלגא. דהיינו ריבעא דיומא הרי [illegible] משה ומפטירין דרשו את ה׳ [illegible].

איפוך

תוספות

נים ולא נים תיר ולא תיר . ״אומר רבי ״נים ולא נים בתוך השינה כשניעור משנתו תיר ולא תיר בתחילה השינה ״לך לא נראה (ה) בערבי פסחים (דף קכ:) דקאמר נתנמנמו יאכלו נרדמו לא יאכלו ואמר רב אשי ה״ד נתנמנמו נים ולא נים וכו׳ והתם מיירי בתחילת השינה בין נים ולא נים בין תיר ולא תיר ״לכנ״ל כפירוש רש״י דאי הוה אמר נים ולא נים הוה אמינא דתיר הוי טפי מנים ואי הוה אמר תיר ולא תיר ה״א דנים הוי טפי מתיר הלכך איצטריך תרוייהו וכולהו בתחילת השינה כדמפרש התם (ו) ובירושלמי מפורש גבי הך ברייתא עד כמה אוכל ושותה עד קרות הגבר וה״ה עד שיעלה עמוד השחר ובד״א שהתנה אבל לא התנה וישן אינו יכול לאכול :

אביי ורבא סיימי אפנתא . פירוש במנעל שאין(ו) שולים שול״א בלע״ז : **דאי** מצי מצער נפשיה עביד אי לא מצי מצער נפשיה לא עביד . ומהאי דקאמר שמואל דלוה תעניתו ופורע דוקא היכי דלא מצי מצער נפשיה אבל היכי דמצי מצער נפשיה לא מצי ללוות תעניתו והכי מסקנא אם אמר הריני בתענית למחר צריך לצעוריה נפשיה ואינו יכול ללוות ופורע בחנם ואפילו אבל בשוגג ישלים אותו והר״י מסופק בדבר אם יכול ללוותו ולפרוע היכי דקביל עליה כבר להתענות והתענה עד חצי היום או רביע יום ואפילו לא מצי לצעורי נפשיה אבל לא התענה ודאי דיכול ללוות אחר בשבילו או אם טעה ואכל בשוגג יאכל וישלים יום אחר ואם התענה בשבת כגון תענית חלום דצריך לפרוע כדאמר ובלבד דיתיב תעניתא לתעניתא אם אירע שיהיה ר״ח אותו יום אז ידחה להעניתו עד יום אחר בשבוע וכן נראה למ״ר שי׳ :

מה אסיפת זקנים ביום אף צום ביום . אבל בלילה לא תימה אמאי אוכלים ושותים מבעוד יום כל הלילה נמי היו יכולין לאכול ולשתות מה אסיפת זקנים ביום אף צום ביום אבל בלילה לא ויש לומר דלא [illegible] מלאכה דוקא מגלגה גמרינן מאסיפה דהא לא כתיב בקרא אלא אספו זקנים וקדשו צום אבל אכילה לא כתיב בקרא :

איפוך

עין משפט נר מצוה

[עמ״ש בס״ו א״ח סי׳ תרל ס״ק ח בגיה סכה קלה בארוכות]

נ א מיי׳ פ״א מהלכות תענית הלכה י טוש״ע א״ח סי׳ תקסח סעיף ו : [ועי׳ תוס׳ נדה סג: ד״ה נים]

נא ב מיי׳ פ״ד מהלכות נדרים הלכה טז סמג עשין רמב טוש״ע שם סעיף ב :

נב ג מיי׳ פ״א מהלכות תענית הלכה יב סמג עשין מד״ס ג טור שו״ע שם סי׳ רכ סעיף ב :

נג ד מיי׳ שם טוש״ע שם סי׳ תקסח סעיף ב :

נד ה ו מיי׳ וסמג שם טוש״ע שם סי׳ רפח סעיף ד :

נה ז מיי׳ פ״ג מהלכות תענית הלכה ג והלכה ד טוש״ע שם סי׳ תקעה סעיף ג :

נו ח מיי׳ שם הלכה ה טוש״ע שם סעיף ד :

נז ט מיי׳ שם הלכה ח וטוש״ע שם סעיף ו :

נח י מיי׳ פ״א שם הלכה יז טוש״ע א״ח סי׳ תקעו סעיף טז :

רבינו חננאל

שנת תרדמה אלא נים ולא נים כגון זה אע״פ שמתנמנם אוכל . (א״א) [אבל] אם ישן שנת קבע ונרדם (לא היא אלא ישן) לגמרי אינו אוכל : ירושלמי ישן ועמד אסיר לא שנו אלא שלא התנה אבל התנה מותר . קיי״ל דלגבי תענית דאכיל בלילה ומפסיק . אם גמר וסלק לא יאכל . אבל אם לא סילק ודעתו עוד ליכל אע״פ שישן [illegible] בתעני׳ שפוסק בו מבע״י אע״פ שפוסק הוזר ואוכל עד שיבא השמש כי הא דאיתא באגדת איכה . ר׳ יהודה בן בתירה אזל לנציבין בערובת צומא רבה אתא ריש כנישתא לשמוניה . א״ל כבר אכלי ופסקי לי . א״ל אשגח עלי דלא לימא הרווא ר׳ לא אשגח עליו אזל עשיה ובסיפא אמרין אכל מן כל עיגול חד פתית ואכל מן כל תבשיל חד פת ושתה מן כל(כוס וכוס) (חבית וחבית) חד כוס . ש״מ דאע״ג דפסק אכיל . ולענין שיתו מיא היכא דאית ליה למיכל. אית ליה למשתי כו׳ . וכן כתב ופירש רבינו הגאון זצ״ל *) . אמר רב יחיד שקבל עליו תענית אמר רבה בר רב שילא לימא הכי מחר אהא בתענית יחיד דאי לא חיישינן שמא תענית צבור קביל על[illegible] בנעילת הסנדל כו׳ . ואסיקנא רבנן דבי רב אשי באלו התעניות השנויות במשנתנו הוו מסיימי מסאנייהו כי אורחייהו ואתו לבי תענית. סברי לה כשמואל דאמר אין תענית צבור בבבל אלא ט׳ באב בל[illegible] הלכה : אמר רב יהודה אמר רב לווה אדם תעניתו ופורע . פי׳ היכא דאיכא צערא או אונס וכיוצא בו . לווה תעניתו ופורע דאמרי לא יהא אלא נדר מי לא פרע למחר וליום אחרא כ״ש תענית . [illegible] הא סברא מדברי שמואל דאמר צערא קבל עליה אי מצי מצער נפשיה כו׳ . מכלל דרב במצטער הוא דאמר : יפה תענית לחלום כאש בנעורת ובו ביום ואפילו בשבת . וכן הלכתא . ויתיב תעניתא [illegible] ומפורש בשבת בפ׳ א׳ : [מתני׳] עברו אלו ולא נענו ב״ד גוזרין ג׳ תעניות כו׳ . ואקשינן בשלמא רחיצה וסיכה ונעילת הסנדל וכיוצא בהן משום תענוג אלא מלאכה אמאי צערא הוא ושנינן [illegible] קדשו צום קראו עצרה . פי׳ קראו עצרה לקידוש (היום) [הצום] . מה עצרת אסור במלאכה אף צום אסור במלאכה . ומאי טעמא איסורו משעת אסיפת זקנים ואימתי אסיפת זקנים ביום . שנאמר תקעו ש[illegible] הריעו בהר קדשי ירגזו כל יושבי ארץ כי בא יום ה׳ . אמר רב כהנא כינופיא מצפרא . היכי עבדינן . אמר אביי מצפרא עד פלגיה יומא מעיינינן ולפניא ריבעא דיומא . קרינן בספרא ובאפטרתא [illegible] בתרא

*) עי׳ בהג״ה כאן שהביא כל דברי רבינו כאן וכתב ראיה לדבריו ע״ש.

רבינו גרשום

ישן שתי אוכל והולך . מי שיש לו להתענות למחר : שלא סילק השלחן : היכי עביד כשקיבל עליו שיהא למחר מותר בנעילת הסנדל דאמר למחר הריני בתענית יחיד : דילמא מיכל נמי אכיל כלומר כי היכי דסיימי סנדל ה״נ יכולין לאכול : סיימי אפנתא שנועלין עליונו של סנדל העור שעל הרגל אבל ה[illegible] הרגל לא היו מניחין. סברי לה כשמואל דאמר אין תענית צבור בבבל לפיכך אין אסורין בנעילת ה[illegible] י״ג

גליון הש״ס

תוס׳ ד״ה נים וכו׳ אומר רבי נים ולא נים בתוך השינה . בתחלת השינה . תיר ולא תיר בסוף השינה כצ״ל : בא״ד לך לא נראה כפ״ם . כאן וכע״ש כצ״ל ע״ז ח״ח סי׳ תרל ס״ק ח :

הגהות הב״ח

(א) רש״י ד״ה יחיד כו׳ אם של צבור אסור כו׳ הס״ד ואח״כ יחה״ד במא ת״נ הבלא אחרונות או [illegible] (ב) ד״ה קאתו כו׳ בפ׳ מקום שנהגו דלאסר בנעילת הסנדל : (ג) ד״ה לצעורי כו׳ ואי לא מצ[illegible] נפשיה הס״ד ואח״כ מה״ד לא יהא אלא נדר יכי אינו משלם (ד) ד״ה ליומא אחרינא : (ד) ד״ה היכי עבדי צ״ל [illegible] קודם ד״ה מעיינין : (ה) תוס׳ ד״ה נים מי׳. לך לא נראה הכי בערבי פסחים : (ו) בא״ד ובירושלמי מפרש גבי הך ברייתא׳ . ר״ל פי׳ דתני בה ישן ועמד כ״ז אוכל : (ז) ד״ה אביי כו׳ שאין לו שולים [illegible]

הגהות מהר״ב רנשבורג א] נפ׳ דלא סגי דלא תשלם . פי׳ ר״ן ורשב״א יתאשם דלא הוי זה כנדיבתם וכבן דתניתא אין אסור פרש״י ותוס׳ ולי״ל נמ״ם כעל אחנה שלם ושמר שמלך :

תורה אור

איפוך אנא לא סלקא דעתך דכתיב °ואלי יאספו כל חרד בדברי אלהי ישראל על מעל הגולה וגו' וכתיב °ובמנחת הערב קמתי מתעניתי ואפרשה כפי אל ה' אמר רפרם בר פפא אמר רב חסדא כל שהוא משום אבל (א) כגון תשעה באב ואבל אסור בין בחמין בין בצונן כל שהוא משום תענוג כגון תענית צבור בחמין אסור בצונן מותר אמר רב אידי בר אבין אף אנן נמי תנינא ונועלין את המרחצאות א"ל אביי ואי בצונן אסור סוכרין את הנהרות מבעי ליה למיתני אמר רב שישא בריה דרב אידי אבא הכי קשיא ליה מכדי תנן אסור ברחיצה נועלין את המרחצאות למה לי אלא לאו ש"מ בחמין אסור בצונן מותר לימא מסייע ליה *כל חייבי טבילות טובלין כדרכן בין בט' באב בין ביוה"כ במאי אילימא בחמין *טבילה בחמין מי איכא [א] שאובין נינהו אלא לאו בצונן וחייבי טבילות אין איניש אחרינא לא אמר רב חנא בר קטינא לא נצרכה אלא לחמי טבריא אי הכי אימא סיפא א"ר חנינא סגן הכהנים כדי הוא בית אלהינו לאבד עליו טבילה פעם אחת בשנה ואי אמרת בצונן מותר ירחץ בצונן אמר רב פפא באתרא דלא שכיח צונן תא שמע *כשאמרו אסור במלאכה לא אמרו אלא ביום אבל בלילה מותר *וכשאמרו אסור בנעילת הסנדל לא אמרו אלא בעיר אבל בדרך מותר הא כיצד יוצא לדרך נועל נכנס לעיר חולץ *וכשאמרו אסור ברחיצה לא אמרו אלא כל גופו אבל פניו ידיו ורגליו מותר וכן אתה מוצא במנודה ובאבל מאי לאו אכולהו ובמאי (ג) עסקינן אילימא בחמין פניו ידיו ורגליו מי שרו והאמר רב ששת אבל אסור להושיט אצבעו בחמין אלא לאו בצונן לא לעולם בחמין ודקא קשיא לך וכן אתה מוצא במנודה ובאבל אשארא קאי תא שמע דאמר ר' אבא הכהן משום ר' יוסי הכהן מעשה ומתו בניו של ר' יוסי בן רבי חנינא ורחץ בצונן כל שבעה התם כשתכפוהו אבליו הוה דתניא *תכפוהו אבליו זה אחר זה הכביד שערו מיקל בתער ומכבס כסותו במים אמר רב חסדא בתער אבל לא במספרים במים ולא בנתר ולא בחול אמר רבא אבל מותר לרחוץ בצונן כל שבעה מידי דהוה אבשרא וחמרא מיתיבי

רש"י

איפוך אנא. דפלגא דיומא קמא האו קרו ומפטרי ובעו רחמי ובאידך פלגא מעייני: על מעל הגולה. ואני יושב משומם עד מנחת הערב ובמנחת הערב קמתי מתעניתי ובקרעי בגדי ומעילי ואכרעה על ברכי ואפרשה כפי אל ה' אלהי: ובמנחת הערב קמתי. אלמא באידך פלגא בעו רחמי עד פניא מכלל דפלגא קמא מעייני במילי דמתא: בנחמיה בן חכליה כתיב בעזרא ואלי יאספו. לי היו מתאספין ובאין טובים שבהן להגיד לפני על מעל וחטא הגולה להפרישם: משומם. אישטורדי"ן בלע"ז על מעלם שמתוודין עד מנחת הערב מחטות ואילך שהגל טמה כדאמרינן במס' יומא (דף כח:) צלותיה דאברהם מכי משחרי כותלי: קמתי מתעניתי. לא שמתענה עד המנחה ואח"כ אוכל אלא כלומר מלצער נפשיה ובקרעי ואם שאני קורע בגדי ומעילי הייתי מתפלל כדי שאתקבלה: כל שהוא משום אבל. כל תענית שאסרו חכמים רחיצה משום אבל כגון ט' באב שהוא משום אבילות חורבן וכל שכן אבל ממש שמתו לפניו דאית ליה צערא טובא אסור בין בחמין וכו': משום תענוג. שמצטערין ואוסרין עצמן בתענוג: ה"ג אמר רב אידי בר אבין אף אנן נמי תנינא ונועלין את המרחצאות וא"ל אביי ואי בצונן אסור סוכרין את הנהרות מיבעי ליה למיתני בתמיה אף אנן נמי תנינא במתני' דקתני גבי תענית צבור ונועלין את המרחצאות דהיינו חמין אבל צונן מותר א"ל אביי כלומר ואי הוה סבירא ליה לתנא דידן דבצונן אסור היכי הוה בעי למיתני סוכרין את הנהרות היכי מצי למיסכרינהו: אבא. רב אידי הכי קא קשיא ליה במתניתין דקאמר שמע מינה דלא אסר אלא חמין מכדי קתני מתני' אסורין ברחיצה וסתם רחיצה בין חמין בין צונן למה לי תו למיהדר ומיתנא ונועלין אלא למימרא דדוקא חמין וכו': לימא מסייע ליה. לרב חסדא דאמר כל שהוא משום אבל אסור אפילו בצונן: כל חייבי טבילות. נדה ויולדת טובלים כדרכן: טבילה בחמין מי איכא. חמי האור הא שאובין נינהו: אלא לאו בצונן. וחייבי טבילות אין משום דטבילה בזמנה מצוה שממהר לטהר עצמו: ה"ג טולי עלמא לא (ג) בחמין ולא בצונן: לא נצרכה אלא לחמי טבריא. והלכך חייבי טבילות אין כולי עלמא לא אבל בצונן שרו: כדי. ראוי הוא בית אלהינו כו': ואם איתא. כדמוקמת לה דבצונן שרי מאי קא מהדר ליה רבי חנינא לתנא קמא מאיבוד טבילה נהי דלא טבלי בחמין משום כבוד בית אלהינו הא מצו טבלי בצונן אלא לאו בצונן נמי אסירי והיינו דאמר לאבד: אמר רב פפא. לעולם בחמי טבריא והיינו דקאמר' חייבי טבילות אין כולי עלמא לא ובצונן כ"ע שרי ומאי לאבד דקאמר ר' חנינא כגון באתרא דלא שכיח צונן: כשאמרו אסור (ד) [במלאכה]. גבי תענית צבור לא אמרו אלא ביום אבל בלילה מותר מהכא *משמע דבלילי תשעה באב מותר במלאכה ואין ביטול אלא ביום אבל אין מפרסמין הדבר: יוצא לדרך. חוץ לעיר: וכן אתה מוצא במנודה ואבל. הכי גרסינן במאי אילימא בחמין מי שרי והאמר רב ששת אבל אסור להושיט אצבעו בחמין אלא לאו בצונן מאי לאו אכולהו כו' הא דקתני וכן אתה מוצא במנודה ואבל אכל הני קאי ואפילו ארחילה ושמע מינה דבתענית צבור אסור לרחוץ כל גופו ואפילו בצונן ותיובתא לרפרם בר פפא: לא אשארא קאי. אנעילה (ה) וסיכה ולעולם הך רחילה בחמין היא אבל בצונן שרי לרחוץ כל גופו והשתא דאמרת במנודה ואבל לאו ארחילה קיימי ליכא לאקשויי כדפרכת לעיל אילימא בחמין מי שרי: ורחץ בצונן בתוך שבעה. גרסינן אלמא בצונן שרי: שתכפוהו אבליו. בזה אחר זה כדקתני שמתו בניו שניהם ולפיכך התירו לו כדאשכחן גבי שיער: מיקל בתער. הסקל פורתא מינייהו: ובתער. דרך שיטוי: נתר. קרקע הוא או אבן כעין שקורין קרי"א בלע"ז: בנתר וחול. דרך לכבס שיתלבן: מידי דהוה אבשרא וחמרא. דתענוג הן בצונן: אין

תוספות

איפוך אנא. פי' דנימא פלגא קמייתא דיומא מצלו ובעו רחמי ואידך פלגא מעיינו במלי דמתא ומשני לא ס"ד:

אמר רב חסדא כל שהוא משום אבל כגון תשעה באב (ו) אסור אפילו בצונן ואבל אסור בין בחמין בין בצונן וכו'. ירושלמי יוסף בריה דרבי יהושע בן לוי בתשעה באב וביוה"כ מרחיץ ידיו ומקנח במפה ומעבירה על גבי עיניו רבי יונה תרי סמרטוטי ויהיב תותי כרעיה פי' היה מניח סמרטוט תחת הכר כדי ללחלחו ומעבירו על גבי עיניו: **וכל** שהוא משום תענוג וכו'. ועכשיו שאין תענית צבור בבבל אלא תשעה באב מותרין אפילו בחמין אפילו י"ז בתמוז וצום גדליה כך פסק ראבי"ה ור' יואל אביו אסר לרחוץ בחמין:

ונועלין המרחצאות. פי' שהן חמין: **אטו** סוכרין נהרות כו'. כלומר אי הוה אסור בצונן מי איכא למיתני סוכרים נהרות פשיטא דלא מצי למסכר כלומר כמו כן לא תידוק מהא דקתני ונועלין המרחצאות: **טבילה** בחמין מי איכא. הא שאובים נינהו מדלא קאמר משכחת לה טבילה (בחמין) דכשירה בחמין כגון שהוחמו והומשכו לבריכה אלא שאמר בחמי טבריא יש להוכיח דכולו שאוב אפילו ע"י המשכה לא מהניא טבילה והא דאמר* דהמשכה כולה כשירה ר"ל לענין שאינה פוסלת את המקוה כשאר מים שאובים אבל טבילה ודאי אינו עולה בהם:

וכן אתה מוצא במנודה ואבל מאי לאו אכולהו. פי' (ז) הא דקאמרינן ובצונן מותר דאבל נמי *מותר בצונן וקשיא לרב חסדא דאמר אבל אסור בין בחמין בין בצונן ומשני אשארא כלומר אשאר דינין (ח) אנעילה וסיכה אבל לא קאי אהא דבצונן:

הכביד שערו מיקל בתער. פי' דרך התיכה אבל לא כדרכו דרך גילוח מדקאמר מיקל ולא קאמר מגלח:

עין משפט נר מצוה

נט א מיי' פ"ה מהלכות תעניות הלכה י סמג עשין מד"ס ג טוש"ע א"ח סי' תקנד סעיף ז:
ס ב מיי' פ"ה מהלכות אבל הלכה ד סמג שם טוש"ע י"ד סי' שפא סעיף א:
סא ג מיי' פ"ג מהלכות תענית הלכה ד טוש"ע א"ח סי' תקעה סעיף ג:
סב ד מיי' פ"ג מהלכות שביתת עשור הלכה ג טוש"ע שם סי' תקנד סעיף ח:
סג ה ו ז מיי' פ"ג מהלכות תענית הלכה ד טור ש"ע שם סימן תקעה סעיף ג:
סד ח מיי' פ"ה מהלכות אבל הלכה ד סמג עשין ב טוש"ע י"ד סי' שפא סעיף א:
סה ט מיי' שם פ"ו הלכה יג טוש"ע י"ד סי' שצ סעיף ג:
סו י מיי' שם טוש"ע שם סי' שפט סעיף א:
סז כ מיי' שם טוש"ע שם סי' שצ סעיף ג:
סח ל מיי' שם טוש"ע שם סי' שפט סעיף א:

רבינו חננאל

בתרא מצלינן ומתודינן [אבל] תפלת התענית בשחרית לא יכלינן למימר דכתיב ואלי יאספו כל חרד בדברי אלהי ישראל על מעל הגולה ואני יושב משומם עד למנחת הערב ובמנחת הערב קמתי מתעניתי ובקרעי בגדי ומעילי [ואכרעה על] ברכי ואפרשה כפי אל ה' אלהי. ש"מ דתפלת התענית באחרית היום הוא ברביעית האחרון אמר רב חסדא כל שהוא משום אבל כגון ט' באב ואבל אסור ברחיצה בין בחמין בין בצונן. אבל כל שהוא משום תענוג כגון תענית צבור בחמין אסור ובצונן מותר. ודייק רב אידי ממתני' מאחר דקתני אסורים ברחיצה למה לי למתנא (כתב) ונועלין את המרחצאות אלא [ה"ק] רחיצה דאסרנא רחיצת במרחץ בחמין הוא דאסיר אבל בצונן שרי ואתינן לסיועיה לר' חסדא מהא דתנ"א כל חייבי טבילות טובלין כדרכן בין בט' באב בין ביוה"כ ואמרי' [בחמין] ליכא לאוקמה דשאיבין נינהו אלא בצונן ואי אמרינן לכ"ע רחיצה בט' באב בצונן שרי אצטריך לאשמעינן טבילה בצונן שהיא מצוה בזמנה דשרי אלא ש"מ רחיצה אפי' בצונן אסור וטבילה דמצוה שרי ולכ"ע אסור ואדחי' לעולם בצונן לכ"ע שרי והא ברייתא בחמין היא. וא"ת מים שאובין הן כגון חמי טבריא דשים חמין הן.
...ן אי הכי סיפא דקתני ר' חנינא סגן הכהנים אומר כדי הוא בית אלהינו לאבד עליו טבילה אחת בשנה. לטבול בצונן דשרי וליכא עבירה. ודחי באתרא דליכא צונן. ורחיצה בחמין אסור משום כבוד ...אלהינו שהרב כדי הוא בית אלהינו לאבד מצות טבילה אחת בזמנה פעם אחת: ת"ש כשאמרו אסור בתענית אסור ברחיצה לא אמרו אלא כל גופו אבל פניו ידיו ורגליו מותר. וכשאמרו אסור במלאכה לא ...אלא ביום אבל בלילה מותר. וכשאמרו אסור בנעילת הסנדל לא אמרו אלא בעיר אבל בדרך מותר הא כיצד יצא לדרך נועל. הגיע לעיר חולץ הסנדל מרגלו ומהלך יחף. וכן אתה אומר במנודה ובאבל.

רבינו גרשום

...ראשונים ז' אחרונים. בשלמא רחיצה וסיכה ונעילת הסנדל ותשמיש המטה. מה אסיפת זקנים ... כנופיא מצפרא ולא מאורתא. אימ' אנא דמצפרא מצלי ולאורתא קרו ומפטרו. במנחת הערב ...עה על ברכי אלמא דרביעית בתרא הוו מצלי: אף אנן נמי תנינא דבתענית צבור אינו אסור אלא ...ן דקתני נועלין את המרחצאות *) אבל היכי איבעי ליה למיתני מי מצי למיתני סוכרין את הנהרות ...שישא בר אבא רב אידי בר אבין הכי קשיא ליה מכדי קתני אסורין ברחיצה דרחיצה משמע ...ן למה לי למתני נועלין את המרחצאות דמשמע נמי חמין לאו למימר דבחמין אסור ובצונן ... והיינו דקאמר אף אנן נמי תנינא כרב חסדא דבתענית צבור בצונן מותר. נימא מסייע ליה ...רשמעינן ליה דאמר תענית צבור אסור בין בחמין בין בצונן:לכולי עלמא לא הרי לך תשעה באב ...שהוא תענית צבור ודייקינן דאפי' בצונן אסור אמר רב חנא מהכא לא תסייעי' לאביי דלא נצרכא ...דקתני טובלין כדרכן אלא לחמי טבריא דמצי למיטבל בהו והכי קאמר טובלין כדרכן בחמין אבל ...לא אבל בצונן אפי' לכ"ע שרי: כדיי הוא בית אלהינו לאבד עליו טבילה אחת שלא יהיה טובל עליו בת"ב כלל. א"א בשלמא דת"ק אמר כל חייבי טבילות טובלין כדרכן בצונן בת"ב אבל כ"ע לא היינו דקא פליג רב חנינא עליה דת"ק דחייבי טבילות אין טובלין בצונן דכדיי הוא בית אלהינו לאבד עליו טבילה אחת אלא אי אמרת בצונן שרי לת"ק והכי קתני חייבי טבילות טובלין כדרכן בחמין אבל כ"ע לא אבל בצונן מותר לכ"ע וקפליג רב חנינא עליה דת"ק דלא מצי לטיפל בחמין א"כ ליכא איבוד טבילה דהא טביל בצונן אע"פ שאינו טובל בחמין דהא שרי בצונן לכ"ע אלא לאו לעולם אסור ת"ק בצונן טובלין אבל כ"ע לא ומסייעא לאביי א"ר פפא לעולם אסור ת"ק טובלין כדרכן בחמין אבל לכ"ע אסור וצונן שרי לכ"ע ודאמר א"כ טבילה בצונן איכא וליכא איבוד טבילה ר' חנינא הוה קאי בדוכתא דלא שכיחא צונן ולעולם מהכא לא תסייעיה לאביי. (כל) אסורו אסור ברחיצה כו' באלו תעניות. מאי לאו הא דקתני וכן אתה מוצא באבל אכולהו אהאי נמי דקתני בסיפא דמילתא בהאי מסכתא באידך פירקא כשאמרו אסור ברחיצה וכו' ורחיצה לא משמע אלא בחמין וקשיא למאן דאמר כל שהוא משום אבל אסור בין בחמין ובין בצונן. לא אשארא לבר מרחיצה קאמר וכן אתה מוצא באבל אבל

*) אולי צ"ל א"ל אביי אלא היכי וכו'. **) לכאורה תמוה דהא גם לר"ח בת"ב אסור בצונן ומאי מייתי מינה ראיה לאביי ואולי דרבינו לא היה גורס כדברי ר"ח כגון ט"ב ועי' ן צ"ע.

הגהות הב"ח

(א) גמ' כל שהוא משום אבל כגון תשעה באב. נ"ב פי' בדרבנן היא לאפוקי בין שהוא משום אבל ובין שהוא משום תענוג אבל ביוה"כ שהוא דאורייתא אע"פ שהוא משום תענוג אסור בין בחמין בין בצונן: (ב) שם מאי לאו אכולהו וכמאי אילימא בחמין כו' כצ"ל ותיבת עסקינן נמחק: (ג) רש"י ד"ה ה"ג כ"ע לא לא בחמין: (ד) ד"ה כשאמרו אסור ברחיצה על ספניו: (ה) ד"ה לא אשארא קאי אנעילה ומלאכה ולעולם: (ו) תוס' ד"ה אמר ר"ח כו' כגון תשעה באב ואבל אסור בין כו' כצ"ל ותיבות אסור אפילו בצונן נמחק: (ז) ד"ה וכן כו' פירוש דקאי אהא דקאמרינן דבצונן מותר: (ח) בא"ד כלומר אשאר דינין קאי אנעילה ומלאכה אבל לא:

הגהות הגר"א

[א] גמ' (שאובין נינהו) קא"מ (ועמ"ש רבינו ביו"ד סי' רא ס"ק קסה וצ"ע):

גליון הש"ס

תוס' ד"ה וכן. מותר בצונן וקשי' לר"ח. ק' לי הא אדרבה כיון דמיירי בצונן ואפ"ה תני כל גופו אסור א"ו דמקשה כמו רש"י דמוכח דבתענית נ"כ אסור בצונן כל גופו וקשיא לר"ח וכמ"ש רש"י:

אין הבוגרת רשאה לנוול את עצמה בימי אבל אביה הא נערה רשאה מאי לאו ברחיצה ובמאי אילימא בחמין אין הבוגרת רשאה והאמר רב חסדא אבל אסור להושיט אצבעו בחמין אלא לאו בצונן לא אביחול ופירכוס לימא מסייע ליה דא"ר אבא הכהן משום רבי יוסי הכהן מעשה ומתו בניו של ר' יוסי בר חנינא ורחץ בצונן כל שבעה אמרי התם בשתכפוהו אבליו זה אחר זה דתניא תכפוהו אבליו זה אחר זה הכביד שערו מיקל בתער ומכבס כסותו במים אמר רב חסדא בתער אבל לא במספרים במים ולא בנתר ולא בחול ולא באהל איכא דאמרי אמר רבא אבל אסור בצונן כל שבעה מאי שנא מבשר ויין התם *לפכוחי פחדיה הוא דעביד לימא מסייע ליה אין הבוגרת רשאה לנוול עצמה הא נערה רשאה במאי אילימא בחמין אין הבוגרת רשאה והאמר רב חסדא אבל אסור להושיט אצבעו בחמין אלא לאו בצונן לא אביחול ופירכוס אמר רב חסדא זאת אומרת *אבל אסור בתכבוסת כל שבעה והלכתא אבל אסור לרחוץ כל גופו בין בחמין בין בצונן כל שבעה אבל פניו ידיו ורגליו בחמין אסור בצונן מותר אבל לסוך אפילו כל שהוא אסור ואם לעבר את הזוהמא מותר צלותא דתעניתא היכי מדכרינן אדבריה רב יהודה לרב יצחק בריה ודרש יחיד שקיבל עליו תענית מתפלל של תענית והיכן אומרה בין גואל לרופא מתקיף לה רב *יצחק וכי יחיד קובע ברכה לעצמו אלא אמר רב יצחק בשומע תפלה וכן אמר רב ששת בשומע תפלה מיתיבי אין בין יחיד לצבור אלא שזה מתפלל שמונה עשרה וזה מתפלל תשע עשרה מאי יחיד ומאי צבור אילימא יחיד ממש וצבור ש"צ הני תשע עשרה עשרין וארבע הוו אלא לאו ה"ק אין בין יחיד דקבל עליו תענית יחיד ליחיד ושקבל עליו תענית צבור אלא שזה מתפלל שמונה עשרה וזה מתפלל תשע עשרה ש"מ יחיד קובע ברכה לעצמו לא לעולם אימא לך ש"ץ צבור ודקא קשיא לך ש"ץ צבור עשרין וארבע מצלי (א) בג' תעניות ראשונות דליכא עשרים וארבע ולא והא אין בין קתני אין בין ג' ראשונות לג' אמצעיות אלא שבאלו מותרין בעשיית מלאכה ובאלו אסורין בעשיית מלאכה הא לכ"ד זה וזה שוין *תנא ושייר מאי שייר דהאי ישייר (ג) ותו והא אין בין קתני אלא תנא באיסורי קא מיירי בתפלות לא מיירי ואי בעית אימא באמצעייתא נמי לא מצלי כ"ד ולא והתניא *אין בין ג' שניות לשבע אחרונות אלא שבאלו מתריעין ונועלין את החנויות הא לכל דבריהן זה וזה שוין וכי תימא הכא נמי תנא ושייר והא אין בין קתני ותסברא אין בין דוקא והא

*) [וע"ע תוספות מגילה ח. ד"ה אין ותוס' ב"ק סב: ד"ה מי קתני ותוס' חגיגה ח. ד"ה אלמי והוספות שבת סג. ד"ה אין]

רש"י

אין הבוגרת. שהביאה שתי שערות רשאה לנוול את עצמה אלא מתקשטת כדי שיקפצו עליה (ג) הא נערה שאינה ראויה להינשא עדיין עד שתבגר רשאה דבת חיוב אבילות היא וקטנה אינה חייבת ולא כלום: בימי אבל אביה. אפילו אירע אבילות לאביה שמת בנו אי נמי שמת אביה ממש אע"פ שהיא בת חיוב אבילות אינה רשאה לנוול: הא נערה. ואפ"ה נערה אינה רוחצת בצונן אלמא דאבל קא בצונן אסור: אכיחול ופירכוס. ולא קא מיירי ברחיצה כלל פירכוס בשיער כמוס בבגדים רחיצה בגוף: זאת אומרת. *מדמוקמינן לה בכיחול ופירכוס הוא הדין להכבוסת: תפלת תענית. עננו: בין גואל לרופא. ברכה בפני עצמה: וכי יחיד. חשוב כל כך שיהו מתקנין לו ברכה בפ"ע להוסיף בתפלתו: בשומע תפלה. שכוללה בתוך הברכה וחותם בשומע תפלה דאותה ברכה והתימתה משמע בין אתענית בין אכל מילי: אין בין יחיד לצבור. גבי תענית: שזה. יחיד מתפלל ביום תעניתו שמונה עשרה וכולל עננו תענית בשומע תפלה: תשע עשרה. דקבע ליה בין גואל לרופא סתם תפלה קרי שמונה עשרה דברכת ולמלשינים ביבנה תקנוה כדאמרינן בברכות (דף כח:): כ"ד הויין. (ד) בפירקין דלקמן (דף טו:) דכ"ד ברכות הוו ביומא דתעניתא והכא קתני י"ט ותו לא: ולצבור. יחיד שקיבל עליו תענית צבור אלמא יחיד קובע ברכה לעצמו כשקיבל תענית צבור: בקמייתא. בג' תעניות ראשונות (ה) דליכא כ"ד כדאמרינן בפרק סדר תעניות כילד בגמ' (שם): דהנו מותרין בעשיית מלאכה וכו'. ראשונות דלא חמירי טלי הלי (ו) הא לכ"ד ברכות זה וזה שוין וקס"ד דאיתנהו לכ"ד באמצעיות מדקמתרצינן קמייתא דליכא כ"ד מכלל דבאמצעייתא איתנהו ולא היא דליתנהו אלא באחרונות כדקרני ההם ומשום דהא מילתא קמייתא מש"ה פריך ליה מכ"ד דליתנהו באמצעיות: תנא ושייר. תנא מילי דאיתנהו בין אמצעיות לראשונות ושייר אין בין לאו דוקא הוא כדמוכח לקמן גבי הידך: ה"ג מאי שייר דהאי שייר אלא דאורויי קא חזינן דתנא לא קא מיירי ומאן דגרים שייר תיבה מוליאין את התיבה כו' שיבוש הוא דאינה אלא באחרונות כדבכמוך ומיפשט פשיטא ליה דאינה אלא באחרונות: מאי שייר דהאי שייר. דלא אורחא דתנא למתני כל מילי ולשיורי חדא אלא לשום כ"ד בקמייתא ליתנהו ולהכי לא חשיב להו באין בין דבתפלה לא קמיירי: באמצעיות נמי ליכא כ"ד. אלא באחרונות כדאמרינן התם: שבאלו. האחרונות מתריעים ונועלין כדתנן נמי במתני' הא לכ"ד זה וזה שוין דבתרוייהו איתנהו:

והא

תוספות

אין הבוגרת רשאה לנוול עצמה. אומר ר"י דהא רשאה לאו דוקא *אלא ה"ק אין הבוגרת חייבת הא נערה חייבת: אלא (ז) בצונן. וקאמר נערה רשאה כלומר דאסורה ולא אמרת דבצונן מותר וקשה לרבא דאמר דבצונן מותר ומשני כי קתני אכיחול ואפירכוס: אלא אמר רב יצחק בשומע תפלה. והכי פסק בשמעתא דתפלת תענית בשומע תפלה ואין יחיד קובע ברכה לעצמו לכך צריך כשאומר עננו בש"ת (דצריך) לאומרו קודם שאומר הברכה כשמגיע לעננו קודם שיתחיל לומר כי אתה ש"ת עמך ישראל ברחמים יאמר עננו ולא יחתום אלא יאמר כי אתה ה' עונה בעת צרה ומושיע ואח"כ כי אתה ש"ת עמך ישראל ברחמים בא"י שומע תפלה אבל שליח צבור אומר גואל ישראל וקובע ברכה וחותם: תנא ושייר. פי' תנא עשיית מלאכה ושייר כ"ד ברכות פי' כ"ד ברכות שבתעניתא היו מוסיפין ו' ברכות כדמפרש לקמן בפ"ב (דף טו.): מאי שייר דהאי שייר כו'. פי' דמשום חדא מילתא לא הוי (ח) לתנא לשייר וא"ת הכא קאמר דלא תנא ושייר דהא אין בין קאמר דמשמע דאין בין זה לזה אלא אלו בלבד וקשה דהא במגילה (דף ח:) קתני אין בין נדרים לנדבות אלא שהנדרים חייב באחריותן ונדבות אינו חייב באחריותן ואנו יודעין דיש (ט) חילוק אחר דנדרים אינן באים אלא מן החולין דכל דבר שבחובה אינו בא אלא מן החולין ונדבות באות מן המעשר כדאמר (דברים כז) וזבחת שלמים ואכלת דכתיב גבי מעשר וי"ל דהתם נמי דזה וזה שוה והני מילי גבי שלמים יש חילוק והא דקתני אין בין מיירי בעולות דאין בין עולות דנדרים לעולות דנדבה אלא שהנדרים חייב באחריותן וזה שאין כן בנדבה דהא אין בין עולות דנדרים לעולות דנדבות אלא חילוק זה דהא כל עולה אינן באין אלא מן החולין*): ותסברא והא שייר תיבה. פי' (י) מפרש לקמן (דף טו:) שמוליאין התיבה ברחוב העיר (אמצעיות) אחרונות ואמצעיות דהא שייר תיבה פי' וליכא למימר דבאיסורא קמיירי דהא דמתריעין ונועלין מאי איסור איכא: להו

עין משפט נר מצוה

[ועי' תוס' קידושין לג. ותוס' חולין כה: ד"ה אין ותוס' ערכין כח: ד"ה אומדין]

סט א מיי' פ"ה מהלכות אבל הלכה א סמג עשין מד"ס ג טוש"ע י"ד סי' ש"פ סעיף א וסי' שפא סעיף א:

ע ב מיי' שם הלכה ד טוש"ע שם סי' שפא סעיף א:

עא ג מיי' שם טוש"ע שם סעיף ב:

עב ד מיי' פ"ב מהלכות תפלה הלכה יד סמג עשין יט טוש"ע א"ח סי' תקסה סעיף א:

עג ה מיי' פ"ג מהלכות תענית הלכה ב טוש"ע א"ח סי' תקעה סעיף ב:

עד ו מיי' שם הלכה ג טוש"ע שם סעיף ג:

רבינו חננאל

[illegible] וכן באבל אנעילת סנדל ואמלאכה קאי אבל (רחיצה לא) [לא אברחיצה] ולעולם בחמין. אמר רבא אבל אסור כל ז' אפי' בצונן ומ"ש מבשר ויין דשרי ליה. ודהי בשר ויין שרינן ליה כדי לפכוחי פחדיה אבל רחיצה דמשום תענוג היא לא התירו. לימא מסייעא ליה אין הבוגרת רשאה לנוול עצמה בימי אבל בית אביה. אבל הנערה שרי לנוול עצמה ושלא לירחוץ אפילו בצונן. וש"מ אבל אפי' בצונן אסור. ודחי לא הבוגרת התירו לכחול ולפרכס. תניא תכפוהו אבליו זה אחר זה שערו מיקל בתער ומכבס כסותו במים. אמר רב חסדא בתער ולא במספרים. במים ולא בנתר. ולא בחול. אמר רב חסדא זאת אומרת אבל אסור בתכבוסת. והלכתא אסור לרחוץ כל גופו כל ז' בין בחמין בין בצונן אבל פניו ידיו ורגליו בחמין אסור ובצונן מותר. ולסוך אפי' כל שהוא אסור. ואם לעבר הזוהמא מות' לסוך שמן טוב. דרש רב יצחק יחיד שקבל עליו תענית מתפלל של תענית בין גואל לרופא ואקשינן עליה וכי יחיד קובע ברכה לעצמו אלא מתפלל עננו בשומע תפלה בכלל הברכה ואינו מתפלל אותה ברכה בפ"ע. ומותבינן עליה מהא דתניא מה בין יחיד לצבור אלא שזה מתפלל שמ"ע ואלו מתפללין י"ט היכי דמי אילימא יחיד המתפלל בינו לבין עצמו עם הצבור וצבור דקתני ש"ץ היורד לפני התיבה האי י"ט ברכות מתפלל בתענית כ"ד מתפלל כדתנן עמדו בתפלה מורידין לפני התיבה זקן ורגיל כו' ואומר לפניהם כ"ד ברכות. ושנינן הכי קתני אין בין יחיד דקאי בצבור כראשון ליחיד המתפלל חוץ לביהכ"נ אלא שזה היחיד העומד בתוך מתפלל י"ח ויחיד המתפלל בכנסת מתפלל י"ט ברכות. אלמא יחיד קובע ברכה לעצמו. ושנינן לעולם יחיד. יחיד דקאי וצבור ש"ץ ממש. וזה ש"ץ המתפלל י"ט ברכות בתעניות ראשונות הוא שאין בה כ"ד ברכות לפיכך זה שמתפלל י"ח וזה מתפלל י"ט. ואקשינן יהא תעניות אמצעיות דקתני בהו ואסור במלאכה וברחיצה ולא קתני כ"ד. ושנינן האי תנא באיסורא קמיירי. כלומר אסור במלאכה וברחיצה כו' הוא דמיירי בתפלות לא קמיירי. אי בעי תימא כ"ד ברכות באמצעייתא נמי ליכא. ואקשינן והא תניא אין בין ג' א[illegible] לז' אחרונות. אלא שבאלו מתריעין ונועלין את החנויות הא לכ"ד זה וזה שוין. לעולם אימא לך באמצעיות נמי אין כ"ד ברכות בהן. ותנא מקצת מה שיש בשבע האחרונות ואינם בג' אמצעיות [illegible]

רבינו גרשום

ברחיצה מחלקן דאילו בתענית קתני ברחיצה דמשמע בחמין אבל לא בצונן ואילו באבל אסור בין בחמין בין בצונן. אין הבוגרת רשאי לנוול עצמה לפי שעומדת על פרקה וראויה לינשא. אילימא בחמין אין הבוגרת רשאי לנוול עצמה כלומר דיכולה לרחוץ בחמין: אלא לאו בצונן קאמר אין הבוגרת רשאה לנוול עצמה אלא רוחצין בצונן הא נערה רשאה לנוול עצמה דאפי' בצונן אינה רוחצת וקשיא לרבא דאמר אבל בצונן מותר. לא כי קתני אין הבוגרת רשאי לנוול הא נערה רשאה אכיחול אבל בצונן מותר אפי' בנערה. התם בבשרא וחמרא ליכא אלא לפכוחי פחדא אבל ליכא תענוג לפיכך שרי. הכא בצונן איכא תענוג לפיכך אסור. אלא לאו בצונן קאמר דנערה רשאה לנוול עצמה [ש"מ] דאבל אסור בין בחמין בין בצונן והוי סיועא לא כי קתני נערה רשאה לנוול בכיחול ופירכוס אבל בצונן מותר ולא הוי סיועא: וכי יחיד קובע ברכה לעצמו. *) יש מברך העונה בעת צרה: בשמע תפלה. שכולל בשומע תפלה ואינו מברך ברכה לעצמו. הני דש"ץ כ"ד הויין כדמפרש לקמן וקתני שזה מתפלל תשע עשרה. אלמא דקובע ברכה לעצמו שמברך העונה בעת צרה: [ודקא קשיא לך דהא] הוויין כ"ד ברכות בדקמייתא בשלש תעניות ראשונות קא מיירי דליכא בהו כ"ד ולא הוי אלא י"ט ולעולם אין [illegible] קובע ברכה לעצמו: אלא שבאלו אמצעיות אסורין במלאכה וראשונות מותרין במלאכה הא [illegible] וארבעה זה וזה שוין כי היכי דבאמצעיות איכא עשרים וארבעה הכא נמי איכא בראשונות כ"ד ול[illegible] להתרוצי דצבור מתפלל י"ט בש"ץ דהא איכא כ"ד אלא ביחיד שקיבל תענית צבור ותישמע דיחיד [illegible] ברכה לעצמו. ה"ג תנא באיסור קא מיירי כלומר לעולם בראשונות ליכא כ"ד והא דלא קתני [illegible] יש כ"ד ובאלו אין כ"ד משום דבאיסורי קא מיירי דהוי אסור בעשיית מלאכה ובתפלה לא [illegible] בברכות ולעולם הא דקתני דצבור מתפלל י"ט מוקמינן בש"ץ אבל לא ביחיד דאין יחיד קובע [illegible] לעצמו. ואיב"א לעולם בראשונות ליכא כ"ד ולהכי לא קתני שבאלו יש כ"ד ובאלו אין [illegible] דבאמצעיות נמי אין כ"ד: **)ה"ג תנא ושייר ולא נמי כלומר שייר כ"ד דבשבע איכא ובאמצעיות [illegible] והא אין בין קתני דמשמע דהוי דוקא כי היכי דאמרינן דאין בין קמא דוקא [illegible] דליכא בינייהו אלא מתריעין ונועלין אבל לכ"ד שוין אלמא דבאמצעיות איכא [illegible].

*) אולי צ"ל וכי יכול לברך וכו'. **) נראה דצ"ל ס"א וכ"ה תנא ושייר ולא גרסינן נמי כלומר וכו'.

הגהות הב"ח

(א) גמ' ודקא קשיא לך ש"צ כ"ד מצלי בקמייתא דליכא כ"ד כצ"ל: (ג) שם מאי שייר דהאי שייר (והא אין בין קתני) תא"מ וכ"ב מפרש"י משמע דלא גרסינן ליה הכא וכ"ש מדקאמר כמקשה ולא והא אין בין קתני ומבני דתני וש"ר כלומר ואין בין לאו דוקא א"כ מאי פריך ליה תו וכה אין בין קתני אבל לכך שייר כתרא דבאמצעייתא נמי לא מצלי כ"ד א"כ הא דקתני אין בין ג' ראשונות כו' דוקא אין בין קתני והכי פריך כמוך וכ"ת הכא נמי תנא ושייר והא אין בין קתני דקס"ד דהאי אין בין נמי דוקא קתני כסכות דריגא ומשני ותסברא כו' כלומר פ"כ ברייתא קתני אין בין דוקא וכשיטא לאו דוקא הוא דהא שייר תיבה פי': (ג) רש"י ד"ה אין הבוגרת וכו' שיקפצו עליה הס"ד ואח"כ מה"ד בימי אבל ואח"כ מה"ב הא נערה: (ד) ד"ה כ"ד הוין כדתנן בפירקין דלקמן: (ה) ד"ה בקמייתא בג' תעניות ראשונות הס"ד ומה"ד דליכא כ"ד: (ו) ד"ה דהנו כו' כולי כאי הס"ד ומה"ד הא כו' מדקמתרצין בקמייתא וכו' ומשום דהא מילתא קמייתא: (ז) תוס' ד"ה אלא לאו בצונן כו' כלומר דאסורה ולא אומרים דבצונן מותר: (ח) ד"ה מאי כו' לא הוי ליה לתנא כו' אלא אלו בלבד וקשה כמג לה דהוי כל"ל ותיבת וקשה נמחק: (ט) באו"ד ואנו יודעין דיש ביניהן חילוק אחר כו' באות מן המעשר דכתיב וזבחת שלמים ואכלת גבי מעשר וי"ל דהתם כמי לכל דבריהם זה וזה שוין מילי דיש ביניהם חילוק גבי שלמים והא דקתני אין בין כצ"ל: (י) ד"ה ותסברא כו' פי' כדמפרש לקמן נרתוב העיר באחרונות אבל לא באמצעיות הס"ד ואח"כ מה"ד ותסברא והא שייר:

מסורת הש"ס

[ז"ל רש"י כ"מ סו: ד"ה לפכוחי פחדיה לפסוק דאגתו וכו']

[שבת נד. וש"נ]

[תוספתא מגילה פ"א] [לעיל יב:]

גליון הש"ס

רש"י ד"ה זאת אומרת מדמוקמינן לה בכיחול כו' [illegible]

עין משפט נר מצוה

עה א מיי' פ"ג מהל' תעניות הלכה ס טוש"ע א"ח סימן תקעה סעיף ס :
עו ב מיי' שם הלכה ז טוש"ע שם סעיף ד :
עז ג מיי' שם פ"ג הל' יג טוש"ע שם סימן תקעו סעיף ס :
עח ד מיי' שם הלכה י טוש"ע שם סעיף :
עט ה מיי' שם הלכה ט טוש"ע שם סעיף ו :
פ ו מיי' פ"א שם הל' ו טוש"ע שם סימן תקעו סעיף יג :

והא שייר תיבה אי משום תיבה לאו שיורא הוא מילי דצינעא קתני מילי דבפרהסיא לא קתני אמר רב אשי מתני' נמי דיקא דקתני *מה אלו יתירות על הראשונות אלא שבאלו מתריעין ונועלין את החנויות אבל בכל דבריהן זה וזה שוין וכ"ת הבא נמי *תנא ושייר והא מה אלו קתני ותסברא מה אלו דווקא הוא והא שייר לה תיבה אי משום תיבה לאו שיורא הוא משום דקא חשיב לה באידך פרקא השתא דאתית להכי עשרים וארבעה נמי לאו שיורא הוא דקתני לה באידך פירקא מאי הוי עלה אמר רב שמואל בר ססרטאי וכן אמר רב חייא בר אשי אמר רב בין גוא"ל לרופא ורב אשי אמר משמיה דרבי ינאי בריה דרבי ישמעאל בשומע תפלה והלכתא בשומע תפלה : תני חדא עוברות ומיניקות מתענות בראשונות ואין מתענות באחרונות ותניא אידך מתענות באחרונות ואין מתענות בראשונות ותניא אידך אין מתענות לא בראשונות ולא באחרונות °אמר רב אשי "נקוט אמצעייתא בידך דמיתרצן כולהו : מה אלו יתירות על הראשונות אלא שבאלו מתריעין ונועלין את החנויות : במאי מתריעין רב יהודה אמר ˂בשופרות ורב יהודה בריה דרב שמואל בר שילת משמיה דרב אמר בעננו קס"ד מאן דאמר בעננו לא אמר בשופרות ומאן דאמר בשופרות לא אמר בעננו והתניא אין פותחין משבע [א] תעניות על הצבור שבהן י"ח התרעות וסימן לדבר יריחו ויריחו שופרות הוה ותיובתא למאן דאמר בעננו אלא בשופרות דכולי עלמא לא פליגי דקרי לה התרעה כי פליגי בעננו מר סבר קרי לה התרעה ומר סבר לא קרי לה התרעה למ"ד בעננו כל שכן בשופרות ולמ"ד בשופרות אבל בעננו לא והתניא *ושאר כל מיני פורעניות המתרגשות כגון ˂חיכוך ˂חגב ˂זבוב וצירעה ויתושין ושילוח נחשים ועקרבים לא היו מתריעין אלא צועקין (א) מרצעקה בפה התרעה בשופרות תנאי היא *דתניא *˂על אלו מתריעין בשבת על עיר שהקיפוה גיים או נהר ועל ספינה המטורפת ביםר' יוסי אמר לעזרה אבל לא לצעקה במאי אילימא בשופרות שופרות בשבת מי שרי אלא לאו בעננו וקרי לה התרעה ש"מ : בשני דר' יהודה נשיאה הוה צערא גזר

רש"י

והא שייר תיבה · דבאחרונות איתא והכא ליתא כדקתני לקמן (דף טו.) סדר תעניות כיצד מוציאין את התיבה כו' ומותבינן בגמרא בהדיא מתיבה דליתא אלא באחרונות ומשני כי קתני נמי מתניתין *בקמייתא : מילי דצינעא · מתריעין בבית הכנסת וכ"ד נמי בבית הכנסת : בפרהסיא · תיבה ברחובה של עיר : דיקא נמי · דלכ"ד זה וזה שוין דקתני מתניתין מה אלו יתירות על הראשונות כו' ואלו כ"ד לא קא חשיב גבי אחרונות : והא מה אלו קתני · דמשמע דווקא : דהא קתני לה באידך פירקין · דמי ששנה מתניתין דהכא תנא נמי דהתם והאי דלא תנא בהאי סמיך אהתם דקתני באחרונות מוציאין התיבה מה שאין כן באמצעיות : השתא דאתית להכי · דמשום דקתני לה באידך פירקין דאמרת דלא הוי שיור כ"ד נמי דאמרת דשוין נינהו איכא למימר דלא הוי שוין דהא אפי' שיורא נמי לא הוי דבהדיא קתני לה באידך פירקין דבאחרונות איתנהו באמצעיות לא והיכא לתרוצי כתירוצא קמא בקמייתא דליכא כ"ד : מאי הוי עלה · היכן אומרה יחיד : נקוט מציעתא בידך · כלומר תרין דבשלש אמצעיות היו מתענין ומתרצא לכולהו הנך מתנייתא הא דקתני בראשונות ולא באחרונות הנך ראשונות לאו ראשונות ממש נינהו אלא אמצעיות דאינהו הוו ראשונות לאחרונות אבל בשבע אחרונות לא מיתענו דכיון דשבע נינהו לא מצו עוברות ומיניקות למיקם בהו והא דקתני באחרונות ולא בראשונות הנך אחרונות אמצעיות נינהו והראשונות ראשונות ממש ואין מתענין בהן דלא תקיף רוגזא כולי האי ולאות לשון הוא להגא למיקרי לאמצעיות ראשונות לאחרונו' והאחרונו' לראשונות : בשופרות · היו עושין ההתרעות ולשון התרעה כמו תרועה וכתם תרועה פשוטה לפניה ולאחריה במסכת ראש השנה (דף לד.) ואהכי מתריעין בשופרות כדכתיב (במדבר י) ותקעתם בחצוצרות וגו' תוקעין בשופרות כדי שיכניעו לבם לקול השופר ויהיו נרתעים מחטאתם ולשם ברכות שהיו מוסיפין ביום התענית היו תוקעין על כל ברכה יבבא אהת שהן י"ח התרעות : רב יהודה אמר · מתריעין עננו בקול רם היו צועקים עננו אבינו עננו עננו אלהי אברהם עננו עננו אלהי יצחק עננו עננו אלהי יעקב עננו הכל כפי שאומרים בסוף הסליחות אבל עננו דתפלת תענית אומר אפי' בראשונות ואפי' יחיד אוקימנא דאומרה בשומע תפלה ותפלה קרי ליה התרעה דאי בשופרות מריעין מיבעי ליה ומאן דמפרש עננו של תפלה תענית משתבש דהא קתני בסמוך שהן י"ח התרעות וקא פריך מן וסימן לדבר יריחו ואם איתא ליפריך בהדיא י"ח הפלות של שמונה עשרה ברכות מי איכא בשבע תעניות : אין פותחין מז' תעניות · באחרונות : שמונה עשרה התרעות · שהן מוסיפין ו' ברכות מי"ח עד כ"ד ולכל אחת שלש תרועות : וסימן לדבר · שלא תטעה אם התרעה הזו תרועה או תפלה : יריחו · דכתיב בה שופרות לישנא אחרינא סימן לדבר כלומר לכך מתריעין כדי שיפלו כדרך שנפלו ביריחו על ידי שופרות דכתיב (יהושע ו) ויתקעו בשופרות וגו' וכתיב (שם) ותפול החומה תחתיה : אלא בשופרות כולי עלמא וכו' · דהא מתריעין דקתני הכא במתניתין דעבדינן בתעניות בשופרות : כי פליגי בעננו · כי פליגי במתריעין דאמריק בעלמא על שאר פורעניות מ"ס עננו נמי התרעה והאי דקתני בעלמא מתריעין בעננו ומאן דאמר בשופרות אבל בעננו לא : חגב · ארבה כתרגומו : צירעה · עוקצת את האדם : יתושין · נכנסין בעיניו ובחוטמו : חיכוך · כמו נתחכך בכותל : הא צעקה בפה היא · אלמא דצעקת פה לא קרי ליה התרעה : תנאי היא · האי תנא דשאר מיני פורעניות סבר צעקה פה לאו שמה התרעה ואידך סבר כו' : גיים · וצרין עליה : נהר · המתפשט ויוצא לחוץ לשטוף את השדה ואת הבתים : המטורפת · כמו בילים טרופות (חולין דף סד.) שהולכת ונדה ועתידה להיטבע במים : לעזרה · צועקין לבני אדם שיבואו לעזרם : ולא לצעקה · תפלה שאין אנו בטוחין כל כך שתועיל תפלתנו לצעוק עליהן בשבת אלמא צעקת פה קרי התרעה מפי מורי נ"א לעזרה דקאמר תנא קמא מתריעין דמשמע בקול רם ואמר ליה רבי יוסי לעזרה שיהו מתפללין כל אחד בביתו לעזרה בעלמא : גזר

תוספות

לאו שיורא הוא דהא קתני לה באידך פירקא · והוא הדין דהוה מצי לתרוצי כדלעיל מילי דבפרהסיא לא קתני :

תני חדא מתענות בראשונות ולא באחרונות ותנא אידך מתענין באחרונות ולא בראשונות ותני אידך לא מתענין לא בראשונות ולא באחרונות (ג) נקוט מציעתא בידך · פירש הקונטרס השלש תעניות אמצעיות בידך דבאותן תעניות עוברות ומיניקות מתענות וה"ק מתענות בראשונות פי' בראשונו' ר"ל אמצעיות דהם ראשונות לאחרונו' שהיו חמורות אבל לא באחרונות דנפישי ולא מצו עבדי להו והא דקתני באחרונות ולא בראשונות האי אחרונו' היינו אמצעיות וקרי להו אחרונות שהם אחרונות מן הראשונות בתחלה גוזרין שלש תעניות וכן בשניה שלש אבל אין מתענות בראשונות שהם קלות והא' דקתני לא בראשונות ולא באחרונות כלומר לא בשלש הראשונות הראשונות ממש ולא בשבע האחרונות האחרונות ממש אלא דווקא באמצעיות :

ורב יהודה בריה דרב שמואל בר שילת משמיה דרב אמר עננו · אומר הר"י (ג) והאי עננו לא ר"ל עננו שבתפלת תענית אלא עניט שאומרים בסליחות וביום הכפורים עננו אבינו עננו אבל עננו דתפלה לא קאמר דהא בשלש ראשונות נמי אמר לה :

ובהן י"ח תרועות וסימן לדבר יריחו · פירוש שביריחו עשו כן שהקיפוה ז' ימים והיו תוקעין בכל יום כמו כן תקנו בתעניות ובכל תענית מוסיפין שש ברכות ועל כל ברכה תוקעין מריעין ותוקעין א"כ הייט י"ח תרועות :

מתריעין לעזרה · פי' שיבואו לעזור העיר וכו' ומתריעין בפה פירוש והאי תרועה ר"ל מתריעין בפה דאין להתיר תרועה בשופר בשבת :

רבי

רבינו חננאל

אחרונות כגון הני כ"ד וכיוצא בהן אמר רב אשי הא דדייקא מתנייתא דייק ממתני' דקתני מה אלו יתירות על הראשונות אלא שבאלו מתריעין ונועלין החנויות הא לכל דבריהן זה וזה שוין · תנא מקצת ושייר מקצת ומאי שייר דהאי שייר [שייר] תיבה דלא קתני ומוציאין התיבה אלא אמרינן תנא ושייר כשם ששייר התיבה שייר כ"ד ברכות ולעולם [אין] מתפללין באמצעיות כ"ד ברכות ודחינן תיבה לאו שיור הוא דקתני באידך פרקין : סדר תעניות כיצד מוציאין התיבה הנה מפרש אכולהו תעניות מוציאין את התיבה . ואמרינן השתא דאתית להכי גם זה השינוי תשני בהא נמי ואימא מוקתני סדר תעניות כיצד וקא מפרש כ"ד ברכות ש"מ אכולהו העניות קסידי וז שנויה היא ולא סמכינן עליה דהא באידך פרקין *) דאין מוציאין התיבה אלא בז' אחרונות : מאי הוה עלה ואסיקנא הלכתא יחיד מתפלל עננו ל"ש יחיד קאי צבור ול"ש יחיד דקאי בעלמא וקי"ל דכל יחיד מזכיר עננו בשומע תפלה · תני חדא עוברות ומיניקות מתענות בראשונות ואין מתענות באחרונות ותניא אידך מתענות באחרונות ואין מתענות בראשונות · ותניא אידך אין מתענות לא באחרונות ולא בראשונות · אמר רב ששת נקוט אמצעייתא בידך כי מתענין בהן דמתרצין כולהו פי' הא דקתני בראשונה מתענות בראשונות בשלש אמצעיות [מייר] ולגבי שבע אחרונות (הני אחרונות) הני שלש אמצעיות ראשונות להני ז' נינהו ואמצעיות דקתני מתענין באחרונות הן ג' אמצעיות דלגבי שלש הראשונות האמצעיות אחרונות מקרו · ובריתא דקתני אין מתענות לא בראשונות [בראשונות] ממש שהן שלש ראשונות ולא באחרונות [באחרונות ממש] שהן ז' האחרונות מכלל דג' הראשונות מתענות לדברי שלשתן ויש לומר דכלהו מודו באמצעיות

[...]נות : ירושלמי עוברות ומיניקות מתענות בט' באב ובג' שניות ולא בז' אחרונות : כתני' אין נוזרין תענית בתחלה בחמישי כו' עד ר' יוסי אומר כשם שאין הראשונות בחמישי כך לא השניות [...]אחרונות : כתני' עברו אלו ולא נענו ב"ד גוזרין עוד כו' · מתריעין דתני בכתני' כיצד הוא רב יהודה אמר התרעה בשופר משמיה דרב אמרו התרעה בעננו ומותבינן [עלה] דרב אין פותחין מז' תעניות [...]צבור ובהן ז' התרעות וסימן לדבר יריחו והתרעות דיריחו בשופר הוו · ושנינן בשופר דברי הכל התרעה היא כי פליגי בעננו רב יהודה סבר עננו לאו התרעה היא ורב סבר עננו נמי התרעה היא · [...]מותבינן עליה ושאר כל מיני פורעניות המתרגשות על העולם כגון חיכוך חגב זבוב צרעה ויתושין ושילוח נחשים ועקרבים לא היו מתריעין אלא צועקין · והנה עננו צעקה היא ואם תאמר שנם [...]התרעה היא נמצא עננו התרעה והיא הצעקה היכי קתני צועקין ולא מתריעין ושנינן תנאי היא יש תנא שקורא עננו התרעה דתנן בפירקין [דחסירא] (קרא) על אלו מתריעין בשבת על עיר שהקיפוה גיים או נהר

*) אולי צ"ל דהא באידך פרקין המריך דאין מוציאין וכו'.

רבינו גרשום

[...]ייר תיבה דבאחרונות איכא ובאמצעיות ליכא אי משום תיבה לאו שיורא הוא דמילי בצינעא [...] כגון מתריעין ונועלין מילי דפרהסיא כגון תיבה שמוציאין לרחוב לא קתני ולעולם איכא תיבה [...]ונות ולא באמצעיות אבל כ"ד דהוי בצנעא אם איתא דליכא באמצעיות הוה קתני שבאילו מתפללין [...]באילו אין מתפללין כ"ד אלא ש"מ דבאמצעיות איכא כ"ד ולא מצית לתרוצי אב"א באמצעיות ליכא [...]ולעולם אמרינן הא דקתני אין בין ג' ראשונות לג' אמצעיות כו' הא לכ"ד שוין דהיכי דבאמצעיות [...] כ"ד ה"נ איכא בראשונות ולא מצית לתרוצי הא דתני שצבור מתפלל י"ם דהא איכא כ"ד אלא [...]ינן ליה ביחיד שקיבל עליו תענית צבור ותפשום דיחיד קובע ברכה לעצמו מתניתין נמי דיקא [...]מצעיות איכא כ"ד מה אילו אחרונות יתירות על הראשונית דהיינו אמצעיות שבאלו אחרונות מתריעין [...]לין אבל לכל דברידם זה וזה שוין אלמא דכי היכי דאיכא כ"ד באחרונות איכא נמי באמצעיות וכי [...]א ת"ל תנא ושייר כלומר דה"נ איבעי ליה למיתני שבאילו יש כ"ד ובאילו אין כ"ד אלא ששירו

הא מה אילו קתני דמשמע דהוי דוקא דליכא בינייהו אלא לרצי דתני בהדיא אר"ל לכ"ד זה וזה שוין דכי היכי דאיכא כ"ד באחרונות איכא נמי באמצעיות . אי משום תיבה לאו שיורא הוא אלא כיון דשייר כ"ד אלמא ש"ם דכי היכא דבאחרונות איכא כ"ד ה"נ איתא כ"ד באמצעיות השתא דאתית להכי התרצית דקתני באידך פרקין דכ"ד לא הוי שיורא כלומר לעולם באחרונות איכא כ"ד ובאמצעיות לא והאי דלא קתני שבאילו יש כ"ד ובאילו אין כ"ד משום דקתני לה באידך פירקא דבאחרונות איכא כ"ד ולא באמצעיות והא דקתני אין בין שלש ראשונות לשלש 'אמצעיות וכו' אמר הא לכל דבריהם זה וזה שוין דכי היכי דבאמצעות ליכא כ"ד ה"נ בראשונות ומצינו לאוקמי הא דקתני שצבור מתפללין י"ם בש"צ בקמייתא דליכא כ"ד ולא ביחיד דאין יחיד קובע ברכה לעצמו : נקוט אמצעייתא בידך כלומר כולהי א:רו דבאמצעייתא מתענות ולא בראשונות ולא באחרונות בראשונות לא דאכתי לא תקיף רוגזא ובאחרונות דקשי עלה להתענות שבעת ימים ומתרצו כולהי הא דקתני מתענות

רבי יהודה נשיאה גזר תלת עשרה תעניות ולא איעני סבר למיגזר טפי אמר ליה ר' אמי הרי אמרו אין מטריחין את הצבור יותר מדאי אמר ר' אבא בריה דרבי חייא בר אבא רבי אמי *דעבד לגרמיה הוא דעבד אלא הכי אמר ר' חייא בר אבא אמר ר' יוחנן לא שנו אלא לגשמים אבל לשאר מיני פורעניות מתענין והולכין עד שיענו מן השמים תניא נמי הכי כשאמרו שליש וכשאמרו שבע לא אמרו אלא לגשמים *אבל לשאר מיני פורעניות מתענין והולכין עד שיענו לימא תיהוי תיובתיה דר' אמי אמר לך רבי אמי תנאי היא דתניא אין גוזרין יותר משלש עשרה תעניות על הצבור לפי שאין מטריחין את הצבור יותר מדאי דברי רבי רשב"ג אומר לא מן השם הוא זה אלא מפני שיצא זמנה של רביעה שלחו ליה בני נינוה לרבי כגון אנן דאפילו בתקופת תמוז בעינן מיטרא היכי נעביד כיחידים דמינן או כרבים דמינן כיחידים דמינן ובשומע תפלה או כרבים דמינן ובברכת השנים 'שלח להו כיחידים דמיתו ובשומע תפלה מיתיבי אמר רבי יהודה *אימתי בזמן שהשנים כתיקנן וישראל שרוין על אדמתן אבל בזמן הזה הכל לפי השנים הכל לפי המקומות הכל לפי הזמן אמר ליה מתניתא רמית עליה דרבי רבי תנא הוא ופליג מאי הוי עלה רב נחמן אמר בברכת השנים רב ששת אמר בשומע תפלה והלכתא בשומע תפלה: בשני מטין עם חשיכה ובחמישי כל היום מפני כבוד השבת: איבעיא להו היכי קתני בב' מטין עם השיכה ובה' כל היום מפני כבוד השבת או דילמא בשני מטין ובחמישי פותחין כל היום כולו תא שמע דתניא 'בשני מטין עד הערב ובחמישי פותחין כל היום כולו מפני כבוד השבת היו לו שני פתחים פותח אחד ונועל אחד היה לו אצטבא כנגד פתחו פותח כדרכו ואינו חושש: עברו אלו ולא נענו ממעטין במשא ומתן ובבנין ובנטיעה: תנא *בבנין של שמחה נטיעה נטיעה של שמחה אי זהו בנין של שמחה זה הבונה בית חתנות לבנו אי זו היא נטיעה של שמחה זה הנוטע *אבורנקי של מלכים: ובשאילת שלום: תנו רבנן 'חברים אין שאילת שלום ביניהן עמי הארץ ששואלין מחזירין להם בשפה רפה ובכובד ראש *והן מתעטפין ויושבין כאבלים וכמנודין כבני אדם הנזופין למקום עד שירחמו עליהם מן השמים *אמר ר' אלעזר 'אין אדם חשוב רשאי ליפול על פניו אלא אם כן נענה כיהושע בן נון שנאמר °ויאמר ה' אל יהושע קום לך למה זה אתה נופל על פניך ואמר ר' אלעזר אין אדם חשוב רשאי לחגור שק אלא אם כן נענה כיהורם בן אחאב שנאמר °ויהי כשמוע המלך את דברי האשה ויקרע את בגדיו והוא עובר על החומה וירא העם והנה השק על בשרו וגו' ואמר ר' אלעזר לא הכל בקריעה ולא הכל בנפילה משה ואהרן בנפילה יהושע וכלב בקריעה משה ואהרן בנפילה דכתיב °ויפל משה ואהרן על פניהם יהושע וכלב בקריעה דכתיב °ויהושע בן נון וכלב בן יפנה קרעו בגדיהם מתקיף לה ר' זירא ואיתימא ר' שמואל בר נחמני אי הוה כתיב יהושע כדקאמרת השתא דכתיב ויהושע הא והא עביד ואמר ר' אלעזר לא הכל בקימה ולא הכל בהשתחויה מלכים בקימה ושרים בהשתחויה מלכים בקימה דכתיב °כה אמר ה' גואל ישראל קדושו לבזה

תורה אור: יהושע ז · מלכים ב ו · במדבר יד · שם · ישעיה מט

רבי יהודה נשיאה גזר תליסר תעניות · על שאר פורעניות (ג) ומיהו קאמר ליה רבי אמי דאין מטריחין דהכי נמי משמע דהוה אשאר מיני פורעניות מדמייתי עלה הא דקאמר רבי יוחנן ל"ש אלא לגשמים אבל לשאר מינים וכו':

שיצאה זמנה של רביעה · דזמן רביעה דיורה הוי במרחשון ויצא מרחשון:

שלח להו כיחידים דמיתו · פירוש ובשומע תפלה תאמרו תפלת (ד) תענית והא דיחיד אומר ותן טל ומטר בברכת השנים אע"ג שמתפלל בעצמו הואיל וזמן צבור הוא אבל בני נינוה הוו יחידים אפי' בתקופת תמוז צריכין למטרא:

הכל לפי השנים · אם צריכים אותה שנה גשמים שהיא שחונה ואם צריכים גשמים כבני נינוה שואלין ותן טל ומטר בברכת השנים:

אור

גזר תליסר תעניתא · כדאמרינן במתניתין (דף טו:) שלש ראשונות ושלש אמצעיות ושבע אחרונות ולשאר פורעניות עביד להו ולא לגשמים: לגרמיה · לעצמו דרש שלא אמר אלא לפי שהוא לא היה רוצה להתענות: לא שנו · דאין גוזרים יותר משלש עשרה: כשאמרו · להתענות שלש ראשונות ושלש אמצעיות ושבע אחרונות: לא מן השם הוא זה · שאין זה (א) טעם שאין מניחין בשביל טורח אלא שכבר יצא זמנה של רביעה של יורה שהרי מרחשון עבר על כולן לסוף התעניות שמקצתן היו בכסליו כדקתני מתניתין ואיכא למשמע מדרבי שמעון דבשאר מיני פורעניות דכל שעתא הוי זימנייהו למיבטלי אפילו טפי גזרינן ורבי דאמר אין מטריחין סתמא אכולהו קאמר והנך דאמרי כרבי: ובשומע תפלה · אמרינן לשאילת מטר כיחיד השואל צרכיו בשומע תפלה דהא דאמרינן שאלה בברכת השנים אפי' ביחיד משום דזמן צבור הוא אבל במילתא אחריתי דהוי ליחיד ולא לצבור כהכא דבתקופת תמוז להו זמן שאילת צבור הוא בשומע תפלה הוא דמדכר ליה ולא בברכת השנים כדאמרינן במסכת ע"ז (דף ח.) ובברכות (דף לא.) אם היה לו חולה בתוך ביתו מזכיר עליו בברכת החולים ולבסוף מוקמינן והלכתא בשומע תפלה כך שמעתי: אימתי · הוא סדר תעניות: בזמן שהשנים כתיקנן · שהיא קציר בניסן וזריעה במרחשון ואין סדר השנים משתנה: וישראל שרוין על אדמתן · שמנהג ארץ ישראל בכך: הכל לפי השנים · אם צריכה אותה שנה למטר כגון שנה שחונה שצריכה לגשמים הרבה: לפי המקומות · כגון נינוה דאפי' בתקופת תמוז בעו מטרא· לא גרסינן לפי הזמן שלא ירדו עדיין גשמים: *בשני מטין עם חשיכה · ולא נועלין ולא פותחין הואיל ולאו *)לכבוד שבת הוא ובחמישי מותרין לפתוח לגמרי: מטין · שלא יראו בני אדם ויצטערו אלא לעת ערב פותחין מקצתן כדי שיהא להם מה לאכול בלילה: או דילמא · פותחין כל היום והכי משמע מתניתין בשני מטין ובה' היו נועלו כדרכו כל היום לגמרי מפני כבוד השבת: איצטבא · כסא דהשתא אין החנות פתוחה לרשות הרבים ואם הוא פתוח אינו נראה כל כך: פותח כדרכו · אפי' בשני (ב): ה"ג תנא בנין בנין של שמחה נטיעה נטיעה של שמחה · בנין דקתני מתניתין לא בנין הצריך לו אלא בנין הצריך לשמחה דבדבר שמחה ממעטינן: בית חתנות · לעשות חופתו: אבוורנקי של מלכים · שכך היו נוהגין כשנולד בן למלך היו נוטעין אילן לשמו ויום שממליכין אותו עושין לו כסא ממנו ליסנא אחרינא אילן גדול המיסך על הארץ לטייל המלך תחתיו ודומה לו בעירובין (דף כה:) ההוא אבוורנקא דהוה ליה לריש גלותא בבוסתניה: של מלכים · דרך מלכים נוטעין אותו לצל הוא לא היא והיא נטיעה של שמחה: ששאל בשלום · תלמיד חכם מחזיר לו משום איבה ובשפה רפה: אבל ומנודה חייבין בעטיפה · °דכתיב ועל שפם יעטה במועד קטן (דף טו.): רשאי ליפול על פניו · לבזות עצמו בפני הצבור שאם לא יענה יתרפוהו כך שמעתי אלא אם כן יודעין בו שהוא חשוב כיהושע שאמר לו הקב"ה קום לך למה זה אתה נופל על פניך: אלא אם כן נענה · שיודעין בו שנענה כיהורם רשע היה אלא שהתענה על רעב שהיה בימיו ונענה דכתיב (מלכים ב ז) ויהי סאה סולת בשקל וסאתים שעורים בשקל: לא הכל · נענין (*בתפלה) ולא הכל נענין בקריעה דיהושע וכלב שלא היו חשובין כמשה ואהרן לא זכו ליענות אלא בקריעה ומקרא בעלמא קא דריש: ויהושע בן נון · כתיב בתריה דההוא דויפל וי"ו מוסיף על ענין ראשון:

*) ולאו לכבוד שבת הוא לא מטין כל היום שיראו בני אדם ויצטערו אלא לעת ערב כצ"ל וכל זה עד לאכול בלילה הוא דיבור אחד :

עין משפט נר מצוה

פא א מיי' פ"ג מהל' תענית הלכה ג טור ש"ע א"ח סימן תקעה סעיף א:

פב ב מיי' פ"ב מהלכות תפלה הלכה יז טוש"ע א"ח סימן קיז סעיף ב:

פג ג מיי' פ"ג מהל' תענית הלכה י טור ש"ע א"ח סימן תקעה סעיף ט:

פד ד מיי' שם הלכה ז טוש"ע שם סעיף ד:

פה ה ו מיי' שם הל' ח טוש"ע שם סעיף י:

פו ז מיי' פ"ה מהלכות תפלה הלכה יג טוש"ע א"ח סימן קלא סעיף ח:

רבינו חננאל

נ"ר ועל הספינה המטורפת בים ר' יוסי אומר לעזרה אבל לא לצעקה והא הכא התרעה בשופר ליכא למימר דהא שבת היא ושופר בשבת אסיר אלא לאו בעננו וקתני מתריעין בשבת ש"מ דקרי לעננו התרעה ש"מ הא דא"ר אמי אין מטריחין על הצבור יותר מדאי ואמרינן לגרמיה הוא דעביד כלומר לא היה יכול להתענות ובשביל עצמו אמר אין מטריחין דתניא כשאמרו י"ג תעניות לפי שאין מטריחין על הצבור לא אמרו אלא לגשמים בלבד אבל לשאר מיני פורעניות מתענין והולכין עד שיענו · ומשני ר' אמי תנאי היא דתניא אין גוזרין על הצבור יותר מי"ג תעניות לפי שאין מטריחין על הצבור יותר מדאי דברי רבי רשב"ג אומר לא מן השם הוא זה אלא מפני שיצא זמנה של רביעה: בני נינוה בעו מר' אנן דאפילו בתקופת תמוז בעי' מטרא אנא נזכיר ותן טל ומטר בברכת השנים או בשומע תפלה כיחיד ששואל צרכיו בשומע תפלה אמר להו בשומע תפלה כיחידים ואותבינן עליה א"ר יהודה אימתי שואלין הגשמים בפרקים הללו בזמן שהשנים כתיקנן וישראל שרוין על ארמתם אבל בזמן הזה הכל לפי השנים הכל לפי המקומות הכל לפי הזמן קשיא לרבי ודחי רבי תנא הוא וחולק על התנאים · מאי הוה עלה ואסיקנא רב ששת אמר בשומע תפלה וקיי"ל כוותיה · ותוב לגבי איסורא הלכתא כרב ששת וזו איסורא היא : פיסקא בשני מטין עם חשכה ומיבעיא לן ופשטנא מתני' דתניא בשני מטין לעת ערב ובחמישי פותחין כל היום מפני כבוד השבת היו לו ב' פתחים פותח אחד ונועל א' היתה לו איצטבא כנגד פתחו פותח ונועל כדרכו ואינו חושש עברו אלו [י"ג תעניות] ולא נענו ממעטין במשא ומתן כו' בנין זה בנין של שמחה : ירושלמי אריב"ל ל"ש אלא בנין של [שמ]חת ממעטין אבל אם היה נוהה סותרו ובונה : ת"ר חבירין אין שאילת שלום ביניהן עמי הארץ ששאלו מחזירין להן בשפה רפה ובכובד ראש · והן מתעטפין ויושבין כמנודין וכאבלים כבני נזופין עד שירחמו

מסורת הש"ס

[ברכות מח. וב"ג] · מגילה כ: · [דיוקי זה שייך לעיל במשנה יב:] · מו"ק טו. · מגילה כב:

הגהות הב"ח

(א) רש"י ד"ה לא מן השם וכו' שאין זה הטעם: (ב) ד"ה פותח כדרכו חשיבנו בשני מה"ד הגה קציר חטים וכו' ודשו ולאו כי רעתכם רבה אלמא סימן קללה הוי הס"ד וכ"כ וכו פי' לסוף משנה דלעיל בדף יב ע"ב: (ג) תוס' ד"ה ר' יהודה כו' בשאר פורענות והכא קאמר ליה כו' והכי נמי משמע: (ד) ד"ה שלח כו' תאמרו תפלת מטר והא דיחיד אומר כו' הוו יחידים ואפילו בתקופת תמוז:

גליון הש"ס

רש"י ד"ה אבל ומנודה דכתיב ועל שפם יעטה תמוה לי הא קרא במצורע כתיב ואבל נפקא לן במו"ק מדאמר ליחזקאל לא תעטה על שפם א"כ אבל צריך עיטוף · ובמנודה לא מייתי קרא כלל והוא איבעיא דלא אפשיטא שם וצ"ע :

[צ"ל בנפילה]

רבינו גרשום

מתענות בראשונות ולא באחרונות היינו אמצעיתא שהן ראשונות לאחרונות ולא באחרונות ממש והאי דקתני מתענות באחרונות היינו אמצעות שהן אחרונות לראשונות ולא בראשונות ממש והאי דקתני אין מתענות לא בראשונות ולא באחרונות היינו ראשונות ממש היינו אחרונות ממש שהן שלש עשרה דהאי שלש שהיחידים מתענין לא חשיב כלום : בעננו והיינו התרעה דהוו בכינופיא וכהן י"ג תרועות כדאמרן בפירקין דלקמן דבברכה ראשונה אמר להם קודם הברכה תקעו ולאחר הברכה תקעו ותוקעין ומריעין ותוקעין וקודם ברכה שניה אומר להם הריעו ומריעין ולאחר ברכות אומר להם הריעו ומריעין ותוקעין ומריעין נמצא בברכה ראשונה מריע אחת ובשניה ג' וכן בכל אלו ז' ברכות בראשונה תרועה אחת ובשניה ג' תרועות נמצא לו' ברכות י"ג תקיעות וסימן לדבר דעבדינן תרועה יריחו הא יריחו בשופרות הוות ומדנקט סימן יריחו ש"מ דתרועה בשופר : החיכוך שחין היה צעקה בפה ומדקתני לא היו מתריעין אלא צועקין אלמא דצעקה בפה ותרועה בשופר : לעזרה ולא לצעקה כל אחד מתפלל בפני עצמו אבל אין שולין כנופיא : ר' יהודה גזר תליסר תעניתא הני וקתני במתניתין רב אמי דאמר אין מתענין יותר מי"ג לגרמיה עבד לא הורה כהלכה : לא שנו שאין מטריחין יותר מדאי אלא לגשמים אבל לשאר פורעניות מתענין והולכין עד שיענו והאי דר' יהודה נשיאה שאר מיני פורעניות הוה : שאין מטריחין את הצבור יותר מדאי דברי רבי אפילו בשאר מיני פורעניות ור' אמי דאמר כר' לא מן השם הוא זה כלומר לאו להכי הוא דבשאר מיני פורעניות אין מטריחין יותר מי"ג אלא לגשמים אין מתענין יותר מי"ג כבר יצאה זמנה של רביעה דבר"ה כסלו הוה ביום ראשון וגזרו תענית בשני ובחמישי ושני דהיינו ט"ו יום בכסליו ומתחיל השניות בשני וחמישי ושני הרי כבר יצא כל כסליו ועכשיו בר"ח טבת מתחילין הז' תעניות חמישי ושני בכל שבוע הרי יצאו בו' תעניות ג' שבועות וגוזרין בשביעי ביום שני בשבוע רביעי הרי יצא כל טבת וי"ג תעניות ואם היו גוזרין עוד תעניות לא היו יכולין לגזור בטבת דאין גוזרין בתחלה אלא ביום שני ושני דטבת כבר עבר אלא היה להם לגזור ביום שני שבשבט וכבר עבר מקצת שבט ובר"ח כבר יצאו זמן רביעה וכבר יצאו רוב גשמי שנה דלהכי הוי *) אמר בשבט ר"ה לאילן דכבר יצאו רוב גשמי שנה : כיחידים דמין ובשומע תפלה ושואלים מטר כיחיד ששואל צרכיו בשומע תפלה א"ר יהודה אימתי סדר כל אילו התעניות הכל לפי השנים דשנה שחונה צריכה לרוב גשמים ושאינה שחונה אינה צריכה גשמים מרובים הכל לפי המקומות כגון נינוה שואלין הגשמים [בתקופת תמוז] ומרכולל הכי ש"מ ושואלין בצבור : מטין עם חשכה לא נועלין ולא פותחין לא נועלין משום בני כפרים שבאין להספיק מים ומזון לאחיהם שבכרכין ולא פותחין הואיל דלאו לכבוד שבת הוא : ובחמישי מותרין לפתוח לגמרי : יש לו שני פתחים בשני פותח אחד לגמרי הואיל ונועל אחר ואם אין לו אלא פתח אחד ולפניו אצטבה פותח [ונועל] כדרכו לגמרי אפילו בשני הואיל דיש לפניו איצטבא דיש היכר · ה"ג תנא·

*) אולי צ"ל אחד בשבט אבל צ"ע דהא"כ שנה מעתו ככ"ש ואפשר דצ"ל ט"ו בשבט וצ"ע ·

לבזה נפש למתעב גוי לעבד מושלים מלכים יראו וקמו ושרים בהשתחויה דכתיב שרים וישתחוו מתקיף לה רבי זירא ואיתימא רבי שמואל בר נחמני אי הוה כתיב ושרים ישתחוו כדקאמרת השתא דכתיב שרים וישתחוו הא והא עבוד אמר רב נחמן בר יצחק אף אני אומר לא הכל לאורה ולא הכל לשמחה צדיקים לאורה וישרים לשמחה צדיקים לאורה דכתיב °אור זרוע לצדיק ולישרים שמחה דכתיב ולישרי לב שמחה:

תהלים צז

הדרן עלך מאימתי

סדר ^א^תעניות כיצד מוציאין את התיבה לרחובה של עיר *ונותנין אפר מקלה על גבי התיבה ובראש הנשיא ובראש אב בית דין וכל אחד ואחד נותן בראשו הזקן שבהן אומר לפניהן דברי כבושין אחינו ^ב^לא נאמר באנשי נינוה וירא אלהים את שקם ואת תעניתם אלא °וירא אלהים את מעשיהם כי שבו מדרכם הרעה ובקבלה הוא אומר °וקרעו לבבכם ואל בגדיכם עמדו בתפלה מורידין לפני התיבה זקן ורגיל ויש לו בנים וביתו ריקם כדי שיהא לבו שלם בתפלה ^ג^ואומר לפניהן עשרים וארבעה ברכות י"ח שבכל יום ומוסיף עליהן עוד שש ואלו הן זכרונות ושופרות °אל ה' בצרתה לי קראתי ויענני °אשא עיני אל ההרים וגו' °)ממעמקים קראתיך ה' °°)תפלה לעני כי יעטוף ר' יהודה אומר לא היה צריך לומר זכרונות ושופרות אלא אומר תחתיהן °°°)רעב כי יהיה בארץ דבר כי יהיה °אשר היה דבר ה' אל ירמיהו על דברי הבצרות ואומר חותמיהן על הראשונה הוא אומר מי שענה את אברהם בהר המוריה הוא יענה אתכם וישמע בקול צעקתכם היום הזה ברוך אתה ה' גואל ישראל על השניה הוא אומר מי שענה את אבותינו על ים סוף הוא יענה אתכם וישמע קול צעקתכם היום הזה ברוך אתה ה' זוכר הנשכחות על השלישית הוא אומר מי שענה את יהושע בגלגל הוא יענה אתכם וישמע בקול צעקתכם היום הזה ברוך אתה ה' שומע תרועה על הרביעית הוא אומר מי שענה את שמואל במצפה הוא יענה אתכם וישמע בקול צעקתכם היום הזה ברוך אתה ה' שומע צעקה על החמישית הוא אומר מי שענה את אליהו בהר הכרמל הוא יענה אתכם וישמע בקול צעקתכם היום הזה ברוך אתה ה' שומע תפלה על הששית הוא אומר מי שענה את יונה ממעי הדגה הוא יענה אתכם וישמע בקול צעקתכם היום הזה ברוך אתה ה' העונה בעת צרה על השביעית הוא אומר מי שענה את דוד ואת שלמה בנו בירושלים הוא יענה אתכם וישמע בקול צעקתכם היום הזה ברוך אתה ה' המרחם על הארץ: מעשה בימי

יונה ג | יואל ב | תהלים קכ | קכא | °)תהלים קל °°)שם קב °°°)מ"א ח | ירמיה יד

רש"י

לבזה נפש למתעב גוי לעבד מושלים · לישראל הבזוים ומתועבים ועבדים מושלין בהן: ולא הכל בקימה · לקראת ישראל לעתיד לבא מלכים יראו וקמו שרים וישתחוו: ה"ג לא הכל לאורה ולא הכל לשמחה דכתיב אור זרוע לצדיק ולישרי לב שמחה · ישרים לשמחה דישרים עדיפי מצדיקים: תורה אור

הדרן עלך מאימתי

סדר תעניות כילד כו': אפר מקלה · אפר ממש ולא עפר אפר סתם הוא עפר דכשם שאפר קרוי עפר דכתיב (במדבר יט) מעפר שרפת החטאת כך עפר קרוי אפר סתם והייט דקתני אפר מקלה אפר שריפה אי הוה תני אפר סתם הוה משמע עפר ואפר מקלה גנאי יותר מעפר סתם ובגמרא מפרש מאי טעמא נותנין אותו: כבושין · לשון עלירה כמו מכבש בלע"ז פריס"א (א) שכובשין את הלבבות להחזירם למוטב ואלו הן דברי כבושין אחינו כו': ובקבלה · שהנביא מלוה לישראל (עמדו בתפלה) והקשה תוספות מאן דהו מאי שנא בהאי קרא דכתיב ביונה וירא האלהים את מעשיהם וגו' ולא קרי ליה דברי קבלה ובהאי קרא דוקרעו לבבכם קרי ליה קבלה ופריק היינו כל מקום שהנביא מלוה ומודיע ומזהיר את ישראל קרי ליה קבלה ובכל דוכתא דלא איתפקד נביא כי האי וירא האלהים שהוא כמספר והולך דיליף מיניה אגב אורחיה מילתא לא קרינן ליה קבלה: (ב) ברחובה של עיר · בגלוי וכי הך דאמרינן במסכת מגילה (דף כה:) בני העיר שמכרו רחובה של עיר והתם מפרש בהדיא *אמר ר' זירא הואיל והעם מתפללים בו בתעניות ובמעמדות: ורגיל · רגיל להתפלל ותפלתו סגורה בפיו ולא יטעה שכל (ג) חזן בטועה סימן רע לשולחיו: וביתו ריקם · משמע דהוא עני ואין לו מחיה בביתו ובגמרא מפרש טעמא אחרינא וגופו נקי מעבירות שלא חטא ולא יצא עליו שום שם רע בשום עבירה כו': זכרונות ושופרות · כל הפסוקים שאומרים בראש השנה: אל ה' בצרתה לי כו' · שלן הן מזמורים: ואומר חותמיהן · על כל פרשה ופרשה אחר זכרונות חתימת זכרונות ואחר שופרות חתימת שופרות וכן אחר כולם מעין הפרשה כדמפרש ואזיל: על הראשונה · בפעם ראשונה הוא אומר מי שענה לאברהם כו' בגואל ישראל היה מתחיל להאריך והולך ואומר לכולן שש ברכות: על השניה · זו היא ברכה ראשונה של שש ברכות כדאמרינן בגמ' והיכך דגואל ישראל זו היא ברכה עלמה של שמונה עשרה והנה מאותן שש אלא שבה היה מתחיל להוסיף ולהאריך על הזכרונות הוא אומר זוכר הנשכחות ועל השופרות שומע תרועה והיא שניה למנינה ועל אל ה' בצרתה לי והיא שלישית למנין שש שומע צעקה(ד) שלישית וכן כולן: ומי שענה את אבותינו על ים סוף · לפיכך אומרה בזכרונות לפי שהיו ישראל נשכחים במצרים כמה שנים ונהייאשו מן הגאולה וזכרם המקום וגאלם דכתיב (שמות ו) ואזכור את בריתי: ובשופרות היה אומר מי שענה את יהושע בגלגל · לפי שנענה בשופרות ביריחו וזהו בעוד שהיו ישראל בגלגל: ואליהו בהר הכרמל · כנגד אשא עיני אל ההרים וכן כולן לפי ענין המזמורים אליהו נענה בהר הכרמל מעין אשא עיני אל ההרים ושמואל במצפה דכתיבי קראתי ומעין אל ה' בצרתה לי: ממעי הדגה · מעין ממעמקים קראתיך ה' ועונה בעת צרה שכן כתיב ביונה קראתי מצרה לי (יונה ב) ובשמואל כתיב ויזעק אל ה' (שמואל א ז) ובאליהו כתיב (מלכים א יח) ענני זו תפלה: ועל השביעית · מפרש בגמרא מאי שביעית מי שענה דוד ויהי רעב בימי דוד שלש שנים שנה אחר שנה (שמואל ב כא): ושלמה · כשהכניס הארון לבית קדש הקדשים אי נמי רעב כי יהיה בארץ וגו' (מלכים א ח) ולפיכך חותם מרחם על הארץ שכן התפללו על ארץ ישראל ותפלה לעני כי יעטוף על דוחק גשמים טפל וכתיב ביה (שם) בהעלר שמים: *בימי רבי חלפתא בלפורי · אביו של רבי יוסי דאמרינן בסנהדרין (דף לב:) אחר רבי יוסי בלפורי [אחר ר' חנניא בן תרדיון] בסיכני: וגומר

[עי' תוספות לקמן ע"ב ד"ה ונותנין]
[לשניי בב בתפלה דגמרא הוא ולא ר' זירא אמרה]
[ברכות לד.]
שייך לע"ב

תוספות

אור זרוע לצדיק ולישרי לב שמחה · פירוש ואין לומר כדלעיל ולישרים האי והאי שמחה ואורה (ה) א"כ דאמרינן דלישרי לב קאי אהא דלעיל כמו כן אמרינן דלדיקים קאי אהא דלאבתריה כיון דסמוך לדיק לישרי לב ובודאי יש הפרש בין זה לזה דאם לא כן לערבינהו ולכתוב לצדיקים ולישרי לב אורה ושמחה אבל ההיא דלעיל לא הוו מלכים ושרים כי הדדי אלא יראו וקמו בינייהו וכמו יראו וקמו דהוי קודם שרים קאי על מלכים דלעיל קאי נמי אשרים דכתיב אבתריה אבל הכא אין לפרש אלא אור זרוע לצדיקים ולישרי לב שמחה:

הדרן עלך מאימתי

עין משפט נר מצוה

א א מיי' פ"ד מהלכות תענית הלכה א ב ג טוש"ע א"ח סימן תקעט סעיף א:

ב ב מיי' שם ס"ו טור א"ח סימן תקעט:

[ועי' תוספו' מנחות יט. ד"ה במקרא]

רבינו חננאל

שירחמו עליהם מן השמים · א"ר אלעזר אין אדם חשוב רשאי ליפול על פניו א)[יחיד בצבור וכן מפורש בתלמוד ירושלמי] [בפ"ב ס"ו] אא"כ נענה כיהושע בן נון שנאמר ויאמר ה' אל יהושע קום לך למה זה אתה נופל על פניך וכן אין אדם חשוב רשאי להעיר שק על בשרו אא"כ נענה כיהורם שנאמר ויהי כשמוע המלך את דברי האשה ויקרע את בגדיו וירא העם והנה השק על בשרו. וא"ר אלעזר משה ואהרן בנפילה · יהושע וכלב בקריעה · ומסקנא יהושע הא והא קא עבד ועוד אמר מלכים בקימה שרים בהשתחויה ואני ב) אומר צדיקים וישרים בשמחה שנא' אור זרוע לצדיק ולישרי לבשמחה:

הדרן עלך מאימתי מזבירין

סדר תעניות כיצד מוציאין את

רבינו גרשום

תנא בנין בנין של שמחה כלומר הא דקתני ממעטין בבנין היינו בבנין של שמחה ג) אבורנקי של מלכים שבשנולד בן נוטעין אילן אחד לשמו וכשמעמידין אותו למלך עושין מבנו כסא מלכות · ומנא לן דיהושע נענה דכתיב ויאמר ה' אל יהושע וגו' ויהושע ר' בוסיף על ענין ראשון דהא והא עבד בנפילה במשה ובקריעה · לא הכל בקימה כלומר לעתיד לבוא שעומדין כנגד ישראל והא והא עביד קימה והשתחויה. ה"ג הכל לאורה ולא הכל לשמחה צדיקים לאורה ולזו לשמחה ישרים אף לשמחה דישרים עדיפי מצדיקים:

הדרן עלך מאימתי

סדר תעניות כו' ואפי' בקמייתא בלימר

הגהות הב"ח

(א) רש"י ד"ה כבושין כו' (שכובשין את הלבבות להחזירם למוטב) תא"מ ונ"ב ס"א שכובשין ודוחקין את הלב לעשות תשובה · וע' ענין אחר שמגלה להם סתרי מעשיהם כמו כבדי כבשי דרחמנא כו' פר"ח: (ב) ד"ה ובקבלה כו' לישראל והקשה כנ"ל ותיבות עמדו בתפלה נמחק: (ג) ד"ה ורגיל כו' שכל ש"ל שטועה: (ד) ד"ה על השניה כו' שומע צעקה וכן כולם כנ"ל ותיבת שלישית נמחק והד"א עם ד"ה מי שענה וד"ה ובשופרות וד"ה ואליהו וכו' ושמואל במצפה כדכתיבי קראתי וכו' וסד"א עד בימי רבי חלפתא: (ה) תוספות ד"ה אור כו' שמחה ואורה דאם כן אמרינן דלישרי לב כו' כמו כן אמרינן דלדיק קאי אהא דלאבתריה כו' ולכתוב לצדיק ולישרי לב אורה ושמחה אבל בפסוק דלעיל לא הוו מלכים ושרים כתובים אהדדי אלא כו' אור זרוע לצדיק ולישרי לב שמחה:

גליון הש"ס

רש"י ד"ה ובקבלה וכו' ולא קרי ליה דברי קבלה · עיין חולין דף קלז ע"א רש"י ד"ה תורת משה:

א) נראה דצ"ל פי' יחיד בציבור וכו'. ב) נראה דחסר כאן וצ"ל אמר רנב"י אף אני אומר צדיקים לאורה וישרים לשמחה שנאמר וכו'. ג) אולי צ"ל ובנטיעה היינו נטיעה של שמחה כגון אבורנקי וכו'.

בימי רבי חלפתא ור' חנניא בן תרדיון שעבר אחד לפני התיבה וגמר את הברכה כולה ולא ענו אחריו אמן תקעו הכהנים [א] ותקעו מי שענה את אברהם אבינו בהר המוריה הוא יענה אתכם וישמע בקול צעקתכם היום הזה הריעו בני אהרן הריעו מי שענה את אבותינו על ים סוף הוא יענה אתכם וישמע בקול צעקתכם היום הזה (א) *וכשבא דבר אצל חכמים אמרו לא היינו נוהגין כן אלא בשער מזרח ובהר הבית שלש תעניות הראשונות *אנשי משמר מתענין ולא משלימין ואנשי בית אב לא היו מתענין כלל שלש שניות ואנשי משמר מתענין ומשלימין ואנשי בית אב מתענין ולא משלימין שבע אחרונות אלו ואלו מתענין ומשלימין דברי רבי יהושע וחכמים אומרים שלש תעניות הראשונות אלו ואלו לא היו מתענין כלל שלש שניות אנשי משמר מתענין ולא משלימין ואנשי בית אב לא היו מתענין כלל שבע אחרונות אנשי משמר מתענין ומשלימין ואנשי בית אב מתענין ולא משלימין אנשי משמר מותרין לשתות יין בלילות אבל לא בימים ואנשי בית אב לא ביום ולא בלילה *אנשי משמר ואנשי מעמד אסורין מלספר ומלכבס *ובחמישי מותרין מפני כבוד השבת כל הכתוב במגילת תענית דלא למספד לפניו אסור לאחריו מותר רבי יוסי אומר לפניו ולאחריו אסור דלא להתענאה לפניו ולאחריו מותר ר' יוסי אומר לפניו אסור לאחריו מותר *אין גוזרין תענית על הצבור בתחילה בחמישי שלא להפקיע השערים אלא שלש תעניות הראשונות שני וחמישי ושני ושלש שניות חמישי שני וחמישי ר' יוסי אומר כשם שאין הראשונות בחמישי כך לא שניות ולא אחרונות *אין גוזרין תענית על הצבור בראשי חדשים בחנוכה ובפורים ואם התחילו אין מפסיקין דברי רבן גמליאל אמר רבי מאיר אף על פי שאמר רבן גמליאל אין מפסיקין מודה היה שאין משלימין וכן תשעה באב שחל להיות בערב שבת: **גמ'** סדר תעניות כיצד מוציאין את התיבה כו' ואפילו בקמייתא ורמינהו שלש תעניות ראשונות ושניות נכנסים לבית הכנסת ומתפללין כדרך שמתפללין כל השנה כולה ובשבע אחרונות מוציאין את התיבה לרחובה של עיר ונותנין אפר על גבי התיבה ובראש הנשיא ובראש אב בית דין ורל אחד ואחד [ג] ונוטל ונותן בראשו רבי נתן אומר אפר מקלה הן מביאין אמר רב פפא כי תנן נמי מתניתין אשבע אחרונות תנן: ובראש הנשיא: והדר תני כל אחד ואחד [ג] (*נוטל ונותן) בראשו איני (*והתנן) *רבי אומר בגדולה מתחילין מן הגדול *ובקללה מתחילין מן הקטן בגדולה מתחילין מן הגדול שנאמר °ויאמר משה אל אהרן ולאלעזר ולאיתמר ובקללה מתחילין מן הקטן (*דאמר מר) *בתחלה נתקלל נחש ואחר כך נתקללה חוה ואח"כ נתקלל אדם הא חשיבותא לדידהו דאמרי להו אתון חשיביתו למיבעי עלן רחמי אכ"ע: (*כל אחד ואחד [ד] (*נוטל ונותן) בראשו: אמר רב אדא) וכל אחד ואחד (*נוטל ונותן) בראשו נשיא ואב בית דין נמי נשקלו אינהו ונינחו בראשייהו מאי שנא דשקיל איניש אחרינא ומנח להו אמר רבי אבא דמן קסרי *אינו דומה מתבייש מעצמו למתבייש

תורה אור

וגומר כל הברכה · כל אותה ברכה עלמה: ה"ג ולא ענו אחריו אמן תקעו בני אהרן תקעו · חזן הכנסת אומר להן על כל ברכה וברכה והוא השמש ולא שליח לבור: לא היינו נוהגין · שלא לענות אמן: אלא בשער מזרח ובהר הבית · כלומר בזמן שבית המקדש קיים כשמתפללין בהר הבית נכנסין בדרך שער המזרח לפי שלא היו עונין אמן במקדש כדאמרינן בגמרא (דף טז:) ואין לומר לא היו נוהגין כן לתקוע אלא במקדש דודאי תוקפין בגבולים כדמוכח בכולה הך מסכת ומסכת ראש השנה (דף כו: כז.): אנשי משמר · של אותה שבת: ולא משלימין · שעדיין אין חמורין כל כך ובגמרא (דף יז:) מפרש שמא תכבד העבודה על אנשי בית אב שהיו עובדין אותו היום ובאים הן לסייעם ואם היו מתענים (נ) לא היה להם כח לעמוד בעבודה: אנשי בית אב · המשמרה מתחלקת לשבעה בתי אבות [illegible] אנשי [מעמד] · אחד כהנים ולוים וישראלים הקבועים ועומדין ומתפללין על קרבן אחיהם שיקבל לרצון ועומדים לשם בשעת עבודה דהיאך קרבנו של אדם קרב והוא אינו עומד על גביו וכולהו מפרש בפרק אחרון (דף כו.): מותרין לשתות יין · לאו גבי תענית איתמר אלא אגב דמיירי בבני משמר מייתי לה: בלילות · אין לחוש שמא תכבד העבודה שהרי לאו מבערב שפסקו הקרבנות ולא כבדה העבודה *שיבואו חיב קרבנות ולא יספיקו בני בית אב של אותו היום וצריכין אלו לסייען והרי אינן ראויין לעבודה משום שכרות: אנשי בית אב אסורין בין ביום בין בלילה · לפי שהיו מעלין כל הלילה אברים ופדרים שפקעו מעל המזבח א"נ לא גמרו ביום גומרים בלילה אבל אנשי משמר אין צריכין לסייע בלילה להפך במזלג דבית אב יכול להספיק לבד היפוך המערכה: אסורים לספר ולכבס · משנכנסו למשמרתם כל אותה שבת אלא מסתפרין קודם לכן וטעמא [illegible] ורחוצין · [illegible] משמרתן מותרים דלך רוב בני אדם להסתפר בחמישי ולא בערב שבת מפני הטורח: כל הכתוב במגילת תענית דלא למיספד · דאיה יומיה דלא להתענאה ומקצתהון דחמירי טפי דלא למיספד ואותן שהן חמורים ואסורים בהספד לפניו אסור בהספד דילמא אתי למיעבד ביו"ט גופיה: ולאחריו מותר · דכיון שעבר יום לא חיישינן ואותן שאינן חמורין ליאסר בהספד אלא דלא להתענאה בין לפניו כו': שלא להפקיע את השערים · כשרואין בעלי חנויות שקונין למוצאי יום חמישי שתי סעודות גדולות אחת (נ) לליל חמישי ואחת לשבת סבורים שבא רעב לעולם ומייקרים ומפקיעים השער אבל משהתחילו להתענות יודעין שאינו אלא מפני התענית: בראשי חדשים · דאיקרי מועד: ואם התחילו · שקיבלו תענית מקודם לכן ונכנס בהן ראש חדש אין מפסיקין דאף על גב דאיקרי מועד לא כתיב ביה יום משתה ושמחה*: שאין משלימין · להתענות כל היום אלא אוכלין סמוך לערב: *מגילת תענית נכתבה בימי חכמים אע"פ שלא היו כותבין הלכות והיינו דקתני כל הכתוב במגילת תענית כאילו היה מקרא: **גמ'** אפילו בקמייתא · מוליאין את התיבה בתמיה: כי קתני נמי מתני' · סדר תעניות כילד בסדר תעניות אחרונות קא מיירי: ה"ג בגמרא ונותנין אפר על גבי התיבה ולא גרסינן אפר מקלה* אפר שריפה עדיף משום אפרו של יצחק כדלקמן: בגדולה · מלוה בעלמא שלא לפורענות וידבר משה אל אהרן ואל אלעזר וגו': הא נמי דיהבינן ברלשייהו דנשיא ואב ב"ד ברישא חשיבותא הוא דאמרי להו אתון חשיביתו טפי כו': דשקיל איניש אחרינא כו' · דקתני ונותנין ע"ג התיבה כו' ועל ראש הנשיא כו' דמשמע על ידי אחר וגבי שאר כל אדם לא תני נותנין אלא כל אחד ואחד (*נוטל) כו':

ואפילו בקמייתא · כלומר ואפי' בג' תעניות הראשונות ובג' שניות קאמר ב...תני' דמוליאין את התיבה לרחובה של עיר ואומר כ"ד ברכות כו' ורמינהו והתניא ראשונות ושניות נכנסין כו' פי' ומתפללין בה כדרך כל השנה כולה כלומר שיאמר י"ח ברכות כדרך שמתפללין כל השנה וקשה דהא לעיל (ד) בפ"ק (דף יג:) קאמרינן אין בין ג' תעניות שניות לשלש ראשונות אלא שבאלו (ה) מתפללין ומותרין בעשיית מלאכה ובאלו אסורין בעשיית מלאכה הא לענין עשרים וארבעה זה וזה שוין דבין בראשונות בין באמלעיות היו אומרים כ"ד ועוד קשה דאמרינן לעיל ואיבעית אימא באמלעיות נמי לא מללו כ"ד ואמאי לא מייתי לה סיועא מהא דהכא וי"ל דהא דקאמר הכא ומתפללין כדרך כל השנה לאו בעשרים וארבע ברכות קאמר אלא קאמר שמתפללין כדרך כל השנה [illegible] לרחובה של עיר:

ונותנין אפר על גבי כו' · ואותו אפר הוי מעלם אדם שהרי (ו) הוא האפר הוי לזכרון העקידה ובעקידה היה עלמות במקוס

עין משפט
נר מצוה

ג א מיי' פ"ד מהלכות תענית הלכה יז טור א"ח סימן תקעט:
ד ב מיי' שם פ"ג ה"ב:
ה ג מיי' שם הלכה ג:
ו ד מיי' שם הלכה ו:
ז ה ו מיי' פ"א מהלכות ביאת מקדש הלכה ו:
ח ז מיי' שם הלכה יב:
ט ח מיי' פ"ו מהלכות כלי המקדש הל' יא:
י ט מיי' פ"א מהלכות תענית הלכה ה טוש"ע א"ח סי' תקעב סעי' א:
יא י מיי' שם פ"ג הל' ג והל' ה טוש"ע שם סי' תקעב סעיף ג ד:
יב כ מיי' שם פ"א הל' ז טוש"ע שם סימן תקעב סעיף ב:
יג ל מיי' פ"ד שם הלכה א טוש"ע שם סימן [illegible]:

[ושייך לעיל במשנה]

רבינו חננאל

התיבה כו' · ואקשינן סדר תעניות מכלל דבכולהו מוציאין את התיבה והתניא שלשה תעניות הראשונות נכנסין לבתי כנסיות ומורשות ומתפללין כדרך שמתפללין כל השנה שבע אחרונות מוציאין את התיבה לרחובה של עיר כו'. ושני רב פפא כי תנן מוציאין את התיבה בז' אחרונות תנן · ואקשינן אמאי אין מתחילין מן הקטן דתניא ר' אומר בגדולה מתחילין מן הגדול שנאמר ויאמר משה אל אהרן *) ואל אלעזר ואל איתמר בניו ובקללה מתחילין מן הקטן דאמר מר בתחלה נתקלל הנחש ואחריו חוה ואחריה אדם ושנינן נתינת אפר על ראש הנשיא חשיבות היא לו דאמרינן ליה חשיבת קסיה דקב"ה למבעי [illegible] מסס וכו'.

*) נ"ל ולאלעזר

רבינו גרשום

ותני בסתם מוציאין את התיבה דמשמע אפילו בראשונות · פאר זו תפילין דכתיב פארך חבוש עליך

מסורת הש"ס

[לעיל יב.]
[מו"ק יד.]
[לקמן כט:]
[כתוספתא ליתא רוב כ"ל וכו' דיבור כפ"ע]
עירובין מא.
נרכות סא.
[כסי' ובקלקלה ו' בכמון]
[שם.]
עירובין יח.
[נ"ל נותן]
[נ"ל נותן]
[סנהדרין מב]
[עי' פרש"י]
הס"ד ואח"כ מד"ה אפר מקלה אפר כו' כנ"ל
[נ"ל נותן]
[ל"ל והתניא] [נ"ל נותן]
[ליתא בברכות וכס מתוללי ככנה]
רש"ל מוחק זה והפיסקא מתחיל מן אידך וכל אחד ואחד וכו'
[גי' רי"ף אדא וגי' רא"ש זירא]
ויקרא י

הגהות הגר"א

[א] במשנה ותקעו · נ"ל תקעו (וכ"ה במשניות): [ב] גמ' וכל אחד ואחד נותן כנ"ל ושבגתיים מוקף: [ג] שם כל אחד נותן כנ"ל: [ד] שם כל א' וא' נותן בראשו אמר כו' כנ"ל ושבנתיים מוקף:

הגהות הב"ח

(א) גמ' את אבותינו על ים סוף כו' היום הזה וכן בכל ברכה וברכה וכשבא הדבר אצל חכמים כו': (ב) רש"י ד"ה ולא משלימין כו' ואם היו מתענים ומשלימין לא היה להם: (ג) ד"ה שלא להפקיע כו' סעודות גדולות אחת ליום התענית לליל חמישי: (ד) תוספות ד"ה ואפילו כו' וקשה דהא לעיל · נ"ב פירוש המקשה קאמר הכי לעיל ואם כן סתרי דברי המקשה אהדדי דהכא קס"ד דאין מתפללין אלא י"ח: (ה) בא"ד אלא שבאלו מותרין בעשיית מלאכה כו' כנ"ל ותיבת מתפללין נמחק: (ו) ד"ה ונותנין כו' שהרי האפר ס כו' כנ"ל ותיבת הוא נמחק:

גליון הש"ס רש"י ד"ה מגילת תענית נכתבה · עיין לעיל דף יב ע"א רש"י ד"ה בגלו:

למתבייש מאחרים והיכא מנח להו אמר רבי יצחק במקום תפילין שנאמר לשום לאבילי ציון לתת להם פאר תחת אפר: רחוב תיבה ושקים אפר אפר קבורה ומוריה סימן: למה יוצאין לרחוב ר' חייא בר אבא אמר לומר זעקנו בצנעא ולא נענינו נבזה עצמנו בפרהסיא ריש לקיש אמר גלינו גלותינו מכפרת עלינו מאי בינייהו איכא בינייהו רגלי מבי כנישתא לבי כנישתא ולמה מוציאין את התיבה לרחובה של עיר אמר ר' יהושע בן לוי לומר כלי צנוע היה לנו ונתבזה בעוונינו ולמה מתכסין בשקים אמר ר' חייא בר אבא לומר הרי אנו חשובין כבהמה ולמה נותנין אפר מקלה על גבי תיבה אמר רבי יהודה בן פזי כלומר עמו אנכי בצרה ריש לקיש אמר בכל צרתם לו צר אמר ר' זירא מריש כי הוה חזינא להו לרבנן דיהבי אפר מקלה על גבי תיבה מזדעזע לי כוליה גופאי ולמה נותנין אפר בראש כל אחד ואחד פליגי בה ר' לוי בר חמא ור' חנינא חד אמר הרי אנו חשובין לפניך כאפר וחד אמר כדי שיזכור לנו אפרו של יצחק מאי בינייהו איכא בינייהו עפר סתם למה יוצאין לבית הקברות פליגי בה ר' לוי בר חמא ור' חנינא חד אמר הרי אנו חשובין לפניך כמתים וחד אמר כדי שיבקשו עלינו מתים רחמים מאי בינייהו איכא בינייהו קברי עכו"ם מאי הר המוריה פליגי בה ר' לוי בר חמא ור' חנינא חד אמר הר שיצא ממנו הוראה לישראל וחד אמר הר שיצא ממנו מורא לעובדי כוכבים: הזקן שבהן אומר לפניהן דברי כבושין: ת"ר אם יש זקן אומר זקן ואם לאו אומר חכם ואם לאו אומר אדם של צורה אטו זקן דקאמרי אף על גב דלאו חכם הוא אמר אביי הכי קאמר אם יש זקן והוא חכם אומר זקן והוא חכם ואם לאו אומר חכם ואם לאו אומר אדם של צורה אחינו לא שק ותענית גורמים אלא תשובה ומעשים טובים גורמים שכן מצינו באנשי נינוה שלא נאמר בהם וירא האלהים את שקם ואת תעניתם אלא וירא האלהים את מעשיהם כי שבו מדרכם הרעה ויתכסו שקים האדם והבהמה מאי הוו עבדי אסרא הבהמות לחוד ואת הוולדות לחוד אמרו לפניו רבונו של עולם אם אין אתה מרחם עלינו אין אנו מרחמים על אלו ויקראו אל אלהים בחזקה מאי אמור אמרו לפניו רבונו של עולם עלוב ושאינו עלוב (א) צדיק ורשע מי נדחה מפני מי וישובו איש מדרכו הרעה ומן החמס אשר בכפיהם מאי ומן החמס אשר בכפיהם אמר שמואל אפילו גזל מריש ובנאו בבירה מקעקע כל הבירה כולה ומחזיר מריש לבעליו אמר רב אדא בר אהבה אדם שיש בידו עבירה ומתודה ואינו חוזר בה למה הוא דומה לאדם שתופס שרץ בידו שאפי' טובל בכל מימות שבעולם לא עלתה לו טבילה זרקו מידו כיון שטבל בארבעים סאה מיד עלתה לו טבילה שנאמר ומודה ועוזב ירוחם ואומר נשא לבבנו אל כפים אל אל בשמים: עמדו בתפלה מורידין לפני התיבה זקן כו': תנו רבנן עמדו בתפלה אע"פ שיש שם זקן וחכם אין מורידין לפני התיבה אלא אדם הרגיל (איזהו רגיל) ר' יהודה אומר מטופל ואין לו ויש לו יגיעה בשדה וביתו ריקם ופרקו נאה ושפל ברך ומרוצה לעם ויש לו נעימה וקולו ערב ובקי לקרות בתורה ובנביאים ובכתובים ולשנות במדרש בהלכות ובאגדות ובקי בכל הברכות כולן ויהבו ביה רבנן עינייהו בר' יצחק בר אמי

היינו

רש"י

למתבייש מאחרים · דהיכא נמצא נפש טפי ומשום תשיעתם הם מתביישים מאחרים אבל שאר בני אדם דלא חשיבי לא מתביישי בנתינת אחרים וסגי להו בנתינת עצמן: פאר תחת אפר · ש"מ במקום תפילין דכתיב ביה (יחזקאל כד) פארך חבוש עליך ואמרינן (ברכות דף יא.) אלו תפילין ומתרגמינן נמי טוטפתך הויין עלך והיכא מניחין תפילין במקום שמוחו של תינוק רופף: בצינעא · בבית הכנסת: גלינו · שיצאנו מכניסתנו: (ב) גלותינו· תהא מכפרת עלינו: דגלו מבי כנישתא לבי כנישתא אחריתא · גלות איכא פרהסיא ליכא: נתבזה בעווניו · וידוי: [ולמה מתכסין]. תוגרות שקין תנינן בירושלמי שהיו חוגרות שקין ויוצאין לבית הקברות ותוקעין בקרנות ובעי ליה מיבעיא שקין למה ובית הקברות למה ותקיעת שופר למה: כבהמה · דמשער בהמה היינו מטלה של עזים: עפר סתם · שאינו אפר מקלה זכירת אפרו של יצחק ליכא התם לא גרסינן אלא איכא בינייהו עפר: קברי עכו"ם · במקום שאין קברי ישראל לבקש רחמים אפי' על עצמן ליכא כל שכן עלינו: מאי הר המוריה וכו' · איידי דאיירי בפלוגתא דרבי לוי ור"ח תנא נמי הא פלוגתא מאי הר מוריה דאברהם קרא למקום העקידה הר יראה וכתיב (בראשית כב) אל ארץ המוריה: חד אמר הר שילא (ג) הוראה · תורה לישראל כי מציון תצא תורה (ישעיה ב) יורו משפטיך ליעקב (דברים לג) ולשכת הגזית שבה עמדו הגבילים המוכיחים לישראל: מורא לעובדי כוכבים. ששומעין גדולות ישראל וירושלים ומתפחדים עליהם שמעתי לישנא אחרינא הר המוריה הר סיני מורא לעובדי כוכבים במתן תורה דכתיב (תהלים עו) ארץ יראה ושקטה: אע"ג דלאו חכם . אלא עם הארץ בתמיהה הא ודאי חכם עדיף: אם יש זקן והוא חכם · אומר זקן והוא חכם: אדם של צורה · בעל קומה שישמעו ויקבלו דבריו להמריך את הלב: מאי אמור · אנשי נינוה דכתיב בחזקה דמשמע בכח וניצוח דין: מי נדחה מפני מי · האי אומר לדיק מפני רשע: אם אין אתה מרחם כו' · כלומר כשם שאתה אומר לרחם על אלו דכתיב (תהלים קמה) ורחמיו על כל מעשיו כן תרחם עלינו: מריש · קורה: בירה · מגדל: שיש בידו עבירה · גזל: ואינו חוזר בו · לכנוס את הגזל למה הוא דומה וכו': נשא לבבנו אל כפים · עם הכפים צריך לישא הלב לשמים כלומר שיחזור מקלקולו: מטופל ואין לו · יש לו טפלים ואין לו במה להתפרנס שלבו דואג עליו [והוא צריך לקרות מקירות לבו עליהן]: ויש לו יגיעה · שמתכוין יותר בתפלת הגשמים: ופרקו נאה · מפרש לקמן: ושפל ברך · עניו: ומרוצה לעם · נוח לבריות ומסכימין לתפלתו: נעימה · בסומי קלא שמושך הלב: ורגיל לקרות כו' · שיהא הפסוקים של תפלה סדורין בפיו:

תוספות

במקום תפילין · פירוש לתת האפר במקום הפאר דהיינו התפילין נקראו פאר כדכתיב לשום לאבילי ציון לתת להם פאר וגו': **איכא** בינייהו דגלו מבי כנישתא לבי כנישתא · פירוש למ"ד משום גלות איכא ולמ"ד משום פרהסיא ליכא דהא בי כנישתא הוי כמו בצנעא:

אפר מקלה · פירוש אותו אפר הוה מדבר הנשרף מעצמות אדם כדי לזכור עקידת יצחק דאלמלא שלא היה בא אלא כדי לומר שהרי אנו לפניך כאפר כמו כן מהני עפר סתם והיינו פירוש איכא בינייהו עפר סתם:

יוצאין לבית הקברות · מכאן נוהגין בכל מקום לילך לבית הקברות בט' באב שהרי ט"ב הוי תענית לצבור כמו שהיו עושין מפני הגשמים:

הר שיצאה ממנו הוראה לישראל · י"מ דזה ירושלם שנקרא על שם אברהם שקראוהו הר ה' יראה (בראשית כב) (ד) והעיר היה נקרא כבר שלם כדכתיב (שם יד) ומלכי צדק מלך שלם ונקרא ירושלם על שם יראה ועל שם שלם לכך אין אנו נותנין יו"ד בירושלם בין למ"ד למ"ס על שם שלם וההר נקרא מוריה על שם תורה כדכתיב (ישעיה ב) כי מציון תצא תורה וכתיב (דברים לג) יורו משפטיך ליעקב והוא לשכת הגזית · המוריה זה סיני ונקרא מוריה על שם שממנו יצא מורא לעובדי כוכבים במתן תורה כדכתיב (תהלים עו) ארץ יראה ושקטה אי נמי רצה לומר דירושלם נקרא מוריה על שם שיש מורא לעובדי כוכבים על גדולתה ומתפחדים:

אדם שיש לו צורה · פירוש בעל קומה כדי שישמעו דבריו ויקבלו ממנו להמריך הלב ופרקו נאה פירוש כשעמד על פרקו אפילו כשהיה בחור היה בלא שם רע:

מאי

עין משפט נר מצוה

יד א מיי' פ"ד מהלכות תענית הלכה א טוש"ע א"ח סימן תקעט סעיף א:

טו ב מיי' שם הלכה ו טוש"ע שם ס"ג:

טז ג מיי' שם הלכה ד טוש"ע שם ס"א:

יז ד מיי' פ"ב מהל' תשובה הלכה ג:

יח ה מיי' פ"ד מהל' תענית הלכה ג טוש"ע א"ח סימן תקעט סעיף א [וסימן נג סעיף ד]:

[כל זה נתבאר במדרש רבה בראשית פ' נ"ו וכמ"ש בילקוט ערך ירושלם]

רבינו חננאל

רחמי אכולי עלמא · ולמה אינו נותן הנשיא ואב ב"ד הן בעצמן על ראשיהם שהמתבייש מן אחרים גדול הוא מהמתבייש עצמו · כלומר בושה גדולה היא כדי שיכוין כל לבו ותיכון מחית ליה לאפר זה בראשו במקום תפילין שנאמר לתת להם פאר תחת אפר: יוצאין לרחובה כדי לשבר הצבור לבם · כלומר צעקנו בצנעא ולא נענינו נבזה עצמנו בפרהסיא ור"ל אמר שתחשב לנו גלות כי הגלות מכפרת עון · ולמה מוציאין את התיבה לרחובה אריב"ל כלי צנוע היה לנו ונתבזה. נתינת אפר על גבי התיבה משום שנאמר בכל צרתם לו צר ולמה מתכסים בשקים לומר כי נחשבנו כבהמה וכל אחד נותן אפר בראשו לומר הנה אנו כאפר (אלי יזכור) [וי"א להזכר] זכות אפרו של יצחק (ופעמים) [וטעם] שיוצאין לבית הקברות כלומר הרי אנו כמתים וי"א שיבקשו מתים עלינו רחמים מאי הר המוריה הר שיצא ממנו הוראה לישראל · וי"א שיצא ממנו מורא לאומות: ירושלמי ונותנין אפר בראש נשיא · ר' אבהו ורבנן חד אמר חפא הנשיא הגדולה במקומה (כל ישראל נשאים) ושפא הצבור נחחית הגדולה וחד אמר לפי שהמא הלמד והמלמד לפיכך יצאו ויתפרסמו על שם והוציא את הפר מחוץ למחנה שירש הכל המאתו של כ"ג: נשא לבבנו אל כפים אל אל בשמים נשות לבבנו לכף ידינו כשם שכף ידינו נקיה כך ניקה לבנו ואח"כ אל אל בשמים י"ג דברים שבטלין רוע גזרה תפלה תשובה צדקה. ושלשתן בפסוק אחד נאמרו (דה"ב ז') ויכנעו עמי אשר נקרא שמי עליהם ויתפללו ויבקשו פני. ויתפללו זו תפלה, ויבקשו פני זו צדקה שנא' אני בצדק אחזה פניך. וישובו מדרכיהם הרעים זו תשובה · מה כתוב תמן ואני אשמע (מן) השמים ולמה יוצאין בין הקברות אם נתחייבנו רעב הרי אנו רעבים ומתענים · ואם נתחייבנו גלות הרי גלינו ממקום למקום · ואם נתחייבנו מיתה הרי אנו בבית הקברות כמתים וקרעו לבבכם ואל בגדיכם אם קרעתם לבבכם בתשובה אינכם קורעין בגדיכם על בניכם כי חנון ורחום הוא מאריך *) חמית: ת"ר אם יש שם זקן וחכם אומר זקן חכם ואם לאו אומר אדם של צורה אחינו לא שק ותענית גורמין אלא תשובה ומ"ט גורמין שלא נאמר באנשי נינוה וירא אלהים את שקם ואת תעניתם אלא וירא אלהים את מעשיהם כי שבו מדרכם הרעה אפילו מי שגזל מריש ובנאו בבירה היה מקעקע הבירה כולה ומחזיר המריש לבעליו: ת"ר אדם שיש בו עבירה ומתודה ואינו חוזר בו דומה למי שיש בידו שרץ שאפילו הוא טובל בכל מימות שבעולם אין טהרה שנאמר מכסה פשעיו לא יצליח זרקו כיון שטובל במ' סאה כו' שנאמר ומודה ועוזב ירוחם: מתני' עמדו בתפלה מורידין לפני התיבה זקן ורגיל: ת"ר אע"פ שאמרו אם יש שם זקן חכם אין מורידין לפני התיבה אלא רגיל רבי יהודה אומר דל שיש לו טף ויש לו יגיעה בשדה

*) פ"ס כאן עיין בירושלמי

רבינו גרשום

ודגלו מבי כנישתא [לבי כנישתא] למ"ד גלות הא איכא למ"ד פרהסיא ליכא: הרי אנו חשובין לפניו כבהמה שהרי לובשין שק שהוא של שיער בהמה: א"ב עפר סתם למ"ד הרי אנו חשובין לפניו כעפר בעפר סתם סגי למ"ד כדי שיזכור אפרו של יצחק מיבעי ליה אפר מקלה: קברי כותים למ"ד הרי אנו חשובין כמתים ה"נ מצי למיפסק לך לקברי אבות של נוים ומ"ד כדי שיבקשו עלינו רחמים איבעי להו למיפק לקברי ישראל: מאי הר המוריה למה נקרא שמה הר המוריה *) דאברהם קרא יראה ומלכי צדק קרא שלם ועשה הקב"ה פשרה ביניהם יקראו ירושלם: הר המוריה שיצאה ממנו הוראה לישראל שכן יושבין סנהדרין בלשכת הגזית ומורין הוראות: דברי כיבושין דברים שאדם סכבש ללבו: מי נדחה מפני מי כלומר דודה גזירתם מלפניו: מריש. קורה: ושוב שחוזר בו: ורגיל להתפלל שצ"ל זכרונות ושופרות לפי שאין זכרונות ושופרות אלא בר"הצ

*) נראה דחסר כאן איזה תיבות ואולי צ"ל דירושלים נקראת על שם אברהם כו' ועי' בתוס' כאן ד"ה הר:

הגהות הב"ח

(א) גמ' עלוב ושאינו עלוב יכול ודאי צדיק ורשע כו' ומחזיר מריש לבעליו ר"כ חמהן ישיב דמי אלא רק ליאוש כמשנה: (ב) רש"י ד"ה גלינו כו' וד"ה גלותינו כו' הד"א: (ג) ד"ה חד אמר הר שילא ממנו הוראה לישראל תורה שנאמר כי מציון: (ד) תוס' ד"ה הר כו' הר ה' יראה וה"ש מתחלה היה נקרא כך שלם כדכתיב ומלכי צדק מלך שלם ואח"כ נקרא ירושלים:

גליון הש"ס

גמרא כדי שיבקשו עלינו רחמים · עיין סוטה דף לד ע"ב תוס' ד"ה אבות:

Marginal notes:

יבעיה סא; תהלים פא; ישעיה סג; (ד"ה ב ג); יונה ג; שם; שם; שם; משלי כח; איכה ג

[גי' הרי"ף אמר רבי לוי בר חמא כו']

[גי' רי"ף ורא"ש ר' לוי בר חמא ור' חנינא]

[בילקוט יונה ר' אלך לי אל הר המור כו' הר המור פליגי בה כו']

[מגילה כט.]

[תוספתא פ"א]

[ליתא בר"ח אלפסי וגם בהרא"ש ע"ש]

היינו מטופל ואין לו היינו ביתו ריקם אמר רב חסדא "זהו שביתו ריקם מן העבירה: ופרקו נאה: אמר אביי "זה שלא יצא (*לו) שם רע בילדותו °היתה לי נחלתי כאריה ביער נתנה עלי בקולה על כן שנאתיה מאי נתנה עלי בקולה אמר מר זוטרא בר טוביה אמר רב ואמרי לה אמר רבי חמא אמר רבי אלעזר זה שליח צבור (*היורד לפני התיבה שאינו הגון): ואומר לפניהם עשרים וארבע ברכות שמונה עשרה שבכל יום ומוסיף עליהן עוד שש: הני שש שבע הוויין כדתנן על השביעית הוא אומר ברוך מרחם על הארץ אמר רב נחמן בר יצחק מאי שביעית שביעית לארוכה כדתניא "בגואל ישראל מאריך ובחותמה הוא אומר מי שענה את אברהם בהר המוריה הוא יענה אתכם וישמע בקול צעקתכם היום הזה ברוך גואל ישראל והן עונין אחריו אמן וחזן הכנסת אומר להם תקעו בני אהרן תקעו [א] וחוזר ואומר מי שענה את אבותינו על ים סוף הוא יענה אתכם וישמע בקול צעקתכם היום הזה ברוך זוכר הנשכחות והן עונין אחריו אמן וחזן הכנסת אומר להם הריעו בני אהרן הריעו וכן בכל ברכה וברכה באחת אומר תקעו ובאחת אומר הריעו: במה דברים אמורים בגבולין אבל במקדש אינו כן "לפי *שאין עונין אמן במקדש ומנין שאין עונין אמן במקדש שנאמר °קומו ברכו את ה' אלהיכם מן העולם עד העולם ויברכו שם כבודך ומרומם על כל ברכה ותהלה יכול על כל ברכות כולן לא תהא אלא תהלה אחת ת"ל ומרומם על כל ברכה ותהלה על כל ברכה תן לו תהלה ואלא במקדש מהו אומר ברוך ה' [ב] אלהים אלהי ישראל מן העולם ועד העולם ברוך גואל ישראל והן עונין אחריו ברוך שם כבוד מלכותו לעולם ועד וחזן הכנסת אומר להם תקעו הכהנים בני אהרן תקעו וחוזר ואומר מי שענה את אברהם בהר המוריה הוא יענה אתכם וישמע בקול צעקתכם היום הזה ברוך ה' אלהי ישראל [ג] זוכר הנשכחות והם עונים ואחריו בשכמל"ו וחזן הכנסת אומר להם הריעו הכהנים בני אהרן הריעו וכו' וכן בכל ברכה וברכה באחת אומר תקעו ובאחת אומר הריעו עד שגומר את כולן וכך הנהיג ר' חלפתא בצפורי ור' חנניה בן תרדיון בסיכני וכשבא דבר לפני חכמים אמרו לא היו נוהגין כן אלא בשערי מזרח ובהר הבית ואית דאמרי כדתניא אומר לפניהן עשרים וארבע ברכות שמונה עשרה שבכל יום ומוסיף עליהן עוד שש ואותן שש היכן אומרן בין גואל לרופא חולי ומאריך בגאולה והן עונין אחריו אמן על כל ברכה וברכה וכך היו נוהגין בגבולין אבל במקדש היו אומרים ברוך ה' אלהי ישראל מן העולם ועד העולם ברוך גואל ישראל ולא היו עונין אחריו אמן וכל כך למה לפי שאין עונין אמן במקדש ומנין שאין עונין אמן במקדש שנאמר קומו ברכו את ה' אלהיכם מן העולם ועד העולם ויברכו (את) שם כבודך ומרומם על כל ברכה ותהלה על כל ברכה וברכה תן לו תהלה: תנו רבנן "על הראשונות הוא אומר ברוך ה' אלהי ישראל מן העולם ועד העולם ברוך גואל ישראל והן עונין אחריו ברוך שם כבוד מלכותו לעולם ועד וחזן הכנסת אומר תקעו כהנים תקעו וחוזר ואומר מי שענה את אברהם בהר המוריה הוא יענה אתכם וישמע בקול צעקתכם היום הזה (והן תוקעין ומריעין ותוקעין) ועל השניה הוא אומר ברוך ה' אלהי ישראל מן העולם ועד העולם ברוך זוכר הנשכחות והן עונין אחריו ברוך שם כבוד מלכותו לעולם ועד וחזן הכנסת אומר הריעו בני אהרן הריעו ואומר מי שענה את אבותינו על ים סוף הוא יענה אתכם וישמע בקול צעקתכם היום הזה והם מריעין ותוקעין ומריעין וכן בכל ברכה וברכה באחת אומר תקעו ובאחת אומר הריעו עד שיגמור את הברכות כולן וכך הנהיג ר' חלפתא בצפורי ור' חנניה בן תרדיון בסיכני וכשבא דבר אצל חכמים אמרו לא היו נוהגין כן אלא בשערי מזרח ובהר הבית: ר' יהודה אומר לא היה צריך לומר זכרונות כו': א"ר אדא דמן יפו מאי טעמא דר' יהודה לפי שאין אומרים זכרונות ושופרות אלא

רש"י

הייתו מטופל ואין לו הייתו ביתו ריקן · היינו כמו (*איזהו): ביתו ריקם מן העבירה · שאין חמס וגזל בביתו: ופרקו נאה · אפילו כשעמד על בחרותו היה נאה בלי שם רע: זה המעמיד חזן שאינו הגון לפני התיבה · רשע שהקב"ה שונא אותו יותר מכולן והוא נותן בקולו לפניו: שביעית לארוכה · שביעית לאותה ברכה שהתחיל להאריך בה ואותה אינה מן התוספת אלא מי"ח ברכות היא כדתניא בגואל ישראל הוא מאריך: הוא אומר לפניהן · אותו הזקן הרגיל ומאריך בגאולה כדקתני מתני': בד"א · דהן עונין אחריו אמן בגבולין: אבל במקדש · אומר אותו הזקן לאחר הפרשיות מי שענה את אברהם הוא יענה אתכם וישמע קול צעקתכם ביום הזה בא"י אלהי ישראל מן העולם ועד העולם ברוך גואל ישראל והן עונים אחריו בשכמל"ו וכן בכל ברכות אדחקדה: לפי שאין עונין אמן במקדש · כדיליף לקמן מקרא: מניין שאין עונין אמן במקדש · דכתיב בתפלת עזרא בבית שני קומו "וברכו את ה' אלהיכם והייתו ברוך ה' אלהי ישראל כו': ויברכו שם כבודך · היינו שעונין אחריו בשכמל"ו כך הוא הפסוק ויברכו שם כבודך ומרומם על כל ברכה ותהלה: ה"ג יכול על כל הברכות כולן תהלה אחת ת"ל על כל ברכה על כל ברכה תן לו תהלה: חזן הכנסת · לא אותו זקן ניהו וחוזר חזן הכנסת ואומר להן מי שענה כו' אע"פ שאמרו אותו זקן: כשמריעין · תחלה הוא אומר להן הריעו בני אהרן וכשתוקעין תחלה הוא אומר להן תקעו בני אהרן כו': וכך הנהיג · כל מנהג זה רבי חלפתא בצפורי: לא היו נוהגין כן · שיהו עונין אחריו ברוך שם כבוד מלכותו לעולם ועד אלא עונין אמן בגבולין: ואית דאמרי כדתני' כו' · כלומר ואיכא דמתני הכי: וכן הנהיג · מנהג זה אמקדש קאי: אלא

תוספות

מאי שביעית שביעית לארוכה · פירוש שמתחילין להאריך ולומר בקשות ותחינות בתוך ברכה של גואל ישראל אבל מ"מ אינה בכלל התוספות בימי תענית דלא היו מוסיפין רק ששה ועל כל הברכות יש טעם על מה הם חותמות בכך הראשונה של גואל אינה מן המנין וכה אומרים מי שענה לאברהם לפי שהיה ראשון לגאולין שניצול מנמרוד ובשניה שהיא ראשונה מן הששה הנוספות אמר מי שענה לאבותנו על ים סוף וחותם ברוך זוכר הברית ולפיכך אומרה בזכרונות לפי שהיו במצרים ונתייאשו מן הגאולה ועליו נאמר (שמות ו) ואזכור את בריתי וכן בשלישית שהיא שניה מן המנין שומע תרועה ביהושע שנענה בירחו דהיינו בעוד ישראל בגלגל בשופרות היה אומר מי שענה ליהושע בגלגל לפי שנענה בשופרות על הרביעית והיא שלישית מן המנין מי שענה לשמואל וכו' ובשמואל כתיב צעקה ותפלה וגבי אליהו כתיב תפלה ענני ה' ענני ואמרינן בגמרא דצעקה גבי שמואל ותפלה גבי אליהו וי"א תפלה גבי שמואל וצעקה גבי אליהו דהא דכתיב ענני גבי אליהו הוא צעקה שמואל במצפה מעין אל ה' בצרתה לי לאליהו בהר הכרמל כנגד אשא עיני אל ההרים וכן כולם:

ברוך מרחם על הארץ · דגבי דוד ושלמה שייך לומר על הארץ דדוד ושלמה התפללו על הארץ דוד גבי מלאך המות בגורן ארונה ושלמה בתפלה דקאמר רעב כי יהיה בארץ ועוד יש לומר משום דאתקין בהמ"ק בארץ ולא קשיא הא דחשיב יונה מקמי דוד אע"ג שהיה קודם משום דבעי למיחתם על הארץ כדמפרש בגמרא:

עין משפט נר מצוה

יט א ב מיי' פ"ד מהל' תענית הלכה ג טוש"ע א"ח סימן תקעט סעיף א [וסימן נג סעיף ד]:

כ ג מיי' שם הלכה ו טור א"ח סי' תקעט:

כא ד ה מיי' שם הלכה טו:

רבינו חננאל

בשדה וביתו ריקם מעבירה ופרקו נאה שלא יצא עליו שם רע בילדותו שפל ברך ומרוצה לעם ויש לו נעימה וקולו ערב ובקי לקרות בתורה ובנביאים ובכתובים ולשנות במדרש בתלמוד בהלכות ובאגדות ובקי בכל הברכות כולן יהבי ביה רבנן עינייהו בר' יצחק בר אמי: היתה לי נחלתי כאריה ביער א"ר אלעזר זה ש"ץ היורד לפני התיבה שאינו הגון: ירושלמי ר' אחא בשם רב אמר אין תענית עכשיו א"ר יוסי הדא אמרה אלין תעניתא דאנן עבדין לית קריין תעניתא · א"ל כן אמיר רבנן כל תענית שאינה נעשית (במצותה) [כתיקונה] עליו הכתוב אומר נתנה עלי בקולה על כן שנאתיה: אומר לפניהם כ"ד ברכות י"ח שבכל יום מוסיף עוד שש. ואלו הן זכרונות ושופרות כו': ואקשינן והתנן על השביעית הוא אומר כו' · הנה ז' ברכות מוסיף ואמאי תנינן ומוסיף עוד שש ושנינן שביעית לארוכה כלומר מוסיף ומאריך בגואל ישראל · נמצאת ברכת גואל ישראל ארוכה שהיא מכלל י"ח ברכות ושש מוסיפין הויין ז' ארוכות ועלה תנן על השביעית הוא אומר ובדתניא בגואל ישראל הוא מאריך ובחותמה אומר מי שענה את אברהם אבינו בהר [המוריה] ··· ק' צ' ב' ה' ב' (ר"ת הוא יענה אתכם וישמע קול צעקתכם ביום הזה ברוך) גואל ישראל · והן עונין אחריו אמן · וחזן הכנסת אומר תקעו בני אהרן תקעו ותוקעין ומריעין ותוקעין וכן בכל ברכה וברכה באחת אומר תקעו בני אהרן תקעו ובא' אומר הריעו בני אהרן הריעו במה דברים אמורים בגבולים אבל במקדש אינו אומר אלא ברוך ה' אלהי ישראל מן העולם ועד העולם ברוך גואל ישראל והן עונין אחריו בשכמל"ו לפי שאין עונין אמן במקדש שנא' קומו ברכו את ה' אלהיכם ואומר ויברכו שם כבודך ומרומם וגו' על כל ברכה תן לו תהלה וכן הנהיג רבי חלפתא בצפורי וכשבא דבר אצל חכמים אמרו לא היו עושין כן אלא בשערי מזרח ובהר הבית בלבד · תניא אומרים לפניהם כ"ד ברכות י"ח שבכל יום ומוסיף עליהן עוד שש והיכן אמרו הני שש ברכות בין גואל לרופא ועונין אמן אחר כל ברכה ותוקעין על כל אחת ואחת כו' על הראשונה הוא אומר מי שענה את אברהם אבינו בהר המוריה כו' · בשניה מי שענה את משה ואבותינו על ים סוף כו' בשלישית מי שענה את יהושע בגלגל ברביעית מי שענה את שמואל במצפה · בחמישית מי שענה את אליהו בהר הכרמל כו'

מסורת הש"ס

[נ"ל זהו וכ"א בר"י שבע"י וכ"א בר"ף וברא"ש]

[נ"ל עליו כך בי' הערוך ערך פרק]

[נ"ל שאינו הגון היורד לפני התיבה וכ"א ברש"י ד"ה זה]

נ"ל ברכו

ברכות סג. סוטה מ:

ירמיה יב

נחמיה ט

הגהות הגר"א

[א] גמרא (וחוזר ואומר) תא"מ: [ב] שם (אלהים) תו"מ: [ג] שם (ה' אלהי ישראל) נ"ב מן העולם ועד העולם:

רש"א מוחק זה

רבינו גרשום

ואומר ואתמיק שחותם בברכה לכל פסוק: מטופל (ובנין) [ואין] לו כלומר שיש לו טיפול בנים ואין לו עושר: ויש לו יגיעה בשדה שעשרותיו וזרועות שצריכין לגשמים: וביתו ריקם שאין לו עושר: שפל ברך ענוי: ויש לו נעימה שיודע לבסם קולו: שבע לארוכות כלומר ודאי אין מוסיפין על שש אלא הא דקתני שבע דארוכות הן שבע דגואל ישראל שבתפלה הוא מאריך ובכאן ואילך אמר אילו שש שהן כמו ארוכות: בד"א שעונין אמן *) קומו וברכו את ה' כן העולם ועד העולם כלומר במקום אמן יש לענות אחר (ברכו) [הברכה] (אמרו) [ולומר] ברוך ה' מן העולם ועד העולם על כל הברכות אין עונה אמן אלא פעם אחת (ת"ל וכו') וכן הנהיג ר' חלפתא בצפורי · לומר שלאחר ברכה זו מי שענה כו': לא היו נוהגין כן אלא בשערי מזרח במקדש אבל בגבולין אומר העניות קודם ברכות כדאמרן לעיל: משום דבעי למיחתם במרחם על הארץ ועיקר א"י בימי דוד ושלמה: ואמר כל הברכות כולן על הסדר וענו אחריו אמן אחר כל ברכה וברכה: וכשבא דבר לפני חכמים שאמרו העניה אחר הברכה אמרו לא היו נוהגין כן אלא בשערי מזרח במקדש אבל בגבולין

*) נראה דחסר כאן וצ"ל כד"א שעונין אמן בגבולין אבל במקדש אינו כן שנאמר קומו כו'.

אלא בראש השנה וביובלות ובשעת מלחמה: על הראשונה הוא אומר מי שענה את אברהם כו' : תנא יש מחליפין צעקה לאליהו ותפלה לשמואל בשלמא גבי שמואל כתיב ביה תפלה וכתיב ביה צעקה אלא גבי אליהו תפלה כתיב צעקה לא כתיב
מ"א יח °ענני ה' ענני לשון צעקה היא : על הששית הוא אומר מי שענה את יונה כו' על השביעית הוא אומר מי שענה את דוד כו' : מכדי יונה בתר דוד ושלמה הוה מאי טעמא מקדים ליה ברישא מש"ם דבעי למיחתם מרחם על הארץ תנא משום סומכוס אמרו ברוך משפיל הרמים : שלש תעניות הראשונות אנשי משמר מתענין ולא משלימין כו' : תנו רבנן "מפני מה אמרו אנשי משמר מותרין לשתות יין בלילות אבל לא בימים שמא תכבד העבודה על אנשי בית אב ויבואו ויסייעו להם מפני מה אמרו אנשי בית אב לא ביום ולא בלילה מפני שהן עסוקין תמיד בעבודה מכאן אמרו כל כהן שמכיר משמרתו ומשמרת בית אב שלו ויודע שבתי אבותיו קבועין שם אסור לשתות יין כל אותו היום במכיר משמרתו ואין מכיר משמרת בית אב שלו ויודע שבתי אבותיו קבועין שם אסור לשתות יין כל אותה שבת אינו מכיר משמרתו ומשמרת בית אב שלו ויודע שבתי אבותיו קבועין שם אסור לשתות יין כל השנה *רבי אומר אומר אני אסור לשתות יין לעולם אבל מה אעשה שתקנתו קלקלתו אמר אביי כמאן שתו האידנא כהני חמרא כרבי : אנשי משמר ואנשי מעמד אסורים לספר ולכבס ובחמישי מותרין מפני כבוד השבת : מאי טעמא *אמר רבה בר בר חנה אמר ר' יוחנן כדי שלא יכנסו למשמרתם כשהן מנוולין ת"ר *מלך מסתפר בכל יום כהן גדול מערב שבת לערב שבת כהן הדיוט אחת לשלשים יום מלך מסתפר בכל יום מ"ט
ישעיה לג אמר רבי אבא בר זבדא אמר קרא °מלך ביפיו תחזינה עיניך כהן גדול מע"ש לערב שבת מ"ט אמר רב שמואל בר יצחק הואיל ומשמרות מתחדשות כהן
יחזקאל מד הדיוט אחת לשלשים יום מגלן אתיא פרע פרע מנזיר כתיב הכא °וראשם לא יגלחו ופרע לא ישלחו וכתיב התם °קדוש יהיה גדל פרע שער ראשו
במדבר ו מה להלן שלשים אף כאן שלשים ונזיר גופיה מגלן אמר רב מתנה *סתם נזירות שלשים יום מגלן אמר קרא יהיה בגימטריא תלתין הוי א"ל רב פפא לאביי ודילמא ה"ק רחמנא לא לירבו כלל אמר ליה אי הוה כתב לא ישלחו פרע כדקאמרת השתא דכתיב ופרע לא ישלחו פרע ליהוי שלוחי הוא דלא לישלחו אי הכי אפילו האידנא נמי דומיא דשתויי יין מה שתויי יין בזמן ביאה הוא דאסור שלא בזמן ביאה שרי אף הכא נמי והתניא *רבי אומר אומר אני כהנים אסורין לשתות יין לעולם אבל מה אעשה שתקנתו קלקלתו ואמר אביי כמאן שתו האידנא כהני חמרא כרבי

תורה אור

מסורת הש"ס

[נ"ל ויזעק שמואל אל ה' בעד ישראל]

הגהות הב"ח
(א) רש"י ד"ה דבעי למחתם כו' על ארץ ישראל (כך שמעתי) תא"מ וג"ב נ"ל דוס פשוט: (ב) ד"ה רבי אומר כו' אבל מה אעשה שתקנתו קלקלתו דהוי כמה שנים שלא חזרה עבודה וקלקלה זו תקנתו : (ג) תוס' ד"ה לא כו' וי"ל · ר"ל נ"ב זה לא גרס שלא כלל :

סנהדרין כב:

[מו"ק יד.]

סנהדרין כב: [כל הסוגיא עד סופו וע"ש כמה וכמה שינוים]

נזיר ה. לט. סנהדרין שם ע"ש מו"ק יט:

סנהדרין שם

הגהות מהר"ב רנשבורג
[א] רש"י ד"ה אסור לשתות יין וכו' והו לא שמא וכו' נ"ב פי' הו לא אסור משום שמא יבנה וכו' ותכבד עבודה דבלי האי לא גזרינן כמ"ש רש"י בד"ה ואינו יודע וכו' ולא חיישינן וכו' עכ"ל ולפיכך אסור רק אותו יום לחוד ולק"מ קושית מהרש"א ודו"ק· שוב ראיתי כן בש"י : [ג] שם ד"ה לא לירבו כלל אלא יסתפרו בכל יום · נ"ב נ"ע דלפ"ז מה יענה לקושי' התוס' ד"ה לא לירבו וביותר יפלא דסוף לשון רש"י הוא כמעט כתירוץ התוספות ונמצאו דברי רש"י סותרים תוך כדי דיבור :

אלא בראש השנה · כדאמרינן בר"ה (דף טז.) אמרו לפני מלכיות וזכרונות וכו' : וביובל · ביום הכפורים של יובל כדתנן התם (דף כו:) שוה היובל לר"ה לתקיעה ולברכות כו' : ובשעת מלחמה · דכתיב (במדבר י) וכי תבאו מלחמה בארצכם על הצר הצורר אתכם וגו' ולא ידעינן מנא איתפרים דאומר ברכות ופסוקי מלכיות זכרונות ושופרות בשעת מלחמה : צעקה לאליהו · על מי שענה את אליהו חותם שומע צעקה ובשמואל שומע תפלה דכתיב ביה תפלה (שמואל א ז) קבצו את כל ישראל המצפתה ואתפלל בעדכם: צעקה · דכתיב (שם טו) ויחר לשמואל ויזעק אל ה' כל הלילה והיכא למימר במצפה הוה ההיא צעקה דבתר פרשת קבצו כל ישראל המצפתה כתיב בפרשת *נחמתי כי המלכתי את שאול וגו' כך שמעתי : גבי אליהו · במעשה דהר הכרמל כתיב תפלה דכתיב ענני ה' ענני דמשמע לשון בקשה ותפלה ולא לשון צעקה ומשני ענני ה' ענני לשון צעקה הוא כך שמעתי : יונה בתר דוד ושלמה · דהוה בימי אמציהו בסדר עולם : דבעי למחתם · בסוף כל ברכות ברוך מרחם על הארץ ולהכי בעי בא תה חתימה דוד ושלמה שהן התפללו על ארץ ישראל (א) כך שמעתי אי נמי משום דאינהו תקון בית המקדש דהוא עיקר הארץ כך שמעתי : ברוך משפיל הרמים · היו אומרים במקום ברוך מרחם שהכניעם במטר ששבו בתשובה : מכאן אמרו · מדקתני הכא דאפילו אנשי משמר שלא היו עובדין באותו היום כלל אפילו הכי אסורין לשתות יין : כהן · בזמן הזה : המכיר משמרתו · היודע מאיזו משמרת הוא מיהויריב או מידעיה או אחת מכ"ד משמרות שיודע שמות אבותיו ואבות אבותיו עד יהויריב ויודע איזה יום ואיזה שבת היו עובדים : קבועין · שיודע ודאי שבית אב שלו עובד במקדש לפי שהרבה היו מבני אבות הכהנים שלא הוקבעו שוב אמר לי רבי קבועין שלא נתחלל בית אב שלו להיות מגואל מן הכהונה ויודע שראוי בית אב שלו לעבוד : אסור לשתות יין כל אותו היום · [א] והו לא שמא יבנה בית המקדש ותכבד העבודה ויהיה זה צריך לעבוד : מכיר משמרתו · שיודע איזה שבת בשנה עובדין : ואינו יודע מאיזה בית אב · דעכשיו אינו מכיר באיזה יום בשבת עובדין ויודע שבתי אבותיו קבועין אסור כל אותה שבת מספיקא בכולהו גרסינן ויודע שבתי אבותיו קבועין הן דאם אינו יודע שבתי אבותיו קבועין לעבוד מותר הוא לשתות יין כל השנה ולא חיישינן שמא יבנה ושמא בית אב שלו יעבדו היום : רבי אומר אומר אני כהן אסור כו' · כלומר אי חיישינן לשמא יבנה יהא אסור לעולם אפי' המכיר משמרתו ומשמרת בית אבותיו דחיישינן שמא ישתנה סדר משמרות ושמא יעבדו כולם לחנוכת הבית בבת אחת ונמצא זה צריך לעבוד אבל מה אעשה (ב) שתקנתו קלקלתו דהוי כמה שנים שלא חזרה בירה וקלקלה זו תקנתו לשתות יין בהדיא ולשמא יבנה לא חיישינן : כשהן מנוולין · שלא יהו סומכין על יום אחד מימי שבת ולא מספרין בשבת שעברה : מסתפר בכל יום · מלוה : מערב שבת לערב שבת · ולא ישהה מלגלח יותר: ומשמרות מתחדשות· בכל שבת ושבת ומשמרה שלא ראתהו עד עכשיו ובאה לראותו הדבר נאה שתראהו ביופיו: לא לירבו כלל· [ג] אלא יסתפרו בכל יום דהכי משמע ופרע דהייט שלשים לא ישלחו אלא יגלחו : שלוחי לא משלחי · הכי משמע פרע שגדלו אינן רשאין לגדל עוד : אי הכי · כיון דמקרא מפקת לה האידנא נמי לא לישלחו ומשני כיין דומיא דיין דכתיב בסמוך להאי ופרע לא ישלחו ויין לא ישתו כל כהן : מה יין בזמן ביאה הוא דאסור · דכתיב (יחזקאל מד) בבואם אל החצר וגו' בזמן שבית המקדש קיים שבאין שם לעבוד : שלא בזמן ביאה · כגון האידנא שהבית חרב ולא זמן ביאה היא : והתניא רבי אומר אומר אני כו' ואמר אביי כו'. מכלל דרבנן אסרי דחיישינן לשמא יבנה ומלי נמי מייתי רישא דברייתא מפני מה אמרו אנשי משמר כו' ואייתי סיפא בלשון קצרה ודייק מינה מכלל דרבנן אסרי :

ויודע שבתי אבותיו קבועין לשם אסור לשתות יין וכו' · פירוש אסור לשתות יין תוך לסעודתו אבל בסעודתו מותר דיין שבתוך הסעודה אינו משכר :

ובחמישי מותרין מפני כבוד השבת מאי טעמא · פי' מאי טעמא אין הכהנים מותרין להסתפר אלא דווקא בחמישי בשבת כדי שלא יכנסו למשמר כשהן מנוולין פי' ולא ימתינו עד יום אחד מימי השבוע הבא ויסתפרו קודם שיכנסו למשמרת דאם לא יסתפרו קודם יהיו אסורין כל השבוע הבא עד יום החמישי ומתוך זה שאסרו לספר כל השבוע הבא יסתפרו קודם שיכנסו למשמרתם ולא יהיו מנוולים :

כהן גדול מסתפר מע"ש לערב שבת וכהן הדיוט אחד לשלשים יום · פירוש שאינו יכול להשהות יותר והאי דקאמר בסמוך השתא דכתיב פרע לא ישלחו פרע ליהוי פי' פרע ליהוי עד שלשים יום אם ירצה :

לא לירבו כלל · פירוש ואפילו עד ל' יום וקשה דאם כן ג"ש דפרע למה לי (ג) וי"ל דשמא ר"ע לא לירבו עד ל' יום אלא יגלח בכ"ט :

שלוחי לא משלחו · יותר משלשים יום :

מכלל

עין משפט
נר מצוה

כב א מיי' פ"א מהל' ביאת מקדש הלכה ב סמג עשין קעו :

כג ב ג ד מיי' שם הלכה ז :

כד ה מיי' שם הלכה יב ופ"ו מהלכות כלי המקדש הלכה יא :

כה ו מיי' פ"ב מהלכות מלכים הלכה ה :

כו ז מיי' פ"ה מהלכות כלי המקדש הל' ו :

כז ח מיי' פ"א מהלכות ביאת מקדש הלכה יא סמג עשין קעב :

כח ט מיי' פ"ג מהל' נזירות הלכה א ופ"א מהלכות ביאת מקדש הלכה יא סמג עשין רכ :

כט י מיי' פ"א מהלכות ביאת מקדש הל' י :

רבינו חננאל

ט' · על הששית מי שענה את יונה במעי הדגה על השביעית מי שענה את דוד ושלמה בנו בירושלים תנא יש שמחליפין צעקה לאליהו וחותמין בברכה החמישית ברוך שומע צעקה ובברכה רביעית שהיא מי שענה את שמואל וחותם ברוך שומע תפלה · ואסיקנא ענני ה' ענני דכתיב ביה באליהו לשון צעקה הוא · ואמאי חותם לדוד ושלמה בנו בסוף והלא אינהו קדימי ליונה משום דבעי למחתם ברוך מרחם על הארץ תנא סומכוס אומר בשביעית הוא אומר ברוך משפיל רמים : מתני' שלש תעניות הראשונות אנשי משמר כו' פי' הכהנים היו חלוקים כ"ד חלקים משמש שבוע ומתחלף יוצא זה ונכנס אחר ואותו החלק המשמש שבוע נקרא משמר וכל המשמר היו חולקין ו' חלקים כל אחד משמש יומו ויצא ונכנס אחר משמש למחר ונקרא חלק שהוא אחד משבעה במשמר בית אב · וכן הוא מפורש בתוספתא (דמכילתין) משמר שיש בו ד' בתי אבות או ו' בתי אבות או ח' או ט' משמר שיש בו ד' בתי אבות ג' מהן מקריבין כל אחד ב' ימים והרביעי מקריב יום אחד ומשמר שיש בו ח' בתי אבות כו' · משמר שיש בו ו' בתי אבות כל אחד משמר יומו וכן כל אחד ואחד ועל זה הסדר שנו בחיצונה אנשי משמר מותרין לשתות יין בלילות אבל לא בימים שמא יזדמנו אותו היום זבחים הרבה ותכבד העבודה על אנשי (בתי דין)בית אב ויסייעו אותן אבל אנשי בית אב אסורין לשתות יין בין ביום בין בלילה מפני שהן תדירין בעבודה ויש באלו כ"ד משמרות שהפילו גורלות מי שעלה גורלו ביום ראשון *)נקבע במשמרתו להיות הוא משמש ביום ראשון לעולם ומי שנקבע ביום שני כמוהו כגון שהיא משמרת יהויריב בתחלת ניסן בית אב פלוני באחד בשבת. בית אב פלוני בשני בשבת. וכן כולן לפיכך אמרו [המכיר] משמרתו באיזה חדש ובאיזה שבוע זמנו ובית אב שלו באיזה היום מן השבוע זמנו והוא מן הקבועים לעולם אסורין לשתות יין בו ביום מ"מ אמרינן שמא יבנה הבית ויהיה שתוי ואינו יכול לשמש בו ביום ומי שאינו מכיר בית אב שלו אבל מכיר באיזה שבוע זמן משמרתו אסור לשתות יין כל אותו שבוע ומי שאינו מכיר [לא] זה ולא זה אבל יודע שבתי אבותיו קבועין בעבודה אסור לשתות יין לעולם דבכל יום חיישינן שמא יומו הוא ר' אומר אומר אני כגון זה אסור לשתות יין לעולם **) אסור דרבנן וכדאמרין (אצל) [אבל] תקנתו קלקלתו וזה השמועה כולה בסנהדרין בסוף פ' כ"ג פי' כיון שנתקלקלה בבית אב שלו הותר שאפילו אם יבנה הבית אינו משמש עד שישב ב"ד של כהונה ויקבעוהו באיזה יום ישמש לפיכך עכשיו מותר וכן כל כהן שאינו בר עבודה ביום ידוע מותר ועל זה אמר אביי כמאן שתי האידנא כהני חמרא כרבי מכלל רבנן סברי

*) נראה דצ"ל ונקבע במשמרתו לגיוס כן הוא משמש וכו' . **) נראה דצ"ל וכדאמרו רבנן אבל תקנתו כו' .

רבינו גרשום

בגבולין אומר העננייה ואח"כ אומר הברכה כדאמר' לעיל : אנשי משמר מתענין ולא משלימין מתענין הואיל ואין עצמן עוסקין בקרבנות ולא משלימין דכיון דמשמר שלהן עוסקין בקרבן היום יו"ט הוא להם לפיכך אין משלימין: אנשי בית אב שמקריבין קרבן היום לא היו מתענין כלל הואיל ועוסקין בקרבן: שלש שניות. שכבר תקפה הצורה: אנשי משמר מותרין לשתות יין בלילות הואיל ואין עוסקין בקרבן היום : אנשי בית אב שעובדין היום לא ביום ולא בלילה הואיל דבלילות מקריבין נמי אברים ופדרים שלא נתעכלו מבערב : כל כהן שמכיר משמרתו ויודע מאיזה משמרה הוא ומשמרת בית אב שלו שיודע באיזה בית אב הוא ויודע שבתי אבותיו קבועין שיודעין באיזה יום עובדין בית אב שלו : אסור לשתות יין כל אותו היום אע"פ שאינו בירושלים אלא הואיל ויודע שהיום עובדין בית אב שלו ואסורין בין הוא נמי אסור : מכיר משמרתו שיודע מאיזה משמרה הוא ואינו מכיר משמרת בית אב שלו שאינו יודע מאיזה בית אב הוא : ויודע שבתי אבותיו קבועין שיודע שמשמרה שלו קבועין ועובדין בשבת [ו] אבל אינו יודע באיזה יום עובד בית אב שלו אסור לשתות יין כל השבת דשמא היום עובד בית אב שלו : ויודע שבתי אבותיו קבועין שיודע שבית אב שלו עובדין יום אחד בשנה שהרי כתיב הן *)ובית המקדש קיים רבי אומר אומר אני אם היה כהן בזמן ביהמ"ק קיים שאין מכיר משמרתו ומשמרת בית אב שלו היה אסור לשתות יין לעולם אבל מה אעשה שתקנתו קלקלתו כלומר חרבן ביהמ"ק שהיא קלקלתם תקנתם לשתות יין כרבי דאמר שתקנתו קלקלתו אבל חכמים אומרים אין מותרין לעולם כדי שלא יכנסו למשמרתם כשהן מנוולין שכשיודעין שאין יכולין לספר ולכבס במשמרתן מספרין ומכבסין קודם שיכנסו למשמרתם

*) ושם עובדין עבודה בזמן שביהמ"ק היה קיים כצ"ל .

עין משפט
נר מצוה

ל א ב מיי' פ"א מהל' ביאת מקדש הלכה ה ופ"ד מהלכות תפלה הל' יז סמג עשין ב ולאוין ש טוש"ע א"ח סימן קמ סעיף ב :

לא ג מיי' פ"א מהל' ביאת מקדש הלכה א סמג לאוין שם :

לב ד מיי' שם הי"ד :

לג ה מיי' שם הל' א :

לד ו מיי' שם הלכה יד :

כרבי מבלל דרבנן אסרי מ"ט מהרה יבנה בית המקדש ובעינן כהן הראוי לעבודה וליכא הבא אפשר דמספר ועייל אי הכי שתוי יין נמי אפשר דגני פורתא ועייל *כדרמי בר אבא דאמר רמי בר אבא °דרך מיל ושינה כל שהוא מפיגין את היין לאו מי איתמר עלה אמר רב נחמן אמר רבה בר אבוה *°לא שנו אלא כששתה שיעור רביעית אבל שתה יותר מרביעית כל שכן שדרך מטרידתו ושינה משכרתו רב אשי אמר °שתויי יין דמחלי עבודה גזרו בהו רבנן °פרועי ראש דלא מחלי עבודה לא גזרו בהו רבנן מיתיבי *ואלו שהן במיתה °שתויי יין °ופרועי ראש בשלמא שתויי יין בהדיא כתיב בהו °יין ושכר אל *תשת אלא פרועי ראש מנלן דכתיב °וראשם לא יגלחו ופרע לא ישלחו וכתיב בתריה ויין לא ישתו כל כהן בבאם אל החצר הפנימית ואיתקיש פרועי ראש לשתויי יין מה שתויי יין במיתה אף פרועי ראש במיתה ומינה אי מה שתויי יין דמחלי עבודה אף פרועי ראש דמחלי עבודה (*°לא כי איתקוש למיתה הוא דאיתקוש אבל לאחולי עבודה לא איתקוש) א"ל רבינא לרב אשי הא מקמי דאתא יחזקאל מאן אמרה א"ל וליטעמיך הא דאמר רב חסדא *) דבר זה מתורת משה לא למדנו ומדברי קבלה למדנו °כל בן נכר ערל לב וערל בשר לא יבוא אל מקדשי (לשרתני) הא מקמי דאתא יחזקאל מאן אמרה אלא גמרא גמיר לה °ואתא יחזקאל ואסמכה אקרא הבא נמי גמרא גמיר לה ואתא יחזקאל ואסמכה אקרא (*כי גמירי הלכה למיתה לאחולי עבודה לא גמירי) : כל הכתוב במגילת תענית דלא למיספד לפניו אסור לאחריו מותר: תנו רבנן *אלין יומיא דלא להתענאה בהון ומקצתהון דלא למיספד בהון מריש ירחא דניסן ועד תמניא ביה איתוקם תמידא דלא למיספד בהון מתמניא ביה עד סוף מועדא איתותב *חגא דשבועיא דלא למיספד בהון אמר מר מריש ירחא דניסן עד תמניא ביה איתוקם תמידא דלא למיספד למה לי מריש ירחא לימא מתרי בניסן ור"ח גופיה יו"ט הוא ואסור אמר רב לא נצרכה אלא לאסור יום שלפניו ושלפניו נמי תיפוק ליה דהוה ליה יום שלפני ראש חדש ר"ח דאורייתא הוא ודאורייתא לא בעי חיזוק דתניא *הימים האלה הכתובין במגילת תענית לפניהם ולאחריהם אסורין שבתות וימים טובים הן אסורין לפניהן ולאחריהן מותרין ומה הפרש בין זה לזה הללו דברי תורה *ודברי תורה אין צריכין חיזוק הללו דברי סופרים *ודברי סופרים צריכין חיזוק אמר מר מתמניא ביה עד סוף מועדא איתותב חגא דשבועיא דלא למיספד למה לי עד סוף מועד לימא עד המועד ומועד גופיה יום טוב הוא ואסור אמר רב פפא כדאמר רב לא נצרכא אלא

*) [במסקנא דגמ' זבחים יח. הצריך ולהבדיל בין הקודש לדרשה אחרינא ושתויי יין דמחלי עבודה יליף התם מג"ש דחוקה חוקה ממחוסר בגדים וקי"ע] **) [וכ"ה בגמרא מנחות סה. לבדיא]

מבלל דרבנן אסרי · פי' מכלל דרבנן אסרי לשתות יין משום דשמא יבנה ביהמ"ק ובעינן כהן ראוי לעבוד וליכא ומשני אפשר דמספר ועייל : בעינן כהנים הראויים לעבודה וליכא · וא"ת והלא כלא יין נמי אסורין בעבודה דטמאי מתים נינהו וצריכין הזאה ג' [וז'] ואמאי אסרי להו יין וי"ל דמ"מ מותרין בעבודת צבור דטומאה הותרה בצבור: פרועי ראש דלא מחלי עבודה · פי' (ה) דלא כתיב בסמוך ולהבדיל וגו' : (דבר תורה) : דבר זה מתורת משה לא למדנו · וא"ת נילף מק"ו ומה בעל מום שמותר באכילת קדשים כדדרשינן במסכת קדושין פרק האיש מקדש (דף נג.) וכל מנחה מחבת וכל מרחשת לכהנים יהיה איש כאחיו ואפ"ה בעל מום אסור לעבוד עבודה ערל שאסור באכילת קדשים דדרשינן פרק הערל (יבמות דף ע.) בג"ש תושב ושכיר מפסח דערל אסור בו אינו דין שאסור לעבודה וי"ל דהלל יוכיח שאינו אוכל בקדשים ואפ"ה כשר לעבודה וכדאמר פרק האומר (קדושין דף סו:) מדכתיב ברך ה' חילו ופועל ידיו תרצה דמשמע אפילו [חולין שבו] הוא רוצה בעבודתו אי נמי מבעל מום לא מצי יליף דאיכא למיפרך מה לבעל מום שכן עשו בו קריבין כמקריבים שכל הקריבין פסולים (ו) שהם בעלי מומים כמו המקריב תאמר בערל שלא עשה בו קריבין כמקריבין דמה ערלות שייך בבהמה : שתויי יין דמחללי עבודה · פי' דכתיב יין ושכר אל תשת וגו' ולהבדיל בין הקודש ובין *) החול : מריש ירחא דניסן ועד תמניא (דהא) [ביה] איתוקם תמידא · פי' כדמפרש במגילת תענית [פ"א] **) שהיו הבייתוסים אומרים שיחיד מתנדב תמיד משום דכתיב תעשה את הכבש אחד תעשה בבקר תעשה משמע יחיד והדרי להו את קרבני לחמי לאשי תשמרו להקריב לשון רבים :

כרבי הא רבנן מיסר אסרי · אפילו שלא בזמן ביאה : ומשני מאי טעמא כו' והכא כו' · מאי טעמא תירוצא הוא כלומר דטעמא מאי גזור רבנן ביין שמא יבנה כו' אבל גבי פרועי ראש לא גזרו דאפשר דמסתפר מיד והדר עייל לבית המקדש לעבודה : דרך מיל ושינה כל שהוא כו' : ושינה משכרתו · והאי שינוי איכא בכך מיהא : שתוי יין דמחלי עבודה · דכתיב יין ושכר אל תשת וסמיך ליה ולהבדיל בין הקדש ובין החול בין עבודה קדושה למחולל' דאי עבד עבודה שתוי יין חילל : פרועי ראש · דלא כתיב ביה חלל דלא נראה חילול : ואילו שבמיתה · בידי שמים במסכת סנהדרין באלו הן הנשרפין (דף פג.) : שתויי יין · במיתה דכתיב יין ושכר אל תשת בבואכם אל אהל מועד ולא תמותו דהייט מיתה בידי שמים מדלא כתיב יומת ואמר בשלמא כו' : ה"ג ומינה מה שתויי יין מחלי עבודה [redacted] לא גרס : כי גמירי הלכה למיתה. לאחולי עבודה לא גמירי : מחלי עבודה · חולין היא כל עבודתו שעבד: אף פרועי ראש · עבודתם מחוללת דלכל מילי איתקוש ותיובתא דרב אשי דאמר פרועי ראש לא מחלי עבודה: דרב חסדא · (א) בפרק שני דזבחים וקא בעי התם כהן ערל שמתו אחיו מחמת מילה מהו ואמר רב חסדא ט' ערל לב וערל בשר : הלכתא גמירי לה · מסיני : (ב) מריש ירחא דניסן עד תמניא ביה · דכל שמונה ימים נשאו ונתנו בדבר עד שנצחו את הצדוקין ועשו אותם יום טוב ודבר זה מפורש במנחות בפרק רבי ישמעאל ובמגילת תענית המטויה אללנו : דלא להתענאה בהון · שסלון אסורין בתענית ומקצתהון שיש בהן קלת חמורין כ"כ שבהספד נמי אסורין: (ג) איתוקם תמידא ואיתותב חגא דשבועיא · בענינים רבים חלקו בייתוסין עם חכמים ומפורשין במנחות ובמגילת תענית [פ"א] וה"ג התם בפ' ר' ישמעאל [ס"ה·] ת"ר אלין יומיא דלא להתענאה בהון ומקצתהון דלא למספד ירחא ניסן וירחא דניסן עד תמניא ביה איתוקם תמידא דלא למיספד ומתמניא ביה עד סוף מועדא איתותב חגא דשבועיא דלא *) למיספד : מריש ירחא דניסן ועד תמניא ביה איתוקם תמידא דלא למיספד· שהיו הצדוקים אומרים יחיד מתנדב ומביא תמיד מאי דרוש את הכבש אחד תעשה בבקר ואת הכבש השני תעשה בין הערבים מאי אהדרו להו את קרבני לחמי לאשי תשמרו להקריב לשון רבים הוא שיהו טולין באין מתרומת הלשכה : מתמניא ביה כו' עד דלא למיספד · שהיו בייתוסים אומרים עצרת אחר השבת הוא שהעומר מתחיל אחד בשבת שנאמר וספרתם לכם ממחרת השבת ניטפל להן רבן יוחנן בן זכאי וא"ל שוטים מניין לכם ולא היה אדם שהחזירו דבר חוץ מזקן אחד שהיה מפטפט כנגדו ואמר משה רבינו אוהב ישראל היה ויודע שעצרת יום אחד הוא עמד ותיקנה אחר שבת כדי שיהיו מתענגים שני ימים וכו' ודחו אותן והלכו להן בייתוסים מכח הפסוקין על כרחן וחזרו בהן (ע"כ הג') איתוקם תמידא דלא למיספד גרסינן ולא גרסינן להתענאה כדמוכח בסמוך דקתני לא נצרכה אלא לאסור את שלפניו ואי גרסינן להתענאה א"כ הייט רבי יוסי דאמר לפניו אסור והא ליכא למימר דרבי יוסי היא דקא פריך כמאן כרבי יוסי בתמיהה מכלל דכרבנן פסיקא ליה : עד סוף מועדא · פסח : חגא דשבועיא דלא למיספד · במגילת תענית [פ"א] מפרש מאי איתוקם : ור"ח יו"ט הוא · דכתיב קרא עלי מועד והוי ראש חודש אב (ד) בהאי מסכתא לקמן (דף כט·) : לאסור

*) ג"י רש"י במנחות להתענאה .

רבינו חננאל

כשמעתייהו ואביי דהוא כהן סבני עלי לא הוה שתי חמרא דהא אמר רבא לדביתהו דאביי ידענא ביה בנחמני דלא הוה שתי חמרא (כתובות סה ע"א) ונהגו [redacted] עכשיו כרבי . הכהנים והלוים אנשי משמר וישראל אנשי מעמד בשבוע המשמשין בעבודה אסורין לספר ולכבס כדי שלא יכנסו במשמרותם מנוולים כיון שיודעין שאסורים (אף) [או] מקריבין ומתקנים את עצמן ובחמישי מותרין לכבס ולספר מפני כבוד השבת : ת"ר מלך מסתפר בכל יום כ"ג מע"ש לע"ש הואיל ומשמרות מתחדשים כהן הדיוט אחד לשלשים יום · שנאמר וראשם לא יגלחו יכול לא יגלחו לעולם אלא יגדלו שערם ת"ל ופרע לא ישלחו לא יתנו שלוח לשער כלו' לא יאריכו שער להיות משלח לפניהם ולאחריהם כסים יכסו את ראשיהם אין להם לגדל אלא כשיעור כסוי הראש והוא שלשים יום כנזירות דכתיב ביה יהיה יהיה בגימטריא ל' וגמרינן פרע פרע מנזיר ואמאי לא גזרו בפרע כמו שגזרו ביין אמר רב אשי שתויי יין דמחלל עבודה גזרו בהו רבנן פרע ראש דלא מחלי עבודה לא [redacted] אלו שבמיתה שתויי יין ופרועי ראש כו' · ואסיקנא דאתקש פרועי ראש לשתויי יין במיתה ומינה מה שתויי יין מחלי עבודה אף פרועי ראש מחלי עבודה ושקלו וטרו ואמרינן האי עד דלא אתא יחזקאל וכתב ופרע לא ישלחו וכתיב בתריה ויין לא ישתו כל כהן תו' דגמרינן מינייהו דאתקוש לשתויי יין [אלא גמרא גמירי להו] ואתא יחזקאל ואסמכא אקראי וכי גמרא גמירי לה דפרועי ראש במיתה אבל לאחולי עבודה לא גמירי גמרא : כתני' כל הכתוב במגלת תענית די לא למספד כו' . ת"ר אלין יומא דלא להתענאה בהון ומקצתהון כו' · אמר מר ריש ירחא דניסן עד תמניא ביה איתוקם תמידא די לא להתענאה *) ואקשינן אמאי לא תני מתרי בניסן דהא ר"ח . נופא לא אצטריך ושני רב לאסור באדר ביום שלפניו ותניא ימים הכתובים במגלת תענית לפניהם ולאחריהם אסור · ואי משום ר"ח דאורייתא איסוריה ואין דברי תורה צריכין חיזוק וכן אקשי אסיפא דקתני מתמניא ביה ועד סוף מועדא איתותב חגא דשבועיא דלא למספד

*) ג"י רבינו כמו שהיתה הג' לפני כתוס' במנחות סה ע"ש.

מסורת הש"ס

[עירובין סד: סנהדרין כב: ע"ש]

עירובין סד: סנהדרין כב:

סנהדרין שם [redacted] [לו:]

[נ"ל אל תשת אתה ובניך ולא תמותו]

[כל זה ליתא בסנהדרין אלא מסיק שם קשיא ע"ש ותוספות שם] [וגם רש"א מוחק כל זה וגרס דמחלי עבודה קשיא] *) יומא עא: מו"ק ה. סנהדרין כב: סג: זבחים יח: כב:

[כל אלו מוחק הרש"ל בסנהדרין כב:]

[מנחות סה. [redacted] הספרים כתוס' ד"ה מריש]

[נתיסב על דינו שנאותן ימים נלחו חכמים את הבייתוסים רש"י שם במנחות] ר"ה יט.

[יבמות סה: [סב]

הגהות הב"ח

(א) רש"י ד"ה דרב חסדא בזבחים פרק שני דקא בעי התם: (ב) ד"ה מריש ירחא כו' נ"ל אחר ד"ה דלא להתענאה כו' : (ג) ד"ה איתוקם תמידא כו' וד"ה מריש ירחא כו' וד"ה מתמניא כו' עד על כרחן וחזרו בהן כד"א ואח"כ מה"ד ה"ג איתוקם תמידא וכו' אלא לאסור את יום שלפניו : (ד) ד"ה ור"ח אב כדאיתא בהאי מסכת : (ה) תוספות ד"ה פרועי כו' פי' דבר תורה דלא כתיב : (ו) ד"ה דבר כו' כשהן בעלי מומין :

רבינו גרשום

למשמרותם כשהן מנוולין הואיל ומשמרות מתחדשות שיראו אותו ביפיותו . ראשם לא יגלחו פרע לא ישלחו ראשם לא יגלחו משמע לא יגלחו כל שערותם לגמרי ופרע לא ישלחו משמע שלא יגדלו שערותם : ודילמא הכי אמרה רחמנא ופרע לא ישלחו דלא לירבו כלל אלא מסתפרין בכל יום: פרע להביא שיגדילו שערם כל שהוא דהיינו ל' יום שלוחי לא ישלחו יותר מדאי . אי הכי הואיל וילפת פרע פרע מנזיר אפילו האידנא נמי יהו אסורין בפרוע ראש נמי כהרי נזירות נוהג בזמן הזה : דומיא דיין דהא איתקש פרוע ראש ליין דכתיב ויין לא ישתו כל כהן וגו' בזמן ביאה למקדש אסור דכתיב יין ושכר אל תשת אתה ובניך אתך בבואכם אל אהל מועד: מכלל דרבנן אסרי בזמן הזה ביין ונימא דפרוע ראש בזמן הזה נמי אסור. תריץ מ"ט אסרי רבנן בזמה"ז מהרה יבנה ביהמ"ק וכו' אבל פרוע לא אסרי: כש"כ ששינה משכרתו ולהכי אסרי בשתויי יין דאי אפשר בתקנה אבל פרוע ראש דאפשר בתקנה לא אסרי: רב אשי אמר להכי אסרי רבנן שתויי יין בזמה"ז הואיל דחמור דהרי מחלל עבודה דאסרינן כתיב בשתויי יין חוקה דכתיב יין ושכר אל תשת וגו' וכתיב בבגדי כהונה חוקה דכתיב (והיתה להם כהונה לחקת עולם אתם] אבנט אהרן ובניו וגו' מה בגדי כהונה שאינו לובשן ושבר מחל עבודה כדאמרינן

גליון הש"ס גמרא ואתא יחזקאל ואסמכה אקרא · עיין יומא דף לב ע"ב וברש"י שם ד"ה מיסיני :

לה א מיי' פ"ב מהלכות מגילה הלכה יג :

אלא לאסור יום שלפניו ה"נ לא נצרכה אלא לאסור יום שלאחריו כמאן כרבי יוסי דאמר בין לפניו בין לאחריו אסור אי הכי בעשרים ותשעה נמי מאי איריא דהוי יומא דמקמי יומא דמיתוקם תמידא תיפוק ליה דה"ל יומא דבתר עשרין ותמניא ביה דתניא *בעשרים ותמני' ביה אתת בשורתא טבתא ליהודאי דלא יעידון מן אורייתא (א) שפעם אחת נגזרה גזירה על ישראל שלא יעסקו בתורה ושלא ימולו את בניהם ושיחללו שבתות מה עשה יהודה בן שמוע וחביריו הלכו ונטלו עצה ממטרוניתא אחת שכל גדולי רומי מצויין אצלה אמרה להם עמדו והפגינו בלילה הלכו והפגינו בלילה אמרו אי שמים לא אחים אנחנו לא בני אב אחד אנחנו לא בני אם אחת אנחנו מה נשתנינו מכל אומה ולשון שאתם גוזרין עלינו גזירות רעות ובטלום ואותו היום עשאוהו יו"ט אמר אביי לא נצרכה אלא לחדש מעובר רב אשי אמר אפילו תימא לחדש חסר א) כל שלאחריו בתענית אסור בהספד מותר וזה הואיל ומוטל בין שני ימים טובים עשאוהו כיו"ט עצמו ואפילו בהספד נמי אסור אמר מר מתמניא ביה ועד סוף מועדא איתותב חגא דשבועיא דלא למספד למה לי למימר מתמניא ביה לימא מתשעה ביה ותמניא גופיה אסור דה"ל יומא דאיתוקם ביה תמידא כיון דאילו מקלע (ליה) מילתא ובטליניה לשבעה תמניא גופיה אסור דה"ל יומא קמא דאיתותב ביה חגא דשבועיא השתא דאתית להכי עשרים ותשעה נמי כיון דאילו מיקלע מילתא ובטליניה לעשרים ותמניא עשרין ותשעה גופיה אסור דה"ל יומא דמקמי יומא דאיתוקם תמידא איתמר ר' חייא בר אסי אמר רב הלכה כר' יוסי ושמואל אמר הלכה כר' מאיר ומי אמר שמואל הכי והתניא רשב"ג אומר ומה תלמוד לומר בהון בהון שתי פעמים לומר לך שהן אסורין לפניהן ולאחריהן מותרין ואמר שמואל הלכה כרבן שמעון בן גמליאל מעיקרא סבר כיון דליכא תנא דמיקל כרבי מאיר אמר הלכה כרבי מאיר כיון דשמעיה לרבן שמעון (ב) דמיקל טפי אמר הלכה כרבן שמעון בן גמליאל וכן אמר באלי אמר רבי חייא בר אבא א"ר יוחנן הלכה כרבי יוסי א"ל רבי חייא לבאלי אסברא לך *כי אמר ר' יוחנן הלכה כרבי יוסי אדלא להתענאה ומי אמר רבי יוחנן הכי והאמר ב) ר' יוחנן הלכה כסתם משנה ותנן ג) *אע"פ שאמרו מקדימין [א] ולא מאחרין מותרין

א) עי' תוס' מנחות סה. ד"ה אלין יומא ב) [שבת מו. וש"נ] ג) מגילה ה.

רש"י

לאסור את שלפניו. להכי נקט מריש ירחא דניסן לאסור את יום שלפני ר"ח בתענית כדתניא בסמוך לפניהן אסורין דאי משום ר"ח לא היה נאסר כדמפרש דדברי תורה אין צריכין חיזוק: כמאן כר' יוסי. דמתני' דאמר אף לאחריו בתמיהה ושבקת רבנן אי הכי דאליבא דר' יוסי מוקמת לה למגילת תענית כ"ט באדר נמי דקתני לעיל דלהכי נקט ר"ח ניסן דהיינו יום שלשים דאדר הסמוך לניסן לעולם חסר מכ"ט יום הוא משום דקא בעי למיסר יום כ"ט תיפוק ליה דבלאו הכי האי אסור יום כ"ט דה"ל יום דבתר כ"ח שהוא י"ט כו' ואסור יום שלאחריו כר' יוסי ואמאי נקט ריש ירחא לאסור את שלפניו: דלא יעידון. שלא יהו צריכין ליבטל מתלמוד תורה שגזר עליהן שלא יעסקו בתורה: הפגינו. צעקו כך מתרגמינן בתהלים כל לשון שועה וצעקה לשון פגינה: אי שמים גרסינן אהה ה' להקב"ה היו צועקים על אותם שגזרו עליהם גזרות קשות והיו אומרים להם לפני הקב"ה וכי לא אחיכם וכו': לא נצרכה אלא לחדש מעובר. בשנה מעוברת שיש בה שני (ג) אדר והאחד חסר *דהשתא כי הוה אדר שני מלא הוה יום שלשים לפני ר"ח ניסן א"נ דעברוה לאדר כגון שלא נראה החדש יום ל' דמשום יו"ט דכ"ח לא מיתסר אלא כ"ט: (ד) רבא אמר אפילו תימא חדש חסר. והאי דנקט מריש ירחא דאי הוה אסר ליה ליום כ"ט משום בתר כ"ח לא הוה אסר ליה אלא בתענית לחודיה: דכל שלאחריו כו'. כלומר כל שאסור משום אחר י"ט בתענית הוא דאסור אבל בהספד מותר והאי דנקט מריש ירחא דלהוי האי כ"ט דנקט מוטל בין שני ימים משום דלאו מיתסר משום דלפני יו"ט אימור לא איתסר בהספד דהאי דנקט כל שלאחריו כו' לאו משום דלפניו נמי אסור בהספד אלא איידי דפריך דליתסר יום כ"ט משום בתר כ"ח הוא דמיהדר ליה כל שלאחריו כו': לימא מתשעה (ה) ותמניא גופיה. י"ט הוא דהא הוה ליה מהנך ימים טובים דאיתוקם בהו תמידא כדכתיב ביה מריש ירחא עד תמניא: ה"ג דאי איקלע מילתא ובטליני' לשבעה תמניא גופיה אסור דהוה ליה יומא (ו) דאיתותב חגי דשבועיא. דאי איקלע מילתא שאם עגר גזירה וצריכין להתענות תוך אלו ימים טובים דתמיד ובטלו אותן להתענות בכולן שאין לבטלה להלאן: אכתי יומא תמניא אסור משום חגא דשבועיא. ואי קשיא אכתי לימא תשעה ואפילו אם אירע מילתא דבטלי אכתי הוא אסור תמניא גופיה משום קמא יומא דחג שבועיא דהוה יום שלפניו לאו פירכא הוא דהא יו"ט גופיה בטיל ואגא ליקום וליגזור קמיה יומא דאיתותב חגא דשבועיא וכה"ג מתרץ לקמן ביום טורייטס: כ"ט נמי. דתנ"לת לה לעיל לא נצרכה כו' להכי נקט בריש ירחא דאי מיקלע כו': כרבי יוסי. דאמר בין לפניו בין לאחריו אסור: כר"מ. סתם מתניתין דקתני לאחריו מותר: מה ת"ל בהון בהון. דלא להתענאה בהון ומקלתהון דלא למספד בהון וקא דריש לה כדדייק לקמן בהון משמע מיעוט: ואמר שמואל גרס: הלכה כרבי שמעון (ז) דמדרבנן נינהו ולא מחמרינן כולי האי: באלי. שם חכם: ה"ג כי אמר רבי יוחנן הלכה אדלא להתענאה. דימים הכתובים במגילת תענית דלא להתענאה לפניהן אסורים ולאחריו מותרין כר' יוסי ולא כר"מ דאמר אף לפניהם מותר אבל אדלא למספד דאין הלכה כרבי יוסי [דאמר] לפניו ולאחריו אסור אלא כר"מ דאמר לפניו אסור לאחריו מותר: ומי א"ר יוחנן הכי. דלפניו מיהא אסור כרבי יוסי: מקדימין. שקראו קודם זמנה: מותרין

תוספות

הלכו והפגינו. הפגינו לשון נהי וצעקה. אי שמים גרסינן פירוש שמים להקב"ה היו צועקין למה יאמרו הגוים איה אלהיכם ולהם אמרו. וכי לאו אחיכם אנחנו וכו': לא נצרכה אלא לחדש מעובר. פירוש דעברוה לאדר שלא נראה הלבנה עד יום ל' והוי ר"ח ניסן יום ל"א פירוש וא"כ האי כ"ט לא מצית לאוסרו *משום יום שלפני ר"ח ניסן דיום ל' מפסיק בינתים משום הכי איצטריך לאוסרו משום יום שלאחר עשרים ותמניא: דאילן אי איקלע וכו'. שום גזרה מריש ירחא וכו' תמניא גופיה אסור דה"ל וכו' והקשה הקונטרס אכתי לימא תשעה ואפילו אי מיקלע שום גזרה ובטלינא לז' ימים וכו' אכתי אסור תמניא גופיה משום דהוי יומא דמקמי יומא דאיתותב חגא דשבועיא ותירץ הקונטרס הא לאו פירכא דהא מיו"ט גופיה דתמיד מבטלינן ליה ואגא ניקום ונגזור משום קמי יומא דאיתותב חגא דשבועיא (ח) וכי האי מתרצינן לקמן ביום טורייטס: רב אמר הלכה כר' יוסי דאמר לפניו אסור אבל לאחריו מותר. וא"ת כיון דאמר הלכה כר' יוסי היאך אנו מתענין לפני הפורים דאי משום דבטלה מגילת תענית מ"מ אחנוכה ואפורים לא בטלו וי"ל דהא דאמר חנוכה ופורים לא בטלו ר"ל הדינין שלהם לעשותן י"ט ודלא להתענאה בהון אבל בדינים דלפניהם בטלו. עוד י"ל (ט) דכיון דיום שלפני הפורים שנתבטל מיו"ט דידהו שהיו רגילין לעשות בהן ונתבטלו יו"ט שלהם ה"נ יש לנו לומר שיבטלו משום טעם לפני הפורים דה"נ אמרינן בסמוך גבי יום שלפני נקנור וכו' וכן גבי יו"ט טורייטס דכיון דבטלו מיוה (י) שלהם לא יאסרו משום יו"ט הבא אחריהם דאסורים משום יום שלפניהם כמו כן ה"נ דכיון דיום שלפני הפורים נתבטל משום עצמו ומותר להתענות לא יאסר משום יום שלפני הפורים: הלכה

רבינו חננאל

ליומא עד המועד. ומועד גופיה יום טוב הוא ולא צריך. ושנינן לאסור שלאחריו כר' יוסי דאמר ימים הללו בין לפניהם בין לאחריהם אסורין. אי הכי רישא דתני מריש ירחא דניסן. ואקשינא דלא תנא ר"ח אלא לאסור יום כ"ט באדר. למה לי תיפוק דהוה לי' יום שלאחר כ"ח באדר ועשאוהו יו"ט. משום דבו בטל שמדא ואתא בשורתא טבא ליהודאי דלא יעידון מן אורייתא. ושני אביי לא נצרכה זו ווו אלא אם יזדמן להתעבר יהיה יום כ"ט אסור בו משום שהוא יום אחר כ"ח בו ויום ל' נמי יהיה אסור משום שהוא יום דמקמי יומא דאיתוקם ביה תמידא. ואקשינן נמי למה לי למימר מתמניא בניסן ימים טובים משום דקבעי דאיתותב חגא דשבועיא. תיפוק ליה דהוה ליה מן הימים טובים דאיתוקם בהו תמידא ושנינן לא נצרכא אלא דאי הדרי ביה רבנן ובטלי לדעי יומי דקבעו משום דאיתוקם תמידא דלא בטלי מניהו אלא ז' יומי ויום ח' אסור מכלל יומא דאיתותב בהו חגא דשבועיא. השתא דאתית להכי כ"ט נמי דאי מקלעא כו' איתוקם תמידא ואיתותב חגא דשבועיא. מפורש במנחות בפרק רבי ישמעאל אומר עומר היה כו' איתוקם תמידא שהיו הצדוקים אומרים יחיד מתנדב ומביא תמיד דהוו דורשי את הכבש תעשה לשון יחיד ואהדרו להו רבנן את קרבני לחמי [תשמרו] שיהיו באין מתרומת הלשכה. והדרו דבריהם. ונתקיימו דברי רבותינו שלא יהיה תמיד בא אלא משל צבור. וכן הוו חולקים ואמרין אין עצרת חלה אלא לאחר שבת. ואהדרו להו רבנן ונדחו החזירו הדבר לירושנו שיהיו סופרים נ' יום ממחרת יו"ט של פסח. ולפי שנדחו דברי צדוקים ונתקיימו דברי חכמים עשאום אותם הימים טובים כימי גאולת מידי צירריהם. רב אמר הלכה כר' יוסי דאמר כל הכתוב במגלת תענית די לא למספד בין לפניו בין לאחריו אסור. [די לא להתענאה לפניו אסור] לאחריו מותר. ושמואל אמר הלכה כת"ק והוא ר"מ. ופתמא דמתני' דיליה היא דא' בדי לא למספד לפניו אסו' לאחריו מותר ובדלא להתענאה בין לפניו ובין לאחריו מותר איני והא' שמואל הלכה כרשב"ג דאמר לפניהם ולאחריהם מותרים. ושמואל הלכה לקולא גמירי. מעיקרא סבר ליכא תנא דמיקל טפי מת"ק דמתני' דהוא ר' מאיר. ואמר הלכתא כת"ק. כיון דחזא רשב"ג דמיקל טפי אמר והלכתא כרשב"ג. אמר באלי א"ר יוחנן

ר"ה יט.

הגהות הב"ח

(א) גמ' דלא יעידון מן אורייתא דלא למספד שפעם אחת כו' ואמרו אי שמים לא אחיכם אנחנו: (ב) שם דשמעיה לרבן שמעון בן גמליאל דמיקל: (ג) רש"י ד"ה לא נצרכה כו' שני אדרים ואחד חסר וכשני אדר חסר דהשתא כי הוי: (ד) ד"ה רבא אמר כו' שם ד"ה דכל שלאחריו וכו' מוטל בין שני ימים טובים דלא קאמר דאסור בהספד משום דהוי יום שלפניו כו' מיתסר כו' והאי דנקט כל שלאחריו: (ה) ד"ה לימא מתשעה ביה ותמניא: (ו) ד"ה ה"ג דאי כו' דהוה ליה יומא דאיתותב ביה חגא כנ"ל וד"ה עם ד"ה דאי וכו' אסור תמניא גופיה ולגזור משום קמייתא יומא דתנא: (ז) ד"ה הלכה כרבי שמעון כו' שמעון דמדרבנן: (ח) תוס' ד"ה דאילן וכו' וכה"ג נמי מתרצינן: (ט) ד"ה רב כו' ועוד י"ל דכיון דיומי שלפני הפורים נתבטלו: (י) בא"ד דכיון דבטלו מיום טוב שלהם אחריהם לאסורים משום:

הגהות הגר"א

[א] גמ' (ולא מאחרין) תא"מ :

רבינו גרשום

עליהם אין בגדיהם עליהם אין כהונתם עליהם אף פרועי ראש מחלי עבודה וכי היכי דאסרי שתויי יין בזמה"ז הכי ליסרו פרועי ראש. ותריצן הא דדייקת מינה לא כלום הוא דא"כ הוא עד שיבא יחזקאל מאן אמרה. בן נכר ערל לב זה כהן משומד בן שנתנכרו מעשיו לאביו שבשמים ערל בשר שמתו אחיו מחמת מילה הכא נמי פרועי ראש מחלי עבודה גמרא גמירי לה ואמאי לא אסרו רבנן פרועי ראש כבשתויי יין תריצן כי גמירי מה שתויי יין במיתה וכו' לאו למימר לא דייקינן האי ומינה אלא לעולם פרועי ראש לא מחלי עבודה להכי לא אסרי רבנן אע"ג דאסרי כשתויי יין: ה"ג מריש ירחא דניסן עד תמניא ביה איתוקם תמידא דלא למספד שהיו צדוקים אומרים מנין מתנדב יחיד תמיד שהיו דורשין את הכבש אחד תעשה שהוא לשון יחיד וחכמים אומרים אינו אלא מתרומת הלשכה שהרי כתיב ביה לאשי דמשמע שבא ממקום ששאר קרבנות באין מתרומת הלשכה. ומריש ירחא דניסן עד תמניא ביה נשאו ונתנו בדבר והודו מינין לחכמים: איתותב חגא דשבועיא דלא למספד שהיו מינין אומרין אין עצרת בא אלא [באחד] בשבת שהיו דורשין ממחרת השבת תספרו חמשים כלומר לאחר שבת בראשית הרי עצרת והכ"א כתיב חמשים יום דמשמע שבא חמשים יום קובע עצרת וכתיב שבע שבתות תמימות תהיינה דמשמע תמימות ממש מאחד בשבת כאן שחל עצרת באמצע שבת והיינו חמשים יום בלא שבע שבתות תמימות מאחד בשבת [כאן שחל עצרת באחד בשבת]: לא נצרכא לאסור שלפניו להכי קאמר דריש ירחא הוי יו"ט דבאדר בתענית ובהספד דאי משום מועד לא הוי אסור דדברי תורה אין צריכין חיזוק. כמאן כר' יוסי די לא למספד בין לפניו בין לאחריו אסור בהספד דאי דרבנן הא אמרו לאחריו מותר. אי הכי כיון כר' יוסי עשרין ותשעה באדר נמי מאי איריא דהוה יומא מקמי דאיתוקם תמידא וקאמר להכי ריש ירחא דניסן לאסור כ"ט באדר שלפניו תיפוק ליה דלהכי הוה אסור דהוה ליה יומא דבתר כ"ח דהוי יו"ט דאסור למספד והוי כ"ט אסור דהוא אמר ר' יוסי בין לאחריו אסור. עדיין פריכנא למה לי למימר מריש ירחא דניסן ליומא מתרי דניסן: והפגינו בלילה כדי שישמע קולם: אמר אביי להכי קאמר מריש ירחא לאסור שלפניו לחודש מעובר דהוי *) ל"א כ"ח קאסר ל' שלפניו דאילו משום כ"ח לא הוי אסור אלא כ"ט: ה"ג רב אשי אמר אפי' תימא בחודש חסר ודפרכת כיון דפוסקים לה כר' יוסי למה לי למימר מריש ירחא דניסן משום כ"ט כדי לאסור [לכ"ט] לאדר שלפניו תיפוק ליה דהוי יומא דבתר כ"ח תריקכל שלאחריו בתענית אסור בהספד מותר כלומר האי דאמר ר' יוסי בין לפניו בין לאחריו אסור לא אסור לאחריו אסור אלא להתענאה אבל בהספד מותר ולהכי איצטריך מריש ירחא דניסן כדי שיהא כ"ט מוטל בין שני ימים טובים **) בין כ"ח לכ"ח דליהוי כיו"ט עצמו דאסור אפי' בהספד וכ"ש בתענית. נפרש מתניתין שלא פי' לעיל כך הורה המורה כל הכתוב במגילת תענית דלא למספד כלומר אותם ימים טובים הכתובים במג"ת שמותרין כל כך דאסור להו למספד וכ"ש להתענאה לפניו אסור ***) בהספד ובתענית הואיל והמור הרבה שביו"ם עצמו אסור אפי' בהספד לאחריו מותר בהספד ובתענית ר' יוסי אומר הואיל וחמור כך שאסור אפי' בהספד נחמיר נמי שבין לפניו ובין לאחריו אסור בין בהספד בין בתענית ודלא להתענאה כלומר ואותן ימים טובים דמג"ת שאינו חמור כל כך שאינן אסורין אלא בתענית אבל בהספד מותרין בין לפניו בין לאחריו הואיל וקל כ"כ [מותרין] ר' יוסי מחמיר מכ"מ אע"פ שקל כ"כ לפניו אסור: ת"ר אלין יומיא דלא להתענאה כלומר כל ימים טובים הכתובים במג"ת אסורין בתענית אבל יש בהן שאין אסורין בהספד ומקצתהן די לא למספד בהן יש מהן שמותרין הרבה שאפי' בהספד אסורין מכשיו נחזור תפרש ההלכה כסדרה. מתמניא ביה עד סוף מועדא איתוקם ביה חגא דשבועיא למה לי למימר מתמניא ביה לימא מט' ביה ותמניא גופיה אסור דהוא אסרינן לעיל מריש ירחא עד תמניא ביה איתוקם תמידא הא תריץ להכי אצטריך למימר מתמניא דאי מקלע מילתא לבטולא יו"ט דתמידא

*) מלשה הנ"ל דסוי ל' יום דמלסר ל' שלפניו וכו'. **) צ"ל בין כ"ח לכ"ח גר"ש ירחא דניסן. ***) הגהה צ"ע דהרי בכה"ג אמר כב"ש לעיל דכל שלפניו או לאחריו אינו אסור רק בתענית.

גליון הש"ס גמ' כי אמר רבי יוחנן הלכה כרבי יוסי אדלא להתענאה. וכעין זה שבועות יג ע"א מנחות לג ע"ב: רש"י ד"ה לא נצרכה וכו' דהשתא כי הוה אדר שני. עי' מג"א סי' תקפח ס"ק ג: תוס' ד"ה לא נצרכה. משום יום שלפני ר"ח ניסן. כלשון הגמרא דסה עיקר מה שאמר הגין הלילה משום יום ל' דהיינו שלאחריו דיום כ"ח:

לז א מיי' פ"ב מהלכות מגילה הלכה יג טוש"ע א"ח סי' תרצ"ו סעיף ג:

לז ב ג מיי' פ"א מהל' תעניות הלכה ו סמג עשין ג טוש"ע א"ח סי' תקעב סעיף ב:

א ד מיי' פ"ב מהלכות תענית הלכה טו יז יח טוש"ע א"ח סי' תקעה סעיף ח:

[בערוך ערך הרג מפרש דשמעיה ואחיו הן הם הרוגי לוד הנזכרים בפסחים נ. וב"ב י: ע"ש]

הלכה מתענה ומשלים. פי' הא דקפסק הלכה מתענה ומשלים אר"ח קאי דאי אחנוכה ואפורים אינו יכול להתענות דיום משתה ושמחה כתיב:

הדרן עלך סדר תעניות קמא

מתריעין עליהם מיד ומתענין כמו כן. ואפילו כראשונות שאומר האחרונות נוהגין בו ואם תאמר (ז) הא דמתריעין משמע דמתריעין ומתענין אמאי צריך לפרש במתני' בסמוך אותה העיר מתענה ומתרעת כיון דסתם מתריעות משמע תרוייהו ויש לומר משום דבעי לאפלוגי ר' עקיבא בסיפא דקאמר מתריעות ולא מתענות:

מותרין בהספד ותענית אימת אילימא בני חמיסר וקא קרו ליה בארביסר ומי שרי והכתיב במגילת תענית *יום ארבעה עשר בו ויום חמשה עשר בו יומי פוריא אינון דלא למיספד בהון ואמר רבא **לא נצרכא אלא לאסור את של זה בזה ואת של זה בזה ואלא בני ארביסר וקא קרי ליה בתליסר יום ניקנור הוא ואלא בני ארביסר וקא קרי ליה בתריסר יום טוריינוס הוא אלא לאו דקא קרו ליה בחדיסר וקתני מותר בהספד ובתענית לא בני ארבעה עשר וקא קרו ליה בתריסר ודקאמרת יום טריינוס הוא יום טריינוס גופיה בטולי בטלוהו הואיל ונהרגו בו *שמעיה ואחיה אחיו כי הא דרב נחמן גזר תעניתא בתריסר אמרו ליה רבנן יום טוריינוס הוא ואמר להו יום טוריינוס [יו] גופיה בטולי בטלוהו הואיל ונהרגו בו שמעיה ואחיה אחיו ותיפוק ליה דהוה ליה יום שלפני ניקנור אמר רב אשי השתא איהו גופיה בטלוהו משום יום ניקנור ניקום וניגזר מאי ניקנור ומאי טוריינוס דתניא ניקנור אחד מאפרכי יוונים היה ובכל יום ויום היה מניף ידו על יהודה וירושלים ואומר אימתי תפול בידי וארמסנה וכשגברה מלכות בית חשמונאי ונצחום קצצו בהונות ידיו ורגליו ותלאום בשערי ירושלים ואמרו פה שהיה מדבר בגאוה וידים שהיו מניפות על ירושלים תעשה בהם נקמה מאי *טוריינוס אמרו כשבקש טוריינוס להרוג את לולינוס ופפוס אחיו בלודקיא אמר להם אם מעמו של חנניה מישאל ועזריה אתם יבא אלהיכם ויציל אתכם מידי כדרך שהציל את חנניה מישאל ועזריה מיד נבוכד נצר אמרו לו חנניה מישאל ועזריה צדיקים גמורין היו וראוין היו ליעשות להם נס ונבוכד נצר מלך הגון היה וראוי ליעשות נס על ידו ואותו רשע הדיוט הוא ואינו ראוי ליעשות נס על ידו ואנו נתחייבנו (א) כליה למקום ואם אין אתה הורגנו הרבה הורגים יש לו למקום והרבה דובין ואריות יש לו למקום בעולמו שפוגעין בנו והורגין אותנו אלא לא מסרנו הקדוש ברוך הוא בידך אלא שעתיד ליפרע דמינו מידך אעפ"כ הרגן מיד אמרו לא זזו משם עד שבאו דיופלי מרומי ופצעו את מוחו בגיזרין:

אין גוזרין תענית על הצבור בתחלה בחמישי כו' אין גוזרין תענית בראשי חדשים כו': וכמה הויא התחלה א) רב אחא אמר שלש רבי אסי אמר ג)אחת אמר ב) רב יהודה אמר רב זו דברי רבי מאיר שאמר משום רבן (שמעון בן) גמליאל אבל חכמים אומרים ד)מתענה ומשלים ג) דרש מר זוטרא משמיה דרב הונא הלכה מתענה ומשלים:

הדרן עלך סדר תעניות כיצד

סדר ה)תעניות אלו ד) האמור ברביעה ראשונה אבל צמחים ששנו מתריעין עליהן מיד וכן שפסקו גשמים בין גשם לגשם ארבעים יום מתריעין עליהן ה) מפני שהיא מכת בצורת ירדו לצמחין אבל לא ירדו לאילן לאילן ולא לצמחין לזה ולזה אבל לא לבורות לשיחין ולמערות מתריעין עליהן מיד וכן עיר שלא ירדו עליה גשמים דכתיב °והמטרתי על עיר אחת ועל עיר אחת לא אמטיר חלקה אחת תמטר וגו' אותה

א) גי' רי"ף רש"י ורא"ש ר' אחא כו' ר' יוסי כו' ועי' מ"מ מהל' תענית פ"א הלכה ז ב) [עירובין מא.] ג) [שם מא:] ד) גי' הרא"ש האמורים וכ"ה ברש"י ברי"ף וכר"ן ה) מיד כ"ה במשנה שבמשניות וברי"ף ורא"ש

תורה אור | [מגילת תענית פ"ב] | [שמות פ"ח] | עמוס ד

מותרין בהספד ובתענית. בני ט"ו (ג) קריאת מגילה דכרכין קודם זמנה כדמפרש התם בי"א בי"ב בי"ג בי"ד בט"ו שהכפרים מקדימין ליום הכניסה מותרין אותן ימים שקראוה קודם זמנה בהספד ותענית: בני חמיסר. דהיינו כרכים המוקפין חומה מימות יהושע בן נון וקא קרי בארביסר כגון שהלך לכפר וקרא עמהן דפרוז בן יומו נקרא פרוז כדאמרינן במגילה (דף יט.): מי שרי. י"ד אפילו לבני ט"ו בהספד ותענית: ואמר רבא לא נצרכה. לכתוב במגילת תענית לגזור הספד ותענית לבני י"ד בי"ד ולבני ט"ו בט"ו דהא קרא כתיב בהדיא להיות עושים את ימי הפורים האלה וגו': אלא לאסור את של זה בזה. כגון בני ט"ו (דקרו) בי"ד ובני י"ד בט"ו: בני ארביסר. כגון כפרים ועיירות: וקא קרי בי"ג. כגון שחל י"ד בג' בשבת ומקדימין ליום הכניסה: יום ניקנור הוא. לקמן מפרש ואסור בהספד ובתענית: אלא בני י"ד וקרו בי"ב. שחל י"ד ברביעי בשבת והקדימו ליום הכניסה דהיינו י"ב: טורייטס. בסמוך מפרשה: בחדיסר. שחל להיות י"ד באחד בשבת וכפרים מקדימין ליום הכניסה דהוו י"א ושמע מינה דאע"ג שהוא יום שלפני טורייטס שרי בהספד ותענית: שמעיה ואחיה. חסידים היו ולא פירש מי הם דאותו שאכלו האריה עידו *היה ולא שמעיה: איפרכי. דוכוס: לולייטס ופפוס אחיו. צדיקים גמורים היו: בלודקי'. היא לוד והיינו דאמרינן בכל דוכתא (ב"ב דף י:*) הרוגי לוד אין כל בריה יכולה לעמוד במחיצתן בגן עדן ויש אומרין שנהרגו על בתו של מלך שנמצאת הרוגה ואמרו היהודים הרגוה וגזרו גזרה על שונאיהן של ישראל ועמדו אלו ופדו את ישראל ואמרו אנו הרגנוה והרג המלך לאלו בלבד: אם מעמו כו': נתחייבנו הריגה. על חטא חייבי מיתות בית דין: דיופלין. שני שרים וכן מטרופולין של מלכים לשון שרים: בגזירין. מקלות כמו גזירי עצים: (ג) שלש. תעניות שני וחמישי ושני; וכמה היא התחלה. שאינו מפסיק לאחר מכאן: רבי אחא ורבי יוסי. (ד) אמוראי נינהו דלאו אורחא דתנאי להשתעויי בגמרא כי האי גוונא: זו דברי ר"מ. ואדברי ר"מ דמתני' קאי דקתני אין משלימין: מתענה ומשלים. עד חשיכה:

הדרן עלך סדר תעניות קמא

סדר תעניות אלו. האמור בפ' ראשון (דף י.) שבתחלה יחידים מתענין (ס) סדר תעניות ואחר כך צבור הולכין ומתענין עד י"ג אם לא נענו: ברביעה ראשונה. אם עבר זמן רביעה ראשונה של יורה ולא ירדו גשמים מתענין והולכין כסדר הזה: אבל צמחים ששנו. שנשתנו ממנהגן תחת חטה יצא חוח תחת שעורה באשה (ו) שלא היו חטים בשבולים או שינוי אחר מתריעין עליהן מיד אפילו בראשונות שכל חומר האחרונות נוהג בהן: בין גשם לגשם. בין רביעה ראשונה לשניה סימן בצורת היא: ירדו לצמחים אבל לא לאילן. מפרש בגמ': לבורות שיחין ומערות. *בבבא בתרא מפרש מאי בור ומאי שיח ומאי מערה וכולן בית כניסות מי גשמים לשתיה: שלא ירדו עליה גשמים דכתיב והמטרתי על עיר אחת ועל עיר אחת לא אמטיר וגו'. כגון שהמטיר בעיר זו ובחבירתה לא המטיר דקללה היא: [גי' בב"ק נ:]

מגילה ה: | [שם]

הגהות הב"ח

(א) גמ' ואנו נתחייבנו כליה למקום ואם אין אתה הורגנו כו' יש לו למקום הרבה דובין ואריות: (ב) רש"י ד"ה מותרין וכו' בני ט"ו וכו' ובני י"ד דכפרים ועיירות שקראו מגילה קודם זמנם כדמפרש התם מגילה נקראת בי"א בי"ב בי"ג בי"ד בט"ו לא פחות ולא יותר כרכין המוקפין חומה מימות יהושע בן נון קורין בט"ו כפרים ועיירות גדולות קורין בי"ד אלא שהכפרים מקדימין ליום הכניסה: (ג) ד"ה שלש כו' נ"ב אחר ד"ה וכמה כו': (ד) ד"ה רבי אחא ורבי יוסי אמוראי נינהו. נ"ב לפי הגירסא שלפנינו דגרס רבי אסי לא היה צריך לפרש דפשיטא דאמוראי נינהו: (ה) רש"י ד"ה סדר תעניות כו' שבתחלה יחידים כך צבור הולכין ומתענין עד י"ג תעניות אם לא נענו כצ"ל ותיבות סדר התעניות נמחק: (ו) ד"ה אבל כו' תחת שעורה באשה או שינוי אחר כו' כצ"ל ותיבות שלא היו חטים בשבולים נמחק: (ז) תוס' ד"ה מתריעין כו' וא"ת כיון דהא דמתריעין משמע:

רבינו חננאל

הלכה כר' יוסי אדילא להתענאה דלפניו אסור איני והאמר ר' יוחנן הלכה כסתם מתני'. ותנן בסתם' מגילה אע"פ שאמרו מקדימין כפרים ליום הכניסה ולא מאחרין. מותרין בהספד ובתענית בו ביום שקורין בו. וליכא לאוקמא להא מתני' בי"ר ובט"ו דקי"ל אע"פ שאין קורין בהן אסורין דתניא בהדיא ארביסר וחמיסר פוריא אינון די לא למספד בהון. ואמר רבא לא נצרכא אלא לאסור את זה בזה ואת של זה בזה. ואפילו מי שאינו יומו ואינו קורא בו אסור בתליסר ובתריסר נמי ליכא לאוקמא דהא יום נקנור ויום טוריינוס אינון וימים טובים נינהו. ליכא לאוקמא אלא כגון שהיה יום הכניסה בי"א וקורין בו ביום. ואע"פ שהוא יום לפני טוריינוס מותר בהספד ובתענית קשיא לר' יוחנן דאמר הלכתא כר' יוסי דאיסר לפניהם ושנינן יום טוריינוס בטולי בטלוה כו'. ושאר השמועה פשוטה היא: מתני' אין גוזרין תענית על הצבור בתחלה בחמישי כו'. אין גוזרין תענית בראשי חדשים בחנוכה ובפורים ואם התחילו כו'. כמה היא התחלה. ר' אחא אמר ג' ר' יוסי אומר אחת וקי"ל כר' יוסי. ואסיקנא אם התחילו כו'. ט' באב שחל להיות ע"ש. פי' הא דתנינן בסוף בכל מערבין ומשתתפין ט' באב שחל להיות בע"ש כו'. קבלה בידינו כי פסח של אותה שנה היה ביום ה'. ובלא' תמוז דההיא שתא ופל ר"ה אב בחמישי. וחל ט' באב להיות בע"ש וחסרו אב ואלול חל להיות ע"ש ור"ה בשבת. דבר ברור הוא שיש לסנהדרין לקבוע חסירין זה אחר זה כפי הססורות שבידם. ובפירוש שנו בענין עצרת (ר"ה ו ע"ב) שניהן מלאין ה' חסרין ו' והם ניסן ואייר *) ור' עקיבא שגמע ביצה מגולגלת מסוכן היה משום שהיה חולה ואמרו לו הרופאים כי גמיעת ביצה טיר בלא מלח באחרית היום היא רפואתו. וכיון שראהו ר' יהודה נרמה לו דסבר המתענה בע"ש אינו משלים **) ט' באב שחל להיות בע"ט. כגון דאקלע פסח דההיא שתא בחמישי בשבת וחל ט' באב בע"ש לפי שהיה תמוז מלא וחיסרו (עוד לתי"ש) [אב ואלול] וחל ר"ה להיות בשבת: ירושלמי אפי' יחיד שקבל על עצמו תענית מתענה ומשלים. ירושלמי (ברכות פ"ד) י"ח ברכות שבכל יום כנגד י"ח מוטודים שמראש תהלים עד יענך ולמה רגשו גוים אינו מן המנין. דברכת המינים ביבנה תקנוה. וכנגד י"ח פעמים שכתוב בתורה אברהם יצחק ויעקב. גם ויקרא בהם שמי ושם אבותי בכלל. וכנגד י"ח צוויים שכתוב בתורה בפרשת המשכן שני מן ואתו אהליאב עד סוף הספר. ז' ברכות של שבת כנגד ז' קולות שכתוב בהבו לה' בני אלים וכנגד ז' אזכרות שכתוב במזמור שיר ליום השבת. ט' ברכות של ר"ה כנגד ט' אזכרות הכתובים בפרש' תנה ובסוף כתיב ה' ידין אפסי ארץ. כ"ד ברכות של תענית צבור כנגד כ"ד רנה תחנה תפלה שכתובים בפרשת שלמה. ר' זירא אמר יחיד בתענית צבור צריך להזכיר עננו ה' עננו כו'. ואסיקנא איכן אומרה בלילי שבת וכיומו. וקי"ל ש"צ אומר בין גואל לרופא חולי. יחיד בשומע תפלה. ר' אחא אמר יחיד בט' באב צריך להזכיר מעין המאורע והוא רחם ה' עלינו ועל ישראל עמך ועל ירושלים עירך ועל ציון משכן כבודך. ועל העיר האבלה התרונה כו' עד ואני אהיה לה נאם ה' חומת אש סביב ולכבוד אהיה בתוכה. והיכן אומרה הכי ר' ירמיה כל דבר שהוא להבא אומרו בעבודה לשעבר אומרו בהודאה כדתנן (ס"ס דברכות) ונותן הודאה לשעבר וצועק לעתיד לבוא. כל הברכות כולן אחר חותמיהן. ואינו אומר בברכה פסוק כלומר אינו מזכיר פסוק לבדו וחותם ברכה. ואלין דאמרי צהלי ורוני יושבת ציון וחותם בברכה אין בו משום ברכת פסוק. ר' זעירא צם תת"ק תענית ולא חשש למגלת תענית. ר' יעקב בר מסקיד לספריא ***) אין אתת בר אנשי שאיל לכון אמרון ליה (הכל) [בכל] מתענין חוץ משבתות וי"ט ור"ח. ותוש"מ וחנוכה ופורים. והלכתא אפילו יחיד שקבל עליו תענית בע"ש מתענה ומשלים (עירובין מא:): הדרן עלך סדר תעניות כיצד

סדר

*) מכאן ועד וחל ר"ה. להיות בשבת הובא בתוס' עירובין דף מ"א ד"ה בילה בשם רבינו ע"ש כאן. **) זה נכלל במ"ש למעלה ואולי ט"ס סיטב. ***) בירושלמי לפנינו הגי' אין אתת איתא מישאל נכון אמרון לה וכו' וע"ש כמפרש.

רבינו גרשום

דיתפידא דלא ניבטיל אלא שבעה אבל תבניא אסור משום דאיתותב בי"ה חנא דשבועיא. השתא דאתת להכי דהרצת משום דאי איקלע מילתא ובטיל ליה עשרין ותשעה נמי רפרכת למה לי' למימר שריש ירחא דניסן משום לאסור כ"ם באדר תיפוק ליה דהוה יומא דבתר כ"ח לעולם להכי אמר מריש ירחי' דניסן כדי לאסור כ"ם באדר שלפניו דאי איקלע מילתא ובטליניה לכ"ח כו': אמר רב הלכה כר' יוסי דאמר דאי לא למספד בין לפניו ובין לאחריו אסור: ושמואל אמר הלכה כר"ם ת"ק דר' יוסי דסתם מתני' ר"ם וקאמר לפניו אסור לאחריו מותר: מי אמר שמואל הכי דאמר לפניו אסור מעיקרא דשמעיה לר"ם דמיקל יותר מר' יוסי דר"ם אינו אוסר אלא לפניו ור' יוסי אוסר בין לפניו בין לאחריו. אדלא להתענאה דקאמר ר' יוסי לפניו אסור לאחריו מותר ולא אדי לא למספד דקאמר אסור בין מלפניו בין לאחריו: מותרין בהספד ובתענית באותן שמקדימין לאסור את של זה בזה וקורין בט"ו אסור בי"ד בהספד ובתענית. יום ניקנור הוא ואין מותרין בהספד ובתענית אלא לאו בחדיסר וקתני מותרין אע"ג דהוי יומא דסקמי

יום טוריינוס ומי אמר ר' יוחנן הלכה כר' יוסי דלפניו אסור לעולם בני ארביסר דקרו בתריסר ולהכי מותרין דלא הוי יומא טבא: תיפוק ליה דתריסר הוי יומא דסקמיה יום ניקנור ולא ליהוי מותר בהספד ובתענית: דיופלי' שלוחים: בגיזירין. קופיץ: וכן בת"ב שחל להיות בע"ש אין משלימין: וכמה היא התחלה דקאמר אם התחילו אין מפסיקין רב אחא אמר שלש שאם היו ג' תעניות קודם ר"ח ורביע' כר"ח אין מפסיקין זו דברי ר"ג דאמר אם התחילו אין מפסיקין אבל אין משלימין:

הדרן עלך סדר תעניות כיצד

סדר תעניות האמור כל אילו תעניות דאמרן לעיל דאין גוזרין לאחר ברביעה ראשונה ולא ירדו גשמים אבל צמחים ששנו שנשתנה מראה שלהן מתריעין עליהן מיד קודם הרביעה שלישית להתענות ומי אמרת לאחר ברביעה ראשונה מתענין. אבל יבשו לא דכיון שיבשו לית להו תקנתא כלל ואי מתריעין עליהן

הגהות הגר"א [א] גמ' אמר להו יום טורייטוס (טוריינוס) תו"מ :

משנה וגמרא

*אותה העיר מתענה ומתרעת וכל סביבותיה מתענות ולא מתריעות רבי עקיבא אומר מתריעות ולא מתענות *וכן עיר שיש בה דבר או מפולת אותה העיר מתענה ומתרעת וכל סביבותיה מתענות ולא מתריעות רבי עקיבא אומר מתריעות ולא מתענות *איזהו דבר עיר המוציאה חמש מאות רגלי ויצאו ממנה ג' מתים בג' ימים זה אחר זה (א) הרי זה דבר פחות מכאן אין זה דבר *על אלו מתריעין בכל מקום על השדפון ועל הירקון ועל הארבה ועל החסיל *ועל החיה רעה ועל החרב מתריעין עליה מפני שהיא מכה מהלכת מעשה שירדו זקנים מירושלים לעריהם *וגזרו תענית על שנראה כמלא פי תנור שדפון באשקלון ועוד גזרו תענית על שאכלו זאבים שני תינוקות בעבר הירדן רבי יוסי אומר לא על שאכלו אלא על שנראו: *על אלו מתריעין בשבת על עיר שהקיפוה נכרים או נהר ועל הספינה המיטרפת בים ר' יוסי אומר (ב) *לעזרה ולא לצעקה שמעון התימני אומר אף על הדבר ולא הודו לו חכמים: על כל צרה שלא תבא על הצבור מתריעין עליהן *חוץ מרוב גשמים מעשה שאמרו לו לחוני *המעגל התפלל שירדו גשמים אמר להם צאו והכניסו תנורי פסחים בשביל שלא ימוקו התפלל ולא ירדו גשמים מה עשה *עג עוגה ועמד בתוכה ואמר לפניו רבש"ע בניך שמו פניהם עלי שאני כבן בית לפניך נשבע אני בשמך הגדול שאיני זז מכאן עד שתרחם על בניך התחילו גשמים מנטפין אמר לא כך שאלתי אלא גשמי בורות שיחין ומערות התחילו לירד בזעף אמר לא כך שאלתי אלא גשמי רצון ברכה ונדבה ירדו כתיקנן עד שיצאו ישראל מירושלים להר הבית מפני הגשמים באו ואמרו לו כשם שהתפללת עליהם שירדו כך התפלל שילכו להן אמר להם *צאו וראו אם נמחית אבן *הטועין *שלח לו שמעון בן שטח אלמלא חוני אתה גוזרני עליך (ג) נידוי אבל מה אעשה לך שאתה מתחטא לפני המקום ועושה לך רצונך *כבן שהוא מתחטא על אביו ועושה לו רצונו ועליך הכתוב אומר *ישמח אביך ואמך ותגל יולדתך: (*מתני') היו מתענין וירדו להם גשמים *קודם הנץ החמה לא ישלימו לאחר הנץ החמה ישלימו ר"א אומר *קודם חצות לא ישלימו לאחר חצות ישלימו מעשה שגזרו תענית בלוד וירדו להם גשמים קודם חצות אמר להם ר' טרפון צאו ואכלו ושתו ועשו יו"ט ויצאו ואכלו ושתו ועשו יום טוב ובאו בין הערבים *וקראו הלל הגדול: **גמ'** סדר תעניות האלו האמור ברביעה ראשונה ורמינהי רביעה ראשונה ושניה לשאול שלישית להתענות אמר רב *יהודה ה"ק סדר תעניות האמור אימתי בזמן שיצאה רביעה ראשונה ושניה ושלישית ולא ירדו גשמים אבל ירדו גשמים ברביעה ראשונה וזרעו ולא צמחו אי נמי צמחו וחזרו ונשתנו מתריעין עליהן מיד אמר רב נחמן דוקא נשתנו *אבל יבשו לא פשיטא נשתנו תנן לא צריכא (ד) *דאקון מהו דתימא אקנתא מילתא היא קמשמע לן: וכן שפסקו גשמים בין גשם לגשם כו': מאי מכת בצורת אמר רב יהודה אמר רב מכה המביאה לידי בצורת אמר רב נחמן נהרא אנהרא בצורתא

רש"י

ה"ג אותה העיר מתענה ומתרעת וכל סביבותיה מתענות ולא מתריעות. ולפיכך מתענות (ה) שאותה העיר שלא ירדו עליה גשמים תלך לקנות התבואה באותה העיר ויהיה בה רעב: או מפולת. שחומותיה והבתים נופלין ברוח: מתריעים בכ"מ. אם (ו) ירצו באספמיא מתריעין בבבל כבבל מתריעין באספמיא כדקתני טעמא בסיפא מפני שהיא מכה מהלכת אם במקום אחד היא מתריעין עליה כל השומעין כדי שלא תבא עליהן: שדפון. בתבואות: ירקון. חולי: חיה רעה. משכלת בני אדם: חרב. חיילות ההולכין להרוג ולהשחית בכל מקום: מלא תנור. מפרש בגמ': לעריהם. בא"י: באשקלון. בארץ פלשתים: ועל שאכלו זאבים. שהיא חיה רעה ומכה מהלכת היא: שנראו. ובאו בעיר: מתריעין. בענט: המטורפת. מלשון טרף אבנא (ברכות דף כח.) ומלשון בילה טרופה (עדיות פ"ב מ"ד) כו' כדמפרש בפרק שלמעלה (דף יד.): שמעון התימני. מתמנה היה: שלא תבא. לישנא מעליא נקט: מרוב גשמים. לאו כגון שירדה על עיר אחת ועל עיר אחת לא ירדה דשם ודאי שתיקן לקללה כדאמר רב יהודה (לעיל ו:) תמטר *מקום מטר שמקלקל תבואה אלא כבר ירדו וטורח הם לבני אדם אבל אינן מקלקלין תבואות וטעמא מפרש בגמרא למה אין מתריעין: תנורי פסחים. שהם בחצרות ושל חרס הן ומטלטלין אותן שלא ימוקו בגשמים: גשמי בורות. שיפוע גשמים למלאות בורות: ונדבות. רצון ועין יפה: אבן הטועין. אבן טועין היתה בירושלים וכל מי שאבדה לו אבידה כו' בבבא מציעא (דף כח:): לנדות. (ז) על כבוד הרב: מתחטא. פורפיי"ש בלע"ז ישמח אביך ואמך ותגל יולדתך: **גמ'** רביעה ראשונה ושניה לשאול. אף על פי שלא ירדו גשמים לא בראשונה ולא בשניה לא היו מתענין אלא שואלין וקשיין מתני' דקתני סדר תעניות אלו האמור ברביעה ראשונה וברייתא אהדדי: הכי קאמר כו'. (ח) וכגון רביעה ראשונה שניה ושלישית דכולי יורה קרי ליה רביעה [א] כך שמעתי: דוקא נשתנו. דכי נשתנו ודאי הוא דמתריעין מיד דצריך להתפלל עליה (ט) שיחזיר ביופי כתקנן: אבל יבשו. לא צריך דמכאן ואילך לא יועיל והוא תפלת שוא אפילו יבשו כשקן חטין עדיין דקין אפילו הכי לא מתריעין: הכי גרסינן פשיטא (י) שנו תנן לא צריכא דאקון מהו דתימא כו': דאקון. שעלו בקנה שנתקשו מעט לאחר שנתייבשו: מהו דתימא אקנתא מילתא היא. דהואיל ונתקשו מעט אם יתפלל מועיל להם קא משמע לן רב נחמן דאקנא לאו מילתא ל"א אבל יבשו לא דממילא חוזרין: לא צריכא דאקון. שעלו בקנה מהו דתימא אקנתא מילתא היא דכיון שעלו בקנה ועדיין לא בשלו כל צרכן ודאי אי לא מתריעין תו לא גדלי קמשמע לן דלאו מילתא היא דאף על גב דאקון אכתי גדלי טפי: נהרא אנהרא בצורתא. בשאין תבואה בעיר אחת ויש בעיירות אחרות ואפשר להביא מזה לזה דרך נהר בספינה:

בצורתא

תוספות

לא צריכא דאקון. פי' לאחר שעלו בקנה נתייבשו מהו דתימא אקנתא מילתא היא פי' דהואיל ועלו בקנה ולא נתבשלו כל צרכם ליבעי התרעה קמ"ל דלאו מילתא היא: **נהרא** אנהרא בצורתא. פי' (כ) (*הכי) בשאין תבואה בעיר ויש הרבה בשאר עיירות ויכולין להביא מזו לזו הייט מקרי בצורת ולא מקרי רעב (ל) ומאחר שיכולין להביא ע"י הנהר דליכא אלא טירחא זעירא ומהאי כלומר מדבר מועט כזה אין מתריעין מדינתא אמדינתא פירוש שצריך להוליך ממדינה למדינה אחרת ע"י חמורים וסוסים ולא מתריעין דאי אפשר להביא בשפע כ"כ כמו בספינות ל"א נהרא אנהרא כלומר אם יבש הנהר זה וצריך להסב נהר אחר לכאן אי נמי צריך להמתין עד שיגדל הנהר האחר ויבא בכאן זה בצורת ולא מתריעין מדינתא אמדינתא אם יבשו כל הנהרות שבזו העיר וצריכין להביא מים מעיר אחרת כפנא וקשה דבמתני' משמע דאבצורת (מ) מתענין דקתני מתריעין עליהן מפני שהיא מכת בצורת ויש לומר דמכת בצורת דמתני' הוי כמו דכפנא כאשר פירשתי שתחת חטה יצא חוח ומשום הכי מתריעין אע"ג דעדיין איט רק בצורת הואיל וסופו רעב מתריעין אע"ג דהשתא לא הוו כפנא אבל לעולם אין מתריעין על מכת בצורת אי לא מצי לבא לידי רעב ולהכי קאמר הכא דנהרא אנהרא דלא הוי אלא כי בצורתא ולא מתריעין:

נהירנא

מסורת הש"ס

לעיל יו.

פסח

[וע"ל רש"י מנחות לד: ד"ה דעג"ל וכו' כדקרינן חוני המעגל על שם עוגה]

ב"מ כח:

[שם איתא הטוען וע"ש תוס' מ"ש בשם הירושלמי]

[רש"י פ"ו לקמן כה:]

[גי' רא"ש ורנא]

[גיטין ל. פ"ש ל"ע על לשון אהרן שכתב רש"י וכן תוס' ד"ה לא צריכא]

[עי' פירש"י לקמן כג. ד"ה עוגה]

[ברכות יט.]

משלי כג

טעות הדפוס

עין משפט נר מצוה

ב א מיי' פ"ב מהלכות תענית ה"ב טוש"ע א"ח סי' תקעו סעיף א וסעיף יב:

סקונטרס כצ"ל

ג ב ג מיי' שם הל' ג והל' ה טוש"ע שם סעיף כ:

ד ד מיי' שם הל' י"א טוש"ע שם סעיף ח ט:

ה ה מיי' שם הלכה ו טוש"ע שם סעיף ו:

ו ו מיי' שם הלכה יא טוש"ע שם סעיף א:

ז ז ח מיי' שם פ"א ה"ו ופ"ב מהלכות שבת הלכה כד סמג עשין ג טוש"ע שם סעיף יג וסי' רפח סעיף ט:

ח ט מיי' שם פ"ב הלכה טו טוש"ע א"ח סי' תקעו סעיף יא:

ט י מיי' שם פ"א הלכה טו טור ש"ע א"ח סימן תקסט סעיף א וסי' תקעה סעיף יא:

י כ מיי' שם טוש"ע א"ח סי' תקעה סעיף יא:

יא ל מיי' שם פ"ב הלכה טו טוש"ע א"ח סי' תקעה סעיף ח:

רבינו חננאל

סדר תעניות האלו האמור ברביעה ראשונה כו'. תרצה רב יהודה הכי סדר תעניות האלו בזמן שיצתה רביעה ראשונה ושניה ולא ירדו גשמים. אבל אם ירדו גשמים וצמחו זרעים וחזרו ושנו. כלומר כמשו מתריעין עליהן מיד ודוקא שנו כעין כמוש אבל יבשו לגמרי אע"ג דחזור אקון אין מתריעין עליהן פי' אקון שחזרו לירוקתן כלומר חזרו לחיותן. ורבותינו הגאונים ז"ל אמרו האי אקון אקנתא לשון חזקה בלשון ארמית ובלשון הזה הוא בגמרא (בפרק מי שאחזו קורדייקוס) [כל הגט דף ל' ע"א *) (פי' פרצידא דתותי קלא. זרע תבואה שהוא תחת אבן צוותה. פי' קלא מלשון (פסחים סב: וש"נ) שקל קלא פתק ביה). מכת בצורת. פי' רב יהודה מכה הבאה לידי בצורת. [או"ל נהרא אנהרא] הוצרכו האנשים המסתפקין מים מזה הנהר לילך לנהר אחר.

*) כל הסגור שייך לעיל בגמרא ריש דף ד'.

בצורת

רבינו גרשום

עליהן הוי תפלת שוא: דאקון שנראה להן קצת תקנה: נהרא אנהרא בצורתא כשצריכין להביא מים מנהר זה להשקות שדות של נהר אחר לפי שאין באותו נהר אחר מים כדי סיפוק להשקות שדותיו והוי סימן בצורת

הגהות הב"ח

(א) גמ' ג' מתים בג' ימים זה אחר זה (הרי זה דבר פחות מכאן אין זה דבר) תא"מ ונ"ב ס"א אין: (ב) שם ר' יוסי אומר לעזרה ולא לצעקה. ג"ב עי' פירושו בדף יד ע"א: (ג) שם אלמלא חוני [...] עליך נדוי אבל מה אעשה: (ד) שם לא צריכא דהדר אקון מהו דתימא: (ה) רש"י ד"ה ה"ג ולפיכך מתענות מפני שאותה העיר וכו' כתבואה באותה שבסביבותיה ויהיו בה רעב: (ו) ד"ה בכ"מ אם נראו באספמיא כו' שהיא מכה מהלכת ולפיכך אף אם במקום אחד: (ז) ד"ה לנדות על כבוד הרב שבקש דברים לומר לא כך שאלתי הס"ד: (ח) ד"ה הכי קאמר כו' כלומר סדר תעניות אלו אמור בשביל רביעה ראשונה כשעברה מכל וכל וכגון רביעה ראשונה: (ט) ד"ה דוקא כו' להתפלל עליהן שיחזרו ביופי כתקנן אבל יבשו לא צריך כו' והוא תפלת שוא הד"א ומה"ד אבל יבשו. כשקן חטין עדיין כו': (י) ד"ה ה"ג פשיטא כשתנו תנן לא צריכא דהדר אקון מהו דתימא כו' דאקון שעלו כו' שנתייבשו מהו דתימא כו' דאקנתא לאו מילתא הד"א וכס"ד: (כ) תוס' ד"ה נהרא כו' כשאין כנ"ל ותיבת הכי נמחק: (ל) בא"ד ולא מיקרי רעב דמאחר שיכולין כו' זעירא ומהאי מילתא כלומר כו' ע"י חמורים וסוסים כפנא פי' ולא מתריעין: (מ) בא"ד דבמתני' משמע דאבצורת מתריעין דקתני מתריעין כו' כאשר פירש"י שתחת חטה

הגהות הגר"א

[א] רש"י ד"ה הכי קאמר כו' ליה רביעה. ל"ב ראשונה:

גליון הש"ס

גמ' כבן שהוא מתחטא. עי' מנחות דף כו ע"ב תד"ה כף תנים:

עין משפט נר מצוה

יב א מיי' פ"ג מהלכות תענית הלכה טו טוש"ע א"ח סי' תקעה סעיף ח :

יג ב מיי' שם הלכה יג טוש"ע א"ח סי' תקעו סעיף ה :

[נ"ל זוכר]

יד ג מיי' שם הלכה י טוש"ע שם סעיף ח :

בצורתא מדינתא אמדינתא כפנא וא"ר חנינא סאה בסלע ושכיחא בצורתא ארבעה (א) ולא שכיחא כפנא א"ר יוחנן לא שנו אלא בזמן שהמעות בזול ופירות ביוקר אבל מעות ביוקר ופירות בזול מתריעין עליה מיד דא"ר יוחנן *נהירנא כד הוו קיימי ד' סאין בסלע והוו נפישי נפיחי כפן בטבריא מדלית איסר: ירדו לצמחין אבל לא לאילן: בשלמא לצמחים ולא לאילן משכחת לה דאתא ניחא ולא אתיא רזיא לאילן ולא לצמחין דאתיא רזיא ולא אתיא ניחא לזה ולזה אבל לא לבורות ולא לשיחין ומערות משכחת לה דאתיא רזיא וניחא *מיהו טובא לא אתיא אלא הא דתניא ירדו לבורות לשיחין ולמערות ואבל לא לזה ולזה הירי משכחת לה דאתיא בשפיכותא ת"ר *מתריעין על האילנות בפרוס הפסח על הבורות ושיחין [א] ומערות (ג) אפילו בפרוס החג ועל כולן אם אין להן מים לשתות מתריעין עליהן מיד ואיזהו מיד שלהן שני והמישי ושני (ג) ועל כולן אין מתריעין עליהן אלא באפרכיא שלהן ואסברא בזמן שיש בה מיתה מתריעין עליה בזמן שאין בה מיתה אין מתריעין עליה ומתריעין על הגובאי בכל שהוא רבי שמעון בן אלעזר אומר אף על החגב ת"ר מתריעין על האילנות בשאר שני שבוע על הבורות ועל השיחין ועל המערות אפילו בשביעית רשב"ג אומר אף על האילנות בשביעית מפני שיש בהן פרנסה לעניים תניא אידך מתריעין על האילנות בשאר שני שבוע על הבורות על השיחין ועל המערות אפילו בשביעית רבן שמעון בן גמליאל אומר אף על האילנות מתריעין על הספיחין בשביעית מפני שיש בהן פרנסה לעניים תניא א"ר אלעזר בן פרטא מיום שחרב בית המקדש נעשו גשמים *צימוקין לעולם יש שנה שגשמיה מרובין ויש שנה שגשמיה מועטין יש שנה שגשמיה יורדין בזמנן ויש שנה שאין גשמיה יורדין בזמנן שנה שגשמיה יורדין בזמנן למה הוא דומה לעבד שנתן לו רבו פרנסתו בא' בשבת נמצאת עיסה נאפית כתיקנה ונאכלת כתיקנה שנה שאין גשמיה יורדין בזמנן למה הוא דומה לעבד שנתן לו רבו פרנסתו בע"ש נמצאת עיסה נאפית שלא כתיקנה ונאכלת שלא כתיקנה שנה שגשמיה מרובין למה הוא דומה לעבד שנתן לו רבו פרנסתו בבת אחת נמצאו ריחים טוחנות מן הכור (ד) מה שטוחנות מן הקב ונמצאת עיסה אוכלת מן הכור כמו אוכלת מן הקב שנה שגשמיה מועטין למה הוא דומה לעבד שנתן לו רבו פרנסתו מעט מעט נמצאו ריחיים מה שטוחנות מן הכור טוחנות מן הקב נמצאת עיסה כמה שנאכלת מן הכור אוכלת מן הקב ד"א בזמן שגשמיה מרובין למה הוא דומה לאדם שמגבל את הטיט אם יש לו מים רבים מים אינן כלין והטיט מגובל יפה אם יש לו מים מועטין מים כלים והטיט אינו מתגבל יפה ת"ר פעם אחת עלו כל ישראל לרגל לירושלים ולא היה להם מים לשתות הלך נקדימון בן גוריון אצל אדון אחד אמר לו הלויני שתים עשרה *מעיינות מים לעולי רגלים ואני אתן לך שתים עשרה עינות מים ואם איני נותן לך הריני נותן לך שתים עשרה ככר כסף וקבע לו זמן כיון שהגיע הזמן ולא ירדו גשמים בשחרית שלח לו שגר לי או מים או מעות שיש לי בידך שלח לו עדיין יש לי זמן כל היום כולו שלי הוא בצהרים שלח לו שגר לי או מים או מעות שיש לי בידך שלח לו עדיין יש לי שהות ביום במנחה שלח לו שגר לי או מים או מעות שיש לי בידך שלח לו עדיין יש לי שהות ביום לגלג עליו אותו אדון אמר כל השנה כולה לא ירדו גשמים

ועכשיו

רש"י

בצורתא. בצורת היא זו ולא רעב הואיל ויכולין לישא בספינות : מדינתא אמדינתא, (ה) וצריכין להוליך ממדינה למדינה על ידי חמרים : כפנא. רעב ורעב קשה מבצורת לפי שאי אפשר להביא בשופי מ"ר (ו) לשון אחר נראה אגמרא אם יבש מעיין זה וצריך להסב מעיין אחר בכאן אי נמי להמתין עד שיגדל נהר אחרת ויבא כאן בצורת הוא זה : מדינתא אמדינתא. אם יבשו כל הנהרות שבתוך העיר וצריכין להביא מים מעיר אחרת כפנא רעב הוא זה תקיפא מבצורתא : סאה בסלע ושכיחא. כי זבני סאה של חיטין בסלע דהיינו יוקר ומטייה לקטוח בכל עת בצורתא : מעות ביוקר. אין מעות מצויות להן: נהירנא. אני זוכר : מדלית איסר. מאין מעות : דאתיא ניחא. ואמרינן בפירקא דלעיל (דף ג:) מיטרא ניחא לפירי ולתבואה ומיטרא רזיא לאילני (ז) דאתיא ניחא לפירי ואתיא רזא לאילנות : בשפיכתא. בכח גדול יותר מדאי דאינה טובה לא לזה ולא לזה שוב אמר רבי שפיכותא מטר דק ועבה יותר מדאי לאילני לא מהניא דלאו רזיא היא לצמחים נמי לא שהגשמים מרובין באין ושוטפין אותן:(ח)בפרוס הפסח. בימי הפסח [א] על בורות שיחין ומערות אע"פ שלא ירדו להן גשמים : [ב] אפילו בפרוס החג.להשקות זרעים ואת בהמתם:אם אין להם (ט) לשתות מתריעין וכו'.· אפילו [ג] בפרוס החג דימות החמה נינהו אפילו הכי מתריעין משום דכולן צריכות לשתות: וכולן . כל אלו : בהיפרכיא שלהן . באותו מלכות שכלו שם מי בורות שיחין ומערות : ואסכרא . בולמ"לע בלע"ז פעמים שנקבע בתוך פיו של אדם ומת לשון כי יסכר פי דוברי שקר (תהלים סג) והיא סרונכה מיתה משונה : בזמן שיש בה מיתה. שהיא (י) משולחת מהלכת ומתים בה : על הגובאי . שמכלה את התבואה כל שהוא אפילו לא נראה אלא קלת בידוע שעתידין לבוא לרוב אבל חגב כל שהוא מצוי הוא ואינו מכלה כל כך כארבה : בשאר שני שבוע. דשמיטה אבל בשמיטה לא דהפקר נינהו : אפילו בשביעית. כל שעה צריכין לשתיה ואע"פ שהגשמים מועילין לקרקע בשביעית : רבן שמעון בן גמליאל אומר. מתריעין על האילנות ואף על הספיחין של שביעית שאינן חשובין כל כך : צמוקין. שיורדין בקושי מלשון ושדיים צומקים (הושע ט) : למה הוא דומה. פרנסתו של כל (כ) השבת טולה : נאפת כתקנה.שיש לו פנאי לאפותה : פרנסתו בבת אחת. פרנסת כל השנה וטוחן אותה ביחד : נמלאת רחיים במה שאוכלת מן הכור כו'. שכן דרך שמשתייר מן הקמח ברחיים וכן כשהגשמים יורדין מרובים ומרביעין את הארץ ומה שהיו טרשים בולעים מן (ל) הרוב בולעין מן המיעוט ומה שהרוח מנשבת ובולעת מן הרוב בולעת מן המיעוט : נמלאת עיסה. עריבה שלשין בה את הבלק שמשתייר בשוליה מן העיסה (מ) אף גשמים כשיורדין מעט מעט נבלעין בטרשי' ואין מרביעין את הארץ: ה"ג מימיו מרובין (נ) אינו כלין וטיט מתגבל יפה מימיו מועטין הטיט אינו מתגבל יפה.מים אינן כלין ויוכלו לגבל טיט הרבה כמה שירלה : נקדימון בן גוריון.עשיר גדול היה:ואני אתן לך י"ב מעיינות מים . כלומר שירדו גשמים ויתמלאו כל המעיינות מים אותן מעיינות לא היו טבעין מים כל כך ואינן מתמלאין מאיליהן כשאר מעיינות :

תוספות

נהירנא. פירוש (*זוכר) אני : **בהפרכיא** שלהן . פי' באותו מלכות : **רבן** שמעון בן גמליאל אומר אף על האילנות בשביעית מפני שיש בהם פרנסה לעניים. פי' הם הספיחים היוצאין מהן וצ"ל דסבר כמ"ד (פסחים דף נא.) ספיחי זרעים אסור דהיינו ר' עקיבא מדקאמר על האילנות ולא קאמר על הספיחים :

נקדרה

רבינו חננאל

בצורת כלומר עצירת מטר מדינה להביא ממדינה אחרת רעב. א"ר יוחנן ל"ש אלא שהמעות בזול ופירות ביוקר כלומר המשא ומתן מצוי ומרויחין בני אדם. אבל מעות ביוקר מתריעין מיד. וא"ר יוחנן נהירנא דהוו ד' סאין בסלע בטבריא והוו [illegible] איסר. גשמי צמחים הבאים בניחותא. גשמי אילן היורדין ברזיא. לא לאילן ולא לזרעים אלא לבורות. כגון דנחתי בשפיכותא שוטפים ויורדין בבורות: ת"ר מתריעין על האילנות בפרוס הפסח ועל מי בורות שיחין ומערות בפרוס החג ועל כולן אינן מתריעין עליהן אלא באיפרכיא שלהן כלומר אנשי מקום בלבד. ואם אין להם מים לשתות מתריעין עליהן מיד ב' וה' וב'. ועל האסכרה כל זמן שהיא ממיתה. ומתריעין על הגובאי ועל החגב [ועל האילנות ועל הספיחין] ובאילנות ובספיחי' בשביעית מפני שיש בהן פרנסה לעניים. ר' אלעזר בן פרטא אומר מיום שחרב ביהמ"ק לא ירדו גשמי ברכה ונעשו צמוקים לעולם. שנה שגשמיה ירדו בזמנן דומה לעבד שנתן לו רבו פרנסתו באחד בשבת כו'. נמצאו טוחנין מן הכור כו'. מדה אחת נשארת בפי הריחיים בכור כמה שנשארת מן הקב. וכך נדבקת מן העיסה בסרקי [illegible] המעט כמו מן הרב. וכן בהגבלת הטיט. אם יש לו מים בבת אחת כדי גיבול שופך ומגביל ואם אין לו אלא מעט שופך מה שבידו ועד שיבואו אחרים יבשו הללו וכאלו לא שפך בהן כלום. *) כך שניא כו': ת"ר פעם אחת עלו ישראל לחג ולא היה [להם] מים לשתות הלך נקדימון כו'

*) אולי צ"ל כולה סוגיא פשוטה.

רבינו גרשום

מדינתא אמדינתא כפנא כשצריכין להביא מים ממדינה למדינה זו הוא סימן רעב : סאה בסלע ושכיחא בצורתא ד' סאין בסלע ולא שכיחא אע"ג דלא הוה יוקר הואיל ולא שכיחא הוי כפנא דאתיא הכי והכי ניחא ורזיא מיהו טובא לא אתא דליהוי לבורות לשיחין ולמערות היכי משכחת לה כיון דאתא לבורות היינו רזיא היינו לאילן: דאתיא בשפיכותא דהוי טפי מרזיא דלא ניחא לאילן אלא לבורות. באיפרכיא שלהן באותן שכונות שצריכין להן בשאר שני שבוע אבל לא בשביעית הואיל ואין אוכלין פירות הגדילין בשביעית : מפני שיש בהן צדקה לעניים דעניים אוכלין פירות הגדילין בשביעית. נעשו מי גשמים מצומקין שאין באין בשפע : נמצא ריחים שאוכלות מן הקב אוכלות מן הכור כלומר שאין קולטין הריחים מן הכור קמח יותר מן הקב דהיינו תקנתו : נמצאת עיסה שאין העריבה אוכלת מן העיסה מן הכור יותר מן הקב : וכן עיר שלא ירדו עליה גשמים ועל האחרת ירדה ואותה העיר שלא ירדה

מסורת הש"ס

כ"ע נא:

[רי"ף ורא"ש ל"ג אפי' פירוח]

[ע' בערוך ערך סקפיון]

מ"ל מעלות

הגהות הב"ח

(א) גמ' ושכיחא בצורתא ארבעה סאין בסלע ולא שכיחא כפנא: (ב) שם ת"ר כו' ושיחין ומערות בפרוס החג ואם אין להם מים כצ"ל ותיבות אפילו ותיבת על כולן נמחק: (ג) שם שני וחמישי ושני וכולן אין מתריעין עליהן ותיבת ועל נמחק : (ד) שם רחיים טוחנות מן הכור כמה שטוחנות מן כו' אוכלת מן הכור כמה שאוכלת מן הקב : (ה) רש"י ד"ה מדינתא אמדינתא דצריכין להוליך : (ו) ד"ה כפנא כו' מ"ר הס"ד : (ז) ד"ה דאתיא כו' לאילני הס"ד : (ח) ד"ה בפרוס הפסח בימי הפסח הס"ד ואח"כ מה"ד על בורות וכו' גשמים הס"ד ואח"כ מה"ד בפרוס ותיבת אפילו נמחק : (ט) ד"ה אם אין להם מים לשתות מתריעין אפי' קודם פרוס החג : (י) ד"ה בזמן כו' שהיא מכה משולחת דמתים בה : (כ) ד"ה למה הוא דומה פרנסתו של כל השנה כולה : (ל) ד"ה נמלאת כו' שהיו טרשים בולעין מן הרוב בולעין מן המיעוט ומה שהרוח מנשבת ובולעת מן המיעוט בולעת מן הרוב : (מ) ד"ה נמלאה עיסה כו' מן העיסה הס"ד ומה"ד טוחנות מן הקב אף גשמים כו': (נ) ד"ה ה"ג מימיו מרובין מים אינן כלין כו' מימיו מועטין מימיו כלין והטיט אינו מתגבל :

הגהות מהר"ב רנשבורג

[א] רש"י ד"ה בפרוס הפסח. בימי הפסח הוא הס"ד :

הגהות הגר"א

[א] גמ' ומערות בפרוס החג ואם אין כו' כצ"ל (וכ"ה בריף ורא"ש ובתוספתא ומלת אפי' ליתא גם בגמ' דפוס [illegible] ג:): [ב] רש"י ד"ה אפילו. רשום קו על מלה זו למחקה: [ג] שם ד"ה אם אין כו' אפי' קודם לפרוס החג. כצ"ל:

ועכשיו ירדו גשמים (א) נכנס לבית המרחץ בשמחה עד שהאדון נכנס בשמחתו לבית המרחץ נקדימון נכנס לבית המקדש כשהוא עצב נתעטף ועמד בתפלה אמר לפניו רבונו של עולם גלוי וידוע לפניך שלא לכבודי עשיתי ולא לכבוד בית אבא עשיתי אלא לכבודך עשיתי שיהו מים מצויין לעולי רגלים מיד נתקשרו שמים בעבים וירדו גשמים עד שנתמלאו שתים עשרה מעינות מים והותירו עד שיצא אדון מבית המרחץ נקדימון בן גוריון יצא מבית המקדש כשפגעו זה בזה אמר לו תן לי דמי מים יותר שיש לי בידך אמר לו יודע אני שלא הרעיש הקב"ה את עולמו אלא בשבילך אלא עדיין יש לי פתחון פה עליך שאוציא ממך את מעותיי שכבר שקעה חמה וגשמים ברשותי ירדו חזר ונכנס לבית המקדש נתעטף ועמד בתפלה ואמר לפניו רבונו של עולם הודע שיש לך אהובים בעולמך מיד נתפזרו העבים וזרחה החמה באותה שעה אמר לו האדון אילו לא נקדרה החמה היה לי פתחון פה עליך שאוציא ממך מעותיי תנא לא נקדימון שמו אלא בוני שמו ולמה נקרא שמו נקדימון (ב) שנקדרה חמה בעבורו תנו רבנן *שלשה נקדמה להם חמה בעבורן משה ויהושע ונקדימון בן גוריון בשלמא נקדימון בן גוריון גמרא יהושע נמי קרא דכתיב °וידם השמש וירח עמד וגו' אלא משה מנלן אמר רבי אלעזר אתיא אחל אחל כתיב הכא °אחל תת פחדך וכתיב התם °אחל גדלך רבי שמואל בר נחמני אמר אתיא תת תת כתיב הכא אחל תת פחדך וכתיב התם °ביום תת ה' את האמרי רבי יוחנן אמר אתיא מגופיה דקרא °אשר ישמעון שמעך ורגזו וחלו מפניך אימתי רגזו וחלו מפניך בשעה שנקדמה לו חמה למשה: וכן עיר שלא ירדו עליה גשמים כו': *אמר רב יהודה אמר רב ושתיהן לקללה °היתה ירושלם לנדה בינהם אמר רב יהודה אמר רב לברכה כנדה מה נדה יש לה היתר אף ירושלים יש לה תקנה °היתה כאלמנה אמר רב יהודה לברכה *כאלמנה ולא אלמנה ממש אלא כאשה שהלך בעלה למדינת הים ודעתו לחזור עליה °וגם אני נתתי אתכם נבזים ושפלים אמר רב יהודה לברכה דלא מוקמי מינן לא רישי נהרי ולא *גזיריפטי °והכה ה' את ישראל כאשר ינוד הקנה במים אמר רב יהודה אמר רב לברכה דאמר רבי שמואל בר נחמני אמר רבי יונתן *מאי דכתיב °נאמנים פצעי אוהב ונעתרות נשיקות שונא טובה קללה שקילל אחיה השילוני את ישראל יותר מברכה שבירכן בלעם הרשע אחיה השילוני קללן בקנה אמר להם לישראל והכה ה' את ישראל כאשר ינוד *הקנה מה קנה זה עומד במקום מים וגזעו מחליף ושרשיו מרובין ואפילו כל הרוחות שבעולם באות ונושבות בו (ג) אין מזיזות אותו ממקומו אלא הולך ובא עמהן דממו הרוחות עמד הקנה במקומו אבל בלעם הרשע בירכן בארז שנאמר °כארזים *(עלי מים) מה ארז זה אינו עומד במקום מים ואין גזעו מחליף ואין שרשיו מרובין אפילו כל הרוחות שבעולם נושבות בו אין מזיזות אותו ממקומו כיון שנשבה בו רוח דרומית עוקרתו והופכתו על פניו ולא עוד אלא שזכה קנה ליטול הימנו קולמוס לכתוב בו ספר תורה נביאים וכתובים תנו רבנן לעולם יהא אדם רך כקנה ואל יהא קשה כארז *מעשה שבא רבי אלעזר **)(בן ר') שמעון ממגדל גדור מבית רבו והיה רכוב על החמור ומטייל על שפת נהר ושמח שמחה גדולה והיתה דעתו גסה עליו מפני שלמד תורה הרבה

נזדמן

*) סנהדרין קה: **) [צ"ל ברבי]

תורה אור

יהושע י · דברים ב · יהושע ג · דברים ב · איכה א · מלאכי ב · מ"א יד · משלי כז · במדבר כד

ועכשיו ירדו גשמים. בתמיה: בוני שמו: נקדרה. זרחה לשון מקדיר שהיתה חמה קודרת ברקיע וזורחת פירטולי"ר בלע"ז: הכי גרסי' נקדימון בן גוריון הא דאמרן: אתיא אחל אחל. כתיב במלחמת יהושע (יהושע ג) אחל גדלך ובמלחמת משה כתיב (דברים ב) אחל תת פחדך מה יהושע (ד) נקדמה לו חמה במלחמתו כדכתיב בהדיא אף משה כן שכן דרך הכתובין למד כתוב מן המפורש ברמז כדיבור דומה לחבירו וגזירה שוה אחת מן י"ג מדות שניתנו לו למשה מסיני ובתחילת סיפרא מפורש: שתיהן לקללה. אקרא קאי הא דכתיב על עיר אחת אמטיר ועל עיר אחת לא אמטיר שניהם לקללה אותה שימטיר עליה רוב גשמים שמקלקלין את התבואה ואת שלא ימטיר אין גשמים ואין תבואה גדילה אשר לא תמטיר עליה מוסב הדבר על העב שהעב בלשון נקיבה דכתיב (מלכים א יח) הנה עב קטנה ככף איש עולה מים: ולא אלמנה גמורה. דהא לא כתיב אלמנה אלא היתה כאלמנה כאשה העומדת באלמנות חיות על בעלה שהלך ועתיד לחזור: דלא מוקמי מינן רישי נהרי. מוכסין: גזיריפטי. סרדיוטין מרוב בזיון: ונעתרות נשיקות שונא. נעתרות לשון הפך כדאמרינן במסכת סוכה (דף יד.) ויעתר לו מה עתר זה מהפך את התבואה פורקא בלע"ז אף כמי נעתרות לשון רבוי וייתור אינקריי"ש בלע"ז כמו העתרתם עלי דבריכם (יחזקאל לה): בירכן בארז. כארזים עלי מים (במדבר כד): ארז זה אינו עומד במקום מים כו'. ואע"ג דכתיב בקרא כארזים עלי מים ההוא לאו בלעם קאמר ליה דבלעם אמר כארזים והמלאך השיבו עלי מים וכן כולהו דבלעם אמר כנחלים דזמינן מתייבשין וקאמר ליה המלאך נטיו דאין יבשין לעולם והיינו דכתיב ויהפוך ה' אלהיך לך את הקללה לברכה על ידי מלאך שהושיבו על ידי מלאך: ואפילו כל הרוחות. שאין קשות: רוח דרומית. היא קשה כדאמרינן (ב"ב ד' כה:) אילמלא בן נץ שמעמידה אין כל בריה יכולה לעמוד מפניה שנאמר המבינתך יאבר נץ יפרש כנפיו לתימן: ומטייל. לשמוח:

נזדמן

נקדרה. כמו מקדר בהרים (עירובין נח:) כלומר שמנקב הרקיע: גזיריפטי. פירוש סרדיוטין ושוטרי הטעם במקל: ונעתרות נשיקות שונא. פירוש (ה) כלומר נאמנים פצעי אוהב וחילופיהן בשונא ונעתרות לשון *הפוך כפתר פורק"א בלע"ז שמהפכין בה את התבואה והכי פשטיה דקרא פצעי אוהב נאמנים שהוא עושה לטובה אפילו כשמכה חבירו מכוין לטובה ונשיקות שונא הם להיפך שעושה הכל לרעה וי"מ פשטיה דקרא הכי נאמנים פצעי אוהב ונעתרות נשיקות שונא כלומר ונעתרות לשון ריבוי כלומר נשיקות שונא דומים הם למשא כלומר הם מרובות ולמשא לעולם וי"מ הכי כשאוהבים עושים מריבה ושונאים זה את זה השנאה נאמנה והכי פירוש נאמנים פצעי אוהב הפצעים זהו השנאה שבין אוהבים הם נאמנות ונעתרות נשיקות שונא פי' דכשהשונאים עושים שלום זה לזה השלום והפשרה שביניהן אמנה וקיימת והיינו נעתרות נשיקות שונא כלומר נשיקות שונא נעתרות: מה ארז זה. פירוש דאע"ג דכתיב ביה בקרא עלי מים ההוא לאו בלעם קאמר ליה אלא מלאך וכן כולהו בלעם אמר כנחלים ומלאך אמר נטיו דאינן מתייבשים וכן עלי נהר:

נזדמן

[סוכה יד. יבמות סג.]

רבינו חננאל

תנא לא נקדימון שמו אלא בוני שמו. ומפני שנקדמה לו חמה נקרא נקדימון. והמטרתי על עיר אחת ועל עיר אחת לא אמטיר. אמרו שתיהן לקללה. זו שגשמיה מרובין יותר מדאי משמשין הארץ ואינה עושה פירות. ומי שגשמיה נעצרים אינה מצמחת. היתה ירושלם לנדה. לברכה שיש לה היתר לבעל כנדה. היתה כאלמנה שנער בה בעלה. לא אלמנה ממש. נבזים ושפלים לברכה שאין מהן שרים למלחמה ולהשתמש אותם לעבודת המלך. קנה במים שרשיו מרובים וגזעו מחליף הולך ובא עם הרוחות כו'. ת"ר מעשה בר' שמעון בן אלעזר

רבינו גרשום

עליו מתענה: שתיהן לקללה. אותה שלא ירדה עליה ואותה שירדה עליה ושתיהן מתענות. דלא מוקמי מינן גזי ריפטי ולא מינרו (פי') [בן]: כארזים עלי מים הוא אמר כארזים *)ורוח הקודש משיבה עלי מים שגזעו מחליף:

*) עי' תוס' ד"ה מה ארז.

הגהות הב"ח

(א) גמ' ועכשיו ירדו גשמים מיד נכנס לבית המרחץ בשמחה ובעוד שהאדון נכנס כו' מעיינות מים והותירו בעוד שיצא האדון כו' חזר ונכנס נקדימון בן גוריון לבית המקדש כו' אהובים בעולמך וכשם שעשית נס כן עשה מיד נכנסה הרוח ונתפזרו העבים: (ב) שם ולמה נקרא שמו נקדימון שעמדה [אולי צ"ל שנקדמה] לו החמה: (ג) שם באות ונושבות בו (אין מזיזות אותו ממקומו) תא"מ ונ"ב ס"א אינו הולך ובא עמהן: (ד) רש"י ד"ה אתיא כו' מה יהושע נקדרת לו חמה: (ה) תוס' ד"ה ונעתרות כו' פירוש נאמנים כו' כצ"ל ותיבת כלומר נמחק:

מסורת הש"ס

ע"ז סה.

לעיל ו:

סנהדרין קה. ע"ש

[ג"י' ערוך ערך גז ו' גזוי דפסאי]

[צ"ל הקנה במים]

במדבר כד [ילקוט ליתא וכן משמע מדברי תוספות ד"ה מה ארז וכו' וכ"מ מהרש"א]

[אבות דר"נ פמ"א מס' ד"א פ"ד ובמס' ר"ש בן אלעזר]

עין משפט נר מצוה

[תוספתא תענית פ"ב ועי' תוס' ב"ק סי' לא סק"ח ...]

מו א מיי' פ"ב מהלכות תעניות הלכה יג טוש"ע א"ח סי' תקעו סעיף ד:

[קידושין עב:]

[וע"ע. תוספות קידושין עב: ד"ה ביום ותוס' כ"ב כג. ד"ה אמר]

נזדמן לו אדם אחד שהוא מכוער ביותר. במסכת דרך ארץ *מפרש דאותו אדם הייט אליהו ולטוב נתכוין כדי שלא ירגיל בדבר: לא צריכא דנפלי מחמת גובהייהו. פי' דהוו בריאות ולא היו ראויות ליפול אלא מחמת גובהן: אמר ליה דאיכא רב אדא בהדן דנפיש זכותיה. ול"צ דהאי רב אדא הוא דהא רב אדא בר אהבה הוה בימי רבא דמליט בכמה מקומות אמר רב אדא בר אהבה אמר רבא (פ) והא רב אדא בר אהבה דהכא משמע דהוה חבר לרב ולשמואל מדקאמר ליה שמואל לרב וקאמר ליה הא איכא רב אדא בהדן ואכן יתעבא דרב יהודה היה תלמיד דרב ושמואל ורבא *הוה נולד ביום שמת רב יהודה ורב אדא היה תלמיד דרבא א"כ ע"כ צ"ל דתרי רב אדא הוו: בהבינתו. פירוש בכינוי שמכנין אותו (י) בן אדם לגנאי בחניכתו פי' כינוי שם משפחתו שם לוי [illegible] עד עשרה דורות (גיטין דף פח·) כגון רבי אברהם אבן עזרא שכל בני משפחתו היו נקראים כך ודוקא לגנאי אבל לשבח מותר:

נזדמן לו אדם. יש ספרים שכתוב בהן אליהו זכור לטוב והוא נתכוון להוכיחו שלא ירגיל בדבר: ה"ג מפולת שאמרו בריאות ולא רעועות שאינן ראויות ליפול ולא שראויות ליפול הי ניהו בריאות והי ניהו שאינן ראויות ליפול הי ניהו רעועות והי ניהו ראויות ליפול הורה אור לא צריכא דקיימן אגודא דנהרא. מפולת שיש שם רוח חזק שמפיל החומות (ה) מפולת שאמרו מתריעין עליהן בבריאות קאמרינן שיהא החומות בריאות ואף על פי כן טפלות מכח נשיבת הרוח אבל אם היו החומות הטפלות רעועות אין מתריעין עליהן וכשאינן ראויות ליפול מתריעין עליהן ולא בראויות ליפול: לא צריכא. הא דקתני שאינן רעועות וראויות ליפול אלא כגון דקאי אגודא דנהרא על שפת הנהר שאע"פ שהיא בריאה ראויה היא ליפול שהמים מפילין אותה שמקלקלין את הקרקע ושוחקין את היסוד: כי ההיא אשיתא רעועה כו': באתרה. במקומה אף על גב דאוגה ראויה ליפול דהא קאה באתרה טולי האי אפילו הכי כיון דרעועה היא לא הוו חלפי תותה אלא היו מקיף סביבותיה: מכנין. ממעטין: ה"ג לא הקפדתי בתוך ביתי (ו) ולא הלכתי בלא תורה. דכל שעתא הוה גרים: בהכינתו. שמכנים לו בני אדם (ז) כגון שם לווי: חניכתו. כמו חניכת אבות בגיטין עד י' דורות (גיטין דף פח·): ביומא דעיבא. יום המעונן דהוי רוח מנשבת ומסתפי דלא תפיל חומות: בגוהרקא. תיבה תלויה בעגלה ושרות יושבות בהן: וסייר. בודק תרגום פוקד (שמות לד) מסער כמו האי טבחא דלא סר סכינא קמיה חכם*: כי הוה ליה מילתא דאסותא רמי ליה אטוא דמיא כו' לא גרסינן: זבין ליה ושדי ליה בנהרא. להכי זבין להו דאי הוה משתייר מידי לגנגין אזלא לאיבוד דמכמשא בשבת ונמלא מכשילן לעתיד לבא דלא מייתי ירקי לסעודת שבת: דסמכא דעתייהו. שנסמכין עניים לאותו ירק ואומרים אין אנו צריכין לקנות ושמא לא ישתייר שם כלום ואין להן מה לאכול בשבת: אין [illegible] אוכלין (ח) ומחזי כבועט בטובה שהשפיע הקב"ה בעולם אי נמי משום דחסה תורה על ממונן של ישראל וזרק לנהר והולכין למקום אחר ומולאין אותם בני אדם ואוכלין אותן כך שמעתי: מילתא דשיבתא. מנהג שדים שמזיקין למי שיאכל ואינו נוטל ידיו דשיבתא כהך דגרסינן במסכת יומא (דף עז:) אמר אביי משום שיבתא והוה תלי ליה להאי כוזא דמיא כי היכי דלימשו ידייהו מינה: בר מהא. חוץ מזו דכל מאן דבעי הוה עייל ואכל: משום

נזדמן לו אדם אחד שהיה מכוער ביותר אמר לו שלום עליך רבי ולא החזיר לו אמר לו ריקה כמה מכוער אותו האיש שמא כל בני עירך מכוערין כמותך אמר לו איני יודע אלא לך ואמור לאומן שעשאני כמה מכוער כלי זה שעשית כיון שידע בעצמו שחטא ירד מן החמור ונשתטח לפניו ואמר לו *נעניתי לך מחול לי אמר לו איני מוחל לך עד שתלך לאומן שעשאני ואמור לו כמה מכוער כלי זה שעשית היה מטייל אחריו עד שהגיע לעירו יצאו בני עירו לקראתו והיו אומרים לו שלום עליך רבי רבי מורי מורי אמר להם למי אתם קורין רבי רבי אמרו לו לזה שמטייל אחריך אמר להם אם זה רבי אל ירבו כמותו בישראל אמרו לו מפני מה אמר להם כך וכך עשה לי אמרו לו אעפ"כ מחול לו שאדם גדול בתורה הוא אמר להם בשבילכם הריני מוחל לו ובלבד שלא יהא רגיל לעשות כן מיד נכנס רבי אלעזר (א) בן רבי שמעון ודרש לעולם יהא אדם רך כקנה ואל יהא קשה כארז ולפיכך זכה קנה ליטול הימנה קולמוס לכתוב בו ספר תורה תפילין ומזוזות: וכן עיר שיש בה דבר או מפולת כו': תנו רבנן מפולת שאמרו בריאות ולא רעועות שאינן ראויות ליפול ולא הראויות ליפול הי ניהו בריאות הי ניהו שאינן ראויות ליפול הי ניהו רעועות הי ניהו ראויות ליפול לא צריכא דנפלו מחמת גובהייהו *אי נמי דקיימן אגודא דנהרא כי ההיא אשיתא רעועה דהואי בנהרדעא דלא הוה חליף רב ושמואל תותה אע"ג דקיימא באתרה תליסר שנין (ב) יומא חד איקלע רב אדא בר אהבה להתם אמר ליה שמואל לרב ניתי מר נקיף אמר ליה לא צריכנא האידנא דאיכא רב אדא בר אהבה בהדן דנפיש זכותיה ולא מסתפינא רב הונא הוה ליה ההוא חמרא בההוא ביתא רעיעא ובעי לפנוייה עייליה לרב אדא בר אהבה להתם משכי' בשמעתא עד דפנייה בתר דנפק נפל ביתא ארגיש רב אדא בר אהבה איקפד סבר לה כי הא *דאמר רבי ינאי לעולם אל יעמוד אדם במקום סכנה ויאמר עושין לי נס שמא אין עושין לו נס ואם תימצי לומר עושין לו נס מנכין לו מזכיותיו אמר רב חנן מאי קרא דכתיב °קטנתי מכל החסדים ומכל האמת מאי הוה עובדיה דרב אדא בר אהבה כי הא דאתמר *שאלו תלמידיו (*את רבי זירא ואמרי לה) לרב אדא בר אהבה במה הארכת ימים אמר להם מימי לא הקפדתי בתוך ביתי ולא צעדתי בפני מי שגדול ממני (ג) ולא הרהרתי במבואות המטונפות ולא הלכתי ד' אמות בלא תורה ובלא תפילין ולא ישנתי בבית המדרש לא שינת קבע ולא שינת עראי ולא ששתי בתקלת חברי ולא קראתי לחבירי *בהכינתו ואמרי לה *)בחניכתו אמר ליה רבא לרפרם בר פפא לימא לן מר מהני מילי מעלייתא דהוה עביד רב הונא אמר ליה בינקותיה לא דכירנא בסיבותיה דכירנא דכל יומא דעיבא הוו מפקין ליה בגוהרקא דדהבא וסייר לה לכולה מתא וכל אשיתא דהוות רעיעתא הוה סתר לה *אי אפשר למרה בני לה ואי לא אפשר בני לה איהו מדידיה וכל פניא דמעלי שבתא הוה משדר שלוחא לשוקא וכל ירקא דהוה פייש להו לגינאי זבין ליה ושדי ליה לנהרא וליתביה לעניים זמנין דסמכא דעתייהו ולא אתו למיזבן ולשדייה לבהמה °קסבר מאכל אדם אין מאכילין לבהמה ולא ליזבניה כלל נמצאת מכשילן לעתיד לבא כי הוה [א] ליה מילתא דאסותא הוי מלי כוזא (ד)דמיא ותלי ליה בסיפא דביתא ואמר כל דבעי ליתי ולישקול ואיכא דאמרי מילתא דשיבתא הוה גמיר והוה מנח כוזא דמיא ודלי ליה ואמר כל דצריך ליתי וליעול דלא לסתכן כי הוה כריך ריפתא הוה פתח לבביה ואמר כל מאן דצריך ליתי וליכול אמר רבא כולהו מצינא מקיימנא לבר מהא דלא מצינא למיעבד משום

מגילה כח.

בראשית לב

רבינו חננאל

שפגע באחד ואמר כמה מכוער כלי זה שמא כל בני עירך מכוערים כמותך. כיון שידע שחטא התחיל לבקש מחילה. נפק ודרש לעולם יהא אדם רך כקנה ואל יהא קשה כארז: מלתא דשיבתא פי' משקה של רפואה:

רבינו גרשום

בריאות טפלות. מתענין: דקמי אגודא דנהרא וה"ק (רעועות)(בריאות) ולא ראויות ליפול לאפוקי דקאי אגודא דנהרא דאע"ג דאין רעועות הואיל וראויות ליפול דאכלה להו מיא אין מתענין עליהן והויא לה *) נמי בריאות ראויות ליפול דקאי באתרא לאותר שהיתה רעועה דהא כיון דקם באתרא הויא כבריאתוכין דהויא רעועה הויא ראויה ליפול. קטנתי מכל החסדים כלומר נתמעטו הזכיות בשביל נסים כי בשקלי וגו'. בהכינתו שכבר קוראין לי ולא **)בחכינתי שאני קריתי לו שם. ביומא דעיבא הדיקא [illegible] דאי יתרי ומספדי לא הוו מייתי בערב שבת אחר: ולא אתו למיזבן ויישבין דלא יתרי להו כלום וסמכו עליה ולא הוה להן מאכל. לשיבתא מילתא דשיבתא הוה גמיר שהיה יודע שרוח רעה שורה (על המים) [על הידים]. ותלי כוזא דמיא (נמי) [כלי] שנוטלין בה את ידיהן ונכנסין. בר מהא דהוה פתח לבבא:

*) נראה מזה דרבינו ה"ה גורס אי נמי כבסיפא אשיתא וכו' והוא נמי פירוש על בריאות וראויות ליפול ולא כפרש"י.

**) נ"י רבינו בחניכתי כי"ד לנסוף וכ"ה בערוך ערך חנך ולפיכן פי' רבינו שאני קריתי וכו' ובערוך כתוב שלא כניתי לו שם ואולי דגם כדברי רבינו צריך להגיה כן וצ"ע.

***) נראה דחסר כאן וצ"ל ודיקא הוה סייר לכלהו מתא וכו' וכל ירקא דהוו פייש להו לגינאי זבין להו וכו'.

מסורת הש"ס

[מגילה כח. וע"ש פרש"י כתובות סו:]

חולין יח.

שבת לג.

[בפי' ליתא]

[גירס' הערוך בחניכתו פי' שלא כינוי לו שם]

*) [פי' הערוך ערך חנך אסי' שם שכינו לו אחרים לא קראוהו]

הגהות הב"ח

(א) גמ' מבני שמעון: (ב) דקיימא באתרה תליסר שנין ולא נפלה יומא חד כו' ניתי מר ונקיף

א"ל: (ג) שם ונפני מי שגדול ממני בחכמה ולא הרהרתי: (ד) שם הוי מלי כוזא מיניה ותלי ליה: (ה) רש"י ד"ה ה"ג מפולת כו' דנהרא הס"ד ואח"כ מה"ד מפולת וכו' החומות הס"ד ומה"ד מפולת שאמרו כו' עליהן הס"ד ומה"ד בבריאות כו' עליהן הס"ד ומה"ד וכשאינן ראויות כו': (ו) ד"ה ה"ג לא כו' ביתי הס"ד ומה"ד ולא הלכתי כו': (ז) ד"ה בהכינתו כו' בני אדם לגנאי כגון: (ח) ד"ה אין מאכילין כו' כיון אוכלין דמיחזי כבועט: (פ) תוס' ד"ה א"ל כו' אמר רבא והאי רב אדא: (י) ד"ה בהכינתו כו' שמכנין אותו בני אדם לגנאי כגון שם לוי בחניכתו פי' כינוי בשם משפחתו ד"ש משפחה שמכנין בני אדם לכל משפחה וקוראין בחניכה שם לוי כמו שם חניכה:

גליון הש"ס

גמ' קסבר מאכל אדם אין מאכילים לבהמה. מג"א סימן קעא ס"ק א:

הגהות הגר"א

[א] גמ' כי הוה ליה. רשום קו על מלת ליה:

משום דנפישי בני חילא דמחוזא אילפא ור' יוחנן הוו גרסי באורייתא דחיקא להו מילתא טובא אמרי ניקום וניזיל וניעבד עיסקא ונקיים בנפשין °אפס כי לא יהיה בך אביון אזלו (א) אותבי תותי גודא רעיעא הוו קא כרכי ריפתא אתו תרי מלאכי השרת שמעיה רבי יוחנן דאמר חד לחבריה נישדי עלייהו האי גודא ונקטלינהו *שמניחין חיי עולם הבא ועוסקין בחיי שעה אמר ליה אידך שבקינהו דאיכא בהו חד דקיימא ליה שעתא רבי יוחנן שמע אילפא לא שמע אמר ליה ר' יוחנן לאילפא שמע מר מידי אמר ליה לא אמר מדשמעי' אנא ואילפא לא שמע ש"מ לדידי קיימא לי שעתא אמר ליה רבי יוחנן איהדר ואוקי בנפשאי °כי לא יחדל אביון מקרב הארץ ר' יוחנן הדר אילפא לא הדר עד דאתא אילפא מליך רבי יוחנן אמרו לו אי אתיב מר וגרים לא הוה מליך מר *אזל *תלא נפשיה באסקריא דספינתא אמר אי איכא דשאיל לי במתניתא דר' חייא ורבי אושעיא ולא פשטינא ליה ממתני' נפילנא מאסקריא דספינתא וטבענא אתא ההוא סבא תנא ליה *האומר תנו שקל לבניי בשבת והן ראויין לתת להם סלע נותנין להם סלע ואם אמר אל תתנו להם אלא שקל אין נותנין להם אלא שקל *אם אמר *מתו ירשו אחרים תחתיהם בין שאמר תנו בין שאמר אל תתנו אין נותנין להם אלא שקל א"ל הא מני ר"מ היא דאמר [ג]מצוה לקיים דברי המת אמרו עליו על נחום איש גם זו שהיה סומא משתי עיניו גידם משתי ידיו קיטע משתי רגליו וכל גופו מלא שחין והיה מוטל בבית רעוע ורגלי מטתו מונחין בספלין של מים כדי שלא יעלו עליו נמלים פעם אחת [היתה מטתו מונחת בבית רעוע] בקשו תלמידיו לפנות מטתו ואח"כ לפנות את הכלים אמר להם בניי פנו את הכלים ואח"כ פנו את מטתי שמובטח לכם כל זמן שאני בבית אין הבית נופל פינו את הכלים ואחר כך פינו את מטתו ונפל הבית אמרו לו תלמידיו רבי וכי מאחר שצדיק גמור אתה למה עלתה לך כך אמר להם בניי אני גרמתי לעצמי שפעם אחת הייתי מהלך בדרך לבית חמי והיה עמי משוי ג' חמורים אחד של מאכל ואחד של משתה ואחד של מיני מגדים בא עני אחד ועמד לי בדרך ואמר לי רבי פרנסני אמרתי לו המתן עד שאפרוק מן החמור לא הספקתי לפרוק מן החמור עד שיצתה נשמתו הלכתי ונפלתי על פניו ואמרתי עיני שלא חסו על עיניך יסומו ידיי שלא חסו על ידיך יתגדמו רגליי שלא חסו על רגליך יתקטעו ולא נתקררה דעתי עד שאמרתי כל גופי יהא מלא שחין אמרו לו אוי לנו שראינוך בכך אמר להם אוי לי אם לא ראיתוני בכך *ואמאי קרו ליה נחום איש גם זו דכל מילתא דהוה סלקא ליה אמר גם זו לטובה *זימנא חדא בעו לשדורי ישראל דורון לבי קיסר אמרו מאן ייזיל ייזיל נחום איש גם זו דמלומד בניסין הוא שדרו בידיה מלא סיפטא דאבנים טובות ומרגליות אזל בת בההוא דירה בליליא קמו הנך דיוראי ושקלינהו לסיפטיה ומלונהו עפרא (למחר כי חזנהו אמר גם זו לטובה) כי מטא התם [שרינהו לסיפטא חזנהו דמלו עפרא] בעא מלכא למקטלינהו לכולהו אמר קא מחייכו בי יהודאי [אמר גם זו לטובה] אתא אליהו אדמי ליה כחד מינייהו א"ל דלמא הא עפרא מעפרא דאברהם אבוהון הוא דכי הוה שדי עפרא הוו סייפיה גילי הוו גירי דכתיב °יתן כעפר חרבו כקש נדף קשתו הויא חדא מדינתא דלא מצו למיכבשה בדקו מיניה וכבשוה עיילו לבי גנזיה ומלוהו לסיפטיה אבנים טובות ומרגליות ושדרוהו ביקרא רבה כי אתו ביתו בההוא דיורא אמרו ליה מאי אייתית בהדך דעבדי לך יקרא כולי האי אמר להו מאי דשקלי מהכא אמטי להתם סתרו לדירייהו ואמטינהו לבי מלכא אמרו ליה האי עפרא דאייתי הכא מדידן הוא בדקוה ולא אשכחוה וקטלינהו להנך דיוראי: אי זו היא דבר עיר המוציאה חמש מאות רגלי כו': ת"ר °עיר (ג)המוציאה חמש מאות ואלף רגלי כגון כפר עכו ויצאו הימנה תשעה מתים בשלשה ימים זה אחר זה הרי זה דבר ביום אחד או בד' ימים אין זה דבר *ועיר המוציאה חמש מאות רגלי כגון כפר עמיקו ויצאו ממנה שלשה מתים בג' ימים זה אחר זה הרי זה דבר

ביום

רש"י

משום דנפישי בני מחוזא. דאיכא עניי טפי וקא מיכלי קרנא: דחיקא להו. עניות: כי לא יהיה בך אביון. בך בעצמך: חיי עולם הבא. תורה: חיי שעה. עולם הזה זה סחורה: קיימא ליה שעתא. עתיד להתגדל ואין זמנו למות: שמע מינה. מדלא שמעתיה איהדר איזיל לתורתי: עד דאתא תורה איר אילפא. ממקום שהלך שם לסחורה: מלך רבי יוחנן. מינוהו לראש ישיבה עליהן מנהג הוא מי שהוא ראש ישיבה היו מגדלין אותו משלהן ומעשירין אותו כדאמרינן גבי כהן גדול בספרא וביומא (דף יח.) והכהן הגדול מאחיו גדלהו משל אחיו: אמרו לו. אנשי המקום לאילפא: אי (ג) אתיב מר וגרים. אם היית יושב ועוסק בתורה היינו ממליכין אותך כמו שעשינו לר' יוחנן דאילפא הוי גמיר טפי מר' יוחנן: תלא נפשיה באסקריא. כלונס עץ ארוך תקוע בגג הספינה שמניחין עליה מכסה וילו"ן בלע"ז: דשאיל לי כו'. כלומר אף על גב דעבדי עיסקא גריסנא אנא טפי מיניה: דבי ר' חייא ודבי ר' אושעיא. דהוו מסדרי מתניתא על פי רבינו הקדוש שהיה רבם: ולא פשיטנא ליה ממתני'. דאשכחנא משנה סותיה דההיא ברייתא: תנא ליה. שנה לפניו כלומר בעא מיניה: האומר תנו שקל לבניי. מי שמת והניח ממונו ביד איש נאמן ואמר תנו שקל חצי סלע לבניי להוצאה בשבוע: וראויין לתת להן סלע. שיש לו נכסים הרבה ואין מסתפקין לשבת בפחות מסלע: נותנין להן סלע. דלאו הוה בדעתיה דלא למיתן להו אלא שקל היה מטה אל תתנו להן אלא שקל והאי דקאמר תנו להן שקל ולא אמר תנו סלע משום דבעי לזרוזינהו כדאמרן בכתובות (דף ע:) כדי לזרזן במשא ובמתן כדי שיטרחו וילמדו דרך ארץ וירויחו: אם מתו ירשו אחרים תחתיהן. אע"ג דאמר תנו שקל ולא אמר אל תתנו אלא שקל גלי בדעתיה דלא בעי למיתב להו אלא שקל בשבת כי היכי דאי מתו ירשו אחרים תחתיהן: אמר ליה. אילפא: הא מני. דקתני אע"ג דלא ספקי בציר מסלע לא יהבינן להו אלא שקל (ד) ר"מ היא דאמר במסכת כתובות במתני' (דף סט:) מצוה לקיים דברי המת דאי לאו מצוה מן הדין נותנין להן כל הראוי להן שהרי כל הממון שלהן הוא ואין בו לאותן אחרים כלום אלא לאחר מיתתן אם יש מותר יש להן ואם לאו לא יטלו ומתוך שרוצין אנו לקיים דבריו שירשו אחרים תחתיהם אנו מקמצין את הממון כדי שיהא שם מותר: והיה מטתו מונחת כו'. רגלי המטה מונחין בספלים מלאים מים שלא יעלו אליו נמלים דרך רגלי המטה מפני שהיה גידם ואם הן עולים אינו יכול ליטלם בידיו ולזורקן: דסלק ליה. כל המאורע לו אפילו רעה: בת בההיא דירא. לן לילה אחת באותו המלון: לסיפטיה. ארגז שלו: לכולהו. שונאיהן של ישראל: כחד מינייהו. כאחד משרי קיסר: מעפרא דאברהם הוא. כשנלחם עם המלכים: גילי. קשין: ביתו. לנו במלון: (ה) כפר עמיקו שלשה מתים בשלשה ימים. מת אחד בכל יום:

ביום

עין משפט נר מצוה

טז א מיי' פ"ו מהלכות זכיה ומתנה הלכה ו טוש"ע ח"מ סי' רנג סעיף יז:

יז ב מיי' פ"ל מהלכות אישות הלכה יד סמג עשין מח טוש"ע אה"ע סי' נד וטוש"ע ח"מ סי' רנג סעיף ג:

יח ג מיי' פ"ב מהלכות תעניות הלכה ה טוש"ע א"ח סי' תקעו סעיף ב:

מסורת הש"ס

[שבת ל. לג: ב"מ פה:]
[כתובות סט:]
[פי' רש"י גיטין נב: ד"ה ואי ובכתובות נ: ד"ה שקל פרש"י]
[ב"ב קמט. כתובות סט:]
[ג"ל אם מתו]
סנהדרין קח:
ע"ש ברכות ס:
ישעיה מא
[מ"ק וכו']

רבינו חננאל

אילפא ור' יוחנן דחיק להו עלמא אמרי ניקום ונעביד עסקא עד דהדר אילפא מלך ר"י. אתא אילפא תלא נפשיה. אמר אי איכא דשאיל לי מתנייתא מדבי ר' חייא ודבי ר' אושעיא ולא פשטנא ליה ממתני'. כלומר כל מה שיש במשניות החיצונות עיקר שלהן במשנתנו ואין כל חכם יודע לפיכך אני גדול מר"י. ולמה זכה לישב בראש ולא זכיתי אני ושאליה ההוא סבא הא דתניא. האומר תנו לבניי שקל בשבת ומת וראויין לתת להן סלע. כי השקל הוא חצי סלע. אם אינו מספיק להן נותן להן סלע. אם אמר בלשון הזה אל תתנו להן אלא שקל אע"פ שאינו מספיק להן אינו נותן להן אלא שקל ואם אמר אם מתו יירשו אחרים תחתיהן כו'. שמעינן מינה דאין אדם רשאי לשנות מדברי המת. ופשט אילפא הא מתניתא אליבא דר' מאיר היא ששנינו במשנתנו בכתובות בפרק מציאת האשה המשליש מעות לבתו והיא אומרת נאמן עלי בעלי יעשה שליש מה שהשליש בידו דברי ר' מאיר. ואוקימנא התם משום דר' מאיר משום דמצוה לקיים דברי המת ואין לשנות מדבריו: אמרו עליו על נחום איש גם זו. שם מקום הוא שנקרא לשם שם אחת העיירות גמזו והוא האמת א) ירושלמי א"ר יוסי בר אבין בזכות ג' דברים גשמים יורדים. בזכות הארץ. ובזכות החסד ובזכות יסורין וכולן בפסוק אחד נאמרו. אם לשבט אם לארצו אם לחסד. מצאנו שבם אלו יסורין. ספני (ג') ד' דברים גשמים יורדין מלמעלה מפני מללים הרעים ומפני בעלי זרוע ושיהא שותה העליון כתחתון ושיתו עיני הכל נשואות לשמים. בעון (ג') ד' דברים גשמים נעצרים בעון ע"ז שנאמר ועבדתם שם אלהים אחרים וכתיב בתריה ועצר את השמים. בעון ג"ע שנאמר ותחניפי ארץ בזנותייכי וכתיב וימנעו רביבים וגו'. בעון ש"ד שנאמר כי הדם הוא יחניף את הארץ. פי' יתן אף על הארץ. (וכתיב וחרה אף ה' בכם ועצר את השמים) ב) בעון פוסקי צדקה ברבים ואינן נותנים דכתיב נשיאים ורוח וגשם אין איש מתהלל במתת שקר. [חמשה] שמות נקרא אד [עב] ענן חזיז נשיא א"ר חנינא מה יעשו גדולי הדור. ואין הצבור נידון אלא אחר רובו. שכן מצינו שכל ל"ח שנים שהיו ישראל כמנודים לשמים לא היה הדבור עם משה. שנאמר ויהי כאשר תמו כל אנשי המלחמה וגו' וכתיב וידבר ה' אלי לאמר. ר' אליעזר עבר תענית ולא נחית מטרא עבר ר' עקיבא תלמידי' ונחית מטרא. עאל ר"ע ואמר מלה"ד למלך שהיו לו ב' בנות אחת חצופה ואחת היתה צנועה. וכשהיתה נכנסת אצלו היה מאריך רוחו עמה כדי שישמע שיחתה שהיה מתאוה לשמוע שיחתה. עשה כן ר"ע בשביל ר' אליעזר רבו כדי שלא יאמרו כי אינו הגון ונמצא חלול שמים. (בירושלמי פ"ג ה"ה) כתיב ויקבצו המצפתה וישאבו מים וישפכו לפני ה' וכי מים שפכו אלא לבם שפכו כמים. ויאמרו שם חטאנו לה' לכש שמואל חלוקו של ישראל אמר לפניו רבש"ע כלום אתה דן את האדם ג) על אמרך לא חטאתי. ואלו אומרים לפניך חטאנו: מתני' איזו היא דבר. עיר המוציאה ת"ק רגלי עיר גדולה המוציאה אלף ת"ק רגלי יוצאי צבא כגון כפר עכו. ויצאו הימנה ט' מתים בג' ימים (בג' ימים אנשים מסש) [וא"ו] הרי דבר בד'

א) עי' בערוך השלם ערך גם זו. ב) בירושלמי לפנינו ליתא זה אך רבינו היה גורס כן בירושלמי ומביא ראיה מכן קרא דכך אף דאידך קרא היינו שיהיה עצירת גשמים. ג) אלא על שאתה אומר לפניך לא חטאתי כנגד נשפט אותך על אמרך לא חטאתי (ירמיה ב').

רבינו גרשום

באסקריא דספינתא: תקם: נותנין להם סלע דאזלינן בתר אומדין דעתי' דלהכי אמר שקל אם אפשר להם לצמצם אבל אם אי אפשר להם נותנין להם סלע *) כיון שאמר תנו אין נותנים להם אלא שקל דאזלינן בתר אומדין דעתיה דכיון דבעי דלירשו אחרים ודאי הוה ליה צר עין על בניו א"ל הא מני ר"מ דמתניתין: מונחת על ארבעה ספלים שלא יעלו עליו הרחש: ביום אחד

*) נ"ל ואם אמר אם מתו ירשו אחרים תחתיהם בין שאמר תנו ובין שאמר אל תתנו אין נותנין להם וכו'.

הגהות הב"ח

(א) גמ' אזלו אותיבו תותי גודא וכו' אי יתיב מר וגרים: (ב) שם ת"ר עיר גדולה המוציאה חמש מאות כו' ועיר קטנה המוציאה כו': (ג) רש"י ד"ה אי יתיב מר וגרים: (ד) ד"ה הא מני כו' אלא שקל בשבת ומה"ד ר"מ היא וכו' שיהא שם מותר בשבת ומה"ד ורגלי מטתו מונחין כו': (ה) ד"ה ביתו לנו במלון בס"ד ואח"כ מה"ד כגון כפר עמיקו ויצאו ממנה שלשה מתים: (ו) תוס' ד"ה אמרו כו'. פי' כתמיה כלומר וכי לא היית:

תורה אור

ביום אחד או בארבעה ימים אין זה דבר דרוקרת עיר המוציאה חמש מאות רגלי הוה ויצאו ממנה שלשה מתים ביום אחד גזר רב נחמן בר רב חסדא תעניתא אמר רב נחמן בר יצחק כמאן כר"מ דאמר *ריחק נגיחותיו חייב קירב נגיחותיו לא כ"ש א"ל רב נחמן בר רב חסדא לרב נחמן בר יצחק ליקום מר ליתי לגבן א"ל תנינא רבי יוסי אומר לא מקומו של אדם מכבדו אלא אדם מכבד את מקומו שכן מצינו בהר סיני שכל זמן שהשכינה שרויה עליו אמרה תורה °גם (שמות לד) הצאן והבקר אל ירעו אל מול ההר ההוא נסתלקה שכינה ממנו אמרה תורה °במשוך (שם יט) [illegible] אמרה תורה °וישלחו מן המתנה כל צרוע *והוגללו הפרוכת הותרו זבין (במדבר ה) והמצורעים ליכנס שם אמר ליה אי הכי (א) ניקום אנא לגבי מר אמר ליה מוטב יבא מנה בן פרס אצל מנה בן מנה ואל יבא מנה בן מנה אצל מנה בן פרס בסורא הוות דברתא בשיבבותיה דרב לא הוות דברתא סברו מיניה משום זכותיה דרב דנפיש איתחזי להו בחילמא רב דנפישא זכותיה טובא הא מילתא זוטרא ליה לרב אלא משום ההוא גברא דשייל מרא וחבילא לקבורה בדרוקרת הוות דליקתא ובשיבבותיה דרב הונא לא הוות דליקתא סבור מינה בזכותא דרב הונא דנפיש איתחזי להו בחילמא האי זוטרא ליה לרב הונא אלא משום ההיא איתתא דמחממת תנורא (ב) ומשיילי לשיבבותיה אמרו ליה לרב יהודה אתו קמצי גזר תעניתא אמרו ליה לא קא מפסדן אמר להו זוודא אייתו בהדייהו אמרו ליה לרב יהודה איכא מותנא בחוירי גזר תעניתא נימא קסבר רב יהודה מכה משולחת (ג) ממין אחד משולחת מכל המינין לא *שאני חוירי דדמיין מעייהו לבני אינשי אמרו ליה לשמואל איכא מותנא בי חוזאי גזר תעניתא א"ל והא מרחק אמר ליכא מעברא הבא דפסיק ליה אמרו ליה לרב נחמן *איכא מותנא בארעא דישראל גזר תעניתא אמר אם גבירה לוקה שפחה לא כל שכן טעמא דגבירה ושפחה הא שפחה ושפחה לא והא אמרו ליה לשמואל איכא מותנא בי חוזאי גזר תעניתא *שאני התם כיון דאיכא שיירתא דלווי ואתיא בהדיה אבא אומנא הוה אתי ליה שלמא ממתיבתא דרקיעא כל יומא ולאביי כל מעלי יומא דשבתא לרבא כל מעלי יומא דכיפורי הוה קא חלשא דעתיה דאביי משום דאבא אומנא אמרו ליה לא מצית למיעבד כעובדיה (ד) ומאי הוו עובדיה דאבא אומנא דכי הוה עביד מילתא הוה מחית גברי לחוד ונשי לחוד ואית ליה לבושא דאית ביה קרנא דהוות בזיעא כי כוסילתא כי הוות אתיא ליה איתתא הוה מלביש לה כי היכי דלא ניסתכל בה ואית ליה דוכתא *דצניעא דשדי ביה פשיטי דשקיל דאית ליה שדי ביה דלית ליה *) לא מיכסיף כי הוה אתרמי ליה צורבא מרבנן אגרא מיניה לא שקיל *ובתר דקאי יהיב ליה פשיטי ואמר ליה זיל בריא נפשך יומא חד שדר אביי זוגא דרבנן למיבדקיה אותבינהו ואבלינהו ואשקינהו ומך להו ביסתרקי בליליא לצפרא

*) כ"א הוה אתי ויתיב ולא

ביום אחד אין זה דבר. דאקראי בעלמא הוא: ה"ג עיר גדולה המוציאה אלף וחמש מאות רגלי יצאו הימנה תשעה מתים וכו' אלף וחמש מאות איש דהיינו פי שלשה בעיר קטנה (ה): כפר עכו דרוקרת נ"א דיוקרא עיר ששמה יו"ד והיא קטנה על שם שיו"ד קטנה באותיות: ה"ג יצאו הימנה ג' מתים *בג' ימים: ריחק נגיחותיו. בשור מועד קאי כבבא קמא בפרק כיצד הרגל מועדת אי זהו תם ואי זהו מועד כל שהעידו בו ג' ימים דברי ר' יהודה ר' מאיר אומר כל שהעידו בו ג' פעמים ביום אחד ר' יהודה סבר כתיב או נודע כי שור נגח הוא מתמול שלשום מתמול הרי שלשום תלת הרי ג' ימים ור"מ סבר ריחק נגיחותיו כשנגח בג' ימים זה אחר זה חייב קירב נגיחותיו שנגח ג' פעמים ביום אחד לא כל שכן: ליקום מר להכא. דרב נחמן בר יצחק הוה יתיב בין גברי דלא חשיבי טלי האי וקאמר ליה רב נחמן בר רב חסדא [illegible] גבאי: תנינא. תני אנא שונה אני ברייתא זו רבי יוסי אומר כו': לא מקומו של אדם מכבדו. ואם אלך ואשב שם אין המקום מכבדני: גם הצאן והבקר אל ירעו. דמשום שכינה היה הר סיני מכובד ומקודש: אל מול ההר ההוא. מדכתיב ההוא משמע כל זמן שהוא בגדולתו שהשכינה עליו (ו) נסתלקה השכינה במשוך היובל וגו' ואע"ג דהאי קרא בלוחות הראשונות כתיב לא נסתלקה שכינה עד לוחות האחרונות שניתנו ביום הכפורים וגם כל ימות החורף שעסקו במלאכת המשכן שהתה שכינה בהר ומשם ניתנו כל המצות בקולי קולות ולפידים ביום קבלת עשרת הדברות עד אחד בניסן שהוקם המשכן ונסעה וחזה שכינה מן ההר וישבה לה על *הכפורת ושם באהל מועד נשנית התורה כללותיה ופרטותיה ועל אותה שעה היה מתיר להם בלוחות הראשונות לעלות כדאמרינן במסכת ביצה (דף ה:) כל דבר שבמנין צריך מנין אחר להתירו וכראש קונטרס רומי אתה מוצא תשובת *רבים בכך: במשוך היובל. [illegible] בסוף השופר כשתסתלק השכינה דרך הוא להאריך ולמשוך התקיעה בשעת סיום: הוגללו הפרוכת. שהיו נגללין בשעת נסיעתן (ז) היו נוטלין טולן ובאין זבים ומצורעים ונכנסין במחנה: פרס. חצי מנה ולשון פרוסה כמו פרס פריסת מלכותך (דניאל ה) שאביו של רב נחמן בר רב חסדא גדול מיצחק אביו של רב נחמן מדמיתקרי בר רב חסדא ואידך רב נחמן בר יצחק מכלל שלא נסמך: דבריתא. דבר: בשיבבותיה. בשכונתו: איתחזי להו בחילמא. להנך אינשי דסברי (ח) משום זכותיה דרב הוא: הא זוטר ליה לרב. נס זה קטן הוא לפי גדולת רב: מרא. פוסויי"ר בלע"ז: זבילי. פלי"א בלע"ז: לקבורה. ומשום זכותיה דקבורה מדדו בו מדה כנגד מדה: ומשיילא לשיבבותה. ומשאילתו לשכנותיה לאחר שהסיקתו משלה לפיכך נמדדת השכר בה במדה: קמצא. ארבה שמכלה את התבואה: לא קא מפסדא. לא בעינן למיגזר תעניתא: זוודא אייתו בהדייהו. בתמיה וכי צידה הביאו עמם שלא יפסידו את התבואה: מעייהו. בני מעיין שלהן שאין להן כרס הפנימי כשאר בהמה וסימן רע הוא: בי חוזאי. מקום במלכות בבל: גזר תעניתא. בעירו: הא מרחק. ואין לחוש שמא יבא עד כאן: אמר להו וכי מעברא פסיק להו. וכי מעברות ושאר מחיצות מפסיקין לפני הדבר שלא יבא: שפחה לא כל שכן. ויש לחוש שמא ישתלח עד כאן: הא שפחה ושפחה. שתי עיירות של חוצה לארץ כגון בי חוזאי ונהרדעא דאתריה דשמואל: שיירתא. דאזלי מבי חוזאי לנהרדעא: דלווי. מתלוה ובא עמהן: שלמא מרקיעא. בת קול אומרת לו שלום עליך: אבא אומנא. מקיז דם: כי הוה עביד מילתא. כשהיה מקיז דם לבני אדם: ודנשים לחודייהו. לצניעותא: דאית ביה קרנא. ויכטוס"א שהיה תקוע בו הקרן שהוא מקיז בו ולנשים הוי מלביש לה: ולא מכסיף. דלאחר *שהכה לא הוה ידע מאן רמי (בכסילתיה) פשיטי להתם ומאן דלא רמי: בריא נפשך. הבריא עצמך: למיבדקיה. לבדקו במעשיו: ומך להו בסתרקי. קיפל תחתיהן תכשיטי צמר טפיד"ו בלע"ז ליטן בהן: לצפרא

יבא מנה בן פרס. כלומר מוטב שיבא גדול בן הדיוט דפרס לא הוה אלא חצי מנה ואל יבא מנה בן מנה דהיינו רב חסדא דהיה מנה כלומר שהיה חשוב ופרס היינו יצחק אבוה דרב נחמן דלא מיקרי רב יצחק: *אמר ליה זוודא אייתי בהדייהו. פירוש וכי צידה הביאו עמהם שיהו אוכלות כלומר אי אפשר שלא יאכלו התבואה והזרעים: אמרו ליה לרב יהודה איכא מותנא בחוירי גזר תעניתא וכו' עד שאני חוירי דדמו מעייהו לבני אינשי. פירוש שבני מעיו של חזיר דומין למעים של בני אדם ויש לחוש שיבא (ט) על בני אדם מכאן נראה שאם יהיה דבר על עובדי כוכבים שיש לחוש ויש להתענות דהא הכא חזינן דגזר תעניתא (י) מדבר שהיה בחזירין משום דדמו מעייהו לבני אדם וכל שכן דנכרים דדמו לישראל: גבירה לוקה. פי' זו ארץ ישראל:

טרפה

נ"א ביום אחד. רש"א

ב"ק כד. ב"מ כט:

[מנחות צט.]

הכפורת באהל מועד ושם נשנית התורה כצ"ל. רש"א

[רבינו ברוך ז"ל]

ס"א מאבראי

ס"א וכי הוי חזי אינש דלא אפשר הוה יהיב ליה כו'

נ"ל צ"ל שסקי

יט א טוש"ע א"ח סי' תקעו סעיף ג:

[נ"ל אמר להו]

כ ב ג מיי' פ"ב מהלכות תענית הלכה ו טוש"ע שם סעיף ב:

רבינו חננאל

בד' ימים או ביום אחד אינו דבר. א"ל רב נחמן בר רב חסדא לרב נחמן בר יצחק ליתי מר יקום הכא. א"ל תנינא לא המקום מכבד את האדם אלא אדם מכבד את מקומו. שכן מצינו בסיני כ"ז שהשכינה עליו כתיב גם הצאן והבקר אל ירעו. נסתלקה שכינה כתיב במשוך היובל המה יעלו בהר. וכן [illegible] נמי כתיב וישלחו מן המחנה כל צרוע וגו' הוגללו הפרוכת הותרו הזבים והמצורעים להכנס. א"ל אבוא אני אצלך. א"ל מוטב יבא מנה בן פרס. פי' חכם בן מי שלא היה אביו חכם אצל חכם בן חכם. בסורא הוה מותנא בשיבבותיה דרב לא הות וכן הות דלקת בדרוקרתא ובשיבבותיה דרב הונא לא הות. ואסיקנא דלאו בזכותייהו דהני אלא בשביל ההוא גברא דמושיל מרא לאינשי לקבורה. ובדיל ההיא איתתא דמחממא תנורא ומושלא לשבבתא. אמרו לר"י איכא מותנא בחוירי אמר כיון דדמיין מעייהו לבני אדם גזרינן תעניתא

רבינו גרשום

אחד אין זה דבר דאקראי בעלמא הוא: או בארבעה מרוחקין: ם מתים דהיינו נמי ג' מתים לג' ימים: ריחק נגיחותיו שנגח בג' ימים הוי מועד. קירב נגיחותיו שנגח ג' ביום [illegible] מפסקי כלומר שיירות מצויין שעוברין במעברות מבי חוזאי להכא כיון דשכיחי שיירתא מבי חוזאי להכא גזר אבל מא"י לבבל דלא שכיחי שיירתא אי לאו משום גבירתה לא הוה גזר. אתי ליה שלמא מכרוז עליה שלמא מרקיעא: דאית ביה קרני כלומר אתרא לקרני.

הגהות הב"ח

(א) גמ' א"ל אי הכי איקום אנא ואיזול לגבי מר: (ב) שם הכיא איתתא דמחממא תנורא מע"ש לע"ש ומשיילא לשיבבותה: (ג) שם מכה משולחת כמין אחד משולחת בכל המינין: (ד) שם למיעבד כעובדיה דאבא אומנא ומאי הוו כו' כי כוסילתא דכי הוות כו' דלא ליסתכל בה והוה ליה דוכתא דצניעא: (ה) רש"י ד"ה ה"ג עיר כו' ויצאו הימנה ט' מתים וכו' כגון כפר עכו אלף וחמש מאות וכו' בעיר קטנה הס"ד ואח"כ מה"ד דרוקרת נ"א יו"ד קרא עיר ששמה יו"ד והיא עיר קטנה על שם כו' כצ"ל ותיבות כפר עכו נמחק: (ו) ד"ה אל מול כו' שהשכינה עליו הס"ד ומה"ד נסתלקה וכו' וכראש קונטרס תשובת רומי: (ז) ד"ה הוגללו וכו' והיו נוטלין וכו' במחנה שכינה הס"ד: (ח) ד"ה איתחזי וכו' דמשום זכותיה: (ט) תוס' ד"ה אמרו כו' ויש לחוש שיבא דבר על בני אדם: (י) בא"ד אדבר שהיה בחזירין. נ"ב וקשה דאמרינן דבשנה כהרי אומי לא שלטה:

בא א מיי׳ פ״ג מהלכות תעניות הל׳ י טוש״ע א״ח סי׳ תקעו סעיף ט :

בב ב ג ד ה ו מיי׳ שם הלכה ז ח טוש״ע שם סעיף ז ז :

בג ז מיי׳ שם הלכה ד טוש״ע שם סעיף א :

לצפרא כרכינהו ושקלינהו וקמו ונפקו לדהו לשוקא ואשכחינהו א״ל לשיימיה מר היכי שוו א״ל הכי והכי א״ל ודלמא שוו טפי א״ל בהכי שקלינהו אמרו ליה דידך נינהו ושקלינהו מינך אמרו ליה במטותא מינך במאי חשדתינן א״ל אמינא פדיון שבויים איקלע להו לרבנן ואכסיפו למימר לי אמרו ליה השתא נשקלינהו מר אמר להו מההוא שעתא אסחתינהו מדעתאי לצדקה הוה קא חלשא דעתיה דרבא משום דאביי (א) אמרו ליה מסתייך דקא מגנית אבולה כרכא ר׳ ברוקא חוזאה הוה שכיח בשוקא דבי לפט הוה שכיח אליהו גביה א״ל *איכא בהאי שוקא בר עלמא דאתי א״ל לא אדהכי והכי חזא להחוא גברא דהוה סיים מסאני אוכמי ולא רמי חוטא דתכלתא בגלימיה א״ל האי בר עלמא דאתי הוא (ג) רהט בתריה א״ל מאי עובדך א״ל זיל האידנא ותא למחר למחר א״ל מאי עובדך א״ל *זנדוקנא אנא ואסרנא גברי לחוד ונשי לחוד ורמינא פורייאי בין הני להני כי היכי דלא ליתו לידי איסורא כי חזינא בת ישראל דיהבי נכרים עלה עינייהו מסרנא נפשאי ומצילנא לה יומא חד הוות נערה מאורסה גבן דיהבו בה נכרים עינייהו שקלי דורדייא דחמרא ושדאי לה בשיפולה ואמרי *דיסתנא היא א״ל מאי טעמא לית לך חוטי (ג) ורמית מסאני אוכמי א״ל עיילנא ונפיקנא ביני נכרים כי היכי דלא לידעו דיהודאה אנא כי הוו גזרי גזירתא מודענא להו לרבנן ובעו רחמי ומבטלי לגזירתייהו ומאי טעמא כי אמינא לך אנא מאי עובדך ואמרת לי זיל האידנא ותא למחר א״ל בההיא שעתא גזרי גזירתא ואמינא ברישא איזיל ואשמע להו לרבנן דלבעי רחמי עלה דמילתא אדהכי והכי אתו הנך תרי *אתי א״ל הנך נמי בני עלמא דאתי נינהו אזל לגבייהו אמר להו מאי עובדייכו אמרו ליה אינשי בדוחי אנן מבדחינן עציבי אי נמי כי חזינן בי תרי דאית להו תיגרא בהדייהו טרחינן ועבדינן להו שלמא: על אלו מתריעין בכל מקום כו׳ : ת״ר על אלו מתריעין בכל מקום על השדפון ועל הירקון ועל ארבה וחסיל ועל חיה רעה *ר׳ עקיבא אומר על השדפון ועל הירקון בכל שהוא *ארבה וחסיל אפילו לא נראה בא״י אלא כנף אחד מתריעין עליהן : ועל חיה וכו׳ : ת״ר חיה רעה שאמרו בזמן שהיא משולחת מתריעין עליה אינה משולחת אין מתריעין עליה אי זו היא משולחת ואי זו היא שאינה משולחת נראית בעיר משולחת בשדה אינה משולחת ביום משולחת בלילה אינה משולחת ראתה שני בני אדם ורצתה אחריהן משולחת *נחבאת מפניהן אינה משולחת טרפה שני בני אדם ואכלה אחד מהן משולחת אכלה שניהן אינה משולחת עלתה לגג ונטלה תינוק מעריסה משולחת הא גופה קשיא אמרת נראתה בעיר משולחת לא שנא ביום ולא שנא בלילה והדר אמרת ביום משולחת בלילה אינה משולחת לא קשיא הכי קאמר נראתה בעיר ביום משולחת בעיר בלילה אינה משולחת אי נמי בשדה [אפילו] ביום [אינה] משולחת (בשדה בלילה אינה משולחת) ראתה שני בני אדם ורצתה אחריהן משולחת הא עומדת אינה משולחת והדר אמרת נחבאת מפניהן אינה משולחת הא עומדת משולחת לא קשיא כאן בשדה הסמוכה לאגם כאן בשדה שאינה סמוכה לאגם טרפה שני בני אדם כאחד ואכלה אחד מהן משולחת שניהם אינה משולחת והא אמרת אפילו רצתה אמר רב פפא כי תני ההיא באגמא: גופא עלתה לגג ונטלה תינוק מעריסה משולחת פשיטא אמר רב פפא כבוכי דציידי : על החרב וכו׳ : ת״ר חרב שאמרו אינו צריך לומר חרב שאינו של שלום אלא אפילו חרב של שלום שאין לך חרב של שלום יותר מפרעה נכה ואעפ״כ נכשל בה המלך יאשיהו שנאמר וישלח

טרפה שני בני אדם אכלה אחד מהן משולחת· והוא הדין לא אכלה אחד מהם משולחת שהרי אם אכלה שניהם אינה משולחת דהא דאכלה שניהם לא הוי מטעם משולחת אלא מטעם דהיא רעיבה והא דנקט אכלה אחד מהם רבותא הוי דאע״ג דאכלה אחד מהן הוי משולחת : כמלא

לצפרא כרכינהו · רבנן לביסתרקי דאבא אומנא ולייתינהו לשוקא לזבנינהו : אמרו ליה · לאבא אומנא לשיימינהו מר והכי נן דמייהו והיו בודקין אותו אם יחשדם כגזלנין או אם יהא שם אותם פחות מכדי דמיהם : במאי חשדתינן · כשלקחתם : וכסיפא. לכו מילתא למימר לי לאמר ליתן אותם ולהכי אתו למינגי גבאי למיעבד טלי האי : לשקלינהו מר · שלא היינו רוצין אלא לנסותך : אלמא דעתיה דרבא אדאביי · דלרבא לא אתי שלמא אלא ממעלי יומא דכיפורי למעלי יומא דכיפורי ולאביי כל מעלי שבתא : אבולא כרכא · על כל בני עירך : רב ברוקא חוזאה · שהיה מבי חוזאי : דבי לפט · מקום : א״ל · רב ברוקא לאליהו מי איכא בהאי שוקא כו׳ : מסאני אוכמי · מנעלים שחורים (ד) שלא כמנהג היהודים : ולא רמי חוטא · לא הטיל ציצית בטליתו : אמר ליה · אליהו לרב ברוקא האי בר עלמא דאתי הוא : קרא ליה · רב ברוקא לההוא גברא: זנדוקנא · שומר בית האסורין (ה) : רמינא פורייאי כו׳ · מטיל אני מטתי בין אנשים לנשים : דיהבי נכרים עינייהו עלה · בעלי בית האסורים : איתרמי נערה כו׳ · דהויא בבית הסוהר: דורדיא דחמרא· שמרים של יין האדומים כדם : בשיפולה · בשולי בגדיה : דיסתנא · דרך נשים לה ומאוסה היא והוא לשון פרסי׳ : אמר ליה · אליהו לרב ברוקא הני נמי בני עלמא דאתי נינהו: בדוחי · שמחים ומשמחים בני אדם : טרחינן . במילי דבדיחותא בינייהו : עד דעבדי שלמא · (ו) שהן דברים שאדם אוכל פירותיהן בעולם הזה והקרן קיימת וכו׳ הבאת שלום בין אדם לחבירו : שדפון וירקון · כיון שנראה כל שהוא מתריעין ומלא תנור דמתניתין להתענות אי נמי מעשה (ז) היה כך : כנף אחד · עוף אחד של אותו מין כעין לפור כל כנף (בראשית ז) : משולחת · מן השמים : בשדה אינה משולחת · דהיינו אורחה : טרפה שני בני אדם · ולא אכלה אלא אחד מהם ודאי משולחת דכיון דלא היתה רעבה אלא לאחד מאי טעמא קטלה ליה לאידך : שניהן אינה משולחת · שמפני הרעב אכלתם : עלתה לגג · רגילין היו להשתמש כל תשמישיהן בגגות שלא היו משופעים אלא חלקים ושוין והוא הדין לבית שתחתיו : עריסה · ברט״ל בלע״ז : הכי קאמר · האי דקתני נראתה בעיר כו׳ הכי קאמר נראתה בעיר כגון שנראתה ביום דכתם נראתה ביום משמע אבל בלילה אינה משולחת והאי דקתני נראתה ביום (ח) א) אשדה קאי דאם נראתה בשדה ביום אינה משולחת : הא עמדה · בשדה דלא רצתה ולא נחבאת : בשדה הסמוכה לאגם · עמדה אינה משולחת דכיון דסמוכה לאגם הייט רביתה ולא ברחה סברה אי אתי בהדאי עריקנא לאגם מיד : בשדה שאינה סמוכה לאגם · עמדה משולחת דכיון דלאו מקום רביתה הוא וקיימא ודאי משולחת גזירה היא : אגם · מרש״ק בלע״ז הסמוך לעיר והוא מלא קנים : כי תניא ההיא · דאכלה אין רצתה לא באגם (ט) דכיון דהייט דוכתה סמכה אדעתה ורהטא אבתרייהו : כבוכא דציידי · כוך קטן של ציידין שיחפרו למארב העופות ואף על גב דלאו בנין קבוע הוא ולא הוה כיישוב הויא משולחת : אין צריך לומר חרב שאינו של שלום · שמתריעין עליה (י) אלא אפילו חרב של שלום · העוברת דרך אותו מלכות לילך להלחם במקום אחרת :

רבינו חננאל

רבא מגנא ובותית אבולא כרכא : א״ל ר׳ ברוקא לאליהו הראיני אדם שהוא מבני העוה״ב א״ל זה הלך אחריו שאלו אמר לו שומר האסורים אני ואסרנא גברי לחוד ונשי לחוד ולא רמינא ציצית כי היכי דלא לתשי דאנא יהודאי . הכי שמענא דנורה של ישראל מהודענא להון וכנו רזמי ומבטלי . דורדיא שמרים של יין . דשתנא נדה . וזה הנראה בבגדיה כבתם דמיה הן . תוב א״ל אליהו הני נמי בני עלמא דאתי נינהו ושאלינהו ואמרו ליה משמחי לב עציבי אנן כלומר יש לנו חן שפה ודברים המסירים עצב מן הלב וכי חזינן נמי צערא בין גברא לחבריה אי בין גברא לאתתיה טרחינן ועבדינן שלמא בינייהו : על אלו מתריעין בכל מקום על השדפון ועל הירקון כו׳ וקי״ל כר׳ עקיבא דברייתא דתני על השדפון ועל [הירקון] (הארבה) בכל שהוא ואוקימנא למתני׳ לקטן דנראה. באשקלון שדפון כמלא פי תנור תבואה כלומר כשיעור פי תנור נשרפה תבואה בשדה תגזרו תענית ואיבעיא לן האי שדפון דמשערינן ליה בשדה שיעור ככיסוי פי התנור הוא . אי כשיעור דרא רפתא דהדר לפומא דתנורא ועלתה בתיקו . וכן נמי א״ר עקיבא וכן בארבה ובחסיל אפילו לא נראה אלא כנף אחד בא״י מתריעין עליהן מיד : פיסקא ועל חיה רעה ת״ר חיה רעה בזמן שהיא משולחת כו׳ ואוקימנא איזו היא משולחת שנראתה בעיר בלילה אי נמי נראתה בשדה ביום אינה משולחת . ראתה שנים ורצתה אחריהן משולחת אבל ראתה איתם ונחבאת מפניהם אי נמי לא נחבאת אלא עמדה בשדה הסמוכה לאגם אינה משולחת טרפה שנים באגם ואכלה אחד מהם משולחת ואם לא אכלה ולא אחד מהם אינה משולחת והני מילי באגם אבל שלא במקום אגם אע״פ שלא אכלה אלא רצתה אליהם משולחת : פיסקא ועל החרב מתריעין . ת״ר אין צ״ל הרב שאינה של שלום שודאי מתריעין אלא אפי׳ חרב של שלום מתריעין שאין לך חרב של שלום יותר מפרעה נכה ואעפ״כ נכשל בה

[גי׳ הערוך זנדוקא] [עי׳ ע״ז כה:]

[נ״ל דישתנא עי׳ ע״ז כה: וכן בג״ערוך]

פ״א אחי

[גי׳ רי״ף ורא״ש ת״ר על השדפון וכו׳]

[גי׳ רי״ף ורא״ש בורחת]

רבינו גרשום

כרכינהו להנו ביסתרקי למכון ואמרו ליה כ״ע לישיימינהו מר . אמר להו הכי והכי שוו דבעי למיהב שוו׳ אילו בסתרקי להנהו ונא דרבנן א״ל ההוא ונא דרבנן חשדתינן דאתינן לוותך לישקלינהו מר לבסתרקי דלא בעינא להו . מסאני אוכמי כנכרים ולא רמו חוטי. ציצית: מפני שהיא סכה מהלכת. שלאחר שנראה כל שהוא אינו מפסיק : שניהם אינה משולחת דאקראי היא מחמת רעבתנותא . א״נ בשדה ביום מסיים הברייתא בשדה הסמוכה לאגם . עמדה אינה משולחת לפי שלבה נסה באגם שהוא מצויה שם . בשדה שאינה סמוכה לאגם עמדה משולחת . באגם נטפיה לא הוה משולחת עד דאכלה מהן . כוכי דאגמא דציידי . צריפין דיוריין קטנים שדרין בהן ציידים ועל אותו גג עלתה דס״ד לא חשיב גג קמ״ל :

הגהות הב״ח

(א) גמ׳ הלשא דעתיה דרבא משום דאביי איתחזי ליה בחלמא אמרו ליה מסתייך : (ב) שם האי בר עלמא דאתי הוא קרא ליה ולא אתא לגביה רהט בתריה א״ל : (ג) שם מ״ט לית לך חוטי וביימת מסאני אוכמי כו׳ דיהודאה אנא דכי הוו גזרי : (ד) רש״י ד״ה מסאני אוכמי כו׳ שלא כמנהג היהודים . נ״ב עי׳ בתוס׳ פרק בן סורר ומורה דף ע״ד וכפ׳ הכונס דף נ״ט : (ה) ד״ה זנדוקנא כו׳ האסורין של מלך כס״ד : (ו) ד״ה עד דעבדי שלמא . דהכאת שלום בין אדם לחבירו כיון אחד מן הדברים שאדם אוכל פירותיהן בעוה״ז והקרן קיימת לעוה״ב הס״ד : (ז) ד״ה שדפון כו׳ אי נמי מעשה שהיה כך היה הס״ד: (ח) ד״ה הכי קאמר כו׳ והאי דקתני נראתה ביום אעיר קאי דאם נראתה בשדה אפילו ביום אינה: (ט) ד״ה כי תניא כו׳ רצתה לא באגם גופה דכיון דהייט : (י) ד״ה אין צריך לומר כו׳ שמתריעין עליה הס״ד ומה״ד אלא כו׳ :

גליון הש״ס

גמ׳ איכא בהאי שוקא . עיין בתורת חיים סנהדרין דף פח ע״ב ד״ה שלחו מתם :

הגהות מהר״ב רנשבורג א) רש״י ד״ה הכי קאמר וכו׳ והאי דקתני נראתה ביום אשדה וכו׳ נמחק מלת אשדה וצ״ל אעיר :

עין משפט
נר מצוה

כד א מיי' פ"ב מהל' תעניות הלכה יא טוש"ע א"ח סימן תקעו סעיף ח:
כה ב מיי' פ"ב מהלכות טומאת מת הל' ד:
כו ג מיי' פ"א מהל' תעניות הלכה ט טוש"ע א"ח סימן תקעח סעיף א:
כז ד מיי' פ"ב מהל' תעניות הלכה כ טוש"ע א"ח סימן תקעו סעיף ג:
כח ה ו מיי' שם הל' טו טוש"ע שם סעיף יא:

°וישלח אליו מלאכים לאמר מה לי ולך מלך יהודה לא עליך אתה היום כי אל בית מלחמתי ואלהים אמר לבהלני חדל לך מאלהים אשר עמי ואל ישחיתך (א) מאי אלהים אשר עמי אמר רב יהודה אמר רב זו ע"ז אמר הואיל וקא בטח בע"ז יכילנא ליה (ב) °ויורו היורים למלך יאשיהו ויאמר המלך לעבדיו העבירוני כי החליתי מאד מאי כי החליתי מאד *אמר רב יהודה אמר רב מלמד שעשו כל גופו ככברה אמר ר' שמואל בר נחמני אמר רבי *(יוחנן) מפני מה נענש יאשיהו מפני שהיה לו לימלך בירמיהו ולא נמלך מאי דרש °וחרב לא תעבור בארצכם מאי חרב אילימא חרב שאינה של שלום והכתיב ונתתי שלום בארץ אלא אפילו (ג) של שלום והוא אינו יודע שאין דורו דומה יפה כי הוה ניחא נפשיה חזא ירמיהו שפוותיה דקא מרחשן אמר שמא ח"ו מילתא דלא מהגנא אמר אגב צעריה גחין ושמעיה דקא מצדיק עליה דינא אנפשיה אמר °צדיק הוא ה' כי פיהו מריתי פתח עליה ההיא שעתא °רוח אפינו משיח ה': מעשה וירדו זקנים מירושלים לעריהם כו': איבעיא להו כמלא תנור תבואה או דלמא כמלא תנור פת תא שמע *כמלא פי תנור ועדיין תיבעי להו כביסויא דתנורא או דלמא כי דרא דריפתא דהדר ליה לפומא דתנורא תיקו: ועוד גזרו תענית על שאכלו זאבים כו': אמר עולא משום ר' שמעון בן יהוצדק *מעשה ובלעו זאבים שני תינוקות והקיאום דרך בית הרעי ובא מעשה לפני חכמים וטיהרו את הבשר וטמאו את העצמות: על אלו מתריעין בשבת כו': תנו רבנן (ד) *עיר שהקיפוה נכרים או נהר ואחד ספינה המיטרפת בים ואחד יחיד שנרדף מפני נכרים או מפני לסטין *ומפני רוח רעה *על כולן יחיד רשאי לסגף את עצמו בתענית רבי יוסי אומר אין היחיד רשאי לסגף את עצמו בתענית שמא יצטרך לבריות ואין הבריות מרחמות עליו אמר רב יהודה אמר רב מ"ט דרבי יוסי דכתיב °ויהי האדם לנפש חיה נשמה שנתתי בך החייה: שמעון התימני אומר אף על הדבר כו': איבעיא להו לא הודו לו רבנן בשבת אבל בחול הודו לו או דלמא לא הודו לו כלל ת"ש דתניא מתריעין על הדבר בשבת ואצ"ל בחול ר' חנן בן פיטום תלמידו של ר' עקיבא משום רבי עקיבא אומר אין מתריעין על הדבר כל עיקר: על כל צרה שלא תבא על הצבור כו': ת"ר על כל צרה שלא תבא על הצבור מתריעין עליה חוץ מרוב גשמים מ"ט אמר ר' (ה) יוחנן *לפי שאין מתפללין על רוב הטובה ואמר רבי יוחנן מניין שאין מתפללין על רוב הטובה שנאמר °הביאו את כל המעשר אל בית האוצר וגו' *)מאי עד בלי די אמר רמי בר *רב(יוד)עד שיבלו שפתותיכם מלומר די אמר (ו) רמי בר רב יוד *ובגולה מתריעין עליה תניא נמי הכי שנה שגשמיה מרובין אנשי משמר שולחין לאנשי מעמד תנו עיניכם באחיכם שבגולה שלא יהא בתיהם קבריהם שאלו את ר' אליעזר עד היכן גשמים יורדין ויתפללו שלא ירדו אמר להם כדי שיעמוד אדם בקרן אפל וישכשך רגליו במים והתניא ידיו רגליו כידיו קאמינא אמר רבה בר בר חנה לדידי חזיא לי קרן אפל דקם ההוא טייעא כי רכיב גמלא ונקיט רומחא בידיה מתחזי (ז) איניבא ת"ר °ונתתי גשמיכם בעתם לא שכורה ולא צמאה אלא בינונית שכל זמן שהגשמים מרובין משטשטין את הארץ ואינה מוציאה פירות דבר אחר בעתם

א) [גי' רי"ף ורא"ש אמר ר' אבא אמר שמואל לפי] ב) [גי' רי"ף ורא"ש ר"י אמר רב וכן גי' רש"א] °)ויקרא כו
ג) [נ"ל יניבא פי' תולעת כדאיתא בחולין סה: ר' חייא נפל ליה יניבא ערוך ערך אנבא]

כמלא תנור תבואה או דלמא כמלא תנור פת · כמלא תנור תבואה הוי פי' כמלא חלל התנור תבואה דהיינו יותר ממלא תנור פת תא שמע כמלא פי תנור פת ואם כן מיירי בפת: **ועדיין** תבעי לך כמלא פי תנור כמלא עגול פי תנור · דהיינו שורה של לחם סביבות פי התנור או דלמא כי דרא דריפתא והדר ליה לפומיה דתנורא שורות שורות של לחם זו למעלה מזו עד פי התנור: **וטהרו** את הבשר · פירוש לפי שנתעכלו במעי הזאבים וטמאו את העצמות דלא מיעכלו: **ועל** כולן רשאי לסגף עצמו בתענית · פי' לענות נפש מתרגמינן לסגפא נפש: **ר'** יוסי אומר אין היחיד רשאי לסגף · וכ"ל דהני תנאי ל"פ בהא דמיירי הני אמוראי בפרקין דלעיל (דף יא:) אם נקרא חוטא או נקרא קדוש וכו' דהאמוראי פליגי במאי דמצערי נפשיה והני תנאי פליגי בהא אי מצערי נפשיה: **לאנשי** (ח) משמר · פי' דהיינו אנשי מעמד דיש בישראל שהיו נחלקים למעמדות להתפלל שיתפללו על אחיהם שבגולה פי' לפי שבגלותיהם שוים ונמוכים מחמת גשמים: **קרן** אפל · פי' שם מקום: **אינבא** · פירוש לגד"א בלע"ז מחמת גובהו של הר: **בלילי** רביעיות ובלילי שבתות · פי' שלא היו בני אדם הולכין בדרכים באותן לילות מפני אגרת בת מחלת כדמפרש במסכת פסחים (דף קיב:): השולה

ושלח אליו מלאכים לאמר מה לי ולך מלך יהודה לא עליך אתה היום כי אל בית מלחמתי ואלהים אמר לבהלני חדל לך מאלהים אשר עמי וגו' לא עליך אני הולך היום · יאשיה יצא לקראתו למלחמה ולא נתנו לעבור בארצו ושלח לו פרעה נכה מלאכים לאמר ט': מאלהים אשר עמי · דקאמר ליה פרעה נכה חדל לך מאלהים אשר עמי (ה): מלמד · מדכתיב ויורו המורים דמשמע יריות רבות יורו המורים: אמר רב יהודה אמר רב מלמד שעשו כל גופו ככברה: הא כתיב ונתתי שלום בארץ · ולמאי הלכתא כתביה רחמנא לאידך קרא וחרב לא תעבור בארצכם אלא אפי' חרב של שלום: שאין דורו דומה יפה · בעיני המקום: איבעיא להו כמלא תנור תבואה · דהיינו שיעור גדול יותר ממלא תנור פת דשיעור קטן הוא שאין דרך למלאות כל חלל התנור פת אלא בדפנות מדביקין אותו: ת"ש · דקתני חדא כי הא לישנא כמלא פי התנור דהיינו פת דהיינו תבואה לא מלי קיימא על פי התנור: או דלמא כי דרא דריפתא · שורה של לחם הדבוקין זה אצל זה כפי התנור או נמי שמדביקין זה למעלה מזה עד פי התנור: ובלען · כשהן שלימין: וטיהרו את הבשר · שהיה מתחלה טומאת מת דמתעכל ונתעכל תוך מעיו וכגון שמתו ישנו פיטול ופירשא בטלמא הוא: וטימאו את העצמות · דלא מתעכלי: מפני רוח רעה · שנכנס בו רוח שידה וכן והולך ושמא יטבע בנהר או יפול וימות: לסגף · לענות נפש מתרגמינן לסגפא נפש (במדבר ל): ילטרך לבריות · כי אין בו כח להרויח ולהתפרנס מיגיעו: דכתיב לנפש חיה · החייה: (ו) חנן בן פטום אומר אין מתריעין על הדבר. אפי' בחול דגזירה היא: רמי בר רב יוד · חכם ששמו יוד: ובגולה · בבבל שהיא במצולת: מתריעין על רוב גשמים · שלא ירדו: שלא יהו בתיהם קבריהן · שעמוקה היא ונטבעים בתיהם במים: אנשי משמר ואנשי מעמד · מפרש בשלשה פרקים לקמן (דף כו·): תנו עיניכם · התבוננו בתפלתכם בתפלות עליהם שלא ירדו רוב גשמים: קרן אפל · שן סלע גבוה וכך שמו: וישכשך רגליו במים · כלומר לעולם אין מתפללין: והתניא ידיו · עד שישכשך ידו (ז): רגלו כידו · וכיון דיכול לשכשך ברגלו או שוחה יכול לשכשך בידו נמי: טייעא · סוחר ישמעאל: ומיתחזי · האי טייעא וגמליה ורומחא לרבה בר בר חנה דהוה על קרן אפל: איניבא · תולעת ל"א כי אנבא ליגדי"א בלע"ז: לא שכורה · לא שתויה יותר מדאי שמשטשטין את הארץ: דכתיב

רבינו חננאל

יאשיהו ונתנו דכתיב ויורו היורים למלך יאשיהו ואמר עשאוה ככברה ולמה נענש מפני שלא נמלך בירמיהו כד חזיה ניה נפשיה שמעיה ירמיהו דהוה קאמר צדיק הוא ה' כי פיהו מריתי פתח עליה ירמיהו רוח אפינו משיח ה': ועוד גזרו תענית על שבלעו זאבים ב' תינוקות בעבר הירדן והקיאום דרך בית רעי וטיהרו הבשר וטמאו העצמות ס"ט כיון דבשר עביד להתעכולי כמעוכל הוא וכפרש הוא חשוב וכגללים שאין להם טומאה אבל העצמות דאקישי מפי לא עבידי לאיתעכלי ובחזקתייהו קיימי לפיכך מטמאי. ומפורש זה כאשר אמרנו במנחות בפ' ר' ישמעאל אומר בבעיא דרמי בר חמא בפיל שבלע כפיפה מצרית והקיאה דרך בית הרעי כו' ואמרינן תפשוט ליה מהא דאמר עולא מעשה שבלעו ב' זאבים ב' תינוקות והקיאום דרך הרעי כו': על אלו מתריעין בשבת על עיר שהקיפוה נכרים כו' ואוקימנא בפרק הראשון דהתרעה זו בעננו. ר' יוסי אומר לשורה ולא לצעקה: ת"ר עיר שהקיפוה נכרים נהר וספינה המטורפת בים. ויחיד הנרדף לפני נכרים מפני רוח רעה או מפני לסטים מתריעין עליהן בשבת. ועל כולן יחיד רשאי לסגף עצמו בתענית ר' יוסי אומר אין היחיד רשאי לסגף עצמו בתענית שמא יצטרך לבריות ואין מרחמין עליו. ואמרי' מ"ט דר' יוסי כתיב ויהי האדם לנפש חיה. נשמה שנתתי בך החייה. שמעון התימני אומר מתריעין אף על הדבר. [משום ר"ע אמרו אין מתריעין על הדבר] כל עיקר. על כל צרה הבאה על הצבור מתריעין עליהן חוץ מרוב גשמים. מעשה שאמרו לחוני המעגל התפלל אלי ירדו גשמים. עוד אמר להם צאו וראו אם נמחית אבן הטועין פי' כדאמרן בפרק אלו מציאות ת"ר אבן הטועין היתה בירושלים כל מי שאבדה לו אבדה נפנה לשם וכל המוצא אבדה נפנה לשם המוצא היה שלה על אותה האבן והיה מכריזו מי שאבדה לו יבא ויתן סימניה ויקח. ומי שאבדה לו אבדה היה נותן סימניה ונוטלה וזו ששנינו צאו וראו אם נמחית אבן הטועין. והוו רבותי מפרשין אם נמחית אבן הטועין מלשון וימח את כל היקום כלומר אם המים כאלו נמחית מן העולם עד שראינו בירושלמי פירוש אחרת כשם שאי אפשר לאבן הזה להמחות כך אי אפשר להתפלל על הגשמים שילכו שלח לו שמעון בן שטח צריך אתה ילהתנדות אלו נגזרת [illegible] אליהו שנשבע שלא יבא מטר אלא לפי דברו ונשבעת אתה שעתה מיד יבא מטר לא נמצאת מביא רבים לידי חטא וחלול השם וכל המביא הרבים לידי חלול השם צריך נדוי וכל המעכב את הרבים [illegible] מצוה צריך נידוי ומניין שאין מתפללין על רוב גשמים שנאמר והריקותי לכם ברכה עד בלי די ואמר רב עד שיבלו שפתותיכם מלומר די. ובגולה מתריעין על רוב גשמים. תניא נמי הכי שנה שגשמיה מרובין [illegible] משמר שולחין לאנשי מעמד תנו עיניכם לאחיכם שבגולה שלא יפלו עליהן בתיהן. יניבא תולעת דגרסינן בכיסוי הדם נפל ליה לר' חייא יאניבא בכיתניה. פי' כאן גירסא כך הוא כינבא תבא ותו [illegible] כגון הא דגרס בפרק (ר' אליעזר אומר תולין) [שמונה שרצים קז:] המפרין וביצי כנים. ועוד בפרק (ב"ש אומר) [שלשה מינים אסורין בנזיר (לט:)] ת"ש מאנבא חיה דמשתכחא בעיקבא ואנבא [illegible] משתכחא ברישא דמוזא ובלשון ישמעאל קורין אותן ציבאן והדעת נוטה על הפירוש שפירשנו אנו. שאלו לר' אליעזר עד מתי יהו הגשמים יורדין ולא יתפללו עליהן שלא ירדו גשמים אמר להן עד כדי [illegible] אדם (במקום אפל) בקרן אפל וישכשך רגלו כידו במים: ת"ר ונתתי גשמיכם בעתם. לא שכורה ולא צמאה אלא בינונית שבזמן שהגשמים רבים משטשטין את הארץ ואינה עושה [illegible]

רבינו גרשום

והכתיב ונתתי שלום ואין צריך לומר חרב שאינה של שלום שאינה עוברת: שאין דורו דומה יפה שאין מעשה ידי הדור יפה שלאיכך הוא בא: כמלא תנור תבואה כמו שהיה קרקע התנור מכוסה מתבואה. כמלא תנור פת היינו מעט. כמלא פי תנור משמע פת שהוא סביב הפה. כי כיסא דתנורא ככיסוי פי התנור דהיינו פת אחד: ומיהרו את הבשר שהרי נתעכל וטמאו את העצמות. שלא נתעכל: לסגף לענות כדמתרגמינן לענות לסגפא: או לא הודו לו כלל. דאין מתריעין על הדבר כלל אפי' בחול בזמן שישנו במקום אחד. מאי טעמא אין מתריעין על רוב גשמים: ובגולה מתריעין על רוב לפי שהן יושבין באגם ורוב גשמים קשה להם. תנו עיניכם שתתפללו. ואשל חד לשטוף במים. סילוא דלא אפשר תלו כידו (למ"ה) תלו או ידו. אינבא. לגמרא: רביעיות שאין בני אדם מצויים לחוץ מפני אגרת בת מחלת. אם נמות נתכסה. צריך להתגרות שמסיח דברים כלפי מעלה:

הגהות

(א) גמ' ואל ישחיתך מאי אלהים אמר רב כו' כצ"ל ותיבות אשר עמי נמחק: (ב) שם יכילנא ליה וכתיב ויורו היורים וכו' כי החליתי מאד אמר רב יהודה אמר רב עשו כל גופו וכו' כצ"ל ותיבות מאי כי החליתי מאד ותיבת מלמד נמחק: (ג) שם שלום בארץ אלא אפילו חרב של שלום כו' כי הוה קא ניחא נפשיה: (ד) שם מ"ד אחד עיר שהקיפוה נכרים: (ה) רש"י ד"ה מאלהים כו' אשר עמי הס"ד ואח"כ מה"ד

הב"ח

אמר ילתבוע הואיל וקא בטח פרעה בע"ז יכילנא ליה וקיים דכתיב ולא כתיב ילתביו לא כפינו כלום ואח"כ מה"ד כל גופו מדכתיב ויורו כו' המורים הס"ד ואח"כ מה"ד כ"א אמר רב יהודה אמר רב [illegible] ככברה הס"ד ותיבת מלמד נמחק: (ו) ד"ה דכתיב כו' החייה הס"ד ואח"כ מה"ד רבי חנן בן פי': (ז) והתניא וכו' ידו כמים הס"ד: (ח) תוס' ד"ה לאנשי משמר פי' היינו אנשי מעמד כו'. ר"ל פי' לקמן [illegible]

תורה אור

בעתם בלילי רביעיות ובלילי שבתות שכן מצינו *בימי שמעון בן שטח *שירדו להם גשמים בלילי רביעיות ובלילי שבתות עד שנעשו חטים ככליות ושעורים כגרעיני זיתים ועדשים כדינרי זהב וצררו מהם דוגמא לדורות להודיע כמה החטא גורם שנאמר °עונותיכם הטו אלה וחטאתיכם מנעו הטוב מכם וכן מצינו בימי הורדוס שהיו עוסקין בבנין בהמ"ק והיו יורדין גשמים בלילה למחר נשבה הרוח ונתפזרו העבים וזרחה החמה ויצאו העם למלאכתן וידעו שמלאכת שמים בידיהם: מעשה ששלחו לחוני המעגל וכו': ת"ר פעם אחת יצא רוב אדר ולא ירדו גשמים שלחו לחוני המעגל התפלל וירדו גשמים התפלל ולא ירדו גשמים עג עוגה ועמד בתוכה כדרך שעשה חבקוק הנביא שנאמר °על משמרתי אעמדה ואתיצבה על מצור וגו' אמר לפניו רבונו של עולם בניך שמו פניהם עלי שאני כבן בית לפניך נשבע אני בשמך הגדול שאיני זז מכאן עד שתרחם על בניך התחילו גשמים מנטפין אמרו לו תלמידיו רבי ראינוך ולא נמות כמדומין אנו שאין גשמים יורדין אלא להתיר שבועתך אמר (א) לא כך שאלתי אלא גשמי בורות שיחין ומערות ירדו בזעף עד שכל טפה וטפה כמלא פי חבית ושיערו חכמים שאין טפה פחותה מלוג אמרו לו תלמידיו רבי ראינוך ולא נמות כמדומין אנו שאין גשמים יורדין אלא לאבד העולם אמר לפניו לא כך שאלתי אלא גשמי רצון ברכה ונדבה ירדו כתיקנן עד שעלו כל העם להר הבית מפני הגשמים אמרו לו רבי כשם שהתפללת שירדו כך התפלל וילכו להם אמר להם כך מקובלני שאין מתפללין על רוב הטובה אעפ"כ הביאו לי פר הודאה הביאו לו פר הודאה סמך שתי ידיו עליו ואמר לפניו רבש"ע עמך ישראל שהוצאת ממצרים אינן יכולין (ב) לא ברוב טובה ולא ברוב פורענות כעסת עליהם אינן יכולין לעמוד השפעת עליהם טובה אינן יכולין לעמוד יהי רצון מלפניך שיפסקו הגשמים ויהא ריוח בעולם מיד נשבה הרוח ונתפזרו העבים וזרחה החמה ויצאו העם לשדה והביאו להם כמהין ופטריות *שלח לו שמעון בן שטח אלמלא חוני אתה גוזרני עליך נידוי [א] שאילו שנים כשני אליהו שמפתחות גשמים בידו של אליהו לא נמצא שם שמים מתחלל על ידך אבל מה אעשה לך שאתה מתחטא לפני המקום ועושה לך רצונך כבן שמתחטא על אביו ועושה לו רצונו ואומר לו אבא הוליכני לרחצני בחמין שטפני בצונן תן לי אגוזים שקדים אפרסקים ורמונים ונותן לו ועליך הכתוב אומר °ישמח אביך ואמך ותגל יולדתך תנו רבנן מה שלחו בני לשכת הגזית לחוני המעגל °ותגזר אומר ויקם לך ועל דרכיך נגה אור ותגזר אומר אתה גזרת מלמטה והקדוש ברוך הוא מקיים מאמרך מלמעלה ועל דרכיך נגה אור דור שהיה אפל הארת בתפלתך כי השפילו ותאמר גוה דור שהיה שפל הגבהתו בתפלתך ושח עינים יושיע דור ששח בעונו הושעתו בתפלתך ימלט אי נקי דור שלא היה נקי מלטתו בתפלתך ונמלט בבור כפיך מלטתו במעשה ידיך הברורין אמר ר' יוחנן כל ימיו של אותו צדיק היה מצטער על מקרא זה °שיר המעלות בשוב ה' את שיבת ציון היינו כחולמים אמר מי איכא דנייים שבעין שנין בחלמא יומא חד הוה אזל באורחא חזייה להוא גברא דהוה נטע חרובא אמר ליה האי עד כמה שנין טעין אמר ליה עד שבעין שנין אמר ליה פשיטא לך דחיית שבעין שנין אמר ליה (ג) האי [גברא] עלמא בחרובא אשכחתיה כי היכי דשתלי לי אבהתי שתלי נמי לבראי יתיב קא כריך ריפתא אתא ליה שינתא נים אהדרא ליה משוניתא איכסי מעינא ונים שבעין שנין כי קם חזייה להוא גברא דהוה קא מלקט מינייהו אמר ליה את הוא דשתלתיה א"ל בר בריה אנא אמר ליה שמע מינה דניימי שבעין שנין חזא לחמריה דאתיילידא ליה רמכי רמכי אזל לביתיה אמר להו בריה דחוני המעגל מי קיים אמרו ליה בריה ליתא בר בריה איתא אמר להו אנא חוני המעגל לא הימנוהו אזל לבית המדרש שמעינהו לרבנן דקאמרי נהירן שמעתתין כבשני חוני המעגל דכי הוי עייל לבית מדרשא כל קושיא דהוו להו לרבנן הוה כפרק להו אמר להו אנא ניהו לא הימנוהו ולא עבדי ליה יקרא כדמבעי ליה חלש דעתיה בעי רחמי ומית אמר רבא היינו דאמרי אינשי או חברותא *או מיתותא אבא חלקיה בר בריה דחוני המעגל הוה וכי מצטריך עלמא למיטרא הוו משדרי רבנן לגביה ובעי רחמי ואתי מיטרא זימנא חדא איצטריך עלמא למיטרא שדור רבנן זוגא דרבנן לגביה למבעי רחמי דניתי מיטרא אזול לביתיה ולא אשכחוהו אזול בדברא ואשכחוהו דהוה קא רפיק (ד) יהבו ליה שלמא ולא

(ה) דכתיב בעתם · זהו בלילי רביעיות ובלילי שבתות דאין טורח לבני אדם דאינם הולכין לדרכים בלילי רביעיות מפני אגרת בת מחלת כפסחים (דף קיב:): שכן מצינו · כלומר ושמא תאמר אין סיפק בגשמים של ב' לילות בשבת מצינו בימי שמעון בן שטח כו': וצררו · קשרו וצררו: הורדוס · סתר בנין דעזרא ובנה בנין יפה ממנו כב"ב (דף ד'): עוגה · שורה עגולה כמו עוגה שהיא עגולה: כדרך שעשה חבקוק · כדמפרש בתרגום של תפלת חבקוק (ו) על משמרתי אעמדה כמין ביב האסורים עשה וישב: ראינוך ולא נמות · כלומר אותך ולא נמות כביאותא המבול שלא נמות ברעב מפני עצירת גשמים: פר הודאה · להודות עליו ועשה (ז) לו סמיכה והביאו שלמים חוני בזמן הבית היה: כמהין ופטריות · בוליי"ן בלע"ז שיצאו מלחלוח הגשמים וידעו כי של ברכה היו: אלמלא חוני אתה · ואדם גדול (ח): לנדות · שמנדין על כבוד הרב שהטיח דברים ואמר לא כך שאלתי: שאלמלא היו שנים כשני אליאו · גזירת עצירת גשמים ומפתח של גשמים בידו של אליהו נרכין: לא נמצא שם שמים מתחלל · בתמיה (ט) שאליהו נשבע חי ה' אם יהיה השנים האלה טל ומטר כי אם לפי דברי (מלכים א יז) ואתה נשבע שאין אתה זז עד שירדו גשמים: נמצא שם שמים מתחלל על ידך · וזה לא זה בא לידי שבועת שוא: מתחטא · לשון הטא כלומר (י) אוי הוגך

וחוטא: לשכת הגזית · סנהדרין: דור שהיה אפל · מרוב לער שלא ירדו גשמים: הושעת בתפלתך · מן המיתה שהבאת עליהם שוכע: של אותו צדיק · חוני המעגל היה מצטער על המקרא הזה: שיר המעלות · לשון פילוי: היינו כחולמים · כחלום נדמה גלות בבל שהיה שבעים שנה: שבעין שני בחלמא · בתמיה מי איתא דנייים שבעין שנין בחלמיה (כ) ויש אדם ישן שבעים שנה בשינה אחת: עד שבעין שנין · לא טעין פירא בטעינא קמייתא: יתיב · חוני המעגל וקא כריך ריפתא: הכי גרסי' הגא עלמא בחרובא אשכחתיה כי היכי דשתלי לי אבהתי אנא נמי אישתיל לבראי: אהדרא ליה משוניתא · עלתה סביבותיו שן סלע: ואיכסי מעינא דאינשי · ולא אשכחוהו התם: רמכי רמכי · וולדי וולדות באלו השנים דניים מעוברת זכר היתה וחזר ובא עליה והולידו: אמר להו · שאל להון בנו של חוני המעגל קיים הוא: נהירנא לן הנך שמעתתא · מוגהת לנו שמועה זו כאילו למדנוה בחיין של חוני המעגל שהיה מפרקה לנו ומניח לנו יפה יפה: או חברותא או מיתותא · ולא גרסינן הכא כחברי דאיוב אלא בבבא בתרא (דף טז:) גבי מעשה דאיוב אם אין חביריו של אדם נוהגין בו כבוד כבתחילה טוב לו שימות אי "נמי משום (ל) הנך בריוני לא כתוב בספרים: רפיק בדברא · עודר בשדה: לא

[פי' תוספות שבת פו: ד"ה דאמר וכו']

רבינו חננאל

בעתם בלילי ד' ובלילי ו'. וכן היו בימי שמעון בן שטח עד שנעשו חטים ככליות שעורים כזיתים ועדשים כדינרין וצררו מהם דוגמא לדורות להודיע כמה החטא גורם שנאמר וחטאתיכם מנעו הטוב מכם. וכן מצינו בבנין בהמ"ק ירדו גשמים בלילות ולמחר נשבה הרוח ונתפזרו העבים וזרחה השמש והשכימו כל אחד ואחד למלאכתן להודיע שמלאכת שמים בידיהם: ת"ר פעם אחת יצא רוב אדר ולא ירדו גשמים שלחו לחוני המעגל להתפלל התפלל ולא ירדו גשמים כו'. מעשה בחוני המעגל דנים ע' שנה כו' ומעשה דאבא חלקיה בר בריה דחוני המעגל דאצטריך עלמא למיטרא ושדרו רבנן לותיה ואשכחוהו רבנן דקא רפיק בדברא יהבו ליה שלמא כו'

רבינו גרשום

ת"ר פעם אחת וכו' היינו (פ"ע) [פ"א] עצמו דמתניתין: עג עוגה וצר צורה: ראינוך ולא נמות בתימא. בשביל שראינוך לא נמות · שאלו היו שנים כשני אליהו שאין מפתחות של מטר ביד הקב"ה לא נמצא שם שמים מתחלל שנמצאת מחלל את שבועתו: משוניתא סלע: רמכי ולדות אי חברא שיהא לו חבר טוב שנוהג בו כבוד:

הגהות הב"ח

(א) גמ' אלא להתיר שבועתך אמר לפניו לא כך שאלתי כו' אלא לאבד העולם אמר לפניו לא תמיהו אמר לפניו: (ב) שם אינן יכולין לעמוד לא: (ג) דחיית שבעין שנין א"ל הגא עלמא בחרובא אשכחתיה: (ד) שם כשנים דהוה קא רפיק בדברא יהבו ליה שלמא: (ה) רש"י בר"ה מעמוד נ"ל ד"א בעתם ותיבת דכתיב נמחק · זהו כו' דאין טורח על בני אדם דאינם: (ו) ד"ה כדרך כו' תפלת חבקוק סס"ד: (ז) ד"ה פר כו' ועשה עליו

הגהות הגר"א

[א] גמרא גוזרני עליך נידוי · ל"ב ולא עוד אלא:

חולין קיט:

ירמיה ה

חבקוק ב

תענית יט.

משלי כג

איוב כב

תהלים קכו

[ב"ב טז:]

(ח) ד"ה אלמלא כו' ואדם גדול אתה סס"ד: (ט) ד"ה לא נמלא כו' בתמיה שלא אליהו היה נשבע חי ה' וכו' שאין אתה זז משם עד שירדו גשמים נמלא כל"ל והד"א: (י) ד"ה מתחטא כו' כלומר טוען ואופה סס"ד והיכה סי נמחק ואח"כ מה"ד כמי לשכת כו': (כ) ד"ה שבעין כו' שבעין שנין בחלמיה כלומר ויש אדם ישן: (ל) ד"ה או חברותא כו' אי נמי משום הנהו בריוני לא כתוב:

ולא אסבר להו אפיה בפניא כי הוה מנקט ציבי דרא ציבי ומרא בחד כתפא וגלימא בחד כתפא כולה אורחא לא סיים מסאני כי מטי למיא סיים מסאניה כי מטא להיזמי והיגי דלינהו למניה (א) כי מטא למתא נפקא דביתהו לאפיה כי מיקשטא כי מטא לביתיה עלת דביתהו ברישא והדר עייל איהו והדר עיילי רבנן יתיב וכריך ריפתא ולא אמר להו לרבנן (ב) תו כרוכו פלג ריפתא לינוקי לקשישא חדא ולזוטרא תרי אמר לה לדביתהו ידענא דרבנן (ג) משום מיטרא קא אתו ניסק לאיגרא וניבעי רחמי אפשר דמרצי הקדוש ברוך הוא וייתי מיטרא ולא נחזיק טיבותא לנפשין סקו לאיגרא קם איהו בחדא זויתא ואיהי בחדא זויתא קדים סלוק ענני מהך זויתא דדביתהו כי נחית אמר להו אמאי אתו רבנן אמרו ליה שדרי לן רבנן לגבי דמר למיבעי רחמי אמיטרא אמר להו ברוך המקום שלא הצריך אתכם לאבא חלקיה אמרו ליה ידעינן דמיטרא מחמת מר הוא דאתא אלא לימא לן מר הני מילי דתמיהא לן מאי טעמא כי יהיבנא למר שלמא לא אסבר לן מר אפיה אמר להו שכיר יום הואי ואמינא לא איפגר ומאי טעמא דרא ציבי אחד כתפיה וגלימא אחד כתפיה אמר להו טלית שאולה היתה להכי שאלי ולהכי לא שאלי מאי טעמא כולה אורחא לא סיים מר מסאניה וכי מטי למיא סיים מסאניה אמר להו כולה אורחא חזינא במיא לא קא חזינא מ"ט כי מטא מר להיזמי והיגי דלינהו למניה אמר להו *זה מעלה ארוכה וזה אינה מעלה ארוכה מאי טעמא כי מטא מר למתא נפקא דביתהו דמר כי מיקשטא אמר להו כדי שלא אתן עיני באשה אחרת מאי טעמא עיילא היא ברישא והדר עייל מר אבתרה והדר עיילינן אנן אמר להו משום דלא בדקיתו לי מאי טעמא כי כריך מר ריפתא לא אמר לן איתו כרוכו משום דלא נפישא ריפתא ואמינא לא אחזיק בהו ברבנן טיבותא בחנם מאי טעמא יהיב מר לינוקא קשישא חדא ריפתא ולזוטרא תרי אמר להו האי קאי בביתא והאי יתיב בבי כנישתא ומאי טעמא קדים סלוק ענני מהך זויתא דהוות קיימא דביתהו דמר לעננא דידיה משום דאיתתא שכיחא בביתא ויהבא ריפתא לענייי *ומקרבא הנייתה [ואנא יהיבנא] זוזא ולא מקרבא הנייתיה אי נמי (ד) הנהו בירוני דהוו בשיבבותן [אנא] בעי רחמי דלימותו והיא °בעיא רחמי דליהדרו בתיובתא [ואהדרו] חנן הנחבא בר ברתיה דחוני המעגל הוה כי (ה) מצטריך עלמא למיטרא הוו משדרי רבנן ינוקי דבי רב לגביה ונקטי ליה בשיפולי גלימיה ואמרו ליה אבא אבא הב לן מיטרא אמר לפני הקב"ה רבש"ע עשה בשביל אלו שאין מכירין בין אבא דיהיב מיטרא לאבא דלא יהיב מיטרא ואמאי קרי ליה חנן הנחבא מפני שהיה מחביא עצמו בבית הכסא אמר ליה רבי זריקא לרב ספרא *תא חזי [מה] בין תקיפי דארעא דישראל לחסידי דבבל חסידי דבבל רב הונא ורב חסדא כי הוה מצטריך עלמא למיטרא אמרי ניכניף (ו) הדדי וניבעי רחמי אפשר דמירצי הקדוש ברוך הוא דייתי מיטרא תקיפי דארעא דישראל כגון ר' יונה אבוה דרבי מני כי הוה מצטריך עלמא למיטרא הוה עייל לביתיה ואמר להו הבו לי גואלקי ואיזיל ואייתי לי בזוזא עיבורא כי הוה נפיק לברא אזיל וקאי בדוכתא עמיקתא דכתיב °ממעמקים קראתיך ה' וקאי בדוכתא צניעא (ז) ומכסי בשקא ובעי רחמי ואתי מיטרא כי הוה אתי לביתיה אמרי ליה אייתי (ח) מר עיבורא אמר להו אמינא הואיל ואתא מיטרא השתא רווח עלמא ותו רבי מני בריה הוו קא מצערי ליה דבי נשיאה אישתטח על קברא דאבוה אמר ליה אבא אבא הני מצערו לי יומא חד הוו קא חלפי התם אינקוט כרעא דסוסוותיהו עד דקבילו עלייהו דלא קא מצערו ליה ותו רבי מני הוה שכיח קמיה דרבי יצחק בן אלישיב אמר ליה עתירי דבי חמי קא מצערו לי אמר ליענו ואיענו אמר קא דחקו לי אמר ליעתרו ואיעתרו אמר לא מיקבלי עלי אינשי ביתי א"ל מה שמה חנה תתייפי חנה ונתייפת אמר ליה קא מגנדרא עלי א"ל אי הכי תחזור חנה לשחרוריתה וחזרה חנה לשחרוריתה הנהו תרי תלמידי דהוו קמיה דרבי יצחק בן אלישיב אמרו ליה ניבעי מר רחמי עלן דניחכים טובא אמר להו עמי היתה ושלחתיה רבי יוסי בר אבין הוה שכיח קמיה דר' יוסי דמן יוקרת שבקיה ואתא לקמיה דרב אשי

יומא

לא אסבר להו אפיה · לא החזיר להם פניו : בפניא · לפנות ערב כשהלך לביתו : דלינהו למניה · הגביה בגדיו אחר כתיפיו כדי שלא יקרעו : כי מיקשטא · בתכשיטין : לאיגרא · עלייה : זויתא · זוית : מזויתא דדביתהו · מאותו הרוח שאשתו שם עלו העבים תחלה שהיא נענית תחלה : לא איפגר · לא אתבטל ממלאכתי כמו יומא דמיפגרי רבנן (שבת דף קכט:) : מ"ט דרא · מדוע נשאת הטלית על כתף אחת ולא נתת בכתף תחת המשאוי : להכי שאלה לי · להתעטף בה : ולהכי לא שאלה לי · להטיל עליה קוצין לקרעה : במיא לא חזינן · מה דאית בה ושמא ישכנו דג או נחש : דלא בדקיתו לי · אם כשרים אם פריצים דאמר מר (במס' דרך ארץ רבה פ"ה) כל אדם יהי בעיניך כלסטים : (ט) טובת הנאה חנם : דאינהו לא הוו קא אכלי דליכא ריפתא וקא מחזקינן בהו טובה חנם : יתיב קאי בבי כנישתא· קמי רביה ולא אתי כולי יומא : דאיתתא שכיחא בביתא · כל יומא וכי מיצטריך עניא מידי אזלה ויהבה (י) : ועוד דמקרבא הנייתה · שדבר אכילה היא נותנת לעני והוא בלא טורח ממה שהיתה נותנת מעות ויטריח העני עד שיקנה : אי נמי · אהכי קדים ענני דידה : משום בירוני · בורים עמי הארץ : ינוקי דבי רב · להמריך לבו ויתכוין בתפלתו : בשיפולי · בשולי בגדיו : אבא אבא · כך רגילים לקרותו כיתום שאומר אבי אבי : שאין מכירין · בין

(כ) *חוני לאבא כסבורין עלי שאני אביהן : ה"ג שהיה מחבא ולא גרסי' שהיה מחבא בבית הכסא · (ל) כי הוה בעי רחמי אמיא היה מחבא עצמו מרוב ענוה ומאן דגרס בית הכסא כלומר מתחבא בבגדיו כשהוא נכנס להסך את רגליו מרוב צניעות : רב הונא ורב חסדא · חסידי דבבל מפרסמין את הדבר ושל ארץ ישראל לצנעין ולא מודיעין שבא המטר בשבילם : תא ליכניף אהדדי · (מ) אלמא משום חד מינייהו לא אתי מיטרא : תקיפי דארץ ישראל רבי יונה · וקא חזינן (נ) דמחמתיה אתי מיטרא : גואלקא· שק"א בלע"ז : ואייתי בזוזא עיבורא· דגן משום כפנא (ס) שאפילו לבני ביתו לא היה מודיע : אייתי לן מר מעיבורא · דבעית למיזבן : רווחא עלמא · דליהוי שובע ואהכי לא זבני ביוקרא דהשתא : הוו קא חלפי · דבי נשיאה : התם · עלויה מערתא דרבי יונה : אינקוט · נדבקו בקרקע שעל גבי מערה ולא היו יכולין לזוז ממקומן (ע) : עתירי דבי חמי · עשירים של בית חמי : ליענו · יהיו עניים : קא דחקו לי · ליתן להן פרנסה : לא מקבלי עלי אינשי ביתי · אין אשתי מקובלת עלי שאינה יפה : מגנדרא · מתגדלת עלי מתוך גבהות יופיה · מגנדרא מלשון מקום הניחו לי אבותי להתגדר בו (חולין דף ז·) : עמי היתה ושלחתיה . (פ) דבר זה היה בידי שכל מה שאני מבקש היו נותנין לי ועכשיו אין תפלתי מקובלת כל כך (צ):דמן יוקרת·מקום:

רבינו חננאל

מעשה בחנן הנחבא בר ברתיה דחוני המעגל (פי' קבלה בידינו הוא שהיו חכמים מתעסקין למנותו פרנס על הצבור ולא קביל והלך ונחבא לפיכך היו קורין אותו חנין הנחבא) דכי הוה אצטריך עלמא מיטרא שדרו רבנן ינוקי דבי רב ומנקטי ליה לגלימיה ואמרי ליה אבא אבא הב לן מיטרא אמר רבון העולמים עשה בשביל אלו שאין יודעין איזה אב נותן מטר · תא חזי חסידי דבבל מיכנפי ובעו רחמי אולי מירצי קב"ה אבל חסידי ארץ ישראל כגון חנין זה וכגון ר' יונה [אבוה דר' מני] כד הוה אצטריך עלמא למיטרא שקיל (אבוה דר' מני) ואלקי . פי' שקים אמר איזיל איזבין חמי אזל קאי בדוכתיה עמיקתא מיכסי שקא בצנעא בעי רחמי ואתי מיטרא כו' . ר' מני בריה הוו מצערי ליה דבי נשיאה אזל אישתטח אמערתא דאבוה הוו מחלפי התם אנקוט כרעיה דסוסוותיהו כו' . הוה שכיח קמיה דר' יצחק בן אלישיב . א"ל עתירי דבי חמוה קא מצערו לי א"ל ליענו ואיענו כו' עד חזרה חנה לשחרוריתה: תרי תלמידי הוו שכיחי קמיה אמרו ליה ליבעי עלן מר רחמי ניחכם . אמר להו עמי היתה אותה תפלה ושלחתיה. ר' יוסי ב"ר אבין

רבינו גרשום

איפגר . איבטל : להכי שאלה להתעטף ולהכי לא שיילה למידר משאוי עלה . מחביא עצמו מתפלל בחשאי: מחביא בבית הכסא צנוע : לחסידי דבבל . שהיו מתפללין בפרהסיא ותקיפי דארעא דישראל מתפללין בצינעא*) וקול התור מכאן שהמלאך דוחק לחור דהיינו זול' קראלקא . גוצלא : דבי חמי . חמיו' לא מקבלי אינשי בית עלי דהויא מבועשת מאי : עמי היתה ושלחתיה . כלומר בתחילה היה לבי לכך אבל כבר קבלתי עלי שלא להטריח את קוני :

*) מתיבות וקול התור עד דכייל עגל לא שייך כאן ומקומו להלן כה ע"כ:

הגהות הב"ח

(א) גמ' להיזמי והיגי דלינהו למניה וסיים מסאניה כי מטא למתא : (ב) שם איתו כרוכו : (ג) שם ידענא דרבנן אמטול מיטרא קא אתו : (ד) שם אי נמי משום דהנהו בריוני כו' . נ"ב עי' פרש"י בסוף עמוד א':

(ה) שם הוה מצטריך : (ו) שם אמרי ניכנף לגבי הדדי וניבעי רחמי : (ז) שם וקאי בדוכתא צניעא וכוס מיכסי בשקא כו' : (ח) שם אמרי ליה אייתי לן מר עיבורא : (ט) רש"י ד"ה דלא כו' כלסטים מכ"ד טובת הנאה כו' : (י) ד"ה דאיתתא וד"ה ועוד הד"א : (כ) ד"ה שאין מכירין בין חנן לאביהן שבשמים כסבורין עלי : (ל) ד"ה ה"ג וכו' · בבית הכסא כלומר מתחבא כו' : (מ) ד"ה תא ליכניף אהדדי אלמא כפרסיא היו שנין ולא בצינעא ל"ש נכניף אהדדי אלמא משום חד מינייהו לא הוה אתי : (נ) ד"ה תקיפי כו' וקא חזינן כו' דמתחמיה בלחוד אתי מיטרא: (ס) ד"ה ואייתי כו' דגן משום כפנא הס"ד ואח"כ מה"ד בדוכתא עמיקתא כעמק לו תחת סלעם כדי שלא ירגישוהו בני אדם שאפילו לבני ביתו : (ע) ד"ה אינקוט כו' לזוז ממקומן שלא הניחם לילך עד שיקבלו עליהם שלא לצער עוד את רבי מני בנו הס"ד ואח"כ מה"ד הוה שכיח ר' מני לפני ר' יצחק בן אלישיב הס"ד : (פ) ד"ה עמי היתה ושלחתיה . נ"ב ס"א כלומר שקבלתי עלי שלא להתפלל על ענין זה שהתפללתי קודם : (צ) בא"ד מקובלת כל כך ומפני שלא רצה להטריח לפני המקום אמר כן הס"ד :

גליון הש"ס

גמ' בעיא רחמי דליהדרו בתיובתא . עיין ברכות דף י ע"א :

[נ"ל קורי עכביש יעב"ץ]

[ב"ק נט:]

[כתובות סו:]

[חולין קכב: מגילה כח:]

תהלים קל

יומא חד שמעיה · רב אשי לרבי יוסי בר אבין ל"א יומא חד שמעיה רבי יוסי בר אבין לרב אשי דקא גרים אמר שמואל השולה דג מן הים בשבת כיון דיבש בו כסלע אע"פ שהוא מפרכס לאחר כן ובעוד שהוא מפרכס השליכו במים חייב משום נטילת נשמה שהיא אב מלאכה דתנן (שבת דף עג·) השוחטו ט' אמר ליה רבי יוסי ובין סנפיריו דודאי לא חי וכשאין מתוכב לידה עסקינן כגון שלדו בתוך הסל והגניתו במים לחיות כדרך ששושין הדייגין : א"ל · רב אשי ולא סבר לה מר דהאי ובין סנפיריו רבי יוסי בר אבין אמרה כלומר מ"ט לא אמרת ליה משמיה שכל האומר דבר

תורה אור

יומא חד שמעיה דקא גריס אמר שמואל *השולה דג מן הים בשבת כיון שיבש בו כסלע חייב א"ל ולימא מר ובין סנפיריו אמר ליה ולא סבר לה מר דההיא רבי יוסי בן רבי אבין אמרה אמר ליה אנא ניהו א"ל ולאו קמיה דר' יוסי דמן יוקרת הוה שביה מר א"ל (*הין) א"ל ומ"ט שבקיה מר ואתא הכא אמר ליה גברא דעל בריה ועל ברתיה לא חס עלי דידי היכי חייס בריה מאי היא יומא חד הוו אגרי ליה אגירי בדברא נגה להו ולא אייתי להו ריפתא אמרו ליה לבריה (א) כפינן הוו יתבי תותי תאינתא אמר תאנה תאנה הוציאי פירותיך ויאכלו פועלי אבא אפיקו ואכלו אדהכי והכי אתא אבוה אמר להו לא תינקטו בדעתייכו דהאי דנגהנא אמצוה טרחנא ועד השתא הוא דסגאי אמרו ליה רחמנא לישבעך כי היכי דאשבעינן ברך אמר להו מהיכא אמרו הכי והכי הוה מעשה אמר לו בני אתה הטרחת את קונך להוציא תאנה פירותיה שלא בזמנה יאסף שלא בזמנו ברתיה מאי היא הויא ליה ברתא בעלת יופי יומא חד חזיא להההוא גברא דהוה כריא בהוצא וקא חזי לה אמר לו מאי האי אמר ליה רבי אם לליקחה לא זכיתי לראותה לא אזכה אמר לה בתי קא מצערת להו לברייתא שובי לעפריך ואל יכשלו ביך בני אדם (ב) הויא ליה ההוא חמרא כדהוו אגרי לה כל יומא לאורתא הוו משדרי לה אגרה אגבה ואתיא לבי מרה ואי טפו לה או בצרי לה לא אתיא יומא חד אינשו זוגא דסנדלי עלה ולא אזלה עד דשקלונהו מינה והדר אזלה אלעזר איש בירתא כד הוו חזו ליה גבאי צדקה הוו טשו מיניה דכל מאי דהוה גביה יהיב להו יומא חד הוה סליק לשוקא למזבן נדוניא לברתיה חזיוהו גבאי צדקה טשו מיניה אזל ורהט בתרייהו אמר להו אשבעתיכו במאי עסקיתו אמרו ליה ביתום ויתומה אמר להן העבודה שהן קודמין לבתי שקל כל דהוה בהדיה ויהב להו פש ליה חד זוזא זבן (ג) ליה חיטי ואסיק שדייה באכלבא אתאי דביתהו אמרה לה לברתיה מאי אייתי אבוך אמרה לה כל מה דאייתי באכלבא שדיתיה אתיא למיפתח בבא דאכלבא חזת אכלבא דמליא חיטי וקא נפקא בציצורא דדשא ולא מיפתח בבא מחיטי אזלא ברתיה לבי מדרשא אמרה ליה בא וראה מה עשה לך אוהבך אמר לה העבודה הרי הן הקדש עליך ואין לך בהן אלא כאחד מעניי ישראל ר' יהודה נשיאה גזר תעניתא בעי רחמי ולא אתא מיטרא אמר כמה איכא משמואל הרמתי ליהודה בן גמליאל אוי לו לדור שכן נתקע אוי לו למי שעלתה בימיו כך חליש דעתיה ואתא מיטרא דבי נשיאה גזר תעניתא ולא אודעינהו לרבי יוחנן ולריש לקיש לצפרא אודעינהו אמר ליה ריש לקיש לרבי יוחנן הא לא קבילנא עלן מאורתא אמר ליה אנן בתרייהו גרירינן דבי נשיאה גזר תעניתא ולא אתא מיטרא תנא להו אושעיא זעירא *דמן חברייא °והיה אם מעיני העדה נעשתה לשגגה משל לכלה שהיא בבית אביה כל זמן שעיניה יפות אין כל גופה צריכה בדיקה עיניה *) טרוטות כל גופה צריכה בדיקה אתו עבדיה ורמו ליה סודרא בצואריה וקא מצערו ליה אמרו (*ליה) בני מאתיה שבקיה דהא נמי מצער לן כיון דחזינן דכל מיליה לשום שמים לא אמרי ליה (ד) מידי ושבקינן ליה אתון נמי שבקוהו רבי גזר תעניתא ולא אתא מיטרא נחית קמיה אילפא ואמרי לה רבי אילפי *אמר משיב הרוח *ונשא זיקא אמר מוריד הגשם ואתא מיטרא אמר ליה מאי עובדך אמר ליה דיירנא בקוסטא דחיקא דלית ביה חמרא לקידושא ואבדלתא טרחנא ואתינא חמרא לקידושא ואבדלתא ומפיקנא להו ידי חובתייהו רב איקלע להההוא אתרא גזר תעניתא ולא אתא מיטרא נחית קמיה שליחא דצבורא אמר משיב הרוח ונשב זיקא אמר מוריד הגשם ואתא מיטרא אמר ליה מאי עובדך אמר ליה מקרי דרדקי אנא ומקרינא לבני עניי כבני עתירי וכל דלא אפשר ליה לא שקלינא מיניה מידי ואית לי פירא דכוורי וכל מאן דפשע משחדינא ליה מינייהו ומסדרינן ליה ומפייסנן ליה עד דאתי וקרי רב נחמן גזר תעניתא בעא רחמי ולא אתא מיטרא אמר שקלוה לנחמן חבוטו מן גודא לארעא חליש דעתיה ואתא מיטרא רבה גזר תעניתא בעי רחמי ולא אתא מיטרא אמרו ליה והא רב יהודה כי הוה גזר תעניתא אתא מיטרא אמר להו מאי אעביד אי משום תנויי אנן עדיפינן מינייהו דבשני דרב יהודה *כל תנויי בנזיקין

*) [פי' רש"י שבת לג.]

בשם אומרו מביא גאולה לעולם : סנפיריו · שפולת בהן : לא הנקמו לי בדעתייכו · אל תחשדוני שלא הבאתי לכם מזונות עד עכשיו : דסגאי · שטרחתי והיתרתי : דהוה כריא בהוצא · סותר גדר הענפים כדי להסתכל דרך הנקב : אמר ליה רבי יוסי מאי האי · מה אתה מעיין כאן: אינשו · שכחו : טשו מפניו · היו מתחבאים : העבודה · שבועה : ביתום ויתומה · לזווג זה לזו : אכלבא · אוצר של חטים : אוהבך · הקב"ה : אלא כאחד מעניי ישראל · משום דמעשה נסים הוא ואסור לאדם להנות ממעשה נסים כדאמר לעיל (דף כ:) ואם עושין לו נס מנכין לו מזכיותיו: רבי יהודה נשיאה. היה בנו של רבן גמליאל בר רבי : לשמואל הרמתי · שהורידו גשמים בשבילו דכתיב *הלא קציר חטים היום ועכשיו באין כל ישראל והפילו על ר' יהודה בן גמליאל דלווח וליכא דמשגח ביה : שנתקע · התקוע : והא לא קבלינן מאתמול · בהדייהו (ה) : גרירין · (גרירנן) גרורין ומשוכין אנו אחריהן וכמי שקבלנו עלינו : זעירא דמן חבריא · לעיר שבישיבה והאי דקרי ליה הכי משום דהושעיה אחרינא הוה התם : מעיני העדה · זקנים מאירי עיני העם: בזמן שעיניה יפות אין כל גופה וכו' · דודאי כל גופה יפה : אין עיניה יפות כו' · הואיל והגאו דבי נשיאה דהוו עיני העדה רשעים דלת העם אין צריכין לבדוק מה מעשיהם לכך לא משגחו בהו מן שמים : אתו עבדי דריש גלותא וקא מצערו ליה · לאושפיזא : אמרו ליה בני מתא · לעבדי דבי נשיאה : מצער לן · מתקף ומגדף אותנו : נחית קמיה · לפני התיבה : נשא · כמו נשב : בקוסטא דחיקא · בכפר רחוק שיש בו עניות ביותר : פירא דכוורי · מחילות של דגים : כל מאן דפשע · דלא בעי (ו) מיקרי משחדינא ליה כו' : ומסדרינא ליה ומפייסנא ליה · מתקן כסדר : ה"ג

השולה דג מן הים · שולה כמו מגביה כיון שיבש בו כסלע (ז) שעדיין הוא מפרכס ובשעה שמפרכס חזר והשליכו לים חייב משום נטילת נשמה שהיא אב מלאכה דתנן (שבת דף עג·) השוחטו והמפשיטו גבי אבות מלאכות : הא

רבינו חננאל

שמע לרב אשי דתני אמר שמואל השולה דג מן הים כיון שיבש בו כסלע חייב . א"ל אימא ובין הסנפירין . א"ל רב אשי הני דרבי ר' יוסי אינון א"ל אנא הוא א"ל רב אשי ואמאי שבקת לר' יוסי דמן יוקרת רבך א"ל גברא דלא חס אבריה ואברתיה עלי דידי חיים · בריה וברתיה מאי היא כו' . כלבא אוצר. ר' יהודה נשיאה גזר תעניתא ולא אתא מיטרא . אמר משמואל הרמתי שאמר הלא קציר חטים היום כו' וכיון שקרא בא המטר הגיע שפלות הדור ליהודה בן גמליאל שהוא פרנס הדור וצועק ואינו נענה . אוי לו לדור הנתקע לכך אוי מי שעלתה בימיו צרה ואין מי שראוי להתפלל ולהשיב חימה · חלש דעתיה [דר"י נשיאה] ואתא מיטרא. רבי נשיאה גזר תענית ולא אודיעינהו לר' יוחנן ולר"ש בן לקיש לצפרא אודיעינהו אמר ר"ל לא קבלנו עלינו מאתמול. א"ר יוחנן ניתיב בתעניתא דאנן בתרייהו גרירינן . דבי נשיאה גזור תעניתא בעו רחמי ולא אתא מיטרא . תנא להו והיה אם מעיני העדה נעשתה לשגגה . משל לכלה בזמן שעיניה יפין אין הגוף צריך בדיקה כו' כלומר פרנסי הדור הוא דלא מעלי . רבי אילפי ירד לפני התיבה לפני ר' אשי אמר משיב הרוח אתא זיקא אמר מוריד הגשם אתא מטרא אמרי ליה מא עובדך אמר להו בקיפא פי' בכפר דחוק דאירנא ופרחנא ומייתינא קדושא ואבדלתא ומפקנא להו ידי חובתייהו . וכן התוא שליחא דצבורא דנחית קמי דרבא דשאלוהו ואמר מקרי ינוקי אנא ומקרינא לבני עניי כבני עתירי ואית לי פירא (דסורי) דכוורי דמפתסנא מיניה כל

רבינו גרשום

שיבש בו כסלע חייב משום צידה ומשום נטילת נשמה: אמר ליה ר' יוסי בר ר' אבין בין סנפיריו א"ל רב יוסף תא בין סנפיריו ר' יוסי היא . כלבא טרון . משמואל הרמתי שהיה מבקש ומביא מטר אפי' בימי קציר חטים דכתיב הלא קציר חטים וגו': בתרייהו דבי נשיאה אזלינן וכי קבילו אינהו הוי כמו קבילו אנו . מעיני העדה עיקר העדה היינו דבי נשיאה . קוסטא אתרא. דחיקא . בני אדם דחוקים :

[נ"ל ונשב וכן לקמן בסמוך וכן לקמן כה: וב"מ פה: איתא ונשב אמנם לפני רש"י היה הגירסא ונשא הלכך פי' רש"י נשא ונשא כמו ונשב]

כט א ב מיי' פי"א מהל' שבת הל' א סמג לאוין סה :

שבת קז·

נ"א הן

שמואל א יב

במדבר

[עי' פרש"י והתו' חולין יב: ד"ה דמן חבריא פרש"י שבת לו. ד"ה זעירא]

[נ"ל להו]

[לקמן כה: ב"מ פה:]

ברכות כ. סנהדרין קו:

הגהות הב"ח

(א) גמ' ליה לבריה כפינן הוו יתבי : (ב) שם ואל יכשלו ביך בני אדם וכן סוף סוף ניה סבוא חמרא : (ג) שם זבן ליה חיטי ואסיק כו' מאי אייתי לך אבוך אמרה : (ד) שם לא אמרי ליה ולא מידי ליה · (ה) רש"י ד"ה והא לא כו' בהדייהו כדאמרינן לעיל מאימתי מקבל רב אמר במנחה ושמואל אמר בתפלת המנחה בס"ד : (ו) ד"ה כל מאן דפשע דלא בעי מיקרי בס"ד ואח"כ מה"ד משחדינא ליה פירי כי היכי דנגמיר בס"ד : (ז) תוס' ד"ה השולה כו' שיבש בו כסלע אע"פ שעדיין הוא מפרכס ובשעה·

תורה אור

בנזיקין הוה ואנן קא מתנינן בשיתא סדרין וכי הוה מטי רב יהודה בעוקצין *האשה שכובשת ירק בקדירה ואמרי לה *זיתים שכבשן בטרפיהן טהורין אמר הויי' דרב ושמואל קא חזינא הכא ואנן קא מתנינן בעוקצין תליסר מתיבתא ואילו רב יהודה כי הוה שליף חד מסאנא אתי מיטרא ואנן קא צווחינן כולי יומא וליכא דאשגח בן אי משום עובדא אי איכא דחזא מידי לימא אבל מה יעשו גדולי הדור שאין דורן דומה יפה רב יהודה חזא הנהו בי תרי דהוו קא פרצי בריפתא אמר שמע מינה איכא שבעא בעלמא יהיב עיניה הוה כפנא אמרו ליה רבנן לרב כהנא בריה דרב נחוניא שמעיה (א) מר דשכיח קמיה ניעשייה דליפוק בפתחא דסמוך לשוקא עשייה ונפק לשוקא חזא כנופיא אמר להו מאי האי אמרו ליה אבוספא דתמרי קיימי דקא מזדבן אמר שמע מינה כפנא בעלמא אמר ליה לשמעיה שלוף לי מסאניי שלף ליה חד מסאנא ואתא מיטרא כי מטא למישלף אחרינא אתא אליהו ואמר ליה אמר הקדוש ברוך הוא אי שלפת אחרינא מחריבנא לעלמא אמר רב מרי ברה דבת שמואל אנא הוה קאימנא אגודא דנהר פפא חזאי למלאכי דאידמו למלחי דקא מייתי חלא ומלונהו לארבי והוה קמחא דסמידא (ב) אתו כולי עלמא למיזבן אמר להו מהא לא תיזבנון דמעשה נסים הוא למחר אתיין ארבי דחיטי *דפרזינא רבא איקלע להגרוניא גזר תעניתא ולא אתא מיטרא אמר להו ביתו כולי עלמא בתעניתייכו למחר אמר להו מי איכא דחזא חילמא לימא אמר להו ר' אלעזר מהגרוניא לדידי אקריון בחלמי שלם טב לרב טב מריבון טב דמטוביה מטיב לעמיה אמר שמע מינה *עת רצון היא מבעי רחמי בעי רחמי ואתי מיטרא ההוא גברא דאיחייב נגדא בבי דינא דרבא משום דבעל כותית נגדיה רבא ומית אשתמע מילתא בי שבור מלכא בעא לצעורי לרבא אמרה ליה איפרא הורמיז אימיה דשבור מלכא לבריה לא ליהוי לך עסק דברים בהדי יהודאי דכל מאן דבעיין ממרייהו יהיב להו אמר לה מאי היא בעין רחמי ואתי מיטרא אמר לה ההוא משום דזימנא דמיטרא הוא אלא לבעו רחמי האידנא בתקופת תמוז וליתי מיטרא שלחה ליה לרבא כוין דעתך ובעי רחמי דליתי מיטרא בעי רחמי ולא אתי מיטרא אמר לפניו רבונו של עולם °אלהים באזנינו שמענו אבותינו ספרו לנו פועל פעלת בימיהם בימי קדם ואנו בעינינו לא ראינו אתא מיטרא עד דשפוך מרזבי *דצפורי לדיגלת אתא אבוה איתחזי ליה בחלמיה ואמר ליה מי איכא דמיטרח קמי שמיא כולי האי °אמר ליה שני דוכתיך שני דוכתיה למחר אשכחיה דמרשם פורייה בסכיני רב פפא גזר תעניתא ולא אתא מיטרא חלש ליביה שרף פינכא דדייסא ובעי רחמי ולא אתא מיטרא אמר ליה רב נחמן בר *אושפזתי אי שריף מר פינכא אחריתי דדייסא אתי מיטרא איכסיף וחלש דעתיה ואתא מיטרא *)ר' חנינא בן דוסא הוה קא אזיל באורחא אתא מיטרא אמר לפניו רבונו של עולם כל העולם כולו בנחת וחנינא בצער פסק מיטרא כי מטא לביתיה אמר לפניו רבונו של עולם כל העולם כולו בצער וחנינא בנחת אתא מיטרא אמר רב יוסף מאי אהניא ליה צלותא דכהן גדול לגבי רבי חנינא בן דוסא דתנן **היה מתפלל תפלה קצרה בבית החיצון *מאי מצלי רבין בר ארא ורבא בר ארא דאמרי תרוייהו משמיה דרב יהודה יהי רצון מלפניך ה' אלהינו שתהא השנה הזו גשומה ושחונה שחונה מעלייתא היא אדרבה גריעותא היא אלא °אם שחונה תהא גשומה ומלולה ואל יכנס לפניך תפלת עוברי דרכים רב אחא בריה דרבא מסיים משמיה דרב יהודה °לא יעדי עביד שולטן מדבית יהודה ואל יהו עמך ישראל צריכין להתפרנס זה מזה ולא לעם אחר אמר רב יהודה אמר רב *בכל יום ויום בת קול יוצאת ואומרת כל העולם כולו ניזון בשביל חנינא בני וחנינא בני דיו בקב חרובים מע"ש לע"ש הוה רגילא דביתהו למיחמא תנורא כל מעלי דשבתא ושדייא אקטרתא

משום

*) יומא נג:

ה"ג בנזיקין הוה · למודם לא היה גדול אלא בסדר נזיקין : שכובשת ירק בקדירה. במסכת [*טהרות] היא בפ' שני (מ"א) גבי ידות מיירי דקיי"ל (עוקצין פ"א משנה א) כל ידות האוכלין אם נגעה טומאה בהן נטמא גם האוכל הצריך לידות דיד מכנים ומוציא כדאמרינן בהעור והרוטב (חולין דף קיח·) מכל האוכל לרבות הידות וקתני התם אשה שהיא כובשת ירק דידות שלהן טהורין דכשהיא עוצרת אותם הידות משתברות וא"א ליטול הירקות בידות שלהן שכשמגו ונפסק האוכל מן היד מחמת כבישה : טובשת · עול"ן בלע"ז עוצרת שילא המשקה שלהן ויבשו דרך אשה בכך טובשת ירק ממים שישתמרו לזמן מרובה: טהורין· העלין והקלחין : ואמרי לה · כי מטא לאידך בפרק שני (דעוקצין משנה א) זיתים שכבשן בטרפיהן כתרגומו עלה טרפא (בראשית ח) עלין שלהן דהיינו ידות : טהורין · הידות להביא טומאה לאוכל דתו לא חזי לנטורי פירי יד : הוויות דרב ושמואל · עומק גדול ולא הוה נהירא ליה: תליסר מתיבתא · שלש עשרה ישיבות איכא בהך מתא דגמרי מסכת עוקצין : כי הוה שליף חד מסאנא · משום עינוי : דחזא מידי · חם ושלום בעובדי בישי : פרצי בריפתא · זורקים אותם זה לזה (ג) : ניעשייה · יעשנו שילא לחוץ : אבוספא דתמרי · על כלי מלא תמרים או פסולת של תמרים : קאימנא אנהר פפא · ההוא יומא דעבד רב יהודה הכי : חלא · חול : דסמידא · סולת והן עומדין מוכרין אותו : אמר להו מעשה נסים כו' · וכמה דאפשר להתרחק ממעשה נסים יותר טוב ונכון : דפרזינא · מקום : אקרון · הקרוני הייתי קורא בחלומי : נגדא · מלקות : איפרא הורמיז · כך שמה איפרא חן יופי שדים היה *לה: מאי היא · מאי עביד להו : אמרה ליה · דכל אימת דבעי מיטרא: זימנא דמיטרא הוא · ואפילו לא בעו נמי אתי מיטרא : שלחה ליה לרבא · דרחמא ליה לרבא : אבותינו ספרו לנו פועל פעלת בימיהם בימי קדם · שהיית מפליא להם נסים (ד): עד דשפיך מרזבי דציפורי · שקילחו מים מן המרזיבות עד ששוטפין בחוצות ויורדין ושופכין : לדיגלת · לנהר חדקל : אשני מטוך · אל תשכב במטתך הלילה : בסכיני · שרצו שדים להורגו וחתכו את מטתו והיינו דאמרי' בשחיטת חולין בפרק הזרוע (דף קלג·) וליקריוה לרבא רבא גזוף היה לא מצינו לו נזיפה בכל הש"ס אלא בזה המעשה כשביקש הגשמים בתמוז שלא לצורך : הכי גרסינן ר"פ גזר תעניתא חלש לביה טעים מידי בעא רחמי ולא אתא מיטרא: אי שריף מר חדא פינכא דדייסא · מלשון שורפה חיה (ע"ז דף כט:) (ה) פינכא מלא כף כמו מלחיך פינכי (פסחים דף מט·) דייסא טריי"ס בלע"ז ולהוכא קאמר ליה הכי חשוב דזוגים בריפתא והקדר בעא רחמי : רבי חנינא בן דוסא תנא הוא : כל העולם כולו בצער · שמבקשין מים לשדותיהן : בנחת · שאני יושב בביתי ואיני צריך לגשמים לפי שאין לי שדות : מאי אהניא ליה צלותיה דכהן גדול · כשהיה מתפלל תפלה קצרה ביום הכפורים שהיה אומר אל יכנס לפניך תפלת עוברי דרכים דר' חנינא מבטל ליה לצלותיה דכהן גדול שאעפ"כ שמע הקב"ה תפלתו ופסיק מיטרא : שחונה · חמה כמו חמותי ראיתי אור (ישעיה מד) תירגם יונתן בן עוזיאל שחינת : אם שחונה תהא גשומה · כשהיא חמה צריכה הארץ לגשמים מאד והדיר : בת קול יוצאת ואומרת כל העולם טעו · ולא גרסי' מהר חורב : קב חרובים מערב שבת לערב שבת · כל השבת היה ניזון בכך חבר לחם היה ומתגלגל היה בחרובין: אקטרתא · דבר במעלה עשן כקיטור הכבשן (ו) :

משום

[ועיין בסנהדרין קו: במהרש"א וע"ע בפי' רש"י בברכות כ.]

ל א ב ג מיי' פ"ד מהל' עבודת יוה"כ הלכה א :

[וע"ע רש"י מו"ק כ: ד"ה איפרא ועי' תוס' גיטין יא. ד"ה הורמין ופי' מקשו על פרש"י]

טהרו' פ"ב מ"א

עוקצין פ"ב מ"א

[גי' הערוך ערך ארן א' דארזנאי פי' בפינות מלאות אורז]

[ברכות ח. יומא כב. יבמות עב. סנהדרין כב.]

תהלים מד

[נ"ל דציפורא וכ"ה בע"י]

[גי' הערוך אושפזתי פי' הוא שם למו של רב פפא]

יומא נג: ע"ש

ברכות יז: חולין פו.

רבינו חננאל

סאן דפסע מסתרינא ליה כתו עד יקרי*) ביסי רב יהודה מצלו ואתי מטרא . אמרי אי משום תורה כולהו תנויי בנזיקין הוה ואנן מתנינן טובא . וכי הוה רב יהודה מטי לאשה שכובשת ירק בקדרה . ואמרי לה זיתים שכבשן בטרפיהן זו היא משנה בעוקצין פ"ב . הוה א' הויה דרב ושמואל קא חזינא הכא כלומר זו קושיא גדולה היא ואנן האידנא מתנינן י"ג מתיבתא בעוקצין אלא מה יעשו פרנסי גדולי הדור שאין דורן יפה : רב יהודה שלף מסאניה למבעי רחמי אמטרא אתחזי ליה חלמא אי שלפת אחרינא מחריב עלמא . ההוא דבעל כותית נגדיה רב יהודה ומית אכלו ביה קורצי. הלשינו עליו שהמית אדם . פי' אכלו קראו עליו מלשינות כדמתרגם קרא בגרון אל תחשוך אכלי · בעא שבור מלכא לצעורייה כו' . ר' חנינא בן דוסא הות אזיל באורחא אתא מיטרא אמר רבון העולמים כל העולם בנחת וחנינא בצער פסק מיטרא כי אתא לביתיה אמר כל העולם בצער בנחת אתא מיטרא אמר רב יוסף כאי אהני צלותא רכ"ג דהוה מצלי ביוה"כ יר"מ שאם תהיה השנה הזאת שחונה תהיה גשומה ואל תכנס לפניך תפלת עוברי דרכים שמתפללין לפסוק המטר הנה ר' חנינא הפסק המטר. ועוד היה מתפלל ואל יעדי עביד שלטן מדבית יהודה, ואל יהיו עמך בית ישראל צריכין זה לזה לפרנסה: בכל יום ב"ק יוצאה כל העולם כולו ניזון בשביל חנינא בני וחנינא בני דיו קב חרובין מע"ש

*) נראה דצ"ל אמרו ליה והא כיפי רב יהודה מצלו ואתי מטרא אמר להו מאי אעביד אי משום הורס וכו' כצ"ל.

רבינו גרשום

האשה שכובשת ירק בקדרה ונגע טומאה לקלח אין מביאין טומאה לירק כיון דנכבש בטיל ליה בתורת יד : זיתים בטרפיהן טרפא נמי הוי ידות : אנא קיימנא בההיא שעתא: דפרזנאי מקום : שחונה :

הגהות הב"ח

(א) גמ' שמעיה דמר דשכיח : (ב) שם ואתו כולי עלמא לאיתבן מיניה ואמינא להו מהא פי' לגרוניא גזר תעניתא כמה רחמי ולא אתא כו' בתעניתייכו כיון למחר אמר להו כו' עת רצון היא למבעי רחמי בעי רחמי : (ג) רש"י ד"ה פרלי כו' זה לזה כמשחקין זה עם זה כס"ד : (ד) ד"ה אבותינו כו' מפליא להם נסים אבל בעינינו לא ראינו כלומר שבימיו שלא לנו נפלאותיך הס"ד : (ה) ד"ה אי שריף כו' מלי שורפה היא מר חדא פינכא מלא כף : (ו) ד"ה אקטרתא כו' כקיטור שכבשן כדי שיהיו פטורין המעשים אלופה נתמר הס"ד :

גליון הש"ס

גמ' א"ל שני דוכתך. עיין חולין דף קלג ע"א רש"י ד"ה מוף :

לא א מיי' פ"ט מהל' נזקי ממון הל' ב סמג עשין סו טוש"ע ח"מ סימן תט סעיף א :

משום כיסופא · שהיו שכינותיה אופות עיסה לכבוד שבת והיא אינה עושה כלום : אגנא · עריבה : מסא · עתר שמוציאין בו הלחם מרדה פאליי"א בלע"ז ומרדה ומסא חדא מילתא היא (ד) : תנא אף היא להביא מרדה נכנסה · פל"א בלע"ז על שם שרודין בה פת מן התנור* שלא היתה שואלת מפני שרגילה בניסין : חזיא · דביתהו בחלמא : מישקל לא שקלי · בתר דיהבי : כל היכא דתני בי שמשי היינו ערב שבת °לא שמעתי טעם* : בחלא דחלא · בכלי שיש בו החומץ ושמתי החומץ בנר ויכבה הנר : עד שנטלו ממנו אור להבדלה · הדליק ממנו נר אחר ליהנות בו ונר של מעשה נסים ליהנה כי היכי דעבד רב יהודה (לעיל דף כד:) בחלא דהוה סמידא : קא מפסדי לן · שדות : דובים · ואבים בשדות : ולא מטו כשורי · אין הקורות מגיעות מכותל לכותל : איכו נימטו כשוריך · יאריכו הקורות : סניפין היו · הקורות של חליות היו במעשה נס נדבקו להן חתיכות קטנות לאורכן : ר"א בן פדת · אמורא היה והוא תקרא מרא דארעא דא"י במסכת נדה (דף כ:) בעל הוראות היה והוא שימש ר' יוחנן *)אחרי מות ריש לקיש והיה דחוק ועני : עבד מילתא · הקיז דם : ברא דתומא · בן השום ללע של שום : חלש ליביה · נתעלפה : צוציתא · ניצוץ : מאפותיה · ממצחו : כולי האי ואפשר · בתמיה כולי האי עבדת ואכתי הך ספיקא דלמא לא מיתרמינא בשעתא דמזוני : דחיי כפישא או דחיינא · ימי חיי שחייתי כבר הם רבים ממה שאני עתיד לחיות : אמר דחיית · מה שכבר חיית מרובים ממה שאתה עתיד לחיות והיינו דקא בכי כי אמר שכינה הכי והאי דחייך משום י"ג נהרוותא לרחוץ בהן ולטייל בהן מזה לזה : אי הכי לא בעינא · דתיחרביה לעלמא : ותו לא · וכי אין אתה נותן לי דברים אחרים : א"ל ולחברך מאי קא יהיבנא · אנא מגברא דלית ליה בעינא לא גרים בספר רבי ובספר שלי כתוב : באסקוטלא אפותאי · היינו טליתא דנפק מיניה שמדביק אצבע צרדה עם הגודל ומכה בצפורן האצבע : איגרו בך גירי · כלומר הכיתי בחיצי לחדווה בעלמא אמר כן : הא אנא והא בר ליואי · הוא איש אחד ואני איש אחד הוא עדיף מינאי : דתברי · שוברים : שיבא מטר בשבילנו · מקבלים אתם עליכם ומסכימין לדעת אחד : כמה עזין · דלא כסין מצטורא : לוי אחוי קידה · טעמן שני גודליו בארץ ושוחה ונושק את הרצפה : הא והא גרמא ליה · החטא גרם לו שנגלע בקידה : ואין

תורה אור

הא והא גרמו ליה · °פי' הראב"ד הא כדעבד דאחוי הקידה קמי רבי איטלע והא דהטיח דברים כלפי מעלה גרמא ליה דאיטלע : שאני

משום כיסופא הוה להך שיבבתא בישתא אמרה מכדי ידענא דלית להו ולא מידי מאי כולי האי אזלא וטרפא אבבא איכספא ועיילא לאינדרונא איתעביד לה ניסא דחזיא לתנורא מלא לחמא ואגנא מלא לישא אמרה לה פלניתא פלניתא אייתי מסא דקא חריך לחמיך אמרה לה אף אנא להכי עיילי תנא אף היא להביא מרדה נכנסה מפני שמלומדת בנסים (א) אמרה ליה דביתהו עד אימת ניזיל ונצטער כולי האי אמר לה מאי נעביד בעי רחמי דניתבו לך מידי* °בעא רחמי יצתה כמין פיסת יד ויהבו ליה חד כרעא דפתורא דדהבא (*חזאי) בחלמא עתידי צדיקי דאכלי אפתורא דדהבא דאית ליה תלת כרעי (*ואת) אוכלת אפתורא דתרי כרעי (*אמרה ליה) ניחא לך דמיכל אכלי כולי עלמא אפתורא דמשלם ואנן אפתורא דמחסר אמרה ליה ומאי נעביד בעי רחמי דנשקלינהו מינך בעי רחמי ושקלוהו תנא גדול היה נס אחרון יותר מן הראשון דגמירי דמיהב יהבי מישקל לא שקלי חד בי שמשי חזייה לברתיה דהוות עציבא אמר לה בתי *למאי עציבת אמרה ליה כלי של חומץ נתחלף לי בכלי של שמן והדלקתי ממנו אור לשבת אמר לה בתי מאי איכפת לך מי שאמר לשמן וידלוק הוא יאמר לחומץ וידלוק תנא היה דולק והולך כל היום כולו עד שהביאו ממנו אור להבדלה ר' חנינא בן דוסא הוו ליה הנך עיזי אמרו ליה קא מפסדן (ב) אמר אי קא מפסדן ניכלינהו דובי ואי לא כל חדא וחדא תיתי לאורתא דובא בקרנייהו לאורתא אייתי כל חדא וחדא דובא בקרנייהו הוה ליה ההיא שיבבתא דקא בניא ביתא ולא מטו כשורי אתיא לקמיה אמרה ליה בניתי ביתי ולא קמטו כשוראי אמר לה מה שמך אמרה ליה איכו אמר איכו נימטו כשוריך תנא הגיעו עד שיצאו אמה לכאן ואמה לכאן ויש אומרין *סניפין עשאום תניא פלימו אומר אני ראיתי אותו הבית והיו קורותיו יוצאות אמה לכאן ואמה לכאן ואמרו לי בית זה שקירה ר' חנינא בן דוסא בתפלתו *ור' חנינא בן דוסא מהיכן הוו ליה עזים [א] והא עני הוי ועוד אמרו חכמים **אין מגדלין בהמה דקה בא"י אמר רב פנחס מעשה ועבר אדם אחד על פתח ביתו והניח שם תרנגולין ומצאתן אשתו של ר' חנינא בן דוסא ואמר לה אל תאכלי מביציהן והרבו ביצים ותרנגולין והיו מצערין אותם ומכרן וקנה בדמיהן עזים פעם אחת עבר אותו אדם שאבדו ממנו התרנגולין ואמר לחבירו בכאן הנחתי התרנגולין שלי שמע ר' חנינא אמר לו יש לך בהן סימן אמר לו הן נתן לו סימן ונטל את העזין והן הן *עיזי דאייתו דובי בקרנייהו רבי אלעזר בן פדת דחיקא ליה מילתא טובא עבד מלתא ולא הוה ליה מידי למטעם שקל ברא דתומא ושדייה בפומיה חלש לביה ונים אזול רבנן לשולי ביה חזיוהו דקא בכי וחייך ונפק צוציתא דנורא מאפותיה כי אתער אמרו ליה מ"ט קבכית וחייכת אמר להו דהוה יתיב עמי הקב"ה ואמרי ליה עד מתי אצטער בהאי עלמא ואמר לי אלעזר בני ניחא לך דאפכיה לעלמא מרישא אפשר דמתילדת בשעתא דמזוני אמרי לקמיה כולי האי ואפשר אמרי ליה דחיי טפי או דחיינא א"ל דחיית אמרי לקמיה א"כ לא בעינא אמר לי בהאי אגרא דאמרת לא בעינא יהיבנא לך לעלמא דאתי תליסרי נהרוותא דמשחא אפרסמון דכיין *כפרת ודיגלת דמענגת בהו אמרי לקמיה האי ותו לא אמר לי ולחברך מאי יהיבנא אמרי ליה ואנא מגברא דלית ליה בעינא מחיין באסקוטלא *אפותאי ואמר לי אלעזר ברי *גירי בך גירי ר' חמא בר חנינא גזר תעניתא ולא אתא מיטרא אמרו ליה והא רבי יהושע בן לוי גזר תעניתא ואתי מיטרא אמר להו הא אנא הא בר ליואי אמרו ליה דניתי וניכוין דעתין איפשר דתברי ציבורא לבייהו דאתי מיטרא בעון רחמי ולא אתי מיטרא אמר להו ניחא לכו שיבא מטר בשבילנו אמרו ליה הן אמר רקיע רקיע כסי פניך לא איכסי אמר כמה עזין פני רקיע איכסי (ג) ואתא מיטרא לוי גזר תעניתא ולא אתא מיטרא אמר לפניו רבונו של עולם עלית וישבת במרום ואין אתה מרחם על בניך אתא מיטרא ואיטלע אמר רבי אלעזר *לעולם אל יטיח אדם דברים כלפי מעלה שהרי אדם גדול הטיח דברים כלפי מעלה ואיטלע ומנו לוי והא גרמא ליה והא לוי אחוי קידה קמיה דרבי ואיטלע הא והא גרמא ליה רבי חייא בר לולייני שמעינהו להנך ענני דקאמרי ניתו וניתבי מיא בעמון ומואב אמר לפניו רבונו של עולם כשנתת תורה לעמך ישראל חזרת על כל אומות העולם ולא קיבלוה ועכשיו אתה נותן להם מטר שדו הכא שריוה אדוכתיהו *דרש רבי חייא בר לולייני מאי דכתיב °צדיק כתמר יפרח כארז בלבנון ישגה אם נאמר תמר למה נאמר ארז ואם נאמר ארז למה נאמר תמר אילו נאמר ארז ולא נאמר תמר הייתי אומר מה תמר

אין

שבת קיז: רש"י ד"ה מרדה | [וכתובות קג. מפרש רש"י בשם ועיין רש"י שבת פו: ד"ה ולימלנו וכו'] | [נ"ל חזיא רש"י] [נ"ל ואיהו אפתורא ע"ש] [*כדאיתא ב"מ פה.] | ב"ק שם: | ב"מ קז. | [גי' הערוך אפותא פי' מצח] | סוטה ג: מגילה כב. | ב"ב פ: תהלים נב

ר"ל מסיבותא דעניא לצדיקי לעלמא דאתי | [נ"ל אמר לה וכן איתא בע"י] | [נ"ל אמאי"כ בדפו"י] | [עי' ערוך ערך סנף] | [עי' בע"י ונה"ל שם דכל זה איתו מן הגמרא מכאן עד דאייתו דובי בקרנייהו] | סיכות כפרת ודיגלת ליתא בע"י | ס"א אגרי [עי' פי' הערוך ערך גר]

רבינו חננאל

חד [בי] שימשא איחלף לברתיה ורמייא חלא לשרגא דשבתא והוות עציבא א"ל אבוה אל תעצבי מי שאמר לשמן וידלוק [יאמר לחומץ וידלוק] תנא [היה דולק] כל השבת עד דשקיל מיניה אור להבדלה: ר' אלעזר בן פדת הוה דחיק ליה עלמא הקיז ולא הוה ליה מידי למיכל אשכח בר תומא שרא לפומא חלש לביה עיילו רבנן לשיוליה ביה ומצאוהו ישן הויה דבכא ואחיך ונפיק ציציתא דנורא מאפותיה כשהקיץ משנתו אמרו ליה מאי היא אמר להו חזאי שכינה בחלמא ואמרי קמיה עד מתי אתנא בהאי דוחקא אתאמר לי מקמיה ניחא לך דליחרב עלמא ואבריה מרישא אפשר דמתיילדת בשעתא דמזוני אמרי קמיה כולי האי ואולי לא בעינא [א"ל בהאי] אגרא [דאמרת] לא בעינא יהיבנא לך לעלמא דאתי י"ג מעיינתא דמשכי אפרסמון דכייא כו' עד מחין באסקוטלא אפותאי כלומר הכהו מלאך באצבעו על מצחו ונראת לו ההכאה כניצוצת של אש כשכופף אדם אצבעו על בוהנו ושומט אותה בכח ומכה את חבירו נקראת-המכה הזאת אסקוטלא . אפותא פדחת · לוי גזר תעניתא ולא אתי מיטרא אמר רבון העולמים אינך משגיח בצער בניך ומרחם עליהם כלומר ראוים הם להתרחם ואינך מרחם ולפי

רבינו גרשום

מרדה לרדות הפת : סניפין שמלאכים האריכום בחתכי קורה : מגביה מן הקרקע שלא יקרץ סמוך לקרקע שיחליף נשו :

הגהות הב"ח

(א) גמ' מפני שמלומדת בניסין היתה אמרה ליה דביתהו כו' אמר לה מאי נעביד אמרה ליה בעי רחמי דניתבו כו' ומאי נעביד אמרה ליה בעי רחמי כו' דגמירי מן שמיא מיהב יהבי : (ב) שם אמרי ליה קא מפסדן עיזך אמר אי כו' אמרה ליה בנאי ביתי ולא קמטו : (ג) שם כמה עזין פני רקיע איכסי כעיבא ואתא מיטרא : (ד) רש"י ד"ה מסא כו' חדא מילתא היא הס"ד ואח"כ מה"ד מרדה פליא בלע"ז על שם שרודין בה פת מן התנור הס"ד ואח"כ מה"ד תנא אף היא להביא מרדה נכנסה שלא היתה שואלת כו' כצ"ל :

הגהות הגר"א

[א] גמ' (והא עני הוי ועוד א"ח א"מ בהמה דקה בא"י) תא"מ :

גליון הש"ס גמרא בעי רחמי יצתה כמין פיסת יד · עי' שמות רבה פ' שמות פ' נ"ב : רש"י ד"ה כל היכא כו' לא שמעתי טעם · עיין ברכות דף כח ע"ב ד"ה מאן שמעת ליה וה"ג : תוספות ד"ה הא וכו' פי' הראב"ד · הנה עוד משמעא דהראב"ד כתוספות יומא דף יח ע"א ע"ו דף לה ע"א :

אין גוזעו מחליף אף צדיק ח"ו אין גוזעו מחליף לכך נאמר ארז אילו נאמר ארז ולא נאמר תמר הייתי אומר מה ארז אין עושה פירות אף צדיק ח"ו אין עושה פירות לכך נאמר תמר ונאמר ארז וארז גוזעו מחליף והתניא **הלוקח אילן מחבירו לקוץ מגביהו מן הקרקע טפח וקוצץ בסדן השקמה שני טפחים בבתולת השקמה שלשה טפחים בקנים ובגפנים מן הפקק ולמעלה בדקלים ובארזים חופר למטה ומשריש לפי שאין גוזעו מחליף הכא במאי עסקינן בשאר מיני ארזים כדרבה בר הונא דאמר רבה בר הונא *עשרה מיני ארזים הן שנאמר °אתן במדבר ארז שטה והדס וגו' ת"ר מעשה ברבי אליעזר שגזר שלש עשרה תעניות על הצבור ולא ירדו גשמים באחרונה התחילו הצבור לצאת אמר להם תקנתם קברים לעצמכם געו כל העם בבכיה וירדו גשמים שוב מעשה בר' אליעזר שירד לפני התיבה ואמר עשרים וארבע ברכות ולא נענה ירד רבי עקיבא אחריו ואמר אבינו מלכנו אין לנו מלך אלא אתה אבינו מלכנו למענך רחם עלינו וירדו גשמים הוו מרנני רבנן יצתה בת קול ואמרה לא מפני שזה גדול מזה אלא שזה מעביר על מדותיו וזה אינו מעביר על מדותיו ת"ר עד מתי יהו הגשמים יורדין והצבור פוסקין מתעניתם כמלא ברך המחרישה דברי רבי מאיר *וחכמים אומרים בחרבה טפח בבינונית טפחיים בעבודה שלשה טפחים תניא *רבי שמעון בן אלעזר אומר אין לך טפח מלמעלה שאין תהום יוצא לקראתו שלשה טפחים והא תניא טפחיים לא קשיא כאן בעבודה כאן בשאינה עבודה א"ר אלעזר כשמנסכין את המים בחג תהום אומר לחבירו אבע מימיך קול שני ריעים אני שומע שנאמר °תהום אל תהום קורא לקול צנוריך וגו' ואמר רבה לדידי חזי לי רידיא דמי לעיגלא (תלתא) ופירסא* שפוותיה וקיימא בין תהומא תתאה לתהומא עילאה לתהומא עילאה א"ל חשור מימיך לתהומא תתאה א"ל אבע מימיך שנא' °הנצנים נראו בארץ וגו': היו מתענין וירדו גשמים קודם הנץ החמה כו': ת"ר היו מתענין וירדו להם גשמים קודם הנץ החמה לא ישלימו לאחר הנץ החמה ישלימו דברי ר' מאיר ר' יהודה אומר קודם חצות לא ישלימו לאחר חצות ישלימו רבי יוסי אומר קודם ט' שעות לא ישלימו לאחר ט' שעות ישלימו שכן מצינו באחאב מלך ישראל שהתענה מתשע שעות ולמעלה שנאמר °הראית כי נכנע אחאב וגו' ר' יהודה נשיאה גזר תעניתא וירדו להם גשמים לאחר הנץ החמה סבר לאשלומינהו א"ל רבי אמי קודם חצות ואחר חצות שנינו שמואל הקטן גזר תעניתא וירדו להם גשמים קודם הנץ החמה כסבורין העם לומר שבחו של צבור הוא אמר להם אמשול לכם [משל] למה הדבר דומה לעבד שמבקש פרס מרבו אמר להם תנו לו ואל אשמע קולו שוב שמואל הקטן גזר תעניתא וירדו להם גשמים לאחר שקיעת החמה כסבורים העם לומר שבחו של צבור הוא אמר להם שמואל לא שבח של צבור הוא אלא אמשול לכם משל למה הדבר דומה לעבד שמבקש פרס מרבו ואמר להם המתינו לו עד שיתמקמק ויצטער ואחר כך תנו לו ולשמואל הקטן שבחו של צבור היכי דמי אמר *משיב הרוח ונשב זיקא אמר מוריד הגשם ואתא מיטרא: מעשה וגזרו תענית בלוד כו': ונימא הלל מעיקרא *)אביי ורבא דאמרי תרווייהו לפי שאין אומרים הלל אלא

*) נ"י רמ"ש רב ושמואל

רש"י

*ואין גזעו מחליף · אם נפסק: אף צדיק · אין לו זכר צדיק אין גזעו מחליף אינו בתחיית המתים: צדיק אינו עושה פירות · אין לו שכר לעתיד: בתולת השקמה · נטיעה שלא נקצצה מעולם: סדן · שכבר הזקין טרונ"ק בלע"ז שנקצץ וחוזר ומתעבה והוא מלשון סדנא בסדניה יתיב (פסחים דף כח.): שני טפחים · שכבר גזעו מחליף: מן הפקק · קשר התחתון: מיני ארזים · שנאמר אתן במדבר ארז שטה והדס וגו' · ובגליר להו תלת וברא"ש השנה (דף כג.) מפרש הוסיפו עליהם אלונים אלמונים אלמוגים: מעשה ברבי אליעזר בן הורקנוס · י"ג תעניות שהתענו והלכו עד שגמרו י"ג כדתנן (לעיל דף יב:) עברו אלו ולא נענו כו': התחילו הצבור לצאת · מבית הכנסת: קברים תקנתם · בתמיה אין לכם אלא לכו קברו עצמכם מפני הרעב: געו · צעקו כמו אם יגעה שור על בלילו (איוב ו) הגוד וגעו (שמואל א ו): ויהיו הצבור פוסקין מתעניתם · דתנן (שם) עברו אלו ולא נענו ב"ד גוזרין עוד כו' אבל נענו שוב אין צריכין להתענות והני מילי לצבור אבל יחיד שהיה מתענה על החולה ונתרפא או על צרה ועברה הרי מתענה ומשלים כדאמרן לעיל (דף י:) כך שמעתי: כמלא ברך המחרישה · אם טשטשו הגשמים בעומק הקרקע כשיעור שורת מענית המחרישה: ברך · הוא הכלי שחורשין בו ומבריכין אותו סמוך לקרקע כשחורשין בו כלומר (א) מילא התלם שירדו המים בתלם מחרישתו שקורין קולטר"א: בחרבה · קרקע יבישה טפח כיון דחריבה היא ונכנסו בה הגשמים טפח ודאי רוב גשמים ירדו: בעבודה · חרושה כגון שדה ניר הנכנסים בה גשמים הרבה ג' טפחים דאפי' בגשמים מועטין נכנסין בה במפח או בטפחיים: אין לך כל טפח · כשנכנסו הגשמים בעומק הקרקע טפח תהום עולה ומתגבר ג' טפחים ואע"ג דמוכחא דארעא אלפא גרמידי בפרק החליל (סוכה דף נג:) אפ"ה רטיבותא מהגייא: [illegible] טפחים: הא דקתני טפחיים ותו לא בעבודה · דאע"ג דנכנסו טפח בקרקע פורתא הוא דנחית והכי לא נפיק בהו לקבליה שלשה טפחים אלא פורתא טפחיים: בשאינה עבודה · דלי נכנסו בה מפח מפי הוא דנחית ונפיק תהום לקבליה ג' טפחים: אבע · לשון נחל נובע: קול שני ריעים · ניסוך המים וניסוך היין: תהום אל תהום קורא · מים עליונים ומים תחתונים: לצנוריך · אותן שני ספלים: האי רידיא · מלאך הממונה על הגשמים כך שמו: דמי לעיגלא · ול"נ תלתא: בין תהומא עילאה לתתאה · בין הרקיע לאוקיינוס היכא דנשקי ארעא ורקיעא: תהומא עלאה · מים העליונים: חשור מימיך · ברקיע: אבע מימיך · למטה בקרקע: הנצנים נראו בארץ · כלומר כשמנסכין מים בחג שהאיסורין נראו בארץ שאין באין אלא משנה לחבירתה כנן זה שאינו יוצא אלא משנה לשנה ועת הזמיר הגיע זמירות החג אז קול התור מלאך דומה לשור תרגום · שור תור שבשעה שמנסכין מים בחג הוא אומר כן לשון אחר כמשמעו הנצנים נראו והזמיר הגיע בשעה שקול התור נשמע: *קודם הנץ החמה לא ישלימו · דאכתי לא חל עלייהו תענית כי נחתי גשמים: קודם חצות · דחצות זמן אכילה היא מחצות ואילך חל התענית כיון שלא סעדו בשעת סעודה: ועשו יו"ט · מתוך שמחה: הלל הגדול · הודו לאלהי האלהים כי לעולם חסדו ומפני שנאמר בו נותן לחם לכל בשר כדאמרינן בשילהי פסחים (דף קיח.): שכן מצינו כו' · כלומר שאין לך אדם בעולם שאין תענית חל עליו מט' שעות ואילך אפי' בני מלכים שדרכן לאכול בט' שעות שעד ג' שעות הן ישנים במטותיהן ושוהין ששה שעות ואוכלין וכדאמרינן בפסחים (דף קז:) אפי' אגריפס המלך שרגיל לאכול בט' שעות ביום לא יאכל עד שתחשך שנאמר הראית כי נכנע אחאב מפני ואחאב לא חלה תעניתו עליו אלא מט' שעות ואילך ועד ט' שעות היה יכול לאכול שלא גמר בדעתו להתענות אלא שבא אליהו אותו היום שנכנס בכרם נבות היזרעאלי ואמר ליה הרצחת וגם ירשת וגו' (מלכים א כא) ילקו הכלבים וגו' (שם) וכתיב ויהי [illegible] שמואל הקטן גזר תעניתא וירדו גשמים קודם הנץ החמה: שבח לצבור הוא · שעדיין לא קראו ונענו: למה הדבר דומה וכו': אלא

רבינו חננאל

שרשיה דברים הללו אישלע ונעשה פיסח · והיינו דאמרינן בכל מקום לעולם לא ישיח אדם דברים כלפי למעלה שהרי אדם גדול הפיח דברים כלפי למעלה ואישלע ומנו לוי. זה שרשו [צדיק כתמר יפרח] כארז בלבנון ישגה · תמר עושה פירות ואין גזעו מחליף ארז גזעו מחליף ואין עושה פירות לפיכך [illegible] לעשות פירות וכארז להחליף גזעו ואקשינן וכי ארז גזעו מחליף והתני' הלוקח (לולב) אילן מחבירו לקוץ מגביהו מן הקרקע טפח בדקלין ובארזין חופר ומשרש לפי שאין גזעם מחליף ושנינן האי ארז שנמשלו בו הצדיקים כגון שטה והדס ועץ שמן וכדרבא דאמר עשרה מיני ארזים הן והללו כולן גזעם מחליף זולתי הארז לבדו. והא דר' אליעזר דירד לפני התיבה ואמר כ"ד ברכות ולא ירדו גשמים וירד אחריו ר' עקיבא ואמר אבינו מלכנו אבינו אתה ואין לנו מלך אלא אתה אבינו מלכנו רחם עלינו ומיד ירדו גשמים הוו מרננו (כ"ע) רבנן יצתה ב"ק ואמרה לא מפני שרבי עקיבא גדול מר' אליעזר אלא ר' עקיבא מעביר על מדותיו ור' אליעזר שומר על מדותיו ואינו מעביר: ת"ר עד היכן גשמים יורדין וצבור פוסקין מתעניתן כמלוא ברך המחרישה · פי' כשיעור חפירת האת בחרישה אם ירדו הגשמים כשיעור הזה ר' יהודה אומר [illegible] טפח בבינונית טפחים בעבודה שלשה טפחים וקיי"ל כר' יהודה: תניא אין לך טפח שיורד מלמעלה שאין תהום עולה לקראתו טפחיים ואם שדה עבודה שלשה טפחים · א"ר אליעזר בשעה שמנסכין מים בחג תהום אומר לחבירו אבע סימך קול ב' רעים אני שומע פי' קול ב' צנורים ניסוך המים וניסוך היין הנסככין מנקבי הספלים של המזבח כדכתיב תהום אל תהום קורא לקול צנוריך · אמר רבה בר בר חנה לדידי חזי לי הא רידיא דמיא לעגלא תלתא פי' בת ג' שנים וקיימי בין תהומא עלאה לתהומא תתאה כדכתיב הנצנים נראו בארץ עת הזמיר הגיע וקול התור נשמע בארצנו פי' קול עגלא הוא קול התור הכתוב בפסוק כי העגל הוא השור: כתני' היו מתענין וירדו גשמים כו' ותנן דסתיא (דשמעתין) דירושלמי הכי סלקן קודם חצות לא ישלימו (והא תנן) (והא אמרינן) נמי בגמרא ר' אמי ור' יהודה נשיאה בתר דאהדריה ר' אמי דאמר אחר חצות שנינו ולכ"ע אין אומרים הלל הגדול אלא על נפש שבעה ואי איכא אתרא דחזישי משום שכרות נוטרין הלל הגדול ואח"כ אוכלין · הלל הגדול *) דכתיב ביה מעלה נשיאים מקצה הארץ ברקים למטר עשה דאמר ר' יוחנן הלל הגדול משעומדין בבית ה' עד סוף הלל הגדול · ואסיקנא שאין שבח לצבור אם ירדו גשמים קודם הנץ החמה אלא אם אמרו משיב הרוח אתא זיקא מוריד הגשם ואתא מטרא וזו שבח צבור והכל פשוטה היא: ירושלמי ר' ארא ור' אבהו בשם ר' יוסי בר' אבין מתניתין היא קודם חצות לא ישלימו עד כדון צפרא הוא לאחר חצות ישלימו עד שש שעות בשבת · א"ר יוסי ב"ר הגינא אסור להתענות [illegible] בקדושה · רב"ו כד הוה בעי דייתות מיטרא הוה אמר לספריה אזל קום קמיה היכלא ואמרו בנין דר' בעי מטרא ולית בחיילי' מטעמ ומיד מיטרא נחית · רב אדא בר אהבה כד הוה שליף מסאניה הוה מיטרא נחית וכד הוה שליף תרווייהו הוה עלמא טייף מטולת בתים הוה תמן והוה רב סייתי חד מן תלמידוי בביתא עד דהוו סמנין ביתא וכיון דהוה נפיק מביתא מיד הוה נפיל ואית דאמרי (א') רב אדא בר אהבה הוה · שאלו לו חכמים מה מעשים טובים יש בידך שלח להם מימי לא קדמני אדם בבית הכנסת ולא הנחתי אדם בבית הכנסת ויצאתי ולא הלכתי ד' אמות בלא תורה ובלא תפלין ולא הזכרתי דברי תורה במקום מטונף ולא הצעתי וישנתי שינת קבע אלא שינת עראי · ולא כיניתי שם לחבירי · ולא צעדתי בין החברים ולא שמחתי בתקלת חבירי · ולא עלה קללת חבירי על מטתי · ולא עברתי בשוק אצל מי שהוא חייב לי · ולא הקפדתי בתוך ביתי לקיים מה שנאמר אתהלך בתם לבבי בקרב ביתי : **) קבלה ביד חכמים כי ביום שנהרג נבות בו ביום הגיע השמועה לאיזבל ובו ביום ירד אחאב אל כרמו לרשתו ובו ביום אמר לו אליהו הרצחת וגם ירשת ומיד נכנע שנאמר ויהי כשמוע אחאב את הדברים האלה ויקרע את בגדיו וישם שק על בשרו ויצום וישכב בשק ויהלך אט · וגמירי דההוא שעתא שעה תשיעית הואי ודם שלש שעות האחרונות מן היום ונחשב צום דכתיב הראית כי נכנע אחאב אבל ראיה ברורה שנתענה אחאב מתשע שעות ולמעלה ליכא :

הדרן עלך סדר תעניות האלו האמור

*) נראה דחסר וצ"ל הלל הגדול צריך להתחיל ממזמור הללו את שם ה' שעומדים בבית ה' וגו' דכתיב ביה מעלה נשיאים וכו' . **) קאי אמ"ש בגמרא שכן מצינו באחאב כו' .

עין משפט נר מצוה

נ"ל אין

לב א מיי' פכ"א מהל' מכירה הלכה טו סמג עשין מב טוש"ע ח"מ סימן ריו סעיף יד:

לג ב מיי' פ"ד מהלכות תענית הלכה יט טוש"ע א"ח סימן תקעה סעיף יא:

מסורת הש"ס

ב"ב פ:

ר"ה כג. סוכה נג. כ"ב פ: [חד"א הוסח עד ד"ה שכן מצינו שייך לפי' המשנה לעיל יט.]

[לעיל יט.]

גי' רי"ף ורא"ש ר' יהודה אומר [תוספתא פ"ב]

מלכים א כא

[לעיל כה. ב"מ פה:]

הגהות הב"ח

(א) רש"י ד"ה כרך כו' כלומר מלוא התלם [illegible]

[ס"א ופריסא]

רבינו גרשום

ארז עצמו אין גזעו מחליף שאר מיני ארזים גזען מחליף: כמלא ברך המחרישה · גומות של מחרישה: כאן בעבודה שהיא מפוררת דרכה ונכנסת בה מים טפח טהרה (אין שוה) מלמטה טפחים ובשאינה עבודה שהיא קשה עד שנכנס טפח מלמעלה שלה ג' טפחים מלמטה: שני ריעים · ניסוך המים וניסוך היין קול צינוריך היינו שני ניסוכין: שנענה מט' שעות ולמעלה שהיה תיל לאכול בט' שכן דרך ארם לאכול בשש והולך שיגן עד שלש שעות אוכל [בט'] ולפי שלא אכל בט' אלא בעשר חשיב תענית: קודם חצות שנינו דאין משלימין ואין צריך לו להשלים: דשכיחא בית שכרות ולא מדי סכוני לאחר אכילה:

הדרן עלך סדר תעניות

אלא על נפש שבעה וכרם מלאה איני והא רב פפא איקלע לבי כנישתא דאבי גובר וגזור תענית וירדו להם גשמים עד הצות ואמר הלל ואחר כך אכלו ושתו שאני בני מחוזא דשכיחי בהו שכרות:

הדרן עלך סדר תעניות אלו

בשלשה *פרקים בשנה כהנים נושאין את כפיהן ארבע פעמים ביום בשחרית במוסף במנחה ובנעילת שערים בתעניות ובמעמדות וביום הכפורים אלו הן מעמדות לפי שנאמר °צו את בני ישראל את קרבני לחמי [במדבר כח] ׳וכי היאך *קרבנו של אדם קרב והוא אינו עומד על גביו התקינו נביאים הראשונים עשרים וארבעה משמרות על כל משמר ומשמר היה מעמד בירושלים של כהנים של לוים ושל ישראלים ׳הגיע זמן המשמר לעלות כהנים ולוים עולים לירושלים וישראל שבאותו משמר מתכנסין לעריהן וקוראין במעשה בראשית (׳ואנשי המעמד היו מתענין ארבעה ימים בשבוע מיום ב׳ ועד יום חמישי ולא היו מתענין ערב שבת מפני כבוד השבת ולא באחד בשבת כדי שלא יצאו ממנוחה ועונג ליגיעה ותענית וימותו) *׳ביום הראשון בראשית ויהי רקיע בשני יהי רקיע ויקוו המים בשלישי יקוו המים ויהי מאורות ברביעי יהי מאורות וישרצו המים בחמישי ישרצו המים ותוצא הארץ בששי ותוצא הארץ ויכלו השמים ׳פרשה גדולה קורין אותה בשנים והקטנה ביחיד בשחרית במוסף ובמנחה נכנסין וקורין על פיהן כקורין את שמע ערב שבת במנחה לא היו נכנסין מפני כבוד השבת ׳כל יום שיש בו הלל אין (א) מעמד בשחרית קרבן מוסף אין בנעילה קרבן עצים אין במנחה דברי ר׳ עקיבא אמר לו בן עזאי ׳כך היה רבי יהושע שונה קרבן מוסף אין במנחה קרבן עצים אין בנעילה חזר רבי עקיבא להיות שונה כבן עזאי זמן עצי כהנים והעם תשעה באחד בניסן בני ארח בן יהודה בעשרים בתמוז בני דוד בן יהודה בחמשה באב בני פרעוש בן יהודה בשבעה בו בני יונדב בן רכב בעשרה בו בני סנאה בן בנימן בחמשה עשר בו בני (ב) זתוא בן יהודה ועמהם כהנים ולוים וכל מי שטעה בשבטו ובני גונבי עלי ובני קוצעי קציעות בעשרים בו בני פחת מואב בן יהודה בעשרים באלול בני עדין בן יהודה באחד בטבת שבו בני פרעוש שניה באחד בטבת לא היה בו מעמד שהיה בו הלל וקרבן מוסף וקרבן עצים °חמשה דברים אירעו את אבותינו בשבעה עשר בתמוז וחמשה בתשעה באב *בשבעה עשר בתמוז

נשתברו

רש״י

אלא בנפש שבעה · מתוך שכתוב בו נותן לחם לכל בשר (תהלים קלו) נאה להאמר על השבע: דאבי גובר · שם אדם או מקום: דשכיח בהו · יין ושכרות ופשעי ולא יאמרו הלל:

הדרן עלך סדר תעניות אלו

תורה אור

בשלשה פרקים במוסף · מפרש בגמרא: נעילת שערים · מפורש בברכות ירושלמי בפרק תפלת השחר אימתי נעילה יש אומרים נעילת שערי מקדש וי״א נעילת שערי שמים שנועלים אותן לעת ערב בגמר תפלה ונוהגין היו להתפלל תפלת נעילה בכל תעניתם כדרך שמתפללין ביוהכ״פ: אלו הן מעמדות · המתענין מתפללין בעריהם שיתקבל ברצון קרבן אחיהם כדלקמן: לפי שנאמר צו את בני ישראל וגו׳ · שהתמיד בא מן השקלים של כל ישראל ואי אפשר שיהו כל ישראל עומדין על גבי קרבנם ומינו מעמדות להיות במקומם: נביאים הראשונים · שמואל ודוד בגמרא מפרש: על כל משמר · ארבעה ועשרים משמרות של כהנים היו ושמואל ודוד תיקנום ועל כל משמר היה מעמד בירושלים שקבועין ועומדין בעיר ועומדין על קרבן אחיהם ולבד אלו הדרים בירושלים היו מעמדות בכל עיר שישראל נחלקו לכ״ד מעמדות כנגד ארבעה ועשרים משמרות כדתניא בברייתא של מ״ט מדות והיינו דתנן היה מעמד בירושלים כהנים לוים וישראלים: כהנים ולוים · של משמר היו עולים (א) בירושלים כהנים לעבודה ולוים לשיר ומכל המעמדות היו קבועין בירושלים לעמוד על קרבן אחיהם: והשאר היו מתכנסין לעריהם · ומתפללין על קרבן אחיהם שיתקבל ברצון ומתענין ומוציאין ספר תורה ביום תעניתם: וקורין במעשה בראשית · ובגמרא מפרש טעמא: ביום הראשון · של שבוע: קורין בראשית כו׳ · פרשה ראשונה ופרשה יהי רקיע לפי שאין בפרשת בראשית לבדה ט׳ פסוקים כדי קריאת כהן לוי ישראל וכן כולן: בששי ותוצא הארץ עד ויכלו · לפי שבפרשת תוצא הארץ אין בה אלא שמונה פסוקים לפיכך אומר ויכלו: פרשה גדולה · שבפרשיות הללו קורין אותה בשנים כגון פרשה ראשונה של בראשית יש בה חמשה פסוקים היו קורין אותה בשנים כדאמרינן בגמרא יהי רקיע באחד וביום השני יהי רקיע באחד יקוו בשנים שיש בה ה׳ פסוקים ביום השלישי יקוו באחד שאין בה אלא ה׳ פסוקים ויהי מאורות בשנים שיש בה ו׳ פסוקים: וקורין אותה על פיהן · כל אחד בפני עצמו ובעי בגמרא מאי קאמר מעיקרא קתני פרשה קטנה כו׳ דמשמע דבספר תורה קורין והדר תנא על פיהם · פרשה בנעילה ליכא: כל יום שיש בו הלל אין בו מעמד (ד) שחרית · אותן שהיו בירושלים לא היו מתפללין על קרבן אחיהם שיש בו הלל לפי שאין להן פנאי לעשות מעמדם שקורין את הלל ומפני ההלל היו דוחין את המעמד: קרבן מוסף · יום שיש בו קרבן מוסף בירושלים אין (ה) מעמד בנעילה בירושלים וכל שכן במנחה הסמוכה למוסף לפי שהיו טרודין במוסף שיש בו להקריב בהמות יותר מתמיד שהוא אחד אין לך מוסף בלא שתי בהמות ולא היה להם פנאי כלל שהכהנים של מעמד טרודים במוסף וישראל שבכן היו טרודים לחטוב עצים ולשאוב מים ודוחה אפי׳ מעמד דנעילה: קרבן עצים · בגמרא מפרש כגון אחד מט׳ זמנים ואותו יום שהיה בו קרבן עצים אפילו לא היה בו מוסף היה נדחה מעמד של מנחה מפני קרבן עצים מפני שקרבן עצים קודם למנחה ודוחה מעמד הסמוך לו [ולא] של נעילה: כך היה רבי יהושע דורש קרבן מוסף אין (ו) במנחה · וטעמא מפרש בגמרא: זמן עצי כהנים והעם · שמתנדבים עצים: תשעה · באלו הט׳ זמנים היו הכהנים והעם מתנדבים להביא עצים והיו מקריבים קרבן אותו היום ואפילו היו עצים הרבה למערכה היו אלו מתנדבין ומקריבין באלו תשעה זמנים: בני ארח בן יהודה · שכשעלו בני הגולה הם התנדבו תחילה באחד בניסן (ז) וספק להם עצים עד כ׳ בתמוז שהתנדבו בני דוד ארח שמואל ומשבט יהודה היה: בני דוד · ממשפחת דוד המלך: סנאה בן בנימין זתוא בן יהודה בני גונבי עלי ובני קוצעי קציעות משפחה אחת הן ובגמ׳ מפרש אמאי מיקרו הכי: בני עדין באחד בטבת שבו בני פרעוש שניה · ובגמרא מפרש אמאי קבעו להן אלו הזמנים: באחד בטבת · שהיה ר״ח [וחנוכה] לא היה בו מעמד כו׳:

נשתברו

תוספות

שאני בני מחוזא דשכיחי בהו שכרות · ולהכי היו אומרים הלל הגדול קודם שיאכלו וישתו ובפסוקי דזמרה נוהגין לומר שחרית ודווקא בפסוקי דזמרה קודם התפלה אבל בשעת תפלה אין אומרים אותו אלא בנפש שבעה וככרם מלאה:

הדרן עלך סדר תעניות אלו

בכל יום שיש בו הלל אין בו מעמד שחרית · פי׳ דהי״ט חנוכה דבשאר יום טוב לא משכחת לה בלא קרבן מוסף:

קרבן מוסף אין בו נעילה · פירוש יום שקרבין בו מוסף אין בו נעילה לפי שטרודין הם במוסף ואין להם פנאי לומר נעילה:

קרבן עצים אין בו מנחה · משום דעד המנחה היו טרודים בקרבן העצים אבל יש בו נעילה דכל כך לא היו מאחרים עד שעת נעילה דאמר בן עזאי כך היה וכו׳:

מנחה

מסורת הש״ס

יומא סו:

[סוטה ח. פ״ש פרש״י]

ירושלמי ג״ג

מגילה כב.

[יומא ד:]

עין משפט נר מצוה

לד א מיי׳ פ״א מהל׳ תענית הלכה טז [וטוש״ע א״ח סימן תקעה סעיף יא]:

א ב מיי׳ פ״ו מהלכות כלי מקדש הלכה א סמג עשין קעב:

ב ג מיי׳ שם הלכה ב:

ג ד מיי׳ שם הלכה ג

ד ה מיי׳ שם הלכה ו:

ה ו מיי׳ שם הלכה ז:

ו ז ח מיי׳ שם הלכה ח:

ז ט מיי׳ פ״ה מהלכות תענית הלכה ב סמג עשין מד״ס ג טור א״ח סימן תקמט:

רבינו חננאל

בשלשה פעמים בשנה הכהנים נושאין את כפיהם כו׳:

רבינו גרשום

בשלשה פרקים כו׳ בתעניות ובמעמדות ודאי מעמדות הן בכל יום אלא לכך חשיב פרק בפני עצמו דלא כל ישראל הן אלא של אותו משמר ובתעניות יש כל ישראל ויש מהן ד׳ פרקים ביום:

הגהות הב״ח

(א) מתני׳ כל יום שיש בו הלל אין בו מעמד בשחרית כו׳ אין בו בנעילה כו׳ אין בו במנחה כו׳ כצ״ל וכן בסמוך: (ב) שם בט״ז בו בני זתוא · נ״ב כ״א זתא: (ג) רש״י ד״ה כהנים כו׳ היו עולים לירושלים כהנים כו׳ על קרבן אחיהם והשאר היו כו׳ כצ״ל וסר״א: (ד) ד״ה כל יום כו׳ אין בו מעמד בשחרית אותן וכו׳ אחיהם ביום שיש בו הלל: (ה) ד״ה קרבן כו׳ אין בו מעמד בנעילה כו׳ שהוא אחד דאין לך מוסף: (ו) ד״ה כך היה כו׳ אין בו במנחה: (ז) ד״ה בני ארח כו׳ באחד בניסן וספקו להם עצים כו׳ בני דוד ארח כך שמו ומשבט יהודה היה כצ״ל ותיבת שמואל נמחק:

עין משפט נר מצוה

ח א מיי' פ"א מהלכות תענית הלכה ו סמג עשין מ"ה ג טוש"ע א"ח סי' תקנב סעיף א:

ט ב מיי' שם וסמג שם טוש"ע א"ח שם סעיף ג:

י ג מיי' שם הלכה ז סמג שם טוש"ע א"ח סימן תקנב סעיף א:

יא ד ה מיי' פי"ד מהל' תפלה הלכה א ג סמג עשין כ טוש"ע א"ח סימן קכט סעיף א:

יב ו מיי' שם פט"ו הלכה ד סמג שם טוש"ע א"ח סימן קכח סעיף לח:

מנחה ונעילה דכל יומא שכיחי בהו שכרות גזרו רבנן · אפילו ביומא דתענית דלית בהו שכרות וקשיא דהכא משמע דבמנחה שייכא שכרות ובפ"ק דשבת (דף י. ושם) קאמר בהדיא דבמנחה לא שייכא שכרות וי"ל דהא דקאמר התם דבמנחה לא שייכא שכרות ר"ל לגבי ערבית שכרות דמנחה לאו כלום (לגבי שבת) דיותר שכיח שכרות בערבית (יותר) מבמנחה אבל לעולם במנחה שייך שכרות לגבי שחרית ומוסף:

ומאן דאמר נהגו אורויי נמי לא מורינן · פירשנו בפ"ק דראש השנה (דף טו: ד"ה וכי):

והאידנא נהוג עלמא דפרסי כהני ידייהו במנחה (ז) כמוך לשקיעת החמה · ולכך לא נהגו העם לומר נשיאת כפים במנחה ביום הכפורים לפי שמתפללין מנחה בעוד היום גדול אבל במנחה בשאר תעניות יש נשיאת כפים אבל מכל מקום בנעילה ביום הכפורים יש נשיאת כפים:

תורה אור

נשתברו הלוחות (א) ובטל התמיד והובקעה העיר ושרף אפוסטמוס את התורה(ב) והעמיד צלם בהיכל בתשעה באב נגזר על אבותינו שלא יכנסו לארץ *וחרב הבית בראשונה ובשניה ונלכדה ביתר ונחרשה העיר *משנכנס אב ממעטין בשמחה *שבת שחל תשעה באב להיות בתוכה אסור מלספר ומלכבס ובחמישי מותרין מפני כבוד השבת *ערב תשעה באב לא יאכל אדם שני תבשילין לא יאכל בשר ולא ישתה יין רבן שמעון בן גמליאל אומר ישנה רבי יהודה מחייב בכפיית המטה ולא הודו לו חכמים *אמר רבן שמעון בן גמליאל לא היו ימים טובים לישראל כחמשה עשר באב וכיוה"כ שבהן בנות ירושלים יוצאות בכלי לבן שאולין *שלא לבייש את מי שאין לו (ג) כל הכלים טעונין טבילה ובנות ירושלים יוצאות וחולות בכרמים ומה היו אומרות בחור שא נא עיניך וראה מה אתה בורר לך אל תתן עיניך בנוי תן עיניך במשפחה °שקר החן והבל היופי אשה יראת ה' היא תתהלל ואומר °תנו לה מפרי ידיה ויהללוה בשערים מעשיה וכן הוא אומר °צאינה וראינה בנות ציון במלך שלמה בעטרה שעטרה לו אמו ביום חתונתו וביום שמחת לבו ביום חתונתו זה מתן תורה וביום שמחת לבו זה בנין בית המקדש שיבנה במהרה בימינו: **גמ'** בשלשה פרקים בשנה כהנים נושאין את כפיהם כו': תעניות ומעמדות מי איכא מוסף חסורי מיחסרא והכי קתני בשלשה פרקים כהנים נושאין את כפיהן כל זמן שמתפללין ויש מהן ארבעה פעמים ביום שחרית ומוסף מנחה ונעילת שערים ואלו הן שלשה פרקים תעניות ומעמדות ויום הכפורים א"ר נחמן אמר רבה בר אבוה זו דברי רבי מאיר אבל חכמים אומרים שחרית ומוסף יש בהן נשיאת כפים מנחה ונעילה אין בהן נשיאת כפים *מאן חכמים ר' יהודה היא דתניא שחרית ומוסף מנחה ונעילה כולן יש בהן נשיאת כפים דברי ר"מ ר"י אומר שחרית ומוסף יש בהן נשיאת כפים מנחה ונעילה אין בהן נשיאת כפים רבי יוסי אומר נעילה יש בה נשיאת כפים מנחה אין בה נשיאת כפים במאי קמיפלגי רבי מאיר סבר כל יומא טעמא מאי לא פרשי כהני ידייהו במנחתא משום שכרות האידנא ליכא שכרות רבי יהודה סבר שחרית ומוסף דכל יומא לא שכיח שכרות לא גזרו בהו רבנן מנחה ונעילה דכל יומא שכיחא שכרות גזרו בהו רבנן רבי יוסי סבר מנחה דאיתה בכל יומא גזרו בה רבנן נעילה דליתה בכל יומא לא גזרו בה רבנן אמר רב יהודה אמר רב הלכה כרבי מאיר ור' יוחנן אמר נהגו העם כרבי מאיר ורבא אמר מנהג כרבי מאיר מאן דאמר הלכה כרבי מאיר דרשינן לה בפירקא מאן דאמר מנהג מידרש לא דרשינן אורויי מורינן ומאן דאמר נהגו אורויי לא מורינן ואי עביד עביד ולא מהדרינן ליה ורב נחמן אמר הלכה כרבי יוסי °והלכה כרבי יוסי (ד) והאידנא מ"ט פרשי כהני ידייהו במנחתא דתעניתא °כיון דבסמוך לשקיעת החמה קא פרשי כתפלת נעילה דמיא דכולי עלמא מידת °שכור אסור בנשיאת כפים מנהני מילי אמר רבי יהושע בן לוי משום בר קפרא למה נסמכה פרשת כהן מברך לפרשת נזיר לומר מה נזיר אסור ביין אף כהן מברך אסור ביין מתקיף לה אבוה דרבי זירא ואמרי לה אושעיא בר זבדא אי מה נזיר אסור בחרצן אף כהן מברך אסור בחרצן א"ר יצחק אמר קרא לשרתו ולברך בשמו מה משרת מותר בחרצן אף כהן מברך מותר בחרצן

אי

נשתברו הלוחות · בגמ' מפרש: ובטל התמיד · לפי שגזרה המלכות גזרה מלהקריב עוד: והועמד צלם בהיכל · שהעמידו מנשה כדמפורש בתרגום ירושלמי בפרשת השמים כסאי וגו' (ישעיה סו): על אבותינו · דור המדבר אם יראה איש באנשים האלה הדור הרע הזה את הארץ וגו' (דברים א): ביתר · עיר גדולה והיו ישראל דרין בה במסכת גיטין פרק הניזקין (דף נז.) אשקא דריספק חרב ביתר: שבת שחל תשעה באב כו' · שבוע: בחמישי מותרין · אם חל תשעה באב בערב שבת מותרין לכבס בחמישי וכשחל ט' באב בד' בשבת לא איצטריך למיתני דמותרין כדאמרינן בגמרא לא שנו אלא לפניו כו': שני תבשילין · *בשר ודגים או בשר וביצים שעליו או דג וביצה שעליו כדאמר בפרק ערבי פסחים (דף קיד:): ישנה · בגמרא מפרש: כפיית המטה · על פניה ולא יישן עליה: שאולין · שכולן שואלות זו מזו אפילו עשירה כדי שלא לבייש כו': טעונין טבילה · קודם שילבשום לפי שאין כל אחת בקיאה בחברתה שמא נדה היתה: וחולות · כמו לחול במחולות (שופטים כא): במלך שלמה · במלך שהשלום שלו: אמו · כנסת ישראל: זה מתן תורה · יום הכפורים שניתנו בו לוחות האחרונות: **גמ'** כל זמן שמתפללין · דהיינו שחרית ומנחה ונעילה: (ה) יש מהן ארבעה פעמים ביום · יום הכפורים שיש בו מוסף: כל יומא מאי טעמא לא פרשי כהני ידייהו במנחה · דכל יומא שכיחא ביה שכרות שכבר סעד וזימנין דמשכא סעודתיה ומשתכר ופריש ידיה בהדי חמריה וכהן שתוי יין אסור לישא את כפיו שנאמר יין ושכר אל תשת בבואכם וגו' (ויקרא י) ונשיאת כפים מעין עבודה כדלקמן: האידנא · בתעניות ובמעמדות לא שכיחא שכרות ובמעמדות נמי מתענין כדלקמן (דף כז:): גזרינן · תענית אטו שאר ימים: נעילה דליתה בכל יומא · אלא ביום התענית: דדרשינן בפירקא · הלכה כרבי מאיר דבעינן דליקום כוותיה עלמא: אורויי אורינן · כרבי מאיר או אחו לקמן אבל בפירקא לא דרשינן דלא פשיטא ליה טובי האי דליהוי הלכה כר"מ ומ"ד נהגו משמע הן נהגו מאיליהן אבל אינו עיקר ומנהג משמע תורת מנהג יש בדבר ומנהג כשר הוא: ורב נחמן אמר הלכה כרבי יוסי והלכה כרבי יוסי · גמרא קא פסיק ומהדר סתמא ומוקי לה הלכה כרבי יוסי ואהכי קא פריך ואלא האידנא כו': כיון דסמוך לשקיעת החמה וכו' · שמאחרין (ו) עד שקיעת החמה ומתפללין כל שעה ואינן הולכין לבית הכנסת משש שעות ומחצה ולמעלה כמו שהיו עושין לאותן הימים: כתפלת נעילה דמיא · דהשתא ליכא למיגזר משום מנחה דכל יומא דמנחתא כי הא ליתא בכל יומא: שכור מיהא אסור בנשיאת כפים · דאפילו ר"מ לא קאמר אלא משום דהאידנא לאו שכרות הוא: פרשת כהן מברך · כה תברכו את בני ישראל אמור להם (במדבר ו): מה משרת כו' · עובד עבודה דלא מיתסר אלא שתויי יין ממש דכתיב יין ושכר אל תשת וגו' הא בחרצן מותר:

מאי

רבינו חננאל

ואקשינן וכי תעניות אית בהו מוסף ותרצינן לה הכי בג' פרקים כהנים נושאין את כפיהם כ"ז שמתפללין ויש מהן ד' פעמים ביום בשחרית במוסף ובמנחה ובנעילה · ואלו הן ג' פרקים תעניות ומעמדות ויוה"כ · ופתח מתני' ר' מאיר היא דלא משכחת לה דנושאין כפיהם כל זמן שמתפללין אלא לרבי מאיר דתני שחרית ומוסף מנחה ונעילה יש בהן נשיאת כפים דברי ר' מאיר וטעמא דר' מאיר מפורש הוא כיון דביום הכפורים ובמעמדות ליכא שכרות במנחה נושאין כפיהם ולא גזרינן · ור' יהודה תני שחרית ומוסף דלרך יש בהן נשיאות כפים דבכל יומא לית בהו שכרות לפיכך לא גזרינן בהו · שמעינן מינה דר' יהודה אין אדם רשאי ליבול אלא אחר תפלת מוסף אבל במנחת דבשאר יומי אית בהו שכרות גזרינן בהו ביוה"כ ובמעמדות [redacted] בה נשיאות כפים משום דאיתא כל יומא ואתי לאחלופי גזרינן אבל נעילה דליתא אלא ביוה"כ ובמעמדות יש בה נשיאות כפים דכיון דליתא כל יומא לא גזרינן · ואסיקנא דהלכתא כר' יוסי דאמר שחרית ומוסף ונעילה יש בהן נשיאות כפים מנחה אין בה נשיאות כפים · והאידנא דלא מצלו מנחה דתעניתא אלא סמוך לשקיעת החמה כדאוקימנא (לעיל יב:) דרביעית היום האחרון הוא דמתפללין בו תפלת תענית כדכתיב ובמנחת הערב קמתי מתעניתי וגו' כנעילה דמיא ויש בה נשיאות כפים· ואע"ג דאמר רב הלכתא כרבי מאיר ודרשינן לה בפירקא ורב הונא אמר מנהג כר"מ אוריי מורינן הכי בפרקא לא דרשי לה (ואף ר') [ור' יוחנן אמר] נהגו כר"מ לא דרשי ולא מורינן כוותיה ואי עביד לא מהדרינן ליה: ודייקי כו' אלמא שכור אסור בנשיאת כפים מנא לן ופשים דכתיב לשרתו ולברך בשמו אתקש (משרת ולו לעביד) [מברך למשרת] ולנזיר מה משרת אסור ביין שנאמר יין ושכר אל תשת אף מברך אסור ביין ושכר דקיימא לן כל המשכר [אסור] ומותר בחרצן אי הכי למאי אתקש לנזיר להכשיר

רבינו גרשום

במוסף דהיינו יוה"כ שיש בו מוסף: אמר רב נחמן זו דקתני נושאין כפיהן בשחרית במוסף במנחה בנעילה ר"מ היא·כל יומא טעמא מאי אין נושאין כפיהן*) האידנא בתענית ובמעמדות וביוה"כ (ובמעמדות) דאית בהו תענית נמי שכיחא שכרות להכי נושאין כפיהן בכל ד' תפלות שבהן: מנחה ונעילה דבשאר יומי שכיחא שכרות גזרו בהו רבנן בהני דלמא אתי למיעבר בשאר יומי נמי: אבל אורויי מורינן כרבי מאיר למאן דבעי כמאן הלכה: והשתא והלכה כרבי יוסי האידנא מאי טעמא פרסי כהני ידייהו ביום הכפורים במנחה כיון דבשקיעת החמה פרסי שהיו מאחרין לתפלת המנחה: שכור אסור בנשיאת כפים דקתני מאי טעמא לא דשכיחא ביה שכרות: **) מהו משרת מותר דכתיב יין ושכר אל תשת אבל אוכל הוא חרצן: אף כהן מברך לא יהא בעל מום והא קיימא לן דבעל מום מברך אלא אם כן יהו מומין שבגלוי · הא איתקש לנזיר מה נזיר בעל מום אף מברך בעל מום: מאי חזית דאקשית לקולא דאקשת ליה לנזיר דבעל מום מותר ואקשת ליה למשרת דבחרצן מותר אקיש לחומרא וניסא מה נזיר אסור בחרצן אף מברך אסור בחרצן ומה משרת בעל מום לא אף מברך בעל מום לא:

אסמכתא

*) אולי צ"ל במנחה משום שכרות האידנא וכו' דהא כמו תענית ליכא שכרות ולכוי וכו'. **) נ"ל מה משרת מותר בחרצן וכו' אף כהן מברך מותר בחרצן: אף כהן וכו'·

מסורת הש"ס

[ר"ס יח:] יבמות מג. [כוונת רש"י בשר מליח דהרי כדאיתא לקמן ל. בברייתא תנא אבל אוכל הוא בשר מליח כו'] [פסחים פב. וש"נ] [פירובין פ. הג"ה]

הגהות הב"ח

(א) במשנה ובוטל התמיד: (ב) והעמידו צלם בהיכל כ"ב רש"י והועמד: (ג) שם את מי שאין לו וכל הכלים טעונין: (ד) גמ' והלכה כר' יוסי ואלא האידנא מ"ט פרסי כו' כיון דסמוך לשקיעת החמה: (ה) רש"י ד"ה ויש מהן: (ו) ד"ה כיון דסמוך לשקיעת החמה כו' שמאחרים עד שקיעת החמה: (ז) תוס' ד"ה והאידנא כו' ידייהו במנחה כיון דסמוך לשקיעת החמה כו' בשאר תעניות יש לומר נשיאת כפים:

אי מה משרת בעל מום לא אף כהן מברך בעל מום לא °הא איתקש לנזיר ומאי חזית דמקשת לקולא אקיש לחומרא אסמכתא נינהו *מדרבנן ולקולא: אלו הן מעמדות לפי שנאמר צו את בני ישראל כו': מאי קאמר ה"ק אלו הן מעמדות ומה טעם תיקנו מעמדות לפי שנאמר °צו את בני ישראל ואמרת אליהם את קרבני לחמי לאשי והיאך קרבנו של אדם קרב והוא אינו עומד על גביו התקינו נביאים הראשונים עשרים וארבעה משמרות על כל משמר ומשמר היה מעמד בירושלים של כהני' ושל לוים ושל ישראלים הגיע זמן משמר לעלות כהנים ולוים עולין לירושלים ת"ר עשרים וארבעה משמרות [א] (א) בארץ ישראל ושתים עשרה ביריחו שתים עשרה ביריחו נפישן להו טובא אלא שתים עשרה מהן ביריחו הגיע זמן המשמר לעלות חצי המשמר היה עולה מארץ ישראל לירושלים וחצי המשמר היה עולה *מיריחו כדי שיספקו מים ומזון לאחיהם שבירושלים אמר רב יהודה אמר שמואל כהנים ולוים וישראלים מעכבין את הקרבן במתניתא תנא ר"ש בן אלעזר (ג) כהנים ולוים וכלי שיר מעכבין את הקרבן במאי קמיפלגי מר סבר *עיקר שירה בפה ומר סבר עיקר שירה בכלי אמר רב (א) חמא בר גוריא אמר רב משה תיקן להם לישראל שמונה משמרות ארבעה מאלעזר וד' מאיתמר בא שמואל והעמידן על שש עשרה בא דוד והעמידן על עשרים וארבעה שנאמר °בשנת הארבעים למלכות דוד נדרשו וימצא בהם גבורי החיל ביעזר גלעד מיתיבי משה תיקן להם לישראל שמונה משמרות ארבעה מאלעזר וארבעה מאיתמר בא דוד ושמואל והעמידן על עשרים וארבע שנאמר °המה יסד דוד ושמואל הרואה באמונתם הכי קאמר מיסודו של דוד ושמואל הרמתי העמידום על עשרים וארבע תניא אידך משה תיקן להם לישראל שש עשרה משמרות שמונה מאלעזר ושמונה מאיתמר וכשרבו בני אלעזר על בני איתמר חלקום והעמידום על עשרים וארבע שנאמר °וימצאו בני אלעזר רבים לראשי הגברים מן בני איתמר ויחלקום לבני אלעזר ראשים לבית אבות ששה עשר ולבני איתמר לבית אבותם שמונה ואומר °בית אב אחד אחוז לאלעזר ואחוז אחוז לאיתמר מאי ואומר וכי תימא כי היכי דנפישי בני אלעזר הכא נמי דנפישי בני איתמר שמנה מעיקרא ארבעה הוו ת"ש בית אב אחד אחוז לאלעזר ואחוז אחוז לאיתמר תיובתא דרב (ג) חמא בר גוריא אמר לך רב (ג) חמא בר גוריא תנאי היא ואנא דאמרי כי האי תנא דאמר שמונה ת"ר (ד) ארבעה משמרות עלו מן הגולה ואלו הן ידעיה [חרים] פשחור ואימר עמדו נביאים שביניהם וחלקום

(א) ס"א חסרא כ ג) ס"א חסרא ד) ערכין יב:

רש"י

מאי קאמר · דקא בעי מאי ניהו מעמדות ומייתי קרא את קרבני לחמי לאשי וגו': הכי קאמר אלו הן מעמדות · דלקמן וטעמא מאי תקון מעמדות לפי שנאמר צו את בני ישראל ואמרת אליהם את קרבני לחמי לאשי וגו': ה"ג תנו רבנן כ"ד משמרות היו בא"י וי"ב ביריחו: י"ב ביריחו בתמיה נפישי להו טובא אלא אימא וי"ב מהן ביריחו · ברישא משמע לבד הכ"ד שבעיירות א"י היו י"ב ביריחו דהוו להו ל"ו וי"ב מהן משמע שמאותן הכ"ד היו י"ב ביריחו · ה"ג הגיע זמן המשמר חצי המשמר עולה לירושלים וחצי המשמר עולה ליריחו כדי שיספקו מים ומזון לאחיהם שבירושלים כלומר כלל היו י"ב ביריחו כשהגיע זמן המשמר לעלות לירושלים בשבת מתחלקים אנשי המשמר חציין הולכין לירושלים לעבודה וחציין הולכין ליריחו הסמוכה לירושלים ומספקין שם מים ומזון לאחיהם וכך עושין כל הכ"ד משמרות נמצא י"ב ביריחו א) לשון אחר נהירא לי: מעכבין את הקרבן · אם אין מעמד עומד בירושלים כדתנן (לעיל דף טו·) על כל משמר היה מעמד בירושלים של כהנים לוים וישראלים כיון דכולהו בעלים בפיקן ליכא (ג) כמותו על גבי עבודה: וכלי שיר מעכבין את הקרבן · פלוגתא בשילהי מסכת סוכה (דף נ:) ובערכין (דף יא·) מפורשת: עיקר שירה בפה · וכלי לבסומי קלא בעלמא וכיון דאיכא לוים לא מעכב משום כלי שיר: עיקר שירה בכלי · אטב וכן בפרק החליל (שם): ארבעה מאלעזר · מבניו של אלעזר עשה מהן ד' משמרות וגמרא גמר לה: המה יסד דוד ושמואל הרואה באמונתם · ותיובתא דרב חמא דאמר שמואל העמידם על י"ו ודוד העמידן על כ"ד דהא שמעי' מינה דתרווייהו בהדי הדדי תקינהו: מיסודו של שמואל הרמתי · שהעמידן על י"ו בא דוד והעמידן על כ"ד איכא ספרים שכתוב בהן מיסודו של שמואל ודוד העמידום על כ"ד כלומר שניהם הועילו בדבר ושמואל העמידם על י"ו ודוד על כ"ד: וימצאו בני אלעזר רבים לראשי הגברים מבני איתמר ויחלקו בני אלעזר ראשים לבית אבותם ששה עשר ולבני איתמר ראשים לבית אבותם שמונה ואומר בית אב אחד אחוז לאלעזר ואחוז אחוז לאיתמר · וימצאו בני אלעזר רבים לראשי הגברים כלומר ראשי הגברים של בני אלעזר היו רבים מאיתמר והאי וימצאו משמע דקודם לכן היו קטנים ועכשיו הוסיפו עליהן ויחלקום לי"ו בית אב אחד אחוז שהיה מתחילה לאלעזר דהיינו ח' אחוז אחד בגורל דהיינו נמי ח' והוו להו י"ו: ואחוז אחוז לאיתמר · מה שהיה מתחילה אחוז לאיתמר אחוזים עתה כבתחילה שלא הרבו עליהם שום בית אב: מאי ואומר · וכי תימא מעיקרא הוו ד' לאלעזר וד' לאיתמר: וכי היכי דנפישי בני אלעזר הכי נמי נפישי בני איתמר · ומיהו בני אלעזר נפישי טפי דהא לאיתמר לא אוקמינהו אלא על ח' ודאלעזר על י"ו: תא שמע ואחוז אחוז לאיתמר · אלמא כדקיימי קיימי ושמע מינה דמשה תיקן להם י"ו ח' מזה וח' מזה וקשיא לרב חמא דאמר ד' וד' והא דכתב לעיל ובשנת הארבעים וגו' המה יסד במה שהוסיפו עליהן עד כ"ד משתעי [אבל] משה תיקן להם י"ו משמרות: תנאי היא · דהא הלכה תנא דלעיל דקתני משה תיקן להן ח' משמרות משניהן ואנא קאימנא כוותיה: עלו מן הגולה · בבית שני והשאר לא עלו שהרבה מישראל נשתיירו ולא רצו לעלות: פשחור ואימר · ומבעיא לי דפשחור (ד) לא כתיב גבי כ"ד משמרות (דה"א כד):

תוספות

אי מה משרת בעל מום לא אף מברך בעל מום לא · פי' כיון דילפינן ג"ש ממשרת נימא כמו משרת דמשרת בעל מום לא אף מברך וכו' ומשני הא איתקש לנזיר וכו' מכאן נראה דבעל מום מברך ברכת כהנים *מדקא חזינן דהש"ס רוצה ללמוד מברך ממשרת ולבעל מום ודחינן ליה אם כן נראה דלענין נשיאת כפים כהן בעל מום נושא כפיו ומכאן יש להוכיח דכהן שהמיר דהוו נושא כפיו וכשר לישא כפיו ולקרות בתורה כמו שלא המיר ורא"ה *מהא דכהנים ששימשו בבית חוניו לא ישמשו במקדש אבל נוטלים חלק עם אחיהם כמו בעלי מומין מדקאמר שהם כבעלי מומין משמע דכל עבודה שבעל מום ראוי לעשות יעשו וכהן בעל מום נושא כפיו* :

ומאי חזית דאקשת לקולא אקיש לחומרא · פי' מאי חזית דמקשת כהן לנזיר להקל ולומר כמו שנזיר הוי בעל מום כמו כן כהן בעל מום כשר ואקשת למשרת מה משרת מותר בחרצן אף כהן מברך מותר בחרצן אקשה לחומרא פירוש ונימא דכמו שנזיר אסור בחרצן אף כהן אסור בחרצן וכמו כהן משרת אסור בעל מום אף כהן מברך בעל מום אסור ומשני אסמכתא וכו':

מר סבר עיקר שירה בפה · ולכך הכל כשרים אפילו פסולים אפילו ממזרים לומר שירה דלא הוי אלא בפה ולמאן דאמר עיקר שירה בכלי אם כן צריך שיהו כהנים או לוים דהא הכלי זמר היה קדוש:

רב

עין משפט נר מצוה

יג א מיי' פט"ו מהל' תפלה הל' ב סמג עשין כ טוש"ע א"ח סימן קכח סעיף ג: [illegible]

יד ב מיי' פ"ג מהל' כלי המקדש הל' ג סמג עשין קע:

טו ג ד מיי' שם [illegible]

[מנחות דף קט: וע"ש בתוס' ד"ה לא]

[וע"ע תוס' סוטה לט: ד"ה כי מגדל ותוס' מנחות קט: ד"ה לא]

רבינו חננאל

להכשיר בו בעל מום להיות כשר לברכה · ואמרינן מה ראית להקשות לקולא אקשתו למשרת להיות מותר בחרצן · ואקשתו לנזיר להיות בעל מום כשר לברכה · אדרבה הקשהו לחומרא · הקשהו למשרת להיות כהן בעל מום פסול בנשיאות כפים והקשהו לנזיר להיות אסור בחרצן · ושנינן אסמכתא בעלמא היא . פי' דרשת סמוכין מדרבנן היא הלכך לקולא דרשינן · וכתיב נמי לעמוד לשרת *) מה משרת עומד אף נשיאות כפים מעומד: פיסקא אלו הן המעמדות · מה טעם תקינו מעמדות לפי שנאמר צו את בני ישראל: ירושלמי א"ר יונה תמידין קרבנן דכל ישראל אינון וא"ת יהיו כל ישראל כל השנה כולה בירושלים עומדים על קרבנן · לא חייבתם התורה אלא ג' רגלים בשנה · ואם יש לומר יהיו יושבין בטילין בעריהם הא כתיב ואספת דגנך הגם כוזהרין לאסוף דגנם ותירושם של כל השנה כולה · התקינו הנביאים הראשונים כ"ד משמרות ועל כל משמר ומשמר היה מעמד בירושלים של כהנים ושל לוים ושל ישראל: ת"ר כ"ד משמרות היו בא"י מהן י"ב ביריחו · הגיע זמן המשמר לעלות חצי המשמר עולה מא"י וחצי משמר מיריחו כדי שיספקו מים ומזון לאחיהם · כלומר חצי המשמר הנותר מספיקין צרכי העולים · ובפעם אחרת מתחלפים · מי שלא עלה יעלה עכשיו · מי שעלה כבר ישב עתה בביתו ויספק צרכי העולים: ירושלמי תני ר' שמעון בן אלעזר ישראל והכהנים והלוים וכלי שיר מעכבין את הקרבן שנאמר כל הקהל משתחוים אלו ישראל · והשיר משורר הלוים והצוצרות מתעכבים אלו הכהנים הכל עד לעלות העולה · הכל מעכבין את הקרבן · אמר רב חסרא אמר רב משה תקן לישראל שמונה משמרות · ד' מאלעזר וד' מאיתמר · בא שמואל והעמידן עד שש עשרה · בא דוד והעמידן עד כ"ד · שנאמר בשנת הארבעים למלכות דוד נדרשו · ואותבינן עליה מהא דתניא משה תיקן להם לישראל ט"ז משמרות · ח' מאלעזר וח' מאיתמר וכשרבו בני אלעזר על בני איתמר חלקום לכ"ד שנאמר וימצאו בני אלעזר רבים לראשי הגברים מבני איתמר ויחלקום לבני אלעזר ראשים לבית אבות ששה עשר · ולבני איתמר לבית אבותם שמונה · היו ח' לאלעזר וח' לאיתמר כנגן שהיו ח' אלפים מזה וח' אלפים [מזה] כל משמר אלף רבו בני אלעזר וכאשר דרשום נמצאו י"ו אלף ובני איתמר ח' אלפים כמו שהיו חלקו בני אלעזר לי"ו [illegible]

*) [illegible]

רבינו גרשום

[illegible]

גליון הש"ס

גמ' מדרבנן ולקולא · [illegible]

הגהות הגר"א

[א] גמ' ת"ר כ"ד משמרות · נ"ב של לוים:

הגהות מהר"ב רנשבורג

א) רש"י ד"ה כ"ג הגיע זמן וכו' לשון אחר נהירא לי · נ"ב ולא נהירא לי:

הגהות הב"ח

[illegible]

עין משפט נר מצוה

טז א מיי' פ"ב מהל' תפלה הלכה ג סמג עשין יט טוש"ע א"ח סימן קלז סעיף ב: יז ב מיי' פי"ג שם ה"ד סמג שם טוש"ע א"ח סי' תכג סעיף ב:

תוספות

רב אמר דולג · פי' הראשון קורא מראש הפרשה ג' פסוקים והשני שאין לו כי אם שני פסוקים מדלג פסוק אחד וקורא ממה שקרא הראשון וכן נמי בראשי חדשים מדלגין והקשה ה"ר יהודה בר נתן ואמאי מדלגין אמאי אינו קורא למעלה בפרשה דהא בשבת בחוש"מ קורא הוא מראה אתה אומר אלי (שמות לג) אע"פ שעיקר הפרשה אינה מתחלת כי אם מפסל לך (שם לד) וי"ל דמ"ה הוא קורא ראה בפרשה של מעלה לפי שכל אותה הפרשה משתעי בחד ענינא אבל פרשה דר"ח לעיל מינה לא משתעי כלל מחד ענינא ולכך אינו קורא בפרשה של מעלה אלא דולג ומזה ראיה למנהגנו אהא דלא קרינן בכל שבת ושבת פרשה של שבת כמו שאנו עושין בי"ט שאנו קורין פרשיות לפי המאורע לפי שאין בפרשה של שבת שלשה פסוקים דאין לומר שנדלג לעיל דלא הוי חד ענינא ·

גזרה משום הנכנסין והיוצאין · פי' שהנכנסין שלא ראו (ה) הראשונים שקרא ג' פסוקים ויראו השני שקורא פסוק אחד מלמעלה יאמרו שהראשון לא קרא אלא שני פסוקים והיוצאין כשהראשון קורא שלשה פסוקים ואינו משייר אלא שני פסוקים איכא גזירת יוצאין דסברי האי שני סגיא ליה בשני פסוקים :

גמרא

וחלקום והעמידום על עשרים וארבעה בללום ונתנום בקלפי בא ידעיה ונטל חלקו וחלק חבריו שש בא [חרים] ונטל חלקו וחלק חבריו שש וכן פשחור וכן אימר וכן התנו נביאים שביניהם שאפי' (*יהוידיב) ראש משמרת עולה לא ידחה ידעיה ממקומו אלא ידעיה עיקר (*ויהוידיב) טפל לו: וישראל שבאותו משמר מתכנסין בעריהן וקורין במעשה בראשית: מנהני מילי א"ר יעקב בר אחא *אמר רב אסי *אלמלא מעמדות לא נתקיימו שמים וארץ שנאמר °ויאמר ה' אלהים במה אדע כי אירשנה אמר אברהם רבש"ע שמא ישראל חוטאין לפניך אתה עושה להם כדור המבול וכדור הפלגה א"ל לאו אמר לפניו רבש"ע הודיעני במה אירשנה א"ל °קחה לי עגלה משולשת ועז משולשת וגו' אמר לפניו רבש"ע תינח בזמן שבית המקדש קיים בזמן שאין בית המקדש קיים מה תהא עליהם אמר לו כבר תקנתי להם סדר קרבנות בזמן שקוראין בהן לפני מעלה אני עליהם כאילו הקריבום לפני ואני מוחל להם על כל עונותיהם ת"ר *אנשי משמר היו מתפללין על קרבן אחיהם שיתקבל ברצון ואנשי מעמד מתכנסין לבית הכנסת ויושבין ד' תעניות בשני בשבת בשלישי ברביעי ובחמישי בשני על יורדי הים בשלישי על הולכי מדברות ברביעי על אסכרא שלא תיפול על התינוקות בחמישי על עוברות ומיניקות עוברות שלא יפילו מיניקות שיניקו את בניהם ובערב שבת לא היו מתענין מפני כבוד השבת ק"ו בשבת עצמה באחד בשבת מ"ט לא אמר ר' יוחנן מפני הנוצרים ר' שמואל בר נחמני אמר מפני שהוא שלישי ליצירה ריש לקיש אמר מפני נשמה יתירה דאמר ריש לקיש *נשמה יתירה ניתנה בו באדם בע"ש במוצאי שבת נוטלין אותה ממנו שנאמר °שבת וינפש כיון ששבת ווי אבדה נפש: ביום הראשון בראשית ויהי רקיע: *תנא בראשית בשנים יהי רקיע באחד בשלמא יהי רקיע באחד תלתא פסוקי הוו אלא בראשית בשנים *)(מ"ט) ה' פסוקי הויין (*ותנן) **הקורא בתורה אל יפחות מג' פסוקים רב אמר דולג ושמואל אמר פוסק ורב דאמר דולג מ"ט לא אמר פוסק קסבר כל פסוקא *דלא פסקיה משה אנן לא פסקינן ליה ושמואל אמר פוסק ומי פסקינן והאמר ר' חנינא קרא צער גדול היה לי אצל ר' חנינא הגדול ולא התיר לי לפסוק אלא לתינוקות של בית רבן הואיל ולהתלמד עשוין *ושמואל התם טעמא מאי משום דלא אפשר הכא נמי לא אפשר ושמואל אמר פוסק מ"ט לא אמר דולג גזירה משום הנכנסין וגזירה משום היוצאין מיתיבי *פרשה של ששה פסוקים קורין אותה בשנים ושל חמשה (א) [ביחיד ואם] הראשון קורא ג' השני קורא שנים מפרשה זו ואחד מפרשה אחרת וי"א ג' לפי שאין מתחילין בפרשה פחות משלשה פסוקין למ"ד דולג לידלוג ולמאן דאמר פוסק ליפסוק שאני התם דאית

*) [ליתא במגילה]

רש"י

והלקום · לכ"ד וכתבו כנוי של כל אחד ואחד בחלק : בללום ונתנום בקלפי · כתבו על כ"ד התיכות קלף ראשי משמרות שחלקו מאותן ד': בא ידעיה · מששה של ידעיה בא אחד מהן ונטל חלקו וחלק ה' חתיכות קלף דהוו להו שש ומי שהיה עולה בידו ראשון היה לשבת ראשונה שבסדר שהיו עולין בידו זו אחר זו כך היו עובדין בשבתותיהן זו אחר זו: וכן התנו · שאפי' יהויריב שהיה במקדש ראשון ראשון למשמרות עולה מן הגולה : לא ידחה ידעיה · הואיל ומתחלה לא עלה יהויריב אלא כל משמרות הנעשות מידעיה קודמות לעבודה ליהויריב ויהויריב בא ועובד אחריהן במקום משמר אחר וששה דידעיה עושין אותן ה' שלא להרבות במשמרות : א"ר אסי לפי שאלמלא מעמדות · עיסקי קרבנות שישראל עושין הן היו כלים בחטאן ומשכן כלין שמים וארץ העומדים בזכותן אין מתקיימין כו': כאנשי דור המבול · שמאחר שהן כלין אין העולם מתקיים והואיל שעל עיסקי קרבן העולם עומד לכך קורין אנשי מעמד בעריהן במעשה בראשית : כבר תקנתי להם כו' · כל זמן שקורין בהן כו' מהיכא יליף לה להאי גמגום : ת"ר אנשי משמר מתפללין על קרבן אחיהן · תמידים שבכל יום : אנשי משמר·(ג)אותן כ"ד שהיו בעריהן : בשני על יורדי הים · דכתיב בשני (בראשית א) יהי רקיע בתוך המים וצריך להזכיר וצרות על הדבר : בשלישי על הולכי מדברות · דכתיב ותראה היבשה תהי ראויה יבשה להולכיה שלא יוזקו מפני חיות רעות : ברביעי על האסכרא · שבו נתלו המאורות וכתיב ביה (שם) יהי מאורות מארת כתיב : ועל עוברות כו' · דכתיב ביה (שם) ישרצו המים שרץ נפש חיה : מפני הנוצרים · שעושים אותו יום טוב שלהם : שלישי ליצירה · דאדם נברא ביום ששי ובכל יום שלישי הוי חלוש כדכתיב (שם לד) ויהי ביום השלישי בהיותם כואבים : נשמה יתירה · שנוטלין אותה ממנו והוי חלש : נשמה יתירה · שמרחיבים דעתו לאכילה ושתיה ... ווי אבדה נפש · וינפש דורש בנוטריקון ווי נפש : בראשית בשנים · כהן ולוי קורין ביום תענית בראשית תלתא פסוקי הוי · וסגיא בהו לחד גברא : רב אמר דולג · הראשון קורא שלשה פסוקים והשני מתחיל בפסוק שסיים בו הראשון והשנים עמו הרי שלשה ומשום אין משיירין בפרשה פחות משלשה פסוקים ליכא משום דלא אפשר : פוסק · מפסיק הפסוק לשנים ראשון קורא שני פסוקים וחצי ולוי משלים חצי אותו הפסוק שקרא הכהן עם שנים הנותרים : ר' חנינא קרא · שהיה בעל מקרא ויודעה בגירסא ובקי בטעמיה : צער גדול · הרבה טרחתי וחזרתי עליו שיתיר לי לפסוק הפסוק לשנים לצורך תינוקות שלומדים לפני שאינן יכולין לקרות פסוק כולו : הכא נמי לא אפשר · גבי ס"ת (ג) ובדילוג אי אפשר משום הנכנסין והיוצאין אם שני דולג ומתחיל בפסוק שסיים בו הראשון בני אדם הנכנסין שלא שמעו קריאת הראשון סבורין לומר שלא קרא הראשון אלא שני פסוקים ונפיק מיניה תורבא וכשהראשון קורא ג' פסוקים ואינו משייר אלא שנים איכא גזרת יוצאין דסברי האי שני דסגיא ליה בשני פסוקים : מיתיבי פרשה של ששה פסוקים · אשאר ימות השנה קאי : ויש אומרים שלשה · מפרשה אחריתי : הכי גרסינן למאן דאמר *)דולג לידלוג למ"ד פוסק ליפסוק. כלומר פרשה של חמשה פסוקין(ד) אמאי קורא שני שלשה פסוקין בפרשה אחרת לידלוג או ליפסוק :

*) [ע' רש"י במגיל' כב· ד"ה למאן וכו"ע]

רבינו חננאל

שמואל ודוד והעמידום על (י"ו) [כ"ד] קשיא לרב חסדא ושנינן הכי מיסוד של שמואל שהוסיף על שתיקן משה· בא דוד והוסיף על מה שתיקן שמואל {והעמידום על כ"ד}שנא' המה יסד דוד ושמואל הרואה באמונתם : ת"ר ד' משמרות עלו מן הגולה · ידעיה חרים פשחור אימר · עמדו הנביאים שביניהם וחלקום לכ"ד משמרות בללום ונתנום בקלפי בא ידעיה ונטל חלקו וחלק חבירו שש וכן חרים וכן פשחור וכן אימר וכן התנו נביאים שביניהם שאע"פ שיהויריב ראש משמרה עולה לא ידחה ידעיה ממקומו אלא ידעיה עיקר ויהויריב טפל לו עמדו ראשי א) משמרות וקבעו עצמן בתי אבות· משמר שהיה בו ה' בתי אבות ג' מקריבין ב) ג' ימים וב' מקריבין ד' ימים · ומי שהיה בו ג)ו' בית אבות כל אחד מקריב יום· וכן כולן · יש מי שקבעו עצמן לעולם · בית אב שהיה בשבת לעולם אינו מקריב אלא בשבת · ומי שהוא ביום ראשון לעולם ביום ראשון · ויש שמגרילין ד) על כל משמר · ויש שהוא מגרילין בכל שבוע ושבוע : ירושלמי ר' הוה מסני(מוציאין) [תרין סניין] אי הוין כדי הוין מתקיימין ואין לא הוו מסתלקין מרדסך · תרגום ויישן ויחלום ודמוך וחלם · (ר') פקיד. לבריה לא תעביר כן אלא סני כולהו לחדא ומני ר' חמא בר' חנינא בראשי' ולמה לא מנייה ר' בגין ... השיבו ר' הוה יתיב מתני [יחזקאל ז] ופלטו פליטיהם והיו אל ההרים כיוני הגאיות כולם (הומה) [הומיות אמר] ליה רבי חנינא (כלם) הומות א"ל חן קריתיה א"ל קומי רב המנונא דבבל · א"ל כד תיחות תמן אמור ליה דמנייתך חכים וידע דלא מיתמני ביומוי · מן דמך ר' א' אני מקבל עד דתמני ר' אפס דדרומא והוה תמן חד סב ה) א"ר חנינא קדמאי אנא תניין וקביל עליה ר' חנינא מתמנן תליתאי שמואל ודבית שילה הוי עיילין שאלין בשלמא דנשיאה כל יומא והוו דבית שילה עלין ויתבין קדמאי פלגו יקר לשמואל ואותיביה קדמאי על רב לתמן פלג ליה שמואל יקר ואותיביה קדמאי אמרו דבית שילה אנן תניין וקביל שמואל עלויה מיתב תליתאי · המה יסד דוד ושמואל הרואה באמונתם אומנות גדולה היתה שאין משמר נוטל ושונה בשדה אחוזה עד שיטול חבירו·תנא בתוספתא· אלו משמרות כהנים לוים וישראלים עמדו נביאים שביניהם וקבעום כ"ד משמרות שנאמר צו את בני ישראל אי אפשר לומר כל ישראל אלא מלמד ששלוחו של אדם כמותו תניא זמן המשמר כהנים ולוים עולין בירושלים וישראל שבאותו משמר שאין יכולין לעלות לירושלים מתקבצין בעריהם וקורין בענין קרבנות ובענין מעשה בראשית ובטלין מן המלאכה (של) [כל] אותה שבת ולמה קורין בקרבנות ובמעשה בראשית ללמדך שאלמלא המעמדות שמתקבצין לא נתקיימו מעשה בראשית שנא' אם לא בריתי יומם ולילה חקות שמים וארץ לא שמתי · וכתיב ויאמר ה' במה ארע כי אירשנה. אמר אברהם לפני הקב"ה רבש"ע מתיירא אני שמא ישראל יחטאו כו' :

א) מכאן עד ויש מהם שמגדילין הוא לשון התוספתא דמכילתין פ"ב וכירושלמי כאן ה"ב . ב) בתוספתא הגי' שלשה מקריבין שני ימים [ור"ל דכל אחד מהנהו אבות מקריבין שני ימים] ושנים מקריבין ... משמר שיש בו ששה חמשה מקריבין חמשה ימים ואחד מקריב שני ימים עכ"ל התוספתא אבל בירושלמי הגי' כמש"כ רבינו וכן צ"ל גם בתוספתא ודו"ק . ג) נראה דצ"ל ומי שיש בו ז' בתי אבות וכ"ה בתוספתא ... ד) בירושלמי הגי' שמגרילין וע"ש במפרש . ה) אמר לי חנינא קדמאי אנא תניין אין ר' אפס ארומא קדמאי אנא תניין כ"ה בירושלמי

הגהות הב"ח

(א) גמ' קורין אותה בשנים ושל חמשה ביחיד ואם הראשון קורא: (ב) רש"י ד"ה אנשי משמר אותן כ"ד שהיו בעריהן מעמד אותן כ"ד שהיו: (ג) ד"ה הכא נמי לא אפשר גבי ס"ת דבדילוג א"א משום ... (ד) ד"ה ס"ג כו' אמאי קורא שני ג' ... (ה) תוס' ד"ה גזירה כו' שלא ראו את הראשון שקרא כו' ויראו את השני:

רבינו גרשום

ושנה מאיתמר וקשיא לרב חסדא אמר לך רב חסדא תנאי הוא דאשכחן תנא דלעיל דתניא משה תיקן ר' מאלעזר ור' מאיתמר ואנא דאמרי כוותיה: בללום ונתנום בקלפי שכשחלקו כל משמר לו' משמרות היה מחלוקת ביניהם שזו אומר אני עולה תחלה וזו אומר אני עולה תחלה מה עשו כתבו שמות ראשי של אותן ה' משמרות שהוסיפו ממשמר ידעיה ובא ידעיה ונטל חלקו וחלק חבריו שהגיח ידיו בקלפי ואומר שם אותה משמורה שעולה בידי תחלה היא עולה תחלה אחרי וכן בשניה וכן בשלישית וכן ברביעית וכן חמישית וכן עשה חרים וכו' שאפי' יהויריב עולה שהוא לא רצה לעלות עם עזרא : מנה"מ דקורין במעמדות מעשה בראשית אמר רב אסי אילמלא מעמדות כלומר קרבנות לא נתקיימו שמים וארץ שנא' ויאמר ה' אלהים במה אדע וגו' קחה לי עגלה משולשת וגו' דהיינו קרבנות לפיכך קוראין במעשה בראשית כשעוסקין בקרבנות לפי שכל מעשה בראשית אינו מתקיים אלא בשביל הקרבנות : אנשי משמר היו מתפללין על קרבן אחיהם שיתקבל ברצון שבו כהנים של משמר נחלק לו' בתי אבות וכל עובד יום אחד וביום שבית אב עובד שאר כל כהנים אנשי משמר ו' בתי אבות מתפללין על קרבן אחיהם בית אב שביעי שיתקבל ברצון : אנשי מעמד היו יושבין ד' תעניות כלו' אותן ישראל כדאמרנו לעיל במשנתנו שמתכנסין בעריהן יושבין ד' תעניות על יורדי הים לפי שנאמר בו והיה ... הים על הולכי מדברות לפי שנאמר בו ותראה היבשה על אסכרא לפי שנאמר בו יהי מאורות ... דמשמע מארה על עוברות ומיניקות לפי שנאמר בו ישרצו המים נפש חיה דהיינו המשוכרות ... לפי שיום חג שלהם באחד בשבת ואם היו ישראל מתענין היו כועסים. שלישי ליצירה שאדם שב...

גליון הש"ס

גמ' אמר רב אסי אלמלא מעמדות · ע' פוריית פ"א מ"ב דאבות :

הגהות הגר"א

[א] גמ' מ"ר· אנשי משמר (רשום עליו אות ב') סיו כו' ואנשי מעמד (רשום עליו אות א')· כלומר דצ"ל ...

הגהות מהר"ב רנשבורג

א] גמ' ת"ר אנשי משמר · כ"כ מגה"ד ז"ל ליפכא ואנשי מעמד היו מתפללין ואנשי משמר מתכנסין לבהכ"נ וכן מוכח במתני' וברמב"ם פ"ז מהלכות כלי מקדש הלכה א' ב' ג' ודו"ק :

דאית ליה רווחא: פרשה גדולה קורין אותה בשנים בשחרית ובמוסף ובמנחה קורין על פיהן כו': איבעיא להו היכי קאמר בשחרית ובמוסף קורין אותה בספר ובמנחה קורין אותה על פה כקורין את שמע או דלמא הכי קתני בשחרית קורין אותה בספר ובמוסף ובמנחה קורין אותה על פה כקורין את שמע תא שמע דתניא בשחרית ובמוסף נכנסין לבית הכנסת וקורין כדרך שקורין כל השנה ובמנחה יחיד קורא אותה על פה אמר ר' יוסי וכי יחיד יכול לקרות דברי תורה על פה בצבור אלא כולן נכנסין וקורין אותה על פה כקורין את שמע: כל יום שיש בו הלל אין בו מעמד כו': מה הפרש בין זה לזה הללו דברי תורה והללו דברי סופרים: זמן עצי כהנים והעם כו': ת"ר למה הוצרכו לומר זמן עצי כהנים והעם אמרו כשעלו בני הגולה לא מצאו עצים בלשכה ועמדו אלו והתנדבו משלהם וכך התנו נביאים שביניהן שאפי' לשכה מלאה עצים יהיו אלו מתנדבין משלהן שנאמר °והגורלות הפלנו על קרבן העצים הכהנים הלוים והעם להביא לבית אלהינו לבית אבותינו לעתים מזומנים שנה בשנה לבער על מזבח ה' אלהינו ככתוב בתורה: ועמהם כהנים ולוים וכל מי כו': תנו רבנן מה היו בני גונבי עלי ובני קוצעי קציעות אמרו פעם אחת גזרה המלכות גזירה על ישראל שלא יביאו עצים למערכה ושלא יביאו בכורים לירושלים והושיבו פרוזדאות על הדרכים כדרך שהושיב ירבעם בן נבט שלא יעלו ישראל לרגל מה עשו כשרין *)(*שבאותו הדור ויראי חטא) הביאו סלי בכורים וחיפום בקציעות ונטלום ועלי על כתפיהן וכיון שהגיעו אצל פרוזדאות אמרו להם להיכן אתם הולכין אומרין להם לעשות שני עיגולי דבילה במכתשת שלפנינו ובעלי שעל כתפינו כיון שעברו מהן עיטרום בסלים והביאום לירושלים: תנא הן הן בני סלמאי הנתופתי ת"ר מה הן בני סלמאי הנתופתי אמרו פעם אחת גזרה המלכות גזירה על ישראל שלא יביאו עצים למערכה והושיבו פרוזדאות על הדרכים כדרך שהושיב ירבעם בן נבט על הדרכים שלא יעלו ישראל לרגל מה עשו יראי חטא שבאותו הדור הביאו גזיריהן ועשו סולמות והניחו על כתפיהם והלכו להם כיון שהגיעו אצלן אמרו להם להיכן אתם הולכין אמרו להם להביא גוזלות משובך שלפנינו ובסולמות שעל כתפינו כיון שעברו מהן פירקום והביאום והעלום לירושלים ועליהם ועל כיוצא בהם הוא אומר °זכר צדיק לברכה ועל ירבעם בן נבט וחבריו נאמר ושם רשעים ירקב: בעשרים בו בני פחת מואב בן יהודה: תנא בני פחת מואב בן יהודה הן הן בני דוד בן יהודה דברי ר' מאיר רבי יוסי אומר הן הן בני יואב בן צרויה: בעשרים באלול בני עדין בן יהודה וכו': תנו רבנן בני עדין בן יהודה הן הן בני דוד בן יהודה דברי רבי יהודה רבי יוסי אומר הן הן בני יואב בן צרויה: באחד בטבת שבו בני פרעוש שניה כו': מני מתני' לא ר' מאיר ולא רבי יהודה ולא רבי יוסי אי ר"מ ליתני שבו בני דוד בן יהודה שניה אי רבי יהודה ליתני שבו בני דוד בן יהודה שניה אי רבי יוסי ליתני שבו בני יואב בן צרויה שניה לעולם ר' יוסי ותרי תנאי אליבא דר' יוסי: באחד בטבת לא היה בו מעמד כו': אמר ליה מר קשישא בריה דרב חסדא לרב אשי מאי

*) [נ"ל ויראי חטא שבאותו הדור]

נחמיה י · משלי י

רש"י

דלית ליה רווחא · שיכול לקרות מפרשה אחרת אבל הכא לית ליה רווחא דהא לא מצי למיקרי אלא בראשית ויהי רקיע: מה הפרש בין זה לזה · מאי שנא דקרבן עצים דחי מעמד דנעילה ומעמד דמנחה לא דחי: הללו דברי תורה · מנחה כדאמרי' בברכות (דף כו:) יצחק אבינו תיקן תפלת מנחה שנאמר ויצא יצחק לשוח בשדה לפנות ערב והנעילה מדברי סופרים · וצריכין חיזוק לא גרסינן [א] הכא: עמדו אלו · זמן דקתני במתני' אהכי הוצרכו למנות משום ההיא תקנה דעבוד להו הנביאים כי היכי דלא לידחינהו מאתרייהו: פרוזדאות · שומרים: בכורים · אדם נכנס לתוך שדהו ורואה אשכול שביכר תאנה שביכרה קושר עליה גמי ועושה אותה בכורים: בקציעות · תאנים יבשים כותשין אותן ועושין מהן עגולין: ה"ג והעלי על כתפיהן · (*בוכיא): במכתשת שלפנינו · שהוא במקום אחר (א) לפני בסמוך וזהו גונבי עלי על שם שמתגנבין מן הפרוזדאות על עסקי עלי: הן הן בני סלמאי הנתופתי · כעין מעשה זה עשו (ב): הן הן בני דוד בן יהודה · דוד מלך ישראל ואהכי קרו ליה פחת מואב שבא מרות המואביה: יואב בן צרויה · שבא מרות המואביה כי צרויה אם יואב אחות דוד היתה שנאמר (דה"א ב) ואחיותיהם צרויה ואביגיל: בני עדין הן הן בני דוד · להכי קרי ליה בספר שמואל (ב כג) עדינו העצני שבשעה שעוסק בתורה מעדן עצמו כתולעת וכשיוצא למלחמה מתקשה כעץ: הן הן בני יואב בן צרויה · פלוגתא היא (*במס' חגיגה) חד אמר עדינו העצני זה דוד *וחד אמר זה יואב: ליתני שבו בני דוד שניה · דהא קאמר ר' מאיר פחת מואב היינו דוד: ולר' יהודה · בני עדין היינו דוד ובמתניתין קתני בהדיא בני דוד והדר קתני בני פחת מואב דלר"מ ולר' יהודה בני עדין היינו דוד שבו שניה מיבעי ליה: ולר' יוסי · דאמר פחת מואב ועדין היינו יואב שבו שניה מיבעי ליה: לעולם ר' יוסי ותרי תנאי אליבא דר' יוסי · דמאן דאמר בני עדין בן יהודה היינו בני יואב לא סבר לה דבני פחת מואב היינו יואב ולהכי לא קתני שבו בני יואב שניה ולא סבירא ליה נמי דהן הן בני דוד דאם כן שבו בני דוד שניה מיבעי ליה למיתני אלא משפחה אחרת הן ומאן דאמר בני פחת מואב היינו בני יואב לא סבירא ליה דבני עדין היינו יואב אלא משפחה אחרת הן: מאי

[נ"ל בוכנא] · [מו"ק טז:] · במו"ק טז: כנ"ל · [לא נמצא שם דחד אמר זה יואב וכתיקוני כלי שרת פקפקתי על נכון]

תוספות

מה הפרש בין זה לזה · כלומר מה הפרש בין קרבן מוסף לקרבן עצים דקרבן מוסף דוחה מנחה וקרבן עצים לא דחי מנחה: הללו דברי תורה · מוסף ולהכי קדחי מנחה דהוי מדברי תורה אבל קרבן עצים דהוי מדברי סופרים והלכך לא דחיא אלא נעילה דהויא מדברי סופרים אבל לא דחיא מנחה דהויא מדברי תורה: בני פחת מואב וכו' הן הן בני דוד · ולכך נקראו בני פחת (ג) שבאו מרות המואביה: הן הן בני יואב בן צרויה · פירוש דצרויה היתה *אחות דוד כדכתיב (דה"א ב) ואחיותיהם צרויה והם באים מזרע רות המואביה: אי ר"מ · דקאמר בני פחת מואב בן יהודה הן הן בני דוד בן יהודה ליתני במתניתין כי קאמר בעשרים בו' בני פחת מואב בן יהודה הוה ה"ל למיתני בני דוד בן יהודה שבו שניה כמו שאומר שבו בני פרעוש שניה אי ר' יהודה דקאמר בני עדין בן יהודה הן הן בני דוד בן יהודה ליתני שבו בני דוד בן יהודה שניה אי ר' יוסי ליתני שבו בני יואב שניה ומשני תרי תנאי ואליבא דר' יוסי וקשיא אמאי לא מוקי אליבא דר"מ ותרי תנאי אליבא דר"מ שהרי טפי יש לן לאוקמא כר"מ דסתמא דמתני' כר' מאיר ונראה לי דלהכי מוקי לה כרבי יוסי משום דרבי יוסי נימוקו עמו ומסתברא כוותיה בכל מקום ואפילו מחבריו:

ויום

נ"ל בת ישי

עין משפט נר מצוה

יח א מיי' פ"ו מהל' כלי המקדש הל' ז:

רבינו חננאל

משמר · מתפללין על קרבן אחיהם שיתקבל ברצון · ואנשי מעמד מתענין ד' תעניות בשבוע · בשני על יורדי הים · שנאמר ויאמר אלהים יהי רקיע בתוך המים וגו' · בשלישי על הולכי מדברות שנאמר יקוו המים ותראה היבשה · בר' על האסכרה שלא תעל בתינוקות שנאמר יהי מאורות · מארת כתיב חסר ו' · בה' על עוברות שלא יפילו ועל המניקות שיגדלו בניהם שנאמר ישרצו המים שרץ [נפש חיה]. בע"ש לא היו מתענין מפני כבוד בשבת וכ"ש שבת עצמה · (א) וסנהדרין לבתי אבות מתענין עמהם · באחד בשבת מ"מ לא · ר' יוחנן אומר מפני הנוצרים · פי' שיו"ם שלהם הוא · ר' שמואל ב"נ אומר מפני שהוא שלישי ליצירה · וכתיב ויהי ביום השלישי בהיותם כאבים · כלומר נברא האדם בששי הנה ששי ושבת ויום ראשון הרי שלש ליצירה והוא עדיין חלש · ר' שמעון בן לקיש אמר מפני נשמה יתירה שנתנת לאדם בשבת כדי לאכול ולשתות ולשמוח ולהתענג כגבור בשתיית היין ואם אין בו כח גדול אין בו יכולת לשתות ובמ"ש ניטלת מן האדם · ונשתייר תשוי כח לפיכך אין בו יכולת · כדכתיב שבת וינפש · כיון ששבת ווי אבדה נפש · כלומר אבדה הנפש היתירה: מתני' וישראל שבאותו משמר מתכנסין בעריהם · פי' קבלנו מרבותינו שהיו בכל יום קורין פרשת קרבנות · ואח"כ היו קורין סדר בראשית · ביום הראשון בראשית ויהי רקיע · תנא בראשית בשנים אמאי בשנים והא ה' פסוקי נינהו · ותנא הקורא בתורה לא יפחות מג' פסוקים · רב אמר דולג · פי' הראשון קורא שלשה · השני חוזר וקורא אחד מאלו השלשה שקראם הראשון והשני פסוקים הנותרים מן הפרשה · ושמואל אמר פוסק הפסוק אחד לשנים כל אחד קורא שלשה · רב אמר דולג · כל פסוקא דלא פסקיה משה אנן לא פסקינן ליה · וקיי"ל כרב וכבר פירשנוהו במגילה · פי' בשחרית במוסף כו' · תנא בשחרית ובמוסף נכנסין בכנסת וקורא בתורה בצבור · ע"ש לא היו נכנסין מפני כבוד השבת: מתני' כל יום שיש בו הלל ואין בו מוסף כגון חנוכה וכיוצא בו לא היה בו בשחרית כלומר לא היה בו מעמד בשחרית לא היו אנשי מעמד נכנסין בכנסת וקורין פרשיותיהן בשחרית וכל יום שיש בו קרבן מוסף כגון ר"ח וחש"מ אין בו לאנשי מעמד קריאה במנחה · כל יום שיש בו קרבן עצים כגון אלו ט' ימים שאנו עתידין לפרשן כדתנא זמן עצי הכהנים והעם ט' אין לאנשי המעמד תפלה בנעילה · אמר בן עזאי משום ר' יהושע כל יום שיש בו קרבן מוסף אין מעמד (ב) בנעילה · קרבן עצים אין במנחה · ואמרינן מה הפרש בין זה לזה · ופרקינן הללו דברי תורה כלומר הימים שיש בהן קרבן מוסף כגון ר"ח וחולו של מועד מן התורה אסורים בתענית ואין צריכין [חיזוק] אלא דוחין המעמד שבנעילה · ואע"פ שאינה תדירה · ואינו דבר ידוע · אבל זמן הכהנים שהוא אסור בתענית מדרבנן צריך חיזוק. לפי' אין בו מעמד במנחה שהוא תדיר והוא ידוע. וכיון שרואין כי דוחה את המנחה נוהגין בו יו"ט. כדתניא [במגלת תענית] ואלו ימים זמן עצי הכהנים והעם אסורין בהספד ותענית: ת"ר למה הוזכרו זמן עצי הכהנים והעם להמנות כשעלו ישראל מן הגולה לא מצאו עצים למערכה ועמדו אלו והתנדבו משלהם · פי' גונבין עלי וקוצעי קציעות גונבין דעת יושבי פרדסאות באמרם להם כי התאנים הבכורות הללו אנו הולכים בהן לכתוש במכתש שלפנינו ובעלי שעל כתפינו לעשותן קציעה של דבילה · פי' עלי יד המכתש כדכתיב אם תכתוש את האויל במכתש בתוך הריפות בעלי · דברים פשוטים הן

א) כן הוא בירושלמי ב) כן היתה גרסת רבינו לפיכך מגרסא שלנו במתני' כדברי ר"ע ור"ע.

הגהות הב"ח

(א) רש"י ד"ה במכתשת כו' במקום אחר לפנינו בסמוך: (ב) ד"ה הן הן כו' עשו כסמוך בס"ד: (ג) תוס' ד"ה בני כו' נקראו בני פחת מואב שבאו מרות:

הגהות הגר"א

[א] רש"י ד"ה הללו · וצריכין חיזוק ל"ג · נ"ב אבל כגאונים גרסי' ופרש"כ:

רבינו גרשום

שבת והוי אחד בשבת שלישי ויש בו חולשא · במוצאי שבת ניטלת ממנו ויש בו חולשא: במוסף במנחה וכו' ופי' בגמ' רב אמר דולג שראשון קורא ג' פסוקים ושמואל אמר פוסק שאינו דולג משום גזרה משום הנכנסין ומשום היוצאין שאם קורא ראשון ג' פסוקים שלמין א' היוצא לאחר כשסיים הראשון שלא נשתייר לשני לקרות אלא ב' פסוקין וכן אם מתחיל השני בפסוק הג' הנכנס לאחר שסיים הראשון כששומע ששני קורא הג' אומר לא קרא הראשון אלא ב' פסוקים: דאית ביה רווחא שיכול לקרות פסוק אחד מפרשה אחרת אבל דלא מצי למקרי מפרשה אחרת דאית לה למיקרא למהר או דולג או פוסק · ובמנחה קורין על פיהן מה שקורין שחרית בספר כדרך שקורין כל השנה בספר: ערב שבת במנחה לא היו נכנסין לקרות בפה לפי שהן עוסקין לכבוד שבת לטרוח בסעודת שבת והאי דקתני בששי ותצא וגו' היינו בשחרית בספר: אין בו מעמד שחרית כלומר אין קורין מה שקורין במעמדות לפי שעוסקין בהלל · קרבן מוסף אין בו נעילה כלומר שיש בו קרבן מוסף אין בו תפלת נעילה ואין קורין במעמדות לפי שעוסקין בקרבן וקסבר דתפלת נעילה קודם לתפלת מנחה ולפי שתפלת מוסף עד הערב עוסקין במוסף בשעת נעילה · קרבן עצים אין במנחה כלומר ביום שמביאין קרבן עצים אין קוראין במעמדות במנחה · לפי שעוסקין בקרבן עצים: קרבן מוסף אין במנחה כלומר מנחה קודם לנעילה ובשעת מנחה עוסקין במוסף ואין פנאי לקרות במעמדות: מה הפרש בין זה לזה כלומר מ"ש דמוסף דוחה מנחה ואין דוחה נעילה וקרבן עצים דוחה אפי' נעילה: הללו קרבן מוסף דברי תורה ואין צריכין חיזוק ואין צריך שיהא דוחה אלא מנחה שסמוך לו אבל קרבן עצים שהן מדברי סופרים וצריכין חיזוק לפיכך עשו בו חיזוק שדוחה אפי' נעילה שאינו סמוך לו: ועמהן עם זתוא שהוא אחרון כהנים ולוים וכל מי שטעה שבטו שאינו יודע מאיזה שבט הוא: שבו בני פרעוש שניה · הן הולכין פעם שניה להביא עצים · באחד בטבת לא היה בו מעמד כל היום שהיה בו הלל בשחרית וקרבן מוסף במנחה וקרבן עצים בנעילה: למה הוצרכו לקבוע הני זמנים להביא עצים למערכה: פרדסאות · ממונים: בקציעות · של דבילה: עיטרום בסלים כמצוה דכתיב ונתת בטנא · פרקום והביאום · עצים של סולמות לירושלים לקרבן עצים · בני פחת מואב הן בני דוד ולהכי קרי ליה מואב משום דאתי מרות המואביה · הן בני יואב דאתי נמי ממואב מאמו: הן בני דוד ועל שם עדינו העצני קרי ליה בני עדין · הן בני יואב ועל שם דוד שהיה ראש משפחותם קרי להו בני עדין על שם דוד · אי ר"מ ליתני נמי שבו בני דוד שניה דר"מ קאמר הני פחת מואב הן בני דוד כיון דתרוייהו קתני להו במתניתין כדתני בני דוד איבעי להו למיתני שבו שניה דכבר קתני דבאו פעם ראשונה דקתני באו בני פחת מואב · אי ר' יהודה ליתני שבו בני דוד שניה נמי דהא תני במתניתין שתי פעמים בני דוד דר' יהודה אמר דבני עדין הן בני דוד אי ר' יוסי ליתני שבו בני יואב שניה · תרי תנאי אליבא דר' יוסי דהאי תנא דאמר אליבא דר' יוסי בני פחת מואב הני בני יואב לא אמר דר' יוסי אמר בני עדין הן בני יואב ומאן דאמר אליבא דר' יוסי בני עדין הן בני יואב לא אמר דר' יוסי אמר בני פחת מואב הן בני יואב ולא תני במתניתין בני יואב אלא פעם אחת להכי לא קתני שבו בני

תורה אור

מאי שנא הלל דדחי דידיה ומאי שנא מוסף דלא דחי דידיה א"ל רב אשי השתא דלאו דידיה דחי דידיה לא כל שכן אמר ליה הכי קאמינא לך לא לידחי אלא דידיה אמר ליה איכא ר' יוסי דקאי כוותך דתניא ר' יוסי אומר כל יום שיש בו מוסף יש בו מעמד מעמד דמאי אילימא מעמד דשחרית הא תנא קמא נמי הכי קאמר אלא מעמד דמוסף דידיה נמי לא דחי אלא דמנחה [א] קרבן עצים דחי אלא לאו דנעילה שמע מינה דידיה דחי דלאו דידיה לא דחי שמע מינה וליתני נמי באחד בניסן לא היה בו מעמד מפני שיש בו הלל וקרבן מוסף וקרבן עצים אמר רבא זאת אומרת הלילא דבריש ירחא לאו דאורייתא דאמר רבי יוחנן משום רבי שמעון בן יהוצדק **שמונה עשר יום בשנה יחיד גומר בהן את הלל ואלו הן שמונת ימי החג ושמונת ימי חנוכה ויום טוב הראשון של פסח ויום טוב (ראשון) של עצרת ובגולה עשרים ואחד יום ואלו הן תשעת ימי החג ושמונת ימי חנוכה ושני ימים הראשונים של פסח וב' ימים טובים של עצרת רב איקלע לבבל חזינהו דקא קרו הלילא בריש ירחא סבר לאפסוקינהו כיון דחזא דקא מדלגי דלוגי אמר שמע מינה מנהג אבותיהם בידיהם תנא יחיד לא יתחיל ואם התחיל גומר: ה' דברים אירעו את אבותינו בשבעה עשר בתמוז כו': נשתברו הלוחות מנלן דתניא *בששה לחדש ניתנו עשרת הדברות לישראל רבי יוסי אומר בשבעה בו מאן דאמר בששה ניתנו בששה ניתנו ובשבעה עלה משה מ"ד בשבעה בשבעה ניתנו ובשבעה עלה משה דכתיב °ויקרא אל משה ביום השביעי וכתיב °ויבא משה בתוך הענן ויעל אל ההר ויהי משה בהר ארבעים יום וארבעים לילה עשרים וארבעה דסיון ושיתסר דתמוז מלו להו ארבעין בשיבסר בתמוז נחית אתא ותברינהו ללוחות וכתיב °ויהי כאשר קרב אל המחנה וירא את העגל וישלך מידיו את הלוחות וישבר אותם תחת ההר: בטל התמיד גמרא: הובקעה העיר בי"ז הוה והכתיב °בחדש הרביעי בתשעה לחדש ויחזק הרעב בעיר וכתיב בתריה °ותבקע העיר וגו' אמר רבא לא קשיא כאן בראשונה כאן בשניה דתניא בראשונה הובקעה העיר בתשעה בתמוז בשניה בשבעה עשר בו: שרף אפוסטמוס את התורה גמרא: העמיד צלם בהיכל מנלן דכתיב °ומעת הוסר התמיד ולתת שקוץ שומם וחד הוה והכתיב °ועל כנף שקוצים משומם אמר רבא תרי הוו ונפל חד על חבריה ותבריה ליה לידיה ואשתכח דהוה כתיב(א) אנת

(שמות כד · שם · ירמיה נב · שם · דניאל יב · שם ט)

מאי שנא הלל דדחי דידיה · מעמד דשחרית: ומאי שנא מוסף דלא דחי דידיה · דקתני יום שיש בו מוסף אין בו (ב) מנחה ולא קתני אין בו מוסף דלא דחי דידיה אלא דמנחה: הכי קאמינא · הכי קא בעינא למימר: אלא דידיה · דמוסף: ה"ג רבי יוסי אומר כל יום שיש בו מוסף יש בו מעמד · ואתאן קמא פליג דאמר יום שיש בו מוסף אין בו (ג) נעילה ואתא ר' יוסי למימר דיש בו מעמד אע"פ שיש בו מוסף: אלא לאו דנעילה הוא · דאמר ר' יוסי דיש בו מעמד ואין מוסף דוחה אותו: באחד בניסן · דאית ביה הלל דראש חדש: (ד) קרבן עצים · (קרבן מוסף) דבני ארח בן יהודה: זאת אומרת · מדלא קתני נמי באחד בניסן אלמא הלל דראש חדש לא דחי ליה למעמד שמע מינה דלאו דאורייתא הוא א] אלא מנהגא כדלקמן: מנהג אבותיהם בידיהן · אבל הלל דחנוכה כגון באחד בטבת ודאי דחי דכיון דנביאים תיקנוהו שיהו אומרים אותו על כל פרק ופרק ועל כל צרה שלא תבא עליהן וכשנגאלין יהו אומרין אותו על גאולתן כדאורייתא דמי: יחיד · כלומר אפי' יחיד גומר בהן את ההלל שכל אחד ואחד חייב לגמור בו את ההלל במסכת ערכין מפורש מאי שנא דגומר כל ימי החג ובפסח לא גומר אלא יום ראשון משום דחג הסוכות חלוק בקרבנותיו וכל אחד ואחד כחג בפני עצמו דמי: ובגולה · שעושין שני ימים טובים משום ספיקא: דמדלגי דלוגי · כגון אנן דמדלגין לא לנו ה' לא לנו ונתחיל מן ה' זכרנו יברך: לא יתחיל · אינו צריך להתחיל בראש חדש: ר' יוסי אומר בשבעה · וטעמייהו מקרא במסכת שבת בפרק ר"ע: בשבעה עלה משה · לקבל הלוחות כלומר ודאי ליכא מאן דפליג עלה דמתני' דקתני די"ז בתמוז נשתברו הלוחות מכלל דכולהו סבירא להו דבשבעה עלה (ה) ואנו מקרא נפקא לן דבשבעה עלה דהאי דכתיב וישכן כבוד ה' על הר סיני ויכסהו הענן ששת ימים ויקרא אל משה ביום השביעי איכא מאן דדריש ליה במסכת יומא כי אחר מתן תורה הוה: משבעה בסיון עד י"ז בתמוז איכא מ' יום כ"ד דסיון שהוא מלא וי"ו דתמוז הרי מ' [illegible] בהר: גמרא · כך קיבלנו מאבותינו: ומעת הוסר התמיד לתת שקוץ שומם וגו' · דבעת שהוסר ונתבטל התמיד באותו היום נתן שקוץ שומם דהיינו הועמד צלם בהיכל: ה"ג והא כתיב על כנף שקוצים · כלומר הא כתיב קרא אחרינא דכתיב ביה שקוצים דמשמע תרי: תרי הוו · שהעמידן מנשה בהיכל: ונפל חד על חבריה וקטעיה לידיה · והנקטע לא קא חשיב והיינו דכתיב שקוץ אחד: אשתכח דכתיב · על ההוא צלם הכי: אנת

ויום טוב הראשון של פסח · הוא גומר הלל אבל שמונה ימי פסח לא משום דלא דמי לחנוכה וסוכות דחנוכה דינא הוא לגמור הלל דכל הח' ימים היה הנס מתגדל והיה כל חד וחד יום טוב וכן בסוכות *כל יומא ויומא הוי י"ט לעצמו לפי שפרי החג מתמעטין והולכין אבל פסח אינו משתנה לא מקרבנות ולא מיום טוב לכך אין גומרים בו ההלל אלא יום הראשון והאידנא דגומרין תרי יומי משום דעבדינן אותו מספק הוי חד יומא לענין קריאת הלל וכן ביום שני של עצרת וכן יום של שמחת תורה ומש"ה יש לנו כ"א יום לגמור הלל:

אמר שמע מינה מנהג אבותיהם בידיהם · י"מ דאמנהג לא מברכינן (ו) מהכא וכן משמע בסוכה בפרק לולב וערבה (דף מד:) דקאמר *אמר אביי הוה קאימנא קמיה דר' יצחק ואייתי ההיא ערבה לקמיה שקל חביט חביט ולא בריך קסבר ערבה מנהג נביאים היא אלמא אמנהג לא מברכינן אבל רבינו תם פסק דמברכינן דהא איתא דלא מברכינן אם כן מאי קאמר בגמרא כיון דשמעינהו דמדלגי ואזלי שמע מינה מנהג אבותיהם בידיהם וכי לא היה לו להכיר אי משום מנהג קרו ליה לא מברכי אי איתא דאמנהג לא מברכינן ואי מברכי לא מנהג הוא וכי תימא דלא בא בתחילת קריאת הלל הא לא מצי אמרת דהא רב איקלע לבבל קאמר דאי איתא דבאמצע תפלה בא הוה ליה למימר איקלע לבי כנישתא ומדלא אמר מדלא ברכי מנהג הוא שמע מינה דאמנהגא נמי מברכינן וההיא דסוכה דמשמע דאמנהגא לא מברכינן היינו דווקא אמנהג דערבה דלא הוי אלא מנהג טלטול בעלמא ואמנהג דטלטול לא מברכינן אבל בשאר מנהג כמו קריאת הלל ואחריני כמו אותו מנהג ודאי מברכינן וכן הלכה למעשה ולפי זה יש ליזהר שלא לדבר באמצע ההלל כיון שבירך דאם כן הוי מפסיק ונראה דאין יחיד מחויב לקרות ההלל אכן אם רוצה לחייב עצמו הרשות בידו*:

ואשתכח דכתיב עילויה · על אותו יד פירוש מלאו כתוב על היד שנחתכה מן הצלם [illegible] של הקב"ה(ז) אשלמת ליה כלומר וכחך נתת לו ויש מפרשים דהכתיבה הוה על הצלם השלם וה"ק אסכחי' עליה על הצלם השלם אנת צבי לאיחרובי ביתיה כלומר אתה רצית להחריב ביתו של הקדוש ברוך הוא וידך אשלמת ליה לכך שלמתי את ידך להקדוש ברוך הוא שחתכתי:

דכתיב

יט א מיי' פ"ג מהל' מגילה וחנוכה הל' ו:

[בספרים מגלו לגדייא בגמרא ערכין י']

כ ב מיי' שם הלכה ו:

[רב אלפס שבת פ"ב דף יא:]

כא ג מיי' שם טוש"ע א"ח סימן תרמד סעיף א:

כב ד מיי' שם טוש"ע א"ח סימן תרפג:

כג ה מיי' שם טוש"ע שם סימן תפח סעיף א:

כד ו מיי' שם טוש"ע א"ח סימן תכב סעיף ב:

כה ז מיי' שם טוש"ע א"ח סימן תכב סעיף ג:

[צ"ל אמר אביי כו' קמיה דרבי אלעזר בר צדוק]

שבת פו: יומא ד:

[ועי' תוס' ברכות יד· ד"ה ימים ותוס' ערכין י· ד"ה יו"ח ותוס' סוכה מד: ד"ה כאן]

ערכין י· [תוספ' סוטה פ"ו ע"ש מס' סופרים פ"כ הל' ט ע"ש]

רבינו חננאל

הן · תנא לפי שמסרו עצמן על המצות נזכרין לברכה · כדכתיב זכר צדיק לברכה · ומן עצי הכהנים והעם תשעה · באחד בניסן בני ארח בן יהודה כו' · מני מתני' אינה לר' מאיר דאמר בני פחת מואב הן הן בני דוד בן יהודה דאי ר' מאיר היא כיון שהקריבו בני דוד בן יהודה (כ"ג)[כ'] בתמוז ובאו בני פחת מואב להקריב בכ' באב היה לו לומר אם בני פחת מואב הן בני דוד בן יהודה שבו בני פחת מואב שניה כמו שאמר בני פרעש שניה · אי מתני' ר' יהודה היא כיון דאמר בני עדין בן יהודה הן בני דוד בן יהודה היה לו לומר שבו בני עדין בן יהודה שניה אי ר' יוסי כיון דאמר בני פחת מואב בן יהודה בני יואב בן צרויה הן ובני עדין הן הן בני יואב בן צרויה היה לו לומר שבו בני עדין שניה · ואוקמיה לר' יוסי ותרי תנאי אליבא דר' יוסי: באחד בטבת לא היה בו מעמד מפני שיש בו הלל שהיא חנוכה והלל דוחה מעמד של שחרית ויש בו קרבן מוסף של ר"ח שדוחה מעמד של נעילה וכ"ש של מוסף דבהדיא תנינן באחד בטבת לא הוה בו מעמד כלל והוא זמן קרבן עצים דתנן באחד בטבת שבו בני פרעש שניה וקרבן עצים דוחה מעמד דמנחה ואוקימנא למתני' דתנא דידן סבר קרבן מוסף דוחה מעמד דנעילה ומעמד דמוסף · ור' יוסי פליג עליה · דתניא ר' יוסי אומר כל יום שיש בו מוסף יש בו מעמד ואוקמנא יש בו מעמד בנעילה · דסבר דידיה והוא מעמד דמוסף דחי דלאו דידיה והוא מעמד דנעילה לא דחי · דייק רבא מדלא קתני באחד בניסן לא היה בו מעמד והנה יש בו קרבן עצים וקרבן מוסף (כגון) [והלל כמו] אחד בטבת (שאי') [ש"מ] הלל דחנוכה הוא כמו הלל של תורה · אבל הלל דר"ח לאו דאורייתא הוא · דא"ר יוחנן משום רבי שמעון בן יהוצדק י"ח ימים בשנה יחיד גומר בהן את ההלל ואלו הן ח' ימי החג וח' דחנוכה · ויו"ט הראשון של פסח ויו"ט של עצרת · ובגולה כ"א יום ט' ימי החג וח' ימי חנוכה וב' ימים של פסח וב' ימים של עצרת · רב אקלע לבבל ושמע דקרו הלל בר"ח בעא למיפסקינהו כיון דשמע להן דפסקי שבק להו · אמר מנהג אבותיהם בידיהם · תנא יחיד לא יתחיל בברכה בזמן שקורין בהן כגון ר"ח וחוש"פ פסח ואם טעה ובירך בא"י אמ"ה אקב"ו לקרוא (והתחיל לגמור) [את הלל גומר] וזהו אם התחיל גומר וקיי"ל הכי דאין הוכה: ה' דברים אירעו את אבותינו וכו' נשתברו הלוחות מנלן לאו שעלה משה למרום בז' בסיון דכתיב ויקרא אל משה ביום השביעי מתוך הענן נמצא שעמד משה במרום כ"ד ימים תשלום סיון וי"ז מתמוז הרי מ' יום · כדכתיב ויהי משה בהר ארבעים יום · למחר ירד ושבר לוחות נמצאת שבירת הלוחות בי"ז בתמוז · בטל תמיד גמרא · *) כר' לוי דאמר אף בימי מלכות הרשעה היו משלשלין להן קופות של זהב · והן היו מעלין להן שני כבשים · ובסוף העלו להן ב' חזירים כו' · אותה שעה גרמו העונות ובטל התמיד ונחרב הבית · והובקעה העיר בחרבן השני י"ז כדתנא בפ' לחדש הרביעי הובקעה העיר בראשונה ובשניה בי"ז שרף אפוסטמוס בי"ז בתמוז את התורה גמרא: בירושלמי היכן שרפה **) העמיד צלם בהיכל מנלן דכתיב ומעת הוסר התמיד · הנה בפירוש כי מעת שהוסר ובטל התמיד ניתן השקץ בהיכל · וכבר אמרנו בי"ז בטל התמיד

*) חסר כאן וצ"ל ובירושלמי ר' סימון בשם ר"י בן לוי בימי מלכות וכו' ולמר ר' אף בימי כו'. **) נראה שחסר כאן ועי' בירושלמי.

רבינו גרשום

בני יואב שניה: מ"ש הלל דדחי דידיה ומ"ש מוסף דלא דחה דידיה התם קאי דקתני במתניתין יש בו הלל אין בו מעמד שחרית קרבן מוסף אין בו במנחה ופריך מר קשישא מ"ש הלל דדחי מעמד בתפלה דידיה דהיינו שחרית ומוסף לא דחי מעמד בתפלה דידיה דקתני מוסף אין במנחה דמשמע אבל במוסף עצמו איכא מעמד. א"ל ומי בעיא לך במוסף דחי דידיה השתא מנחה דלא הוה דידיה דחי ליה מוסף ממעמד דידיה דמוסף מיבעיא אמאי*) דחי נמי במנחה הא הלל לא דחי אלא דידיה דשחרית להודית: ר' יוסי קאי כוותך · דמוסף לא דחי אלא מעמד דמוסף ולא דמנחה: דידיה נמי לא דחי · תמי' וכי מוסף לא דחי מעמד שבמוסף: י"ח יום גומרין את ההלל ולא קתני ר"ח · לא יתחיל הלל בר"ח:

ובשבעה(עשר)(עלה)ואותו יום לא חשבינן אלא מכן ואילך חשיב מ' יום כ"ג דסיון שהוא מלא וי"ז בתמוז הרי מ' נמצא שבמ' ירד ושבר את הלוחות· מעת הוסר התמיד לתת שקוץ כלומר ביום שהוסר התמיד הקים צלם וכבר אמר בי"ז בטל התמיד (דכתיב עולה לליצנותא)כמ' באב נגזרה גזרה על אבותינו שלא יכנסו לארץ ובערב ט"ב חזרו מרגלים ולמחר קבעו ט"ב:דרך שלשת ימים הרי כ"ב דיום עשרים עצמו דאייר הוא מחשבון הג' ימים וכתיב עד חדש ימים דהיינו כ"ט ימים וחשוב ז' דאייר לפי שהוא חסר וכ"ב דסיון הרי החדש ימים ועדין נשתיירו ח' דסיון לפי שהוא מלא וכתיב ותסגר מרים שבעת ימים הרי כ"ט דסיון ובאותו יום עצמו שלח מרגלים וכתיב וישובו מקץ ארבעים יום חשוב ב' דסיון וכ"ט דתמוז הרי ל"א וח' דאב דאמרו דבערב

*) חסר כאן וצ"ל א"ל הכי קאמינא לך לא לדחי אלא דידיה ואמאי דחי וכו'.

הגהות הב"ח

(א) גמ' ואשתכח דהוה כתיב עליה אנת צבית לאחרובי ביתיה וידך אשלמת ליה: (ב) רש"י ד"ה מוסף כו' אין בו במנחה ולא קתני אין בו במוסף דלא: (ג) ד"ה ואתא ר' יוסי כו' אין בו בנעילה ואתא: (ד) [illegible] (ה) [illegible] (ו) תוס' ד"ה אמר כו' לא מברכינן [illegible] (ז) [illegible]

הגהות הגר"א

[א] גמ' אלא דמנחה ודנעילה ש"מ כו' · כצ"ל:

הגהות מהר"ב רנשבורג

א] רש"י ד"ה זאת אומרת וכו' אלא מנהגא כדלקמן מנהג וכו' · נ"ב הכל דבור אחד וק"ק:

אנת צבית לאחרובי ביתא ידך אשלימת ליה בתשעה באב נגזר על אבותינו שלא יכנסו לארץ מנלן דכתיב °ויהי בחדש הראשון בשנה השנית באחד לחדש הוקם המשכן ואמר מר *שנה ראשונה עשה משה את המשכן שניה הקים משה את המשכן ושלח מרגלים וכתיב °ויהי בשנה השנית בחדש השני בעשרים בחדש נעלה הענן מעל משכן העדות וכתיב °ויסעו מהר ה' דרך שלשת ימים אמר רבי חמא בר חנינא *אותו היום סרו מאחרי ה' וכתיב °והאספסוף אשר בקרבו התאוו תאוה וישובו ויבכו גם בני ישראל וגו' וכתיב °עד חדש ימים וגו' דהוו להו עשרין ותרתין בסיון וכתיב °ותסגר מרים שבעת ימים דהוו להו עשרין ותשעה בסיון וכתיב °שלח לך אנשים ותניא בעשרים ותשעה בסיון שלח משה מרגלים וכתיב °וישובו מתור הארץ מקץ ארבעים יום הני ארבעים יום נכי חד הוו אמר אביי *תמוז דההיא שתא מלויי מליוה דכתיב °קרא עלי מועד לשבור בחורי וכתיב °ותשא כל העדה ויתנו את קולם ויבכו העם בלילה ההוא *אמר רבה אמר ר' יוחנן (א) (*אותו היום ערב) תשעה באב היה אמר להם הקב"ה אתם בכיתם בכיה של חנם ואני קובע לכם בכיה לדורות חרב הבית בראשונה (ג) דכתיב °ובחדש החמישי בשבעה לחדש היא שנת תשע עשרה [שנה] למלך נבוכדנצר מלך בבל בא נבוזראדן רב טבחים עבד מלך בבל ירושלם וישרוף את בית ה' וגו' וכתיב °ובחדש החמישי בעשור לחדש היא שנת תשע עשרה [שנה] למלך *נבוכדנצר מלך בבל בא נבוזראדן רב טבחים עמד לפני מלך בבל בירושלם וגו' ותניא אי אפשר לומר בשבעה שהרי כבר נאמר בעשור ואי אפשר לומר בעשור שהרי כבר נאמר בשבעה הא כיצד בשבעה נכנסו נכרים להיכל ואכלו וקלקלו בו שביעי שמיני *ותשיעי סמוך לחשכה הציתו בו את האור והיה דולק והולך כל היום כולו *שנאמר °אוי לנו כי פנה היום כי ינטו צללי ערב והיינו דאמר רבי יוחנן (ג) אלמלי הייתי באותו הדור לא קבעתיו אלא בעשירי מפני שרובו של היכל בו נשרף ורבנן אתחלתא דפורענותא עדיפא ובשניה מנלן דתניא *מגלגלין זכות ליום זכאי וחובה ליום חייב אמרו [א] כשחרב בית המקדש בראשונה (ד) אותו היום ערב תשעה באב היה ומוצאי שבת היה ומוצאי שביעית היתה ומשמרתה של יהויריב היתה והלוים היו אומרי' שירה ועומדין על דוכנם ומה שירה היו אומרים °וישב עליהם את אונם וברעתם יצמיתם ולא הספיקו לומר יצמיתם ה' אלהינו עד שבאו נכרים וכבשום *וכן בשניה נלכדה ביתר גמרא *נחרשה העיר תניא *כשחרב טורנוסרופוס הרשע את ההיכל נגזרה גזרה על רבן גמליאל להריגה בא אדון אחד ועמד בבית המדרש ואמר בעל החוטם מתבקש בעל החוטם מתבקש שמע רבן גמליאל אזל טשא מינייהו אזל לגביה בצנעא א"ל אי מצילנא לך מייתית לי לעלמא דאתי א"ל הן א"ל אשתבע לי אשתבע ליה סליק לאיגרא נפיל ומית וגמירי דכי גזרי גזירתא ומית חד מינייהו מבטלי לגזרתייהו יצתה בת קול ואמרה אדון זה מזומן לחיי העולם הבא תנו רבנן משחרב הבית בראשונה נתקבצו כיתות כיתות של פרחי כהונה ומפתחות ההיכל בידן ועלו לגג ההיכל ואמרו לפניו רבונו של עולם הואיל ולא זכינו להיות גזברין נאמנים יהיו מפתחות מסורות לך וזרקום כלפי מעלה ויצתה כעין פיסת יד וקיבלתן מהם והם קפצו ונפלו לתוך האור ועליהן קונן ישעיהו הנביא °משא גיא חזיון מה לך איפוא כי עלית כולך לגגות תשואות מלאה עיר הומיה קריה עליזה חלליך לא חללי חרב ולא מתי מלחמה אף בהקב"ה נאמר °°מקרקר קיר ושוע אל ההר: משנכנס אב ממעטין בשמחה כו': אמר רב יהודה בריה דרב שמואל בר שילת משמיה דרב כשם שמשנכנס אב ממעטין בשמחה כך משנכנס אדר מרבין בשמחה

אמר

°) ישעיה כב °°) שם

רש"י

אנת צבית לאחרובי ביתיה וידך אשלימת ליה · הגלס אומר לחבירו אתה רצית להחריב ביתו של מקום שהטית ישראל אחריך ואני פשיתי בך נקמה ושלמתי לך ידי ל"א אנת צבית לאחרובי ביתא וידך [אשלים] לי לשון שאילת [כלים] כלומר ועלה בידי :. ואמר רבי חמא בר חנינא אותו היום וכו' · מהר לשון מהר עכשיו כשנסעו י"ט ימים מחדש אייר קודם עליית הענן פשו להו י' והנהו י' היו בין דרך שלשת ימים וז' דהסגרת מרים וחדש (ה) של כ"ט ימים שאכלו בשר הוה ל"ט והשתא אשתכח דמשה שלח מרגלים בכ"ט דסיון : הני ארבעים נכי חד · ב' מסיון וכ"ט מתמוז הוה ל"א וח' מאב הוה ל"ט : וחובה על ידי חייב · היינו תשעה באב דרגילין לבוא בו רעות : הכי גרסינן מגלגלין זכות ע"י זכאי : מוצאי שבת · יום ראשון : מוצאי שביעית · שמינית : דוכן · מקום עשוי כעין איצטבא ועליו לוים עומדין לשורר : וישב עליהם את אונם וברעתם יצמיתם ה' אלהינו · במזמור אל נקמות ה' והוא שיר של יום רביעי והאי דאמרי ליה ביום ראשון איליא בעלמא (ו) הוה דנפל בפומייהו כדאמרינן בערכין (דף יב·) פי' אילייא קינה שכן תרגום יונתן בן עוזיאל שא קינה (יחזקאל כח) טול אילייא וכמו אלי כבתולה חגורת שק על בעל נעוריה (יואל א) שפירושו קונני ובכי : נחרשה העיר · כדכתיב (מיכה ג) ציון שדה תחרש שנחרשה כולה ונעשית כשדה חרושה: בעל החוטם · בעל קומה וצורה ל"א גדול הדור : מתבקש · ליהרג ברמז אמר ליה שלא יכירו בו אנשי המלך : טשא · נחבא כמו טשו במערתא (שבת דף לג:) : אזל · האדון אצל רבן גמליאל בצנעא : ומית חד מינייהו · מן היועצין וכסבורין שאירע להן על שהרעו לגזור : גיא חזיון · ירושלים שהכל מסתכלין שם : מקרקר · לשון יללה : קיר ושוע · מקונן וזועק לשון הגה קול שועת בת עמי (ירמיה ה) קיר כמו קירי דבשחיטת חולין (דף *קלט:) : אל ההר · בשביל הר ציון ששמם : משנכנס אדר · ימי נסים היו לישראל פורים ופסח:

תוספות

(ז)דכתיב עד חדש ימים הוו להו כ"ב בסיון· פי' חשוב מעשרים ימים של ר"ח אייר עד סופו תמלא ט' ימים נמלא בכ' בסיון כ"ט ועד חדש. ימים· הוי שלשים ימים אם כן לפי זה תמלא מעשרים ושנים לחדש השני דזה אייר חדש שלם עד כ"ב דסיון וג' ימים שנסעו מהר ה' הרי ל"ג דל מינייהו ב' ימים דבעשרים בחדש נעלה הענן ואייתר להו שני ימים פשו כ"ג דל יומא מן שלשה שהאחד מן הג' ימים היה בכלל החדש (ח) שאייר חסר פש להו כ"ב* :

אמר אביי תמוז דההיא שתא מלויי מליוה · ועשו אותו משלשים ימים כדי שיכלו המ' ימים בתשעה באב שלשים יום דתמוז ואחד דסיון דבכ"ט שלח המרגלים ותשעה באב הרי ארבעים ימים וביום תשעה באב שבו המרגלים מתור הארץ : וישב עליהם את אונם וברעתם יצמיתם ולא הספיקו לומר יצמיתם ה' אלהינו עד שבאו האויבים וכו' · פי' באותו פסוק יש ב' פעמים יצמיתם ולא הספיקו לומר השני עד שבאו וכבשום ואומר ר"י *אע"ג דאין אותו פסוק כלל במזמור שיר של מול"ש אירע להם כך שאמרו אותו פסוק ובירושל' מפרש אילייא נקט פירוש אילייא הוי כמו אלי כבתולה דהוי לשון קינה כמו שקורין העולם ריאוכי"א בלע"ז :

מסורת הש"ס / עין משפט / הגהות

כו א טוש"ע או"ח סימן תקנא :

פי' מהרש"א

[סנהדרין סט: זבחים קיח: ערכין יג·]

[כל זה איתא בערכין יא: ומצבי רבא ואיתימא רב אבי איליא בעלמא ט'ן]

[נ"ל אותה לילה ליל וכן איתא בע"י]

[לפנינו בקרא נבוכדראצר]

נ"א של עשירי

ערכין יא:

תהלים צד

[ע"ש ברש"י ז"ע ולפנ"ד נ"ל כמו מקרקרן דבשחיטת חולין נג·]

[ר"ה יח:]

[כשחרש כצ"ל ועיין תי"ט]

גי' עין יעקב נחרשה העיר נמי נגמרא · תניא כשחרש כו' וכטור סי' תקמט מעתיק נחרשה העיר שחרש טורנוסרופוס כו'

רבינו חננאל

וה' דברים אירעו את אבותינו בט' באב נגזר על אבותינו שלא יכנסו לארץ מנא לן · דתניא בכ"ט בסיון שלח המרגלים הנה שני ימים העותרים בסיון ול' יום של תמוז שאיתה שנה תמוז מלא היה · כדכתיב קרא עלי מועד לשבור בחורי הרי ל"ב וח' ימים באב הרי מ' יום שלמים · נמצאו שהגיעו ט' באב . אמר רבא אותו היום ט' באב היה והיו ישראל יושבים ובוכים · אמר הקב"ה אתם בכיתם בכיה של חנם אני אקבע לכם בכיה לדורות · חרב הבית בראשונה שנאמר בחודש החמישי בעשור לחדש בא נבוזראדן וגו' וכתיב קרא אחרי' וישרוף את בית ה' ואת בית המלך וכתיב קרא אחרינא בחדש החמישי בשבעה לחדש היא שנת תשע עשרה בא נבוזראדן רב טבחים עבד מלך בבל וישרוף את בית ה' ואת בית המלך · אי אפשר לומר בשבעה שכבר נאמר בעשרה ואי אפשר לומר בעשרה שכבר נאמר וכו' ואכלו ושתו וקרקרו עד ט' בו בערב (באב) הציתו סמוך לחשכה והיה דולק והולך כל היום שנא' אוי לנו כי פנה היום כי ינטו צללי ערב· א"ר יוחנן אלמלא הייתי באותו הדור לא קבעתיו אלא בעשירי מפני שרובו של היכל בעשירי נשרף · ותנא דידן תחלת פורענותא עדיפא · ובשניה דתניא ר' יוסי אומר מגלגלין זכות ליום זכאי וחובה ליום חייב . כשחרב הבית בראשונה ט' באב היה ומ"ש ומוצאי שביעית היתה ומשמרת יהויריב היתה כו' · נלכדה ביתר ונחרשה העיר נמרא · פי' שאמר הנביא

לתת

הגהות הב"ח

(א) שם אותו היום ערב · תא"מ וכ"כ ס"א אותו היום תשעה באב היה : (ב) שם חרב בית בראשונה מנלן דכתיב וכתיב: (ג) שם דאמר ר' יוחנן אלמלי· כ"כ ע' ר"ש סקולא עומד כתוס' ד"ה אלמלא: (ד) שם כשחרב בהמ"ק בראשונה (אותו היום ערב ת"ב היה) תא"מ וכ"כ ס"א אותו היום תשעה באב היה: (ה) רש"י ד"ה אמר רבי חמא כו' וחדש של כ"ט ימים · כ"כ מפרש"י מבואר דמפרש עד חדש ימים וגו חדש של לבנה דהיינו כ"ט י"ב תשצ"ג ונמצא שלשה ימים שסרו הן כ' וכ"א וכ"ב מאייר כשאכלו שבעה מאייר וכ"ב מסיון שבו כלה חדש ימים שאכלו בשר דהיינו כ"ט יום עוד ס"ל לרש"י דהמרגלים באו בסוף שמיני לאב שהרי ל"ל ט' בכו בכיה של חנם והוקבע לדורות אבל התוס' נחלקו עליו וס"ל דעד חדש ימים וגו' הוא חדש שלם של שלשים יום שלמים ונדחקו לפרש דיום ג' שסרו דהיינו כ"ב מאייר נחשב לכאן ולכאן דיום הג' שסרו הוא עצמו היום הראשון מהחדש שאכלו בשר ועוד נחלקו וס"ל דכ"ט דסיון שבו שלח מרגלים אינו מחשב בחשבון מ' יום דמרגלים אלא הוא נחשב מז' ימים דהסגרת מרים ולא נשאו המרגלים רגליהם אלא ביום ל' דסיון ולפי זה צריך לפרש דלא שבו המרגלים אלא בט' באב בסוף היום בכו בכיה של חנם ונקבע עליהם בכיה לדורות כי לעת הערב סמוך לחשיכה הציתו בו האש ולפי זה לא גרסינן אותו היום ערב תשעה באב היה כו' אלא ה"ג אותו היום ט' באב היה: (ו) ד"ה וישב כו' אילייא בעלמא הוא דנפל: (ז) תוס' ד"ה וכתיב כו' מעשרים ימים של חדש אייר וכו' הוי שלשים יום א"כ: (ח) בא"ד היה בכלל החדש פש להו כ"ב כצ"ל ותיבות שאייר חסר נמחק:

רבינו גרשום

דבערב ט"ב חזרו א"כ לא הוו בדרך אלא מ' נכי חדא וקרא אמר ארבעים : תמוז מליוה ואיכא ל' דתמוז נמצא בערב ט"ב מ' מלאים ולמחר קבעי לט"ב . קרא עלי מועד שקבעו תמוז של שלשים . וחובה ע"י חייב לפי שבט"ב היה כבר חייב ששרף בו בראשונה . כשחרש משמע נחרש : בעל החוטם כלומר עין שבהם חשוב שבהם . רבפלי קצרי · לכבס ולגלח מאי כבוד שבת איכא במאי ולבוש בחמישי אלא לאו להניח וללבוש בשבת דהיינו כבוד שבת טעמא דבחמישי לפי שהוא קרוב לשבת אבל שאר יומי אפילו להניח וקשיא לרב התנא :

הגהות מהר"י לנדא א] גמ' כשחרב בכמ"ק בראשונה אותו היום תשעה באב היה כצ"ל :

אמר רב פפא *הלכך בר ישראל דאית ליה דינא בהדי נכרי לישתמיט מיניה באב דריע מזליה ולימצי נפשיה באדר *דבריא מזליה °לתת לכם אחרית ותקוה אמר רב יהודה בריה דרב שמואל בר שילת משמיה דרב אלו דקלים וכלי פשתן °ויאמר ראה ריח בני כריח שדה אשר ברכו ה' אמר רב יהודה בריה דרב שמואל בר שילת משמיה דרב כריח שדה של תפוחים: שבת שחל תשעה באב להיות בתוכה אסורין לספר ולכבס: אמר רב נחמן לא שנו אלא לכבס וללבוש אבל לכבס ולהניח מותר ורב ששת אמר אפילו לכבס ולהניח אסור אמר רב ששת תדע דבטלי קצרי דבי רב [illegible] (א)*בחמישי מותרים מפני כבוד השבת למאי אילימא לכבס וללבוש מאי כבוד שבת איכא אלא להניח ובחמישי הוא דשרי אבל השבת כולה אסור לעולם לכבס וללבוש וכשאין לו אלא חלוק אחד *דאמר רב אסי א"ר יוחנן ג'מי שאין לו אלא חלוק אחד מותר לכבסו בחולו של מועד איתמר נמי אמר רבי בנימין אמר ר' אלעזר לא שנו אלא לכבס וללבוש אבל להניח מותר מיתיבי ד'אסור לכבס לפני תשעה באב אפילו להניח לאחר תשעה באב וגיהוץ שלנו ככיבוס שלהן וכלי פשתן אין בהם משום גיהוץ תיובתא ה'שלח רב יצחק בר גיורי משמיה דרבי יוחנן אע"פ שאמרו כלי פשתן אין בהן משום גיהוץ אבל אסור ללובשן בשבת שחל תשעה באב להיות בתוכה אמר רב לא שנו אלא לפניו ו'אבל לאחריו מותר ושמואל אמר אפילו לאחריו נמי אסור מיתיבי שבת שחל תשעה באב להיות בתוכה אסור לספר ולכבס ובחמישי מותרין מפני כבוד השבת כיצד חל להיות באחד בשבת מותר לכבס כל השבת כולה בשני בשלישי ברביעי ובחמישי לפניו אסור לאחריו מותר חל להיות בערב שבת מותר לכבס בחמישי מפני כבוד השבת ואם לא כבס בחמישי בשבת מותר לכבס בערב שבת מן המנחה ולמעלה *לייט עלה אביי ואיתימא רב אחא בר יעקב אהא *חל להיות בשני ובחמישי קורין שלשה ומפטיר אחד בשלישי וברביעי קורא אחד ומפטיר אחד רבי יוסי אומר ולעולם קורין [illegible] דתניא *ז'תשעה באב שחל להיות בשבת וכן ערב תשעה באב שחל להיות בשבת אוכל ושותה כל צרכו ומעלה על שולחנו אפילו כסעודת שלמה בשעתו ואסור לספר ולכבס מר"ח ועד התענית דברי רבי מאיר רבי יהודה אומר כל החדש כולו אסור רשב"ג אומר אינו אסור אלא אותה שבת בלבד ותניא אידך ונוהג אבל מראש חדש ועד התענית דברי ר' מאיר רבי יהודה אומר כל החדש כולו אסור רשב"ג אומר אינו אסור אלא אותה שבת בלבד אמר ר' יוחנן ושלשתן מקרא אחד דרשו דכתיב °והשבתי כל משושה חגה חדשה ושבתה מאן דאמר מר"ח ועד התענית מחגה

תורה אור: ירמיה כט · בראשית כז · הושע ב

רש"י

ניזיל בהדיה · בערכאות שלהן: *ונתתי לכם אחרית ותקוה · איידי דאיירי רב יהודה לעיל נקיט ואזיל: דקלים · להתפרנס מהן שיש מהן בבבל הרבה כדאמרינן בפ"ק (דף ט:) עולא איקלע לבבל חזה מלא צנא דתמרי כו': כלי פשתן · ללבוש: לא שנו · במתני' שכל השבוע אסור לכבס: אפילו לכבס ולהניח · כדי שילבוש לאחר זמן לאחר ט' באב אסור דנראה כמסיח דעתו שעוסק בכיבוס בגדים: אמר רב ששת תדע · דאפי' לכבס ולהניח אסור: קצרי · כך שמם *בלשון ישמעאל והם כובסין שמעתי אומרים על שם שמקצרין בגדי צמר כשדורסין אותן ברגליהן במים שקורין פורלוי"ר והיינו דמתרגמינן עין רוגל (שמואל ב יז) עינא דקצרא: אילימא לכבס וללבוש · מיד בחמישי מאי כבוד שבת איכא: אלא · לאו לכבס ולהניח עד השבת: לעולם לכבס וללבוש · מיד בחמישי (ב): וכמי שאין לו אלא חלוק אחד · דאין לו להחליף ומאי מפני כבוד השבת דחי [illegible] מכבס השתא בחמישי תו לא מצי לכבס ליה: (ג)חולו של מועד · שאין לו אלא חלוק אחד דלא סגיא דלא מכבס מפני הכנימה ואפי' כיבס לפני המועד מותר לכבסה במועד: וגיהוץ שלנו · אינו יפה אלא ככיבוס שלהן ואסור נגהן לפני תשעה באב אפילו להניח לאחר תשעה באב אבל כיבוס שלנו מותר: כלי פשתן אין בהן · ליאסר משום גיהוץ אלא בכלי מילת לושקי"ש בלע"ז: לא שנו · שאסור ללובשו בשבוע שחל תשעה באב להיות בתוכה אלא בימים שלפני תשעה באב שאם חל ביום רביעי אסור ללובשו ראשון ושני ושלישי: אבל לאחריו · חמישי ושביעי א] ובשישי מותר: חל להיות באחד בשבת מותר לכבס כל השבת כולה · דהיינו לאחריו: חל להיות בשני או בשלישי ברביעי ובחמישי כו': לייט עלה אביי ואיתימא רב אחא בר יעקב אהא · המכבס בתשעה באב אפילו מן המנחה ולמעלה ואדקאי בברייתא מפסיק לה למילתא וקאמר לייט עלה אביי [illegible] דההיא ברייתא גופה היא: ומפטיר · (ה) מאותן שלשה אחרון מפטיר מתוך שאין מוסיפין בחול יותר מג' אנשים ולא כר"ח על ד' שאין לנו להוסיף אלא בשבת וי"ט כדמפרש במגילה (דף כא·) ולפיכך קורין ג' דזמן ספר תורה הוא וכלאו הכי הוו קרו שלשה שהוא מתקנת עזרא לקרות בשני ובחמישי כהן ולוי וישראל: קורא אחד ומפטיר אחד · אחד קורא והוא עצמו המפטיר קתני מיהת לאחריו מותר תיובתא דשמואל: וכן ערב תשעה באב שחל להיות בשבת · *אינו מפסיק סעודתו ואינו ממעט בתבשילין אלא אוכל כל צרכו ומעלה על שולחנו אפי' כסעודת שלמה בשעתו דפלוגתא היא במסכת גיטין בפרק [מי שאחזו] (דף סח:) דאיכא למאן דאמר מלך והדיוט ומלך ואיכא למ"ד מלך והדיוט כלומר כשנטרד שוב לא חזר למלכותו לפיכך הולך לומר בשעתו בעת מלכו ותקפו שהיה אוכל הוא ושריו ס' כור סולת כו': ועד התענית · אלמא דסבירא ליה לרבי מאיר לפניו אסור לאחריו מותר ורבי יהודה ורבן (*גמליאל) סבירא להו דאפילו לאחריו נמי אסור: [נ"ל שמעון בן גמליאל]

תוספות

אמר רב פפא הלכך האי בר ישראל דאית ליה דינא בהדי נכרי לישתמיט וכו' · פירוש משום דאמר לעיל מגלגלין חובה ליום החייב: של תפוחים · י"מ תפוחים *כריח אתרוגים: קצרי דבי רב · פירוש כובסין הבגדים ולכך קרי להו קצרי על שם שמקצרין הבגדים ע"י רחילת המים: מי שאין לו אלא חלוק אחד מותר לכבס במועד · (*ובטבול יום) ובפ' אלו מגלחין (מו"ק דף יד·) דקאמר וליטעמיך הא דאמר רבי אבי אמר רבי יוחנן מי שאין לו אלא חלוק אחד וכו' דפריך יאמרו כל החלוקים אסורים לכבס בחול המועד וחלוק זה מותר ומתרץ זה אזורו מוכיח עליו שאין לו אלא חלוק אחד וא"כ דוקא להם אבל לנו ודאי אסור אפי' אין לנו אלא חלוק אחד שאין אנו אוגדין אזור על חלוקות שלנו ולא הוי אזורו מוכיח עליו וכן צריך ליזהר שלא לכבס המלכפת בחול המועד אע"ג שאין לנו אלא אחת אבל מ"מ יש נגשים לכבס בגדי התינוקות כדי לשכוב דהוי כמי שאין לו אלא חלוק אחד שיש רגילות להחליף בגדיהם וכל שעה צריך לו כל בגדיו ועל זה נהגו העולם לכבסם בחול המועד:

בשני ובחמישי קורין שלש ומפטיר אחד · מכאן מוכיח רבינו תם דמפטיר עולה למנין שבעה מדקאמר קורין שלש ומפטיר אחד שמפטיר אחד מן הג' דקא מיבעיא ליה במגילה (דף כג· ושם) מפטיר עולה למנין שבעה או לא משמע מהכא דעולה ותרוייהו

עין משפט נר מצוה

כו א טוש"ע א"ח סימן תקנא סעיף א:

[עי' תוס' שבת פה·ד"ה פריו קודם]

כח ב מיי' פ"ז מהל' י"ט הלכה כא סמג לאוין עה טוש"ע שם סימן תקלד סעיף א:

[נ"ל ובחולין דף קז:]

כט ג ד מיי' פ"ה מהל' תענית הלכה ו סמג עשין מד"ס ג טוש"ע שם סימן תקנא סעיף ג:

ל ה מיי' שם טוש"ע שם סעיף ד:

לא ו מיי' פי"ב מהל' תפלה הלכה טו טור א"ח סימן תקנט:

לב ז מיי' פ"ה מהל' תענית הלכה ח טוש"ע א"ח סימן תקנב סעיף י:

[לעיל טו:]

מ"ק יד· יח· חולין קז:

רבינו חננאל

לתת לכם אחרית ותקוה · אמרינן משמיה דרב אלו דקלין וכלי פשתן · ראה ריח בני כריח שדה · כריח שדה של תפוחין: בגדים מגוהצין אסור ללובשן בשבת שחל ט' באב להיות בתוכה עד יום תענית ואפילו הן בגדים של פשתן. פי' גיהוץ בלשון ישמעאל צקל והוא מעברי ליה תומרתא (כתובות יז:) שבת שחל להיות ט' באב בתוכה אסור לספר ולכבס · ובחמישי מותר [illegible] איקימנא בזמן שחל ט' באב בע"ש בה' שמקודם יום ט' באב התירו לו לכבס וללבוש כשאין לו אלא חלוק אחד ומותר לכבס אפילו בחוש"מ. כבוס*) חלוקת רב נחמן ורב ששת היא וקיי"ל בהא כרב ששת דא' אפילו לכבס ולהניח אחר ט' באב אסור תדע דקא בטלי קצרי דבי רב ומותבינן מהא דתניא אסור לכבס לפני ט' באב ואפילו להניח לאחר ט' באב וגיהוץ של בני ארץ בבל כבוס של בני א"י · וכלי פשתן אין בהן משום גיהוץ · אבל אסור ללובשן בשבת שחל ט' באב להיות בתוכה: [שבת שחל ט"ב להיות בתוכה] אסורין לספר ולכבס ובחמישי מותרין מפני כבוד השבת כיצד חל להיות באחד בשבת מותרין לכבס כל השבת כולה חל להיות ט' באב בב' או בג' או בד' או בה' לפניו אסור לאחריו מותר · חל ט' באב להיות בע"ש מותרין לכבס בחמישי · פי' מי שאין לו אלא חלוק אחד ואם לא כיבס בה' יכבס בע"ש בט' באב עצמו מן המנחה ולמעלה · לייט אביי מי שהצריך ודחק עצמו לכך · ובקריאת הספר קיי"ל כר' יוסי דאמר לעולם קורין ג' בט' באב ומפטיר

*) נראה דצ"ל וכבוס להניח לאחר ת"ב.

מסורת הש"ס

[נ"ל לאו]

[גירסת רא"ש דתקיף מזלי"]

[ע' ב"ק קיט: ובפרש"י שם]

[קדושין לג: וש"נ]

[מגילה כב:]

עירובין מ:

[עי' נא"מ בא"ח סי' תקנב ס"ק יב כוונת רש"י במ"ש אינו מפסיק סעודתו]

הגהות הב"ח

(א) גמ' ובחמישי מותרין מפני כבוד השבת מאי מותרין אילימא לכבס כו' אלא [illegible] השבת כולה: (ב) רש"י ד"ה לעולם כו' מיד בחמישי וכמי שאין לו כו' כד"ל: (ג) ד"ה בחולו של מועד דכיון שאין לו אלא חלוק אחד לא סגי דלא מכבס ליה מפני הכנימה: (ד) ד"ה ומפטיר אחד מאותן שלש:

הגהות הגר"א

[א] רש"י ד"ה אבל ושביעי · רשום קו עליו (למחקו):

רבינו גרשום

לעולם לכבס וללבוש בחמישי ודאמרת מאי כבוד שבת איכא דלית ליה אלא אותו חלוק ולא מצי למשתרך עד שבת והיינו כבוד שבת דמכבס ליה ולהכי שאר יומי אסור אבל להניח לא הוי אסור וגיהוץ שלנו אסור · לייט עלה אביי במאן דכבים בע"ש בט' באב מן המנחה ולמעלה קורין ג' הואיל וכל חמישי ושני קורין ג' ומפטיר אסוף אסיפה תיובתא דשמואל הא דקתני מותר לכבס כל השבוע ושמואל אמר

הגהות מהר"ב רנשבורג א] רש"י ד"ה אבל לאחריו וכו' ושביעי · נמחק מלת ושביעי:

רש"י

מתגה · כלומר יליף טעמא מן חגה דהיינו ר"ח שנקרא חג כדאמרי' לעיל (דף כט·) קרא עלי מועד : הלכה כר"מ · דלפניו אסור ולאחריו מותר: הלכה כרבן שמעון בן גמליאל · דאין איסור נוהג אלא באותה שבת: תרוייהו לקולא · כדמפרש ואזיל דכלפניו מוקי הלכה כר"מ דלפניו ולא לאחריו ובאותה שבת אבל קודם אותה שבת אפילו לפניו מותר : משש שעות ולמטה · כלפי השחר: המפסיק בה · דשוב אינו אוכל עוד מאותה סעודה והילך : ה"ג כיצד ישנה א"ר יהודה אם הוא רגיל כו' : בעשרה · שהיו סועדין עמו לכבודו : וחכ"א ישנה · אשני תבשילין קיימי (א) בשר ויין ימעט : מליח · דג או בשר מליח דאין בו טעם כל כך אחר ששהה שלשה ימים במלח כדלקמן (ב) כשלמים והנותר מבשר זבח השלמים וגו' שפי לא אשכחן דמקרי בשר : כל שהוא משום ט' באב · כגון סעודה המפסיק בה : כל שאינו משום ט"ב · כגון סעודה המפסיק בה בתענית צבור אי נמי סעודה שאינו מפסיק בה : ה"ג ר' ישמעאל בר' יוסי אומר משום אביו כל שעה שמותר לאכול מותר לרחוץ ולא גרסינן בשר כלומר אפי' בשעת סעודה המפסיק מותר לרחוץ הואיל ומותר לאכול : אסור באכילה ובשתיה · הני אין נוהגין באבל דקא חשיב נמי איסורים שנוהגין בו לבד מהני דנהיגי באבל רחיצה סיכה ונעילה כו' : ואסור לקרות בתורה כו' · דכתיב בהו משמחי לב (ג) : במקום שאינו רגיל לקרות · דכיון דלא ידע אית ליה צערא : עד כמה · הוי בשר גמור דלא הוי בשר מליח כל זמן שהוא כשלמים שלא שהה במלחו אלא שני ימים ולילה אחד כזמן אכילת שלמים והכי נקט כשלמים דבזמן אכילת שלמים אשכחן דאקרי בשר דכתיב (ויקרא ז) והנותר מבשר זבח השלמים וגו' טפי לא אשכחן דמקרי בשר שהטעם נפסל אחרי ב' וג' ימים : יין מגתו · חדש ומתוק ואינו טוב כיין ישן ומשלשל ומזיק : תוסס · רותח : אין בו משום גילוי · שאין נחש שותהו כי יברח מרתיחתו :

תוספות

ותרוייהו לקולא · כלומר תרוייהו כדר"מ דאמר מר"ח ועד התענית וכרשב"ג דאמר אינו אסור אלא אותה שבת בלבד הלכה כתרוייהו לקולא כלומר דאינו אסור אלא אותה שבת בלבד כרשב"ג ודוקא [עד] התענית אבל לאחר התענית מותר דהלכה כר"מ דאמר דאינו אסור אלא עד התענית ואע"ג דשלחו משמיה דר' יוחנן דכלי פשתן מותר לכבס במועד מ"מ החמיר לנו מורינו רש"י לאחר סדינין שלנו לכבס אותה שבוע שהיה בה ט"ב קודם התענית [ג] אבל היכא דחל ט"ב בה' בשבת מותר לכבס ולספר מחלות ואילך מפני כבוד השבת דאין להמתין עד ערב שבת מפני טורח השבת° :

ערב ט"ב לא יאכל אדם ב' תבשילין · פירוש ב' תבשילין ר"ל בשתי קדירות כגון שקורין העולם אכלנו ב' מינים שקורין מיישו"ן אבל אין לאסור לאכול תבשיל שעושין מבללים ומגבינה ומבילים דאע"ג דאין רגילין העולם לאכול בללים חיין כדאמר בעירובין (ד' כט·) אכל בלל והשכים ומת וכו' שקשין לכל גופו של אדם כחרבות אעפ"כ מאחר שאין עושין מהם תבשיל בעצמו אם לא ישימו (ד) או שומן או שום דבר שנותן בהם טעם אינו קרוי תבשיל כדי לאסור הבילים שמשימין עמהם אבל מן גבינה המבושל בקדירה אין חששא לאכול דכל דבר שהוא נאכל כמו שהוא חי כמו חלב כמו גבינה כמו תפוחים אין בהם תורת בשול כלל וכלל : **ואם** היה רגיל לסעוד בעשרה יסעוד בחמשה · צריך למעט בכבודו : **ואע"ג** דקאמר הש"ס דבשר מליח מותר כל זמן שאינו כשלמים כלומר שעבר יותר מב' ימים משחיטתו אפ"ה לדידן אסור לאכול בשר אפי' מלוח מזמן מרובה כיון דאנו רגילים לאכול בשר מליח וכן צריך למעט בשתייתו שאם היה רגיל לשתות עשרה כוסות מסכר או ממשקה אחר לא ישתה כי אם חמשה וצריך לשנות מקומו שהוא רגיל לאכול בו כמו שהיה מנהגו של רבי יהודה בר' אילעאי שישב ואכל ערב ט"ב בין התנור לכיריים מקום שהיה מנוול :

גמרא

תורה אור

מתגה ומ"ד כל החדש כולו אסור מחרשה ומ"ד כל השבת כולה אסור משבתה אמר רבא הלכה כרשב"ג ואמר רבא הלכה כרבי מאיר ותרוייהו לקולא וצריכא דאי אשמועינן הלכה כר' מאיר הוה אמינא אפי' מר"ח קמ"ל הלכה כרשב"ג ואי אשמועינן הלכה כרשב"ג הוה אמינא אפילו לאחריו קמ"ל הלכה כרבי מאיר : ערב תשעה באב לא יאכל אדם ב' תבשילין כו' : אמר רב יהודה לא שנו אלא משש שעות ולמעלה אבל משש שעות ולמטה מותר ואמר רב יהודה לא שנו אלא בסעודה המפסיק בה אבל בסעודה שאינו מפסיק בה מותר °ותרוייהו לקולא וצריכא דאי אשמעינן בסעודה המפסיק בה הוה אמינא אפי' משש שעות ולמטה קמ"ל משש שעות ולמעלה ואי אשמעינן משש שעות ולמעלה הוה אמינא אפי' בסעודה שאינו מפסיק בה קמ"ל בסעודה המפסיק בה תניא כלישנא קמא תניא כלישנא בתרא תניא כלישנא בתרא הסועד ערב תשעה באב אם עתיד לסעוד סעודה אחרת מותר לאכול בשר ולשתות יין ואם לאו אסור לאכול בשר ולשתות יין תניא כלישנא קמא ערב תשעה באב לא יאכל אדם שני תבשילין לא יאכל בשר ולא ישתה יין רבן שמעון בן גמליאל אומר ישנה אמר רבי יהודה כיצד משנה אם היה רגיל לאכול שני תבשילין יאכל מין אחד ואם היה רגיל לסעוד בעשרה בני אדם סועד בחמשה היה רגיל לשתות עשרה כוסות שותה חמשה כוסות במה דברים אמורים משש שעות ולמעלה אבל משש שעות ולמטה מותר תניא אידך ערב תשעה באב לא יאכל אדם שני תבשילין לא יאכל בשר ולא ישתה יין דברי ר"מ וחכ"א ישנה וממעט בבשר וביין כיצד ממעט אם היה רגיל לאכול ליטרא בשר יאכל חצי ליטרא היה רגיל לשתות לוג יין ישתה חצי לוג יין ואם אינו רגיל כל עיקר אסור רשב"ג אומר אם היה רגיל לאכול צנון או מליח אחר סעודתו הרשות בידו תניא אידך כל שהוא משום תשעה באב אסור לאכול בשר ואסור לשתות יין ואסור לרחוץ כל שאינו משום ט"ב מותר לאכול בשר ולשתות יין ואסור לרחוץ ר' ישמעאל בר' יוסי אומר משום אביו כל שעה שמותר לאכול [א] בשר מותר לרחוץ ת"ר כל מצות הנוהגות באבל נוהגות בט' באב [ב]אסור באכילה ובשתיה *ובסיכה ובנעילת הסנדל ובתשמיש המטה ואסור לקרות בתורה בנביאים ובכתובים ולשנות במשנה בתלמוד ובמדרש ובהלכות ובאגדות אבל קורא הוא במקום שאינו רגיל לקרות ושונה במקום שאינו רגיל לשנות וקורא בקינות באיוב ובדברים הרעים שבירמיה ותינוקות של בית רבן *)[ג]בטלין משום שנאמר °פקודי ה' ישרים משמחי לב ר' יהודה אומר אף אינו קורא במקום שאינו רגיל לקרות ואינו שונה במקום שאינו רגיל לשנות אבל קורא הוא באיוב ובקינות ובדברים הרעים שבירמיהו ותינוקות של בית רבן בטלים בו משום שנאמר פקודי ה' ישרים משמחי לב : לא יאכל בשר ולא ישתה יין : תנא *[ד]אבל אוכל הוא בשר מליח ושותה יין מגתו בשר מליח עד כמה אמר רב חיננא בר כהנא משמיה דשמואל [ה]כל זמן (*שאינו) כשלמים ויין מגתו עד כמה כל זמן שהוא תוסס תנא **)[ו]יין תוסס אין בו משום גילוי [ז]וכמה תסיסתו ג' ימים אמר רב [ח]כך היה מנהגו של רבי יהודה ברבי אילעאי ערב תשעה באב מביאין לו פת חריבה במלח ויושב בין

*) [גירס' הרי"ף והרא"ש אינן בטילין בו דברי ר"מ ר' יהודה אומר אף אינו קורא במקום וכו' ותינוקות של בית רבן בטילין בו משום שנאמר פקודי ה' ישרים משמחי לב ועי' טור א"ח ר"ס תקנד] **) [סנהדרין ע. ע"ז ל· תוספתא תרומות פ"ז]

עין משפט נר מצוה

לג א מיי' פ"ה מהל' תענית הלכה ו סמג עשין ג טוש"ע א"ח סימן תקנב סעיף א וסעיף ט:

לד ב מיי' שם הלכה י סמג שם טוש"ע שם סי' תקנד סעיף א :

לה ג ד מיי' שם הלכה ז סמג שם (טוש"ע שם סי' תקנב סעיף ב):

לו ה ו מיי' פ"א מהל' רוצח ושמירת נפש הלכה ח סמג עשין לט וטור י"ד סימן קטז :

[עי' ב"י בא"ח סי' תקנא מה שתמה על דברי תוס' אלו]

לז ז מיי' פ"ה מהל' תענית הלכה ט טוש"ע א"ח סימן תקנב סעיף ו :

רבינו חננאל

ומספיר אחר · ואסיקנא הלכתא (כר' יוחנן) כרשב"ג דאמר אינו נוהג אלא אותה שבת בלבד שחל ט' באב להיות בתוכה · והלכתא כר' מאיר דאמר עד התענית · אבל לאחר התענית שאר א) שבוע מותר · וזהו פי' הלכתא כתרוייהו לקולא : ערב ט' באב לא יאכל ב' תבשילין כו' ואפילו אורז ועדשים · אבל אוכל תבשיל אחד בלבד שלא יהיה אותו תבשיל בשר ואם הוא בשר בן ג' ימים מותר · דא' כל בשר שאינו כשלמים בן ב' ימים ולילה אחד כדכתיב ביום זבחכם יאכל וממחרת וגו' אינו קרוי בשר אלא מליח ויין תוסס נמי כגון שנסחט בתוך ג' ימים מותר שאינו עדיין יין · אמר רב יהודה אמר רב ל"ש לא יאכל ב' תבשילין ולא יאכל בשר ולא ישתה יין בערב ט' באב משעה שיעברו שש שעות מן היום כגון שיקבע סעודתו משעה שביעית ולמעלה · והני מילי בסעודה שהוא מפסיק בה כלומר בתענית · אבל אם ברעתו לאכול עדיין פעם אחרת או קודם שעה ששית מותר ב) (מתשתא מיברדי) · הני מילי פשוטות הן . רשבג"א אם היה רגיל לאכול אחר סעודתו צנון או מלח הרשות בידו : ת"ר כל שהוא משום ט' באב אסור לאכול בשר ולשתות יין ואסור לרחוץ ג) משעה שאסור לאכול אסור לרחוץ . ואע"ג דתנינן נוהג אבל עד התענית ואמרינן הלכתא אבל אסור לרחוץ כל גופו בין בחמין בין בצונן כל ז' אבל פניו ידיו ורגליו בחמין אסור בצונן מותר · הא גרסינן בפסחים פרק מקום שנהגו (דף נד:) אין בין ט' באב ליוה"כ כו' מסייע ליה לר' אלעזר דאסור לארם שירשים אצבעו במים בט' באב כדרך שאסור ביוה"כ . אע"ג דמותבינן עליה הא משני רב פפא חסורי לא קתני · וגרסינן בפ' יוה"כ (יומא עח·) מטפחת היה לו לריב"ל (ביוה"כ) [עיוה"כ] מקנח פניו ידיו ורגליו לטהר מעבירה ע"ג עיניו ואינו חושש. ערב ט' באב שורה במים ועושה כמין כלים נגובים למחר מעביר ע"ג עיניו ואינו חושש ש"מ מהני כלהו דרחיצת פניו ידיו ורגליו בט' באב אפילו בצונן אסור אלא אם היו מטונפות : ת"ר כל מצות הנוהגות באבל נוהגות בט' באב · אסור ברחיצה ובסיכה ובנעילת הסנדל ובתשמיש המטה · שלח רב ד) הגאון בלשון הזה יהא בנדוי כל מי שעושה אחת מכל אלו בט' באב כל היום ואסור לקרות בתורה בנביאים ובכתובים ולשנות במשנה בתלמוד כו' · ר' יהודה ה) אומר אינו קורא אלא במקום שאינו רגיל לקרות מפני שצער הוא לו וקורא באיוב ובקינות פי' איכה ובדברים הרעים שבירמיה ותינוקות של בית רבן בטלים משום פקודי ה' ישרים משמחי לב · תנא יין תוסס אין בו משום גילוי · וכמה תסיסתו ג' ימים לפיכך בערב ט' באב מותר :

א) אולי צ"ל כל שאר ימי השבוע מותר . ב) אולי צ"ל מחלוקת ר"מ וחכמים פשוטות הן . ג) אולי צ"ל ר' ישמעאל בר"י אמר משעה שמותר לאכול מותר לרחוץ . ד) אולי צ"ל רב האי גאון . ה) נראה דצ"ל ר' יהודה אומר אף אינו קורא במקום שאינו רגיל וכו' .

רבינו גרשום

אבל לאחריו נמי אסור: מתגה מה חגה ח' ימים אף כיעום שמחה ח' ימים : ותרוייהו לקולא הלכה כר"מ דאמר אין אסור אלא עד התענית והלכה כרשב"ג דאין איסור אלא אותה שבת והוא שלפני ט' באב : בסעודה המפסיק סעודה אחרונה שמקבל עליו תענית · אבל בסעודה שאין מפסיק כגון סעודה שאוכל קודם לכן שעדיין יאכל אחריה . כל שהוא משום ת"ב היינו ט' באב עצמו כל שאינו משום ת"ב שאר תעניות . קורא הוא במקום שאינו רגיל לקרות לפי שמצטער : כל זמן שהוא כשלמים שני ימים ולילה אחד אינו אוכל בערב ת"ב אבל אחר כן אוכל שבטל מתורת בשר.

הגהות הב"ח

(א) רש"י ד"ה ותכ"א ישנה אשני תבשילין קיימי אבל בשר ויין : (ב) ד"ה מליח כו' כדלקמן הס"ד והשאר נמחק : (ג) ד"ה ואסור לקרות כו' משמחי לב במקום שהוא רגיל הס"ד : (ד) תוס' ד"ה ערב כו' אם לא ישימו בו שומן או :

הגהות הגר"א

[א] גמרא כל שעה שמותר לאכול (בשר) תו"מ (וכן מחקו רש"י וכן בתוספתא ליתא) : [ב] שם ותינוקות של ב"ר אינן בטלין ר' יהודה כו' · כצ"ל (וכ"ה ברי"ף ורא"ש וכא"ז וגירסתם כת"ק דברי ר"מ וכ"ד הפוסקים שפסקו כר' יהודה) : [ג] תוס' סד"ה ותרוייהו · (אבל היכא כו' עד טורח השבת) תא"מ (וכבר תמה הב"י ע"ז) :

לח א מיי' פ"ה מהל' תענית הל' י סמג עשין ג טוש"ע א"ח סי' תקנד סעיף כב:
לט ב מיי' שם טוש"ע שם סעיף כד:
מ ג ד טוש"ע שם סעיף כה:
מא ה מיי' פ"ה מהל' אבל הלכה יא טור י"ד סימן שפו:

בין תנור לכיריים ואוכל ושותה עליה קיתון של מים ודומה כמי שמתו מוטל לפניו תנן התם *מקום שנהגו לעשות מלאכה בט' באב עושין מקום שנהגו שלא לעשות אין עושין ובכל מקום ת"ח בטלים רשב"ג אומר לעולם יעשה כל אדם עצמו כתלמיד חכם תניא נמי הכי רשב"ג אומר לעולם יעשה אדם עצמו כתלמיד חכם כדי שיתענה תניא אידך *רשב"ג אומר כל האוכל ושותה בט' באב כאילו אוכל ושותה ביוה"כ ר"ע אומר כל העושה מלאכה בתשעה באב אינו רואה סימן ברכה לעולם וחכ"א כל העושה מלאכה בט' באב ואינו מתאבל על ירושלים אינו רואה בשמחתה שנא' °שמחו את ירושלם וגילו בה כל אוהביה שישו אתה משוש כל המתאבלים עליה מכאן אמרו *כל המתאבל על ירושלים זוכה ורואה בשמחתה ושאינו מתאבל על ירושלים אינו רואה בשמחתה *תניא נמי הכי כל האוכל בשר ושותה יין בט' באב עליו הכתוב אומר °ותהי עונותם על עצמותם: רבי יהודה מחייב בכפיית המטה ולא הודו לו חכמים: תניא אמרו לו לרבי יהודה לדבריך עוברות ומניקות מה תהא עליהן אמר להם אף אני לא אמרתי אלא ביכול תניא נמי הכי מודה ר' יהודה לחכמים בשאינו יכול ומודים חכמים לרבי יהודה ביכול מאי בינייהו איכא בינייהו שאר מטות כדתניא *כשאמרו לכפות המטה לא מטתו בלבד הוא כופה אלא כל המטות כולן הוא כופה אמר רבא הלכתא כתנא דידן *ולא הודו לו חכמים כל עיקר: א"ר שמעון ב"ג לא היו ימים טובים לישראל כחמשה עשר באב וכיוה"כ: *בשלמא יום הכפורים משום דאית ביה סליחה ומחילה יום שניתנו בו לוחות האחרונות אלא ט"ו באב מאי היא אמר רב יהודה אמר שמואל יום שהותרו שבטים לבוא זה בזה מאי דרוש °זה הדבר אשר צוה ה' לבנות צלפחד וגו' דבר זה לא יהא נוהג אלא בדור זה אמר רב יוסף אמר רב נחמן יום שהותר שבט בנימן לבוא בקהל שנאמר °ואיש ישראל נשבע במצפה לאמר איש ממנו לא יתן בתו לבנימן לאשה מאי דרוש אמר רב ממנו ולא מבנינו (*אמר) רבה בר בר חנה א"ר יוחנן יום שכלו בו מתי מדבר דאמר מר עד שלא כלו מתי מדבר לא היה דבור עם משה שנאמר °ויהי כאשר תמו כל אנשי המלחמה למות וידבר ה' אלי אלי היה הדבור עולא אמר יום שביטל הושע בן אלה *פרוסדיות *שהושיב ירבעם בן נבט על הדרכים שלא יעלו ישראל לרגל ואמר לאיזה

(ישעיה סו; יחזקאל לב; במדבר לו; שופטים כא; דברים ב)

כל העושה מלאכה בתשעה באב אינו רואה סימן ברכה לעולם · כלומר באותה מלאכה שרגיל לעשות בתשעה באב אינו רואה סימן ברכה לעולם וחייב אדם לנער ולמעט בכבודו ובהגהותיו שאם היה רגיל לשכב על שני כרים לא ישכב כי אם על אחד אבל עוברות ומניקות אינן חייבות כולי האי שאינם יכולות להצטער בעצמן ואוכלין סעודה המפסקת מבעוד יום וכן נמי ביום הכפורים (נמי) צריך לסעוד מבעו"י דתוספת יום הכפורים מן התורה כדכתיב (ויקרא כג) מערב ועד ערב וכתיב בעצם היום הזה (שם) אבל מכל מקום אין לאסור לשתות · משאכל סעודה מפסקת ועדיין הוי היום גדול *כדמשמע בירושלמי דר' יוסי איקלע לבצרה אכל סעודה מפסקת אתא לגבי דריש כנישתא והוה סעיד אמר ליה ההוא ריש כנישתא סעוד אללי אמר ליה אכלית ואפסקית אמר לו אחות חלו דלא לוחרין רדין ודרא לא אשגח עליה אבל מכל עיגול פחית ואכל מכל תבשיל ותבשיל חד פת ושתה מכל חבית חד כסא והכי הלכתא אם עדיין היום גדול לאחר שאכל סעודה המפסקת מותר לשתות אפילו ערב יוה"כ וכל שכן ערב תשעה באב:

אמר רבא הלכה כתנא דידן ולא הודו לו חכמים · פירוש שאין צריך לכפות המטה והאידנא דחיישינן לכשפים לא עבדינן כפיית המטה ואפילו בא"ב:

יום שהותרו השבטים לבא זה בזה · פירוש דהיינו י"ט:

יום שבו כלו מתי מדבר · כדאמרי' (במדרש איכה) כל ט' באב היו עושין קבריהן ושוכבין בתוכן ולמחר הכרוז יוצא הבדלו החיים ואותה השנה שכלתה הגזרה קמו כולם והיו סבורים שמא טעו בחודש עד שראו הלבנה מלאה ואז ידעו שכלתה הגזרה ועשו יו"ט ופרשב"ם (בב"ב דף קכא·*) כל המ' שנים לא היו מתים אלא בט' באב *ובכל ט' באב היו מתים *כ"א אלף ופרוטרוט ומפרש התם דאותו פרוטקוט עולה למ' שנים ט"ו אלף וי"מ שהיו מתים בכל יום אך רוב המתים היו לעולם בתשעה באב ובחמשה עשר באב פסקה הגזרה ולא מתו כלל ועשו י"ט: בחשבון החדש חזרו ושכבו בקבריהן בלילות עד ליל חמשה עשר וכיון שראו שנתמלאה הלבנה בט"ו ולא מת אחד מהם ידעו שחשבון חדש מכוון וכבר מ' שנה של גזרה נשלמו קבעו אותו הדור לאותו היום יו"ט: דאמר מר כו' · לפיכך יו"ט הוא: לא היה הדבור עם משה ביחוד ותיבה דכתיב וידבר ה' אלי לאמר אלי נתייחד הדיבור ולע"ג דמקמי הכי כתיבי קראי בהו וידבר היכא דאמרי לא היה פה אל פה אלא בחזיון לילה גמגום:

תיקט

בין תנור לכיריים · מקום מטול שבבית: אינו רואה סימן ברכה · מאותה מלאכה: כל האוכל בשר ושותה יין בתשעה באב עליו הכתוב אומר ותהי עונותם על עצמותם · בתשעה באב כלומר בסעודה המפסקת בה: עוברות ומניקות · שאינן יכולות לישן על גבי קרקע: ביכול · שאפשר לו: מאי בינייהו · כיון דזה מודה לו ביכול וזה מודה לו בשאינו יכול: שאר מטות · שבבית שאינו שוכב בהן ר' יהודה דמחייב במתני' בכפיית המטה קמחייב נמי ביכול בשאר מטות ורבנן סברי מטתו כופה ולא שאר מטות וכדתניא גבי אבל: שניתנו בו לוחות אחרונות · שבי"ז בתמוז ירד משה מן ההר תחלה ושיבר את הלוחות ובי"ח שחן את העגל ודן את הפושעים ועלה למרום נשתהה שם שמונים יום ארבעים יום עמד בתפלה דכתיב (דברים ט) ואתנפל לפני ה' ארבעים יום וארבעים לילה וארבעים יום עמד כבראשונה חשוב מי"ז בתמוז עד יום הכפורים והוו להו שמונים יום שנים עשרה שנשתיירו מתמוז דהוא חסר ושלשים דאב ותשעה ועשרים דאלול הרי אחד ושבעים ותשעה דתשרי הרי שמונים יום וליל לוס (א)השלים כנגד לילו של י"ז תמוז דלא הוה בחושבניה דהא נפק ליה כבר בשעה שעלה השתא הוי להו פ' שלמין לילה ויום ובוקר יום כפור ירד שהוא עשרה בתשרי ואותו היום נקבע ליום כפור להודיע שמחל וניחם על הרעה אשר דבר לעשות לעמו ועל כן נקבע לום כפור בעשרה בתשרי כך שמעתי: שהותרו שבטים לבא זה בזה · דרחמנא אמר וכל בת יורשת נחלה וגו' (במדבר לו) וכתיב (שם) ולא תסוב נחלה ממטה למטה אחר כי איש בנחלתו ידבקו בני ישראל ועמדו והתירו דבר זה בחמשה עשר באב: זה הדבר אשר צוה ה' לבנות צלפחד וגו' · זה מיעוט הוא כלו' לא יהיה דבר זה נוהג אלא בדור זה בדור של בנות צלפחד: לבא בקהל · לישא נשים לפי שנשבעו ישראל מלהוציא ורוח רדרמוד בשופטים (כא): ממנו · מיעוט הוא דכתיב איש ממנו לא יתן בתו לבנימין לא גזרו אלא מהם (ממנו) אבל מבניהם לא גזרו: שכלו מתי מדבר · דתניא כל ארבעים שנה שהיו במדבר בכל ערב תשעה באב היה הכרוז יוצא ואומר צאו לחפור והיה כל אחד ואחד יוצא וחופר לו קבר וישן בו שמא ימות קודם שיחפור ולמחר הכרוז יוצא וקורא יבדלו חיים מן המתים וכל שהיה בו נפש חיים היה עומד ויוצא וכל שנה היו עושין כן ובשנת ארבעים שנה עשו ולמחר עמדו כולן חיים וכיון שראו כך תמהו ואמרו שמא טעינו

תורה אור

[ברכות יז: פסחים נה:]
[כרי"ף ובר"א"ש מהוספים דברי ר"ע להרבה ודברי רשב"ג לר"ע]
[ב"ב ב:]
מו"ק כו: נדרים כ: סנהדרין כ:
בס"י אי' דקאמר ולא הודו
ב"ב קכא: פ"ש
[בב"ב קכא: איתא רב דימי בר יוסף אמר רב נחמן יום וכו']
[גיר' הערוך פרוזראות פי' שומרים ועי' לעיל כתי' והושיבו פרוזדאות כו']
[גיטין פח:]
[וכם הגי' פרדסיות וכן הגי' בב"ב קכא:]
[פ"ש בהשב"ם ופי' מהרש"א]
מתים מה"ר אלף בפרוטרוט כב"ל
גיטין ו:
ברי"ף וברא"ש ליתא תניא

הגהות הב"ח

(א) רש"י ד"ה שניתנו כו' הרי שמונים יום וליל פס כפור השלים כנגד:

רבינו חננאל

ר' אומר כל האוכל ושותה בט' באב כאלו אוכל ושותה ביוה"כ · ר' עקיבא אומר העושה מלאכה בט' באב אינו רואה סימן ברכה לעולם · וחכ"א העושה מלאכה בט' באב אינו רואה בשמחת ירושלים שנאמר שמחו את וגו' שישו אתה משוש כל המתאבלים עליה · כל שאינו מתאבל על ירושלים אינו רואה בשמחתה · וכל האוכל בט' באב עליו הכתוב אומר ותהי עונותם על עצמותם · עונותיו הקיקים על עצמותיו · ר' יהודה מחייב בכפיית המטה ולא הודו לו חכמים · תנא מודה ר' יהודה לחכמים בשאינו יכול כגון עוברות ומיניקות וכיוצא בהן שאין כופין מטותיהן · ומודים חכמים לר' יהודה שכופה כל אדם מטתו מי שהוא יכול לישן על הקרקע ואמר רבא הלכתא כתנא דידן דקתני לא הודו לו חכמים · מנהגו של ר' יהודה ברבי אלעאי בערב ט' באב היה יושב בין תנור לכיריים ואוכל פת חריבה במלח · ושותה קיתון של מים ודומה כמי שמתו מוטל לפניו: ארשב"ג לא היו ימים טובים לישראל כט"ו באב וכיוה"כ · בשלמא יוה"כ משום שהוא יום שנתנו לוחות האחרונות לפי שכשתחשב מז' בסיון שעלה משה לקבל לוחות הראשונות מ' יום עד י"ז בתמוז שנא' ואתנפל לפני ה' וגו' עד כ"ט באב וסיד א"ל הקב"ה למשה עלה אלי ההרה · ועלה ביום ל' של אב (עשה ג') [עמד מ'] יום וירד בלוחות האחרונות והוא יוה"כ לפיכך ראוי להיות יו"ט · אלא ט"ו באב מפני מה הוא יו"ט ואמרי' יום שהותרו שבטים לבוא זה בזה · דדרוש זה הדבר שכתוב בענין ולא תסוב נחלה ממטה למטה אחר · לא יהא נוהג אלא באותו דור שנכנסו לארץ · ולהם נחלקה הארץ בלבד · ור' יוחנן אמר שהותר שבט בנימין דדרוש · איש ממנו לא יתן בתו לבנימין ממנו ולא מבנינו · רב נחמן אמר יום שכלו בו מתי מדבר · ומצינו בפירוש בירושלמי ר' אבון אמר שבטל בו החפירה רא"ר לוי בכל ערב ט' באב היה משה רבינו מוציא כרוז במחנה ישראל צאו לחפור היו יוצאין (עצכן) וחופרין קברות וכל אחד ישן בקברו · ובשחר מי שנמצא חי חזר לאהלו והמתים נשארו בקבריהן ומוצאין עצכן בכל שנה חסרים ט"ו אלף ופרוטרוט בשנת ל"ח שנה עשו כמנהג כל השנים עמדו כולן לא מת אחד מהן · אמרו טעינו בחשבון אני היום ט' באב וכן אמרו בי"א בי"ב ובי"ג ובי"ד כיון שהגיע ט"ו באב וראו הלבנה מלאה

רבינו גרשום

מחייב בכפיית המטה לכוף מטתו כאבל: עוברות ומניקות · שאי אפשר להם בלא כפיית מה תהא עליהן: שאר מטות שאינו שוכב עליה דר' יהודה מחייב לכוף כל המטות שבבית והכ"א אינו חייב לכוף אלא מטתו בלבד: כל הכלים המשאולות ו לוו מעונית מבילה שמא דנדה היו · יום שכלו מתי מדבר וקבעו יום טוב לפי שחזר הדיבור למשה. יום שפוסקין מלכרות עצים למערכה ומיכן ואילך מוסיפין לעסוק בתורה:

גליון הש"ס תוס' ד"ה כל העושה וכו' כדמשמע בירושלמי בעירובין דף מא ע"א בתוס' ד"ה לא אכם כתבו כן בשם מדרש איכה רבתי: שם ד"ה יום שבו וכו' ובכל ט"ב היו מתים · עיין תשובת תום יו"ט בסוף ספר תשובו' של הגאון מוהר"ר וז"ל נכוסו:

מב א מיי' פ"ב מהל' ברכות הל' א:

לאיזה שירצה יעלו · הושע בן אלה רשע היה דכתיב (מלכים ב יז) ויעש הרע בעיני ה' רק לא כמלכי ישראל והיינו דקאמר רק שבטל את הפרוסדאות ואמר לאיזה שירצו יעלו: הרוגי ביתר · בפרק הניזקין (גיטין דף נז): מלכרות · לפי שכן לאין ומאותו הזמן אין כח בחמה לייבשן וחיישינן מפני התולעת לפי שעץ שיש בו תולעת פסול למערכה כדאמרינן (מדות פ"ב מ"ה): יום תבר מגל · שבירת הגרזן שפסק החוטב מלחטוב עצים: מכאן ואילך · מחמשה עשר באב ואילך דמוסיף לילות על הימים לעסוק בתורה יוסיף חיים על חייו: דלא יוסיף · לעסוק בתורה בלילות: תקבריה אימיה · כלומר ימות בלא עתו: בת מלך · אף על פי שהיה לה שואלת מבת כהן גדול כו' שלא לבייש את השואלת מתוך שאין לה: מבת כהן גדול · שהוא קרוב וסמוך למלכות: סגן · כהן חשוב ממונה תחת כהן גדול להיות תחתיו ביום הכפורים אם יארע פסול בכהן גדול ביום הכפורים ישמש זה הסגן תחתיו: משוח מלחמה · הוא הכהן המכריז במלחמה *מי האיש הירא ורך הלבב וגו' (דברים כ): אפילו מקופלין ומונחין בקופסא · אישקורייי"ן: צריכין טבילה · כולן שלא לבייש את שצריכה טבילה: שאין אשה אלא לבנים · אם בניך יהיו מיוחסין הכל קופלין עליהם בין זכרים בין נקבות: על מנת שתעטרונו בזהובים · שאחרי הנישואין תתנו לנו תכשיטין ומילתא בעלמא הוא דאמרי כלומר ובלבד שתתנו לנו מלבושים נאים: מחול · סביב לשון מחול הכרם (כלאים פ"ד מ"א): מראה באצבעו · ואומר זה ה' קוינו לו ויושיענו זה ה' קוינו לו נגילה ונשמחה בישועתו:

תיקנו ביבנה הטוב והמטיב · פירוש בברכת המזון ומש"ה תקנו יותר על היין הטוב והמטיב שפי מבשאר דברים לפי שהיו [כמו] גדר בכרם ולא נסרחו: יום תבר מגל · פירוש שמוטעין מלכרות עצים למערכה פירוש משום שחלש כחה של חמה ומגדלין התולעים באילנות ועצים מתולעים פסולים למערכה כדאמר [במדות] (פ"ב מ"ה) שהכהנים בעלי מומין הם מנקרים העצים ומסירין העצים מתולעים שפסולות למערכה:

דלא מוסיף יאסף · פי' אותו שאינו מוסיף מן הלילות על הימים יאסף: מאי יאסף תקבריה אימיה · תימה וכי היה מסופק מאי יאסף אלא נראה לומר דלא מוסיף יוסיף(א) ומיהא קבעי גמרא מאי יסיף אבל לעולם הוה ידע דיאסף הוא לשון מיתה כדכתיב (בראשית מט) ויגוע ויאסף אל עמיו: כל אחד ואחד מראה הקדוש ברוך הוא באצבעו שנאמר הנה אלהינו זה קוינו לו וגו' נגילה ונשמחה בישועתו:

הדרן עלך בשלשה פרקים
וסליקא לה מסכת תענית

לאיזה שירצו יעלו *רב מתנה אמר יום שנתנו הרוגי ביתר לקבורה ואמר רב מתנה *אותו יום שנתנו הרוגי ביתר לקבורה *תקנו ביבנה הטוב והמטיב הטוב שלא הסריחו והמטיב שנתנו לקבורה רבה ורב יוסף דאמרי תרוייהו יום שפסקו מלכרות עצים למערכה (*תניא)רבי אליעזר הגדול אומר מחמשה עשר באב ואילך תשש כחה של חמה ולא היו כורתין עצים למערכה לפי שאינן יבשין אמר רב מנשיא וקרו ליה יום תבר מגל מכאן ואילך דמוסיף יוסיף ודלא מוסיף (*יאסף) (*תני רב יוסף) מאי יאסף אמר רב יוסף תקבריה אימיה: שבהן בנות ירושלים כו': ת"ר בת מלך שואלת מבת כהן גדול בת כהן גדול מבת סגן ובת סגן מבת משוח מלחמה ובת משוח מלחמה מבת כהן הדיוט וכל ישראל שואלין זה מזה כדי *שלא יתבייש את מי שאין לו: כל הכלים טעונין טבילה: אמר רבי אלעזר אפילו מקופלין ומונחין בקופסא: בנות ישראל יוצאות וחולות בכרמים: תנא מי שאין לו אשה נפנה לשם: *מיוחסות שבהן היו אומרות בחור וכו': תנו רבנן יפיפיות שבהן מה היו אומרות תנו עיניכם ליופי שאין האשה אלא ליופי מיוחסות שבהן מה היו אומרות תנו עיניכם למשפחה לפי *שאין האשה אלא לבנים מכוערות שבהם מה היו אומרות קחו מקחכם לשום שמים ובלבד שתעטרונו בזהובים אמר עולא ביראה אמר רבי אלעזר עתיד הקדוש ברוך הוא לעשות מחול לצדיקים והוא יושב ביניהם בגן עדן וכל אחד ואחד מראה באצבעו שנאמ' °ואמר ביום ההוא הנה אלהינו זה קוינו לו ויושיענו זה ה' קוינו לו נגילה ונשמחה בישועתו:

הדרן עלך בשלשה פרקים וסליקא לה מסכת תענית

הדרן עלך בשלשה פרקים וסליקא לה מסכת תענית

רבינו חננאל

מלאה אמרו ודאי כשל הקב"ה אותה גזרה לפיכך עשאוהו יו"ט · רב מתנה אמר יום שנתנו הרוגי ביתר לקבורה בו ביום תקנו הט"ב והמטיב הטוב שלא הסריחו והמטיב שנתנו לקבורה · יום שפוסקין בו לכרות עצים למערכה כדתניא ר"א הגדול אומר מט"ו באב תשש כחה של חמה ולא היו כורתים עצים למערכה מפני שאין יבשים וכיון שאין יבשים מתליעין וקרו ליה יום תבר מגל · כלומר מעתה אין אנו צריכין מגל לחתוך בו עצים · [מכאן ואילך] פי' מט"ו באב מי שמוסיף מן הלילה ליום כלומר עוסק בלילה ושונה שכבר האריך הלילה · ומי שלא יוסיף תקבריה אימיה שאינו מן החכמים שמנדרין שנה מעיניהם בעולם הזה וחיים לעוה"ב: הדרן עלך בשלשה פרקים

רבינו גרשום

תשש כחה של חמה · ואינה מייבשת העצים. יום תבר מגל כלומר מיכן ואילך אין צריכין המגל לכרות עצים: ודלא מוסיף לילות על הימים לעסוק בתורה [יסיף] לפי שכבר גדולין הלילות: אפי' מקופלין חיישינן שמא ישבה עליהן נדה · לעשות מחול להצדיקים שהצדיקים עושין מחול והקב"ה יושב באמצע ומראין זה לזה ואומרים הנה אלהינו זה קוינו לו ויושיענו זה ה' קוינו לו נגילה ונשמחה בישועתו:

הדרן עלך בשלשה פרקים וכולה מסכתא ופרקיהון ארבעה וסימניהן הזכרת סדר תעניות שלשה:

פסקי תוספות ממסכת תענית

מאימתי

א אסור להזכיר משיב הרוח עד שיזכיר שליח ציבור: נהגו לשאול לכך אומר ותן טל ומטר. ד"ה כרא"ש [סימן כ]:
ב אמר משיב הרוח בימות החמה גוערין בו ומוחין לבל יעשהו עוד: שם
ג בימות הגשמים לא אמר מוריד הגשם מחזירין אותו לראש הברכה ואם לא חזר עד אתה חונן א) אומר ברוך אתה מוריד הגשם וכו' ותן טל ומטר ודיו:
ד כגולם לשנים יום שואלין מטר: ב) ד"ה הלכתא: דף י
ה ביום שמיני בחג אחרון מזכיר גשם ולא ראשון וביום טוב ראשון של פסח להפך וכיון שפוסק שוב אינו מתחיל: ד"ה בגמרא: דף ד
ו עוללות שאין להן כתף פסיגין זה על גב זה כתף תלויות בשדרה ויורדות ולא נתבשלו: (זה נמצא בירושלמי דפאה פ"ז):
ז בישתבח ברוך אתה ה' אל מלך גדול בתשבחות אל ההודאות גדול בתשבחות זהו רוב ההודאות:
ח מ"מ כל אחד מודה לחבירו בין על האמת בין על השקר:
ט ברחוקים מנהר פרת כגון בני בבל לא היו עולין לרגל:
י תענית ציבור אסור ברחיצה וכל שכן גיהון ותספורת ואבל אסור רק שבעה ותספורת וגיהון שלשים יום:
יא יום שנים כלאחריו:
יב ירושלמי פרנס בעינן נאמן ותשוב ושהגילה משום גזרה:
יג המתענה על החולה ונתרפא או מת מתענה ומשלים: ד"ה בגמרא: דף י ע"ב
יד ההולך למקום שמתענין מתענה עמהם וכשיוצא משם אוכל בין דעתו לחזור בין אין דעתו לחזור: שם בד"ה ההולך
טו שכח ואכל יפרוש מיד ולא יאכל כדי שוכתו וכן עוברות ומניקות וחולים: שם
טז תשובי נכים מתמהים כבני רעבון וכליל שטבלה: ד"ה אסור: דף יא
יז אין תענית ציבור בבבל לפי שאין הנשיא עמהן: ד"ה כרא"ש: סי' ס'
יח קבל להתענות שני ימים אוכל בלילה שביניהם אם לא פירש: שם סימן יא
יט מתענין לשעות אם אמר הריני בתענית למחר עד חצות ואחר כך נמלך וגומרו: שם סי' יב
כ אין אומרים עננו לא בערבית שרוצה להתענות למחר ולא בשחרית:
כא בטלה מגילת תענית הימים שנקבעו לומר על הניסים אבל יום טוב *) כגון תשעה באב לא בטלו:
כב לא קבל תענית מותר לאכול ומיהו אם התענה אומר עננו כמו בתענית חלום ג)
כג קבלת תענית אומר בשומע תפלה הריני בתענית למחר ותרצני כי אתה שומע תפלת עמך:
כד קבל עליו תענית בני וחמישי ובני קודם שקבעו חודש ביום שלשים **) אלא בשלשים ואחד ואל שלשים ואחד ביום שני וחמישי מקיים קבלתו:
כה ד) המקבל תענית יחיד אומר מבערב הריני בתענית יחיד למחר:
כו המקבל עליו תענית סתם אין נאסר אלא בתענית יחיד:
כז ציבור שגזרו תעניות ואירעו בהן ראש חדש או פורים ולא בטלו על דעתם מפסיקין אותו יום ואין מתענין ועכשיו ציבור הוי כיחיד לענין תענית וצריכין לפרוע אותו יום שמפסיקין: שם
כח גמר בערב מלאכול מותר כל זמן שלא ישן ואוכל עד שיעלה עמוד השחר ה). מתנמנם אינו בישן:
כט נהגו לשתות אחר שינה דהוי כתנאה דמותר ואין יחיד מתפלל עננו אלא במנחה:
ל מתענין לשעות ומתפללין עננו:
לא קבלת תענית בע"ה ובתענית חלום מתפלל עננו:
לב אחר שקיעת החמה אוכל ואין צריך להמתין עד צאת הכוכבים:
לג לוה אדם תעניתו ופורע ודוקא אם יארע לו אונס ·
לד כשהציבור מתענין אין יכולין ללות אפילו על מנת לפרוע:
לה נוגרת שהגיע זמנה ליכנס עליה ליפות עצמה בימנאו לה קופלים וכן נוגרה נשואה:
לו אבל אסור לרחוץ כל גופו בין בחמין בין בצונן אבל פניו ידיו ורגליו בצונן מותר בחמין אסור אפילו אצבעו לסוך אסור ואם אין מתכוין לתענוג אלא להעביר זוהמא מותר או מלוכלך רוחץ בצונן להעביר זוהמא ואפילו ביום הכיפורים שרי בכך:
לז אפילו מלאכה מותרת בשבת משום סכנת נפשות:
לח יחיד רשאי לומר בכל ברכה מעין הברכה ו):
לט צריך פרנסה בברכת השנים וכה"ג:
מ עכשיו רבים הצריכים מטר קובעים בש"ת ולא בברכת השנים יחיד אין אומר עננו בין גואל לרופא אלא בשומע תפלה ובתענית ציבור שלנו רבים הן קובעים ברכה בין גואל לרופא:

סדר תענית כיצד

מא נשא לבבנו אל כפים כאילו טובל שרץ בידו ז) שאין שרץ בידו שאין טבילה מועלת: [בירושלמי פ"ב הלכה א']:
מב להוריד לפני התיבה רגיל בתיבה ואגדה ומבין בכל הברכות דאפילו הרגיל בגמרא ובאגדות סוטה · כשמתפלל ברבים:
מג בחתימה אחת אין ח) להיות ברוך פעמים:
מד יוצאין לקבורה לרחובה של עיר כגולים ואם נתחייבנו מיתה הרינו כמתים ואם גלות הרינו גלינו ואם רעב הרינו רעבים:
מה כהן המכיר משמרתו ומשמרת בית אביו אסור לשתות יין באותו יום:
מו חנוכה ופורים לפניו ולאחריו אסור בהספד ובתענית:
מז אין מתחילין להתענות ביום חמישי:

סדר תענית אלו

מח אפילו יחיד המקבל עליו תענית מתענה ומשלים:
מט שביב מרע שאמר אל תתנו לבני אלא שקל נותנין להן כל צורכן:
נ הר הבית היה מקורה ולא היו הגשמים יכולין ליכנס:
נא התראת ספק הויא שמחוסר אחריו מעשה הדא המדביק פת בתנור חייב אם לא רדה מיד:
נב נתן נכסיו לעניים אף אתו העניים מונית מהן:
נג כשמקבלין תעניות אחר הפסח ושבועות לא צריך כל יחיד לקבל עליו מבעוד יום:
נד קבלו הציבור תענית ונענו הדבר קודם חצות לא ישלימו אחר חצות ישלימו:
נה כלל הגדול מפני הגשמים יתחילו העומדים בבית ה' בלילות ט) שבירות גשמים בלילה וכתיב מעלה נשיאים וגו':

בשלשה פרקים

נו נשיאת כפים שחרית מוסף ונעילה ולא בלילה:
נז כהנים של משמר הן שעולין למעמדן:
נח מותר לאכול ולשתות קודם תפלת מוסף ולא להשתכר:
נט בעל מום בסתר נושא כפיו ואף בגלוי כשרגילין בו בני עירו:
ס אין מפסיקין בפרשה פחות משלשה פסוקים ובהתחלה פליגי:
סא לא היו מתפללין על קרבן אחיהם בתמידים. כל יום שיש בו הלל אין בו מעמד:
סב אין מברכין על הלל דראש חדש דמנהגא הוא:
סג נ"ל ראשון של פסח חובה ליחיד לגמור הלל מכל מקום הא דקאמר יחיד לא יתחיל ואם התחיל גומר אראש חדש קאי על ידי דילוג גומר ומיהו לשון גומר משמע בלא דילוג:

*) נ"ל שא"ל כגון ר"ח חנוכה ופורים וכ"ע לייתב הני' אלפניו: **) [נ"ל ולא בשלשים ס'] : סליקא לה פסקי תוספות ממסכת תענית

הגהות ב"ח א) אומר לראש לא אמר כי אם מוריד הגשם ותן טל ומטר דיו: ב) ...

[מגילה ו.] [גיטין נ"ז] [ברכות מח:] [גיר' ע"י דתניא] [נ"ל יוסף כן א"י בכ"ב וע"ש ברש"ל] [ב"ב קכא.] [פסחים סב: וש"נ] [ע"י הגיר' בפ"י] [ישעי' כה]

הגהות הב"ח (א) תוס' ד"ה מאי כו' דלא מוסיף יוסיף ומשום הכי קבעי גמרא מאי:

אִלֵּין יוֹמַיָּא דִּי לָא לְהִתְעַנָּאָה בְּהוֹן וּמִקְצָתְהוֹן דִּי לָא לְמִסְפַּד בְּהוֹן:

מִן רֵישׁ יַרְחָא דְנִיסָן וְעַד תְּמָנְיָא בֵּיהּ אִתּוֹקַם תְּמִידָא דִּי לָא לְמִסְפַּד בְּהוֹן; וּמִתְּמָנְיָא בֵּיהּ וְעַד סוֹף מוֹעֲדָא אִתּוֹתַב חַגָּא דְשָׁבוּעַיָּא דִּי לָא לְמִסְפַּד.

בְּשִׁבְעָה בְּאִיָּר חֲנֻכַּת שׁוּר יְרוּשְׁלֶם דִּי לָא לְמִסְפַּד; בְּאַרְבְּעַת עֲשַׂר בֵּיהּ נְכִיסַת פִּסְחָא זְעֵירָא דִּי לָא לְמִסְפַּד; בְּעֶשְׂרִין וּתְלָתָא בֵּיהּ נְפַקוּ בְּנֵי חַקְרָא מִירוּשְׁלֶם.

בְּעֶשְׂרִין וְשִׁבְעָה בֵּיהּ אִתְנְטִילוּ כְלִילָאֵי מִיהוּדָה וּמִירוּשְׁלֶם.

בְּאַרְבְּעַת עֲשַׂר בְּסִיוָן אֲחִידַת מִגְדַּל צוּר : בְּחַמְשַׁת עֲשַׂר בֵּיהּ וּבְשִׁתַּת עֲשַׂר בֵּיהּ גְּלוֹ אֱנָשֵׁי בֵית שְׁאָן וֶאֱנָשֵׁי בִקְעֲתָה ; בְּעֶשְׂרִין וַחֲמְשָׁה בֵּיהּ אִתְנְטִילוּ דֵימוֹסָנָאֵי מִיהוּדָה וּמִירוּשְׁלֶם.

בְּאַרְבְּעַת עֲשַׂר בְּתַמּוּז עֲדָא סְפַר גְּזֵירְתָא דִּי לָא לְמִסְפַּד.

בַּחֲמְשַׁת עֲשַׂר בְּאָב זְמַן אָעֵי כָהֲנַיָּא דִּי לָא לְמִסְפַּד ; בְּעֶשְׂרִין וְאַרְבְּעָה בֵּיהּ תַּבְנָא יי לְדִינַנָא.

בְּשִׁבְעָה בֶּאֱלוּל יוֹם חֲנֻכַּת שׁוּר יְרוּשָׁלֶם דִּי לָא לְמִסְפַּד; בְּשִׁבְעַת עֲשַׂר בֵּיהּ אִתְנְטִילוּ רוֹמָאֵי מִיהוּדָה וּמִירוּשְׁלֶם; בְּעֶשְׂרִין וּתְרֵין בֵּיהּ תַּבְנָא לְקַטָּלָא רַשִׁיעַיָּא;

בִּתְלָתָא בְּתִשְׁרֵי אִתְנְטִילַת אַדְכָּרְתָא מִן שְׁטָרַיָּא .

בְּעֶשְׂרִין וּתְלָתָא בְּמַרְחֶשְׁוָן אִסְתַּתַּר סוֹרֵיגָה מִן עֲזָרְתָא; בְּעֶשְׂרִין וַחֲמְשָׁה בֵּיהּ אֲחִידַת שׁוּרַת שְׁמְרוֹן ; בְּעֶשְׂרִין וְשִׁבְעָה בֵּיהּ תָּבַת סָלְתָּא לְמִסַּק עַל מַדְבְּחָא .

בִּתְלָתָא בְּכִסְלֵו אִתְנְטִילוּ סֵימָוָתָא מִן דָּרְתָא; בְּשִׁבְעָה בֵּיהּ יוֹם טָב יוֹם שֶׁמֵּת הוֹרוֹדוֹס; בְּעֶשְׂרִין וְחַד בֵּיהּ יוֹם הַר גְּרִיזִים דִּי לָא לְמִסְפַּד; בְּעֶשְׂרִין וַחֲמְשָׁה בֵּיהּ יוֹם חֲנֻכַּת תְּמָנְיָא יוֹמִין דִּי לָא לְמִסְפַּד.

בְּעֶשְׂרִין וּתְמַנְיָא בְּטֵבֵת יְתֵיבַת בֵּי כְנִישְׁתָּא עַל דִּינָא.

בִּתְרֵין בִּשְׁבָט יוֹם טָב וְדִי לָא לְמִסְפַּד; בְּעֶשְׂרִין וּתְרֵין בֵּיהּ בְּטֵילַת עֲבִידְתָא דַּאֲמַר סָנְאָה לְהֵיתָאָה לְהֵיכְלָא דִּי לָא לְמִסְפַּד; בְּעֶשְׂרִין וּתְמָנְיָא בֵּיהּ אִתְנְטִיל אַנְטִיוֹכוֹס מַלְכָּא מִן יְרוּשְׁלֶם.

בִּתְמָנְיָא וּבְתִשְׁעָה בַּאֲדָר יוֹם תְּרוּעַת מִטְרָא; בִּתְרֵין עֲשַׂר בֵּיהּ יוֹם טִירְיוֹן; בִּתְלַת עֲשַׂר בֵּיהּ יוֹם נִיקָנוֹר; בְּאַרְבְּעַת עֲשַׂר בֵּיהּ וּבַחֲמְשַׁת עֲשַׂר בֵּיהּ יוֹמֵי פוּרַיָּא אִנּוּן דִּי לָא לְמִסְפַּד; בְּשִׁתַּת עֲשַׂר בֵּיהּ שָׁרִיו לְמִבְנֵי שׁוּר יְרוּשְׁלֶם דִּי לָא לְמִסְפַּד; בְּשִׁבְעַת עֲשַׂר בֵּיהּ קָמוּ עַמְמַיָּא עַל פְּלֵיטַת סָפְרַיָּא בִּמְדִינַת כַּלְקִיס וּבֵית זַבְדִּין וַהֲוָה פֻרְקָן לְבֵית יִשְׂרָאֵל; בְּעֶשְׂרִין בֵּיהּ צָמוּ עַמָּא לְמִטְרָא וּנְחַת לְהוֹן; בְּעֶשְׂרִין וּתְמַנְיָא בֵּיהּ אֲתַת בְּשׂוֹרְתָא טָבְתָא לִיהוּדָאֵי דְּלָא יֶעְדּוּן מִן אוֹרָיְתָא דִּי לָא לְמִסְפַּד.

לָהֵן כָּל אֱנָשׁ דִּיהְוֵי עֲלוֹהִי מִן קַדְמַת דְּנָא יֶאֱסַר בִּצְלוֹ.